Communications in Computer and Information Science 896

Commenced Publication in 2007
Founding and Former Series Editors:
Phoebe Chen, Alfredo Cuzzocrea, Xiaoyong Du, Orhun Kara, Ting Liu, Dominik Ślęzak, and Xiaokang Yang

More information about this series at http://www.springer.com/series/7899

Xabier Larrucea · Izaskun Santamaria
Rory V. O'Connor · Richard Messnarz (Eds.)

Systems, Software and Services Process Improvement

25th European Conference, EuroSPI 2018
Bilbao, Spain, September 5–7, 2018
Proceedings

Springer

Editors
Xabier Larrucea
Tecnalia Bizkaia
San Sebastián
Spain

Izaskun Santamaria
Tecnalia Bizkaia
San Sebastián
Spain

Rory V. O'Connor
School of Computing
Dublin City University
Dublin
Ireland

Richard Messnarz
I.S.C.N. GesmbH
Graz
Austria

ISSN 1865-0929 ISSN 1865-0937 (electronic)
Communications in Computer and Information Science
ISBN 978-3-319-97924-3 ISBN 978-3-319-97925-0 (eBook)
https://doi.org/10.1007/978-3-319-97925-0

Library of Congress Control Number: 2018950532

This Springer imprint is published by the registered company Springer Nature Switzerland AG
The registered company address is: Gewerbestrasse 11, 6330 Cham, Switzerland

Preface

Systems, Software and Services Process Improvement – 25th European Conference, EuroSPI^2 2018, September 5–7, 2018

This textbook comprises the proceedings of the 25th EuroSPI Conference, held during September 5–7, 2018 in Bilbao, Spain.

At EuroSPI 2018 new workshop communities were formed based on the cooperation with the EU Blueprint for Automotive project DRIVES (2018–2021) and the medical device industry. Therefore, we have extended the scope of the conference from software process improvement and systems, software and service-based process improvement, as well as systems and product improvement, to include and cover the whole life cycle of products. Since 2008, EuroSPI partners have packaged SPI knowledge in job role training and established a European certification association (www.ecqa.org) to transport this knowledge Europe wide using standardized certification and exam processes.

Conferences were held in Dublin (Ireland) in 1994, in Vienna (Austria) in 1995, in Budapest (Hungary) in 1997, in Gothenburg (Sweden) in 1998, in Pori (Finland) in 1999, in Copenhagen (Denmark) in 2000, in Limerick (Ireland) in 2001, in Nuremberg (Germany) in 2002, in Graz (Austria) in 2003, in Trondheim (Norway) in 2004, in Budapest (Hungary) in 2005, in Joensuu (Finland) in 2006, in Potsdam (Germany) in 2007, in Dublin (Ireland) in 2008, in Alcala (Spain) in 2009, in Grenoble (France) in 2010, in Roskilde (Denmark) in 2011, in Vienna (Austria) in 2012, Dundalk (Ireland) in 2013, in Luxembourg in 2014, in Ankara (Turkey) 2015, in Graz (Austria) in 2016, and in Ostrava (Czech Republic) in 2017.

EuroSPI is an initiative with the following major action lines http://www.eurospi.net:

- Establishing an annual EuroSPI conference supported by software process improvement networks from different EU countries.
- Establishing a social media strategy with groups in LnkedIn, Facebook, Twitter and online statements, speeches, and keynotes on YouTube, and a set of proceedings and recommended books.
- Establishing an effective team of national representatives (from each EU country) growing step by step into more countries of Europe.
- Establishing a European Qualification Framework for a pool of professions related to SPI and management. This is supported by European certificates and examination systems.

EuroSPI has established a joint newsletter with the European Certification and Qualification Association (www.eurospi.net, in the menu "About EuroAsiaSPI"), the SPI Manifesto (SPI = Systems, Software and Services Process Improvement), a set of social media groups including a selection of presentations and keynotes freely available on YouTube, and access to job role-based qualification through the European Certification and Qualification Association (www.ecqa.org).

A typical characterization of EuroSPI is reflected in a statement made by a company: "... the biggest value of EuroSPI lies in its function as a European knowledge and experience exchange mechanism for SPI and innovation."

Since its initiation in 1994 in Dublin, the EuroSPI initiative has outlined that there is not a single silver bullet with which to solve SPI issues, but that you need to understand a combination of different SPI methods and approaches to achieve concrete benefits. Therefore, each proceedings volume covers a variety of different topics, and at the conference we discuss potential synergies and the combined use of such methods and approaches. These proceedings contain selected research papers under six headings:

- Section I: SPI Context and Agility
- Section II: SPI and Safety Testing
- Section III: SPI and Management Issues
- Section IV: SPI and Assessment
- Section V: SPI and Safety Critical
- Section VI: Selected Keynotes and Workshop Papers

Section I presents three papers related to the issue of the context of SPI and the agile context in particular, and the impact context has on the software process. Section II explores the issues of both safety and testing from an SPI perspective. Section III presents three papers dealing with issues surrounding the topic of management issues as it relates to SPI, including change management, knowledge management, and project management. Section IV discusses issues surrounding assessment of software process, including cultural awareness and improvement planning. Section V explores the theme of safety-critical software from an SPI viewpoint and also combining safety and security.

Section VI presents selected keynotes from EuroSPI workshops concerning the future of SPI. From 2010 onwards, EuroSPI invites recognized key researchers to publish their thoughts about new future directions of SPI. These key messages are discussed in interactive workshops and help create SPI communities based on new topics.

The first set of papers relates to the GamifySPI workshop and explores Gamification and Persuasive Games for Software Process Improvement, Information Technology, and Innovation Management. The second collection of papers relates to the topic of SPI in Industry 4.0 – The Digitalization of Design and Manufacturing and elaborates a set of best practices and success factors for the implementation of industry 4.0. The third collection of papers surrounds the topic of Best Practices in Implementing Traceability. The fourth collection discusses the topic of Good and Bad Practices in Improvement with key contributions from European initiatives, which developed best practices for SPI. The fifth collection of papers relates to the topic of Functional Safety and addresses best practices from automotive industry to cope with cyber security and functional safety. The sixth collection addresses experiences with Agile and Lean and examines a series of success factors and examples of being lean and agile. The seventh collection of papers addresses the topic of Standards and Assessment Models and examines different ISO standards and assessment models will be introduced, explained, and discussed. The eighth collection of papers addresses Team Skills and Diversity Strategies and examines a varierty of organizational and human factors as they relate to SPI. The ninth set of papers deals with the critical domain of SPI in Medical Device Industry. Finally the tenth set of papers covers Empowering the Future Infrastructure and specifically skills and improvements needs.

September 2018

Xabier Larrucea
Izaskun Santamaria
Rory V. O'Connor
Richard Messnarz

Recommended Further Reading

In [1] the proceedings of three EuroSPI conferences were integrated into one book, which was edited by 30 experts in Europe. The proceedings of EuroSPI 2005 to 2017 inclusive have been published by Springer [2–14].

References

1. Messnarz, R., Tully, C. (eds.): Better Software Practice for Business Benefit – Principles and Experience, 409 pages. IEEE Computer Society Press, Los Alamitos (1999)
2. Richardson, I., Abrahamsson, P., Messnarz, R. (eds.): Software Process Improvement. LNCS, vol. 3792, p. 213. Springer, Heidelberg (2005)
3. Richardson, I., Runeson, P., Messnarz, R. (eds.): Software Process Improvement. LNCS, vol. 4257, pp. 11–13. Springer, Heidelberg (2006)
4. Abrahamsson, P., Baddoo, N., Margaria, T., Messnarz, R. (eds.): Software Process Improvement. LNCS, vol. 4764, pp. 1–6. Springer, Heidelberg (2007)
5. O'Connor, R.V., Baddoo, N., Smolander, K., Messnarz, R. (eds): Software Process Improvement. CCIS, vol. 16, Springer, Heidelberg (2008).
6. O'Connor, R.V., Baddoo, N., Gallego C., Rejas Muslera R., Smolander, K., Messnarz, R. (eds): Software Process Improvement. CCIS, vol. 42, Springer, Heidelberg (2009).
7. Riel A., O'Connor, R.V. Tichkiewitch S., Messnarz, R. (eds): Software, System, and Service Process Improvement. CCIS, vol. 99, Springer, Heidelberg (2010).
8. O'Connor, R., Pries-Heje, J. and Messnarz R., Systems, Software and Services Process Improvement, CCIS Vol. 172, Springer-Verlag, (2011).
9. Winkler, D., O'Connor, R.V. and Messnarz R. (Eds), Systems, Software and Services Process Improvement, CCIS 301, Springer-Verlag, (2012).
10. McCaffery, F., O'Connor, R.V. and Messnarz R. (Eds), Systems, Software and Services Process Improvement, CCIS 364, Springer-Verlag, (2013).
11. Barafort, B., O'Connor, R.V. and Messnarz R. (Eds), Systems, Software and Services Process Improvement, CCIS 425, Springer-Verlag, (2014).
12. O'Connor, R.V. Akkaya, M., Kemaneci K., Yilmaz, M., Poth, A. and Messnarz R. (Eds), Systems, Software and Services Process Improvement, CCIS 543, Springer-Verlag, (2015).
13. Kreiner, C., Poth., A., O'Connor, R.V., and Messnarz R. (Eds), Systems, Software and Services Process Improvement, CCIS 633, Springer-Verlag, (2016).
14. Stolfa, J, Stolfa, S., O'Connor, R.V., and Messnarz R. (Eds), Systems, Software and Services Process Improvement, CCIS 633, Springer-Verlag, (2017).

Acknowledgments

Some contributions published in this book have been funded with support from the European Commission. European projects (supporting ECQA and EuroSPI) contributed to this Springer book include: DRIVES – BLUEPRINT Project, InnoTEACH (LET'S BE INNOVATIVE! Development of Creativity, Innovation and Entrepreneurship), ELIC – Engineering Literacy, and EMVOI (ISO 17024 Certification for EU Project Managers).

In this case the publications reflect the views only of the author(s), and the Commission cannot be held responsible for any use that may be made of the information contained therein.

Funded by the
Erasmus+ programme
of the European Union

Organization

General Chair and Workshop Chair

Richard Messnarz	ISCN GesmbH, Graz, Austria

General Co-chair

Micheal Mac an Airchinnigh	ISCN, Ireland

Scientific Chair

Rory V. O'Connor	Dublin City University, Ireland

Organization Chair

Eva Christof	ISCN GesmbH, Graz, Austria

Local Organization Chairs

Xabier Larrucea	Tecnalia, Spain
Izaskun Santamaria	Tecnalia, Spain

GamifySPI Workshop Co-chairs

Murat Yilmaz	Cankaya University, Turkey
Rory V. O'Connor	Dublin City University, Ireland

Industry 4.0 Workshop Co-chairs

Andreas Riel	Grenoble INP, France
Michael Reiner	University of Applied Sciences Krems, Austria

Best Practices in Implementing Traceability Workshop Co-chairs

Rainer Dreves	Continental Automotive, Germany
Bernhard Sechser	Methodpark, Germany

Good and Bad Practices in Improvement Workshop Co-chairs

Eva Breske	Robert BOSCH Engineering, Germany
Tomas Schweigert	SQS, Germany

Functional Safety and Cybersecurity Workshop Co-chairs

Alexander Much	Elektrobit, Germany
Miklos Biro	SCCH, Austria
Jenny Gorner	KnowIT, Sweden
Richard Messnarz	ISCN GesmbH, Austria

Agile and Lean Workshop Co-chairs

Alexander Poth	Volkswagen AG, Germany
Susumu Sasabe	JUSE, Japan
Antonia Mas	University of the Balearic Islands, Spain

Standards and Assessment Models Workshop Co-chairs

Gerhard Griessnig	AVL, Austria
Timo Varkoi	FiSMA, Finland
Klaudia Dussa Zieger	IMBUS, Germany

Team Skills and Diversity Strategies Workshop Co-chairs

Gabriele Sauberer	Termnet, Austria
Mirna Munoz	CIMAT, Mexico

SPI in Medical Device Industry Workshop Co-chairs

Armin Riess	BBraun, Germany
Alastair Walker	Lorit Consultancy, UK
Marion Lepmets	Softcomply, Ireland

Empowering the Future Infrastructure Workshop Co-chairs

Svatopluk Stolfa	VSB Ostrava, Czech Republic
Jakub Stolfa	VSB Ostrava, Czech Republic
Peter Dolejsi	ACEA, the European Automobile Manufacturers Association

Board Members

EuroSPI Board Members represent centers or networks of SPI excellence having extensive experience with SPI. The board members collaborate with different European SPINS (Software Process Improvement Networks). The following have been members of the conference board for a significant period:

Rory V. O'Connor	Dublin City University, Ireland
Miklós Biró	Software Competence Center Hagenberg, Austria

Ricardo Colomo-Palacios	Ostfold University, Norway
Michael Reiner	IMC FH Krems, University of Applied Sciences, Austria
Gabriele Sauberer	TermNet, Austria

EuroSPI Scientific Program Committee

EuroSPI established an international committee of selected well-known experts in SPI who are willing to be mentioned in the program and to review a set of papers each year. The list below represents the Research Program Committee members. EuroSPI also has a separate Industrial Program Committee responsible for the industry/experience contributions.

Miklós Biró	Software Competence Center Hagenberg GmbH, Austria
Jose Antonio Calvo-Manzano	Universidad Politécnica de Madrid, Spain
Paul M. Clarke	Dublin City University, Ireland
Ricardo Colomo Palacios	Ostfold University College, Norway
Darren Dalcher	University of Hertfordshire, UK
Anca Draghici	Politechnic University of Timisoara, Romania
Elli Georgiadou	Middlesex University, UK
Pasi Kuvaja	University of Oulu, Finland
Dieter Landes	University of Coburg, Germany
Timo Mäkinen	Tampere University of Technology, Finland
Wolski Marcin	University of Poznan, Poland
Paula Ventura Martins	University of Algarve, Portugal
Antoina Mas	Universitat de les Illes Balears, Spain
Fergal Mc Caffery	Dundalk Institute of Technology, Ireland
Antoni Mesquida	Universitat de les Illes Balears, Spain
Mirna Muñoz	CIMAT-Zacatecas, Mexico
Rory V. O'Connor	Dublin City University, Ireland
Efi Papatheocharous	SICS Swedish ICT AB, Sweden
Michael Reiner	University of Applied Sciences Krems, Austria
Andreas Riel	Grenoble INP, France
Miran Rodic	University of Maribor, Slovenia
Tomas San Feliu	Universidad Politécnica de Madrid, Spain
Kerstin Siakas	Thessaloniki Institute of Technology, Greece
Jakub Stolfa	Technical University of Ostrava, Czech Republic
Svatopluk Stolfa	Technical University of Ostrava, Czech Republic
Dietmar Winkler	University of Technology Vienna, Austria
Murat Yilmaz	Cankaya University, Turkey

Contents

SPI and Assessment

SPI and Safety Critical

Selected Keynotes and Workshop Papers

GamifySPI

Experiences with Agile and Lean

Standards and Assessment Models

SPI Context and Agility

Maturity Models for Agile Software Development: What Are They?

Rafaela Mantovani Fontana[1(✉)], Regina Albuquerque[2], Rosmar Luz[2], Ana Carolina Moises[2], Andreia Malucelli[2], and Sheila Reinehr[2]

[1] Federal University of Paraná, R. Dr. Alcides Vieira Arcoverde, 1225, Curitiba, PR, Brazil
rafaela.fontana@ufpr.br, carol.moises@gmail.com

[2] Pontifical Catholic University of Paraná, R. Imaculada Conceição, 1155, Curitiba, PR, Brazil
{regina.fabia,sheila.reinehr}@pucpr.br, rosmar.luz@pr.senai.br, malu@ppgia.pucpr.br

Abstract. Aiming at process maturity and agility, various studies have proposed combinations of CMMI-DEV with agile methods. Yet other studies have proposed maturity models founded on agility, focused on agile process improvement. These agile maturity models define different structures, approaches and underlying concepts for agile maturity. This study aims at presenting them in a unified manner by identifying the studies, analyzing the proposed models and comparing them. The research approach was the systematic literature review on scientific databases. Based on the 14 models found, we analyzed levels' structures, maturity concept, assessment methods and mature practices. Our results show that current maturity models do not agree in some aspects but converge in others. Based on these findings, we suggest future studies to enrich process improvement knowledge in agile methods.

Keywords: Agile methods · Maturity models · Process improvement

1 Introduction

Maturity in software development has currently been defined in terms of the Capability Maturity Model Integration for Development – CMMI-DEV [4] or the international standard ISO/IEC 15504, now revised by ISO/IEC 33002 [10]. These models define levels for organizations to gradually increase process definition and control and, thus, their maturity in developing software. High-maturity is achieved when processes are quantitatively managed and optimized [4].

Due to the relevant adoption of agile methods in the last decade [5], several studies have been presented combining agile with CMMI-DEV [27]. The

This research project is supported by CNPQ (National Council for Scientific and Technological Development) – Process Number 311176/2015-1.

X. Larrucea et al. (Eds.): EuroSPI 2018, CCIS 896, pp. 3–14, 2018.
https://doi.org/10.1007/978-3-319-97925-0_1

goal in these initiatives is to accomplish process maturity with the benefits of agility. With the same purpose, another group of studies have also been proposed: the ones that present agile maturity models [3]. These models intend to guide improvements with agile methods. Differently from the consolidated CMMI-DEV reference model, the approaches for agile maturity models are still diverse and little consensus exists among them [9,13].

In this context, this study aims at presenting currently proposed agile maturity models and deeply evaluating them. Our research approach was the systematic literature review on scientific databases. The findings are relevant to software engineering researchers in the sense that they provide insight into directions in the agile maturity field; and to practitioners, as current maturity models are consolidated, enabling elucidating practical approaches for agility assessment.

This paper is organized as follows. Section 2 presents other reviews on agile software development maturity and their results. Section 3 describes our research approach. Section 4 presents the answers to our research questions and Sect. 5 discusses the results. Section 6 concludes the paper with future work challenges.

2 Related Work

Some years ago, Buglione [3] stated that the discussions on agile software methodologies should trigger the need to better define maturity in agile software development. Based on the analysis of agile maturity models, [3] concluded that an agile maturity assessment should be cheap, fast and provide enough details to provide the basis for an improvement plan.

Leppänen [13] complemented the view of [3] and showed that models define different agile practices for different maturity levels. He also found that current models do not define maturity from the view point of successful agile software development, and all of them were created based on a single experience or on conceptual models. According to [13], there is still a need for properly validating the models.

In the same year, two other studies presented analysis of agile maturity models: Schweigert et al. [24] and Özcan-Top and Demirörs [17]. The work by Schweigert et al. [24] aimed at presenting the state of the art of agile maturity models. They verified that current agile maturity models either have a structure based on CMMI-DEV; have a level structure; or do not use explicit levels. The authors derived the same conclusion as [13], saying that there is no unique approach to make models results comparable. The work by [17] analyzed agile maturity models to identify their strengths and weaknesses. Their conclusion on the study was similar to the other authors' in the sense that current maturity models are too different and do not provide enough guidance to agile process adoption or agile process improvement. The most recent review we found on agile maturity models was the one by Schweigert et al. [25], which seems to complement the same authors previous work [24] stating that agile maturity involves – besides processes – values, emotions and culture.

These five reviews on maturity models for agile software development presented by Buglione [3], Leppänen [13], Schweigert et al. [24], Özcan-Top and

Demirörs [17] and Schweigert et al. [25] provided a first view of the models being proposed and an initial analysis of their structure. In this study, we aim at updating previous studies and deeply analyzing the models to answer research questions on agile maturity, as stated in the next section.

3 Research Approach

The research objective that guided our work was to *present current agile maturity models and to evaluate them to provide a basis for future studies.* To answer that, we applied the systematic literature review approach [11]. The approach comprises three phases: planning, execution and report.

3.1 Phase 1 – Planning

In the planning phase, we defined the research protocol. The objective was to specify the procedures that would be taken in the review and to reduce research bias [11], as explained in the next subsections.

Objective and Research Questions. The objective of this systematic literature review study was to present current agile maturity models and to evaluate them to provide a basis for future research. Based on the gaps left by current available reviews, we defined the following research questions to be answered by the primary studies found:

- RQ1: Which are the maturity models proposed for agile software development?
- RQ2: What is maturity in agile software development?
- RQ3: How is an assessment performed with agile software development maturity models?
- RQ4: Which agile practices are considered mature by such models?

Search Strategy. We searched studies related to the research question by using the following search string: ("maturity model" OR "agile maturity") AND ("agile" OR "agility" OR "scrum" OR "lean software" OR "extreme programming"). This search was performed in full-text papers in the databases: ACM Digital Library, ScienceDirect, IEEE, Scopus and SpringerLink. We searched for papers published in journals and conferences from 2001 through 2017. The start date was set due to the publication of the Agile Manifesto.

Exclusion Criteria. Our exclusion criteria (EC) were defined according to the reading step (title, abstract or full-text), as listed below:

- Title reading
  - EC1: Papers with repeated title;

- Abstract reading
  - EC2: Secondary studies (systematic reviews or systematic mappings) that do not approach maturity models in agile software development;
  - EC3: Articles not related to agile maturity models;
- Full-text reading
  - EC4: Papers that do not present clear information about the creation of a maturity model for agile software development;
  - EC5: Papers with repeated results (we considered the paper with a more detailed description of results).

3.2 Phase 2 Execution

We followed our research protocol to search for papers by following four main steps: search, title reading, abstract reading and full-text reading.

In the first step, we conducted the search for the studies over each database, using the string and time period defined. This procedure resulted in 3,468 papers. During the second step – title reading – EC1 was applied (3,380 papers left). Next, during the abstract reading, EC2 and EC3 were applied (74 papers left). These three first steps were performed by two authors. For the last step, two other authors read the full-text of remaining papers (applying EC4, there were 13 papers left and for EC5, 11 papers left).

Finally, 11 papers were chosen as the ones related to maturity models in agile software development. During full-text reading, we identified other important studies cited by the selected papers and included them [20,23,26], resulting in 14 papers to be analyzed in the report phase.

The selected papers were Nawrocki et al. [16], Lui and Chan [14], Packlick [19], Sidky et al. [26], Qumer and Henderson-Sellers [23], Patel and Ramachandran [20], Patel and Ramachandran [21], Benefield [2], Fontana et al. [7], Silva et al. [28], Özcan-Top and Demirörs [18], Stojanov et al. [30], Soares and Meira [29] and Fontana et al. [8].

3.3 Phase 3 - Report

The analysis of the papers' content was performed by the first author. The data obtained in the selected studies were analyzed according to the research questions.

To answer RQ1 (*which are the maturity models proposed for agile software development?*), we analyzed the models proposed in the papers according to the directions presented by [15, p. 149], which states that maturity models should present the following characteristics:

- Audience: definition of the expected users of the model;
- Aim: the model may be applied to either one of two aims - analysis or benchmarking. The first aim helps determine the necessary improvements, while the second presents best practices for comparison by other organizations;
- Scope: defines if the model is generic or domain-specific;

- Success criteria: [15] suggest that models must have criteria to define if the application was successful;
- Process areas: according to [15, p. 150], process areas uncover the conceptual foundation used in the development of the model;
- Maturity levels: Maturity levels must be based on a rationale that, according to [15], may be existence and adherence to a structured process, modification of organizational structure, emphasis on people, or emphasis on learning;
- Cell texts: The model must provide the characteristics at the intersection of process areas and maturity levels;
- Administration mechanism: definition of the mechanisms used for applying the model.

For research questions RQ2 (*what is maturity in agile software development?*) and RQ3 (*how is an assessment performed with agile software development maturity models?*) we used the same approach. We directly extracted statements from the texts, identifying, respectively, highest maturity levels and assessment approaches.

To answer the last question, RQ4 (*which agile practices are considered mature?*) our analysis approach was based on the thematic networks proposed by [1]. When performing this analysis, the full-text is systematically read to identify: (i) basic themes, which are the evidences in the text that directly answer the research question; (ii) organizing themes, which are categories of basic themes grouped to facilitate understanding; and, finally, (iii) the global theme, which encapsulates organizing themes in a higher-order understanding.

3.4 Threats to Validity

Considering the construct validity, we defined an all-embracing search string to be able to retrieve research papers related to all aspects respecting the objective of this review. Regarding the internal validity, we applied a pair review scheme for paper selection, either for title and abstract reading and for the full-text reading. To reinforce external validity, we included primary and secondary papers in our analysis.

4 Results

To accomplish the objective of this study, 14 agile maturity models were analyzed according to the research questions. The answers are presented next.

4.1 RQ1 - Which Are the Maturity Models Proposed for Agile Software Development?

We analyzed each of these models according to the directions presented by [15, p. 149], as described in Sect. 3.3. The result of our analysis is summarized in Fig. 1.

	Audience	Aim	Scope	Success criteria	Process areas	Maturity levels	Cell texts	Administration mechanism
Nawrocki et al. (2001)	Organizations implementing XP	Analytic	Only for XP	No evidence	Yes, based on intersections between XP and CMM	4 levels, based on existence an adherence to a structured process	Yes, defined through practices	Partial. Concludes that the assessment is subjective
Lui and Chan (2005)	Inexperienced XP teams	Analytic	Only for XP	No evidence	Yes, based on visual data mining of XP practices	4 levels, based on learning	No evidence	No evidence
Packlick (2007)	Agile teams at Sarbre Airline Solutions	Benchmarking	Agile in general	Yes. Defined acceptance criteria for goals areas	Yes, based on goals	5 levels, based on people	Yes, defined through user stories	Yes, presents how they implemented it in the company
Sidky et al. (2007)	Agile teams	Analytic	Agile in general	Yes. Defined project and organizational assessment	Yes, based on Agile Principles	5 levels, based on existence and adherence to a structured process	Yes, defined through practices	Yes, defines a four-stage process for agile adoption
Qumer and Henderson-Sellers (2008)	Agile teams	Analytic	Agile in general	No evidence	No evidence	6 levels, based on existence and adherence to a structured process	No evidence	Partial. Describes two implementation cases
Patel and Ramachandran (2009)	Agile teams	Analytic	Agile in general	Yes. Defined the assessment process	Yes, based on Agile Practices	5 levels, based on existence and adherence to a structured process	No evidence	Yes, exemplifies how to perform the assessment
Patel and Ramachandran (2009b)	Agile teams	Analytic	Story Cards	Yes. Defined the assessment process	Yes, based on Agile Practices	4 levels, based on existence and adherence to a structured process	Yes, defined areas for improvement for each practice	Yes, exemplifies how to perform the assessment
Benefield (2010)	XP teams at British Telecom	Benchmarking	Only for XP	Yes. Defined the assessment method	No, but defines 7 dimensions for assessment	5 levels, based on existence and adherence to a structured process	No evidence	Yes, exemplifies how to perform the assessment
Fontana et al. (2014a)	Agile Teams	Analytic	Agile in general	No evidence.	No. Suggests agile practices	3 levels, but they mention adherence to a process should not be measured	No evidence.	No evidence.
Silva et al. (2014)	Organizations with CMMI and Agile	Analytic	Quality Assurance	Yes. The model was evaluated against its feasibility, completeness and adequacy	Yes. Based on CMMI and agile	5 levels, based on existence and adherence to a structured process	Yes. Describes purpose, results and work products	No evidence.
Özcan-Top and Demirörs (2014a)	Organizations implementing agile	Analytic	Agile in general	Yes. Present the assessment method	Yes, named as generic and aspect practices	4 levels, based on existence and adherence to a process (practices)	Described in the technical report	Yes, exemplifies how to perform the assessment
Stojanov et al. (2015)	Organizations scaling agile	Analytic	SAFe	Yes. The model was evaluated using Delphi sessions against understandability, practicality and necessity	Yes. Based on Sidky's model and SAFe principles and practices	5 levels, based on existence and adherence to a structured process	Yes. Provides a supplementary on-line document	Yes, exemplifies how to perform the assessment
Soares and Meira (2015)	Organizations with CMMI and Agile	Analytic	Agile project management	No evidence.	Yes. Based on CMMI and agile	5 levels, based on existence and adherence to a structured process	Yes. Briefly describes processes areas	No evidence.
Fontana et al. (2015)	Agile Teams	Analytic	Agile in general	No evidence.	Yes. Based on outcomes	No levels, based on categories of outcomes to be pursued	Yes. Defines a check list in a supplementary on-line document	Yes. Suggests a check-list as an assessment method.

Fig. 1. Agile maturity models' characteristics

Figure 1 allows observing that most of the models have an analytic purpose, as they focus on enabling the evaluation of an entity. Most of them address agile in general [7, 8, 18–20, 23, 26], but some of these models were developed for specific purposes such as extreme programming (XP) [2, 14, 16], quality assurance [28], story cards [21], SAFe (Scaled Agile Framework) [30] and project management [29]. Except for one model [8], all of them present 4 to 5 maturity models, in a CMMI-DEV style. The influence of CMMI-DEV is also observed in the maturity levels based on existence and adherence to a structured process. This influence is not explicitly stated in the papers – as Fig. 1 shows, only two models explicitly declare to be targeted at organizations with CMMI-DEV and agile.

4.2 RQ2 - What Is Maturity in Agile Software Development?

We identified how authors see maturity in agile software development by understanding their highest maturity levels. Abstracting the details of each model, maturity was defined as *practices adoption, continuous improvement, sustaining agility, project performance or highly productive teams*:

- Practices Adoption: the studies that claimed that maturity is gained when new practices are adopted by the team [7,14,21];
- Continuous Improvement: the studies that described that maturity in agile is similar to the maturity concept defined by the CMMI-DEV reference model [28,29];
- Sustaining agility: comprises the studies that defined that mature teams have lean processes and keep agile [23,26,30];
- Project performance: the studies that defined maturity as a way of obtaining results in the projects [16,20];
- Highly productive teams: the studies that provided mature characteristic for three models [2,18,19], which pose teams as a central role for maturity in agile software development.

One exception was the model proposed by [8], which does not describe maturity levels. For the authors, maturity is obtained when results are accomplished in various aspects of software development and team.

4.3 RQ3 - How Is an Assessment Performed with Agile Software Development Maturity Models?

In the studies we evaluated, we identified four different ways to perform the assessment in agile maturity models: (i) evaluation of indicators as Not Achieved (NA), Partially Achieved (PA), Largely Achieved (LA) or Fully Achieved (FA); (ii) based on CMMI-DEV; (iii) adoption of practices; or (iv) evaluation of achievement of outcomes/goals/capabilities:

- Evaluation of indicators: the majority of the agile maturity models present this type of assessment. Models [18,20,21,26,30] propose indicators that should be evaluated regarding the extent at which they were achieved;
- Based on CMMI-DEV: these models [28,29] propose process areas that should be evaluated against their evidences;
- Adoption of practices: models [14,16] uncovered this category of assessment because they propose that assessment should evaluate the practices adopted by the team;
- Evaluation of the achievement of outcomes/goals: studies by [2,8,19,23] present elements such as goals or outcomes that must be present to asses maturity.

The only paper that did not mention assessment, was the one by Fontana et al. [7] as the authors only used a maturity model to describe the process of maturing in agile teams.

4.4 RQ4 - Which Agile Practices Are Considered Mature?

Our last research question identified which agile practices are considered mature in current maturity models for agile software development. The global theme "mature practices in agile software development" and the organizing themes "software, customer, organization, people, process and requirements" were the ones that emerged from the thematic network analysis.

When we were analyzing the practices suggested by the models for each of these themes, we verified that some of them represented practices itself, that is, activities that the team might perform. On the other hand, some authors described the results that the teams might achieve in a context of mature software development with agile practices. For example, the software basic theme "automated builds" was identified as a practice, and "agile coding" was identified as a result of applying a number of practices that lead to coding in agile ways. Thus, the basic themes derived from the analysis represented either practices or results described in the papers.

The greatest number of basic themes was grouped in the *software* organizing theme. This means that maturity in agile software development is mainly described by practices related to the software itself. The list below shows the basic themes (practices and results) identified for all organizing themes.

- Software: basic themes related to the software being developed.
  - Practices: Concurrent testing, automated builds, automated tests, efficient coding, integrated tools, daily builds, automatic deploy, test-driven development, pair programming, continuous integration and code review;
  - Results: Agile testing, agile coding, high-level software, high-level source code and agile engineering techniques;
- People: basic themes related to people involved in the development of the software.
  - Practices: Team leads to continuous improvement, embrace change, face-to-face interaction, shared responsibility and collaborative work;
  - Results: Having experienced people, an assertive team, improved productivity, learning culture, improvement culture and agile leadership;
- Processes: basic themes related to acting on the working processes.
  - Practices: Removing waste, continuous improvement, collecting measures and estimating in agile ways;
  - Results: Light processes, understand their situation and keep a sustainable pace;
- Customer: basic themes related to relationship with the customer.
  - Practice: On-site customer;
  - Results: Customer satisfaction and confidence;

- Organization: basic themes related to the organizational structure and support.
  - Practices: Agile physical setup and agile prioritized in the organization;
  - Results: None;
- Requirements: basic themes related to the definition of the requirements of the software.
  - Practices: Using metaphors;
  - Results: Requirements discovery;

These data show current maturity models differ in structure but, nevertheless, agree on emphasizing software product and people practices. These results are in accordance with the value from the SPI Manifesto [22], which states that software process improvement must involve people actively.

5 Discussion

Previous literature reviews on maturity models for agile software development showed that models structures are diverse, and their validation is still in its early stages [3,13,17,24,25]. These studies also showed that most models are not academically created and, thus, their empirical validity is not confirmed.

We have furthered the analysis of current reviews on maturity models to answer questions regarding their content and their representations of maturity in agile software development. We answered our first question "which are the maturity models proposed for agile software development?", by presenting 14 papers published in academic databases and their diverse structures. Our results confirm previous findings by showing that we are still a long way from getting to a consensus on a path to maturity in agile software development.

We believe, however, that this path to maturity in agile software development might not even be a single standardized one [9]. Recognizing a pattern in the evolution of agile practices and developing a model of maturity based on that might not even be possible, once agile teams usually tailor their development process [9]. Nevertheless, a maturity model seems necessary. We have evidence from previous studies [7] that shows that agile practitioners need guidance for evolvement and want to characterize their agility.

Our second research question investigated what maturity is in agile software development. Maturity models must have an underlying concept of maturity to guide improvements [12]. Nevertheless, we missed a unified view on what maturity is for agile software development. Although previous studies tried to define maturity in agile software development [6], there is still room for empirical studies to theoretically base maturity models in the field.

The third research question we investigated regarded how an assessment is performed with agile software development maturity models. We found evidence that agile academics are divided regarding the way to evaluate agility. On the one hand, ISO/IEC 15504 is an actual standard for software process assessment. On the other hand, there are claims and evidence that assessment in agile software development should be lighter [3,7]. Gren et al. [9] showed that quantitative evaluations in agile software development may not reflect agility. We agree with the authors that there is a trade-off between answering practitioners' need for a measurement tool and creating an in-depth way to characterize agility.

When analyzing the data that answered our last research question, we identified the practices considered mature by the current agile maturity models. Although there is evidence that agile teams tailor their practices and that practices distribution among levels is not a consensus [9], we identified that current models relate mature practices mainly to the software product and to people.

Our results uncover the diversity of possibilities to reach agile maturity. There are different structures, assessment modes, underlying concepts of maturity and mature practices. Nevertheless, some of them converge, showing that the agile maturity model might be not a unique solution to all contexts, but a set of possibilities that should be applied dependent on the organizations' purposes. This conclusion converges to the SPI Manifesto principle that states that software improvement should use dynamic and adaptable models as needed [22].

6 Conclusions

This paper presented a systematic literature review on maturity models for agile software development. Our study showed that models structures, underlying concepts of maturity and assessment modes are still diverse. Nevertheless, current maturity models agree on the practices related maturity. The analysis of the papers showed that we need future studies focusing on:

1. Empirically validating the structure of current approaches: our results on RQ1 showed that there are different models, with different structures and they are not still properly validated. They should be tested through action research to empirically define their application contexts;
2. Testing the context in which different assessment modes should be applied: our analysis on RQ3 showed that different assessment types might be used in agile maturity models. Traditional or lighter assessment modes seem to be needed in different contexts and research should test and show when each one should be used;
3. Creating practical ways to apply existing models in the industry: as the models found in literature are not extensively validated, we need empirical applications to be able to propose industry-friendly models, that respond to agilists needs to light measurements;
4. Theoretically elaborating what maturity is in agile software development: our analysis showed that current models seem to be built over simple observations or combinations of current approaches. We still need a theory that creates a foundation for agile maturity.

References

1. Attride-sterling, J.: Thematic networks: an analytic tool for qualitative research. Qual. Res. **1**, 385–405 (2001). https://doi.org/10.1177/146879410100100307

2. Benefield, R.: Seven dimensions of agile maturity in the global enterprise: a case study. In: Proceedings of the 43rd Hawaii International Conference on System Sciences, Honolulu, HI, pp. 1–7 (2010). https://doi.org/10.1109/HICSS.2010.337
3. Buglione, L.: Light maturity models (LMM): an agile application. In: Proceedings of the 12th International Conference on Product Focused Software Development and Process Improvement, PROFES 2011, June 2011
4. CMMI Product Team. CMMI for Development, Version 1.3 (CMU/SEI-2010-TR-033). Software Engineering Institute, Carnegie Mellon University (2010). http://www.sei.cmu.edu/library/abstracts/reports/10tr033.cfm
5. Dingsoyr, T., Nerur, S., Balijepally, V., Moe, N.B.: A decade of agile methodologies: towards explaining agile software development. J. Syst. Softw. **85**(6), 1213–1221 (2012). https://doi.org/10.1016/j.jss.2012.02.033
6. Fontana, R.M., Fontana, I.M., Garbuio, P.A.R., Reinehr, S., Malucelli, A.: Processes versus people: how should agile software development maturity be defined? J. Syst. Softw. **97**, 140–155 (2014). https://doi.org/10.1016/j.jss.2014.07.030
7. Fontana, R.M., Reinehr, S., Malucelli, A.: Maturing in agile: what is it about? In: Cantone, G., Marchesi, M. (eds.) XP 2014. LNBIP, vol. 179, pp. 94–109. Springer, Cham (2014). https://doi.org/10.1007/978-3-319-06862-6_7
8. Fontana, R.M., Reinehr, S., Malucelli, A.: Agile compass: a tool for identifying maturity in agile software-development teams. IEEE Softw. **32**(6), 20–23 (2015). https://doi.org/10.1109/MS.2015.135
9. Gren, L., Torkar, R., Feldt, R.: The prospects of a quantitative measurement agility: a validation study on an agile maturity model. J. Syst. Softw. **107**, 38–49 (2015). https://doi.org/10.1016/j.jss.2015.05.008
10. ISO/IEC - International Organization for Standardization/ International Electrical Committee. ISO/IEC 33002:2015. Information technology - Process assessment - Requirements for performing process assessment (2015)
11. Kitchenham, B.: Procedures for performing systematic reviews. Keele University, Technical report (2004). http://goo.gl/iJ84Z5
12. Kohlegger, M., Maier, R., Thalmann, S.: Understanding maturity models results of a structured content analysis. In: Proceedings of the I-KNOW 2009 and ISE-MANTICS 2009, 2–4 September 2009. http://goo.gl/hnw7uh
13. Leppänen, M.: A comparative analysis of agile maturity models. In: Pooley, R., et al. (eds.) Information Systems Development: Reflections, Challenges and New Directions, pp. 329–343. Springer, New York (2013). https://doi.org/10.1007/978-1-4614-4951-5_27
14. Lui, K.M., Chan, K.C.C.: A road map for implementing eXtreme programming. In: Li, M., Boehm, B., Osterweil, L.J. (eds.) SPW 2005. LNCS, vol. 3840, pp. 474–481. Springer, Heidelberg (2006). https://doi.org/10.1007/11608035_38
15. Maier, A.M., Moutrie, J., Clarkson, J.: Assessing organizational capabilities: reviewing and guiding the development of maturity grids. IEEE Trans. Eng. Manag. **59**(1), 138–159 (2012). https://doi.org/10.1109/TEM.2010.2077289
16. Nawrocki, J., Walter, B., Wojciedhowski, A.: Toward maturity model for eXtreme programming. In: Proceedings of the 27th Euromicro Conference, pp. 233–239 (2001). https://doi.org/10.1109/EURMIC.2001.952459
17. Ozcan-Top, O., Demirörs, O.: Assessment of agile maturity models: a multiple case study. In: Woronowicz, T., Rout, T., O'Connor, R.V., Dorling, A. (eds.) SPICE 2013. CCIS, vol. 349, pp. 130–141. Springer, Heidelberg (2013). https://doi.org/10.1007/978-3-642-38833-0_12

18. Top, Ö.Ö., Demirörs, O.: Assessing software agility: an exploratory case study. In: Mitasiunas, A., Rout, T., O'Connor, R.V., Dorling, A. (eds.) SPICE 2014. CCIS, vol. 477, pp. 202–213. Springer, Cham (2014). https://doi.org/10.1007/978-3-319-13036-1_18
19. Packlick, J.: The agility maturity map - a goal oriented approach to agile improvement. In: Proceedings of the Agile Conference 2007, 13–17 August, pp. 266–271 (2007). https://doi.org/10.1109/AGILE.2007.55
20. Patel, C., Ramachandran, M.: Agile maturity model (AMM): a software process improvement framework for agile software development practices. Int. J. Softw. Eng. IJSE **2**, 3–28 (2009)
21. Patel, C., Ramachandran, M.: Story card maturity model (SMM): a process improvement framework for agile requirements engineering practices. J. Softw. **4**(5), 422–435 (2009)
22. Pries-Heje, P., Johansen, J.: SPI Manifesto (2010). http://2018.eurospi.net/images/eurospi/spi_manifesto.pdf
23. Qumer, A., Henderson-sellers, B.: A framework to support the evaluation, adoption and improvement of agile methods in practice. J. Syst. Softw. **81**(11), 1899–1919 (2008). https://doi.org/10.1016/j.jss.2007.12.806
24. Schweigert, T., Vohwinkel, D., Korsaa, M., Nevalainen, R., Biro, M.: Agile maturity model: a synopsis as a first step to synthesis. In: McCaffery, F., O'Connor, R.V., Messnarz, R. (eds.) EuroSPI 2013. CCIS, vol. 364, pp. 214–227. Springer, Heidelberg (2013). https://doi.org/10.1007/978-3-642-39179-8_19
25. Schweigert, T., Vohwinkel, D., Korsaa, M., Nevalainen, R., Biro, M.: Agile maturity model: analyzing agile maturity characteristics from the SPICE perspective. J. Softw.: Evol. Process **26**, 513–520 (2014). https://doi.org/10.1002/smr.1617
26. Sidky, A., Arthur, J., Bohner, S.: A disciplined approach to adopting agile practices: the agile adoption framework. Innov. Syst. Softw. Eng. **3**(3), 203–216 (2007). https://doi.org/10.1007/s11334-007-0026-z
27. Silva, F.S., Soares, F.S.F., Peres, A.L., Azevedo, I.M., Vasconcelos, A.P., Kamei, F.K., Meira, S.R.L.: Using CMMI together with agile software development: a systematic review. Inf. Softw. Technol. **58**, 20–43 (2015). https://doi.org/10.1016/j.infsof.2014.09.012
28. Silva, F.S., Soares, F.S.F., Peres, A.L., Azevedo, I.M., Pinto, P.P., Meira, S.R.L.: A reference model for agile quality assurance: combining agile methodologies and maturity models. In: Proceedings of the 9th International Conference on the Quality of Information and Communications Technology, pp. 139–144 (2014). https://doi.org/10.1109/QUATIC.2014.25
29. Soares, F.S.F., Meira, S.R.L.: An agile strategy for implementing CMMI project management practices in software organizations. In: Proceedings of the 10th Iberian Conference on Information Systems and Technologies (CISTI), Portugal, 17–20 June 2015. https://doi.org/10.1109/CISTI.2015.7170402
30. Stojanov, I., Turetken, O., Trienekens, J.J.M.: A maturity model for scaling agile development. In: Proceedings of the 41st Euromicro Conference on Software Engineering and Advanced Applications (2015). https://doi.org/10.1109/SEAA.2015.29

Agile Development and Operation of Complex Systems in Multi-technology and Multi-company Environments: Following a DevOps Approach

Gorka Benguria(✉), Juncal Alonso(✉), Iñaki Etxaniz(✉), Leire Orue-Echevarria(✉), and Marisa Escalante(✉)

TECNALIA, Parque Tecnológico de Bizkaia Ed: 700, 48160 Zamudio, Spain
{Gorka.Benguria, Juncal.Alonso, Inaki.Etxaniz, Leire.Orue-Echevarria, Marisa.Escalante}@tecnalia.com

Abstract. Big innovation and research projects usually require merging contributions form organizations with expertise in different domains. Managing and participating in multi-company projects that use multiple state-of-the-art technologies constitute a challenging activity due to many factors such as integration inexperience, evolving components, tentative requirements, independent teams or independent management centers. In the late nineties and in the early years of 2000, several methodologies arose with the focus on fast releases of working software, commonly known as agile, that aimed to address many of the challenges that this kind of projects face. However, in most cases, these methodologies were not fully adoptable as the automation investment was too high and it was not recoverable during the duration of the project. The global servitization trend and the appearance of approaches, such as DevOps, to support the continuous and fast adjustment of those services to stay in business has also impacted innovation and research projects. On one hand, matured technologies that reduce the automation investment have arisen. On the other hand, whenever it makes sense, services which benefit from the application of DevOps approaches are required to be implemented. This paper explains the implementation of DevOps approaches to support the agile development in the context of innovation and research projects. It also describes two practical implementation cases where such approaches were implemented and how they evolved in the course of the time.

Keywords: DevOps · Continuous integration · Continuous delivery Agile

1 Introduction

Globalization and the increase of competition is pushing organisations to deliver new products and features at increasing rate to stay attractive for their customers base. In the software domain, this implies to be able to faster and more frequent release features to the final users. To increase the releasing capability, software organisations have been

X. Larrucea et al. (Eds.): EuroSPI 2018, CCIS 896, pp. 15–27, 2018.
https://doi.org/10.1007/978-3-319-97925-0_2

forced to adopt DevOps [1, 2] approaches to reduce the time required to develop, integrate, test, and deploy. The DevOps philosophy attempts to use automated systems to bridge the information gap between project team entities (Development and Operations teams) with the main objective of fostering their collaboration in the development and operation stages of a software application [3]. The DevOps philosophy incorporates some principles, methods and practices related with the agile methodologies [4] such as continuous delivery, continuous integration and collaboration.

Agile methodologies [5, 6] have afforded many companies a much-needed tool in the digital era: a collaborative and flexible way to develop software. Considering Agile manifesto [7] as compendium of principles, it can be concluded that they represent an attitude towards change that is common for both Agile and DevOps. In essence, DevOps is Agile applied beyond the software team. A DevOps approach takes agile a step further and applies it beyond the plan, design, build, and test stages of software development to the rest of the software lifecycle: deployment, release, operation, and monitoring [8].

Innovation and research projects usually require involving different organizations with expertise in different areas. The number of organizations is variable depending on the scope and domain of the project (for example, fi-ware project [9] was participated by close to 90 companies), but usually the number varies between five and ten. These organizations work together during years towards a common objective. During that time, a subset of these organizations can be required to work together to produce and validate a software solution that solves a set of needs. This kind of collaboration has some challenges to consider:

- Non-collocated Information Technology (IT) teams from different organizations with different technologies, cultures, languages, working calendars, priorities, quality standards, etc.
- Disperse development effort to be leveraged with research, reporting, dissemination, and other parallel production-oriented activities.
- Tentative requirements, integration inexperience and evolving components.
- Solutions or demonstrations should be repeatable long after the project's end based on commercial or audit requests.

With the global servitization trend, innovation and research projects are required to implement services with similar challenges that match most of the situations given also in projects with distributed teams. This increase the development and operation complexity as it introduces additional requirements to the applications such as servers, domains, networks, platforms, authorization, authentication, certificates, and so on. Fortunately, more and more features of those services are being packaged as easily reusable open source assets, which enable an easier and faster management of that complexity.

Nowadays, provided that the required resources are available, it is feasible and affordable to deploy a service together with its corresponding platform in few minutes. However, a few years ago, this was simply cumbersome.

The current paper presents a DevOps approach implemented in Tecnalia to enable the agile development of applications, especially service oriented ones, in multi-technology and multi-company environments.

2 A DevOps Framework for Agile Development

Agile methodologies include characteristics that make them interesting for innovation and research projects. For example, one of the principles of the agile methodologies is to "Deliver working software frequently, from a couple of weeks to a couple of months, with a preference to the shorter timescale" [7]. This may help in the clarification of tentative requirements and integration approach. Besides, it may also help with the evolution of the components.

But on the other hand, agile methodologies have certain principles that make them incompatible with this kind of projects. For example, the principles related to "Business people and developers must work together daily throughout the project" and "The most efficient and effective method of conveying information to and within a development team is face-to-face conversation" are totally incompatible with the facts that the teams are not collocated and that the effort should be leveraged with other activities.

Therefore, more than establishing a DevOps Framework to enable an agile methodology at project level, our objective was to establish a DevOps Framework that enable the organizations participating in the project to be agile in their own terms.

2.1 DevOps Framework Approach

In the same way that there is no standard definition of DevOps, there is no agreement about what a DevOps framework should consist of. For us, a DevOps framework is a set of tools that facilitate the transition and interactions between the application development and its exploitation.

The DevOps framework that we are currently using in different projects such as OPERANDO [10], CITADEL [11] or DECIDE [12] was not designed as a holistic solution to be applied in all projects of Tecnalia. Indeed, this approach started in OPERANDO based on the lessons learned from a previous project, MOVEUS [13].

MOVEUS [13] was a project in the smart cities domain that provided a set of mobility services that encouraged sustainable transport. In that project, Tecnalia was the partner responsible for the infrastructure. During the development, more than thirty servers were used, some were virtual, some were physical. Servers were split between two environments, integration and piloting. Integration was supported with an on-premise Open Stack cluster for cost constraint requirements, while piloting was supported in AWS [2] for reliability and performance requirements. From that project there were several lessons learned:

- Infrastructure migration can happen, and it will happen several times
- Following the installation guidelines is time consuming, and finding problems is very common
- The domain strategy is important as the number of servers and environments grow
- An improper use of cloud services may generate many expenses
- Non-root users are configured by default with contracting capabilities by AWS
- The virtual machines created using the AWS images cannot be exported later on
- The storage of the application and the demonstrations is an issue in the long term
- Integration infrastructure also requires some reliability

So, when the project OPERANDO started in which Tecnalia was also in charge of the infrastructure, it was decided to change the approach to be able to deal with some of the abovementioned problems. Our principles were as presented next.

The first set of requirements for our framework were to use reliable platforms in all environments, to control the expenses on the selected cloud environments, to support the replication of the platform, and to facilitate the deployment of new features. From those requirements, the first version that included a subset of the components of OPERANDO was developed. From that version and through a very simple process (Fig. 1), the platform continued to evolve.

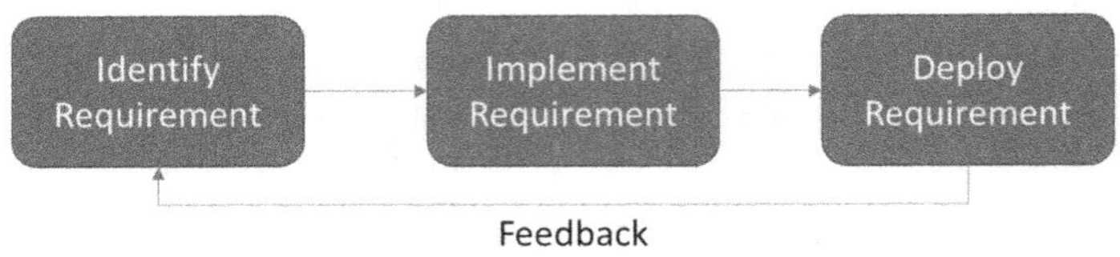

Fig. 1. DevOps framework approach

Most of the changes that had to be performed in a later stage consisted of minor adjustments. Nevertheless, certain changes involved the introduction of new requirements such as adding monitoring capabilities over the framework, supporting guidelines over the platform (with the knowledge necessary to adjust them), supporting pilots or making the infrastructure instantiable to other projects.

2.2 DevOps Framework Configuration Process

The DevOps Framework is adapted to each project following the generic process described in the Fig. 2.

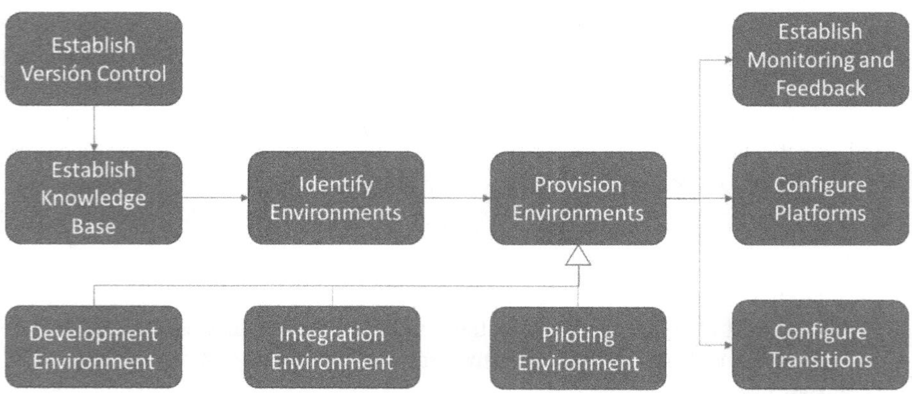

Fig. 2. DevOps framework configuration process

All these activities can be grouped into four categories: Knowledge Management, Environments establishment, Transitions configuration and Feedback Management.

2.3 Knowledge Management

The first set of activities are oriented to ensure that the knowledge of the project is reliably stored and provided in the best way possible to all participants: developers, pilot owners, managers or external contributors.

The main requirement pursued by the knowledge management is to support the replication of the platform. This support should enable, even external people, to replicate the platform from scratch.

The Knowledge management in our approach is made differently depending on the project assets being managed. Application development projects make use of different assets which are subject of storage in the long term. Among others, the following can be cited:

- Code, including configuration, formal specifications, scripts, …
- Sensible information such as access passwords, private certificates, and licenses keys.
- Documents such as guidelines or reports, etc.
- Data for testing, such as anonymized data from pilots.
- External compiled libraries.
- Images of virtual machines and containers.
- Releases.

The Knowledge management in our DevOps framework include two mandatory components: the version control system and the knowledge storage.

The version control system is supported by Git [14]. It is of course possible to use other technologies such as subversion [15] or cvs [16]. However, git was selected because nowadays it is the one that is most widely used (about 87% as demonstrated in the last Stack Overflow Survey [17]). Depending on the project, different Git implementations such as Github [18], BitBucket [19] or Gitlab [20] can be used. Depending on the implementation between external SaaS (Software as a service) [21] or on-premise installation can also be chosen.

The first component in our DevOps framework, the version control system, is used as the communication channel from development to operation. Developers store the code along with the necessary resources for their components in the version control system and the operators retrieve them from there. In addition to that, the version control system is also used to store the code and scripts necessary to quickly build the different environments required to develop and deploy the application.

The second component in our DevOps framework, the knowledge storage, is focused on collecting the guidelines to help project participants during their development and deployment activities. The knowledge storage aims to contain information about how the technologies have been used and configured in order to support all aspects of the application. As a guidelines repository, we require a central content management system with strong search capabilities. With that thought in mind, a WordPress CMS [22] linked to a Solr [23] indexing system to enhance the WordPress searching mechanisms was implemented.

These two mechanisms cover most, but not all, of the assets of an application development project. The remain assets are stored locally. These include sensitive information, big binary data sets for testing, external compiled libraries, images (of virtual machines and containers). However, depending on their relevance to the project additional mechanisms such as keepass [24] for sensible information, or archiva [25] for external libraries, could be established.

2.4 Establishment of Environments

The establishment of environment is another set of activities that needs to be covered. This involves the identification of environments, the configuration of environments and the configuration of platforms.

Development and operation constitute two different environments, but depending on the characteristics of the application, it can make sense to introduce additional environments to ensure aspects such as the interoperability, performance or the behavior in a real environment. Figure 3 shows an example of environments between development and production.

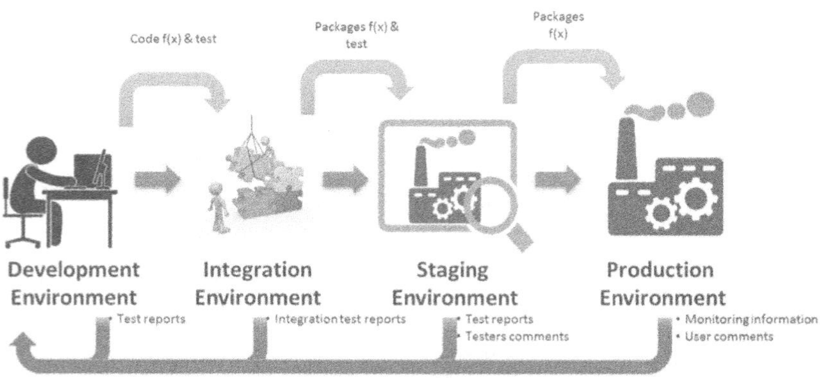

Fig. 3. Environments in an application development

In Innovation and research projects the environments shown above vary slightly. In this case, instead of having staging and production environments, these kinds of projects present a (or several) piloting environment. The current DevOps Framework deployed in Tecnalia provides support in the provisioning of the development, integration and piloting environments.

The support for the development environment is focused on two aspects: speed in setting it up and standardization. The first aspect, speed in setting it up aims to reduce the time required to configure a machine to start with the development. Depending on the complexity, a development environment may require multiple tools, each with different installation and activation procedures. Installing, activating, and configuring them, one by one could take days. Whenever possible, portable and activation independent technologies are prioritized. The objective is to create a folder that contains all the tools required to start working in the project properly configured. This has reduced the development environment setup to less than one hour. Standardization aims to share exactly the same development environment among all the developers with the goal of avoiding the "it works on my machine" syndrome. The portable approach, where we even include the java version, largely reduced this effect among the development environments. Technologies that have been packaged in the development environment for windows 64 bits include eclipse [26], mysql [27], git [18], squirrel [28], nodejs [29], Vagrant [30], Cygwin [31], Maven [32], gradle [33] or notepad ++ [34]. The only installation requirement is VirtualBox [35] but only in case Vagrant is needed.

The support for the integration environment is focused on the assurance that all components can be built and work seamlessly together from scratch. The integration environment is configured in a way that every 24 h, it is reset and all the components built again taking the last version stored in the master branch. After building the components, the environment is able to start all of them automatically and run some integration tests to ensure that they interoperate as expected. For the integration environment, we make use of the Docker [36] technology. Docker is a container technology that allows to simulate multiple independent operating systems over the same machine. This reduces heavily the infrastructure requirements in the integration environments. For instance, in the project MOVEUS previously referred, more than ten servers in AWS were used. This could have been reduced notably if Docker had been used. As a comparison, in OPERANDO only one server with 25 containers is used.

Finally, we have the piloting environment. The support in this environment is focused on the assistance to external companies in the instantiation of the components of the project in their own premises. In previous projects, the transference of the technical developments required getting the compiled libraries somehow and make them work in some preconfigured platform. This was highly error prone. As part of our DevOps Framework we provide two elements: a Docker registry from which the companies can download the last version of the components of the project packaged as Docker images, and a script that configures and runs those Docker images in a Docker server.

Another activity performed in relation to the establishment of the environments has been the configuration of platforms. In innovation and research projects involving multiple companies, components are often programmed with different technologies that require a diverse terrain of platforms. The DevOps framework of Tecnalia includes an increasing set of preconfigured elements to be integrated in different environments, and platforms such as tomcat, mono, nodejs, python [37], mysql, mongodb [38], Hadoop [39], cas [40], ldap [41], liferay [42], jhipster [43], Jenkins [44], …

2.5 Transitions Configuration

Transitions Configuration support the automation of the deployment of new features from the development environment to the operation one. In our DevOps Framework we provide support for the transition between development, integration and piloting.

To support these transitions, we use a continuous integration software and build automation tools. Specifically, as continuous integration software, we use Jenkins and as a build automation tool, we use Maven.

Nevertheless, the focus in our case is on the transition between the development and the integration environments. As shown in Fig. 4, Jenkins includes tasks for the provisioning of pre-requisites to compile the components, tasks to package the components (services and integration tests) as Docker images, tasks to run the services, and tasks to perform the integration tests over the running services.

Fig. 4. Jenkins tasks categories

Each of these Jenkins tasks is specified in a *Jenkinsfile* stored in the version control system (in our case, git). The task is split in stages as shown in Fig. 5 for a task on service package. Among those stages, we can see stages in charge of gathering the source code provided by the developers, stages in charge of gathering the DevOps source code that describe how to build the necessary infrastructure for the component, stages to compile the code, stages to create the Docker image with the platform and with the component, and stages in charge of pushing the created Docker image into the Docker registry for their later use by the pilots.

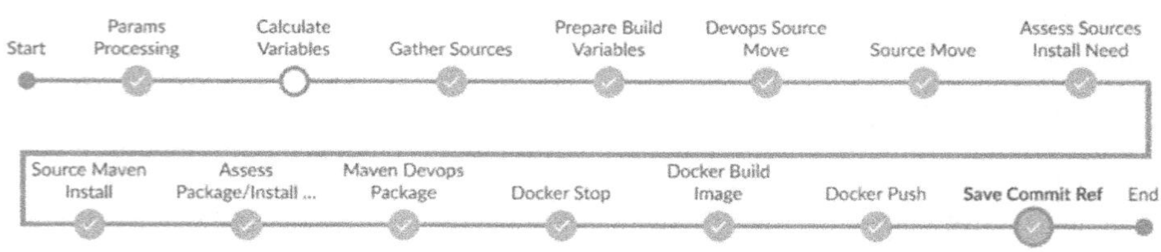

Fig. 5. Jenkins tasks stages

The usage of Maven, apart from building java components, is to fill some gaps or difficulties that we faced with Jenkins. In particular, we use Maven to enable the use of Docker in Jenkins. To save time in the deployment of the DevOps Framework, we decided to use Jenkins packaged in Docker, which is as easy to deploy as:

```
Docker run -p 8080:8080 Jenkins
```

Since we found the installation of a Docker inside so complex, we decided to use the Maven plugin for Docker from frabric4io [45]. Moreover, it facilitated the usage of common properties when instantiating the Docker components such as service end-points. We aggregated all of them in a common Maven project that is referenced in each of the service and integration test running tasks.

2.6 Management of Feedback

The final set of activities are those related with the management of feedback. This covers the collection of information from the different environments. Currently, the support for the management of feedback in our DevOps Framework is limited. Two mechanisms have been implemented: Automatic monitoring mechanisms and a ticket based system to be able collect feedback from testing activities.

Automatic monitoring mechanisms are based on state of practice of monitoring platforms, that collect information about the services running at the integration platform. Figure 6 shows how Nagios is used to monitor the status of the services of the OPERANDO project in the integration platform.

Fig. 6. Nagios monitoring of integration platform

For the ticket based system, different technologies depending on the project and the preferences of the participants are being used. Among others, Jira and GitLab issues.

3 Practical Implementation of DevOps Philosophy in Multi-technology Environments

The DevOps Framework introduced previously has been applied in different projects during the last two years. The DevOps Framework applied in each project present differences taking into consideration the continuous improvement of the platform.

3.1 OPERANDO Ecosystem

OPERANDO project aims to implement and validate an innovative privacy enforcement framework that will enable the Privacy as a Service (PaS) business paradigm and the market for online privacy services.

OPERANDO project is being carried out by nine companies from seven different countries. The architecture requires to leverage technologies such as Back end REST technologies (Jaxrs/Python Flask/Spring), single sign on mechanisms (cas), directory services for access control (ldap), relational databases (Mysql), non-relational databases (e.g. MongoDB), front end technologies (Html 5/css/Javascript/.Net), Reporting frameworks (Birt [46]) or Monitoring Frameworks (Nagios [47]).

The OPERANDO Ecosystem was the first project in which the DevOps Framework was applied. The project duration has been three years and is almost at its closure. We have been applying and adjusting the DevOps Framework for a timeframe of two and a half years. During this period, a lot of feedback and improvement suggestions about the DevOps Framework that has led to some fine-tuning has been acquired. This includes:

- The developer project should not be bothered with DevOps details as DevOps details should be contained in a separate project. i.e.: how the code is packaged in a Docker container.
- During the project, we were required to migrate the integration environment twice. The first time, the migration time needed was two weeks which was acceptable when comparing to MOVEUS, that took several months. In any case, lessons learned were gathered and the migration process improved. The second migration took just a couple of hours.
- Developers require feedback, therefore, we implemented a new profile of observer users to enable them to check the results of their deployment in the integration platform. However, that was not enough as they also required logs access which was later on integrated.
- Developers want to test things quickly. They require a certain degree of control over the integration process to enable them to trigger the compilation process at any time. They also require to be able to take a look inside the component. This is a more complex issue that is currently under analysis.

3.2 CITADEL Ecosystem

CITADEL project is focused on transforming Public Administrations (PAs) to deliver more efficient, inclusive and citizen-centric public services. For this, the project captures data to understand how satisfied citizens are with digital public services, identifies new or unsatisfied needs and allows citizens to take active part in the creation of new public services to increase their uptake.

CITADEL project is composed of eleven organizations from four countries. The architecture requires to leverage technologies such as user registries for citizens, single sign on mechanisms (OpenId Connect), directory services for access control (ldap), front-end technologies (Html 5/css/Javascript), Back-end REST technologies [48] (Jaxrs), databases (Mysql), and Intranet Portals (Liferay) in an integrated set of services, named ecosystem in the jargon of the project.

The duration of the CITADEL project is also three years. We have been applying the DevOps Framework during almost one year. During that period, we have learned some additional lessons that will drive future improvements. These include:

- "it works on my machine" Syndrome also happens between environments; therefore, it could be interesting to bring the real (or almost real) infrastructure to the development environment. We are exploring the usage of Vagrant to enable the instantiation of the integration containers in the developers' machines. This may require powerful development equipment.

- The continuous creation and destruction of Docker images and container leave behind garbage that should be automatically cleared out. Thus, we need garbage collection mechanisms for Docker.
- Development with http to avoid the creation of certificates is bringing more problems than benefits. Therefore, we need to consider certificates when configuring platforms and at the same time, we need to support its creation.
- As we increase the number of independent DevOps Frameworks, we are more in need of a homogeneous and integrable ways to monitor them. For this we are exploring monitoring alternatives such as Grafana [49] that allow to easily define dashboards for each of the frameworks, environments and services.

4 Conclusions and Future Work

The current paper documents practical implementations of the DevOps approach in diverse software-based environments, where multi-disciplinary distributed teams are co-developing and co-deploying software assets (often using immature technologies) to achieve a medium TRL [50] solution (usually TRL 5-6). The peculiarities of these collaborative developments imply several challenges and shortcomings that can be addressed setting up a proper DevOps approach with the corresponding enabling technologies and tools.

The solution proposed by the authors covers the "traditional" DevOps cycle, focusing mainly on the continuous integration, and continuous deployment phases of the Software Development Life Cycle (SDLC). Nevertheless, the advent of cloud-computing offerings, which is witnessing a growing trend by the increasing diversity of cloud service offerings leading to hybrid and multi-cloud infrastructures, are available for complex software applications which can profit from these variaty of offers and features. This new situation opens up a world of possibilities for increasing the efficiency of software applications by selecting a combination of the most appropriate resources on-demand and re-adapting the application on-the-fly to meet the working conditions of the software. The presented DevOps approach, can be therefore, adapted to support this upcoming scenario, where "multi-cloud" based applications can be (re-) adapted, considering their Non-Functional Requirements. This can be achieved trough the extension of the *"traditional"* DevOps cycle in what the authors call *"Extended DevOps"*. The authors will extend the concepts and approach presented in this paper in the context of the DECIDE [12] project which proposes an extension of the "traditional" DevOps approach on the two axis: Dev and Ops.

For the Dev axis, the authors propose to extend the development phase with previous and subsequent activities that cover: (1) the architectural design for multi-cloud applications (at generic level and specific to non-functional requirements), (2) the election of the best deployment configuration based on theoretical simulations. For the Ops axis, the extension will cover: (3) The orchestration of heterogenous cloud resources (4) The continuous re-deployment of software components to maintain the working conditions.

Acknowledgements. The projects leading to this paper have received funding from the European Union's Horizon 2020 research and innovation programme under grant agreements No. 731533, 726755 and 653704.

References

1. DevOps, Wikipedia, 18 April 2018
2. What is DevOps? - Amazon Web Services (AWS), Amazon Web Services, Inc. https://aws.amazon.com/devops/what-is-devops/. Accessed 23 Apr 2018
3. "DevOps" an Extension of Agile Methodology – How It will Impact QA? AFourTech : Software Development Company | Software Testing Services, 25 Apr 2014
4. Navigating DevOps - What it is and why it matters to you and your business (2017)
5. Sutherland, J., Schwaber, K.: The Scrum Papers: Nut, Bolts, and Origins of an Agile Framework, p. 224, April 2012
6. Beck, K.: Extreme Programming Explained: Embrace Change. Addison-Wesley Professional (2000)
7. Beck, K., et al.: Agile Manifesto (2001)
8. DevOps Takes Agile Further - What is DevOps? https://www.bcg.com. https://www.bcg.com/agile/devops/default.aspx. Accessed 19 Apr 2018
9. FI-WARE: Future Internet Core Platform: Project and results. https://cordis.europa.eu/project/rcn/99929_en.html
10. OPERANDO CONSORTIUM. https://www.operando.eu/servizi/notizie/notizie_homepage.aspx. Accessed 19 Apr 2018
11. CITADEL H2020 (2016)
12. Home | DECIDE: Multicloud Applications Towards the Digital Single Market. https://www.decide-h2020.eu/. Accessed 16 Apr 2018
13. MoveUS | ICT cloud-based platform and mobility services available, universal and safe for all users | MoveUS. http://www.moveus-project.eu/. Accessed 19 Apr 2018
14. Git. https://git-scm.com/. Accessed 20 Apr 2018
15. Apache Subversion. https://subversion.apache.org/. Accessed 20 Apr 2018
16. CVS - Open Source Version Control. http://www.nongnu.org/cvs/. Accessed 20 Apr 2018
17. Stack Overflow Developer Survey 2018, Stack Overflow. https://stackoverflow.com/insights/survey/2018/?utm_source=so-owned&utm_medium=social&utm_campaign=dev-survey-2018&utm_content=social-share. Accessed 20 Apr 2018
18. Build software better, together, GitHub. https://github.com. Accessed 20 Apr 2018
19. Bitbucket | The Git solution for professional teams. https://bitbucket.org/. Accessed 20 Apr 2018
20. Gitlab. https://about.gitlab.com/
21. Software as a service, Wikipedia, 10 Apr 2018
22. WordPress. https://en.wordpress.com
23. Apache Solr. http://lucene.apache.org/solr/. Accessed 20 Apr 2018
24. Reichl, D.: KeePass Password Safe. https://keepass.info/. Accessed 20 Apr 2018
25. Archiva – The Build Artifact Repository Manager. https://archiva.apache.org/index.cgi. Accessed 20 Apr 2018
26. Open Innovation Community - Eclipse IDE | The Eclipse Foundation. http://www.eclipse.org/. Accessed 23 Apr 2018
27. MySQL. https://www.mysql.com/. Accessed 23 Apr 2018
28. SQuirreL SQL Client Home Page. http://squirrel-sql.sourceforge.net/. Accessed 23 Apr 2018

29. Node.js Foundation: Node.js, Node.js. https://nodejs.org/en/. Accessed 23 Apr 2018
30. Vagrant by HashiCorp, Vagrant by HashiCorp. https://www.Vagrantup.com/index.html. Accessed 13 Apr 2018
31. Cygwin. http://www.cygwin.com/. Accessed 23 Apr 2018
32. Maven – Welcome to Apache Maven. https://Maven.apache.org/. Accessed 13 Apr 2018
33. Gradle Build Tool. https://gradle.org/. Accessed 23 Apr 2018
34. Notepad++ Home. https://notepad-plus-plus.org/. Accessed 23 Apr 2018
35. Oracle VM VirtualBox. https://www.virtualbox.org/. Accessed 23 Apr 2018
36. Docker, Docker. https://www.Docker.com/. Accessed 11 Apr 2018
37. Welcome to Python.org, Python.org. https://www.python.org/. Accessed 23 Apr 2018
38. MongoDB for GIANT Ideas | MongoDB. https://www.mongodb.com/. Accessed 23 Apr 2018
39. Welcome to ApacheTM Hadoop®! http://hadoop.apache.org/. Accessed 23 Apr 2018
40. CAS | Apereo. https://www.apereo.org/projects/cas. Accessed 11 Apr 2018
41. Lightweight Directory Access Protocol, Wikipedia, 02 April 2018
42. Liferay: Software de experiencia digital adaptado a tus necesidades. https://www.liferay.com/. Accessed 23 Apr 2018
43. JHipster - Generate your Spring Boot + Angular/React applications! https://www.jhipster.tech/. Accessed 23 Apr 2018
44. Jenkins, Jenkins. https://Jenkins.io/index.html
45. Docker-Maven-plugin: Maven plugin for running and creating Docker images. fabric8 (2018)
46. BIRT Home. http://www.eclipse.org/birt/. Accessed 23 Apr 2018
47. Nagios - The Industry Standard In IT Infrastructure Monitoring. https://www.nagios.org/. Accessed 13 Apr 2018
48. Representational state transfer, Wikipedia, 13 April 2018
49. Grafana - The open platform for analytics and monitoring. https://grafana.com/. Accessed 13 Apr 2018
50. Technology readiness level, Wikipedia, 04 April 2018

The Impact of Situational Context on Software Process: A Case Study of a Very Small-Sized Company in the Online Advertising Domain

Görkem Giray[1(✉)], Murat Yilmaz[2], Rory V. O'Connor[3,4], and Paul M. Clarke[3,4]

[1] Kokteyl Corporation, Istanbul, Turkey
gorkem.giray@kokteyl.com
[2] Çankaya University, Ankara, Turkey
myilmaz@cankaya.edu.tr
[3] School of Computing, Dublin City University, Dublin, Ireland
{rory.oconnor,paul.m.clarke}@dcu.ie
[4] Lero – The Irish Software Research Centre, Limerick, Ireland

Abstract. A primary concern of software development is selecting a suitable methodology to implement a software project. However, this selection is affected by many factors, with evidence suggesting that a specific set of factors defines a specific situational context for a project. This situational context leads to a project-specific software process. In this paper, we report on our analysis of a very small-sized company's current software process based on a reference framework that identifies the factors of a situational context. The outcome of our case study confirms the earlier findings that a software process is highly dependent on situational factors. The company has a suitable situational context (such as very small-sized, experienced, skilled, cohesive team with low turnover) to apply agile practices and its software process is more close to an agile rather than plan-driven approach. Moreover, the company is continuously adopting its software process to the situational factors changing from project to project and over time.

Keywords: Software process · Software development process
Situational context · Situational factor · Process selection · Process tailoring

1 Introduction

Central to the entire discipline of software engineering is the concept of software process and the improvement of that process. Therefore, selecting and tailoring a software process plays a critical role that guides the transformation of ideas into software products [1–3]. A software process consists of a set of interrelated practices, each of which is a systematic and repeatable way of achieving a predefined objective [4]. There have been many practices proposed over the last 20 years, each adding some value to software engineering discipline [5]. It has now become a complex problem to tailor a suitable software process for a given specific project. In general, a software

X. Larrucea et al. (Eds.): EuroSPI 2018, CCIS 896, pp. 28–39, 2018.
https://doi.org/10.1007/978-3-319-97925-0_3

process is designed by making some decisions implicitly and using some tacit knowledge [6].

Recently, some efforts have been allocated to make the factors affecting software process explicit [7–9] and associate these factors with the practices selected [10]. A software process depends on many situational factors, which are sometimes interrelated as well. Ensuring the harmonization between a set of situational factors and a software process is a complex problem [11]. To help to solve this problem, some case studies were conducted to understand how some successful organizations achieve this harmonization [12–14]. Moreover, [10] consolidates situational factors and the corresponding software process tailoring actions proposed in software engineering literature.

In this paper, we report on our analysis of a very small-sized software development company in Turkey, named Kokteyl (which resides in Istanbul, Turkey) based on the situational factors reference framework described in Clarke et al. [7]. Software processes of small-sized companies have started to gain interest recently since small and medium sized enterprises dominate software development sector in all countries worldwide. In line with this, ISO/IEC 29110 [15] introduced the term "very small entities," defined as "an enterprise, an organization, a department, or a project having up to 25 people" [16]. According to the Scientific and Technical Research Council of Turkey, half of the software development companies in Turkey have less than 10 employees and 35% of them have 10–50 employees. Our objective is to understand the implicit relationships between the situational factors and the software process adopted by this very small-sized company. By doing so, we aim to contribute to the development of a suite of case studies including commonalities and differences in various types of situational contexts. We believe that such a suite will help to reduce challenges in harmonizing situational context and software process.

Section 2 presents a review of situational factors in the literature. Section 3 briefly discusses the case study research method used in this work. Section 4 presents an overview of the online advertising domain, the case study company operating in this domain, and the current software process of this company. Section 5 provides our analysis of the situational factors that shape the software process of the case study company. Section 6 includes the discussion and threats to validity. Section 7 concludes the paper.

2 Situational Factors

A software development setting is a part of a bigger whole that is made up of human, technologies available for software development, external factors, etc. In such a setting, a software process guides a software development team in translating user needs into a software product [17]. There are many approaches (generally positioned within a plan-driven and agile spectrum nowadays) that form a software process. It is generally accepted that software process is shaped by considering factors which make up the situational context for a project and heavily affects the formation of a software process. Many researchers have remarked the importance of assessing some of these factors as listed in Table 1.

Table 1. A partial list of situational factors identified in the literature.

Factor	Description	References
Team experience	Denotes the degree of team experience	[7, 10, 18, 19]
Team size	Denotes number of members in development team	[7, 10, 18–22]
Management commitment [26]	Denotes the level of commitment of high-level decision makers foe project (such as senior management, project sponsor)	[7, 10, 19]
Feasibility of requirements	Denotes how much feasible to implement requirements are (technologically, economically, etc.)	[7]
Volatility of requirements	Denotes how much requirements are changing during the project	[7, 10, 19, 22]
Criticality	Denotes the impact of failures, such as loss of human life, financial loss, etc.	[7, 10, 18, 20, 22]
Number of stakeholders	Denotes the number of stakeholders in the project	[7, 10, 19]
Stakeholders availability	Denotes how much stakeholders of the project are readily accessible	[7, 10, 19]

Boehm and Turner identify five critical decision factors to have a properly balanced software process in plan-driven and agile spectrum for a specific project [18]. Cockburn proposes three variations of Crystal method family based on the assessment of team size and criticality (magnitude of potential loss) [20]. Xu and Ramesh conducted an empirical study to identify the factors that play a key role in software process tailoring [19]. Ambler and Lines identify eight scaling factors a team may need to address to adapt a software process [21]. Kruchten proposes two sets of factors making up a situational context: organization level and project level factors [22]. Kalus and Kuhrmann built up a catalog of 49 factors [10].

Recently, two of the authors have produced and published an initial reference framework [7] to better guide process designers to tailor project specific processes as well as to understand the underlying decisions behind software process tailoring. The reference framework comprises 44 factors classified into 8 main categories and further elaborated into 170 sub-factors.

Using the reference framework, we have investigated the situational factors affecting the software process in the case study company. We used case study research method, which is briefly explained in the next section.

3 Research Method

The case study method has been proposed as a research method in software engineering to investigate a phenomenon in its real-life context [23]. Yin states that case study method should be used especially when the boundaries between phenomenon and context are not clearly evident [23]. As we stated before, a software process is shaped in a situational context. We consider that a case study [24] is proper research method to build a qualitative understanding of how a software process is shaped in a particular situational context [25]. We have used observation and interview techniques to collect data. We analyzed these qualitative data considering the literature and reported our results. To understand the context of this case study better, the next section briefly presents the domain, the case study company, and the software process currently adopted by the company.

4 Case Study Background

In this section, we present the important concepts of online advertising domain; introduce the case study company and its software products; and explain the software process used in the company.

4.1 Online Advertising Domain

The digital age has provided new ways for organizations for interacting with consumers. With the rise of the Internet along with the increased use of computers and mobile devices; online advertising has become one of the preferred advertising forms. Online advertising is a form of advertising, which uses the Internet to deliver marketing messages to consumers. Figure 1 illustrates the main stakeholders in online advertising domain and the relationships among them.

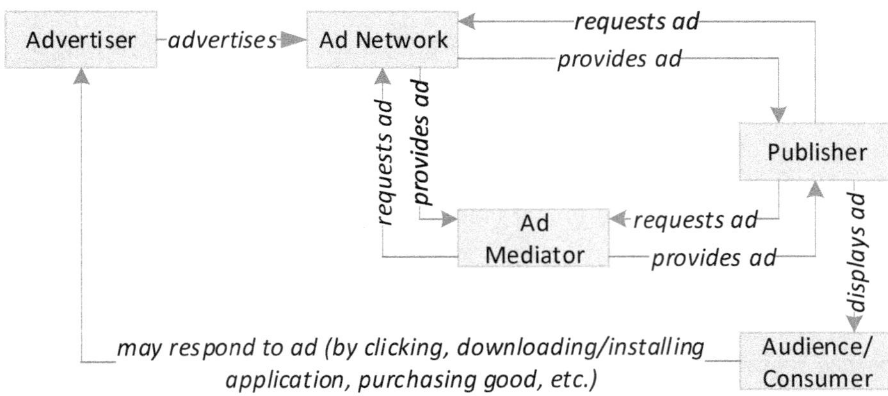

Fig. 1. Main stakeholders in the online advertising domain.

An advertiser is a person, organization or company that places advertisements to communicate a message to audiences/consumers. An ad network aggregates advertisement demand and delivers proper ads to publishers according to their requests. An ad mediator provides access to multiple ad networks (hence multiple ad demand pools) from one central platform. Publishers can maximize revenue by receiving most appropriate ads from a much larger ad demand pool through ad mediators. Moreover, the publisher can increase their fill rate, which denotes the ratio of a number of ad requests in relation to the number of ads provided. From a technical perspective, publishers integrate with only ad mediator's platform and the complexity of integrating with many ad networks is hidden behind ad mediator's platform. A publisher receives ads from ad networks and/or ad mediators and displays ads to audiences/consumers. Common publishers in the online advertisement are web sites and mobile apps. Kokteyl, which is the case study organization in this work, is operating in online advertising domain and is briefly introduced in the next sub-section.

4.2 Case Study Company

Kokteyl is a very small-sized software development company founded in 2002. Shortly after the establishment, they launched a website and a mobile application providing up-to-minute live scores and statistics for football games over the globe. In 2008, they entered to online advertisement sector and started to develop ad mediation software. Moreover, the company is developing and maintaining mobile games. Figure 2 illustrates the software product portfolio of the company.

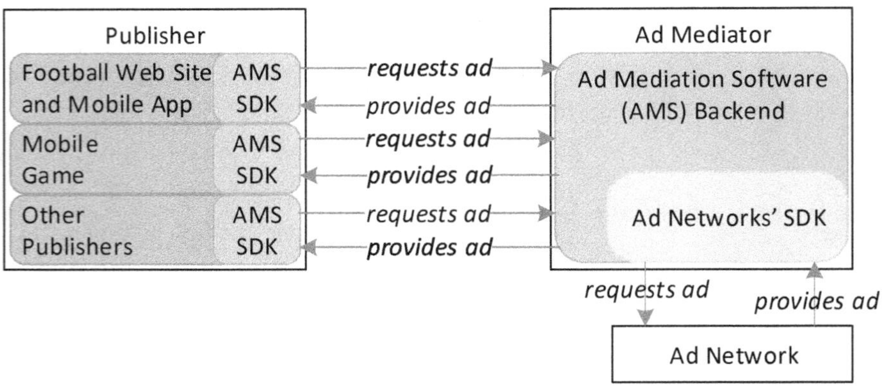

Fig. 2. Company's software product portfolio.

The company owns an ad mediation software (AMS), which has two main components, backend services and an SDK (Software Development Kit) to be integrated with the publisher's software. AMS backend is integrated with more than 40 ad networks through each ad network's SDK. Publishers can receive ads from all of these ad networks only by integrating AMS SDK (one of the benefits of using an ad mediation software as stated above).

The company also developed and maintained a football web site and mobile application with millions of users. A UK-based company has acquired this web site and mobile application in 2016. This football web site and mobile application are still using AMS for displaying ads.

The company also develops and maintains 5 mobile games, which are also publishers for AMS. There is also other publishers' software (which are the customers of Kokteyl) that are using AMS to display ads. As of now, the company's main business is built on AMS. They are trying to convince more publishers with high page views and active users to use AMS. Their revenue is coming from commission fees out of ad revenues of these publishers.

The company employs a software development team, which are organized around two software products as shown in Table 2. Five developers are creating and maintaining AMS backend, including server-side services, data persistency, and report development. 5 developers are developing and maintaining AMS SDK for Android and iOS operating systems. Backend side and mobile app for the games are being developed by 1 and 2 developers respectively and 1 graphic designer is designing the user interfaces for the games. No team member has been assigned to develop football web site and mobile app anymore as a UK-based company acquired them.

Table 2. Team organization per software product.

Software product	Component	Number of team members
AMS	Backend	5 developers
	Android SDK	3 developers
	iOS SDK	2 developers
Mobile games	Backend	1 developer
	Mobile app	2 developers
	UI	1 graphic designer

The team is employing a software process that is more close to agile paradigm (less focus to documentation and more focus to working software; less focus to process and more focus to individuals and collaboration; less focus to plan according to contracts and/or long-term constant requirements) as briefly explained in the next sub-section.

4.3 The Software Process of the Case Study Company

Figure 3 illustrates the software process from eliciting requirements to deployment. For the sake of simplicity, we eliminated the iterative steps and showed the main flow of the process. This process depicts the steps taken for the implementation of one requirement; therefore the company adopts an approach much more close to agile rather than waterfall. The company does not adopt any software process standard.

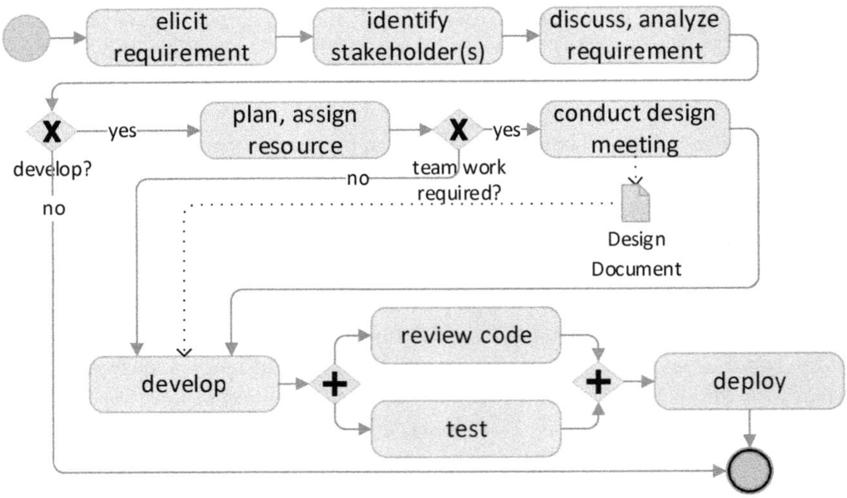

Fig. 3. High-level software process of case study organization.

The details of the process are as follows classified as the main phases of software development:

Requirements Engineering: The members of the team elicit a requirement from customers, competitors' products, and improvement opportunities (mainly from problems) identified by the team. The team leads identify relevant team member(s); discuss and analyze this requirement. If they consider this requirement worth developing, the required resources are assigned; otherwise, the requirement is discarded. The requirements are tracked using a project management tool, Asana, and undergo the following statuses: (1) Ice box: the requirement is not yet decided to be developed and may be discarded; (2) Backlog: the requirement is decided to be implemented; (3) In progress: the requirement is being analyzed and implemented; (4) Test: tests are being conducted; (5) Done: the relevant implementation has been completed.

Design: If the development needs team work rather than one member, a design meeting is conducted. The output of this meeting is a design document, which defines the solution. Moreover, an owner is assigned to this requirement, who takes full responsibility to involve relevant stakeholders based on the analysis and design conducted and follows up the implementation until the end of the deployment.

Development: Relevant members complete development tasks sequentially and/or in parallel.

Test: The team is organized so that there are at least two team members who are responsible for a component and code changes made by a member are reviewed by the corresponding peer. Each member conducts unit, integration, and system tests. User acceptance test is also done within the team. No regression testing practice and test automation are applied.

Deployment: The team prefers a rollout to a small group of users for evaluation and testing. At the first step, the team members receive and start to use the new version. Afterwards, the users of a mobile game (generally 100 s of users) are receiving the new version. When a new version of AMS SDK is being deployed, the evaluation is being made by a restricted pool of users (1000 s of users) of publishers. At the last step, the new version is deployed for all of the users.

The next section analyzes the situational factors that have led the software process explained in this section, using the reference framework [7].

5 Application of Situational Factors Reference Framework

Two techniques have been employed for applying situational factors reference framework to the case study company: (1) Observation; (2) Interview. One of the authors, who is knowledgeable about the situational factors, has worked in the company's office and conducted both silent and interactive observations [26] for 4 days. Occasionally, the author asked questions about the current software process to find out why such a process is being applied. The author also conducted two interviews with 3 team leads. The author introduced the situational factors reference framework to the leads and asked questions to them by using the sub-factors listed in the framework [7]. Table 3 lists the dominant situational factors affecting Kokteyl's software process.

Table 3. Situational factors identified in the case study.

Category	Sub-factors identified in the case study
Personnel	*Team size:* The team consists of 19 members: 13 developers, 2 analysts, 1 project manager, 1 graphic designer, 2 user support personnel
Personnel	*Experience:* The average experience of the team is 7.2 years. The leads/senior members of the team have a working experience of more than 15 years
Personnel	*Skill:* The team is highly skilled in software development. Each of the senior members is specialized in a key area, namely development on Android or iOS, and backend development. These senior members are providing on-the-job training and guidance to the junior members. Moreover, the team is experienced in large-scale data management, distributed computing, and concurrent computing
Personnel	*Cohesion:* The team is working together in an open office and has successfully completed many projects in the past. A newcomer has to complete a trial period in which her/his harmony with the team is observed. As a result, the cohesion of the team is high
Personnel	*Turnover:* Turnover, especially with key developers, is low. 5 developers out of 12 are working in the company for more than 8 years
Organization	*Size:* With around 25 employees Kokteyl is a very small-sized organization. This allows efficient information exchange through conversations and face-to-face meetings

(*continued*)

Table 3. (*continued*)

Category	Sub-factors identified in the case study
Operation	*End users:* All the end users are outside the organization, mobile game users and publishers' owners. The users of AMS (publishers' owners) are strategically much more important than mobile game users since publishers are reaching thousands, millions of users. Some of the users are cooperative while some are demanding
Operation	*Prerequisites:* AMS SDK is integrated with every single mobile application. Its integration should be easy and smooth
Application	*Deployment profile:* When a new version of AMS SDK is ready, all the publishers should adapt their application accordingly and launch a new version. While some publishers update their application quickly, some prefer to stay with the old version for any reason. Therefore, AMS backend and SDK should be backward compatible with a number of old versions, which are still being used by publishers
Application	*Component reuse:* The team prefers to reuse components if its quality has been proved. They try to validate its quality by checking who are using that component and what their comments are. If the references and comments are positive, they validate the component by using it
Application	*Performance:* There is a significant requirement for very high performance from AMS. AMS should respond to thousands of requests per second and the response time should stay in a couple of milliseconds
Business	*Business drivers:* The company's sustainability relies upon mainly the success of AMS, hence most of the efforts are dedicated to the improvement of this product
Business	*Payment arrangements:* The company does not make money by delivering software products based on fixed or time and materials based contracts. The revenue relies on commission fees out of ad revenues of the publishers
Business	*Customer satisfaction:* The strategically important customers are publishers. It is very important to provide high quality software to these publishers since they can easily switch to another as mediation product. Moreover, there are not too many publishers, therefore it is important to try to keep all of them satisfied in order not to lose revenue

6 Discussion

Kokteyl can be considered as a successful very small-sized company since it has been working for software industry for 16 years and managed to develop a software product that has been acquired by a large-scale company based in the UK. Based on this business success, we can conclude that the company has applied a proper software process and managed to adapt it according to changing situational factors. Kokteyl has not designed and adapted its software process using situational factor reference framework explicitly. On the other hand, we can observe that they evaluated many situational factors and selected the proper practices implicitly.

The company does not adopt any process framework (e.g. Scrum), instead a process expert selects a set of practices to tailor a software process close to an agile approach. There are some minor differences between the practices applied by the teams developing AMS and mobile games. While mobile game development team has a fixed release cycle of 4 weeks, AMS development team does not have a fixed release cycle. Since AMS is the software product on which the company's revenue relies on, the team has to respond to new requests and problems very quickly. Therefore, they release a new version of AMS when a significant and urgent change has to be made and deployed. Not fixing the release cycles ensures to keep high customer satisfaction (AMS customers, which are strategically important).

The acquisition of football web site and mobile app by the UK-based company is an important development that has affected some of the situational factors. The company used to be a publisher with a very high traffic and was making money from publishing ads. The team was focused on developing a web site and a mobile app. They were neglecting regression testing and test automation because of their overhead. When a problem is observed, they were fixing it by updating the web site and/or sending a new version of the mobile app to the relevant store. With the AMS, the deployment has become a two-step process whose second part is done by publishers. When a new version of AMS is released, all the publishers should update their applications by including the new AMS SDK. Therefore, Kokteyl started to assess including regression testing in their software process. To decrease the overhead of regression testing, test automation is also being considered.

The customers of the football web site and mobile app used to be satisfied by providing data timely along with a good user experience. On the other hand, the development of AMS requires the design of complex algorithms whose outputs cannot be validated precisely. The team tracks realized revenues to try to understand whether they have improved an algorithm. Design of such algorithms is related to recent research areas, such as machine learning. Therefore, the team considers to include practices regarding research and development in their software.

The situational factors identified during this case study are already included in the situational factors reference framework. This is an additional evidence on the wide coverage of this framework. On the other hand, it does not seem to be practically possible to have a complete framework on situational factors, as pointed out in [7, 10]. We aim to conduct more case studies in various sectors and try to extend the framework and improve the content, language, and structure. In addition, we can also provide scales to evaluate situational factors, such as creating a taxonomy of organization size along with intervals (i.e. very small organizations have less than 25 employees). Moreover, adding the associations between situational factors and software development processes to the framework would contribute to software engineering discipline. Such associations would especially contribute to situational method engineering discipline, whose objective is creating a software process for a specific situation [27].

Our discussion is subject to some validity threats, which are briefly described. During the data collection, we used one researcher who has conducted observations and interviews. Although we tried to mitigate this threat by crosschecking observation and interview outputs and prolonged involvement [24] (by making several visits to the case study company), there is still a potential risk that a single researcher can draw wrong conclusions. Regarding external validity, it is not possible to generalize the findings based on just this one case study. To reduce the impact of this threat, we evaluated the findings based on the literature and other case studies to explore some common patterns.

7 Conclusions and Future Work

To investigate how companies design a project-specific software process, we conducted a case study in a very small-sized software development company, named Kokteyl, in Istanbul, Turkey. The company does not adopt any process framework or standard. We have observed that they have formed a suitable software process based on the situational context the company and its projects reside. There are also some differences between the software processes used for different projects. We have identified that these differences are based on the situational factors identified in the literature [7, 10]. Moreover, the company constantly fine-tunes its software process based on the changes in the situational factors.

Further work is required to confirm and validate these findings. To this end we propose the following: (1) we will continue to conduct such case studies to form a suite of case studies to help practitioners in reducing challenges in harmonizing situational context and software process; (2) we plan to guide Kokteyl for improving their company-wide a research and development skills by analyzing changes in situational factors and proposing corresponding actions for adopting the software process accordingly.

References

1. MacCormack, A., Verganti, R.: Managing the sources of uncertainty: matching process and context in software development. J. Prod. Innov. Manag. **20**, 217–232 (2003)
2. Jones, C.: Development practices for small software applications. CrossTalk J. Defense Softw. Eng. **21**(2), 9–13 (2008)
3. Rong, G., Boehm, B., Kuhrmann, M., Tian, E., Lian, S., Richardson, I.: Towards context-specific software process selection, tailoring, and composition. In: Proceedings of the 2014 International Conference on Software and System Process (ICSSP 2014), pp. 183–184. ACM, New York (2014)
4. Jacobson, I., Ng, P.W., McMahon, P.E., Spence, I., Lidman, S.: The Essence of Software Engineering: Applying the SEMAT Kernel. Addison-Wesley Professional (2013)
5. Kennaley, K.: SDLC 3.0: Beyond a Tacit Understanding of Agile. Fourth Medium Press, (2010)
6. Ryan, S., O'Connor, R.V.: Acquiring and sharing tacit knowledge in software development teams: an empirical study. Inf. Softw. Technol. **55**, 1614–1624 (2013)
7. Clarke, P., O'Connor, R.V.: The situational factors that affect the software development process: towards a comprehensive reference framework. J. Inf. Softw. Technol. **54**(5), 433–447 (2012)

8. Jeners, S., O'Connor, R.V., Clarke, P., Lichter, H., Lepmets, M., Buglione, L.: Harnessing software development contexts to inform software process selection decisions. Softw. Q. Prof. **16**, 35–36 (2013)
9. Ng, P., Huang, S., Wu, Y.: On the value of essence to software engineering research: a preliminary study. In: 2nd SEMAT Workshop on a General Theory of Software Engineering (GTSE 2013), pp. 51–58 (2013)
10. Kalus, G., Kuhrmann, M.: Criteria for software process tailoring: a systematic review. In: Proceedings of the 2013 International Conference on Software and System Process - ICSSP 2013, pp. 171–180. ACM Press, New York (2013)
11. Clarke, P., O'Connor, R.V., Leavy, B.: A complexity theory viewpoint on the software development process and situational context. In: Proceedings of the 2016 International Conference on Software and System Process (ICSSP 2016) (2016)
12. Marks, G., O'Connor, R.V., Clarke, P.M.: The impact of situational context on the software development process – a case study of a highly innovative start-up organization. In: Mas, A., Mesquida, A., O'Connor, R.V., Rout, T., Dorling, A. (eds.) SPICE 2017. CCIS, vol. 770, pp. 455–466. Springer, Cham (2017). https://doi.org/10.1007/978-3-319-67383-7_33
13. Clarke, P.M., et al.: Exploring software process variation arising from differences in situational context. EuroSPI **748**, 29–42 (2017)
14. O'Connor, R.V., Elger, P., Clarke, P.M.: Exploring the impact of situational context – a case study of a software development process for a microservices architecture. In: Proceedings of the International Workshop on Software and Systems Process – ICSSP 2016, pp. 6–10 (2016)
15. O'Connor, R.V., Laporte, C.: The evolution of the ISO/IEC 29110 set of standards and guides. Int. J. Inf. Technol. Syst. Approach **10**(1), 1–21 (2017)
16. Larrucea, X., O'Connor, R.V., Colomo-Palacios, R., Laporte, C.Y.: Software process improvement in very small organizations. IEEE Softw. **33**(2), 85–89 (2016)
17. Systems and software engineering –Vocabulary, ISO/IEC/IEEE 24765:2010(E) (2010)
18. Boehm, B., Turner, R.: Observations on balancing discipline and agility. In: Agile Development Conference, pp. 32–39 (2003)
19. Xu, P., Ramesh, B.: Using process tailoring to manage software development challenges. IT Prof. **10**(4), 39–45 (2008)
20. Cockburn, A.: Crystal Clear A Human-Powered Methodology for Small Teams. Addison Wesley Professional (2004)
21. Ambler, S.W., Lines, M.: Disciplined Agile Delivery: A Practitioner's Guide to Agile Software Delivery in the Enterprise, 1st edn. IBM Press (2012)
22. Kruchten, P.: Contextualizing agile software development. J. Softw.: Evol. Process **25**(4), 351–361 (2013)
23. Yin, R.K.: Case Study Research - Design and Methods. SAGE Publications (2003)
24. Runeson, P., Host, M., Rainer, A., Regnell, B.: Case Study Research in Software Engineering: Guidelines and Examples, 1st edn. Wiley Publishing (2012)
25. O'Connor, R.V.: Using grounded theory coding mechanisms to analyze case study and focus group data in the context of software process research. In: Mora, M., Gelman, O., Steenkamp, A., Raisinghani M. (eds.) Research Methodologies, Innovations and Philosophies in Software Systems Engineering and Information Systems, chap. 13, pp. 1627–1645. IGI Global (2012)
26. Basri, S., O'Connor, R.: Organizational commitment towards software process improvement an irish software VSEs case study. In: Proceedings of 4th International Symposium on Information Technology 2010 (ITSim 2010), Malaysia, June 2010
27. Henderson-Sellers, B., Ralyté, J., Ågerfalk, P., Rossi, M.: Situational Method Engineering. Springer, Heidelberg (2014). https://doi.org/10.1007/978-3-642-41467-1

SPI and Safety Testing

From Certifications to International Standards in Software Testing: Mapping from ISQTB to ISO/IEC/IEEE 29119-2

Mary-Luz Sánchez-Gordón and Ricardo Colomo-Palacios(✉)

Østfold University College, 1757 Halden, Norway
{mary.sanchez-gordon, ricardo.colomo-palacios}@hiof.no

Abstract. In today's software development industry, software testing allows one to ensure the quality but it cannot be done exhaustively and it requires selective and careful planning. That means a test process which is not only time-consuming but also useful and crucial because today, more than ever software is becoming part of our personal and professional life. Software testing is gradually gaining relevance among software practitioners and researchers. Due to that, several organizations, which offer personal certifications, have emerged and international standards have been developed. However, there is still a need to support software practitioners in gaining awareness and understanding about them. The aim of this study is to perform a mapping from all major activities of ISTQB Foundation Level Certification (CTFL), to corresponding processes of ISO/IEC/IEEE 29119-2. Thus an analysis has performed to identify the differences and overlap between the two approaches, which allows a better understanding of them. The findings show that the test process of ISTQB CTFL is largely covered by the ISO/IEC/IEEE 29119-2. In addition, a tailored conformance was also outlined to ISO/IEC/IEEE 29119-2.

Keywords: Software testing · ISTQB CTFL · ISO/IEC/IEEE 29119
Mapping

1 Introduction

Today, software is ubiquitous —software is everywhere— [1, 2]. Software is affecting all aspects of our personal and professional life [3]. As a consequence, software testing has become a mandatory part of software development [4]. Its importance is widely recognized [5, 6] and there is a growing concern in how to improve the accomplishment of this process [7]. Over the time, practitioners have been forced to develop and adopt better testing practices software due to code's rising size and complexity, greater demands regarding development speed and agility, increased heterogeneity and geographic distribution of software teams and their components [4]. Beginning in the early 1970 s, the level of professionalism associated with software testing was gradually increased [8] until "Software Tester" became a profession and special qualification schemes have been emerged (e.g. ISTQB, see Table 1). Regarding standards of software testing, there was a gap because they were either partial (such as ones proposed by IEEE and BSI) or were specific to particular and highly regulated sectors (such as ones

X. Larrucea et al. (Eds.): EuroSPI 2018, CCIS 896, pp. 43–55, 2018.
https://doi.org/10.1007/978-3-319-97925-0_4

related to aviation or health). This gap is intended to be covered by ISO/IEC 29119 Software Testing standard [9], which was published in 2013 and closely-supported by IEEE and BSI. Another standard that is relevant and defined specifically for ISO/IEC 29119-2 is ISO/IEC 33063 Process Assessment Model for Software Testing [10]. Additionally, a number of approaches has been specifically developed for that purpose but many of them have been adapted or extended from Test Maturity Model integration (TMMi) and/or Test Process Improvement (TPI) [11, 12]. Among the approaches that used other models, Test Spice deserves to be mentioned because it conforms to the ISO/IEC 15504 [13].

Despite decades of work by researchers and practitioners, test management (encompasses activities related to test management, e.g., planning, control, monitoring, etc.) had been reported by practitioners as a big challenge [5], and one of the areas of most importance to the practitioners, which requires further research [5, 6]. Although there are already available mappings, —such as ISO/IEC 12207:2008 to ISO/IEC/IEEE 29119-2 mapping [9] and a complete mapping between ISO-29119-2 and TMMi [14] — as far as the authors know, none of them are not focused on understanding the better of two worlds: personal certifications and international standards in software testing. Therefore, this paper aims to contribute to fill this research gap by presenting results of a process mapping study between the well-known ISTQB Certification and the ISO/IEC/IEEE 29110 standard. The authors targeted this study only for the software testing process by delimiting an adequate scope.

The remainder of this paper is structured as follows: Sect. 2 presents the background of this study and the ISO 29119 and ISTQB CTFL. In Sect. 3 authors outlines the research method and report on the results of the mapping while Sect. 4 summarizes a conclusion and future research.

2 Background

2.1 Certifications

Due to the growing importance of professionalism in software testing several organizations, which offer certifications, have emerged such as QAI Global Institute, American Society for Quality, International Software Quality Institute, International Software Testing Qualification Board, and International Institute for Software Testing (see Table 1). However, one of them has been gaining popularity among practitioner: ISTQB. According to its website, as of December 2016 the ISTQB certification is becoming popular in the global scale, having over 740,000 exams and issued more than 535,000 certifications in over 120 countries world-wide. This certification schema considers three levels: foundation [15], advanced [16] and expert [17].

Table 1. Software testing certifications.

Organization	Certifications
QAI Global Institute	Certified Associate in Software Testing (CAST) Certified Software Tester (CSTE) Certified Manager of Software Testing (CMST)
American Society for Quality (ASQ)	Certified Software Quality Engineer (CSQE) Quality Assurance Management Professional (QAMP)
International Software Quality Institute (iSQI)	Certified Agile Tester (CAT) Certified Agile Test Driven Development Mobile App Testing - Foundation Level (CMAP) CMAP Mobile App Test Automation CMAP Mobile App Performance Testing
International Software Testing Qualification Board (ISTQB)	Foundation Level and its extensions (Agile Tester, Model-Based Tester) Advanced Level (Test Manager, Test Analyst, Technical Test Analyst, Security tester, Test Automation Engineer) Expert Level (Improving Test Process, Test Management)
International Institute for Software Testing (IIST)	Professional Testing Certifications (CSTP) Agile Testing Certifications (CASTP) Test Automation Certification (CSTAS) Test Manager Certifications (CSTL) Mobile Test Certifications (CMSTP) Quality Management Certifications (CSQM)
European Certification & Qualification Association (ECQA)	Provisional Assessor TestSPICE Competent Assessor TestSPICE

2.2 ISTQB Fundamental Test Process

The ISTQB is a world-wide organization widely accepted among practitioners which provides a fundamental test process. The following briefly describes the fundamental test process [15]: planning and control; analysis and design; implementation and execution; evaluating exit criteria and reporting; and test closure activities.

- Test planning is the activity of defining the objectives of testing and the specification of test activities in order to meet the objectives and mission. Test planning takes into account the feedback from monitoring and control activities. Test control is the ongoing activity of comparing actual progress against the plan, and reporting the status, including gaps.
- Test analysis and design is the activity in which general testing objectives are transformed into tangible test conditions and test cases. The first task is to review the specification of what should be tested. The specification should be concrete and clear enough to develop test cases and test procedures. Other key tasks are to evaluate testability of the requirements and system, and design the test environment.
- Tests implementation and execution is the activity where test procedures or scripts are specified by combining the cases in a particular order and including any other

information needed for test execution. Furthermore, the environment is set up and the tests are run.

- Evaluating exit criteria is the activity where test execution is assessed against the defined objectives. Exit criteria should be set and evaluated for each test level. Finally, a test summary report for stakeholders should be written.
- Test closure activities collect data from completed test activities to consolidate experience, including checking and filing testware, facts and numbers. For instance, when a particular milestone is achieved or when software system is released.

These activities in the test process may overlap. Testing also comprises reviewing documents (including source code) and carrying out static analysis.

2.3 ISO/IEC/IEEE 29119

The aim of ISO/IEC/IEEE 29119 is to define a generic process model for software testing that can be used within any software development life cycle [9]. The model specifies test processes that can be used to govern, manage and implement software testing in any organization, project or testing activity. Currently, there are five parts but this study is focused in the second part (29119-2-2013). It describes the software testing process that is composed of several layers; the top layer is the Organizational Test Process Level, which defines the testing policy and the testing strategy of the entire organization. The second layer is the Test Management Processes, which defines the test activities in projects. On this level, test plans are defined and maintained based on the given organization level policies and strategies. The last level is the Dynamic Test Processes, which defines the actual testing work [18].

3 Method: Mapping

This section outlines the research method implemented for this study. Model mapping or gap analysis is the key component of the proposed approach. An understanding of the differences between the models involved in the assessment is a must-have to conduct a complete assessment and get valuable results. Thus, a mapping allows the detection of differences and similarities between these approaches. Two researchers were involved in this study and discussed the reliability threats early in the design phase and agreed on the procedure, considering activities to mitigate the effect of one researcher's bias. Consequently, an protocol was adapted from the guidelines proposed by Baldassarre et al. approach [19], it is also worthy to note that the guidelines had been followed in previous studies [20–22].

The protocol describes the plan for the review and ensures that the study is undertaken as planned while reduces the possibility of researcher bias. It includes the steps of: (1) Analyze the models; (2) Design the mapping; (3) Carry out the mapping; (4) Present the outcomes and analyze the results. In what follows, the mapping performed is described using the method provided.

3.1 Models Analysis

The first activity is to analyze each reference model involved in a mapping process. ISTQB CTFL and ISO/IEC/IEEE 29119 were chosen for this study based on their relevance. Both of them were studied in detail and an overview of them is described in the background section of this paper.

3.2 Mapping Design

The purpose is to perform a step-by-step comparison and a mapping of the reference models. To do that, authors carried out the following activities:

1. Identification of elements to be compared: all major tasks of ISTQB CTFL, and the clauses of each requirement of ISO/IEC/IEEE 29119-2 standard. There are a different number of clauses by requirement, e.g. 6.2.4.1 in Table 2 has four clauses (a, b, c and d) and 7.2.4.1 has only three (a, b and c).
2. Direction of the comparison: The direction is from ISTQB CTFL to ISO/IEC/IEEE 29119-2.
3. Comparison scale definition: The scale has been used in previous works [19, 20]. It contains the following four elements: strongly, partially, weakly and non-related.
   - Strongly related (●), the process is especially named in the standards and the process has many concepts in common and many of them have the same process steps.
   - Partially related (◑), the process is not especially named, but there are one or more activities in the standard which lead to the implementation of the process defined in the other standard.
   - Weakly related (◔), the process is not especially named, but there is a process or a process concept which can/should be adapted in an activity in the other standard.
   - Non-related (○), no relationship can be identified.
4. Comparison template definition: All these values are analyzed and checked from a holistic point of view and authors determine to what extent ISO/IEC/IEEE 29119-2 activities and tasks are fulfilled.

3.3 Mapping Execution

This mapping is an iterative process in which authors analyze the ISTQB process against ISO/IEC/IEEE 29119 process. The first step to do when comparing both processes is to map their basic, constituent components. For each process all activities are studied. The objective is not to set a naïve approach between activities' names. In this mapping, authors also analyze whether specific activities and task are also met. In order to carry out the mapping, a first high level relationship between the reference models is defined. Then, a drilling down process analyzing in detail these relationships helps the authors to identify fine grained relationships. In order to check the consistency of the results, a test-retest approach and re-evaluation were carried out as well. All these mapping are managed by using several spreadsheets where ISTQB activities are displayed as rows, and ISO/IEC/IEEE 29119 clauses are displayed as columns. However, due to the limited space of this paper, the outcomes are presented in five tables (see Tables 2, 3, 4, 5 and 6) where each of them is represented one of the ISTQB activities and their tasks are described in the text but not displayed in the table.

3.4 Outcomes

Coverage of Testing Practices. As already stated above, a detailed and extensive study has been performed. The first step in the study was done starting from the test processes defined by ISTQB CTFL and trying to find a corresponding layer within ISO/IEC/IEEE 29119. Figure 1 shows the layers of the test process model which include varying numbers of test process. Certainly, finding a corresponding process does not imply they provide the same level of coverage on test practices, but it can be a good first step towards comparing both processes and provides a structure for subsequent studies to be carried out. Figure 1 provides an overview of ISTQB fundamental process to ISO/IEC/IEEE 29119-2 high-level mapping. The five activities of ISTQB fundamental process are drawn-up in the middle section and the corresponding process of ISO/IEC/IEEE 29119-2, are provided (with arrows) in gray on the left and right side.

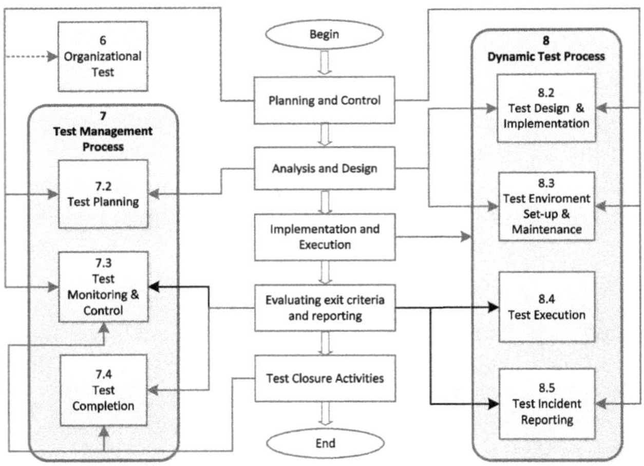

Fig. 1. ISTQB CTFL to ISO/IEC/IEEE 29119-2 high-level mapping.

Figure 1 shows an important finding regarding coverage relationship (arrows). Basically, the layers of Test Management and Dynamic Test (ISO/IEC 29119-2 standard) are required to provide coverage of the ISTQB CTFL. The clauses of the Organizational Test Process of ISO/IEC 29119-2 are hardly dealt with within ISTQB CTFL. The aim of the Organizational Test Process is to define a process for the creation and maintenance of organizational test specifications, such as organizational test policies, strategies, processes, procedures and other assets. One can therefore conclude that ISTQB CTFL does not address test practices at this layer but one of the tasks of the test leader in its syllabus points out "write or review a test strategy for the project, and test policy for the organization". Therefore, Planning and Control is very weakly related to ISO/IEC 29119-2 (dotted line) and the scope of ISTQB is fundamentally limited to Test Management and Dynamic Test.

ISTQB CTFL is largely covered by the ISO/IEC 29119-2. Consequently, a more detailed analysis was carried out. The analysis was extended to a study on the level of detailed test practices. Just having a corresponding ISTQB CTFL process does not mean that all clauses and requirements (i.e. shall statements) of ISO/IEC 29119-2 are covered by ISTQB CTFL process. The study of the five activities of the fundamental test process within ISTQB CTFL is described in more detail in what follows.

Planning and Control. Table 2 presents the "Planning and Control" to ISO/IEC/IEEE 29119-2 mapping. This activity, which is defined in Chapter 5 of ISTQB CTFL syllabus, includes six major sections: "Test Organization", "Test Planning and Estimation", "Test Progress Monitoring and Control", "Configuration Management", "Risk and Testing" and "Incident Management". Each of them is described below.

Table 2. Planning and control (ISTQB) to ISO/IEC/IEEE 29119-2 mapping

ISO/IEC/IEEE 29119-2 clause		a	b	c	d	e	f	g	h	i	J
6.2.4.1	Develop organizational test specification	○	◔	○	○						
7.2.4.1	Understand context	●	◑	○							
7.2.4.2	Organize test plan development	●	○	○	○						
7.2.4.3	Identify and analyze risks	●	●	●	●	●	●				
7.2.4.4	Identify risk mitigation approaches	◑	●								
7.2.4.5	Design test strategy	◑	◑	●	●	○	◑	◑	◑	○	○
7.2.4.6	Determine staffing and scheduling	◑	●	○							
7.2.4.8	Gain consensus on test plan	●	○	○	○						
7.3.4.1	Set-up	◑	◑	◑							
7.3.4.2	Monitor	●	●	◑	◑	○					
7.3.4.3	Control	●	○	●	◑	○	○	○	○		
7.3.4.4	Report	◔	○								
8.2.4.3	Derive test coverage items	◑	○	○	◑						
8.3.4.1	Establish test environment	◑	◔	○							
8.5.4.1	Analyze test results	◑	●	◑							
8.5.4.2	Create/update incident report	●	●								

"Test Organization" is strongly related to 7.2.4.5 Design Test Strategy (d) and it is very weakly related to 6.2.4.1 Develop Organizational Test Specification (b), as already mentioned in the Sect. 3.4. Moreover, "Test Organization" indicated that "...the effectiveness of finding defects by testing and reviews can be improved by using independent testers..." and it provides options for independence but this approach is not contemplated within the ISO/IEC 29119-2 standard.

"Test Planning" is strongly related to 7.2.4.1 Understand Context (a). The above is also supported by the next two sentences within ISTQB CTFL syllabus: "… tailoring these main activities within the context of the system and the project is usually required" and "Principle 6 Testing is context dependent". Furthermore, "The Psychology of Testing" within ISTQB CTFL syllabus points out that "… People tend to align their plans with the objectives set by management and other stakeholders, for example, to find defects or to confirm that software meets its objectives. Therefore, it is important to clearly state the objectives of testing". In consequence, it is strongly related to 7.2.4.8 Gain Consensus on Test Plan (a) and it is partially related to 7.2.4.1 Understand Context (b). Additionally, "Test Organization" highlights tasks of the Test Leader and Tester and "Test Planning Activities" states that "… making decisions about what to test, what to test, what roles will perform the test activities, how the test activities should be done, and how the test results will be evaluated" therefore it is partially related to 7.2.4.6 Determine Staffing and Scheduling (a) and, when considering "Entry Criteria and Exit Criteria", it was found that it is strongly related to 7.2.4.2 Organize Test Plan Development (a) as well.

"Test Planning and Estimation" is partially related to 7.2.4.5 Design Test Strategy (a) and it is strongly related to 7.2.4.6 Determine Staffing and Scheduling (b). Likewise, "Test Strategy, Test approach" is strongly related to 7.2.4.5 Design Test Strategy (c) and it is partially related to 7.2.4.5 Design Test Strategy (f and h).

"Test Progress Monitoring and Control" is strongly related to 7.3.4.2 Monitor (a and b) and 7.3.4.3 Control (a and c). It is also partially related to 7.3.4.1 Set-Up (a, b and c), 7.3.4.2 Monitor (c) and 8.2.4.3 Derive Test Coverage Items (a). And it is weakly related to 7.3.4.4 Report (a).

"Configuration Management" is partially related to 8.3.4.1 Establish Test Environment (a) and it is weakly related to 8.3.4.1 Establish Test Environment (b). In turn, "Incident Management" is strongly related to 8.5.4.1 Analyze Test Results (b) and it is partially related to 8.5.4.1 Analyze Test Results (a and c). And it is also strongly related to 8.5.4.2 Create/Update Incident Report (a and b).

"Risk and Testing" is strongly related to 7.2.4.3 Identify and Analyze Risks (a, b, c, d, e and f) and 7.2.4.4 Identify Risk Mitigation Approaches (b), while it is partially related to 7.2.4.4 Identify Risk Mitigation Approaches (a) and 7.2.4.5 Design Test Strategy (b). It is also weakly related to 7.3.4.2 Monitor (d) and 7.3.4.3 Control (d).

Furthermore, the test development process of ISTQB CTFL syllabus points out that "… can be done in different ways, from very informal with little or no documentation, to very formal …" and "… establishing traceability from test conditions back to specifications and requirements enables both effective impact analysis when requirements change, and determining requirements coverage for a set of test…", that means it is partially related to 7.2.4.5 Design Test Strategy (g) and 8.2.4.3 Derive Test Coverage Items (d), respectively.

Test Analysis and Design. This activity has seven major tasks. Only one of them "evaluating testability of the test basis and test objects" is apparently non-related to any particular clause within the ISO/IEC/IEEE 29119-2 because the term "testability" is not made explicit on it. However, it could be achieved by the ways that the requirements of ISO/IEC/IEEE 29119-2 standard are fulfilling.

Table 3. Test analysis and design (ISTQB) to ISO/IEC/IEEE 29119-2 mapping.

ISO/IEC/IEEE 29119-2 clause		a	b	c	d	E	f	g	h	i	j
7.2.4.5	Design test strategy	○	○	○	○	●	○	○	○	○	○
8.2.4.1	Identify feature sets	●	○	○	○	○	○				
8.2.4.2	Derive test conditions	◑	◑	●	○	○					
8.2.4.4	Derive test cases	◑	◑	●	◑	○					
8.2.4.6	Derive test procedures	○	◑	○	○	○	○				
8.3.4.1	Establish test environment	●	○	○							

The tasks "Reviewing the test basis (such as requirements, software integrity level* (risk level), risk analysis reports, architecture, design, interface specifications)" and "Designing the test environment set-up and identifying any required infrastructure and tools" are strongly related to 8.2.4.1 Identify Feature Sets (a) and 8.3.4.1 Establish Test Environment (a). Likewise, the task "Identifying necessary test data to support the test conditions and test cases" is linked with four requirements: one of them is strongly related to 7.2.4.5 Design Test Strategy (e), two of them is partially related to 8.2.4.4 Derive Test Cases (a) and the 8.2.4.6 Derive Test Procedures (b), and the last task is strongly related to 8.3.4.1 Establish Test Environment (a). While, the task "Identifying and prioritizing test conditions based on analysis of test items, the specification, behaviour and structure of software" is partially related to 8.2.4.2 Derive Test Conditions (a and b). In turn, "Creating bi-directional traceability between test basis and test cases" is partially related to 8.2.4.4 Derive Test Cases (d) and "Designing and prioritizing high level test cases" is partially related to 8.2.4.4 Derive Test Cases (a and b) as well. According to ISTQB "…the 'Standard for Software Test Documentation' (IEEE STD 829-1998) describes the content of test design specifications (containing test conditions) and test case specifications" therefore it is strongly related to 8.2.4.2 Derive Test Conditions (c) and 8.2.4.4 Derive Test Cases (c) as Table 3 shows.

Test Implementation and Execution. This activity presents ten major tasks. Table 4 shows, as might be expected that "Dynamic Test Process" in ISO/IEC/IEEE 29119-2 is related to them. At first glance, Test Execution (8.4) is more related than other clauses (8.2, 8.3 and 8.5). On the one hand, there are four tasks that support it. Moreover, one of them "Reporting discrepancies as incidents and analyzing them in order to establish their cause (e.g., a defect in the code, in specified test data, in the test document, or a mistake in the way the test was executed)" is also partially related to 8.4.4.2 Compare Test Results (b) and 8.5.4.1 Analyze Test Results (a), and it is also strongly related to 8.5.4.2 Create/Update Incident Report (a).

On the other hand, the task "Repeating test activities as a result of action taken for each discrepancy, for example, re-execution of a test that previously failed in order to confirm a fix (confirmation testing), execution of a corrected test and/or execution of test in order to ensure that defects have not been introduced in unchanged areas of the software or that defect fixing did not uncover other defects (regression testing)" is partially related to 8.5.4.1 Analyze Test Results (a and b). The remainder tasks are also partially related to 8.2.4.4 Derive Test Cases (b and d), 8.2.4.5 Assemble Test Sets (a),

Table 4. Test implementation and execution (ISTQB) to ISO/IEC/IEEE 29119-2 mapping.

ISO/IEC/IEEE 29119-2 clause		a	b	c	d	e	f	g	h	i	j
8.2.4.4	Derive test cases	○	◑	○	◑	○					
8.2.4.5	Assemble test sets	◑	○	○							
8.2.4.6	Derive test procedures	◑	◑	◑	●	○	○				
8.3.4.1	Establish test environment	◑	○	○							
8.3.4.2	Maintain test environment	●	○								
8.4.4.1	Execute test procedures	●	●	●							
8.4.4.2	Compare test results	●	◑								
8.4.4.3	Record test results	●									
8.5.4.1	Analyze test results	◑	◑	○							
8.5.4.2	Create/update incident report	●	○								

8.2.4.6 Derive Test Procedures (a, b and c) and 8.3.4.1 Establish Test Environment (a). Additionally, according to ISTQB "…during test implementation the test cases are developed, implemented, prioritized and organized in the test procedure specification (IEEE STD 829-1998) …", so it has a strongly relationship with 8.2.4.6 Derive Test Procedures (d) as well.

Evaluating Exit Criteria and Reporting. This activity includes three major tasks. Table 5 shows, as one of them "Checking test logs against the exit criteria specified in test planning" is strongly related to 7.3.4.2 Monitor (b) and it is partially related to 7.3.4.3 Control (h). Whereas other task "Assessing if more test are needed or if the exit criteria specified should be changed" is partially related to 8.5.4.1 Analyze Test Results (b) and the 8.4.4 Test Execution (particularly see NOTE 2). The last task "Writing a test summary report for stakeholders" is also partially related to 7.4.4.4 Report Test Completion (a and b).

Table 5. Evaluating exit criteria and reporting (ISTQB) to ISO/IEC/IEEE 29119-2 mapping.

ISO/IEC/IEEE 29119-2 clause		a	b	c	d	e	f	g	h	i	j
7.3.4.2	Monitor	○	●	○	○	○					
7.3.4.3	Control	○	○	○	○	○	○	○	◑		
7.4.4.4	Report test completion	◑	◑	○	○						
8.4.4	Test execution - note 2	◑									
8.5.4.1	Analyze test results	○	◑	○							

Test Closure. This activity has seven major tasks but only one of them is not made explicit in the ISO/IEC/IEEE 29119-2: "handing over the testware to the maintenance organization". The task "finalizing and archiving testware, the test environment and the test infrastructure for later reuse" is strongly related to 7.4.4.1 Archive Test Assests (a and b) (see Table 6). However, it is worth noting that this task could be considered related to 7.4.4.2 Clean Up Test Environment (a) "the test environment shall be restored to a pre-defined state on completion of all testing activities" if it is being taken into account when "finalizing … the test environment …". Likewise, the task "Checking which planned deliverables have been delivered" is strongly related to 7.3.4.2 Monitoring (b) and the task "Analyzing lessons learned to determine changes needed for future releases and projects" is partially related to 7.4.4.3 Identify Lessons Learned (a and b). Also, the task "using the information gathered to improve test maturity" has been considered partially related to 7.4.4.3 Identify Lessons Learned (a) because this could be achieved by recording "recommended improvements to the testing and other processes". Regarding the task "Closing incident reports or raising change records for any that remain open" and "Documenting the acceptance of the system", they are strongly related to 7.4.4.4 Report Test Completion (a, c and d) and they are partially related to 7.4.4.4 Report Test Completion (b). Finally, 7.4.4.1 Archive Test Assets (c) could be achieved if "the availability of reusable test assets shall be recorded and communicated to the relevant stakeholders".

Table 6. Test closure activities (ISTQB) to ISO/IEC/IEEE 29119-2 mapping.

ISO/IEC/IEEE 29119-2 clause		a	b	c	d	e	f	g	h	i	j
7.3.4.2	Monitor	○	●	○	○						
7.4.4.1	Archive test assets	●	●	○							
7.4.4.2	Clean up test environment	○									
7.4.4.3	Identify lessons learned	◑	◑								
7.4.4.4	Report test completion	●	◑	●	●						

4 Conclusions

This paper studies two well-established software testing process paradigms, namely ISTQB CTFL and ISO/IEC/IEEE 29119 standard. The mapping is defined following Baldassarre et al. approach [19]. In fact, a protocol was made which includes a test-retest approach and re-evaluation in order to gain reliability. As a result, the test process of ISTQB CTFL is largely cover by the ISO/IEC 29119-2. However, key concerns about "Handing over the testware to the maintenance organization" and "improving the test process by using independent testers" is not directly aligned with the ISO/IEC/IEEE 29119-2 standard. Furthermore, "evaluating testability of the test basis and test objects" seems to be overlooked because the term "testability" is not made explicit within the ISO/IEC/IEEE 29119-2 standard but it could be achieved by the ways of its requirements are fulfilled. Despite the fact that "the test development process [ISTQB] can be done in different ways, from very informal with little or no documentation, to very formal …", it would not be so obvious what to do. Although this current mapping does not cover 100% of the ISTQB CTFL syllabus the insights of this study indicate that an approach like this can be designed for achieving tailored conformance to the ISO/IEC/IEEE 29119-2. However, justification should be provided whenever a process defined in Clauses 6, 7, and 8 of ISO/IEC/IEEE 29119-2 is not followed. In fact, all tailoring decisions should be on the one hand recorded with their rationale, including the consideration of any applicable risks, and on the other hand, it should be agreed by the relevant stakeholders. This paper may contribute to a better understanding ISTQB CTFL and ISO/IEC/IEEE 29119-2 and therefore gain clarity regarding their relevance. In addition, it might help practitioners to use either of the two approaches for improving their software projects if they do not use these approaches as a checklist without sense [23]. Consequently, practitioners can use it as a source of inspiration, where each model represents a tool box as it points out by SPI Manifesto [23], to enrich their test processes by adopting the relevant test practices of the previous approaches. For organizations, it provides a more complete view on test process in general. For researchers, this paper provides an analytical deconstruction of both approaches through a systematic method, including a comparison and the identification of gaps, differences and overlaps. As further work, the authors are currently interested in the extension of the mapping presented here to test design techniques.

References

1. van Genuchten, M., Hatton, L.: Compound annual growth rate for software. IEEE Softw. **29**, 19–21 (2012)
2. O'Connor, R.V., Colomo-Palacios, R.: Security awareness in the software arena. In: Engemann, K. (ed.) Routledge Companion to Risk, Crisis and Security in Business. Routledge, Abingdon (2018)
3. Colomo-Palacios, R., Casado-Lumbreras, C., Soto-Acosta, P., Misra, S., García-Peñalvo, F. J.: Analyzing human resource management practices within the GSD context. J. Glob. Inf. Technol. Manag. **15**, 30–54 (2012)
4. Spinellis, D.: State-of-the-art software testing. IEEE Softw. **34**, 4–6 (2017)
5. Garousi, V., Felderer, M., Kuhrmann, M., Herkiloğlu, K.: What industry wants from academia in software testing?: hearing practitioners' opinions. In: Proceedings of the 21st International Conference on Evaluation and Assessment in Software Engineering, pp. 65–69. ACM, New York (2017)
6. Garousi, V., Mäntylä, M.V.: A systematic literature review of literature reviews in software testing. Inf. Softw. Technol. **80**, 195–216 (2016)
7. Orso, A., Rothermel, G.: Software testing: a research travelogue (2000–2014). In: Proceedings of the on Future of Software Engineering, pp. 117–132. ACM (2014)
8. Gelperin, D., Hetzel, B.: The growth of software testing. Commun. ACM **31**, 687–695 (1988)
9. ISO: Software and systems engineering – Software testing – Part 2: Test processes, Geneva (2013)
10. ISO: ISO/IEC 33063 Information technology — Process assessment — Process assessment model for software testing, Geneva (2015)
11. Garcia, C., Dávila, A., Pessoa, M.: Test process models: systematic literature review. In: Mitasiunas, A., Rout, T., O'Connor, R.V., Dorling, A. (eds.) SPICE 2014. CCIS, vol. 477, pp. 84–93. Springer, Cham (2014). https://doi.org/10.1007/978-3-319-13036-1_8
12. Garousi, V., Felderer, M., Hacaloğlu, T.: Software test maturity assessment and test process improvement: a multivocal literature review. Inf. Softw. Technol. **85**, 16–42 (2017)
13. TestSPICE - intacs.info. http://www.intacs.info/index.php/testspice
14. van Veenendaal, E.: TMMi and ISO/IEC 29119: Friends or Foes? TMMi Foundation (2016)

15. Müller, T., Friedenberg, D.: Foundation level syllabus. In: ISTQB (2011)
16. Bath, G., Smith, M., Black, R., McKay, J.: Advanced level syllabus. In: ISTQB (2012)
17. Bath, G., Evans, I., van Veenendaal, E.: Expert level syllabus. In: ISTQB (2011)
18. Kasurinen, J., Taipale, O., Smolander, K.: How test organizations adopt new testing practices and methods? In: IEEE Fourth International Conference on Software Testing, Verification and Validation Workshops, pp. 553–558 (2011)
19. Baldassarre, M.T., Caivano, D., Pino, F.J., Piattini, M., Visaggio, G.: Harmonization of ISO/IEC 9001:2000 and CMMI-DEV: from a theoretical comparison to a real case application. Softw. Qual. J. **20**, 309–335 (2011)
20. Haufe, K., Colomo-Palacios, R., Dzombeta, S., Brandis, K., Stantchev, V.: Security management standards: a mapping. Procedia Comput. Sci. **100**, 755–761 (2016)
21. Larrucea, X., Santamaría, I., Colomo-Palacios, R.: Assessing ISO/IEC29110 by means of ITMark: results from an experience factory. J. Softw. Evol. Proc. **28**, 969–980 (2016)
22. Sanchez-Gordón, M.-L., Colomo-Palacios, R., Herranz, E.: Gamification and human factors in quality management systems: mapping from octalysis framework to ISO 10018. In: Kreiner, C., O'Connor, R.V., Poth, A., Messnarz, R. (eds.) EuroSPI 2016. CCIS, vol. 633, pp. 234–241. Springer, Cham (2016). https://doi.org/10.1007/978-3-319-44817-6_19
23. Pries-Heje, J., Johansen, J.: SPI Manifesto. http://www.iscn.com/Images/SPI_Manifesto_A.1.2.2010.pdf

Integrating SEooC Components in Highly Automated Vehicles

Georg Macher[1(✉)], Markus Bachinger[1], Andreas Kager[1], Michael Stolz[1], and Christian Kreiner[2]

[1] AVL List GmbH, Graz, Austria
{georg.macher,markus.bachinger,andreas.kager,michael.stolz}@avl.com
[2] Graz University of Technology, Graz, Austria
christian.kreiner@tugraz.at

Abstract. From its early beginnings, the automotive industry has always been known for creating fascinating, innovative new solutions and concepts. Today's vehicles are evolving from computers-on-wheels towards the internet of everything and data-on-wheels. Automotive systems currently exhibit increased levels of automation as well as ever tighter integration with other vehicles, traffic infrastructure, and cloud services. As a result, a shift of the value creation in the automotive domain toward information and communications technology (ICT) domain can be observed over the years.

This can be perceived as boon or bane - it greatly increases complexity and uncertainty, but at the same time opens up new opportunities for realizing innovative safety functions. Novel advanced driver assistance systems features or automated driving functions drive the need for advances and novel safety and security solutions, while highly relying on existing components developed in the traditional automotive development landscape.

Novel constraints coming from highly automated and distributed driving functionalities which can not be supervised by drivers must therefore be considered as an integral part of the development of modern vehicles. But within these terms a lack of experience with development approaches for automated driving and safety engineering of such automated functionalities still exist. In the current phase, more and more highly automated driving functions become integrated in conventional vehicles relying on safety components developed for conventional passenger vehicle usage. This paper will concentrate on the constraints and additional points to be considered when developing or integrating existing safety-related components developed as SEooC in the context of highly automated vehicles.

Keywords: ISO 26262 · Automotive · HARA · Safety analysis
Autonomous vehicles · SEooC

1 Introduction

The European automotive industry generates 12.6 million (direct and indirect) jobs in the EU with a total trade balance of 96.1 billion € [4] and is the EU's

X. Larrucea et al. (Eds.): EuroSPI 2018, CCIS 896, pp. 56–67, 2018.
https://doi.org/10.1007/978-3-319-97925-0_5

top investor in R&D, with 50.1 billion € invested per year. At the same time, the market is highly competitive and currently being strongly reorganized by emerging markets (e.g., BRICS countries) and new market entrants (e.g., Tesla) and is highly impacting different major societal challenges such as reduction of pollutant emissions, reduction of traffic fatalities, or increased mobility for an ageing population. These societal challenges are also strongly supported by advanced driver assistant systems (ADAS) and autonomous driving functions (ADF), with the purpose of taking over specific driving manoeuvres and finally eliminating the demands for driver intervention. While the technology trends are strongly supported and even enabled by cyber-physical systems and Industrial Internet-of-Things (IIoT) to improve connectivity and generate meaningful information and knowledge out of the available data.

As a result, the complexity of embedded automotive systems has grown significantly in recent decade and a shift of the value creation in the automotive domain toward ICT domain could be observed over the years. In terms of complexity, current premium vehicles are equipped with more than 100 ECU's being responsible for an added value of up to 75% for electric and hybrid vehicles and making up 25% of the vehicle costs [19]. Further, also relying more and more on external cloud-based services to handle the necessary control SW system for automated vehicle operation. In terms of shift of the value creation, vehicles evolved from pure mechanical product to (a) vehicle as mechatronics product (providing advanced local control strategies), further to (b) connected vehicle to provide context information, and (c) advanced cyber-physical systems (CPS) introducing ADAS and autonomous driving functions. Next steps envisioned include (d) capability to deploy knowledge discovery, data analytics, machine learning algorithms and finally (e) ad-hoc connected and trusted ad-hoc systems of systems, where external information could be used to influence safety critical decision (e.g., traffic light information from the infrastructure used to influence torque demands of approaching vehicles) [13].

ADAS and ADF drive the need for advances and novel approaches for safety-related features, while highly relying on existing components developed in the traditional manner. The common sense of safety-related development has to be justified to now consider additional constraints coming from highly automated and distributed driving functionalities which can (in near future) no longer be controlled by drivers. Unfortunately, there is currently still a lack of available best practices and standards which are geared specifically for safety engineering of automated driving functionalities, which have no driver in the loop for monitoring. In the current transition phase, more and more automated driving functions become integrated in conventional vehicles and thus relay on safety components developed in the context of conventional passenger vehicle usage rather than in the light of automated driving.

In this paper, we concentrate on the constraints and additional points to be considered when developing or integrating existing safety-related components developed as safety-element-out-of-context (SEooC) in the context of highly automated vehicles. One of the main challenges of the current SEooC component development is to identify additional requirements and needs that will appear when using the component in an automated vehicle instead of a conventional. To remediate this problem, we propose a systematic approach to support an ISO 26262 [10] safety-related development of SEooC for application in autonomous vehicle. The aim of this work is to provide an exemplary automatic transmission unit system which has been developed for conventional vehicles application and shall now be analysed for safe reuse in a highly automated vehicle.

This paper is organized as follows: Sect. 2 reviews recommendations and guidelines related to automotive safety engineering and state-of-the-art automotive development approaches. In Sect. 3 a generic concept for the review of the SEooC system development assumptions is given to help to ensure that the assumptions do not base on wrong driver controllability assumptions or rely on the driver-as-monitor principle for the usage in context of highly automated driving. Before Sect. 4 describes the exemplary transmission system and the architectural design analysis for delta-constraints related to autonomous vehicles. Finally, Sect. 6 concludes the work.

2 Automotive Engineering Approaches

Automotive engineering approaches are subject to several ISO standards.

Safety engineering is an integral part of automotive engineering and safety standards, such as the road vehicles - functional safety norm ISO 26262 [10] and its basic norm IEC 61508 [7]. The ISO 26262 standard defined not only the engineering of functional safety in the automotive domain, but was also taken as a template how the lifecycle for automotive systems can be structured. The scope is set to a system which implements a function on the vehicle level, and for which function and item hazards are identified and a safety concept is developed. For the identification of these hazards safety assessment techniques, such as failure mode and effects analysis (FMEA) [8] and fault tree analysis (FTA) [9], are also specified, standardized, and integrated in the automotive development process landscape. Currently efforts on second editions of IEC 61508 and ISO 26262 are taken and first approaches of enhancing an integration of safety and security are considered.

Currently the working draft of ISO/SAE AWI 21434 "road vehicles - cybersecurity engineering" is in its finalization phase. It is a partial evolution of SAE J3061 [20]. The main focus is on cybersecurity for road vehicles but other attributes are also considered. Safety is on the one side considered as one of the assets which need to be protected by cybersecurity and safety engineering is considered as a related discipline. The generic approach is similar to ISO 26262, the scope is on a cybersecurity critical system in the vehicle and the next hop outside of the vehicle.

ISO/WD PAS 21448 Road vehicles - Safety of the intended functionality is also still in development and defines safety engineering which out of scope of functional safety ISO 26262 context. There is still an ongoing discussion how such systems with their undefined environment and conditions can be analysed.

Besides this several OEM standards (such as BMW group standard GS 95014 or VWs KGAS standard) state their own requirements for cyber-security and functional safety engineering. The SS 7740 [11] provides an assessment model for functional safety processes within the automotive industry, supporting ISO-26262. The main purpose of the SS 7740 assessment model is to standardize assessments of functional safety processes including well-defined capability levels i.e. an ISO 26262 functional safety audit with standardized capability levels known from Automotive SPICE. This approach has also been focused by the SoQrates assessment model presented in [14] and further been extended for the assessment of cyber-security related system development.

A guide to the functional safety of automotive systems according to ISO 26262 can be found in the SafEUr functional safety manager trainings [17] and literature [2,5]. Also numerous funded projects, to mention only the most recent one, the PRYSTINE project [3], focus on ADV and safety and security issues.

A specific term and concept of the ISO 26262 standard is the safety element out of context (SEooC), which is described in ISO26262 part 10. This SEooC development concept is geared towards development of an element which is to be integrated in an unknown environment or is supposed to be integrated into different products. For this approach safety requirements for the integration and assumptions on the design and environment of the element are assumed and are later to be taken in to account for the integration. Thus, the integrator of the SEooC component has to assure that the assumed requirements and constraints are not violated.

The SEooC concept is frequently used for automotive micro-controller development and system components (such as gearboxes, electric steering systems, etc.) which can be used in different vehicle variants. Therefore, several works exist in this context; e.g. Schneider et al. [18], which provides a practical approach for a SEooC device driver for electric motors. Ruiz et al. [16] presented an experience report of the application of the SEooC concept from ISO 26262 to an electric parking system.

In contrast to this, the works regarding SEooC development and autonomous driving vehicles is quite limited. The work of Bergenhem et al. [1] is a position paper solely, claiming that for autonomous vehicles, the safety requirement hierarchy of ISO 26262 implies semantic gaps and ISO 26262 needs to be enhanced in this regards. The works of Kocsis et al. [12], Hoerwick and Siedersberger [6], and Reschka [15] deal with safety concepts, strategies, and architectures for autonomous driving systems in general, but do not provide further details regarding SEooC concepts.

Considering that Advanced driver assistant systems (ADAS) and autonomous driving vehicles (ADV) approaches are highly relying on existing components developed in a traditional manner and not especially developed for autonomous vehicles raises the awareness, that a lack of available best practices and publications which are geared specifically for SEooC development of automated driving functionalities exists. In the SEooC context it is not possible to perform a complete hazard analysis and risk assessment without knowledge of the item level hazards. Therefore, it is useful to also consider possible hazards that may occur in the specific operation environment and document them along with the predicted ASIL rating of the assumed requirements the SEooC shall have to comply with. Current industry practice and information from potential customers can be used as sources for identifying hazards, and then estimating the appropriate ASIL for the assumed requirements. But in the context of highly automated driving such assumptions many base on wrong driver controllability assumptions or relying on the driver-as-monitor principle.

3 SEooC Review Concept for Highly Automated Driving Application

Today's ADAS and highly automated vehicles fully rely on existing components developed in a traditional manner for conventional vehicles. Since, in today's best practices many hazards and hazardous situations are assumed less critical, because it can be assumed that average driver can handle such situations or other systems actuated by the driver can prevent critical situations (driver-as-monitor), dangerous situations in the context of highly automated driving may be mistakenly omitted. Therefore, this section provides a generic concept for the review of the SEooC system development assumptions in the context of highly automated driving.

1. Situations with **Controllability C** $<$ **3** shall be re-analysed for their argumentations and related safety goals.
   (a) $C = 2$ & $C = 1$: a dual-channel design is most probably required.
   (b) $C = 0$: might not be considered in further ASIL considerations, but need to be analysed for side-effects in automated vehicle context.
2. Situations with an **Exposure E=0** should be cross-checked with and covered by SotIF analysis.
3. **Severity S=0** situations may still not be safety related, but need to be analysed carefully to prevent from reputation losses.

These principles will be exemplified in the following section by an exemplary automatic transmission unit system which is planned to be reused in a highly automated vehicle.

4 Automatic Transmission Unit Use-Case Delta Analysis

This section presents an exemplary automatic transmission unit use-case and the application of the generic concept presented. The system has been developed for conventional vehicles application and will now be safely reused in a highly automated vehicle. The use-case and its interacting systems is depicted in Fig. 1 and is a training example, not intended to be complete or represent state-of-the-art technologies. The general application use-case is that the driver selects a driving mode via the gear shift lever and communicates torque requests to the hybrid control unit (HCU). The HCU translates these inputs to control the available torque sources (e-motor(s) and combustion engine) to provide the requested torque via the gearbox to the wheel. Based on the selected driving mode, the provided torques and the brake actuation the transmission control unit (TCU) controls the gearbox accordingly and (pre-)selects the adequate gear(s). The state-of-the-art hazard and risk analysis (HARA) of the high level design transmission item (consisting of control unit, software, electronic elements and their interfaces) results in assigning Automotive Safety Integrity Levels (ASILs) to hazardous events and the formulation of safety goals. According to ISO 26262 the ASIL ratings are based on tables which help to rate S (Severity) 0–3, E (Exposure) 0–4, and C (Controllability) 0–3 of the situations. Table 1 shows the example rating of such a conventional transmission system HARA of the most hazardous events.

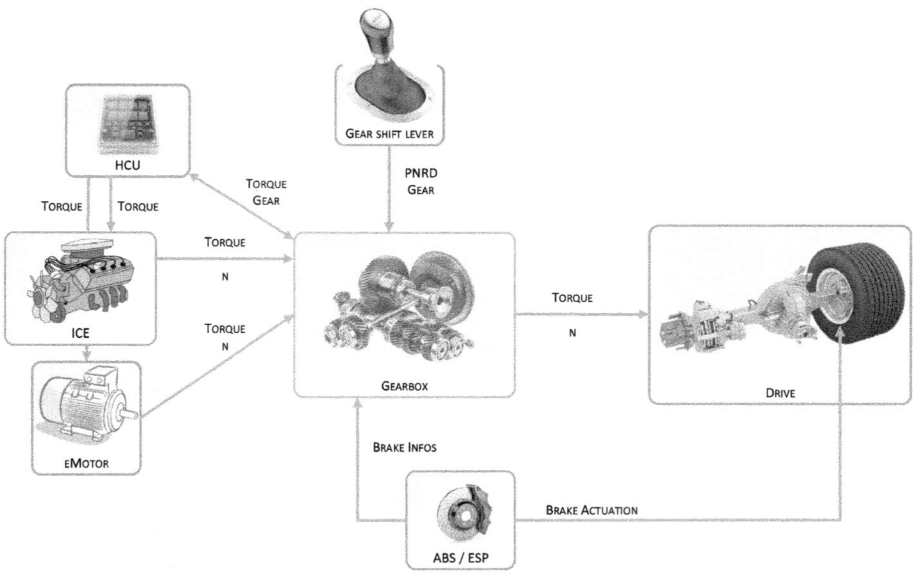

Fig. 1. Item definition of the automatic transmission system example

During the further development of the system, these safety goals are broken down to system safety requirements. Therefore, the safety experts and system analyst usually search for those potential faults that can lead to critical failures (e.g. using the FMEA as a source) and define requirements to diagnose and avoid these faults.

4.1 Automated Vehicle Context

As mentioned in the previous section, in the context of automated driving functions the ratings for the definition of the ASIL must be re-evaluated, since the

Table 1. Excerpt of the automatic transmission system HARA

Hazard		External Measures	ASIL	ID Safety goal	Safety goal	Safe State
ID	Description					
H01a	Unintended forward/backward acceleration	Not Present	B	SG_01	Avoid acceleration of the vehicle if not requested by the driver	Drivetrain open
H02	Unintended deceleration	ESP	B	SG_02	Avoid vehicle deceleration ≥ Dec_safety_threshold if not requested by the driver when vehicle speed > vSpeed_Safety_Threshold	Drivetrain open
H06	Acceleration in the wrong direction	Not Present	A	SG_03	Avoid acceleration in the wrong direction	Drivetrain open
H04	Blocking of driving wheels	Not Present	D	SG_04a	Avoid blocking of driving wheels when vehicle speed > vSpeed_Safety_Threshold	Drivetrain open
H04	Blocking of driving wheels	Not Present	A	SG_04b	Avoid blocking of driving wheels when vehicle speed is ≤ vSpeed_Safety_Threshold	Drivetrain open
H10	Sudden movement of the vehicle	Not Present	C	SG_05	Avoid Park Pawl disengagement if not requested by the driver	Park pawl engaged

controllability (C) factor may vary. To further detail this, three automated driving functions scenarios are taken into account for the following system HARA delta analysis of the transmission system.

Highway Pilot (L3): The function takes over driving functionalities (acceleration, de-acceleration, and lane keeping) in a less constraint environment (highway), at higher speeds, but with driver having the possibility to supervise and take back the control. This function is conforming SAE automation level L3.

Piloted Parking Via App (L4): For this scenario the driver is outside the vehicle and controls the vehicle via an App on the mobile phone. The environment is also less constraint (limited to parking lots) and the vehicle speed is very low. For such functionality, specific concepts are required that overrule the gear shift lever and parking lock mechanisms. This scenario conforms SAE automation level L4.

Fully Autonomous (L5): The vehicle is fully autonomous and has probably no steering, braking or throttle pedal at all for the driver to intervene. This scenario is the most complex one and complying a SAE automation level L5.

4.2 Delta-Analysis for Automated Vehicle Application

Table 1 describes the resulting re-evaluated safety goals and ASIL ratings in the context of these automated driving scenarios.

SG_02"‘avoid vehicle deceleration if not requested"’, **SG_04a**"‘avoid blocking of driving wheels (higher speeds)"’, and **SG_04b** "‘avoid blocking of driving wheels (lower speeds)"' are related to internal functions of the transmission system only and will therefore not be affected by the application in an automated vehicle.

SG_05 "'avoid park pawl disengagement if not requested"' is also related to a transmission system internal function only and not effected, but an additional SEooC constraint of the transmission for vehicle integration arises. The constraint requires an electrically actuated parking brake, which assures that sudden movement of the vehicle can be prevented according to ASIL C quality requirements. This results from the 'Piloted parking via App' scenario, which requires a specific concept that can overrule the gear shift lever and parking lock mechanisms.

SG_03 "'avoid acceleration in the wrong direction"' is also affected by the 'Piloted parking via App' scenario, since this scenario reduces the controllability to C3. In this scenario the driver is not in the car, which results in combination with S3 (low speed) and E3 (parking manoeuvre) in an ASIL C instead of ASIL A quality requirements for this safety goal.

SG_01 "'avoid acceleration if not requested"' will be affected by all fully automated driving scenarios and the App parking scenario, since in any case the controllability is reduced to C3 (driver is either not in the car or has no driver input interface). This, in combination with maximum severity (S3) and maximum exposure (E4), results in an ASIL D instead of ASIL B quality requirement.

5 Automatic Transmission Unit Application for Automated Driving

As mentioned, it is expected that also fully automated driving cars (currently estimated to be available in 2030 the latest) being based on reused systems which are originally designed in an SEooC manner for conventional vehicle application. Therefore, it is most likely that the effort for re-design and re-assessment of these components is kept as low as possible. The delta analysis done in Sect. 4.2 reveals that automation nevertheless may have some impact and an initial re-assessment of the SEooC will be required. But to keep component development changes low, additional constraints for the SEooC may be mentioned for automated vehicle application and the component development of the transmission itself may then not require to be change for the component's functional safety concept. Aside from this, some functionalities (such as hill-hold or creep function) must be analysed for park pilot or other ADF functions in general. Here a redesign of such functionalities would be probably required, depending on the specific implementation of the functionality, since automated driving functionalities will be more context-aware and thus easier to predict and manage.

The described delta analysis revealed the following additional constraint for transmission SEooC integration in a highly automated vehicle, if no changes to the SEooC itself are done:

- The control unit for the highly-automated driving functionalities (HAD) must be able to actuate the vehicle brakes (required by decomposition of SG_01

(ASIL D) to initial SG_01 (ASIL B(D)) for the transmission unit and SG_01 (ASIL B(D)) for the HAD)
- Sudden movement of the vehicle and unintended deactivation of parking lock SG_05 (ASIL C) must be prevented by electric parking brake also (controlled by HAD, ASIL C)
- ESP must be fail-operational to ensure a redundant control path for HAD
- Creep function may be implemented solely via e-drive
- Shut-down and parking procedures must be kept also for HAD
- Ready-to-drive procedures must be kept also for HAD (to ensure initial system self-test)
- routines which driver is required to follow to dependably shut down the car(a.k.a. 'Verlassenskonzepte') have to be analysed for novel automated driving functionalities.

For each integration of a SEooC component an analysis of situations which have a controllability argumentation $C < 3$, an adequate support by the HAD

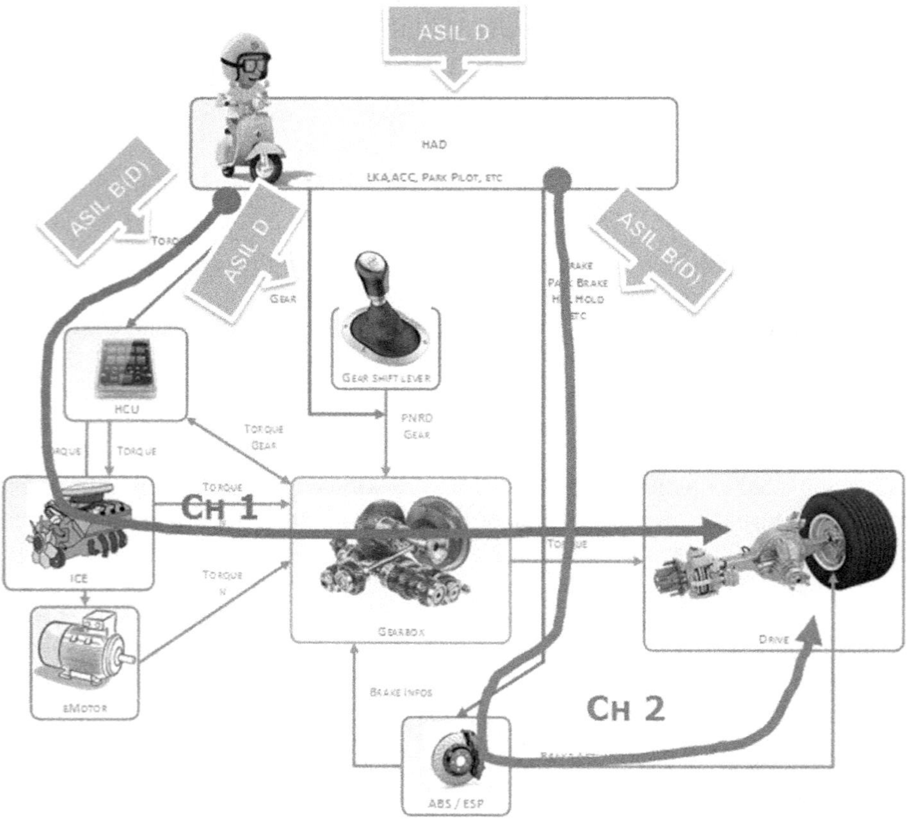

Fig. 2. HAD and automatic transmission system interaction depiction

concept must be provided (according to generic review concept). The use-case's HAD concept and the interaction with the automatic transmission unit is depicted in Fig. 2, which also highlights the required two channels for ASIL B(D) decomposition.

6 Conclusion

In Sect. 3 a generic concept for the review of the SEooC system development assumptions is given to help to ensure that the assumptions are not based on wrong driver controllability assumptions or rely on the driver-as-monitor principle for the usage in context of highly automated driving. Before Sect. 4 describes the exemplary transmission system and the architectural design analysis for delta-constraints related to autonomous vehicles. Finally, Sect. 6 concludes the work.

In this paper we focused on SEooC systems developed for conventional vehicles and the constraints and additional points to be considered when integrating such systems in highly automated vehicles. Autonomous driving vehicles require advances and novel safety and security solutions, but will highly rely on existing components developed in the traditional automotive development landscape. Therefore, one main challenge is to identifying additional requirements and needs that will appear when using a component in an automated vehicle instead of a conventional.

In this publication a generic concept for the review of the SEooC system development assumptions is given and an exemplary automatic transmission unit system (developed for conventional vehicle application) has been analysed for safe reuse in a highly automated vehicle. The paper presented a systematic analysis approach, a delta-analysis for automated vehicles and an approach for safe integration in autonomous vehicle context. Further, an exemplary integration approach geared towards keeping the transmission SEooC changes to a minimum (ideally requiring no changes), but instead identify additional constraints for the integration was described.

Acknowledgments. This work is dedicated to our co-author late Christian Kreiner, who was impressive for many reasons and has been a wonderful teacher, co-worker, leader and friend. You have been everything one could look for in a good mentor, the real-world Master Yoda, and made working with you an exciting, inspiring and memorable experience. We will always be grateful to you for your support and kindness. May the force still be with you.

The authors would like to thank for the support by the *PRYSTINE* project. The research leading to these results has received funding from the Austrian national funding authorities and ECSEL Joint Undertaking under grant agreement nr 783190 (project *PRYSTINE*).

References

1. Bergenhem, C., et al.: How to reach complete safety requirement refinement for autonomous vehicles. In: CARS2015 - Critical Automotive applications: Robustness and Safety (2015)
2. Boehringer, K., Kroh, M.: Funktionale Sicherheit in der Praxis, July 2013
3. Druml, N., et al.: PRYSTINE - PRogrammable sYSTems for INtelligence in automobilEs. In: Under Review at DSD2018 (2018)
4. European Automobile Manufacturers Association: The automobile industry pocket guide 2016–2017. Technical report, European Automobile Manufacturers Association (2016)
5. Gebhardt, V., Rieger, G., Mottok, J., Giesselbach, C.: Funktionale Sicherheit nach ISO 262626 - Ein Praxisleitfaden zur Umsetzung, vol. 1. Auflage. dpunkt.verlag (2013)
6. Hoerwick, M., Siedersberger, K.-H.: Strategy and architecture of a safety concept for fully automatic and autonomous driving assistance systems. In: 2010 IEEE Intelligent Vehicles Symposium University of California (2010)
7. ISO - International Organization for Standardization: IEC 61508 Functional safety of electrical/electronic/programmable electronic safety-related systems
8. ISO - International Organization for Standardization: IEC 60812 Analysis techniques for system reliability - Procedure for failure mode and effects analysis (FMEA) (2006)
9. ISO - International Organization for Standardization: IEC 61025 Fault tree analysis (FTA), December 2006
10. ISO - International Organization for Standardization: ISO 26262 Road vehicles Functional Safety Part 1–10 (2011)
11. ISO - International Organization for Standardization: SS 7740 Road vehicles - Functional Safety Process Assessment Model (2012)
12. Kocsis, M., Sussmann, N., Buyer, J., Zoellner, R.: Safety concept for autonomous vehicles that operate in pedestrian areas. In: Proceedings of the 2017 IEEE/SICE International Symposium on System Integration (2017)
13. Macher, G., Armengaud, E., Schneider, D., Brenner, E., Kreiner, C.: Towards dependability engineering of cooperative automotive cyber-physical systems. In: Stolfa, J., Stolfa, S., O'Connor, R.V., Messnarz, R. (eds.) EuroSPI 2017. CCIS, vol. 748, pp. 205–215. Springer, Cham (2017). https://doi.org/10.1007/978-3-319-64218-5_16
14. Messnarz, R., Kreiner, C., Riel, A.: Implementing Functional Safety Standards has an Impact on System and SW Design - Required Knowledge and Competencies (SafEUr). Software Quality Professional (2015)
15. Reschka, A.: Safety concept for autonomous vehicles. In: Maurer, M., Gerdes, J.C., Lenz, B., Winner, H. (eds.) Autonomous Driving, pp. 473–496. Springer, Heidelberg (2016). https://doi.org/10.1007/978-3-662-48847-8_23
16. Ruiz, A., Melzi, A., Kelly, T.: Systematic application of ISO 26262 on a SEooC: support by applying a systematic reuse approach. In: 2015 Design, Automation Test in Europe Conference Exhibition (DATE), pp. 393–396, March 2015
17. SafEUr Training Material Committee: ECQA Certified Functional Safety Manager Training Material. training dossier, April 2013
18. Schneider, R., et al.: Safety element out of context - a practical approach. In: SAE International Technical Papers, no. 2012-01-0033, April 2012

19. Scuro, G.: Automotive industry: innovation driven by electronics (2012). http://embedded-computing.com/articles/automotive-industry-innovation-driven-electronics/
20. Vehicle Electrical System Security Committee: SAE J3061 Cybersecurity Guidebook for Cyber-Physical Automotive Systems

The Shell Model – A Method for System Boundary Analysis

Walter Sebron(✉), Hans Tschürtz, and Peter Krebs

Vienna University of Applied Sciences, 1100 Vienna, Austria
{walter.sebron,hans.tschuertz,
peter.krebs}@fh-campuswien.ac.at

Abstract. The application of analysis methods in systems and safety engineering depends on the available depth of knowledge about a system in the respective lifecycle phases. However, the analysis method chain shows gaps as it should support system analyses during the whole lifecycle of a system. The aim of this paper is to discuss the Shell Model Analysis method, which aims at closing a gap in early system lifecycle phases, like the concept phase. The Shell Model Analysis is a graphical method that splits up a system and groups its parts into concentric shells, built around a selected system part under consideration. A set of rules and guidelines has been defined in order to enable a proper shell build-up. Originally, the method was intended to assist the analysis of electronic system parts, like e.g. an embedded control unit for a braking system, by supporting the definition and analysis of the system's boundary and its environment only. Meanwhile, it has been extended to also produce results that can be starting points for consecutive analysis methods.

Keywords: Analysis methods · System and safety engineering
System boundary definition

1 Introduction

A variety of different analysis methods is applied in systems and safety engineering, in order to ensure the correct functioning and safety of a system. These analysis methods are usually intended for a specific phase in the engineering lifecycle, depending on what minimal depth of knowledge about the system is necessary.

In [1] (ch. 4.2), the "hazard filter" shows how typical hazard analysis methods – like PHA, HAZOP. FMEA, etc. – are used depending on the according lifecycle phases of a system. The more a system development advances, the more sophisticated the necessary analysis methods become. These methods need deeper details about the system in order to produce meaningful results. Especially the classical (safety) analysis methods (e.g. FMEA, FTA, HAZOP) need detailed knowledge about a system [2] (p. 27). Only the early method types during conceptual design can be applied with a low level of system detail knowledge [1] (ch. 4.3.1).

In order to apply an analysis method to a system correctly, it is necessary to first understand its basic requirements and design [1], (ch. 5.2.2), and to have clearly defined system boundaries [1] (p. 20). Without those boundaries, the system cannot be

X. Larrucea et al. (Eds.): EuroSPI 2018, CCIS 896, pp. 68–79, 2018.
https://doi.org/10.1007/978-3-319-97925-0_6

distinguished exactly from its environment. It also becomes difficult to define the scope of analyses.

System engineering and system safety should look at all aspects of a system as an integrated whole, rather than looking at individual components in isolation from the system [1] (p. 4). This is often termed holistic approach and is also advocated in [2] (p. 19). Though, most, if not all, of the analysis methods applicable at an early lifecycle stage exhibit at least one of the following shortcomings:

- Not following a structured and systematic approach (e.g. brainstorming)
- Not defining the system boundaries (e.g. PHL, PHA)
- Not defining a system structure (e.g. HAZOP)
- Not supporting a holistic view (e.g. FMEA, checklists).

But when analyzing a (sub-)system-to-be-built at a very early stage, it is almost inevitable to come across the need for a structured method that aides in defining the overall system boundaries and its environment, but also allows to focus upon the specific (sub-)system as it is embedded in the overall system.

2 The Basic Idea

2.1 Motivation

Experiences from conducting safety analyses for industrial projects showed several issues, such as:

- different and often divergent viewpoints on the systems-to-be-analyzed,
- incomplete understanding of the boundaries of a system, and therefore of the system environment,
- ambiguities about the newly intended functioning of a system and its components.

This showed the need for a method that supports and emphasizes the understanding of a system as a whole, the definition of its boundaries and environment. Such a method should be applicable already at a very early project stage with only brief knowledge on the system itself and the overall system that it is embedded into. It should facilitate a description of the components and their relationships within the overall system. It should foster awareness of possible environmental influences which may vary due to different usage scenarios. This method should serve as an entry point for further system and safety analyses; its focus on the setting of boundaries of and within a system is key for being able to conduct a variety of analysis methods afterwards.

However, looking into different descriptions [4–6] and collections [1, 3, 7] of analysis methods, no method was found that would satisfy the above mentioned needs, indicating the need for a new method.

2.2 Methodical Background

As stated in [2] (ch. 2.3), when developing a (safety critical) system, understanding of the system, its environment, its workings, its failure modes, etc., is crucial. The main obstacle in this context is the ever-increasing complexity of newly developed systems. Again, according to [2], "[simplicity] is the only real way to ensure understanding, or understandability, of the systems being produced." This simplicity can be achieved by use of appropriate structure. This is why the Shell Model Analysis uses the concept of simplification by focusing on one element of interest, called the "system under consideration" (SUC) and its interactions with other system elements. This way, "unnecessary" details are omitted, thus limiting the efforts for modelling while still allowing purposeful input to subsequent analyses.

Additionally, structuring is achieved by placing the different elements of the overall system into different layers, the so-called "shells." These layers are arranged in a concentric manner; hence a Shell Model (SM) is generated. Furthermore, the structure gets enhanced via displaying the relationships of the different components via arrows, thus defining also their basic interfaces. A preliminary version of the Shell Model Analysis was described in [8], and used as basis for the method defined in this paper.

2.3 Goals of the Method

Since the basic idea for the method was to support the build-up and structure of a system, its boundaries and influencing factors, the main goals of the method are:

- Definition of a system's external boundary
- Depicting the inner structure of a system and the relationship between components
- Consideration of environmental influences
- Definition and consideration of use cases, usage scenarios and situations
- Applicability at a very early lifecycle phase, e.g. pre-concept phase.

Additional goals were identified during development of the Shell Model Analysis method, in order to support, and provide input to, subsequent analysis methods:

- Definition and consideration of the top level functions
- Listing and considering modes of the components and their influences on functions
- Listing of communication types between components and defining their interfaces
- Supporting the discovery and definition of preliminary hazards
- Providing a holistic picture of the system.

3 The Shell Model Analysis Method

3.1 Prerequisites

As the Shell Model Analysis should be applicable at a very early lifecycle stage, little input is required:

- A basic idea or rough concept of the overall system

- The selection of the SUC itself
- Basic functional requirements of the SUC.

3.2 Basic Concepts of the Shell Model Analysis

The Shell Model Analysis represents the structural and functional relationship between the SUC and its surrounding systems graphically as an interconnected structure, organized into a series of concentric stratums, or "shells". The elements of the structure depict the individual elements of a larger system which communicate with one other to execute functions. In addition, relevant influences from the environment and usage scenarios complement the view. A complete structure represents a system in its environment and is termed a shell model for the system.

Figure 1 depicts the elements of the Shell Model Analysis. A component is a part of a larger system and can be clearly delineated (e.g. a dedicated HW element, such as a sensor or actuator). Each component is identified by an arbitrary component identifier (such as a name or numerical ID) that must be unique over the whole SM.

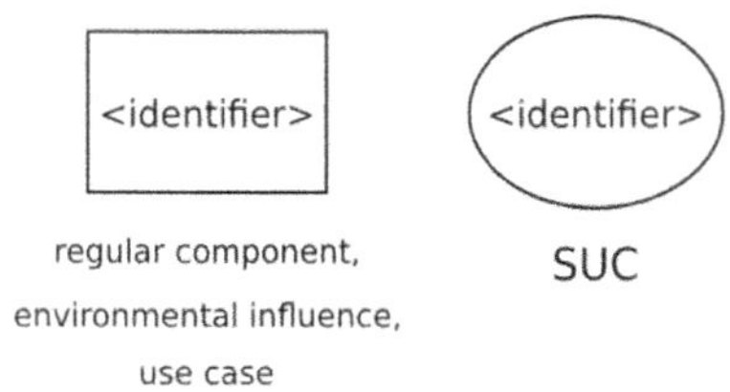

Fig. 1. Elements of the Shell Model Analysis

The SUC is as a special kind of component and exists exactly once in a shell model - hence a unique symbol is reserved for it. Definition of an SUC and its identifier forms the initial step in creating an SM.

In addition to the SUC, a shell model can contain an arbitrary number of regular (i.e. non-SUC) components, or even none at all. The regular components form the "inner" or SUC environment which directly influence or depend on its behavior.

Direct communication between components is symbolized by arrows in between the component symbols for the exchange of messages. Messages include transfer of energy (e.g. electricity) or information (e.g. analogue or digital signals) - either uni-directional or bidirectional. Additionally, regular components can assert an indirect influence on the SUC (e.g. via heat or EMI) which is represented by a "fringe" at the component symbol, including a suitable label. Figure 2 shows the arrows for direct communication and an indirect influence.

Components are grouped into the eponymous shells to convey further information on the logical or physical structure of a system and to facilitate the definition of the analysis scope. Shells are (with one exception) depicted as closed curves of dashed lines which are aligned in a concentric fashion. Each shell must possess a unique and meaningful identifier. Therefore, the Shell Model Analysis shells are non-empty sub-sets of components (i.e. each shell must contain at least one component) that form a hierarchy, starting from the innermost to the outermost shell.

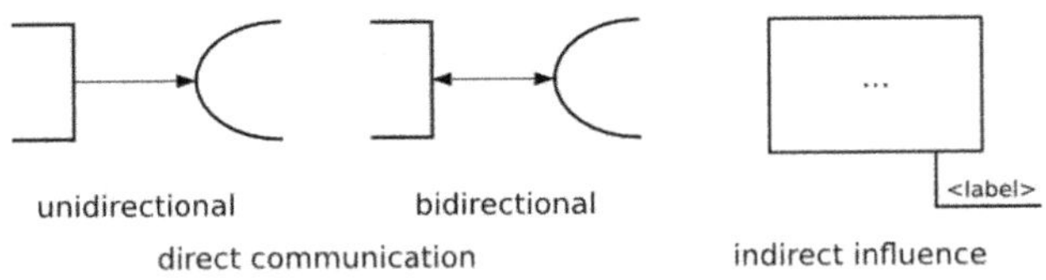

Fig. 2. Arrows for direct communication and notation for indirect influence of component

3.3 Defining Shells

After selection of the SUC, all components that directly communicate with the SUC have to be identified. This includes:

- Components that provide input to the SUC (e.g. sensors, user input elements)
- Components that receive output of the SUC (e.g. actuators, user output elements)
- Components that communicate bidirectionally with the SUC (e.g. clients, servers).

Each of the identified components directly impacts or is impacted by the SUC and is termed an "adjacent component" (AC) of the SUC. The SUC and its ACs are grouped into one shell which is used as the innermost shell of the shell hierarchy as the SM is further developed. As the ACs are situated at a "hop distance" of 0 from the view point of the SUC, this initial shell is termed the zero shell (Z-shell). A well-formed SM must contain exactly one Z-shell which must consist of only the SUC and its ACs linked by respective communication arrows.

Figure 3 shows a typical example of a Z-shell with a generic Programmable Logic Controller (PLC) as SUC, together with its surrounding components (the ACs). Note the communication to the component "Communication Bus", which is defined as an AC although it could physically extend from the SUC by quite a distance.

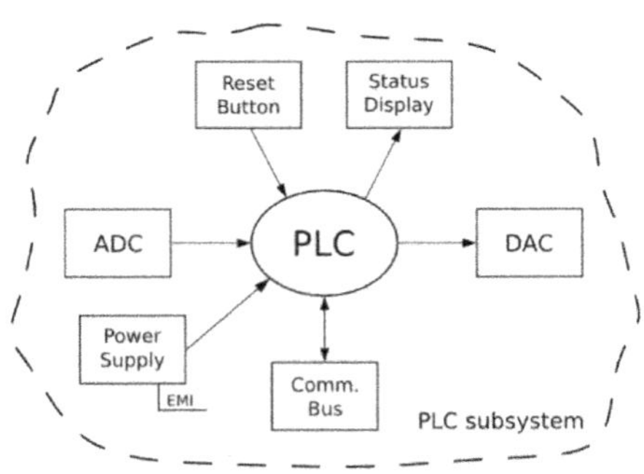

Fig. 3. Example of a zero shell depicting a Programmable Logic Controller (PLC) and its ACs

After definition of the Z-shell, further analysis might identify components that provide input or receive output from the ACs of the SUC, i.e. communicate only indirectly with the SUC. These "next order components" are placed outside the Z-Shell and are grouped together into a new shell that fully encloses the Z-shell. This outer shell (O-shell) of order one (O_1-shell) therefore contains only components with a distance of "one hop" from the SUC.

Figure 4 shows how the running example of the PLC is extended by an O_1-shell containing components that provide/receive indirect input (Sensor) or output (Actuator) to/from the SUC. Note that some ACs might not have a corresponding component in the O_1-shell.

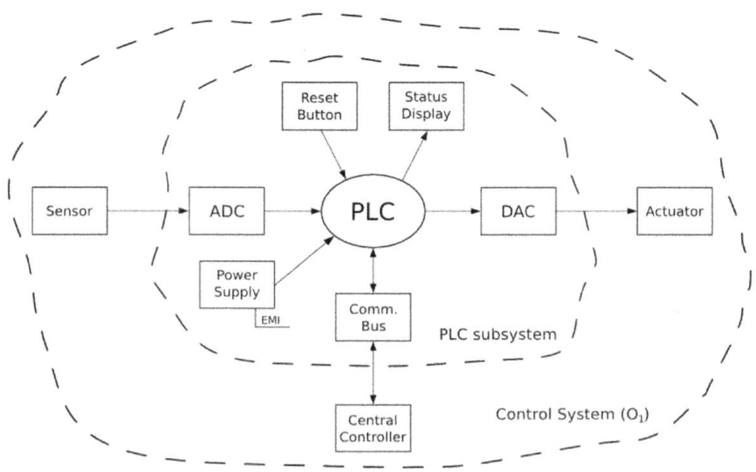

Fig. 4. Adding the first O-shell with indirectly communicating components

The principle of identifying indirect senders/receivers and adding them by means of outer shells can be repeated an arbitrary number of times. This results in a hierarchy of shells with increasing order. The amount of O-shells depends mainly on the complexity of the analyzed system and the intended scope of the analysis. After adding the last O-shell, this outermost O-shell is designated as the border of the system and is termed the system border shell (S-shell). To facilitate visual recognition, the border of the S-shell is drawn with a solid line.

Figure 5 shows the addition of a second O-shell (O_2-shell) with a component "Operator" representing the user interacting via some user interface elements with the SUC. As the construction should end at this point, the O_2-shell is marked as S-shell by its solid line. Of particular note is that the "Operator" communicates directly with two ACs, effectively "skipping" the O_1-shell. The order of an O-shell should therefore not be conflated with the "hop order" of its components. Note however, that only O-shells might be skipped in this way - direct communication between the SUC and a component of an O-shell is not allowed.

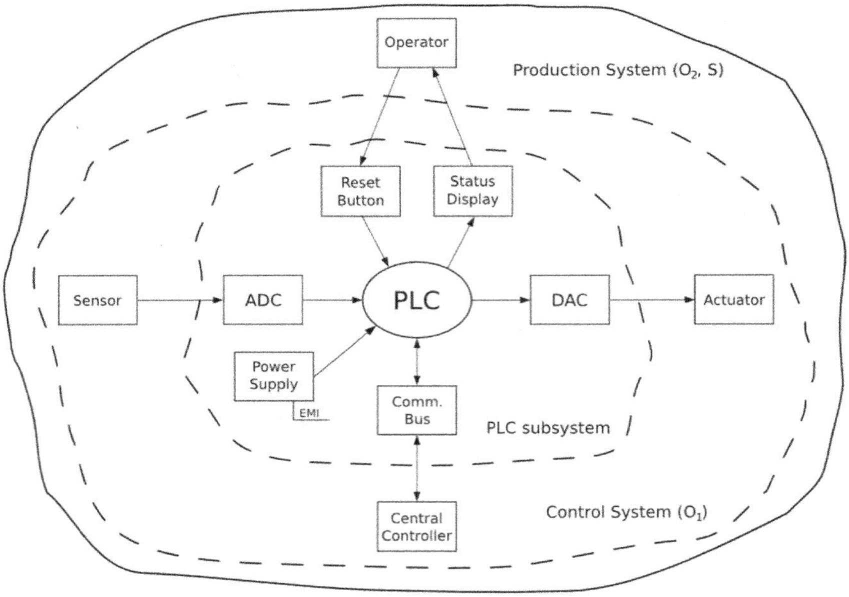

Fig. 5. Adding a second O-shell (O_2-shell) as the S-shell of the example system

3.4 Further Shells

The shells contained within the system border describe the structure of the analyzed system and can be considered as an "internal" environment for the SUC. Information on the environment external to the system is added via two specialized shells.

The first one, the environment shell (E-shell) encompasses the S-shell and contains elements that represent environmental influences that might plausibly affect the SUC or regular components. A typical example is the influence of high or low temperature on the performance of electronic components. Environmental influences differ from the indirect influences exerted by regular components in that they originate from outside the system and are not limited to E/E/PE-related phenomena. Each environmental influence is identified by a suitable identifier (e.g. "heat", "moisture", "vibration").

The second one, the use case shell (U-shell) encircles the E-shell and contains use case elements that represent usage scenarios or situations that are relevant to the overall system and the SUC (usually during operation). The intention is to define a set of disjoint "profiles" for further analyses, which can be used to analyze the SUC under different circumstances (e.g. low vs. high demand).

A complete SM for the running example is depicted in Fig. 6. Note that no communication arrows originate or end at elements of the E- and U-shell.

3.5 Complementary Information

The information conveyed by the elements of an SM is, in general, not enough to fully understand the workings of a system. This is deliberate in order to avoid overloading

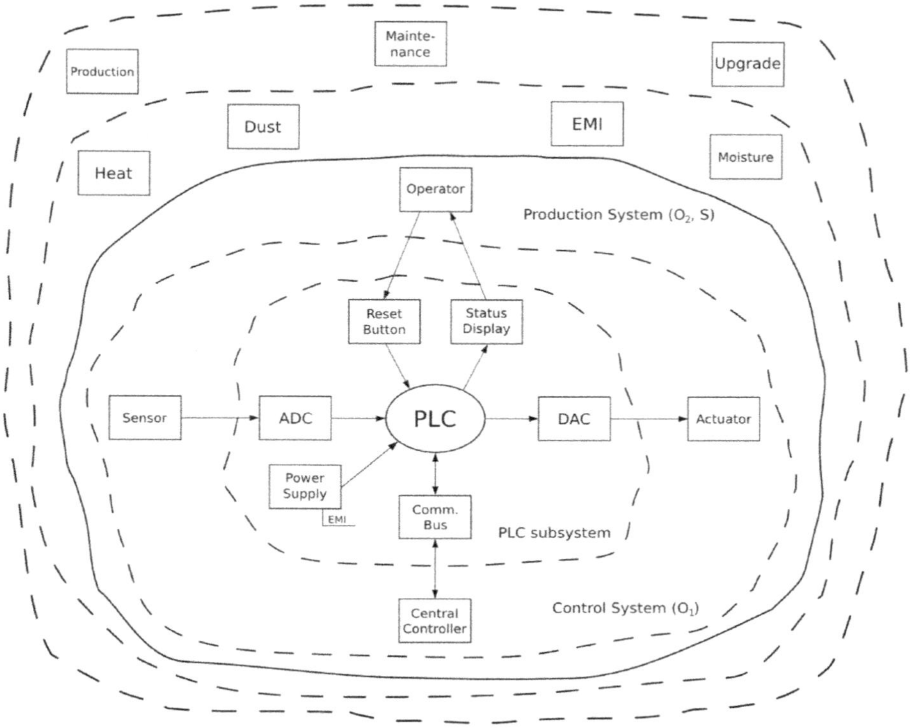

Fig. 6. Complete PLC example with added E-shell and U-shell

the graphical depiction. However, for a thorough understanding of the system, additional information is necessary. Specifically, the following complementary data should be specified for an SM:

- For each component, including the SUC, a description of the component's purpose in the system and its interfaces for direct communication
- For each regular component with indirect influences, a description of each indirect influence asserted by the component and detailed constraints (e.g. exact thresholds for temperature, EM field strength, etc.)
- For each communication arrow, the set of messages that can be exchanged between the communicating components
- For the Z-shell and each O-shell, a description of the shell's meaning (i.e. the criterion for choosing this shell)
- For each environmental influence, detailed constraints similar to indirect influences
- For each use case, a description focusing on important influences on the system and SUC (e.g. expected demand rate).

The formal representation of the complementary information is not prescribed by the Shell Model Analysis. One possibility is to use a "data dictionary" - basically a set of simple tables with references to the elements of an SM. An excerpt of the data dictionary for the running example can be seen in Fig. 7. It is suggested to use a configuration management system for maintaining an SM and its associated data dictionary.

COMPONENT LIST		
Identifier	**Description**	**Interfaces**
PLC (SUC)	PLC for machine control	Input: Digital In x2, Power In (24Vdc) Output: Digital Out x2 Bidirectional: RS-485 interface
Reset Button	External, debounced reset button	Input: User action Output: Digital Out
...	...	...

SHELL LIST	
Shell	**Description**
PLC subsystem (Z)	PLC inside PLC cabinet
Control system (O_1)	PLC cabinet plus control elements
Production system (O_2, S)	Control system plus operator
...	...

ENVIRONMENTAL INFLUENCES	
Identifier	**Description**
Heat	Heat buildup in PLC cabinet due to thermal radiation of nearby machines, maximum expected temperature +60°C
Dust	Accumulation of metal particles in PLC cabinet from metal-cutting work, grain sizes of 50-100µm
EMI	Radiation EMI from nearby machines and wireless networks, limits acc. to ISO 62061, Annex E
...	...

USE CASES	
Identifier	**Description**
Production	Default use case, continuous demand on PLC for control purposes
Maintenance	Maintenance of machines, no demand on PLC, MTTR = 1d
Upgrade	Upgrade and/or replacement of PLC
...	...

COMMUNICATIONS			
Unidirectional			
Sender	**Receiver**	**Type**	**Message Set**
ADC	PLC	Digitised measurement value	{Digitised measurement value}
Reset Button	PLC	Reset signal	{No Reset, Reset}
...	...	...	...
Bidirectional			
Peer	**Peer**	**Type**	**Message Set**
PLC	Comm. Bus	Control commands/responses	{'Execute Test' Command, 'Test OK' Response, ...}
...	...	...	...

Fig. 7. Excerpt tables of the data dictionary for the example in Fig. 6.

3.6 Derivation of System Functions

A shell model is a static depiction of a system's structure. However, it is possible to describe the dynamic behavior from the relationships between communicating components. This allows further analyses of a system's intended and, more importantly, unintended behavior.

A system function (or simply, function) is defined as an alternating sequence of components and unidirectional communications between them. The most basic function consists of one component, the sender, communicating some energy or information to another component, the receiver. Obviously, only components linked by a communication arrow in the SM can be part of a function and the communication must match the direction and definition of the arrow. The communication between sender and receiver can consist of a non-empty subset of messages defined for the communication arrow. By prefixing a proper message subset with a '!', the subset consisting of the set difference between the given subset and the complete set of messages for this arrow can be stated for convenience. In addition, a '*' symbol represents the complete set of messages.

In order to specify changes in the status of a component in response to communications or as part of a function execution, each component is augmented by a mode. To symbolize an internal mode change, a dashed arrow is used that links two instances of the same component with differing modes.

Figure 8 depicts a basic function (a) and an internal mode change (b) in a graphical and sequence-based notation, where the latter represents a function/mode change as a sequence of (component, mode) tuples and {message} subsets. By chaining basic functions and mode changes, complete functions over the components of an SM can be defined. The component at the start of the chain is termed "trigger", the component at the end of the chain is termed "terminator" of a function. Thus a complete function (from trigger to terminator) is represented via a sequence of functional steps and messages, a "function-message chain" (FMC).

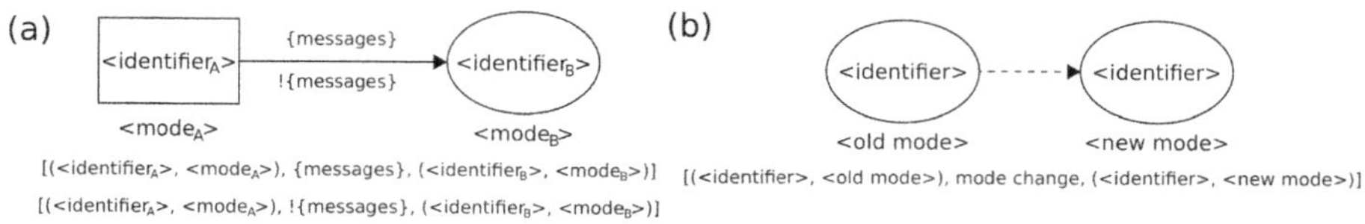

Fig. 8. (a) Basic function and (b) internal mode change in graphical and sequence notation

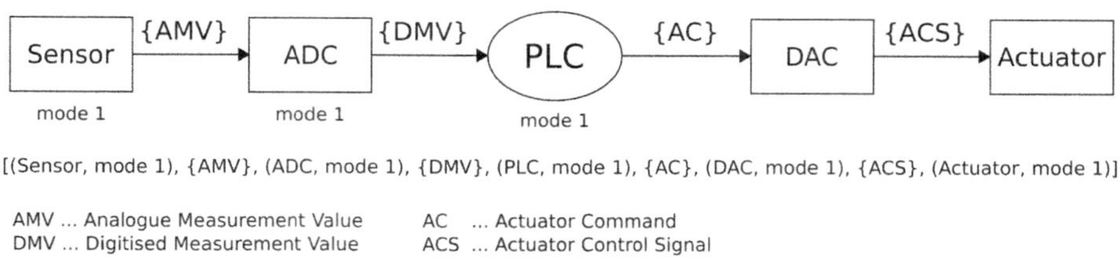

Fig. 9. A simple example function for the PLC shell model

Figure 9 shows the FMC for a simple example function for the "PLC" SM with the components "Sensor" and "Actuator" as the trigger and terminator, respectively. Note that the mode is omitted for some components - in this case, the component is understood to assume its default mode which must be defined for each component.

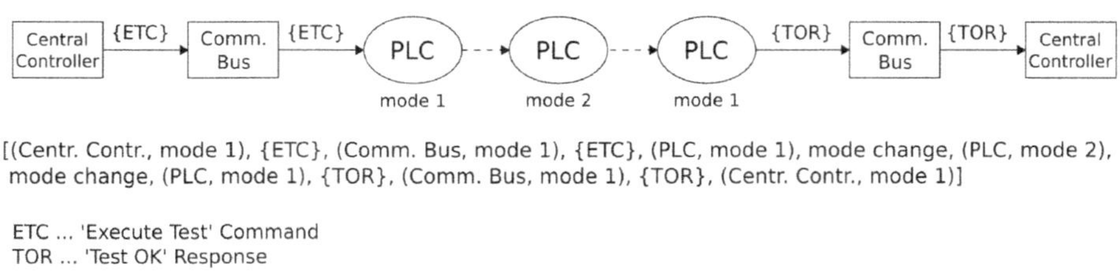

Fig. 10. Example PLC function with an internal mode change of the SUC

A more elaborate example function is depicted in Fig. 10. Here, the "PLC" undergoes a mode change in response to a communication from the "Central Controller", reverting to the original mode afterwards (supposedly after executing the command). Note that only the order of function steps can be modelled - the real time behavior of functions is out of scope of the notation.

4 Modelling Guidelines

Following the syntactical rules of the Shell Model Analysis leads to well-formed shell models but does not guarantee maximum readability and suitability for further analyses. In the following, a sample of important aspects and advice concerning the construction of practically usable shell models is given.

4.1 Placement of ACs

In many cases, ACs assume clearly defined roles in their communication with the SUC. By consistently placing ACs according to their role at certain positions relative to the SUC, the amount and ratio of interfaces of the SUC can be easily discerned. The following placement is suggested:

- ACs which only provide input, to the left of the SUC (e.g. sensors)
- ACs which only receive output, to the right of the SUC (e.g. actuators)
- ACs which represent user interface elements, to the top of the SUC (e.g. buttons)
- ACs which communicate bidirectionally with the SUC, to the bottom (e.g. busses).

4.2 Functional Relevance of Communication

When adding communication arrows, the choice should be guided by the relevance of the communication for subsequent analyses. A principle rule is that only communication paths that include the SUC should be added. This excludes arrows between regular components that are not a part of a function where the SUC is involved.

For functions where the SUC is included, the scope of communication must be limited to a reasonable amount in order to balance completeness of the system view against complexity of further analyses. For example, a communication between the "Power Supply" and the "Sensor" could be added to the "PLC" example and the derived function in Fig. 9. This would allow an analysis to consider failures of the power supply and its consequences on the function.

4.3 Logical Versus Structural Definition of Shells

Shells can be defined in a variety of ways, with the "ideal" choice depending on the system and the choice of subsequent analyses. Often, the most suitable choice is based on logical distance of regular components to the SUC. In this case, an outer shell's order is synonymous with the amount of components that must be traversed over communication arrows in order to reach the SUC. The O_1-shell in the "PLC" example was defined in this way.

An alternative to logical order is to define shells according to a system's physical layout. In this case, shells of higher order contain components which are situated at a further physical distance from the SUC. By aligning shells with physical demarcations (e.g. containments, fire barriers), analyses regarding the impact of environmental influences on the system components can be facilitated.

5 Conclusion and Further Considerations

As the Shell Model Analysis is representing a method at a very early lifecycle stage, its findings and results can be used as inputs for further analysis methods. This way, the Shell Model Analysis closes the method gap at this stage, providing input to e.g. a HAZOP Analysis, an FMEA, a qualitative FTA (limited to single component level), a further requirements analysis, a use-case and scenario analysis, and further functional analyses.

The Shell Model Analysis only supports qualitative analysis, as quantification is infeasible at such an early lifecycle stage. Also, the Shell Model Analysis is not suitable for describing or handling parallel structures in the sense of redundant solutions. As of now, the Shell Model Analysis is restricted to electrical, electronical, and programmable electronic (E/E/PE) systems.

The application of the Shell Model Analysis to technologies other than E/E/PE systems (such as mechanics, hydraulics, and pneumatics) and other extensions to the method are under investigation. Furthermore, the method would clearly benefit from a tool or tool chain supporting the graphical modelling effort, the definition of the data dictionary, the derivation of the FMCs (graphical and/or tupel notation), and even parsing the FMC tupels of the FMCs for ambiguities or other discrepancies.

References

1. Ericson II, C.A.: Hazard Analysis Techniques for System Safety, 2nd edn. Wiley, New Jersey (2016). ch. 5.2.2
2. McDermid, J.: Issues in Development of Safety-Critical Systems, Safety-Critical Systems, First ed., pp. 16–42. Chapman & Hall, London (1993)
3. IEC: IEC 61508-6 Functional safety of electrical/electronic/programmable electronic safety-related systems, ed. 2.0, part 6. IEC, Geneva (2010)
4. IEC: IEC 60812 Analysis techniques for system reliability – Procedure for failure mode and effects analysis (FMEA), ed. 2.0. IEC, Geneva (2006)
5. U.S. Nuclear Regulatory Commission: NUREG-0492 - Fault Tree Handbook. U.S. Government Printing Office, Washington (1981)
6. Ericson II, C.A.: Fault Tree Analysis Primer, 2nd edn. CreateSpace Independent Publishing Platform, Charleston (2011)
7. Preiss, R.: Methoden der Risikoanalyse in der Technik. Edition TÜV Austria, Vienna (2009)
8. Tschürtz, H.: Safety-Vorgehensmodell zur Konzeption und Entwicklung von sicherheitskritischen Systemen. Dtechn Thesis, Institute for Engineering Design and Logistics Engineering, Vienna University of Technology, Austria (2016)

SPI and Management Issues

Improving the Choice of Organizational Change Strategy

Jan Pries-Heje[1(✉)], Peter H. Carstensen[2], Jørn Johansen[3], and Otto Vinter[1]

[1] Department of People and Technology, Roskilde University, 4000 Roskilde, Denmark
{janph, otv}@ruc.dk
[2] Department of Computer Science, University of Copenhagen, 2200 Copenhagen, Denmark
peter.h.carstensen@di.ku.dk
[3] Whitebox Aps, 2970 Hørsholm, Denmark
jj@whitebox.dk

Abstract. At the strategic level in ISO/IEC 33014 you identify the scope of change and choose change strategy; possibly using the Organizational Change Nexus for doing so. The Nexus-model takes into account the contingencies in an organization and can be used to derive a recommendation for how to organize the change process. In this paper we present a new and improved Nexus version 2 solving three problems that were in the original Nexus: (1) Over-sensitivity to the answer of a few statements. (2) A bias in the questionnaire leading to certain strategies being recommended too often. (3) New research on organizational change that ought to be included. Further, we can present the first results from using the Nexus in 51 companies in 2017–18 Based on a first analysis of these results we conclude that Nexus 2.0 works better and has overcome the three problems we identified.

Keywords: Organizational Change Nexus · ISO/IEC 33014
Recommending change strategy · ImprovAbility · Process improvement

1 Introduction

Organizational change, change management, process improvement and other attempts to change existing structures and processes in organizations is highly complex [1]. Whether we want to make changes in order til improve the organization's effectiveness, efficiency or flexibility, or whether we aim at improving our product quality, customer satisfaction etc. the actual planning of the changes and carrying out the required activities are highly complicated and require a lot of effort from both management, the change agents and the involved actors.

Due to this, huge amounts of literature exist on strategies and suggestions and recommendation for undertaking the change. Famous authors like Kotter [2], Hammer [3], Mintzberg [4], Drucker [5], Senge [6], Huy [7] and many other have published series of book and papers for how to cope with the challenges of organizational change.

X. Larrucea et al. (Eds.): EuroSPI 2018, CCIS 896, pp. 83–94, 2018.
https://doi.org/10.1007/978-3-319-97925-0_7

Thirteen years ago we developed a framework that we named the Organizational Change Nexus [8, 9]. Central was the identification of 10 different overall types of strategies. These 10 types of strategies have later been included as a core part of the ISO/IEC 33014 standard (Guide for Process Improvement) [10]. In Table 1 the 10 types of overall change strategies are presented along with a short explanation of each.

Table 1. The ten overall change strategies defined in ISO/IEC 33014 (re. Table 4 in [10]).

Change strategy	Definition and literature examples
Attitude-driven	Change is driven by a focus on organizational learning, individual learning and what creates new attitudes and behavior
Commanding	Change is driven and dictated by (top) management. Management takes on the roles as owner, sponsor and change agents
Employee-driven	Change is driven from the bottom of the organizational hierarchy when needs for change arise among employees
Exploration	Change is driven by the need for flexibility, agility, or a need to explore new markets, technology or customer groups
Measures-driven	Change is driven by metrics and measurements used to identify change areas and to measure improvements in the areas identified
Optionality	Change is driven by the motivation and need of the individual or group. It is to a large degree optional whether the individual takes the innovation into use
Production-organized	Change is driven by the need for optimization, economics of scale and/or cost reduction
Reengineering	Change is driven by fundamentally rethinking and redesigning the organization to achieve dramatic improvements
Socializing	Change in organizational capabilities is driven by working through social relationships. Diffusion of innovations happens through personal contacts rather than through plans and dictates
Specialist-driven	Change is driven by specialists, either with professional, technical, or domain knowledge

Part of the Nexus development was the creation of a questionnaire-based tool for identifying which (combination of) strategies would be most suitable for a specific change in a specific organizational context. The Nexus has proven very useful for deciding how to organize the overall strategic planning for change, i.e. decide which strategies to apply. The value of the approach has been tested many times cf. [11, 12].

However, over the last more than ten years research on organizational change and change strategies has come up with important new contributions and new trends on for example lean management and relational coordination. Furthermore, we have observed a tendency for some strategies to come out as recommendable too often when using the questionnaire-based tool, which led us to the hypothesis that the questionnaire was too sensitive to a few specific statements.

Based on these observations we initiated a research project with the overall aim of answering the following questions:

- Which trends and developments in research on change strategies are relevant for, and should be incorporated in an updated version of the Organizational Change Nexus?
- How can we create an updated version of the Nexus that ensures a more proper balance (and thereby applicability) of the strategies recommended by the questionnaire-based tool?

The remainder of this paper will first introduce the original Organizational Change Nexus in some more detail as well as some findings from practical use of this. Then we describe the work involved in developing version 2 of the Organizational Change Nexus. A summary and overview of the new version 2 will be provided and we offer a first set of findings from applying the new version. We end this paper with a discussion on to what extent we have managed to overcome the deficiencies we set out to cope with.

2 The Organizational Change Nexus

Too many software developing organizations fail when they try to improve. They may go through an assessment and they may start one or more improvement initiatives; But somehow, they never close the "learning cycle" [13] where they continuously measure, improve, evaluate and learn. In fact, figures from Denmark show that more than half of the companies that goes through an assessment never manage to improve successfully.

To cope with this high "mortality rate" a research project was initiated in January 2003 named Talent@IT. The word "talent" in the title emphasized the role of people and individuals, their skills, competencies and capabilities. The research project resulted in a new framework, an ImprovAbility model [14], to enhance the success rate with improvement initiatives. This framework is now part of the ISO/IEC 33014 [10] standard for process improvement in IT organizations which was published in November 2013.

As a part of the ImprovAbility model we developed a framework that contains 10 different overall types of strategies for managers to choose from. The strategies were selected based on a systematic study of change management literature looking for characteristics of successful use.

The idea pursued was to compare the characteristics of a specific change situation with the characteristics in which each strategy worked well. The aim was to identify the optimal solution to the question of which change strategy should be recommended. However, it turned out that there were nearly no common characteristics between the schools of thinking. It was a truly wicked problem [15]. Instead, we decided to derive a design theory for each school of thinking. Hence, the Nexus framework consist of 10 different design theories formulated as technological rules [16]. Each design theory has as a result a "fit" which then as a whole can be used to derive recommendations on which specific change strategy to choose.

For example, in relation to deriving the design theory on the change approach called "Optionality" (See Table 1) it was found that it would fit well in the following situation:

- When you have employees that are self-aware and have an opinion
- When you have very knowledgeable employees that know their work domain areas well
- When there are vast differences between the tasks of different employees so that they best can decide themselves whether to change or not.

To support the selection of a change strategy we also developed a questionnaire-based tool to guide managers in assessing and selecting which (combination) of the 10 overall change strategies that would be most appropriate in a specific organizational setting. The tool calculates a *fit* for each of the strategies based on contingencies of the situation today and the wished-for change.

Such a fit for a wished-for change in a specific organization could look as Table 2. Fit is calculated on a scale going from −100% up to +100% fit. In Table 2, the Specialist-driven change strategy has a nearly perfect fit of 92% and the Optionality change strategy is nearly as good with a fit of 84%. Using a combination of these when executing the change would therefore be advisable. On the other hand the Commanding change strategy has the worst fit (−84%) and should definitely not be used in this change situation.

Table 2. Example of a strategic fit for a wished-for change in a specific organization.

Change strategy	Calculated fit
Attitude-driven	38
Commanding	−84
Employee-driven	−54
Exploration	−58
Measures-driven	16
Optionality	**84**
Production-organized	26
Reengineering	−40
Socializing	64
Specialist-driven	**92**

3 Analyzing the Use of Nexus Version 1

Since its development in 2005–08 we have used the Organizational Change Nexus in more than 200 organizations (164 using the old version 1 of the Nexus) – private and public, It-developing and – applying – with very positive reactions from the managers using the Nexus.

The majority of the uses have been performed by managers enrolled in an Executive Master Program at Roskilde University in Denmark. The managers used the Nexus for planning organizational change projects in their home organizations. This ensured that the Nexus was used in real projects and not just university-adapted projects. All the participating managers had responsibility for organizational change at project level or higher in their own organization.

Before using the framework the managers were trained for three days in organizational change in general and in using the Nexus specifically. Specifically the project managers were asked to do the following with the Organizational Change Nexus:

1. Choose and describe an organizational change in your context.
2. Fill out the Nexus questionnaire from that contextual perspective.
3. Calculate the fit for each of the 10 strategies using the Nexus tool.
4. Document the recommendation to the organization – what change strategy (combination) to follow.
5. Create a detailed organizational change plan and document the rationale for the plan.
6. Discuss the utility of the Nexus framework.

As a result 164 reports were gathered each 5–6 pages long. The reports were analyzed by one of the authors of this paper using Grounded Theory (GT) techniques. Specifically the Strauss and Corbin [17] school of thought was used ending up with a "core story" which in this case was about which change strategies were chosen? With what outcome? How did the plans look? And was the situated implementation useful?

In Table 3 it can be seen for each of the 10 change strategies which change strategy came out as the best fit and which came out as the worst fit.

Table 3. Best and worst fit for each of the 10 strategies when using version 1.

Change strategy	Number of best fit	Number of worst fit
Attitude-driven	10	17
Commanding	11	12
Employee-driven	4	14
Exploration	1	38
Measures-driven	2	33
Optionality	73	3
Production-organized	17	8
Reengineering	4	36
Socializing	10	0
Specialist-driven	39	2

Optionality was clearly the most popular change strategy recommended as the best fit in 73 out of 164 organizations. A Specialist-driven strategy was the second most popular strategy coming out with the best fit in 39 out of 164 cases. The Production-organized strategy was the third most popular with 17 recommendations.

Three strategies came out as worst fit in most cases. Exploration was only the recommended best strategy in 1 case and the worst in 38 cases. Reengineering was only a best fit in 4 cases and worst fit in 36 cases, probably because the companies assessed were not having an eminent crisis. This indicates a potential bias in the data analyzed here. Finally, Measures-driven also shows a large number of worst fits, probably because the questions in version 1 may have a bias towards not selecting it. This will be discussed below.

In each and every one of the 164 cases we have first coded and analyzed the translation of the recommended change strategy to the plan for change in the specific organization. Second, we coded for comments and experiences on the facilitation process. Many questioned or discussed who should participate in the scoring process. E.g. "The three scorings illustrate the need for a discussion where all participates". "In general you have to carefully select who is to fill out the questionnaire?" "Is it required that top-management is involved in doing it? And maybe you should even have some questions clarifying who they are?"

This line of thought was combined with an identified need for more knowledge on the persons being involved in the scoring. One said: "I would add a dimension characterizing the person that is scoring and their pre-understanding as well as their position in relation to change". Further, there were even some people noticing that: "The tool does not take into account feelings and individual personal preferences".

Third, our coding grouped a number of people pointing critically at the calculation of fit for the change strategies captured by the tool (scoring spreadsheet). One comment was that some assertions/statements can be interpreted very differently. E.g. statements using the words 'always' or 'complex' are probably too strongly formulated.

Another outcome of the coding was the identification of a need for adding more assertions/statements in the questionnaire. E.g. "I would like the scoring tool to be enhanced with some clarifying questions to better paint a view of the organization". "I believe the questions and the filling out of the template could be influenced by: Where I am in the organizational hierarchy; what tasks I take care of; other cultural values than the Danish ones".

Fourth, comments to the scoring and calculation of fit were about the sensibility caused by relatively few assertions to some of the change strategies. E.g. "The scoring of a particular strategy depends on 2–4 parameters which don't seem like adequate grounding for making decisions. Thus it will not be advisable to choose a strategy based alone on the model's recommendation". The conclusion here is that two-to-three assertions do not seem to be enough to form a solid recommendation about a specific change strategy. This applies in particular to the Measures-driven strategy, which had only two assertions/statements in the questionnaire.

4 How We Developed Nexus Version 2

As stated in the introduction and in the section above, version 1 of the Organizational Change Nexus had a number of deficiencies. Some of the change strategies were too sensitive to a few specific questions, which we suspected resulted in some strategies being recommended too often and some not being recommended as often as they should have been. The managers who were subjected to the Nexus questionnaire had also expressed problems interpreting the meaning of a few questions. Finally, research on organizational change had moved on in the 10 years passed and produced new findings that we felt needed to be included. E.g. using a lean approach [18] to change had become quite popular as well as looking at relational coordination [19] for change.

We therefore set out to create a version 2 dealing with these deficiencies and include the new research on lean management and relational coordination. A little over a year ago version 2.0 was ready for trial by managers enrolled in the Executive Master Program at Roskilde University using the Nexus for real change projects in their home organizations.

In this section we describe the process that moved the Nexus from version 1 to version 2 as it exists today after having been used in more than 50 companies. Figure 1 shows the content of version 1 and the process leading to version 2 described below.

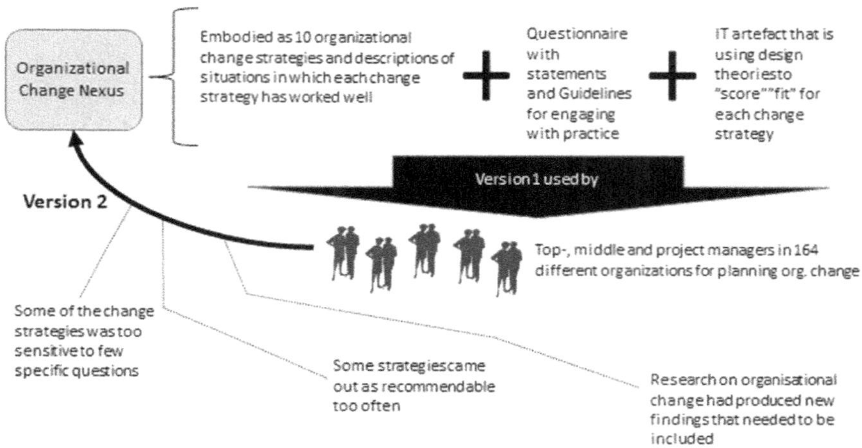

Fig. 1. The content of the Organizational Change Nexus version 1 (at the top) and the process leading to version 2 (lower part of figure).

From the beginning we were aware that the 10 overall strategies on which the Nexus is based had been promoted to the ISO/IEC 33014 standard [10]. Thus, in order to remain consistent with the standard, we were not able to delete or add new strategies – or even change their names. The new findings on organizational change had to be confined to (re)interpretations of the description in one or more of the now standardized overall strategies.

However, when it came to redefining questions in the questionnaire that we used to determine the fit of the overall strategies, we had more freedom to define new or reformulate old questions. This meant that we could aim at solving the deficiencies of sensitivity and suspected biases. The sensitivity was evident as the number of assertions/statements that determined the fit of a strategy ranged from two to four questions.

At our first meeting two more issued were brought to the table. The first was that managers in companies that had used version 1 often requested more concrete advice on how then to execute the recommended strategies in practice. A parallel track to the updating of the Nexus was then established headed by two of us. The result of this work has been published [20, 21].

Issues about how to perform the Nexus scoring process was also brought up. One issue was the need for standardizing the Nexus scoring process when managers in the consensus meeting had differing views on the score for a question and consensus therefore hard to reach. Another issue was about defining the scope of the organizational change so that the right participants were involved in the scoring. We ended up deciding that it was very important to initiate the interaction with the organization by clearly defining the scope, e.g. describing what the target group for change would do differently when the change process reach the end; the so-called "desired future state".

In order to solve the sensitivity issue, we quickly decided that the number of questions related to each strategy should be the same, and in order to keep the size of the questionnaire to one page, we agreed on having exactly four statements per strategy in the questionnaire.

The new field of relational coordination [19, 22] was quite natural and easy to include under the Socializing strategy and the questions were modified to reflect this new field.

Including the new field of lean management [18, 23] under the Production-organized strategy proved to be more challenging, however. The original idea behind this strategy was based on Taylor's scientific management [24, 25] and lean management is designed for similar production environments where you aim for smooth processes and economics-of-scale. However, there is a slight difference in the lean philosophy and application in practice. After reviewing the literature on lean management we developed and agreed on some new statements (assertions) for the Nexus questionnaire to encompass lean.

As soon as we had completed a draft Nexus version 2 questionnaire we started validating it through the Executive Master Program where the participating managersall had more than 3 years of practical experience in organizations. We received valuable feedback on the formulation and relevance of the statements/assertions, which we integrated in the questionnaire.

We then performed a final evaluation and check of the questionnaire to find out how well the questions covered the 3 important issues described in a technological rule [16]: "If your current state is X, your desired future state is Y, then you should perform Z to get there." This led to organizing the questions in the following groups: (1) The Organization today; (2) The Employees today; (3) Experiences with Organizational Change; (4) The Organizational Change; and (5) The Result of Organizational Change (desired future state).

Validation of the new questionnaire in real-life assessments in organizations started immediately after and seemed to confirm that sensitivity to a few statements was no longer an issue. There were also fewer problems with the understandability of the individual statrements. We therefore consider the current version 2 as the completion of our work on updating the nexus and the accompanying questionnaire.

5 Changes in Nexus Version 2

As described in the previous section the development of the Organizational Change Nexus version 2 led to a number of changes and enhancements. The main changes/enhancements are described in this section.

New theory on lean management [18, 23] was added to the Production-organized strategy, and new theory on relational coordination [19, 22] was added to the Socializing strategy. This was done after a re-analysis on the evolving knowledge base of international state-of-the-art papers and books.

For the production-organized and lean strategy the statements in the questionnaire ended up being (agree => better fit for this strategy unless otherwise stated):

- The organizational context is very dynamic and demands frequent changes (disagree => better fit for this strategy)
- We have knowledge and skills that could be used in a more optimal way through economy-of-scale and uniform processes
- It is primarily simple and well-understood workflows and – processes that will be changed
- Existing workflows have bottlenecks and needs to be more effective.

For the socializing and relational coordination strategy the statements in the questionnaire ended up being:

- Today the target group for change has common goals, common knowledge and considerable mutual respect
- It is primarily attitudes and social relations that needs to be changed in the future
- Until now it is the work with social relations that has created change
- In the future the work of the target group for change is very dependent on each other; they need to work closely together.

The Nexus questionnaire and tool wherein the knowledge on the calculation of fit is embedded were changed to make sure that there were at least four assertions/statements for scoring the fit of each of the 10 strategies in order to reduce the sensitivity of a few or a single question.

Furthermore the tendency for the Optionality strategy to very frequently come out as recommended was countered by adding a situation-descriptive assertion on whether the change at hand is mandatory/enforced e.g. because of new legislation from outside the organization. A new assertion determining whether the Optionality strategy has a good fit was added: “The change ahead of us is unavoidable; we have to change.” This assertion requires disagreement for the Optionality strategy to have an optimal fit.

To the knowledge on the facilitation process when using the Nexus was added a recommendation to include in the group scoring the key stakeholders: Owner, User, Project/Change Manager, and Process Improver. This was added because the original facilitation process had shown that only having managers involved could lead to a too narrow view on the current state and organizational change.

6 Findings from Using Nexus Version 2

The new Nexus 2.0 was tried in 34 companies in the spring of 2017 and 2018 by managers attending the Executive Master Program at Roskilde University.

Furthermore another 17 groups of graduate students at the IT University of Copenhagen following a course on Digital Change Management used the Organizational Change Nexus version 2 for changes in 17 Danish and International companies such as Maersk and Novo.

In short the results were good. Again the managers in the Executive Master Program participants evaluated the utility to be very high and they reported that many companies followed the organizational change plan derived from using the Nexus.

In Table 4 it can be seen which of the 10 change strategies came out as the best fit and which came out as the worst fit when using Nexus version 2 in the 34 companies from which the Executive Master students came.

Table 4. Best and worst fit for each of the 10 strategies when using version 2 in 34 companies.

Change strategy	Number of best fit	Number of worst fit
Attitude-driven	7	1
Commanding	5	3
Employee-driven	5	2
Exploration	7	0
Measures-driven	1	13
Optionality	5	1
Production-organized	4	1
Reengineering	0	6
Socializing	5	1
Specialist-driven	4	6

7 Discussion and Conclusion

If we now look at the three problems we were trying to address we can see the following outcome. The first problem we tried to address in the Change nexus version 1 was the over-sensitivity to the answer of a few statements. We addressed that by adding statements – still based solidly in empirical findings and literature – so that the scoring of the fit of every change strategy was based on at least four assertions/statements. This addition of more questions seems to have worked out quite well. By adding more questions there was a risk that the total questionnaire had become too long and tedious. But not a single report mentions this as a problem. In fact there are 2 or 3 of the Executive Master Program participants that would have liked to have even longer and therefore deeper questionnaires with more statements/assertions.

The second problem was whether bias in the questionnaire was leading to certain strategies being recommended too often. The two "suspects" were Optionality and Specialist-driven. From Table 4 (compared with Table 3) we can clearly see that the new and updated set of statements have taken care of that bias. Neither Optionality nor Specialist-driven is coming out as the best change strategy any more. However, a closer look at Table 4 indicates that we may have added another bias towards Measures-driven change. 13 out of 34 end up having Measures-driven as the least recommendable strategy. We will have to look further into that.

The third problem was that new ideas in the change management field materialize over time and new and relevant research has appeared since we "froze" version 1 of the Nexus in 2008. Specifically we saw the need for adding lean management and relational coordination. In the concrete we added lean to the production-organized strategy and relational coordination to the socializing strategy. Based on the comments we received from the 51 applications of Nexus 2.0 we conclude that we have included these new fields of organizational change research successfully.

Hence, our final conclusion is that Nexus 2.0 works better and has overcome the three deficiencies we set out to cope with.

References

1. Clarke, P., O'Connor, R.V., Leavy, B.: A complexity theory viewpoint on the software development process and situational context. In: 2016 IEEE/ACM International Conference on Software and System Processes (ICSSP). IEEE (2016)
2. Kotter, J.P.: Leading change: why transformation efforts fail. Harv. Bus. Rev. **73**, 59–67 (1995)
3. Hammer, M.: Reengineering work: don't automate, obliterate. Harv. Bus. Rev. **68**, 104–112 (1990)
4. Mintzberg, H., Ahlstrand, B., Lampel, J.: Strategy Safari: A Guided Tour Through the Wilds of Strategic Management. Financial Times, Prentice Hall, London (2002)
5. Drucker, P.: Innovation and Entrepreneurship. Routledge, Abingdon (2014)
6. Senge, P.M.: The fifth discipline, the art and practice of the learning organization. Perform. Improv. **30**(5), 37 (1991)
7. Huy, Q.N.: Time, temporal capability, and planned change. Acad. Manag. Rev. **26**(4), 601–623 (2001)
8. Pries-Heje, J., Vinter, O.: A framework for selecting change strategies in IT organizations. In: Münch, J., Vierimaa, M. (eds.) PROFES 2006. LNCS, vol. 4034, pp. 408–414. Springer, Heidelberg (2006). https://doi.org/10.1007/11767718_36
9. Pries-Heje, J., Baskerville, R.: The design theory nexus. MIS Q. **32**, 731–755 (2008)
10. ISO: ISO/IEC/TR 33014. In: Information Technology – Process Assessment – Guide for Process Improvement, Geneva, Switzerland (2013)
11. Pries-Heje, J., Johansen, J.: Change strategy for ISO/IEC 33014: a multi-case study on which change strategies were chosen. In: Barafort, B., O'Connor, R.V., Poth, A., Messnarz, R. (eds.) EuroSPI 2014. CCIS, vol. 425, pp. 317–330. Springer, Heidelberg (2014). https://doi.org/10.1007/978-3-662-43896-1_29
12. Pries-Heje, J., Johansen, J.: Choosing change strategy for ISO/IEC 33014. J. Softw.: Evol. Process **27**(8), 573–583 (2015)
13. Matsuo, M., Nakahara, J.: The effects of the PDCA cycle and OJT on workplace learning. Int. J. Hum. Resour. Manag. **24**(1), 195–207 (2013)
14. Pries-Heje, J., Johansen, J.: ImprovAbility-Success with Process Improvement. DELTA, Borough Park (2013)

15. Rittel, H.W., Webber, M.M.: Dilemmas in a general theory of planning. Policy Sci. **4**(2), 155–169 (1973)
16. Aken, J.E.V.: Management research based on the paradigm of the design sciences: the quest for field-tested and grounded technological rules. J. Manag. Stud. **41**(2), 219–246 (2004)
17. Corbin, J., Strauss, A., Strauss, A.L.: Basics of Qualitative Research. Sage, Thousand Oaks (2014)
18. Poppendieck, M., Poppendieck, T.: Lean Software Development: An Agile Toolkit. Addison-Wesley, Boston (2003)
19. Gittell, J.H.: How interdependent parties build relational coordination to achieve their desired outcomes. Negot. J. **31**(4), 387–391 (2015)
20. Carstensen, P.H., Vinter, O.: Developing action plans based on strategy–aspects to consider. Softw. Qual. Prof. Mag. **20**(2) (2018)
21. Carstensen, P.H., Vinter, O.: Aspects you should consider in your action plan when implementing an improvement strategy. In: Mas, A., Mesquida, A., O'Connor, R., Rout, T., Dorling, A. (eds.) SPICE 2017. CCIS, vol. 770, pp. 467–480. Springer, Cham (2017). https://doi.org/10.1007/978-3-319-67383-7_34
22. Hoffer Gittell, J.: Coordinating mechanisms in care provider groups: Relational coordination as a mediator and input uncertainty as a moderator of performance effects. Manag. Sci. **48** (11), 1408–1426 (2002)
23. Womack, J.P., Jones, D.T.: Lean thinking—banish waste and create wealth in your corporation. J. Oper. Res. Soc. **48**(11), 1148 (1997)
24. Taylor, F.W.: Scientific management. Sociol. Rev. **7**(3), 266–269 (1914)
25. Taylor, F.W.: Scientific Management. Routledge, Abingdon (2004)

An Analysis of IT Project Management Across Companies in an International Scenario

Paulo Roberto Martins de Andrade(✉) and Samira Sadaoui

University of Regina, Regina, SK S4S 0A2, Canada
{martinsp,sadaouis}@uregina.ca

Abstract. With the growing recognition of the importance of Project Management (PM), new solutions are still researched to improve PM practices in environments where there is a restriction on the project types. PM is becoming more widespread in business and academia but without enough information about the course of actions to be taken to archive success. This is principally true in the IT sector where the impact of new technologies is felt faster than in any other areas. This present study reviews the actual state of IT project management based on an online survey that we conducted with worldwide companies. Our aim is to provide insights and recommendations on how to increase the projects' success rate based on the results of the survey analysis.

Keywords: Project management · Agile · Survey analysis
Risk management · IT projects

1 Introduction

As stated by [1], the concept of Project Management (PM) refers to *"the application of knowledge, skills, tools and techniques to the project activities with the purpose of attending its requirements"*. This concept along with the company culture and other business processes (e.g. IT, marketing, financial and commercial) produce what we call the outputs (artifacts) for the PM process. Outputs are generated from different departments across the business, and are part of the company's culture. They facilitate the execution of PM throughout its cycle: initiation, planning, control and closure. Examples of such outputs are payment schedule, team member information, company hierarchy, stakeholders' list and technologies adopted in the company.

Nowadays, to increase the success rate of projects, it is necessary for businesses to learn from past PM practices that have been tested in different environments. Although managing the PM process is one of the crucial parts for the success of any project, especially when developing new systems or saving time and money, there is no study that depicted the actual picture of companies and their methodologies [1]. This situation is true especially for projects in the

X. Larrucea et al. (Eds.): EuroSPI 2018, CCIS 896, pp. 95–107, 2018.
https://doi.org/10.1007/978-3-319-97925-0_8

IT sector, as there is a lack in the literature about PM in the IT sector [2–5]. Consequently, in this paper, we examine the PM standards and tools used by worldwide companies and assess their impact on IT projects.

Albeit there is a considerable literature about PM, it is however very general with predetermined implementation formulas and without any insights on the project successes and failures and their implications. Additionally, there is a very limited accumulated knowledge on the management of IT projects. Most of the research focus on Agile frameworks and how they can be used to improve the PM practices [1]. The very essence of our study requires empirical investigation.

Thus, we developed a robust survey with the intention of determining the characteristics of PM practices in the IT domain. Numerous companies, local and international, participated in the survey. As a result, based on real-world scenarios, we will present the actual picture of the PM field (what these companies are doing and archiving). IT Project Management (ITPM) is undoubtedly an emerging theme among professionals as well as in the Project Management Institute (PMI). To date, limited information can be found addressing the profiles of projects along with the profiles of professionals and companies in a synthesized way and under several angles that this research sought to address. Through the conducted data analysis in this paper, we will determine, in the future work, what are the best PM practices (what companies should be doing more) as well as the contributing factors to the success rate of projects from different angles. The outcome of this research will provide valuable lessons from the PM field, and insights for other areas, like engineering, business, medical and social.

2 Related Work

We are facing changes in different aspects of human life (social, cultural, political, technological, and economic) and it is happening at an increasing speed. Usually is common to associate results of projects with these significant changes [6]. Consequently, managing projects in an efficient way for an era of changes is a difficult challenge of modern-day management [7]. Overcoming this challenge is being prepared to manage projects in a planned and professional manner.

In the last 60 years, several standards have risen, and they have contributed to increasing the level of PM professionalism. The IPMA (International Project Management Association), which represents associates of many national corporations (mainly in Asia, Africa, and Europe), created its own standards (formed by national programs developed by members of the association, the quality assurance process, and a central framework) and certification program. The Australian Institute of Project Management (AIPM) issued in 1996 the *"National Standard of Competence for Project Management"*. The Government of Australia approved it as a piece of the country's national qualification system [8]. Furthermore, The Association for Project Management in England established norms of competence for PM too. The same happened across the globe, like the Project Management Institute (PMI) that published the PMBOK Guide and the British Central Computer and Telecommunications Agency (CCTA) that published its own method. Other organizations with national-scale projects are eagerly involved in the advancement of the project manager ocupation in China, Japan and South Africa [6].

In 2015, Bonnie performed a search about the view and use of PM in the world. This study was based on data collected from important companies (i.e. PMI and the Harvard Business Review). Each one did their search with different industries and published their results. Table 1 provides an overview of the most relevant data from Bonnie's study [2].

Table 1. Project management statistics in 2015

Key performance indicator	Level reached
% of companies used PM in the entire organization	59%
% of companies used PMBOK	41%
% of companies used others methodologies	33%
% of companies used a PM software	77%
% of companies conducted risk management	64%
% of companies used Agile Frameworks	38%
% of companies used Agile and choose Scrum for their process	16%
% of projects led by a certified project manager	80%
% of project managers that break up larges projects into smaller ones	30%
% of IT projects that ran over budget	45%
% of IT projects that ran over time	70%
% of IT projects that delivered less aggregated value than expected	56%
% of companies were unclear on the IT projects' business objectives	45%
% of IT projects that met their goals	64%
% of project requirements that were usually out of sync with the business	78%

From Table 1, we can observe that the situation of the projects in the world is not the best and this is why researchers investigate these issues. A failure in a project means that companies will expend more time and more money to achieve their goals or even worst, they will fail as a business. For example, the *"% of IT projects that ran over budget"*. We can see that almost half of all projects expend more money that was planned to get it completed. This issue can happen from poor planning or for risks that were not managed right. We also noticed that not all organization use PM according to *"% of companies that used the project management in the entire company"*. With the value of 59%, we can conclude that this discipline needs to be more widespread in the culture of organizations. However, simply adopting a process is not a solution, as we can see in *"% of project requirements are usually out of sync with the business"*. The latter means that 78% of the interviewed people think that the project requirements should be reviewed because they do not aim the business goals.

In addition, the Project Manager has been cited by some authors as a relatively new and emerging profession. It is because several organizations, public and private, research and education institutions, and others, are frequently seeking to study, propagate, put into practice, and envolve the knowledge, tools, models, and methodologies employed in this field and profession [1,9,10]. The authors of these papers were aligned with the data from Table 1. This shows the great necessity of more studies in the ITPM field.

3 Survey Design and Process

3.1 Survey Design

In October 2016, we interviewed local IT businesses in Canada to determine what problems they face in their projects. We conducted an informal survey with five companies from three sectors (software development, real estate, and education), with a total of eight interviewees. From the survey, we noticed that all companies were having similar problems despite the use of different approaches (e.g. lack of documentation, teams were not really involved in all phases, miscommunication, and unexpected changes). If these problems occur in small companies where adaptations are easier to implement [11], so what could we expect from larger businesses? So, we developed a study based on an online survey with the goal of investigating the current PM situation of worldwide companies: what are they doing right and wrong? who is in charge for PM; and how are they managing the projects? These questions were fundamental in the survey design.

We structured the survey into four parts: (1) profiles of the participant and companies; (2) profile of PM processes; (3) profile of projects; (4) organizational performance and risk management. The first three parts (they are presented in this paper as Sects. 4, 5, and 6 respectively) are used to profile the participant, the company, processes, and projects. Based on these profiles, we will conduct a qualitative analysis using crossed information. For instance, what companies with an income of more than 500 K with high-risk projects do differently from companies with low-risk projects? The last part assesses how risk management impacts the projects and also exposes the metrics used to measure the success of projects. This part of the survey and its data will be analyzed in a future publication. We will cross information obtained from part 4 with the other sections to conduct a qualitative analysis and compare some possible scenarios. We know for fact that these metrics change from company to company but we can find some intersection points that could be used by anyone [12].

We created the survey with the anonymous participation with the purpose of determining the best practices in the market and to develop a new approach with regard to the investigation results of the survey aligned with the literature review. The survey was published as a technical paper and can be accessed on [13]. This study was approved by the University of Regina Ethics Board.

3.2 Survey Process

In March 2017, we invited companies to participate in the survey and distribute it to their partners. At the beginning, we chose companies located in the city of Regina (Canada). This was the first round of invitations to get feedback from the interviewed about the research. Based on the feedback, we extended the survey by including more options in the questions and improving their descriptions, and then posted it online. Next, we sent an invitation to the Project Management Institute (PMI) Chapters to disseminate our survey. From the PMI Global, we had support from chapters of Houston, Central Virginia, Metrolina, Costa Rica, Quad City Area, Central Italy, Ivory Coast, Norway, and Southern Italy. From the PMI Brazil, we had support from chapters of Amazonia, Rio Grande do Sul, Pernambuco, Sergipe, and Rio de Janeiro. Considering the large number of companies and professionals affiliated with PMI Chapters, it was necessary to determine a sample with respect to the criteria of accessibility and representability (with close connection to PM in the IT sector). Then, we created several distribution lists to institutions and researchers that are related to our subject. These lists have helped the research to reach a more diversified and multicultural public. The survey remained open until May 2017. In summary, the total number of invitations was 3,439 people. From this number, we had 1,262 accesses to the survey where 157 responses were obtained (around 12.4% of the accesses).

4 Profiles of Participant and Company

Knowing the profile of employees and companies is an important step before adopting any PM approach [14]. This step is crucial because each business domain (banking, education, telecommunication, government, etc.) has it own particularities. Thanks to the profiles, it is possible to understand the PM standards and then compare them between companies. The goal here is to determine why a certain approach was a successful or a failed practice. The profile analysis is a fundamental principle before the development of best market practices.

4.1 Participant

The primary goal here is to identify what kinds of professionals are working with ITPM and their qualifications. One of the factors is to check how the status of a qualified professional or his knowledge of a specific approach (though certifications and experience) can influence the project success rate. According to our data, 52% of participants are between 36 and 50 years old. This information could tell us that more than a half of the participants are in an advanced position in their careers and with more expertise to share. Another useful information that we observed is the degree level. We found out that 76% of the sample has a degree higher than the Bachelor level. This could demonstrates a necessity in the market for the continuous professional improvement since, in PM, a professional needs to go beyond the undergraduate degree to hold a good position.

Regarding the professional experience with general projects, we have eight participants (5.3% of the sample) that never managed a project. These people are basically team members or have another position in the company. In another hand, 71.4% of participants managed more than 6 projects in the past. This data is significant for this kind of study since it brings assertive practices gained through time and experience. We also asked about the professional certification and the answers brought some surprises. According to [7,15], most of people who work in IT projects possess the Agile certification CSM (Certified ScrumMaster). However, our data shows that 58.7% of participants holding the Project Management Professional Certification (PMP), 28.7% the ITIL Certification, 20.7% the CSM, 11.3% the COBIT Certification, 10.7% a Six Sigma Certification, and 7.3% the PRINCE2 Certification (an acronym for PRojects IN Controlled Environments). Some other certifications were mentioned but they do not have an expressive number.

Next, we extracted information about the professional experience with IT and Agile projects. Our data shows that 74.7% of our sample have more than six years of experience in PM. Within this set, 91.1% have more than one year of IT experience and 81.6% have more than six years (68% of the global sample). Inside the sample, we selected people that is less than 25 years old and with at least one year of experience with IT projects, from where we obtained the amount of 71.6% using Agile (48.7% of the sample). 28.6% of people with more six years of experience with IT projects have used Agile. We can conclude that Agile principles have become more important in recent years and its adoption has been growing among the professionals in the PM field [1]. This statement is true since the PMI created an agile certification (PMI-ACP) and in its new publication, "AGILE Practice Guide", PMI aligns PMBOK PM best practise with the principles and values of the Agile Manifesto [15,16].

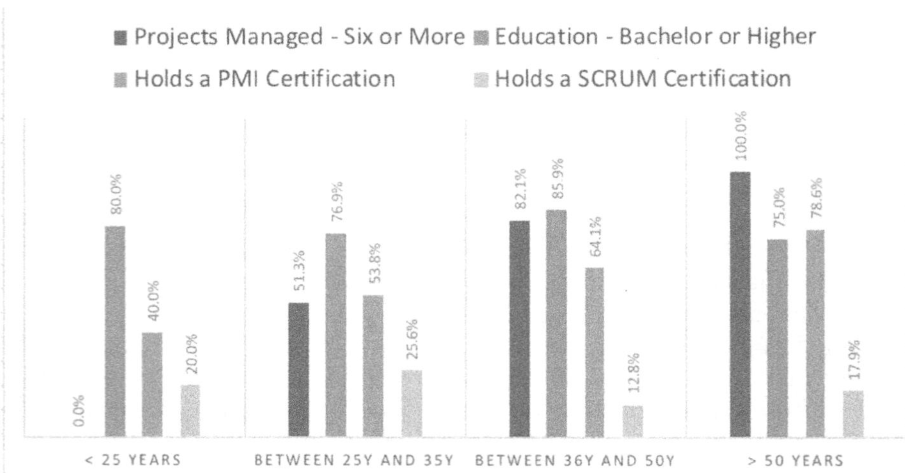

Fig. 1. Profile of participants by age

Moreover, Fig. 1 summarizes the data discussed previously using the age as a division. It also includes the two primary professional certifications for project managers: PMI (PMP, PM-ACP, and CAPM) and Scrum (Scrum Master and Product Owner). With this view, we can evaluate the reality and experience of each group. One intriguing data here is the link between the number of people that managed six projects or more and the number of people that holds a PMI Certification. If we look people with more than 25 years, are really close, what means, according to [17], a necessity for certified professionals in advanced PM positions. In other words, these certifications help the companies to ensure that their professionals are more prepared to take care of their projects and to have more responsibilities for high risk and complex projects. Another information that we can observe here is the low adoption of the Agile Certifications. For the our research propose (and listed in the survey as options) we are considering the following Agile Certifications: PMP-ACP, CSM, CSPO, and CSP.

4.2 Company

Here, we identify the companies where we are getting the results from, such as the type of industry, country, annual income, and size. With these information, we can analyze which techniques work better for which kinds of companies. We can also check if the industry or the location (both influences the business culture) has an impact on the choice of methodologies. This will helps us to better understand the universe of our study. First, we looked into the location of each company, and we can observe that most of the participants came from Brazil (with 40.7%). Other countries with a good participation are Cote d'Ivoire (15.3%), Canada (11.3%), United States (8.7%) and Italy (8%). The diversity of countries brings a rich multicultural view to the study.

Moreover, we categorized the industries of each company. We noticed that the ITPM field is present in all kinds of industries. We have, among the participant, a total of 30.6% of companies specifically from the IT industry, 28.7% from Education, 11.3% from Consulting, 9.3% from Government, and 20.1% from other kinds, such as Business Administration, Law Firms, Hospitality and Commerce. So, we can deduce what types of practices are more present. For example, we can state from that only 63% of companies from the IT Industry employs Agile frameworks in their projects. This means that besides the proven benefits of using Agile in the ITPM [18], not all companies agree that it is the best option. Despite that, 91.3% of the IT industry from our sample have someone with knowledge and experience with Agile frameworks.

5 Profile of Project Management Processes

Now, we need to go deeper about how the PM field works on the daily basis. A robust PM process is a key to the success of any projects [16]. Having this in mind, we can state that managerial and administrative decisions have a big impact on the projects since they create the enterprise culture, and consequently define how the PM area will be handled.

5.1 Formal Approaches

One of the first points to investigate is whether the company has a formal PM approach (well defined and internalized in the business culture) or not. This is important because if companies do not have an approach, they are considered just makers: they proceed with each project using a different process, not thinking about the standards and project constraints or about the RM. This will create uncertainty about the success of the project. In other words, they do not plan ahead their projects and just follow the orders from someone else, thus making it difficult for projects to be successfully completed. From the sample, 70.7% of companies have a formal approach to manage their projects. This is unexpected since in the market there is a pressure for faster delivery of new products and services, and at the same time companies need to save money [11,12]. This is a difficult task without the help of a PM approach. Another interesting data is that from companies that have a formal PM approach, 80.2% have the PMBOK has one the components for their approach, 45.3% have a Agile Framework as a component, 15.1% use PRINCE 2, and only 7.5% have they own specific PM methodology. Moreover, we noticed that only 51.3% of companies checked the project complexity. It was a surprise since we know that is necessary to check the project complexity before its launch in order to chose the right tools and process to achieve success [16].

We also identified a low rate of companies having a risk verification method. Risk management is an important sub-field of PM since it can contribute to the success or failure of a project [19]. A risk could be harmful (a threat), such as a team member leaving the company, late payment, late approval, or problems with suppliers. It can also be beneficial, such as new technologies or frameworks to implement to reduce the job amount, quick approval, or low exchange currency rate to pay for resources. Therefore, it is necessary to manage risks to avoid threats and take advantage of opportunities. From the data, only 60.7% of companies have a proper method to manage risks. According to [1], anything below 70% is considered as a low adoption value and as a signal that we need to improve PM in business.

Moreover, the survey data show that 43.3% of companies have a portfolio management. The latter is a step forward to the PM because it takes care of all the company's projects and prospects. From our study, we can notice that Italy is the most thoughtful in managing project complexity, with 75% of its companies having an underlying methodology. Following is Cote dÍvoire with 52.17%, Brazil with 49.18%, and Canada with 47.1%.

5.2 Business Model for Project Management

When we think about PM, support and guidelines from the administrative board are needed to make the process flow well. Here, 70% of companies have this support. Still, there are companies where their IT departments did not get the necessary help to make their projects happen because they are resilient to new projects and technologies [11]. We have some examples in the literature about big companies that resisted the changes, making their projects be late or archived [5]. When companies create their own Project Management Office (PMO), they recognize the importance of PM and the need of a different department to provide all the necessary support and centralize processes and projects. According to [15], *"Strategic PMOs enable strategic change in organizations. (...). Some serve as a means to standardize project-related governance processes (...). Others serve as centers of excellence (...)"* [16]. From the survey data, only 53.3% of companies have a PMO, which could impact the projects' standards and how the projects are conducted. Regarding the big companies, with the annual income more than 100 million of US dollars, the number goes to 71.2%. Although the advantages of the PMOs, not all companies are prepared to take this step further in their organizational architecture.

In short, the importance of a well-defined PM process is crucial. However, if we consider only the companies with a defined formal methodology, we note that there is still room for improvement in their process. For example, 68.2% of these companies have a portfolio management approach, and 67.9% do a complexity study before starting the projects to obtain the rights resources. If we consider the historical database, 58.7% have something similar and 76.5% have a methodology to manage risks. Among the companies with a formal PM process, 79.3% use a specialist software to manage their projects and 12.3% use only electronic spreadsheets and text editor to do their work.

6 Profile of Projects

With the "Profile of Projects", we can obtain information about the project (results, approaches, success and failure rates, problems) and underlying methodologies. So, it is possible to evaluate which approach helped more the companies to attain project success or to predict incidents (threats and opportunities). The efforts of the project team and manager should be spent on managing what many authors and researchers call the"triple constraint" (cost, time and scope) of project needs [1,16]. We can also include the project quality as a fourth piece, that can be affected by the balance of the triple constraint. These four "forces" maintain a natural balance between each other in a project, which we establish through the creation of baselines (snapshots of the project) for the scope, time, and cost. From this point where the baselines were creates, changes in a constraint (e.g. costs) will be reflected in one or more of other factors. For example, to meet a customer request for reducing the project cost, the project deadline should be increased or the project scope should be decreased. Otherwise, we will end up having a negative impact on the quality of the project because we will need to hire cheaper and less experienced teams, or to use cheaper and possibly lower quality materials, or to reduce the number of tests.

6.1 General View of Projects

Considering the triple constraint, our sample show that only 22.7% of companies consider more than 80% of their projects as a success (accomplished the initially planned scope, time and cost) and 31.3% had a success rate between 45% and 80%. We consider this as a good range since the Chaos Report pointed the average of success in IT projects in 2016 as 38% [20]. This also means that companies that had more than 80% of success rate could be viewed with an excellent performance.

For companies with more than 80% of their successful projects, 29.4% created their own approach, 41.2% used the Agile/Scrum or an approach based on this methodology, and 70.6% used an approach based on PMBOK. If we consider companies with a success rate between 45% and 80%, we have a reduction in the adoption of Agile frameworks (only 28.2% uses Agile/Scrum). We can observe that the adoption of Agile could help to improve the success rate, but it is necessary to analyze other factors such as the experience of who is managing the project, company and project size, company culture and PM process. With this analysis, we can state that Agile has contributed with 9% in the success of large size companies, and 23% for medium size companies. We got this percentage after crossing the information about the success rates and data from the previous section.

Moreover, the RM contributed to 41% in the success of large companies, 20% for medium-sized, and 37% for small-sized. The complexity is another factor that we considered, but instead of the company size, we adopt the project size. With this comparison, a methodology to check the complexity before the project could start can have an influence of 39% in the success rate for large projects (more than one year) and 24% for medium projects (between six months and one year). If we based the statics on the experience of who is managing the project for the same context (same size of project and company), there is only 7% of the difference in the impact of the success rate. It means that with the right support and methodologies, the experience with projects will have a small impact in the general success rate of a project but its come as a significant impact in the context of risk management (since this discipline becomes easier with experience and a project/lessons learned database).

In addition to this information, Table 2 demonstrates that all analyzed factors have a close range, which means, inside of our sample, these factors do not have a direct influence if a project is challenging or not. Different of our expectation, this analysis shows that we need to have new ways to identify a challenging project besides with we already have in the literature. We could consider other factors such: if the company has the right approach for that kind of project; if there is all the necessary information for the scope; the culture of the company; the right and necessary definition for the product quality; and others. We analyzed, for each range of Challenging Projects percentage, the Complexity Approach (CA), Project Management Office (PMO), Risk Management (RM), Historical Database (HDB), Board Support (BS) and Training for Teams (TT).

Table 2. Challenging projects analysis

Challenging projects	Data analysis					
	CA	PMO	RM	HDB	BS	TT
0%	50%	50%	75%	50%	63%	25%
1%–15%	29%	47%	47%	71%	76%	41%
16%–45%	55%	61%	59%	71%	77%	41%
46%–80%	60%	60%	76%	76%	80%	40%
>80%	50%	50%	55%	73%	78%	41%

7 Conclusion

By examining pragmatically whether a company has expectations about the success of its projects, it is interesting to get as much information as possible about other projects inside (historical basis) or outside (best market practices and literature) the company. This way we can minimize the risk, optimize the operations and even save money. This paper presents the initial results of our ongoing study of providing insights on how to increase the project's success rate. Our ultimate goal is to create a new PM approach, focused on risk management, and based on the best practices identified in this research. In this work, we already identified some crucial decisions for companies.

Management. According to our data, as an average, less than 50% of the companies have a complexity approach, which combine with other factors such as the training for teams (average of 40%) influences the challenge of a project (how difficult it will be to manage and archive success). Is also possible to notice low adherence to risk management. From the data presented, where only 22.7% of the companies had success in more than 80% of their projects, we can verify from the general analysis that the adoption of a well-known standard (such as the PMBOK or an Agile Framework) is not a guarantee of success. The companies need to put more effort to the Risk Management, and they need to include the CA and TT as essential parts to the success.

We can conclude that most of the large companies are putting effort into the PM discipline. However, some areas that can influence the success of projects are still left out. This research is still not conclusive regarding the impact that each factor cited in this study (e.g. complexity, methodology, training, and others) can have on PM. As a future work, we will verify the data collected using the fourth part of the survey and realize an in-depth qualitative analysis. We will cross the information found in this new analysis with the previous information presented on this paper to suggest a new practices to solve the identified issues.

Acknowledgment. The CNPq (Conselho Nacional de Desenvolvimento Cientifico e Tecnologico - "National Counsel of Technological and Scientific Development") and the University of Regina support this work. The University of Regina Ethics Board had approved this work through the certificate posted on https://goo.gl/OOYZHj.

References

1. Andrade, P.R.M., Albuquerque, A.B., Frota, O.F., da Silva Filho, J.F.: PM5: one approach to the management of IT projects applied in the Brazilian public sector. In: Proceedings of 13th International Conference on Software Engineering Research and Practice - SERP, WorldComp, pp. 49–54 (2015)
2. Bonnie, E.: Complete collection of project management statistics 2015 (2015). https://www.wrike.com/blog/complete-collection-project-management-statistics-2015. Accessed 28 Mar 2018
3. Garwood, D.A., Poole, A.H.: Project management as information management in interdisciplinary research: "lots of different pieces working together". Int. J. Inf. Manage. **41**, 14–22 (2018)
4. Cavarec, Y.: Revisiting the definition of project success. In: 2012 PMI Global Congress Proceedings, Vancouver, Canada, pp. 10–18. Project Management Institute (2012)
5. Marinho, M., Sampaio, S., Lima, T., de Moura, H.: Overcoming resistance to change in business innovation processes. Int. J. Eng. Technol. (IJET) **04**, 148–161 (2012)
6. Bierwolf, R.: Towards project management 2030: why is change needed? IEEE Eng. Manag. Rev. **45**(1), 21–26 (2017)
7. Prikladnicki, R., Lassenius, C., Carver, J.C.: Trends in agile updated: perspectives from the practitioners. IEEE Softw. **35**(1), 109–111 (2018)
8. Padalkar, M., Gopinath, S.: Six decades of project management research: thematic trends and future opportunities. Int. J. Proj. Manag. **34**(7), 1305–1321 (2016)
9. Killen, C.P., Hunt, R.A., Kleinschmidt, E.J.: Project portfolio management for product innovation. Int. J. Qual. Reliab. Manag. **25**(1), 24–38 (2008)
10. Heising, W.: The integration of ideation and project portfolio management - a key factor for sustainable success. Int. J. Proj. Manag. **30**(5), 582–595 (2012)
11. Andrade, P.R.M., Albuquerque, A.B., Araujo, R.G., Filho, J.C., Pereira, T.R., Mendonca, N.C.: Improving business by migrating applications to the cloud using cloudstep. In: Procedering for the 29th International Conference on Advanced Information Networking and Applications Workshops, pp. 77–82. IEEE, Gwangju (2015)
12. Andrade, P.R.M., Sadaoui, S.: Improving business decision making based on KPI management system. In: 2017 IEEE International Conference on Systems, Man, and Cybernetics (SMC), pp. 1280–1285. IEEE, Banff (2017)
13. Andrade, P.R.M., Sadaoui, S.: Survey questions for a study of the project management behavior in the IT sector. Technical report, University of Regina, April 2018. https://doi.org/10.13140/RG.2.2.20010.11209
14. Marinho, M., Sampaio, S., Lima, T., de Moura, H.: A guide to deal with uncertainties in software project management. Int. J. Comput. Sci. Inf. Technol. (IJCSIT) **06**, 1–20 (2014)
15. Project Management Institute: About us (2018). https://www.pmi.org/about. Accessed 29 Jan 2018
16. Project Management Institute: A Guide to the Project Management Body of Knowledge (PMBOK® Guide), 6th edn. Project Management Institute, Newtown Square (2017)
17. Silva, L.A., Damian, I.P.M., Padua, S.I.D.: Process management tasks and barriers: functional to processes approach. Bus. Process Manag. J. **18**(5), 762–776 (2012)

18. Eickhoff, F.L., McGrath, M.L., Mayer, C., Bieswanger, A., Wojciak, P.A.: Large-scale application of IBM design thinking and agile development for IBM z14. IBM J. Res. Dev. **62**(99), 1–9 (2018)
19. Waterman, M.: Agility, risk, and uncertainty, part 1: designing an agile architecture. IEEE Softw. **35**(2), 99–101 (2018)
20. TSG International: Chaos report 2016 (2017). http://www.standishgroup.com/outline. Accessed 12 Feb 2018

An Approach to Investigating Proactive Knowledge Retention in OSS Communities

Mehvish Rashid[1,2], Paul M. Clarke[1,2], and Rory V. O'Connor[1,2(✉)]

[1] Dublin City University, Dublin, Ireland
Mehvish.Rashid2@mail.dcu.ie, {Paul.M.Clarke, Rory.OConnor}@dcu.ie
[2] Lero, The Irish Software Research Centre, Limerick, Ireland

Abstract. Open Source Software (OSS) is the manifestation of software developed and released under an "open source" license, meaning that under certain conditions; it is openly available for use, inspection, modification, and for redistribution free of cost, or with cost based on the license agreement. The transient nature of work force results in turnover induced knowledge loss in OSS projects. Knowledge loss phenomenon refers to loss of experience and expertise in OSS projects due to leaving contributors, whose knowledge remains unshared with other contributors. The outcome of this work is the research methodology, to contribute towards the formation of proactive knowledge retention practices in OSS projects to transform contributor's use of knowledge and engagement in knowledge relevant activities including knowledge sharing and knowledge transfer.

Keywords: Open source software · Knowledge loss
Proactive knowledge retention · Mixed methods research

1 Introduction

Contributors in Open Source Software (OSS) projects interact on technology-mediated channels to acquire and to share knowledge such as mailing lists, forums, and Internet Relay Chat (IRC). The contributors who are skilled and experienced in a specific module of the project and may not explicitly share their acquired knowledge on their leaving, and therefore the project suffers from a knowledge gap. In contrast to contributors in OSS projects, employees in traditional software development organisation may be under contractual obligation to notify their employer before leaving the organisation and to fulfil a notice period during which knowledge transfer concerns can be addressed. The workforce in OSS projects is of a transient nature due to inevitable high turnover fate [1, 2] and further, departing contributors may not provide notice and in an instant, may no longer be available for the purpose of formal knowledge transfer activities.

OSS projects have a hierarchical onion-like structure (see Fig. 1), consisting of core, co-developer, active users, and passive users [3–5]. The knowledge distribution among contributors in OSS projects is not uniform and absence of a contributor who is the original owner of the files or system in the project to perform maintenance tasks

X. Larrucea et al. (Eds.): EuroSPI 2018, CCIS 896, pp. 108–119, 2018.
https://doi.org/10.1007/978-3-319-97925-0_9

results in risking files to abandonment [6]. A small subset of contributors, typically 20%, called core members, make major code contributions of about 80% in OSS projects [3]. These 80% of the contributors, who make knowledge contributions in the form of the code, can be considered the most knowledgeable ones on the project. As depicted in Fig. 1 of the onion model, knowledge distribution in OSS projects is non-uniform with a higher concentration of code contributors in the centre of the onion than in the outer layers. The focus of this research is on the uniform distribution of knowledge among contributors, by the introduction of continuous knowledge transfer techniques and practices, which we refer to as a proactive knowledge retention strategy for OSS projects. This paper presents the research methodology to investigate the knowledge loss problem in OSS projects articulated in [7]. The research methodology discusses the overall research approach to be employed to devise a proactive knowledge retention strategy in OSS projects.

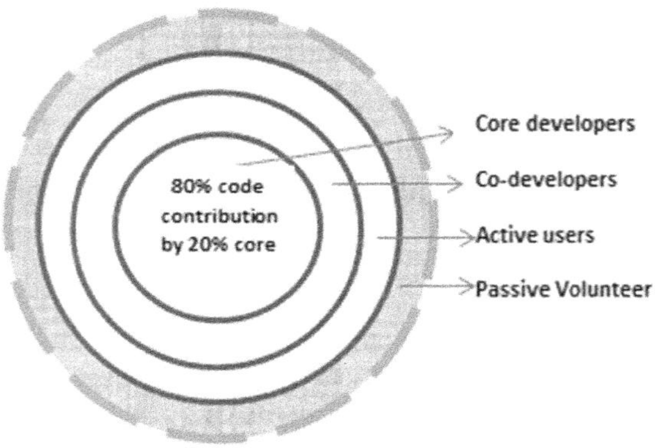

Fig. 1. Onion model representing contributors in OSS projects users [3–5]

2 Background

"Knowledge is information combined with experience, context, interpretation and reflection" [8]. In OSS projects knowledge generation is continuous through the process of knowledge creation and sharing and is cyclic in nature. There are two kinds of knowledge generated, namely tacit and explicit, where tacit knowledge being that has not been made explicit, that may for example be in the mind of one or more individuals but not documented [9]. Both tacit and explicit knowledge are inevitably created as software is produced, and the advent of agile software development [10] has placed an emphasis on reducing explicit documented knowledge. The impact of this development suggests a heightened demand to address tacit Knowledge Retention (KR) in software development projects.

The research on knowledge management in OSS projects have focused on knowledge shared and knowledge reuse, cross boundary learning in open communities, knowledge sharing involving strategic interaction, learning theory on knowledge creation and sharing in online communities, learning driven by criticism and error correction, a social view of learning that have overcome problem of tacit knowledge transformation. However, the research community has overlooked KR in OSS projects so far. In order to reduce the impact of knowledge loss on the organisation's productivity and on product's quality, organisations invest in KM processes.

The knowledge loss due to the loss of experience and expertise on the project impacts productivity and additional time is required to learn the workings of the project when original contributors are no longer accessible [11]. The central hypothesis of this work states that: The knowledge loss in OSS projects due to contributor turnover can be reduced by introducing proactive knowledge retention practices in OSS projects that can transform contributor's use of knowledge and engagement in knowledge relevant activities including knowledge sharing and knowledge transfer.

In OSS projects inevitable turnover due to the transient nature of contributors [2] and absence of contractual bindings for notification before contributors leave, make it difficult to enable any reactive knowledge transfer activity. Therefore, the reactive approach of knowledge retention that may be practised in a traditional software organisation may prove entirely ineffective for OSS projects. The central hypothesis stresses the need for proactive knowledge retention practices in OSS projects arising from the difference of organisational and governance structure between OSS and traditional software organisations. The central hypothesis leads to the first research question: **RQ1. What practices can enable effective proactive knowledge retention strategy in OSS projects?**

OSS projects are dynamic, dispersed, with transient contributors concurrently performing tasks in different roles, and collaborating through technologically mediated channels. The challenge is to formulate the strategy for proactive knowledge retention, which can resonate with the idiosyncratic nature of OSS projects without causing an overhead to the productivity of the project and contributors. The OSS communities focus on self-direction and favour intrinsic value system and therefore imposing a strategy that calls for contributors to limit their freedom will lower their enthusiasm of doing well for the society. The next step after identification of retention practices requires their incorporation with the OSS projects work settings, which leads to the second research question: **RQ2. How to incorporate proactive knowledge retention strategy with established work practices in OSS projects?**

3 Research Philosophy

Worldviews provide a general philosophical direction to research with common elements having different stances [12]. Philosophical worldviews shape the approach taken for research by influencing research designs and research methods [13]. Worldviews differ in: ontology which is the nature of reality; epistemology which refers to how we gain knowledge about what we know; axiology which explains role of values in research; methodology determines the process of research; and rhetoric is the language of research [14].

3.1 Three Worldviews

The three worldviews reflected as different philosophical concerns in research are positivism (also called post positivism), interpretivism, and pragmatism. Underlying philosophical concerns further determine the selection of the research method to conduct any research.

Positivism. The positivists advocate in the quantification of their learning through numbers and the use of statistical equations to predict human behaviour [15]. A positivist believes that social life is pretty stable and constant [16]. In such an approach, if the learning of a concept is not possible through quantifiable methods it is generally ignored. The positivists extract simple relationships from a complex real world in numbers without considering the context [16]. Positivists stress deterministic philosophy, reductionism, observation and measurement, and theory verification [13]. In deterministic philosophy, causes determine the effects or outcomes. Reductionism is about reducing ideas into small discrete tests consisting of variables based on hypothesis and research questions. Knowledge development by positivist is through observing and measuring objective reality in numbers, and by verification of laws and theories that govern the world.

Interpretivism. Interpretivist focuses more on human thoughts and actions in social and organisational contexts [17]. Interpretivists (also called constructivists) believe in understanding the context and meaning by taking into account the real setting of the world in which they live and work. Interpretivist led research tends to develop subjective, varied, and multiple meanings about an object enabling them to unfold complex views [13]. The views on the situation being studied are collected from as many participants as possible [13]. For example, in open-ended questioning, a researcher carefully listens to the views of participants and shapes his or her interpretation from cultural and historical experiences [13]. Research led by an interpretivist generates or inductively develops a theory or pattern from the interpretation [13].

Pragmatism. Advocates an alternative world view to positivism and interpretivism and primarily focuses on the problem to be researched and the consequences of the research [12]. Pragmatism offers a middle position or mixed methods research movement with a practical and outcome-oriented method of inquiry based on action and leads by enabling researchers to have better answers to their research questions [18]. Furthermore, pragmatism takes a value-oriented approach to research and reach an agreement about importance of culturally derived values and desired conclusion [18]. Pragmatism as a philosophical underpinning for mixed methods studies, focuses on the research problem [19]. Pragmatism uses pluralistic approaches to derive knowledge about the problem [19] and is concerned with real-world practice.

3.2 Research Philosophy Adopted for the Current Study

The philosophical position adopted in this research is that of pragmatism, with a focus on the research problem and enabling empirical research to find answers to the research questions. The pragmatist worldview reflects the direct action oriented approach of a researcher towards the investigation of the research problem at hand. We suggest that this research would benefit by adopting pragmatism and approaching the problem by understanding it in a practical manner and by using multiple methods in research. The goal of this research is to devise a systematic strategy on the use of proactive knowledge retention practices in OSS projects. The development of an overarching proactive knowledge retention strategy requires understanding of the phenomenon and exploration in real life with multiple contexts and with the ability to quantify the concepts.

The view taken in this research is that of taking a middle position between two extremities of being a positivist or an interpretivist. Solely being an interpretivist or positivist is inadequate in terms of addressing the objective of this research. The insights provided by the use of qualitative and quantitative research in a mix method can be integrated into a workable solution under pragmatism [18]. The goal of mixed methods research is not to replace either qualitative or quantitative approach but to use their strengths and minimize the weaknesses of both in single research studies and across studies [18].

4 Eliciting Empirical Research Methodology

Empirical studies are emphasised to provide a scientific basis for software engineering [20] and to investigate the social and cognitive processes surrounding complex software systems [21]. Empirical methods allow for informed and well-grounded decisions and allow the investigation of a phenomenon by experimenting and experiencing it in the real world settings [20]. Methodology is defined as "the collection of methods or rules by which a particular piece of research is undertaken" and the "principles, theories and values that underpin a particular approach to research" [22]. Another definition states: "methodology is the overall approach to research linked to the paradigm or theoretical framework" [23]. In general, research methodology is a systematic approach to achieve particular goals of the research. The pragmatist worldview adopted in this research lays the foundation to the research methodology including the research design. Pragmatically inclined researchers focus more on the desired outcomes and solution to the problem. Mixed methods research applies pragmatist system of philosophy where "the researcher mixes or combines quantitative and qualitative research techniques, methods, approaches, concepts or language into a single study" [18]. Research designs under each research approach provide specific directions and guidelines to conduct research [13]. The discussion on research design continues in Sect. 4.1. The research method refers to "systematic modes, procedures or tools used for data collection and analysis." [23]. A method is mainly a set of principles through which empirical data is collected and analysed [24]. Research methods can be classified as qualitative, quantitative or both [20].

4.1 Research Design

The research designs are the strategies of inquiry employed under a specific research approach. In this section, the research designs employed by three research approaches: qualitative, quantitative, and mixed methods are discussed.

Quantitative Approach. "The quantitative research mainly focus on deduction, confirmation, theory or hypothesis testing, explanation, prediction, standardized data collection, and statistical analysis." [18]. Quantitative research is based on the use of statistical methods and establishes relationships between variables [25] or quantifies a relationship by comparing two or more groups [13]. The aim is to identify a cause-effect relationship. Quantification is the confirmation of a hypotheses rather than the formation of the hypothesis [26]. Quantitative research employs numbers to capture or describe some phenomenon but may be limited in the sense that it can overlook certain important information [15]. The strategies of inquiry employed in quantitative research are experimental designs such as true experiments and quasi-experiments, and non-experimental design such as surveys [13].

Experiments determine that if special treatment to a group can influence an outcome. Controlled experiments are quantitative in nature since they measure different variables and attain varying results. The variables are repetitively changed and measured again [20]. The variables to be measured in quantitative research are identified based on the theory [24]. In controlled experiments a cause and effect relationship is studied by manipulating independent variables and observing the effect on dependent variables [24]. Controlled experiments are sometimes referred to as research in small [27] and have a limited scope. The controlled experiments have a fixed design and the procedure to run an experiment is a formal one. In surveys, the primary means of gathering data are interviews or questionnaires which are sent to a large number of representing population [20]. When conducting a survey, a sample of a representative population is selected based on criteria and results may be generalised for the sample population. The survey has to be designed carefully ensuring that the questions are understandable by the participant and the data collected from the target population is valid and useful for the study.

Qualitative Approach. Qualitative research refers to the study of objects in their natural setting [20]. A qualitative researcher tries to understand the causes while interpreting a phenomenon by accepting that there are multiple interpretations of the explanations given to them by the subjects in the study [28]. The subject is the person who takes participates in the study to evaluate an object [20]. Qualitative research believes in a range of different ways of interpretation and understanding views of the subjects on the concerned problem at hand [20]. Case studies, ethnographies, post-mortem analysis, action research [21], phenomenology, grounded theory, and narrative [13] are primarily qualitative in nature.

A case study investigates a contemporary phenomenon in a real life context and the control is lower than with experiments. Case studies provides the richer and deeper description of the studied phenomenon [25]. A case study is an observational study on an ongoing project, while experiment is a controlled study [24]. It has been noted that case studies can combine data collection by using methods such as interviews, questionnaires, archives, and observations [29]. Similarly, a case study can also embed other research methods e.g. a survey may be conducted within a case study [25]. The use of mixed method approach explains that survey can be used within a case study. Ethnography is another research method applied in a participant-observer manner [21]. The researcher participates with the team members to observe and understand the social interaction taking place in the community [24]. In action research, the researcher applies an iterative problem solving approach to a current situation to improve it [24]. The action research method requires an agreement from the problem owner(s) to collaborate and identify the problem.

Phenomenological research is a design originating from philosophy and psychology where the researcher describes the experiences of participants about a phenomenon as provide by participants [13]. The details provided on experiences of several participants about a phenomenon develops into a core description of a phenomenon under study [13]. Phenomenological design strongly underpins the philosophical attributes of a research topic and involves conducting interviews [31]. Grounded theory is another qualitative research design of inquiry from sociology, which facilitates the researcher in deriving a general, abstract theory about a process, action, or interaction grounded in the views of participants [13]. The data collection involves using multiple stages until a data saturation point is reached and no new information is found, the data refinement is through interrelationship of categories of information [32].

Mixed Methods Approach. "Mixed methods research is formally defined as the class of research where the researcher mixes or combines quantitative and qualitative research techniques, methods, approaches, concepts or language into a single study" [18]. Mixed methods involves combining qualitative and quantitative research by the collecting qualitative data, which is open-ended and without predetermined responses, and quantitative data, which is closed-ended in nature and the selection of responses is from predetermined list of answers [13]. The mixed methods are valued and thought to neutralize the weakness and bias that arises in research by the usage of just one method [13].

4.2 Research Design for the Current Study

In this work, mixed method research will be employed to investigate the research questions stated in Sect. 2. The objective of this research is to identify a proactive knowledge retention strategy, which will elaborate a set of effective knowledge retention practices in OSS projects. Mixed method research emerges from pragmatism, a worldview that offers to combine the positivist view of quantifying the object of research and the interpretivist view of interpreting different meanings associated with it. Therefore, both research types, qualitative and quantitative, which merge in mixed method research design, will serve the purpose of understanding the phenomenon of knowledge retention in OSS projects and generalizing the results to a larger community of OSS projects. This research will adopt a mixed method approach with qualitative and quantitative data collection and an independent data analysis for each data type. The findings from analysis will be merged to understand and elaborate the phenomenon of proactive knowledge retention in OSS projects.

In this research, the rationale of using mixed methods is related to triangulation, complementarity and expansion. Using qualitative and quantitative methods will facilitate a triangulation of results from different perspectives of knowledge retention in OSS projects. Complementarity will further play an essential role to use one method to elaborate and clarify the results obtained from the other method i.e. complementing the results of quantitative methods with the help of the qualitative method. Using different methods for different inquiry components will also expand the breadth and range for descriptive research. At a practical level, mixed methods has its strength, for utilising both qualitative and quantitative research to overcome the limitation of each approach; at a practical level the mixed method approach is complex and sophisticated; and at a procedural level, a mixed method approach provides offers the potential to establish a more rounded understanding of the problem [13].

4.3 Research Methods

This section elaborates the research methods employed for empirical data collection and the selection of research method considered suitable for this research.

- **Quantitative Method:** Focus on data collection that is largely of a numeric type and the required information is specified in advance and data is gathered using scaled instruments while interpretations are made on the basis of the statistical results [13]. The use of a questionnaire most likely includes a numerical rating scale for quantitative data collection [18]. In order to collect data, researchers can employ an instrument or test, which has a set of questions to evaluate the confidence towards an approach, or use checklist to identify and observe people involved in some task [13].
- **Qualitative Method:** Data collection involve observing the behaviour of individuals and conducting interviews with individuals where they can talk about a topic openly mostly without the use of specific questions. Researchers make interpretations from the themes or patterns that emerge from the data. Qualitative research theory may be applied after the data collection while following the process of coding (data analyses by labelling and categorising) [30].
- **Mixed Method Data Collection:** Here data collection comprises of both types of data quantitative and qualitative, to measure the concepts, parallel variables, or constructs, under study [13]. Both kinds of data is collected such as qualitative, which is open-ended and quantitative, which is closed-ended data to investigate research questions or hypotheses and the procedures for both qualitative and quantitative data analysis are detailed to perform analysis with adequate sampling, sources of information, data analysis steps.

The data collection for the current study is by using mixed methods that involve both qualitative data and quantitative data. A survey instrument will be employed for qualitative and quantitative data collection. The purpose of the data collection using mixed methods will be to analyse and evaluate the proposed practices based on the feedback from the OSS community. Furthermore, the collected feedback from the OSS community will be utilised for improving the proposed practices for proactive knowledge retention in OSS projects. The questionnaire for survey interview will be prepared after examining the literature on practices and developing a set of proposed practices for proactive knowledge retention in OSS projects. Rather than using one type of data collection the combination of both quantitative data (close-ended questions with a larger sample) and qualitative data (open-ended questions with a smaller sample) overcomes the weakness arising from the use of only one data type. The analysis for each type of data collection will be performed separately and then results will be combined to understand the knowledge retention phenomenon in OSS projects.

4.4 Data Analysis

There are different possible ways in a mixed methods design, to converge or to merge the data from two different types of data collections. The two data collections are analysed separately and then results are explained. The two data collections can be merged by a side-by-side comparison, by transformation procedure and by table or graph [13]. In side-by-side comparison, the results from both types of data collection are reported separately and then findings are compared. In transformation procedure, the qualitative data is transformed to quantitative data by changing the qualitative themes into quantitative variables. The two types of data collection can also be merged in the form of tables and graph while display. In this research, the data analysis for quantitative and qualitative data will be performed independent of each other. The findings from both types of analysis will be combined to understand and elaborate the phenomenon. The results from the analysis of two data collections will be interpreted and produced in writing.

4.5 Validity Concerns

There are three key validity concerns while using the mixed method research. The first one is of unequal sample size when qualitative and quantitative data is collected [13]. Generally quantitative sample size is larger than qualitative sample size to perform statistical tests. The sample size for a qualitative data collection is small since the intension is to study the sample extensively and gain an in-depth perspective. The second concern is that it can be problematic to compare the findings from two data types with different variables and merge them will lead to incorrect strategy for inquiry [13]. In case of divergence, it can be difficult to explore the results any further. The third concern is to have the same participants in qualitative and quantitative data collection for a better comparison [13].

The qualitative and quantitative data collection will be conducted in such a way that both types of data are represented equally in the sample size of the survey questionnaire. The two types of data collection will be analysed separately by using side-by-side comparison. The results of both analyses will be merged and reported collectively. The design of the survey questionnaire will ensure that same concepts are measured in collection of both qualitative and quantitative data by removing any inconsistencies. The responses on qualitative and quantitative data will be collected simultaneously through survey questionnaire from each participant. The summary of the research methodology is illustrated in Fig. 2, where rectangles represent survey design, data collection, or data analysis, while an oval represents merging the findings, interpreting, or incorporating them in OSS KR practices.

Fig. 2. The Research Methodology to investigate proactive knowledge retention in OSS projects

5 Future Work

The main goal of this research is to develop an overarching proactive knowledge retention strategy in OSS projects, something that we suggest is warranted based on a review of the literature and on the volatile nature of the OSS workforce. The mixed method research described in this paper establishes the baseline of the research methodology for the investigation of proactive knowledge retention in OSS projects. Moving onto the next phase to implement the research methodology, we will shift our focus to survey design. The research objectives will underpin the survey design and will align with the data collection in order to accomplish the research goals. In order to design the survey, selection of appropriate data components is required to develop a questionnaire and gather valuable information from OSS communities. A streamlined process is required to identify the data components with a close examination of known and unknown information leading to the formation of an elaborative set of knowledge retention practices suitable for OSS projects. The analysis of the data collected through the anticipated surveys will facilitate in assessment, refinement and improvement of the knowledge retention practices in OSS projects based on the feedback from OSS community. The objective of this research is to improve proactive knowledge management as a counter-balance to the transient and sometimes uncommitted nature of OSS personnel. We suggest that the research methodology identified herein is appropriate to this research and that it will deliver tangible benefits for both contributors to OSS projects and consumers of OSS.

Acknowledgments. This work was supported, in part, by Science Foundation Ireland grant 13/RC/2094 to Lero, the Irish Software Research Centre (www.lero.ie).

References

1. Michlmayr, M.: Quality Improvement in Volunteer Free and Open Source Software Projects: Exploring the Impact of Release Management. University of Cambridge (2007)
2. Yu, Y., Benlian, A., Hess, T.: An empirical study of volunteer members' perceived turnover in open source software projects. In: 2012 45th Hawaii International Conference on System Science (HICSS), pp. 3396–3405. IEEE (2012)
3. Mockus, A., Fielding, R.T., Herbsleb, J.D.: Two case studies of open source software development: apache and mozilla. ACM Trans. Softw. Eng. Methodol. **11**, 309–346 (2002)
4. Crowston, K., Annabi, H., Howison, J., Masango, C.: Effective work practices for software engineering: free/libre open source software development. In: Proceedings: ACM Workshop on Interdisciplinary Software Engineering Research, pp. 18–26. ACM, USA (2004)
5. Crowston, K., Howison, J.: The social structure of free and open source software development. First Monday 2 (2005)
6. Rigby, P.C., Zhu, Y.C., Donadelli, S.M., Mockus, A.: Quantifying and mitigating turnover-induced knowledge loss: case studies of chrome and a project at Avaya. In: Proceedings of the 2016 International Conference on Software Engineering (2016)
7. Rashid, M., Clarke, P.M., O'Connor, R.V.: Exploring knowledge loss in open source software (OSS) projects. In: Mas, A., Mesquida, A., O'Connor, R.V., Rout, T., Dorling, A. (eds.) SPICE 2017. CCIS, vol. 770, pp. 481–495. Springer, Cham (2017). https://doi.org/10.1007/978-3-319-67383-7_35
8. Davenport, T.H., Prusak, L.: Working Knowledge: How Organizations Manage What They Know. Harvard Business Press, Boston (1998)
9. Ryan, S., O'Connor, R.V.: Acquiring and sharing tacit knowledge in software development teams: an empirical study. Inf. Softw. Technol. **55**, 1614–1624 (2013)
10. Beck, K., et al.: Manifesto for agile software development (2001)
11. Izquierdo-Cortazar, D., Robles, G., Ortega, F., Gonzalez-Barahona, J.M.: Using software archaeology to measure knowledge loss in software projects due to developer turnover. In: 42nd Hawaii International Conference on System Sciences, pp. 1–10. IEEE (2009)
12. Creswell, J.W., Clark, V.L.P.: Designing and Conducting Mixed Methods Research. SAGE Publications, Thousand Oaks (2011)
13. Creswell, J.W.: Research Design: Qualitative, Quantitative, and Mixed Methods Approaches. SAGE Publications, Thousand Oaks (2014)
14. Lincoln, Y.S., Lynham, S.A., Guba, E.G.: Paradigmatic controversies, contradictions, and emerging confluences, revisited. In: The Sage Handbook of Qualitative Research (2011)
15. Rubin, H.J., Rubin, I.S.: Qualitative interviewing: The Art of Hearing Data. SAGE, Thousand Oaks (2011)

16. Denzin, N.K.: The Research Act: A Theoretical Introduction to Sociological Methods. Transaction Publishers, Piscataway (1973)
17. Klein, H.K., Myers, M.D.: A set of principles for conducting and evaluating interpretive field studies in information systems. MIS Q. **23**, 67–93 (1999)
18. Johnson, R.B., Onwuegbuzie, A.J.: Mixed methods research: a research paradigm whose time has come. Educ. Res. **33**, 14–26 (2004)
19. Tashakkori, A., Teddlie, C.: SAGE Handbook of Mixed Methods in Social & Behavioral Research. SAGE, Thousand Oaks (2010)
20. Wohlin, C., Höst, M., Henningsson, K.: Empirical research methods in software engineering. In: Conradi, R., Wang, A.I. (eds.) Empirical Methods and Studies in Software Engineering. LNCS, vol. 2765, pp. 7–23. Springer, Heidelberg (2003). https://doi.org/10.1007/978-3-540-45143-3_2
21. Shull, F., Singer, J., Sjøberg, D.I.: Guide to Advanced Empirical Software Engineering. Springer, London (2008). https://doi.org/10.1007/978-1-84800-044-5
22. Somekh, B., Lewin, C.: Research Methods in the Social Sciences. SAGE, Thousand Oaks (2005)
23. Mackenzie, N., Knipe, S.: Research dilemmas: paradigms, methods and methodology. Issues Educ. Res. **16**, 193–205 (2006)
24. Easterbrook, S., Singer, J., Storey, M.-A., Damian, D.: Selecting Empirical Methods for Software Engineering Research. In: Shull, F., Singer, J., Sjøberg, D.K. (eds.) Guide to Advanced Empirical Software Engineering, pp. 285–311. Springer, London (2008). https://doi.org/10.1007/978-1-84800-044-5_11
25. Runeson, P., Höst, M.: Guidelines for conducting and reporting case study research in software engineering. Empir. Softw. Eng. **14**, 131–164 (2009)
26. Sharif, K.Y., English, M., Ali, N., Exton, C., Collins, J.J., Buckley, J.: An empirically-based characterization and quantification of information seeking through mailing lists during open source developers' software evolution. Inf. Softw. Technol. **57**, 77–94 (2015)
27. Kitchenham, B., Pickard, L., Pfleeger, S.L.: Case studies for method and tool evaluation. IEEE Softw. **12**, 52–62 (1995)
28. Denzin, N.K., Lincoln, Y.S.: The SAGE Handbook of Qualitative Research. SAGE, Thousand Oaks (2011)
29. Eisenhardt, K.M.: Building theories from case study research. Acad. Manag. Rev. **14**, 532–550 (1989)
30. O'Connor, R.: Using grounded theory coding mechanisms to analyze case study and focus group data in the context of software process research. In: Mora, M., et al. (eds.) Research Methodologies, Innovations and Philosophies in Software Systems Engineering and Information Systems, pp. 256–270. IGI Global (2012)
31. Giorgi, A.: The Descriptive Phenomenological Method in Psychology: A Modified Husserlian Approach. Duquesne University Press, Pittsburgh (2009)
32. Strauss, A., Corbin, J.: Basics of Qualitative Research: Techniques and Procedures for Developing Grounded Theory. SAGE Publications, Thousand Oaks (1998)

SPI and Assessment

Integrating Culture Awareness and Formalisation in Software Process Assessment and Improvement for Very Small Entities (VSEs)

Tatsuya Nonoyama[2(✉)], Edward Kabaale[2], Lian Wen[1,2], David Tuffley[1,2], and Zhe Wang[1,2]

[1] Institute for Integrated and Intelligent Systems, Griffith University, Brisbane, Australia
[2] School of Information Communication Technology, Griffith University, 170 Kessels Road, Brisbane, Qld 4111, Australia
{t.nonoyama, e.kabaale, l.wen, d.tuffley, z.wang}@griffith.edu.au

Abstract. Software process assessment and process improvement are fundamentally essential if software companies are to improve their development processes and perform at best practice level. However, established software process assessment models (PAMs) like SPICE or CMMI are scaled to be applicable to Small and Medium Enterprises (SMEs) all the way up to very large companies. So far, there is no mature PAM applicable to Very Small Entities (VSEs), which are usually defined as companies with 25 or less employees. As the majority of software companies are classified as VSEs, the lack of a mature PAM is a glaring omission in the Software Engineering domain in need of rectification. A major challenge with producing a VSE-appropriate PAM is the cultural diversity of VSEs. It is not amenable to a one size fits all solution suitable for all VSEs. Another challenge is the high human resource cost of a SPICE or CMMI process assessment. It is often cost-prohibitive for VSEs. This paper therefore proposes a model to meet the need; the *Culture Impact on Software Assessment* (CISA). CISA facilitates the development of PAMs that are both lightweight, making them easy and cheap to apply, while also being highly relevant to individual VSE, thereby significantly increasing the efficiency of PAMs. Additionally, this paper introduces a formal specification (ontology) of CISA to enable future development of software process semi-automatic assessment tools that will greatly reduce the cost for software process assessment for VSEs.

Keywords: Process assessment model · Process improvement Ontology · Culture evaluation · Very small enterprise · VSE

X. Larrucea et al. (Eds.): EuroSPI 2018, CCIS 896, pp. 123–135, 2018.
https://doi.org/10.1007/978-3-319-97925-0_10

1 Introduction

Software Engineering (SE) standards are by necessity being adopted in software company of all sizes. ISO/IEC 29110 [1, 2] has been introduced particularly for Very Small Entities (VSEs) with less than 25 employees [3]. It has reduced the number of software processes from more than 50 as defined in ISO/IEC 12207: Systems and Software Engineering-Software Life Cycle Processes down to two most important software processes [4]). However, what is still lacking is a predefined software assessment model for ISO/IEC 29110. Where VSEs are interested in certification and recognition, the requirement for assessors still makes assessment a prohibitively expensive exercise [6]. The development of deployment packages (DP) helps VSEs to understand the details of ISO/IEC 29110 and facilitate the implementation thereof. Boucher [6] argues that process reference models still need to be tailored to the situational background of adopting VSEs.

Among the factors that influenced the design of ISO/IEC 29110 standard for VSEs was that it was supposed to be compliant with ISO/IEC 15504 standard (aka SPICE) that is transiting to ISO/IEC3300xx series to accommodate more domains and other process characteristics other than process capability [7]. This factor led to the development of ISO/IEC 29110 part 3 that provides guidelines for using and tailoring ISO/IEC 15504 to assess software development following the ISO/IEC 29110 standard. However, these guidelines and ISO/IEC 15504, do not address the divergent cultural issues of VSEs while carrying out assessment in VSEs, except the emphasis of the guidelines is put on the number of processes and capability levels selected from the parent standard.

Several studies have proposed process assessment models (PAMs) for a VSE based on ISO/IEC 29110 [8] using the part 3 guidelines to tailor ISO 15504 usage in VSEs; The study [9] proposed a PAM and method for VSEs based on ISO/IEC 29110 using the guidelines in part 3 to tailor ISO/IEC 15504 for use in VSEs. As a result, an exemplar PAM for VSE is suggested. This PAM limits its scope on the process dimension (capability level 1) of ISO/IEC 15504. Their justification is that the current profiles of ISO/IEC 29110 are currently limited to only process dimension of ISO/IEC 15504. In the same line [10] proposed another PAM still tailoring ISO/IEC 15504 using ISO/IEC 29110 part 3 guidelines. However, none of these PAMs consider the cultural situations of a VSE during assessment. According to Jaakkola [11], there are several culture sensitive processes that must be fine-tuned for VSEs to adopt. This is especially true in VSEs where resources are limited.

The well-accepted PAM as defined by ISO/IEC 15504 is too heavy and expensive for VSEs to adopt. VSEs need the PAMs to be cost-efficient and to address their common issues. Furthermore, the lack of cultural acknowledgement may lead to a failure to detect desirable inputs, outputs and work products of the VSE [4]. To acknowledge cultural diversity of VSEs, we need to design cost-efficient PAM that is applicable to evaluate the culture of a VSE.

Therefore, in this paper, we proposed CISA framework that takes into consideration cultural diversity of VSEs while carrying out process assessment. We have critically compared our framework with existing frameworks such as the culture sensitivity assessment model (CSAM) developed in the STEP project [11]. We have additionally formalised the framework in a form of ontology to lay a first stone towards developing semi-automated process assessment tools. Section 2 introduces the necessary literature background for our study. In Sect. 3, we introduce the proposed CISA framework and its formalisation using ontologies. In Sects. 4 and 5, we provide a brief discussion, conclusion and sketch future directions for our work.

2 Background

2.1 ISO/IEC29110 and ISO/IEC15504

In 2011, ISO/IEC29110: Software Engineering Lifecycle Profiles for Very Small Entities (VSEs) was published to help small software companies (VSEs) with 25 employees or less [9, 12]. It provides suitable software processes, process improvement and assessment guidelines for VSEs. In ISO/IEC 29110, project management process (PM process) and software implementation process (SI process) holds the key to a successful software company. In comparison to ISO/IEC12207, with 50 software processes, a lightweight ISO/IEC29110 has been compressed and selected only two software processes for VSEs.

The current PAM guideline of ISO/IEC 29110 reflects upon the six-point measurement scale system which derived from ISO/IEC 15504. Both standards use the concept of six-point measurement scale to determine process capability for future process improvement. Although, there is no mature PAMs for a VSE, the assessment guideline was published to help them assess software processes. ISO/IEC 29110-3 is reflected on specific assessment indicators from selected process outcomes in ISO/IEC 15504. The objectives of ISO/IEC 29110 software processes are associated with ISO/IEC 12207 process outcomes.

ISO/IEC 15504: Information Technology Process Assessment is the reference model for assessing software processes. The six-point scale consists of 0-incomplete, 1-performed, 2-managed, 3-established, 4-predictable and 5-optimized (ISO/IEC 15504, 2008). Each level indicates the maturity of process improvements with the scale being determined by a set of objectively assessed process attributes. For most VSEs, it is only expected to reach capability level 2 with basic work products and outcomes [7]. Some researchers argue that measurement scale of ISO/IEC 15504 takes a significant amount of financial resources to make an adjustment for VSEs.

For large software companies, formalizing a defined software assessment scheme is financially feasible. However, VSEs do not have the time or financial resources to establish formalised assessment methods. Apart from financial gaps between VSEs and large software companies, their process assessment practices are more influenced by cultural factors than large software companies [4, 13–15] For VSEs, it is vital to avoid major modification on PAMs. The strategic response to this limitation is to design the PAM that fit the software environments of a VSE.

2.2 Culture and Process Assessment Models (PAMs)

In general, culture is a collection of ideas, customs and social behaviours of a particular group of people [16, 17]. Culture is a generic form of how people behave in certain circumstances. The concept of culture can be divided into two broad components such as national and organisational culture. National culture can be defined as a set of norms, behaviours, beliefs and customs that inform the character of a country [18]. The component of national culture is large and there is a sub-component called organisational culture. The organisational culture can be related to values and behaviours that reflects upon the working environment of an organisation [16]. Furthermore, organisational culture can be decomposed into smaller sub-cultures such as working culture which associates with behaviors and attitudes.

The culture impacts on software process is difficult to evaluate especially for VSEs. Due to size differences, many researchers have argued that most culture evaluations are only applicable for a large organization. A PAM that supports the idea of Competing Values Theory (CVT) is a good example of culture evaluation for larger organisations. CVT allows comparing values using multiple assessment questions [21]. Furthermore, the Culture Sensitivity Assessment Model (CSAM) was developed for measuring the sensitivity level of a software company. This model would be the closest PAM with cultural consideration in process assessment. However, it is also intended for large enterprises. The ideal PAM should cover a diverse cultural and technical issues of a VSE [10, 15, 19]. We could scale down CSAM and implement simple but, it may be less effective culture evaluation for VSEs.

2.3 Culture Evaluations by Neeley and Trompenaars

The five work attitudes and behaviors proposed by Tsedal Neeley [20] to enhance cross-cultural collaboration. Based on Neeley's findings, a large Japanese enterprise Rakuten has successfully implemented these work patterns and attitudes. As the result Rakutan's approach to managing cross-cultural issues has proven efficacious. The communication is a vital part of process assessment and can lead into a major issue, if neglected [4]. Neeley's theory is useful to establish the basic procedure of process assessment in different cultural backgrounds.

(1) Embrace positive indifference.
(2) Seek commonality between cultures.
(3) Identify with the global organisation rather than your local office.
(4) Seek interaction with other, geographically distant subsidiaries.
(5) Aspire to a global career.

During an assessment VSEs are likely to encounter the 3 layers of culture. Dutch organisational theorist Fons Trompenaars and his research team acknowledged and improved on Edger Schein's ideas of multi-layered culture. In Trompenaar's perspective, culture is like an onion with different layers [22]. The deeper the layer is, the more difficult it is to be measured. The layer (1) The outside of the onion is how people perceive the surface of the onion. In other words, the artifacts of culture which includes the way we dress and how we conduct ourselves. The layer (2) The second layer consists of norms and values. Layer (3) The third and deepest layer contains the shared assumptions among the members of that culture.

To apply the 3 layers of culture into SE perspective, a VSE can be divided into two layers of culture and this allows the VSE to evaluate. For example: most VSEs should consider assessing the impacts on national and organisational cultures of software development. This is because, different VSEs are more culturally diverse than large organisations which influenced by national and organisational policies [22–24]. Evaluating different layers of culture can determine the best approach to improve their practice.

2.4 Ontology Support for Culture Aware Software Process Assessment

Due to their powerful knowledge representation formalism and associated inference mechanisms, ontology-based approaches have been increasingly adopted to formally represent software engineering domain knowledge. Ontologies aim at capturing domain knowledge in a formal generalised way and provide a commonly shared understanding of a domain. This domain understanding can be reused, shared and standardised across applications [26]. A formal ontology is a tool independent and explicit representation of a domain in a human and machine understandable way that is amenable to computer inferences.

The Web Ontology Language (OWL) is a W3C standardised language for modeling ontologies on the semantic web. OWL is underpinned by Description Logics (Baada, 2003), a knowledge representation language for its formal semantics and interpretation. OWL comes in different flavours and in this study we consider OWL DL, a flavour that optimises the trade-off between expressivity and decidability. Moreover, OWL is well supported by optimised off the shelf inference engines such as *Pellet* and open source modeling environments like *Protege* from Stanford University. The need to support standards compliant software development with ontologies especially for small software companies has been recently evaluated in (Colomo-Palacios, 2016). In this evaluation, it was established that there is an evident gap in ontology support for the standardisation of software development processes especially for VSEs. While ontologies have been used to support software process standardisation before [25, 26], few studies such as [27] have utilised ISO/IEC 29110 in standards tailoring of software processes to VSEs. Moreover, we note from the preceding discussion that there is currently no publicly available formalised framework that supports culture aware software process assessment for VSEs. This motivates us to provide one that will enable the development of semi-automated process assessment tools for VSEs.

3 Introduction of Culture Impact on Software Assessment (CISA) Framework

In this section, we present the Culture Impact on Software Assessment (CISA) framework visualised in the Fig. 1. The purpose of CISA is to highlight the impact of culture difference on the software process implementation. CISA is developed in accordance with the guidelines prescribed for process descriptions by ISO/IEC TR

24774 where a process is defined through its purpose and outcomes. Process definition through its purpose and outcomes that has been used successfully in process assessment and improvement [28] has its roots in ISO/IEC 15504 which also provides a list of possible practices and work products that are used to prove that the process is able to achieve its purpose through the demonstration of process outcomes. The cultural dimension is derived from [20, 22].

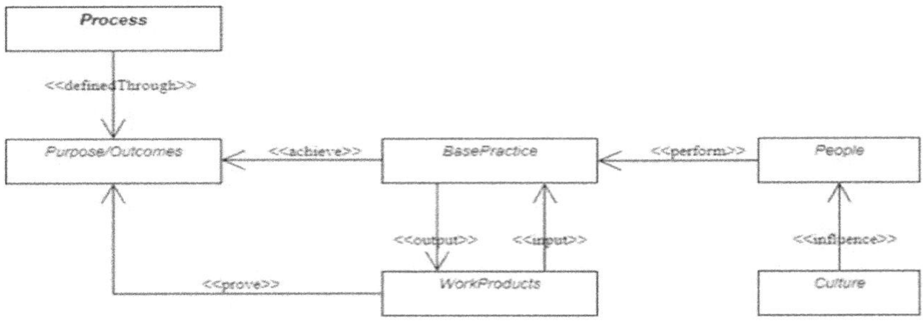

Fig. 1. CISA framework

In CISA framework, a process is defined through its intended purpose and evidenced by the objective achievement of the process outcomes. Process outcomes are sufficient and necessary conditions to achieve the software purpose. In ISO/IEC 29110, process objectives are mapped to process outcomes in ISO/IEC 12207 [29]. To achieve the process outcomes, base and generic practices are performed by roles (people) to produce work products. Work products are also inputs to the practices that are used to achieve the process outcomes. Work products are used to prove that the process outcomes are being achieved.

For example, in software requirements analysis process, the software requirements specification (SRS) can be used to prove that the analysis process was carried out. People perform practices to achieve the process outcomes, however, people are different, given that they can come from different backgrounds and cultures. Different cultures will influence the way people carry out their activities to meet the process outcomes. While the process outcomes may be the same, different people can use different practices to achieve the same outcomes. The outcomes simply say what the successfully performed process will look like, not how to go about performing it, thus allowing individuals to devise their own optimum methods.

3.1 Examples of How CISA Can Be Applied to Different Culture Types

Figure 2 shows the concept of CISA in a simple way. Suppose One Software Process is implemented by two different teams (Team A & Team B) with two different culture types (A & B as well). For example, let Team A as individualist VSE based in U.S and B as Collectivist VSE based in Japan. These two teams (A and B) have different practices in software requirement analysis process. Alternatively, we can assume the final goal is to secure the software contract but, they are more likely to have different approaches to reach the same goal. The outcomes of the process may be fixed, but the two teams are likely to achieve the outcomes through different practices and work products. The culture type A and B influencing the teams that carry out practices based on their cultures to produce the work products that prove the process outcomes. While the two different teams can use different practices, they will nonetheless achieve the same process outcomes.

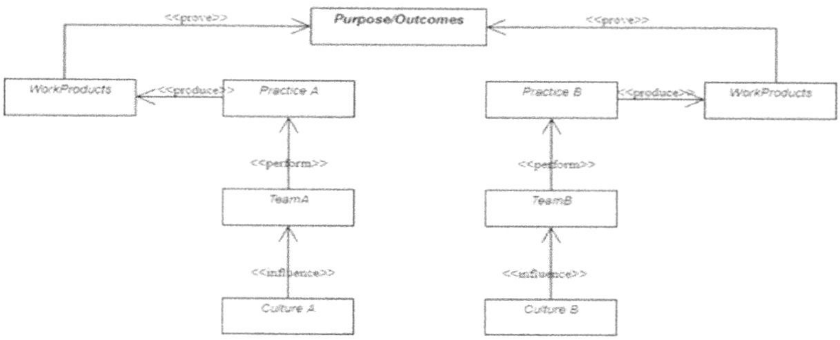

Fig. 2. Practices based on two different culture types

Table 1 illustrates the characteristics of two culture types. We use the characteristics of culture type A and B to produce different sets of practices. The allocation of culture types can help VSEs to examine their characteristics of software process without abandoning traditional ways of producing software. Once the characteristics are defined, a VSE can follow the assessment tips to help achieve the same process outcome. CISA is an appropriate culture framework to assess Software Requirement Analysis in SI process. Many software practitioners and software developers can, on occasion underestimate the culture impacts on PAMs. Therefore; we want to highlight that the process of achieving the outcome (the goal) is different based on the culture of a VSE.

Table 1. Characteristic comparison between individualist and collectivist

Characteristic	Individualist VSE (A)	Collectivist VSE (B)
Adopting new features in software process	Only accepts features with a detailed analysis & facts	Accepts features if the manager wants it
The interaction between an employee and a consumer	When it's necessary	Frequent interaction is acceptable
Software requirement approval	Detailed plan is needed	Less detailed plan but, flexibility is expected
The impact on software process	Work equality is important	Consumer needs
Country	America	Japan

To make assessment easier for VSEs to adopt, we recommend both culture types A and B to use culture evaluation such as Neeley (N) and Trompenaars (T) in their workplace. VSEs from both culture types can use the assessment tips to kick start the culture evaluation. **(1) Assessment Tip for Trompenaars**: provides 3 layers of culture. This theory is important when the VSE wants to examine the culture deeply. It is also useful to analyze and compare other software company's culture from the same country. **(2) Assessment Tip for Neeley:** can help standardize communication channels and networks. This concept is very useful once the VSE have established an ideal organisational culture of assessment process.

3.2 Onto-CISA: An OWL Formalisation of CISA

Even though the developed CISA framework enhances and tailors VSE's software development activities according to their operational culture, it still needs formal enhancement to enable process automation and verification [25, 30]. A formal software process specification is a specification expressed in a language whose vocabulary, syntax and semantics are formally defined and well understood. Software process formalisation supports formal software process definition and assessment, automated analysis, verification and validation, and aiding in choosing the appropriate process for a given project [30]. Formal methods such as OWL ontologies and composition trees (CT) have been used in modeling and formalising software processes before. For example, composition trees have been used to formally model and compare software processes in [19, 31]. Ontology based approaches (Tarhan 2017) have also been proposed to model, validate, constraint and query software process descriptions.

Due to the great diversity and complexity of software processes from different standards and process models coupled with varying situational contexts, in earlier work [30], we developed an axiom based metamodel for process formalisation where key process concepts were grounded in a metamodel. The rationale for a metamodel for process formalisation is to provide a uniform underpinning for the various process concepts during their formalisation. This is in line with the upper ontology developed for ISO software engineering standards [32] to provide a uniform and consistent terminology for all ISO present and future software engineering standards.

A formal defined process serves as a standard by enabling collaboration and cooperation between teams. They also enable process automation, dynamic assembly and tailoring of process elements, formal reasoning and queries about activity specifications and reusable workproducts. It also creates the opportunity to measure the process usage and ensures process compliance [25]. Ontologies are primarily used in standards compliant software development approaches to formally and unambiguously represent the concepts in the domain or as a basis to construct conceptual models of different elements in software organisations [27] such elements include processes, activities, tasks, roles, artefacts and roles. We provide a formalisation of the developed CISA framework based on the translation algorithm and metamodel for software process formalisation developed in our earlier studies [25, 30]. We also make use of concepts and properties in earlier developed ontologies for the SE domain such as the Software Lifecycle Ontology (SLO) and Software Implementation Process Ontology (SIP) developed in the ALIGNED project. Our ontology development follows a similar approach like the one for CISA framework development. For example, we model CISA classes as ontology concepts, CISA relations as ontology object properties and CISA individuals as the instances in the ontology. For brevity we use DL [33] notation for our CISA framework formalisation in Fig. 1.

$$\text{Process} \sqsubseteq \exists \text{defined Through.ProcessPurpose} \tag{1}$$

$$\text{ProcessPurpose} \equiv \text{ProcessOutcomes} \tag{2}$$

$$\text{Practices} \sqsubseteq \exists \text{achieve.ProcessOutcomes} \tag{3}$$

$$\text{WorkProducts} \sqsubseteq (\exists \text{inputOf} \sqcap \text{outputOf}).\text{Practices} \tag{4}$$

$$\text{WorkProducts} \sqsubseteq \exists \text{prove.ProcessOutcomes} \tag{5}$$

$$\text{People} \sqsubseteq \exists \text{peform.Practices} \tag{6}$$

$$\text{Culture} \sqsubseteq \exists \text{influence.People} \tag{7}$$

We have implemented the CISA framework in Protege. Protege is a free open source ontology building tool from Stanford university and is widely used in ontology building for both academic and commercial purposes. Importantly its embedded with reasoning services provided by FaaCT++ and Hermit reasoners. In Fig. 3, we visualise the formalisation of CISA framework in Protege. OWL-DL facilitates different reasoning services both at the class and instance level. In our example, we have used consistency and instance checking to make sure that all the ontology classes and instances are consistent.

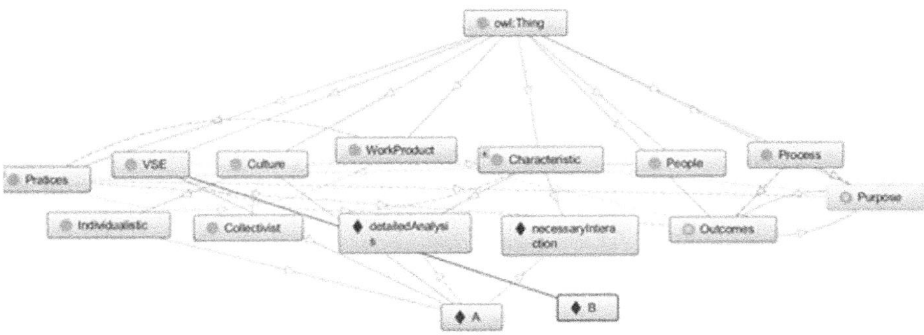

Fig. 3. Excerpt of Onto-CISA in Protégé

On the other hand, our proposed formalisation can help in recommending a set of practices for a given VSE based on a given set of cultural characteristics exhibited by a VSE. For example, if a VSE exhibits characteristic like only accepting new process features with a detailed analysis and facts, interactions between customers and developers can only happen when necessary, software requirements approval needs a detailed plan, then such a VSE is likely to be an individualistic one and therefore individualistic practices would suit such a VSE. We use SWRL to formalize such rules that enhance the expressivity of the ontology.

$$\text{VSE }(?\text{x}) \wedge \text{hasCharaterisctics}(?\text{x}, ?\text{y}) \wedge \text{Characteristics}(?\text{y}) \rightarrow \wedge \text{Individualistic}(?\text{x}) \tag{8}$$

This rule enables VSE classification based on cultural characteristics exhibited. This enables the VSE management to align their culture sensitive processes to individualist practices as identified in Table 1 above. Based on this, we used instance checking via the DL query tab to check if culture type individualistic entails any instance. The Query retrieves A (see Fig. 1), an instance of VSE that has the characteristics highlighted above. We hope to expand on the range of reasoning services that the ontology can provide to various VSEs depending on their characteristics.

4 Comparison Between CISA and Other Culture Evaluations

In this paper, we have stressed the importance of culture impacts on the PAMs and formalizing of the developed CISA framework for VSEs. The differences were significant when comparing CISA to other culture based PAMs. Due to cultural diversity of VSEs, culture based PAMs were too complex for VSEs. Based on our evaluation, a single culture evaluation of Hofstede is not enough to cover software environments of a VSE. Biiro et al. [34] proposed a third dimension to CMMI. This model was based on Hofstede's cultural framework where CMMI was extended with a third cultural dimension. Related to the above model, CSAM was proposed in STEP project [11] where organizational processes drawn from ISO/IEC 15504 were integrated with Hofstede's cultural dimension. In this model, each process is assessed to take into account the cultural effects. However, these two models were meant for large organizations without considering the unique features of VSEs. As opposed to the above culture models for software process analysis, CISA has been developed following a lexical analysis [11] of the process descriptions in ISO/IEC 29110 a standard specifically developed for VSEs with appropriate number of processes and work products to fit the unique features of VSEs. To ease the uptake of CISA by VSEs, it has been formalized in an ontology creating a foundation for its automation. While, other PAM supports the idea of CVT to evaluate work values of an organization, using assessment questions [21]. Both CVT and CASM contains a rich amount of information on culture evaluations yet, there is only a limited support on modifications for VSEs. These two models consume time and money which made it difficult for VSEs to consider. We therefore propose a PAM called CISA to support simplified and effective culture assessment for VSEs. At this stage of research, CISA framework is still in prototype stage, our plan is to enhance the content of assessment support and two given cultural concepts (the 3 layers of culture and five attitudes and behaviors).

5 Conclusion

To conclude this paper, VSEs are still facing difficulties in adopting available PAMs like ISO/IEC 15504 that are met for large organizations. While ISO/IEC 29110 provides guidelines for adopting ISO/IEC 15504 in VSEs, these are not yet well utilised in VSEs due to the cultural diversity of VSEs. Based on our research evaluation, the culture impacts on PAMs and a formalized scheme are significantly important for process improvement. To address cultural issues of a VSE, we have proposed a simple culture framework called CISA and a formalized it into an ontology to enable future semi-automated software process assessment tools. We compared our framework against CSAM model an existing model for assessing the level of culture sensitivity in a large organisation. As earlier stated, CSAM is a model for large organisations and therefore not suitable for VSEs. In general, VSEs are much more diverse in their culture as compared to large software companies. The developed CISA is still in an early stage with promising results and provides suggestions for different culture types [35]. As part of our future work, we intend to extend CISA to include other suitable sets of practices for both culture types to accomplish the same software outcomes of ISO/IEC 29110. We also intend to fine tune the formalisation of the CISA and extend it with more rules and perform comprehensive evaluations in different VSE types.

References

1. O'Connor, R.V., Laporte, C.Y.: Deploying lifecycle profiles for very small entities: an early stage industry view. In: O'Connor, R.V., Rout, T., McCaffery, F., Dorling, A. (eds.) SPICE 2011. CCIS, vol. 155, pp. 227–230. Springer, Heidelberg (2011). https://doi.org/10.1007/978-3-642-21233-8_27
2. O'Connor, R., Laporte, C.: The evolution of the ISO/IEC 29110 set of standards and guides. Int. J. Inf. Technol. Syst. Approach **10**(1), 1–21 (2017)
3. O'Connor, R.V., Laporte, C.Y.: An innovative approach to the development of an international software process lifecycle standard for very small entities. Int. J. Inf. Technol. Syst. Approach **7**, 1–22 (2014)
4. Nonoyama, T., Wen, L., Rout, T.: Current challenges and proposed software improvement process for vses in developing countries. In: Clarke, Paul M., O'Connor, R.V., Rout, T., Dorling, A. (eds.) SPICE 2016. CCIS, vol. 609, pp. 437–444. Springer, Cham (2016). https://doi.org/10.1007/978-3-319-38980-6_33
5. Nonoyama, T., Wen, L., Rout, T., Tuffley, D., O'Connor, R.V.: The Impact of cultural issues on the software process of very small entities. Softw. Qual. Prof. **20**(2), 59–68 (2018)
6. Boucher, Q., Perrouin, G., Deprez, J.-C., Heymans, P.: Towards configurable ISO/IEC 29110-compliant software development processes for very small entities. In: Winkler, D., O'Connor, Rory V., Messnarz, R. (eds.) EuroSPI 2012. CCIS, vol. 301, pp. 169–180. Springer, Heidelberg (2012). https://doi.org/10.1007/978-3-642-31199-4_15
7. Rout, T.: The evolving picture of standardization and certification for process assessment. In: Proceedings of the 7th QUATIC, pp. 63–72. IEEE (2010)

8. O'Connor, R.V., Sanders, M.: Lessons from a pilot implementation of ISO/IEC 29110 in a group of very small Irish companies. In: Woronowicz, T., Rout, T., O'Connor, R.V., Dorling, A. (eds.) SPICE 2013. CCIS, vol. 349, pp. 243–246. Springer, Heidelberg (2013). https://doi.org/10.1007/978-3-642-38833-0_23
9. Varkoi, T., Makinen, T.: Process assessment in very small entities - An ISO/IEC 29110 based method. In: QUATIC, pp. 436–440 (2010)
10. Ribaud, V., O'Connor, R.V.: Blending process assessment and employees competencies assessment in very small entities. Systems, Software and Services Process Improvement. CCIS, vol. 543, pp. 206–219. Springer, Cham (2015). https://doi.org/10.1007/978-3-319-24647-5_17
11. Jaakkola, H.: Culture sensitive aspects in software engineering. In: Düsterhöft, A., Klettke, M., Schewe, K.-D. (eds.) Conceptual Modelling and Its Theoretical Foundations. LNCS, vol. 7260, pp. 291–315. Springer, Heidelberg (2012). https://doi.org/10.1007/978-3-642-28279-9_20
12. Laporte, C.Y., O'Connor, R.V.: Software process improvement in graduate software engineering programs. In: Proceedings 1st International Workshop Software Process Education, Training and Professionalism (SPEPT 2015), CEUR Workshop Proceedings, pp. 18–24 (2015)
13. Suryaningrum, D.H.: Knowledge management and performance of small and medium entities in Indonesia. IJIMT **3**(1), 35–41 (2012)
14. Sánchez-Gordón, M.-L., O'Connor, R.V., Colomo-Palacios, R., Sanchez-Gordon, S.: A learning tool for the ISO/IEC 29110 standard: understanding the project management of basic profile. In: Clarke, Paul M., O'Connor, R.V., Rout, T., Dorling, A. (eds.) SPICE 2016. CCIS, vol. 609, pp. 270–283. Springer, Cham (2016). https://doi.org/10.1007/978-3-319-38980-6_20
15. Roldan, M.D.: Sustaining "Lilliputs" in the global knowledge-based economy: prospects for micro, small, and medium scale enterprises in the developing world. Eur. J. Sustain. Dev. **4** (2), 269–274 (2015)
16. Abraham, L.R.: Cultural differences in software engineering (2009)
17. Yilmaz, M., O'Connor, R.V., Colomo-Palacios, R., Clarke, P.: An examination of personality traits and how they impact on software development teams. Inf. Softw. Technol. **86**, 101–122 (2017)
18. Norbury, P.: A Traveller's Guide to Custom and Culture, 1st edn. Graphic Arts Center, London (2003)
19. Wen, L., Rout, T.: Using composition trees to validate an entry profile of software engineering lifecycle profiles for very small entities (VSEs). In: Mas, A., Mesquida, A., Rout, T., O'Connor, R.V., Dorling, A. (eds.) SPICE 2012. CCIS, vol. 290, pp. 38–50. Springer, Heidelberg (2012). https://doi.org/10.1007/978-3-642-30439-2_4
20. Neeley, T.: How to successfully work across countries, languages, and cultures. Harvard Business Magazine, pp. 1–3 (2017)
21. Muller, S.D., Kraemmeergaard, A., Mathiassen, L.: Managing cultural variation in software process improvement: a comparison of methods for subculture assessment. IEEE Trans. Eng. Manag. **56**(4), 584–599 (2009)
22. Trompenaars, F., Hampden-Turner, C.: Riding the Waves of Culture. McGraw-Hill, New York (1998)
23. Hofstede, G.: Motivation, leadership, and organization: do American theories apply abroad? Organ. Dyn. **9**(1), 42–63 (1980)

24. Nonoyama, T., Wen, L., Rout, T., Tuffley, D.: Cultural issues and impacts of software process in very small entities (VSEs). In: Mas, A., Mesquida, A., O'Connor, R.V., Rout, T., Dorling, A. (eds.) SPICE 2017. CCIS, vol. 770, pp. 70–81. Springer, Cham (2017). https://doi.org/10.1007/978-3-319-67383-7_6
25. Kabaale, E., Wen, L., Wang, Z., Rout, T.: Representing software process in description logics: an ontology approach for software process reasoning and verification. In: Clarke, Paul M., O'Connor, R.V., Rout, T., Dorling, A. (eds.) SPICE 2016. CCIS, vol. 609, pp. 362–376. Springer, Cham (2016). https://doi.org/10.1007/978-3-319-38980-6_26
26. Tarhan, A., Giray, G.: On the use of ontologies in software process assessment: a systematic literature review. In: EASE (2017)
27. Eito-Brun, R.: Ontology-based tailoring of software process models. In: Terminology and Knowledge Engineering (2014)
28. Rout, T., et al.: SPICE in retrospect: developing a standard for process assessment. J. Syst. Softw. **80**(9), 1483–1493 (2007)
29. Marks, G., O'Connor, R.V., Yilmaz, M., Clarke, P.M.: An ISO/IEC 12207 perspective on software development process adaptation. Softw. Qual. Prof. **20**(2), 48–58 (2018)
30. Kabaale, E., Wen, L., Wang, Z., Rout, T.: An axiom based metamodel for software process formalisation: an ontology approach. In: Mas, A., Mesquida, A., O'Connor, R.V., Rout, T., Dorling, A. (eds.) SPICE 2017. CCIS, vol. 770, pp. 226–240. Springer, Cham (2017). https://doi.org/10.1007/978-3-319-67383-7_17
31. Wen, L., Tuffley, D., Rout, T.: Using composition trees to model and compare software process. In: O'Connor, R.V., Rout, T., McCaffery, F., Dorling, A. (eds.) SPICE 2011. CCIS, vol. 155, pp. 1–15. Springer, Heidelberg (2011). https://doi.org/10.1007/978-3-642-21233-8_1
32. Gonzalez-Perez, C., Henderson-Sellers, B., McBride, T., Low, G.C., Larrucea, X.: An ontology for ISO software engineering standards: 2) Proof of concept and application. Comput. Stand. Interfaces (2016)
33. Baader, F., Horrocks, I., Sattler, U.: Description logics. In: Staab, S., Studer, R. (eds.) The Handbook on Ontologies in Information Systems. Springer, Berlin (2003). https://doi.org/10.1007/978-3-540-24750-0_1
34. Biro, M., Messnarz, R., Davison, A.G.: The impact of national cultural factors on the effectiveness of process improvement methods: the third dimension (2002)
35. Larrucea, X., O'Connor, R.V., Colomo-Palacios, R., Laporte, C.Y.: Software process improvement in very small organizations. IEEE Softw. **33**, 85–89 (2016)

Designing a Process Assessment Model Based on Multiple Sources - A Procurement Case

Samuel Renault(✉), Stéphane Cortina, and Philippe Valoggia

Luxembourg Institute of Science and Technology,
5 Avenue des Hauts-Fourneaux, 4362 Esch-sur-Alzette, Luxembourg
{samuel.renault, stephane.cortina, philippe.valoggia}@list.lu

Abstract. This paper relates the design of a procurement processes assessment model based on multiple sources. The authors explain the literature on procurement processes, procurement capability determination and maturity models, and the related published frameworks. The paper describes the selected sources and compares them together. Then the Transformation Process used to design the process assessment model, based on the use of goal trees and requirements derivation is detailed and then further discussed. A part of the resulting process assessment model is presented. The originality and the main explorative part of the works resides in the combined use of several sources to build the model.

Keywords: Procurement · Process assessment model
Requirement engineering · Transformation process · ISO

1 Introduction

Procurement is a necessary activity for many organisations, should they be public or private. Dealing with the establishment of contractual relationships between organisations for the provision of works supplies or services, procurement is in the scope of both Regulatory Compliance and Governance, although it tends to be ignored or minimized; for example very few Process Assessment Models (PAM) focused on procurement exists. Among these few, no model is fully compliant with the requirements of the ISO/IEC 33004 standard [1]. Such PAM would allow organisations to determine their capability with regards to their procurement practices, to support the implementation of new practices or processes, or to determine process-related risks.

This paper presents an attempt to design a PAM that is compliant with the ISO/IEC 33004 requirements, that addresses public or private organisations, with the widest possible procurement scope so as to cover either services, supplies or both, and that is not limited to the domain of Information Technology (IT). Previous works related to the elaboration of process assessment models are usually based on a single or a main source. The source is either the reference for the business sector (e.g. the exemplar PAM of the ISO/EC 15504-5 [2] is based on ISO/IEC 12207 standard [3], the TIPA for ITIL PAM [4] is based on the latest version of the IT Infrastructure Library [5]), or, when the PAM is built on purpose, the framework used by the organisation under assessment. In the specific case of procurement, no single or main standard exists, but

X. Larrucea et al. (Eds.): EuroSPI 2018, CCIS 896, pp. 136–146, 2018.
https://doi.org/10.1007/978-3-319-97925-0_11

several frameworks and sources provide partial and complementary views on procurement. The question raised by this paper is then: *how to build a generic PAM, based on multiple sources?* The application case is the domain of procurement.

Section 2 describes the works carried out by the authors and their peers in the fields of procurement and process assessment. Section 3 details the main sources used to build the procurement PAM. Section 4 describes the Transformation Process that we followed in order to build the procurement PAM. Section 5 discuss the variations in the application of the Transformation Process and the limits of the current works.

2 Related Works

A recent literature review [6] shows that the determination of organisations' procurement capability is not sufficiently addressed by the research. Although research has been carried out to develop maturity models for outsourcing [6] or IT procurement capability determination models [7], most stayed at the design or at the experimentation levels. Up to the authors knowledge [8] only few frameworks oriented towards procurement process have been taken up by the market. These few address mainly mature organisations and the IT domain. This led the authors to build a specific IT procurement process framework for small organisations whose deployment was described [9] and whose usage was later analysed [10]. Though, neither this framework proposal for small organisations nor the ones identified in the literature, and further described in the following Sect. 3, do address the capability determination of an organisation with regards to its procurement processes in a domain-independent context and embracing both public and private procurement.

For the International Organization for Standardization (ISO), in the domain of process assessment, the ISO/IEC 330xx series of standards [11] is the reference. It is composed of several documents, both normative (i.e. those providing requirements), and informative (i.e. guidance and examples). Recently revised, the latest version of this standard is now generic, and can been used to assess any quality characteristic (such as capability, security, or safety) of any process of any kind of domains [12–14]. For that, the assessment method relies on well-defined PAMs whose content and structure comply with the requirements defined in ISO/IEC 33004 [1].

In 2008, The Luxembourg Institute of Science and Technology – LIST (previously known as Public Research Centre Henri Tudor) published its own Transformation Process [16] for building ISO-compliant process reference, process assessment, and organizational maturity models from a collection of requirements. Based on Goal-Driven Requirements Engineering techniques [17], this Transformation Process has been widely used to build various process models, such as: a PAM for Management Systems Standards [18], a PAM for ITIL v3 [19], a PAM for ITIL 2011 [4], a PAM for assessing Medical IT networks [20], or a Maturity Model for ISO/IEC 20000-1 [21].

The application of this Transformation Process to several procurement-related frameworks will be described in detail in Sect. 4.

3 Source Documents for Building the PAM

In order to carry out the building of a procurement PAM, the procurement-related frameworks were watched and candidates were identified to be used as sources.

The Information Services Procurement Library (ISPL) [22] is a set of five books published by EXIN (Dutch editor) in 1999. The aim of ISPL is to define a framework (processes, deliverables, good practices) formalizing the acquisition of IT services. ISPL addresses well-structured organisations performing large-scale IT acquisitions. The main procurement processes described in ISPL are: Acquisition initiation, Procurement that is subdivided into three sub processes (Tendering, Contract monitoring, and Contract completion) and Acquisition completion.

In 2000, the Software Engineering Institute of the Carnegie Mellon University, based on its generic Capability and Maturity Model (CMMi) [23], issued both the e-Sourcing Capability Model and an adaptation of the CMMi for Acquisition projects (CMMi–Acq) [24]. While CMMi-Acq follows the main principles of CMMi but considers the case where the organisation purchases third party components rather than develops in-house, eSCM was built with a view to assess both the capability of suppliers and purchasers in the scope of IT services outscoring. Thus eSCM is published in two versions: one dedicated to services providers (eSCM-SP) [25] and one dedicated to purchasers or so-called clients (eSCM-CL) [26]. Considering the procurement point of view (rather than the point of view of propositions and services provision), the clients' version of eSCM (eSCM-CL) is more relevant for designing the PAM.

In 2016, the Institute of Electrical and Electronics Engineers (IEEE) published 'Recommended Practice for Software Acquisition', under reference IEEE-1062:2015 [27]. Although not a standard, this document provides description of practices for software acquisition that follows the principles of the process description in other IEEE and ISO standards with descriptions of processes, purposes, outcomes and activities.

A last meaningful source of information is the European public procurement directive, whose last version dates back to 2014. The Directive 2014/24 EU [28] establishes the legal and regulatory background for public procurement. It describes requirements in term of Obligations and Rights. Some of them are organized according to the main stages of a procurement process (particularly in the *Chapter III*).

In order to comply with the objective of a PAM addressing organisations either public or private, with the widest possible procurement scope, these four sources should be used together for the design of the PAM.

4 Designing the Process Assessment Model for Procurement

4.1 Analysing the Source Documents

We started the design of our PAM for procurement by comparing the four documents described in Sect. 3. For that, we highlighted their main differences and similarities with regards to their scope, targeted audience, and structure. Thus, the scope was analysed by considering both the purchasing goal (acquisition vs. outsourcing) and the purchasing object. Indeed outsourcing, compared to acquisition, implies a deeper approach since some activities of the organisation are delegated to a third party in a longer term customer-supplier relationship. Table 1 below provides a comparison overview of the four sources.

Table 1. Main characteristics of the sources used for the procurement PAM

Date	Source	Scope: goal	Scope: object	Audience	Structure
1999	ISPL [22]	Acquisition	Information services	Purchasers	Processes groups/process/ activities
2000	e-SCM [23]	Outsourcing	Services	Purchasers Suppliers	Processes group/process/purpose/ outcome/practice
2016	IEEE 1062:2015 [27]	Acquisition	Software (supplies & services)	Purchasers	Process/purpose/outcome/ activities
2014	Directive 2014/24 EU [28]	Acquisition	Works, Supplies, Services	Public purchasers Member states	Rights and obligations Conditions Exceptions

In summary, ISPL is a domain-specific (IT) procurement processes framework not aiming at capability determination; e-SCM is a domain-specific (IT) procurement process capability model, whose capability determination model is not based on the ISO/IEC 3300x series of standards; IEEE 1062:2015 is a domain-specific (software) procurement processes framework not aiming at capability determination; The Directive 2014/24/EU is a public procurement law (domain independent), but not structured around processes and not aiming at capability determination. As one can notice from the overview of the sources, our sources are quite complementary to each other and no single source emerges as the main source for our PAM.

As explained above, our sources cover slightly different topics and have each a different structure. Therefore we applied a qualitative analysis method by coding each source in order to be able to analyse each source's content on a same basis. We used the NVIVO software [29] to code each source. The purpose of coding is to identify categories from raw text content, so as to be able to later analyse properties, and detect concepts and relationships. Coding requires to have a common coding grid for all sources.

We drafted this grid by identifying a set of phases and processes that would be the common denominator. Such identification was based on expert judgement [15] and consensus among the research team. From the structure of each source, we summarized the main concepts and proposed a set of process groups and processes. This common set, (depicted in Fig. 1), was then used as a coding grid to code the text of each source. An example of the results of the coding for two sources is presented in Fig. 2.

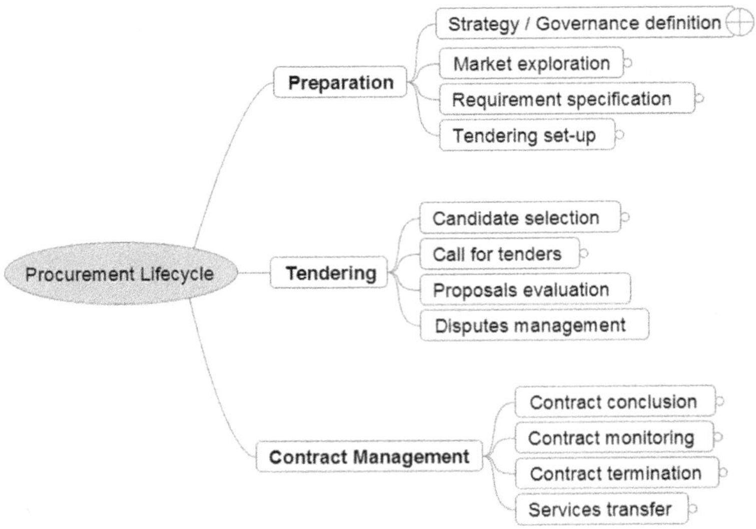

Fig. 1. The candidates' common process groups and processes

4.2 Applying the Transformation Process

For building our PAM, we followed the 9 steps of the Transformation Process described in [16]. The activities conducted during these steps are described below.

Step 1 – Identify Elementary Requirements in a Collection of Requirements. The identification of the elementary requirements were performed during the coding of our selected sources. Indeed, as introduced in Sect. 4.1, we first analysed the content of each document. Thus, during this step, we assigned each individual task, practice, activity, and/or requirement to one of the twelve common processes.

Step 2 – Organize, and Structure the Requirements. For the organization and structuration step, we created one requirement tree per process. With the help of a mind map tool, we obtained a graphical view of all the components coming from our different sources. We also paid attention to keep a record of the origin of each requirement in terms of chapter/section/area. Thus a strict traceability between the elements composing our future procurement PAM and the source document(s) will be ensured. An example of a part of one requirement tree is shown on Fig. 3.

Step 3 – Identify Common Purposes Upon Those Requirements and Organize Them. This step consisted in the semantical analysis of all the requirements attached to a process in order to understand the meaning of each of them. We thus grouped the requirements by common goal, by paying a particular attention to the misalignment of the vocabulary used in the different documents. This allowed us to draft a first version of the overall purpose, and to characterize the scope, of each process.

Step 4 – Identify and Factorize Outcomes from the Common Purposes and Attach Them to the Related Goals. Based on the groups of requirements created during the

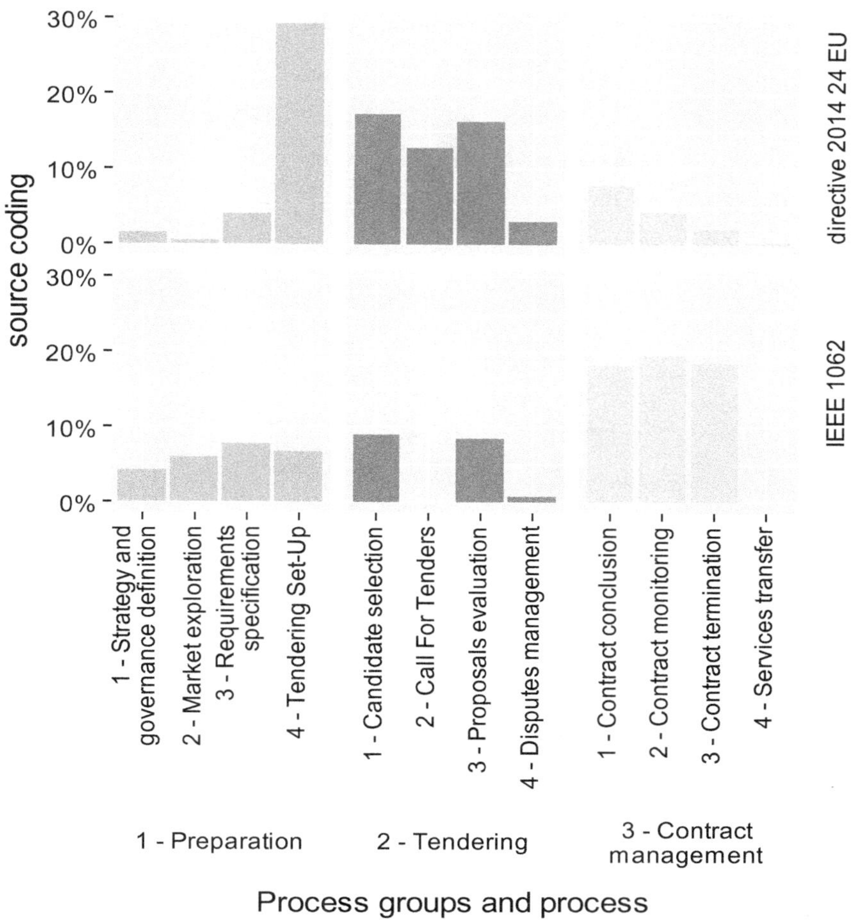

Fig. 2. Example of coding distribution for two sources: % of the coded source text (y) coded to the process (x)

step 3, we drafted the process outcomes. We factorized and/or divided them in order to have between 3 and 7 observable expected results per process (as recommended by ISO/IEC 24774 [30]). Moreover, we designed them in such a way that the whole set of outcomes is necessary and sufficient to ensure the achievement of the process goal.

Step 5 – Group Activities Together Under a Practice and Attach It to the Related Outcomes. For each outcome, we grouped together the tasks and activities that were considered as indicators of the presence of this outcome. For that, we created base practices, by paying attention to exclude the duplicated ones (i.e. similar activities and tasks, coming from our multiple source documents, and using close but different vocabulary).

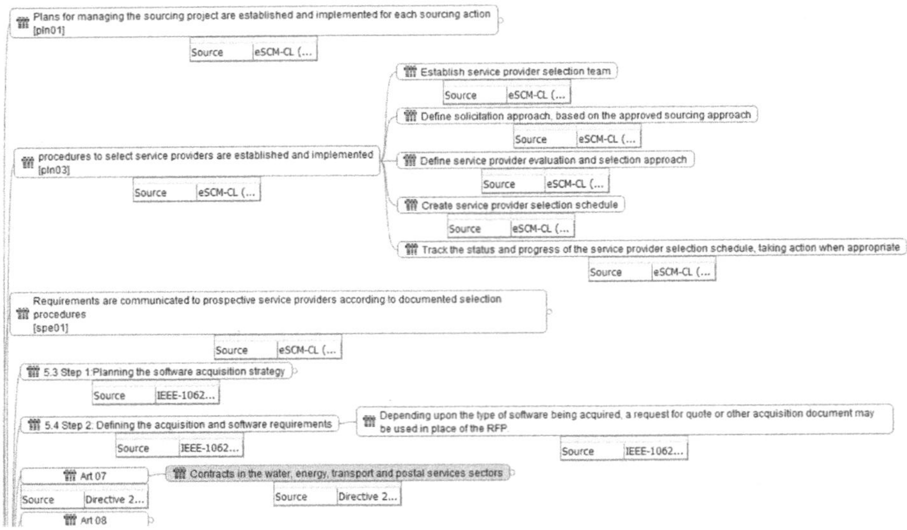

Fig. 3. An example of a part of a requirement tree

Step 6 – Allocate Each Practice to a Specific Capability Level. We analysed the practices designed during step 5, in order to find those that were not directly contributing to the achievement of the process goal. Such practices, which are in fact indicators of a capability attribute above the process performance, were allocated to a level higher than one on the capability scale used in our procurement PAM.

An example of such a higher level indicator is the following practice, coming from the e-SCM framework: *"Establish team for evaluating potential service providers"* and which was allocated to the capability level 2 (Performance Management Attribute).

Step 7 – Phrase Outcomes and Process Purpose. We formulated the process purpose and process outcomes as recommended by the ISO/IEC 24774 standard [30]. Thus, the purpose was expressed using a single verb at the active form and describing the high level objective of the process. Then, the outcomes were phrased at the passive form, using one or more verbs, and describing measurable expected results (such as the production of an artefact, a significant change in state, or the meeting of specified constraints, e.g., requirements, goals, etc.).

Step 8 – Phrase the Base Practices Attached to Outcomes. During this step, we phrased the base practices in a generic way, each starting with an action verb at the infinitive. We avoided the use of vocabulary specific to one of the selected sources. For each practice, we also listed the outcome(s) to which it contributes, and we displayed the source documents from which it was derived.

Step 9 – Determine Work Products Among the Inputs and Outputs of the Practices. The inventory of all the inputs and outputs of each process has not been done yet.

4.3 Resulting Model

The design of the procurement PAM, described above, is still ongoing. For the time being, we have completed the description of three processes out of twelve. We have not started the inventory and description of the process inputs and outputs yet. In its current state, our PAM includes all the references to the source documents(s) at the origin of the different process components (purpose, outcomes, base practices). One example of process description is shown below, on Fig. 4, for the "Market Exploration" process.

Process ID	MAEX
Process Name	Market exploration
Process Purpose	The purpose of the Market exploration process is to decide on whether or not to initiate the procurement based on the understanding of the market opportunities.
Process Outcomes	As a result of successful implementation of the Market exploration process: 1. High level acquisition objectives are defined; [eSCM-CL opa03] 2. Market opportunities (suppliers and their works/services/products) are identified; [eSCM-CL opa04][IEEE 1062 Step 3] 3. Market opportunities are analyzed; [eSCM-CL app04] 4. Decision on whether or not to initiate the procurement is taken and communicated. [eSCM-CL app05][Directive 2014/24/EU Art 40]
Base Practices	**MAEX.BP1: Identify potential sourcing areas.** [Outcome 1] [eSCM-CL opa03] **MAEX.BP2: Define objectives for sourcing in potential sourcing areas.** [Outcome 1] [eSCM-CL opa03] **MAEX.BP3: Gather information on market opportunities** [Outcome 2] [IEEE 1062 Step 3] [Directive 2014/24/EU Art 40] **MAEX.BP4: Filter market opportunities with regards to the high-level acquisition objectives** [Outcome 2] [eSCM-CL opa04] **MAEX.BP5: Analyze risks related to market opportunities** [Outcome 3] [eSCM-CL app04] **MAEX.BP6: Assess potential impact of works / services / products with regards to the high level acquisition objectives** [Outcome 3] [eSCM-CL app04] **MAEX.BP7: Verify if market opportunities answer high-level acquisition objectives within reasonable risks exposure and positive impact** [Outcome 4] [eSCM-CL app05] **MAEX.BP8: Decide to pursue the procurement** [Outcome 4] [eSCM-CL app05] **MAEX.BP9: Communicate the decision to relevant stakeholders** [Outcome 4] [Directive 2014/24/EU Art 48]

Fig. 4. An example of process description

5 Discussions

Transformation Process is a thematic analysis of qualitative data. Such analysis looks across all qualitative materials available to identify common themes. It can be achieved by using different reasoning methods. The ones that structures Transformation Process is inductive reasoning. Also referred as Grounded Theory [31], it consists in making broad generalization from specific observations. Applied to PAM design, Themes (step 3) should emerge from elementary requirements identification and analysis (steps 1 and 2). Inductive reasoning have been successfully applied to the design of PAM from single source [18–20], but does not really fit where there is multiple sources. Procurement PAM is built from 4 distinct sources hence elementary requirements to be processed are numerous (we counted more than 2000) and their analysis requires long effort (step 2). In order to ensure Transformation Process efficiency, it is necessary, prior to elementary requirements extraction (step 1), to define a first version of the expected Process map (step 3). From a methodological point of view, this Process Map is a coding scheme [32]; and introducing such kind of scheme refers to deductive reasoning. It implies to begin with thinking up a theory about the topic of interest and then continue with testing it by collecting evidences from qualitative materials. Procurement PAM design has started by defining a coding scheme that illustrates procurement process mapping as defined by expert judgement [15] (3 groups, 12 processes).

On the other hand, the team could have chosen to use one of the source as a reference for the groups and processes and to map the other sources to this reference. Two facts prevented the team to do so: first the vocabulary discrepancy, second the risk of bias in the Transformation Process. Indeed each source uses its own terminology to name concepts (like actors, work products, activities …) that seem common within the scope of the procurement PAM. Within each source, some concepts are referred to with specialized terms while other concepts are referred to with more generic terms. So using a common set of groups and processes helped to identify under the same umbrella concepts expressed with different terms in each source. Also should one source had been used as the reference to code the other sources, the steps of the transformation would have probably been interpreted primarily from the perspective of the coding source, thus resulting in a risk of bias (favouring the reference source and lowering the differences of perspective provided by the other sources). In summary, defining a common and specific set of groups and processes helped to generalise both the vocabulary used in the PAM and then to make the design decisions with such genericity in mind.

Procurement PAM's coding scheme has just been used to cluster elementary requirements in order to avoid having to process too large volume of requirements together. But, the deeper analysis of each cluster has been conducted according to inductive reasoning methods. The reasoning method that might be used to design PAM from multiple sources is a combination of deductive and inductive reasoning, also called abductive reasoning method. Abductive reasoning usually starts with incomplete knowledge about a topic and proceeds to its extension through evidences collected at the ground. PAM Procurement Design actually leads to the extension or, at least, to the consolidation of knowledge about procurement.

6 Conclusion and Next Steps

This paper presented the design of a generic procurement PAM, based on several complementary source documents. For the time being, the design work is ongoing, and the expected PAM is thus still under development. In the coming weeks, the authors plan to finalize a first version of this process assessment model. Then, they plan a review and validation phase, where experts in the process assessment domain (members of ISO/JTC/SC7/WG10) will be appealed to make comments and to suggest improvements. After that, a first experimentation is expected, in order to test the procurement process assessment model in a real case study. Last, both the procurement process assessment model and the feedback from the experimentation will be analysed and presented to the community of interest active in the field of procurement for validation. Because the number of sources related to a field of application (i.e. a topic) will continue to increase, the PAM design method have to be adapted accordingly. As discussed in the previous section, analysis of a large volume of elementary requirements implies to modify the step-by-step procedure in order to comply with abduction reasoning principles. But, it also requires to adopt technologies to support the PAM designers in carrying out the analysis process. Achieving PAM design "digitalization" supposes to define and explore function and features of existing and emerging technologies as Natural Language Processing.

References

1. ISO/IEC: ISO/IEC 33004. Information Technology—Process assessment—Requirements for process reference, process assessment and maturity models (2015)
2. ISO/IEC 15504-5:2012. Information Technology—Process assessment—An exemplar software life cycle process assessment model (2012)
3. ISO/IEC/IEEE 12207:2017. Information Technology—Systems and software engineering—Software life cycle processes (2017)
4. TIPA for ITIL 2011 r2 v4.1 (2015). http://bit.ly/23camL4. Accessed 21 Mar 2018
5. The Cabinet Office: ITIL Lifecycle Publication Suite. TSO Edition (2011)
6. Ahmad, E.A.: Maturity models of IT outsourcing: a systematic literature review. Int. J. Adv. Appl. Sci. **4**(12), 52–56 (2017)
7. Dalberg, V., Angelvik, E., Elvekrok, D.R., Fossberg, A.K.: Cross-cultural Collaboration in ICT Procurement. In: Proceedings of the 2006 International Workshop on Global Software Development for the Practitioner, New York, pp. 51–57 (2006)
8. Renault, S.: IT systems and services procurement: a framework-based support for buyers in retrospect. In: Presented at the Eurospi^2 2014, Luxembourg (2014)
9. Renault, S., Barafort, B., Dubois, E., Krystkowiak, M.: Improving SME trust into IT consultancy: a network of certified consultants case study. In: EuroSPI 2007 Industrial Proceedings, Potsdam, pp. 10.1–10.8 (2007)
10. Renault, S.: Organisational software and IT services purchasing. In: Presented at the 25th International Purchasing and Supply, Education and Research Association Conference, Dortmund (2016)
11. ISO/IEC: ISO/IEC 330xx. Information Technology - Process Assessment (2013, 2017)

12. Automotive Spice. http://www.automotivespice.com/fileadmin/software-download/Automotive_SPICE_PAM_30.pdf
13. Lepmets, M., Clarke, P., McCaffery, F., Dorling, A., Finnegan, A.: Development of MDevSPICE® - the medical device software process assessment framework. J. Softw.: Evol. Process (2015). (Special Issue - EuroSPI 2014)
14. Enterprise SPICE (2010). http://enterprisespice.com/page/publication-1. Accessed 21 Mar 2018
15. An introduction to public procurement, Office of Government Commerce, UK (2008)
16. Barafort, B., Renault, A., Picard, M., Cortina, S.: A transformation process for building PRMs and PAMs based on a collection of requirements – example with ISO/IEC 20000. In: 8th International SPICE 2008 Conference, Nuremberg (2008)
17. Rifaut, A.: Goal-driven requirements engineering for supporting the ISO 15504 assessment process. In: Richardson, I., Abrahamsson, P., Messnarz, R. (eds.) EuroSPI 2005. LNCS, vol. 3792, pp. 151–162. Springer, Heidelberg (2005). https://doi.org/10.1007/11586012_15
18. Cortina, S., Mayer, N., Renault, A., Barafort, B.: Towards a process assessment model for management system standards. In: Mitasiunas, A., Rout, T., O'Connor, Rory V., Dorling, A. (eds.) SPICE 2014. CCIS, vol. 477, pp. 36–47. Springer, Cham (2014). https://doi.org/10.1007/978-3-319-13036-1_4
19. Cortina, S., Picard, M., Valdés, O., Renault, A.: A challenging process models development: the ITIL v3 lifecycle processes. In: The International Conference SPICE (2010)
20. MacMahon, S.T., McCaffery, F., Eagles, S., Keenan, F., Lepmets, M., Renault, A.: Development of a process assessment model for assessing medical IT networks against IEC 80001-1. In: Mas, A., Mesquida, A., Rout, T., O'Connor, R.V., Dorling, A. (eds.) SPICE 2012. CCIS, vol. 290, pp. 148–160. Springer, Heidelberg (2012). https://doi.org/10.1007/978-3-642-30439-2_14
21. Picard, M., Renault, A., Barafort, B.: A maturity model for ISO/IEC 20000-1 based on the TIPA for ITIL process capability assessment model. In: O'Connor, R., Umay Akkaya, M., Kemaneci, K., Yilmaz, M., Poth, A., Messnarz, R. (eds.) Systems, Software and Services Process Improvement. CCIS, vol. 543, pp. 168–179. Springer, Cham (2015). https://doi.org/10.1007/978-3-319-24647-5_14
22. EXIN, Ed.: Introduction to ISPL, vol. 1 (5 vols). SDU, The Hague (1999)
23. Chrissis, M.-B., Konrad, M., Shrum, S.: CMMI: Guidelines for Process Integration and Product Improvement. Addison-Wesley, Boston (2006)
24. Ritcher, K.: CMMI® for Acquisition (CMMI-ACQ) Primer, Version 1.2. Software Engineering Institute, May 2008
25. Hyder, E.B., Heston, K.M., Paulk, M.C.: ESourcing Capability Model for Service Providers (eSCM-SP). Van Haren Publishing, Zaltbommel (2010)
26. Hefley, B., Loesche, E.A.: ESourcing Capability Model for Client Organizations (eSCM-CL). Van Haren Publishing, Zaltbommel (2010)
27. IEEE Recommended Practice for Software Acquisition, IEEE Computer Society, Standard IEEE-1062-2015, February 2016
28. Directive 2014/24/EU of the European Parliament and of the Council of 26 February 2014 on public procurement and repealing Directive 2004/18/EC Text with EEA relevance (2014)
29. http://www.qsrinternational.com/nvivo/what-is-nvivo. Accessed 26 Mar 2018
30. ISO/IEC TR 24774. Systems and software engineering – Life cycle management – Guidelines for process description (2010)
31. Glaser, B.G., Strauss, A.L.: The Discovery of Grounded Theory: Strategies for Qualitative Research. Aldine, Chicago (1967)
32. Timmermans, S., Tavory, I.: Theory construction in qualitative research: from gounded theory to abductive analysis. Sociol. Theor. **30**(3), 167–186 (2012)

Eight Aspects of Actions in Improvement Plans

Peter H. Carstensen[1] and Otto Vinter[2(✉)]

[1] Department of Computer Science, University of Copenhagen, 2200 Copenhagen, Denmark
peter.h.carstensen@di.ku.dk

[2] Department of People and Technology, Roskilde University, 4000 Roskilde, Denmark
otv@ruc.dk, vinter@ottovinter.dk

Abstract. Process improvement planning and managing changes in general are highly complex and demanding activities. To establish an overview of recommended actions in such plans, we performed a thorough study of a comprehensive set of change strategy literature. For each author we extracted their main recommendations for action. The result was a list of recommendations for action containing 233 recommendations. Through analytic induction we identified eight generic aspects that managers, process consultants and change agents should consider when planning and executing changes and process improvements. In this paper we present and discuss the eight aspects. We provide some reflections on how these aspects could be used for inspiration, or as checklists, when designing action plans in practical change management situations. Finally, we relate the eight aspects to the values and principles in the SPI Manifesto and the guidelines for process improvement in ISO/IEC 33014.

Keywords: Action plans · Aspects of change · Change strategies ISO/IEC 33014 · Process improvement · SPI Manifesto

1 Introduction

Process improvement is a challenge irrespective of whether you seek formal assessment of your general maturity through one of the prominent frameworks like CMMI [1], ISO/IEC 15504 (SPICE) [2], or merely want to improve those processes you feel are in most urgent need. Process improvement is, however, only one type of organizational change. They are all about changing people's way of working and consequently inherently complex, difficult and often prone to failure.

Our research interest has been to address (part of) this issue by examining which recommendations can be extracted from the existing change management literature and investigate the applicability of these as advice for those planning and executing a change. To do so, we have performed a thorough study of the literature that is the foundation for the 10 overall change strategies defined in ISO/IEC 33014 [3]. We have extracted statements from this material that represent recommended actions to support a change. We have primarily focused on the (top) management perspective.

During this process we have identified and validated 8 aspects that can be seen as overall headings or categories for the actions. The aspects thereby reflect our

X. Larrucea et al. (Eds.): EuroSPI 2018, CCIS 896, pp. 147–158, 2018.
https://doi.org/10.1007/978-3-319-97925-0_12

aggregation of what a series of prominent authors consider essential. The eight aspects are listed in Table 1 and described in detail in Sect. 4.

Table 1. The 8 aspects of recommended actions for executing a change.

Aspect	Short explanation
Communication	Types of information that should be communicated, to/by whom, when/through which channels
Competences and training	The competences management and change-team should have before the work on the change is initiated, or which should be built up on the way
Culture	The culture that should be established/changed/supported in the organization to secure the success
Decision-making	Decisions and commitments it is important to make and achieve before and during the work on the change, who should make them, when and within what scope
Knowledge acquisition	The knowledge that should be obtained/gained/collected before and during the work on the change
Methods and techniques	Concrete methods and techniques that should be used in order to execute the change
Organizing	How the change-team as well as all involved or affected by it should be organized/structured
Processes and plans	Concrete plans and processes that management and change-team establish for the work

The work on arriving at the 8 aspects and how they are related to the 10 overall change strategies in ISO/IEC 33014 has been reported in Carstensen and Vinter [4]. We believe that these 8 aspects can be supportive for the management, process consultant or change agent when developing and executing a specific action plan for a change in a particular context. We have described our suggested way of doing so in Carstensen and Vinter [5].

The aim of this paper is first to describe and exemplify the 8 aspects further, and then to reflect upon the applicability and coverage of the aspects in a specific change context, namely that of software process improvement (SPI).

To do so, we first set the stage by mentioning what others have done with respect to defining frameworks similar to our aspects for change (Sect. 2). Then follows a brief presentation of our process of extracting relevant recommended actions from the change management literature and how we arrived at identifying the eight aspects (Sect. 3). Details of this process can be found in [4].

We then present each of the aspects in detail in Sect. 4, and in order to put our work into a specific SPI context of change, we relate the aspects to the 3 values and 10 principles in the SPI Manifesto [6] (Sect. 5) and briefly also to the Guidelines for process improvement in ISO/IEC 33014.

Finally we reflect over some potential biases and discuss the usability of the aspects in practice (Sect. 6).

2 What Have Others Done

There is a huge body of literature on change strategies and general recommendations on how to organize and conduct strategic changes. Among the widely known and broadly recognized can be mentioned: Kotter focusing on an eight point plan for a change [7]; Hammer and Champy arguing for reengineering the whole corporation [8]; Mintzberg's overall conceptual frameworks for understanding and changing different organization structures [9]; Rogers' deep analyses of adoption and diffusion of changes [10]; Senge's approach to change organizations through socializing and learning [11]; and Huy focusing on structuring and sequencing of strategies over time [12]. Most of these have been central in setting the scene for the research reported in this paper.

Finally, the ISO/IEC standards mentioned above [2, 3] have also contributed to defining the steps in planning and executing a change, especially within the area of process improvement. In addition, the SPI Manifesto [6] presents a set of values and principles specifically for the SPI context.

In his influential book on strategy safaris [13] Mintzberg and his co-authors suggest a set of 'strategy schools' approaching the strategy formation process as: a conception, a negotiation, a transformation, or as being a formal, analytical, visionary, mental, emergent, collective or reactive process. These 10 distinct schools might be supportive for characterizing a specific change process or categorizing an approach or methodology.

Balogun and her co-authors [14, 15] provide a diagnostic framework called the 'change kaleidoscope' for identifying appropriate 'design choices'. This framework consists of three layers: The organizational strategic change context referring to the broader strategic analysis conducted; 8 essential features of the change context (time, scope, preservation, diversity, capability, capacity, readiness, and power); and 6 dimensions of choices open to the change agent (path, start-point, style, target, levers and roles).

Next to the academic literature lots of consultants, bloggers, consultancy companies etc. have provided their lists of suggestions and recommendations, for example strategy + business that provides 10 principles for leading change management [16] focusing on culture, how to involve all layers in the organization, how to engage and lead etc.

Throughout the literature are mentioned aspects like: motivating people and sharing the vision. But the main focus in the literature remains on how to structure and plan the change and the processes to be followed. To our knowledge, however, very few attempts have been made to define a framework of common aspects to be considered by managers, process consultants and change agents in their planning and design of the actions to be performed. We believe that our 8 aspects represent such a framework and will describe the aspects in details in Sect. 4.

3 Our Research Approach

Our research approach is based on analytic induction. We began by extracting recommended actions from the literature behind 2 of the 10 ISO/IEC 33014 [3] strategies. We read the texts from end-to-end and extracted statements by the author(s) that seemed characteristic for the strategy. One of us was reading the texts and the other was reviewing the extracted recommendations for action.

We kept the recommendations as close to the original statements in the texts as possible. Our main intervention was to make the statements actionable i.e. put them into imperative form. An example of such a reformulation of a statement is: "Leadership of change belongs to one small group of people, typically located at the top of the formal hierarchy" ([12] p. 605), which was reformulated to a recommended action: "Ensure that leadership of the change belongs to one small group of people typically located at the top of the formal hierarchy".

When we looked at the resulting recommended actions we could see that some of the recommendations were addressing the same aspect of the change (e.g. culture). We identified 8 such aspects and then hypothesized that these 8 aspects would be applicable also to the recommendations for the remaining 8 strategies. We discussed each aspect and defined them properly.

We quickly realized that the aspects were not completely orthogonal, which was never our intention. We regard the aspects as a kind of check-list for management or process consultant, who develops and executes a change process. Their applicability in practice is more important to us than whether they are 100% precise. The 8 aspects are listed in Table 1.

To validate the hypothesis we repeated the same process for the rest of the 10 strategies defined in ISO/IEC 33014 [3]. The extracted statements from the corresponding literature were now analyzed whether they could be allocated to the previously identified aspects. We found this rather easy, which confirmed our hypothesis. We performed other types of validations too, the details of which can be found in [4].

4 The Eight Aspects to Be Considered in a Change Plan

The approach mentioned in the previous section involved a careful review of in total 32 books and articles. This review identified 665 recommendations for action when organizing and carrying out strategic changes. This number was later refined to 233 recommendations that were the most clearly indicative of the strategies. Through analytic induction we identified 8 generic aspects that managers, process consultants and change agents need to consider when planning and executing changes. An overview of the aspects is presented in Table 1.

The 8 aspects cover all the central themes that should be considered and included in a change plan. Some aspects cover how the work should be planned and undertaken i.e. Plans and Processes, and Methods and Techniques.

Other aspects have to do with ensuring that the relevant information is collected, how the work should be organized and how decisions should be made – ahead of the actual change activities as well as while the change is being undertaken i.e. Knowledge acquisition, Organizing and Decision-making.

Finally some aspects have to do with the people involved in the actual change: Culture, Communication, and Competences and Training.

In the rest of this section each of the 8 aspects will be described in detail. First we present a definition of the aspect, then some example recommendations from literature, and finally some reflections over the distribution across the overall change strategies.

4.1 Communication

Definition: About the types of information that should be communicated, to whom, by whom, when and through which channels. This includes documents and artefacts required for supporting and evaluating the change.

Example Recommendations from Literature:

- "Promote communication between communities of practice" ([17] p. 69).
- "Meet employees face to face and communicate your vision" ([12] p. 612).
- "Communicate often and focus on the opportunities" ([18] p. 6).
- "Develop and publish clear documented corporate beliefs and purpose - a mission statement" ([19] p. 36).

The Communication aspect is not evenly distributed over the 10 overall change strategies in the ISO/IEC 33014 standard. Communication issues are mentioned most often when a strategy of dictating change or reengineering the processes or structures in the organization is adopted. The vision must be clear, shared and reinforced often.

In cases of more exploratory or employee-driven changes communication is performed more informally and therefore not mentioned often by the authors.

4.2 Competences and Training

Definition: About the competences management and change-team should have before the work on the change is initiated, or which should be built up on the way, as well as competences and education/training that should be established for the parts of the organization included in the change.

Example Recommendations from Literature:

- "Ensure that the local adopters are sufficiently educated/trained to understand the big picture about the available innovation/change" ([10] p. 399).
- "Train change agents to become competent in interpersonal inquiry" ([12] p. 608).
- "Develop leadership skills among middle managers to install new values in them" ([12] p. 620).

Most authors addressing the Competences and training aspect focus on changes involving the attitude of employees and learning organizations. The aspect is also mentioned for types of changes with particular emphasis on developing the competences of the persons driving the change, like change agents, middle managers or selected groups in the target audience.

For changes in highly specialized organizations this aspect is ignored in the literature, presumably because the competences are expected to be present already.

4.3 Culture

Definition: About the culture, that should be established/changed and supported in the organization in order to secure the success of the desired change. It could be directed at the whole (or specific parts of the) organization, including management, the change-team as well as the parts of the organization included in the change.

Example Recommendations from Literature:

- "Engage in recurrent rituals to build shared meanings" ([12] p. 608).
- "Encourage people to challenge and examine alternatives" ([12] p. 619).
- "Encourage individuals to establish improvement goals for themselves and their groups" ([19] p. 19).

This aspect is often mentioned by authors dealing with changes in attitude of the employees or organizational learning, and also in cases of changes involving relational coordination, and changes taking place through social networks. The focus of the recommendations is on creating situations where the employees can open up for new changes in their environment e.g. through discussion fora where current practices (culture) are questioned and improved.

The Culture aspect is not addressed in the literature where dictating change or reengineering the processes or structures in the organization is the goal.

4.4 Decision-Making

Definition: About the types of decisions and commitments it is important to make and achieve before and during the work on the change, who should make them, when and within what scope, they can be made; specifically the delegation of authority.

Example Recommendations from Literature:

- "Shift power to the experts (specialists) by virtue of their knowledge" ([9] p. 106).
- "Enable the diffusion and adoption of the change by making alternatives clear" ([10] p. 6).
- "Base your management decisions on a long term philosophy, even at the expense of short term financial goals" ([20] p. 5).

The number of recommendations associated with this aspect is relatively uniformly distributed across the 10 overall strategies in ISO/IEC 33014. This seems natural as all types of change must establish some form of clarity about how decisions should take place e.g. who is responsible for what, and what authoritative power is distributed to different layers or persons in the organization.

The approach to how decision-making is defined, however, differs among the overall strategies. The more dictating strategies recommend maintaining the power of authority at the top of the organization, whereas other strategies where the participation of employees is desired, authoritative power is distributed more widely e.g. to change agents.

4.5 Knowledge Acquisition

Definition: About the types of knowledge, that should be obtained/gained/collected before and during the work on the change. This could comprise knowledge about the preconditions for the change, or clarification of the specific conditions about the (part of the) organization that should undergo the change. Also knowledge on whether the activities seem to have had the expected effects and whether it might be relevant to consider changing the strategies applied.

Example Recommendations from Literature:

- "Study norms and conventions that provide the implicit context for performing practices" ([17] p. 23).
- "Ensure that the impact of existing initiatives are evaluated and considered carefully before starting another series of improvement initiatives" ([19] p. 159).
- "Analyze constraints and evaluate specifications" ([21] p. 189).

Strangely enough this aspect is not very well addressed by the authors when it comes to giving recommendations for action. It seems as if most authors have fixed their minds on executing a change and therefore do not address the prerequisites and context that defined the change in the first place. Nor do the authors seem to take much interest in giving recommendations on how to collect and use feedback from the organization as the change activities are progressing.

Except for changes in highly specialized organizations, the majority of the 10 overall change strategies in ISO/IEC 33014 have less than 3 recommendations given by the authors.

4.6 Methods and Techniques

Definition: About the concrete methods and techniques, that should be used in order to execute the change. How they should be performed and by whom.

Example Recommendations from Literature:

- "Co-ordinate, advise and manage instead of keeping control centrally" ([17] p. 39).
- "Set the stage, step back a bit, allow patterns to emerge, and determine which ones are desirable" ([12] p. 615).
- "Forget the past, break rules and traditions in order to create variation" ([22] p. 251).

This aspect is by far the most popular when it comes to giving recommendations, and the recommendations are evenly distributed over the 10 overall strategies in ISO/IEC 33014. The recommendations cover a wide set of issues and are at several levels of abstraction.

We have asked ourselves whether this aspect should be split in two or more aspects, but we have not yet been able to find a good division and relevant definitions for such aspects.

4.7 Organizing

Definition: About the organizing of the change. How the team responsible for the change as well as all involved in it or affected by it should be structured, their roles in the change defined, and which groups and fora should be formed.

Example Recommendations from Literature:

- "Ensure that leadership of the change belongs to one small group of people typically located at the top of the hierarchy" ([12] p. 605).
- "Establish and cultivate communities of practice" ([17] p. 22).
- "Form quality improvement teams with representatives from each department" ([19] p. 19).

The number of recommendations from the literature is relatively uniformly distributed across the 10 overall strategies in ISO/IEC 33014. This seems natural as all types of change must establish some form of clarity about how a change should be organized.

It is noticeable, however, that the number of recommendations dealing with exploratory changes is much higher than for other types of changes and this may be because the authors want to emphasize that such activities must be organized separately from the normal operations in the organization.

4.8 Processes and Plans

Definition: About the concrete plans and processes that management and change-team establish for the execution of the whole and/or specific parts of the work.

Example Recommendations from Literature:

- "Overhaul processes which create a vicious cycle of overload, stress, burnout and low morale" ([12] p. 612).
- "Use comprehensive strategic planning including competitive analysis and portfolio management" ([12] p. 604).
- "Ensure control at all stages of planning and operationalization of the strategy" ([13] p. 55).

We had expected that change management authors would present many recommendations about which processes and planning was needed for executing a change. But the aspect received fewer recommendations than many other aspects e.g. Methods and Techniques.

Recommendations for this aspect are most often given for changes aimed at optimizing operations or restructuring the organization using quantitative measurements as drivers.

Only few recommendations are presented for changes where the employees are the prime drivers or mediators in the change.

5 The Aspects in Relation to Software Process Improvement

As mentioned previously the 8 aspects we have identified are to some extent recognizable in many authors' recommendations and reflections on 'general' issues to consider when planning and executing change activities.

In this section we focus on the 8 aspects in relation to a prominent process improvement framework: The SPI Manifesto [6]. Hereby we can evaluate the coverage of the aspects in a software process improvement (SPI) context and vice versa.

The SPI Manifesto states that SPI is based on 3 values: People, Business and Change. These values are supported by 10 principles ([6] p. 1). The People value is supported by 4 principles. The Business value and Change value are supported by 3 principles each.

The People value states: "We truly believe SPI must involve people actively and affect their daily activities" ([6] p. 3). This means increasing the competitiveness through the knowledge and active involvement of people in improvement actions. When we look into the recommendations associated with the two aspects: Culture, and Competences and training, we find a number of recommendations that address the active involvement of people as well as providing the involved people with sufficient and relevant competences and training. Other aspects like: Communication, Decision-making and Methods and Techniques also contain recommendations addressing this value.

The Business value states: "We truly believe that SPI is what you do to make business successful" ([6] p. 4). This means that the processes you improve must fit the needs of your business. Many of the recommendations associated with the aspects focus on setting and communicating goals for the change that are dictated by the needs of the business; typically reflected in the aspects: Communication, Knowledge acquisition, Methods and techniques, and Processes and plans.

The Change value states: "We truly believe that SPI is inherently linked with change" ([6] p. 5). This means that accepting and adopting change throughout the organization is essential. As a consequence the organization must ensure that its infrastructure has a change management component in it. This aligns with the recommendations associated with the aspects: Culture, Organizing, Methods and techniques, and Processes and plans.

We therefore claim that there is – not surprisingly – a fine compliance between the core values in the SPI Manifesto and the recommendations associated with the eight aspects.

In order to fully relate the SPI Manifesto to our aspects our approach has been to treat the document as we previously did in our literature review. We carefully read the text, extracted recommendations and assigned them to aspects.

We found that the most common aspect in recommendations across the SPI Manifesto is: Methods and techniques. This result is common for all the literature we have reviewed. However, we also found that the aspects: Decision-making and Organizing were assigned to only 1 recommendation each, which is not the case for the general literature on change. We think that this issue represents a weakness in the SPI Manifesto.

If we only look at the 10 principles and their meaning (i.e. not the full text) and relate them to the aspects, we get the result shown in Table 2.

Table 2. The 10 SPI Manifesto principles and related aspects.

Manifesto principles	Related aspects
1. Know the culture and focus on needs	Culture, knowledge acquisition
2. Motivate all people involved	Culture
3. Base improvement on experience and measurements	Competences and training, culture
4. Create a learning organization	Culture, competences and training
5. Support the organization's vision and objectives	Methods and techniques, processes and plans
6. Use dynamic and adaptable models as needed	Methods and techniques, knowledge acquisition
7. Apply risk management	Methods and techniques
8. Manage the organizational change in your improvement effort	Processes and plans, methods and techniques
9. Ensure all parties understand and agree on process	Communication
10. Do not lose focus	Methods and techniques, Processes and plans

In Table 2 we observe that the Culture aspect is very much present in the People value principles (1–4). The aspect of Competences and training is also common, but we also observe that the principles focus more on using and including the actors' experiences, not so much on the establishment of new competences.

The principles associated with the Business value (5–7) and Change value (8–10) are dominated by the aspects: Methods and techniques and Processes and plans, which was to be expected.

From the above it is clear that the principles can be related to the aspects and vice versa. This is not very surprising as the literature and sources of inspiration to a large extent are the same.

But we also observe that the aspects: Communication, Decision-making, and Organizing are not as frequently represented as in the other literature we have reviewed. Again this is not very surprising as the basis for our aspects is the general change management literature which is broader and covers more than recommendations for software process improvement.

On the other side we found that business-related recommendations in the Manifesto like "process improvement goals must reflect business goals" were all assigned to the aspect: Methods and techniques. Separating such recommendations from the Methods and techniques aspect should be considered by us in the future.

We have performed a similar analysis of the Guidelines for Process Improvement in the ISO 33014 standard. Space limitations, however, prevent us from giving a full review here. Suffice to say, that the standard also gives few recommendations for the

Decision-making aspect. For the aspects of Communication, Culture, and Competences and training few recommendations are presented also.

6 Conclusion

This paper has presented 8 aspects that, together, establish a set of areas that needs to be addressed in change activities, both with respect to management, planning and carrying out the actual change activities. Based on the literature behind the 10 strategies defined in ISO/IEC 33014 [3] we extracted statements representing the authors' recommended actions for change and from this synthesized the 8 aspects presented here (Sect. 4).

To demonstrate the relevance of the 8 aspects in a software process improvement context we have compared them with the values and principles in the SPI Manifesto [6]. This showed that the SPI Manifesto contains recommendations for all of the 8 aspects, although the aspects of Communication, Organizing and Decision-making have only a very limited representation compared to the general change management literature. This could call for further investigations into whether this is due to the nature of the SPI Manifesto (focusing very much on values and opinions), or whether the SPI Manifesto could be improved if these aspects were more explicitly incorporated.

We are aware that our research into the change management literature has some methodological weaknesses which mean that the validity and the applicability of the aspects should be investigated further. E.g. we realize that we have not included all relevant literature on change management and process improvement. It is furthermore quite obvious that further validation of the usefulness of the aspects can only take place on real-life cases. A third issue has to do with the fact that we are the only two persons who have (1) identified the recommendations from the literature, (2) selected the recommendations to be included in the final list for each strategy, and (3) conducted the analytic induction and abstraction leading to the 8 aspects.

In our research approach we have continuously aimed at getting our findings and selections validated, but there is still a risk of a methodological weakness and a source for bias in our results. Thus, future research should aim at investigating other relevant sources for recommendations on change strategies; seek to get the aspects tested and validated on other sets of recommendations; and possibly validate whether other readers of the same literature would extract a similar set of recommendations, and select a similar set as the most important.

Given the reservations above, we are confident of the usefulness of the aspects we have found. We firmly believe that when planning and executing changes in your specific context and case, you should carefully consider the aspects when developing your action plan. In the literature we have found many indications that the 8 aspects cover relevant facets and ingredients in change management and process improvement. Careful consideration of the 8 aspects when designing a specific action plan will therefore constitute a good platform for ensuring that all relevant facets have been addressed.

Acknowledgments. We wish to thank Professor Jan Pries-Heje (Roskilde University) and Partner Jørn Johansen (Whitebox) for thoughtful discussions and review of the 8 aspects. We also wish to thank the change management master students at Roskilde University for their contribution in the validation process.

References

1. Chrissis, M.B., Conrad, M., Shrum, S.: CMMI for Development: Guidelines for Process Integration and Product Improvement, 3rd edn. CMU/Software Engineering Institute, Westford (2012). ISBN 978-0321711502
2. ISO: ISO/IEC/TR 15504-4. Information technology–process assessment–guidance on use for process improvement and process capability determination, Geneva, Switzerland (2013)
3. ISO: ISO/IEC/TR 33014. Information technology–process assessment–guide for process improvement, Geneva, Switzerland (2013)
4. Carstensen, P.H., Vinter, O.: Aspects you should consider in your action plan when implementing an improvement strategy. In: Mas, A., Mesquida, A., O'Connor, R.V., Rout, T., Dorling, A. (eds.) SPICE 2017. CCIS, vol. 770, pp. 467–480. Springer, Cham (2017). https://doi.org/10.1007/978-3-319-67383-7_34
5. Carstensen, P.H., Vinter, O.: Developing action plans based on strategy – aspects to consider. Softw. Qual. Prof. J. **20**(2), 4–15 (2018)
6. Pries-Heje, J., Johansen, J.: SPI Manifesto (2010). www.iscn.com/Images/SPI_Manifesto_A.1.2.2010.pdf
7. Kotter, J.P.: Leading Change. Harward Business Review Press, Boston (1996)
8. Hammer, M., Champy, J.: Reengineering the Corporation; A Manifesto for Business Revolution. Harper Business, New York (1993)
9. Mintzberg, H.: Structure in Fives - Designing Effective Organizations. Prentice-Hall, Englewood Cliffs (1983)
10. Rogers, E.M.: Diffusion of Innovations, 5th edn. Free Press, New York (2003)
11. Senge, P.M.: The Fifth Discipline: The Art and Practice of the Learning Organization. Doubleday, New York (1990)
12. Huy, Q.N.: Time, temporal capability, and planned change. Acad. Manag. Rev. **26**(4), 601–623 (2001)
13. Mintzberg, H., Ahlstrand, B., Lampel, J.: Strategy Safari: A Guided Tour Through the Wilds of Strategic Management. Financial Times/Prentice Hall, London (2002)
14. Balogun, J., Hailey, V.H., Gustafsson, S.: Exploring Strategic Change. Pearson, Harlow (2015)
15. Balogun, J., Hailey, V.H.: Devising context sensitive approaches to change: the example of glaxo wellcome. Long Range Plan. J. **35**, 153–178 (2002)
16. www.strategy-business.com. Accessed 12 May 2017
17. Ciborra, C.U., and Associates: From Control to Drift. The Dynamics of Corporate Information Infrastructures. Oxford University Press, Oxford (2000)
18. Bashein, B.J., Markus, M.L., Riley, P.: Preconditions for BPR success: and how to prevent failures. Inf. Syst. Manag. **11**(2), 7–13 (1994)
19. Oakland, J.S.: TQM – Text with Cases, 3rd edn. Butterworth-Heinemann, Newton (2003)
20. Liker, J.K.: The Toyota Way. Tata McGraw-Hill, New York (2004)
21. Simon, H.A.: The structure of ill structured problems. Artif. Intell. **4**, 181–201 (1973)
22. Benner, M., Tushman, M.: Exploitation, exploration, and process management: the productivity dilemma revisited. Acad. Manag. Rev. **28**(2), 238–256 (2003)

SPI and Safety Critical

Method of Evaluating the Influence Factor of Safety in the Automated Driving System: The Chasm Between SAE Level 2 and Level 3

Masao Ito(✉)

NIL Software Corp., 2-17-7 Kinuta, Setagaya, Tokyo, Japan
nil@nil.co.jp

Abstract. Recently vehicle control system becomes have the automated feature. In this situation, the analysis based on malfunction of a system is not enough. We have to consider other hazard types such as the hazard originated from threats, the hazard that comes from the misinterpretation on using sensor. In this paper, we provide several hazard types that we have to think and explain the consistent approach to analyse the system in the concept phase.

Keywords: Safety · Security · ADS · ISO 26262 · J3016 · J3061
CARDION · SOTIF

1 Introduction

The embedded system of the automobile is improving every year especially from the viewpoint of safety, comfort, energy consumption and so on. Notably, the introduction of automated control, like Advanced Driver Assistance System (ADAS), provides the safe car to the users.

The progress of automated control means that the control of a car moves from the driver to the machine. This movement creates a new problem. Usually, the driver recognises the environment, making decision and control. The automated control implies to include the entire recognition and right decision. Those two of three parts (i.e. recognition and decision) is not deterministic ones because the environment with moving objects like other cars or pedestrians is very complicated and each object moves independently. It implies that we have to think the other elements to keep car safe besides the functional safety provided by the standard ISO 26262.

Currently, the central target of the automated driving system (ADS) becomes beyond the level 2 (partial driving automation) of SAE definition [1]. Between the level 2 and level 3 (conditional driving automation), there is an essential difference on the subtask of the dynamic driving task (DDT), that is who is responsible for the object and event detection and response (OEDR). In the level 2 the driver does the OEDR, but in the level 3, the system will do it instead.

It is difficult to sense object fully under the various circumstances, so the critical characteristic of OEDR is the probabilistic one even if we use the excellent approach to find the objects and events [7, 8]. This non-systematic feature may lead us to safety where the discussion of functional safety is hard to cover.

X. Larrucea et al. (Eds.): EuroSPI 2018, CCIS 896, pp. 161–172, 2018.
https://doi.org/10.1007/978-3-319-97925-0_13

There are several factors to consider other than functional safety when we examine safety. In this paper, we discuss two issues. One is security and the other is multiple ADAS subsystem.

If security problems occur when the system is in charge of control, there might introduce an accident. As for automobile embedded system, there is the cyber security guidebook, SAE J3061 [2]. This guidebook provides the process that is comparable to ISO 26262. So, we can easily understand it if we know the ISO 26262 standard. But both don't have the dedicated concrete method.

Secondly, we have to think the multiple ADAS subsystem. It may cause safety concerns, particularly when we develop them at different timings. To depict the all driving scenes is hard work, and it becomes more difficult for consolidating the behaviour of the multiple ADAS subsystems.

We summarize the influence factors for safety in Table 1.

Table 1. Influence factors

Influence factor	Safety category	Standard
Malfunction	Functional safety	ISO 26262 [5]
Misinterpretation of sensor signals	Safety of the intended functionality (SOTIF)	ISO PAS 21448 [18]
Attack	Automotive cybersecurity	ISO/SAE AWI 21434, SAE J3061 [2]
Decision of ADS	Safety of the decision	N/A

In the survey [19], it says there are three major activities in the safety-relating standardisation. That is the top three records in Table 1. It does not have the last record: "Decision of ADS". The cover of SOTIF is not currently clear, but it is relating to the detection part of OEDR. The 'R' of OEDR is the response to the detection and recognition of objects and events. Also, the system decides to response the recognised them. Currently, there is no existing or planned standard for the decision of ADS.

In this paper, we take account of the four influence factors in Table 1. Note that we do not consider whole security matter. We only think the cybersecurity relating to safety. As for the lifecycle phase, we will focus on the concept phase of system development and explain how to solve safety-related factors based on activities that the ISO 26262 Part 3 says. In Sect. 2 we explain issues we would like to answer. Section 3 describes our approach. Finally, we will summarise them.

We use the following terms. The term 'automated driving system (ADS)' includes 'driver assistance system (DAS)' and 'advanced driver assistance system (ADAS)'. The distinction between these two follows the definition in the eSafety project [3]. The general driving support system is DAS, and if it includes the environmental recognition and judgment, i.e. OEDR, it is called ADAS. We use ADS when referring to both, or when it is hard to say 'driver' support.

2 Issues

2.1 Hazards Coming from Threats

We concentrate on safety, so intrusion for privacy information and physical theft by key unauthorized access are outside the scope of this paper. We first try to find hazards and then find the threats that are relating to hazards. For example, in the adaptive cruise control (ACC) system, we consider a hazard that the time to collision (TTC) with the forward car cannot be maintained properly. This hazard might be caused by the failure of the equipment and the delay of detection of a failure. At the same time, we also think that there may be a security breach to falsify the TTC calculation.

In this paper, we call the hazard caused by the threat H_{THR}. And the normal hazard that comes from the malfunction of the system is called H_{MAL}.

2.2 ADS: Level 2 and Level 3 and Above

First, we consider an example of the car that has multiple ADAS subsystems. From this example, we will propose the principal in ADS of Level 3 or higher.

Example of Multiple ADAS Operation Scenarios

Let's consider an example where multiple ADSs operate (Fig. 1)[1]. It is an example combining the control in the longitudinal direction and the control in the lateral direction. This scenario has modified the case in NHTSA's report [4]. This report shows research results on appropriate HMI when multiple ADSs are used.

The scenario here is as follows: (1) the self-vehicle S follows the forward vehicle F by ACC. Since the preceding vehicle F finds an obstacle O ahead and changes the lane. (2) The driver of the self-vehicle S visually observes that there is an obstacle and at the same time the collision warning and braking (CWB) enacts and know the distance is too short to avoid the collision. (3) The driver of the self-vehicle S intends to change the lane and the active lane change with the assistance of Active Lane Change Assistance (ALCA). However, as the high-speed vehicle X is approaching from the left rear side, so ALCA steers to original lane with the warning to avoid collision with vehicle X. This situation is an ambivalent one if the only escape path is an acceleration to go in front of the vehicle X.

At level 2, this relates to the Human-Machine Interface (HMI) issue how effectively the system notifies the situation to the driver. With multiple warnings from the CWB and ALCA, it is essential to avoid the confusion of the driver. We already described this type of issue with the controllability of the driver in the paper [14]. We define this type of hazard that is relating to HMI as H_{HMI}.

At level 3, there is another problem, since the system is responsible for OEDR. That is, we cannot expect the entirely correct recognition of OEDR. Of course, the driver cannot always identify the object and make a correct judgement, either. But he is responsible for that. If the system is in charge of OEDR, it is necessary to grasp the degree of how OEDR can correctly do its work for keeping the system safe because the

[1] The issue shown in this example is categorized in the last one of Table 1 (i.e. "decision of ADS").

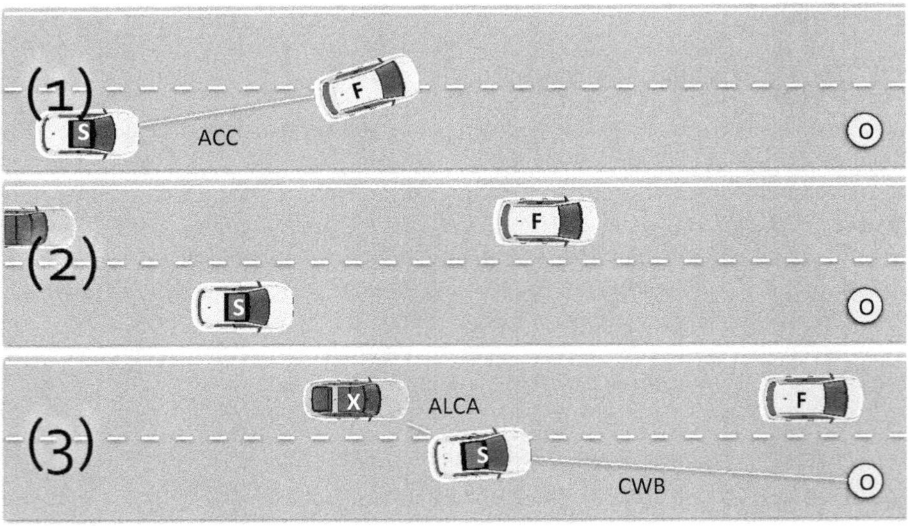

Fig. 1. A scenario shows the difficult situation of the car with multiple ADS systems.

system in charge of judgement. Let the hazard associated with this type relating to OEDR be H_{OEDR}. We describe the principle of ADS in the next clause.

ADS Principles

Substitution Principle

ADS should have the freedom of detection and the freedom of manoeuvre equal to or higher than that of a human being. The degree of detection freedom is the range and precision of detection of the object under the current environment. The degree of manoeuvre freedom refers to longitudinal and lateral available manoeuvring that can be taken in the current vehicle state.

Route Selection Principle

The system should select only the route with sufficient confidence to avoid danger under a current vehicle condition, environmental situation and both degrees of freedom.

At the level 3 or higher, the substitution principle can be considered a reasonable principle, because the machine performs environmental recognition (including other vehicles, etc.) instead of human beings. Route selection principles are principles for clarifying the responsibility of ADS.

Those principles are applied as follows. For example, the self-vehicle runs along the lane, and the nearby lane is opposing one. At this time, the vehicle travels within the range of degree of detection freedom. If there is a relationship between the preceding vehicle and the following vehicle, acceleration/deceleration is performed within the range of manoeuver freedom. If the oncoming car enters the lane of interest, it searches for an appropriate avoidance route. In the above example of multiple ADSs, the system might select the route when the path changing the lanes with acceleration operation has sufficient reliability under the route selection principle.

2.3 Relationship with ISO 26262

ISO 26262 aims at ensuring safety against hazards caused by malfunction of the system. Of course, malfunction is the problem for us to always consider. However, even when the function is working correctly, safety may not be maintained. In other words, we need to think about safety, even where the original ISO 26262 doesn't cover. The hazard H_{HMI} and H_{OEDR} cited above are examples. The latter is a case where there is a gap between demand and realization in the first place if the safety goal says that the system always recognizes target correctly. The realization concerning the recognition of the object itself has a danger, and the software also requires stochastic treatment similar to hardware ("In this case, the consequences are comparable to those of HW and SW failures and may also be safety critical." [7]). Of course, ISO 26262 is a comprehensive approach. We think of a method that can treat other hazards type other than the malfunction of the system.

According to the above discussion, there are two points we have to discuss.

As ISO 26262 covers a single item, we have the special care to the system that has multiple ADSs. For example, consider the previous ALCA as an item in the previous scenario (Fig. 3). ALCA performs control of lateral movement and longitudinal braking. According to the standard, we do the 'item definition (3–5)[2]', 'start the safety lifecycle (3–6)', and 'hazard analysis and risk assessment (HARA, 3–7)'. Suppose that there is a combination with CWB and ACC that are also categories of ADAS. We have to consider those items as the tightly relating subsystems. In the standard, we do this as part of the item boundary description in the item definition stage (3–5.4.2). However, it does not explicitly appear in hazard analysis and risk assessment.

When considering the hazards relating to braking, the braking control of ALCA is different from the control in CWB and ACC. We will think the hazard event that 'unintended braking occurs' in the HARA of item ALCA. For this hazard event, we assess the risk of the target item of ALCA. But, of course, we think the effect of other items: CWB and ACC. It is necessary to perform HARA individually and also including mutual interference. That is, we need to consider not only the influence on other items of ALCA but also whether hazards in ALCA will affect other items that has the braking control [8]. Of course, it is also necessary to consider the influence on the item ALCA from other existing items. In other words, if you have a connection in terms of function, you need to think about the effect mutually.

The second point is that ADS will replace the human recognition function (especially at the level of automation of Level 3 or higher). If this is right, the software safety of ADS truly comes from the consideration of "systematic failure". Regarding faults, as well known, it is treated as the systematic failure concerning software. And regarding hardware, we handle it stochastically [5]. On the other hand, as we saw in the previous principle when machines substitute for humans, the system has to process the information from many sensors under the complicated conditions of the surrounding environment. The judgment there always includes stochastic elements.

[2] We use the pointing system to refer a description: P-CH.SC.CL, where P is the part number, CH is a chapter number, SC is a section number and CL is a clause number of ISO 26262.

For example, when recognizing a forward vehicle, whether it is an image or a point group by LIDAR, there is no definitive correct answer. Depending on a certain threshold, it is a forward vehicle or false image unrelated to it [6]. For the recognition of the environment including the target; the system always has to calculate the result stochastically. If the safety goal is systematic only, there will be a gap called 'functional insufficiency' between the safety target, and the design and implementation [7, 8]. We can describe the goal declaratively, but we have to write design and coding procedurally and include some probabilities.

3 Method

We have proposed a method to analysis safety and security in the conceptual phase by the approach called CARDION [9]. We extend this method and deal with the problem mentioned in the previous section.

3.1 CARDION Method

It is a method to support the conceptual stage of ISO 26262. It corresponds to Part 3 of ISO 26262. The difficulty in the conceptual phase is that it is hard to use the safety and security methods normally used in design and implementation. If the structure is clear, Fault Tree Analysis (FTA) or Failure Mode and Effect Analysis (FMEA) can be used, However, for an item which is an abstract representation of the system, its structure and failure mode is not clear, so apply It is difficult. Nevertheless, it is important to analyse intrinsic safety and security by examining hazards and threats at an early stage. Therefore, a method suitable for the concept stage is required. Regarding security, the process of SAE J3061 has the almost same structure of ISO 26262, as it is "(t)he process framework described in this document is analogous to the process framework described in ISO 26262" ([2], p. 6).

The central part of the CARDION method is the next process. Usually, it repeats several times.

- Create an item sketch.
- Create a goal model for the item and simultaneously refine the item sketch.
- Apply the guideword to each goal description.
- Use item sketches to identify hazards and threats of the item.
- Establish safety and security goals and describe the (safety and security) requirements.

First, using the item sketch, we describe the target item according to ISO 26262 3-5.4.11 (function/non-functional of the item and description of the boundary). The item sketch includes static representation Static representation can be given using schema (e.g. UML class diagram, internal block diagram of SysML [10], or specification type representation of CATALYSIS approach [11]).

A part of the example in the ACC is shown in the lower left of Fig. 2 and the left in Fig. 3.

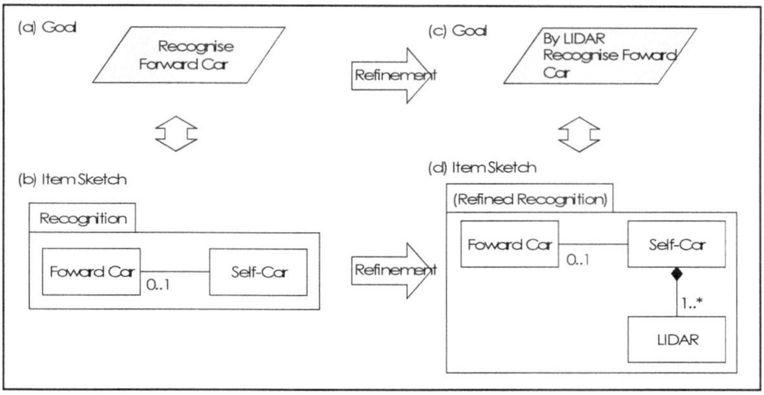

Fig. 2. Item sketch (structure)

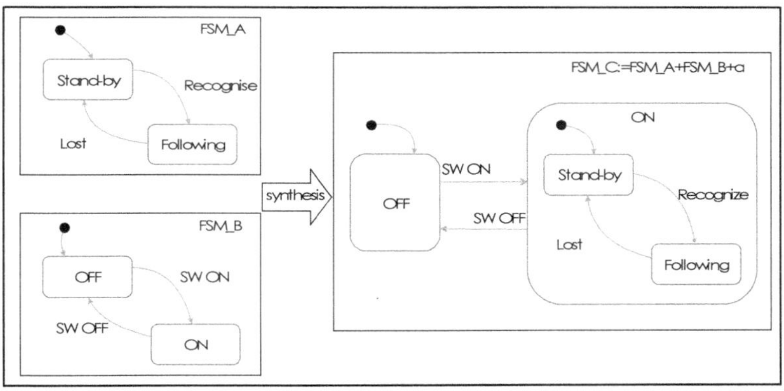

Fig. 3. Item sketch (behaviour)

The goal model of the item corresponds to the function/non-functional requirements that the item should have. As the base modelling method, we use the goal model of the KAOS approach [12] (see Fig. 4), but our approach does not rely only on the KAOS method. Any method can be used as long as we can clearly describe the distinction between the functional requirement and the non-functional requirement, and the relation between the requirements (for example, refinement relationship). Anyway, it is important to describe requests themselves for an item as natural language (NL) sentences. At this stage, natural language description is more suitable than formal description [15]. Moreover, in our method, it is necessary to describe requirements as an NL sentence to manipulate them to be described later. Herein, each request sentence is called a goal description sentence. Also, if necessary, we create new versions by refining or synthesizing the current item sketches. In Fig. 2, the lower right shows the refinement process from the lower left. The right finite state machine can be obtained by synthesizing the two finite state machines shown on the left of Fig. 3.

Next, we apply the guideword of HAZOP [13] to the previous goal description sentence and obtain a hazard candidate. The guidewords are following: NO or NOT (negation), MORE (quantitative increase), LESS (quantitative decrease), AS WELL AS (qualitative increase), PART OF (qualitative decrease), REVERSE (logically inverse), OTHER THAN (fully substitution), EARLY/LATE (clock time) and BEFORE/AFTER (order or sequence).

If the goal descriptive sentence is "system recognizes a forward car" and we apply the guideword NOT, the new sentence is "system does not recognise the preceding vehicle". And this new one is the hazard candidate. Alternatively, by applying LATE, we can obtain "system late recognise the forward car."

The advantage of this operation is exhaustive one by using guidewords extending time and space.

Elements that impede the achievement of the goal are called obstacle nodes in KAOS. Here, we use the four hazard types mentioned up to now: hazard H_{HMI} for HMI, hazard H_{OEDR} for OEDR, and hazard H_{MAL} for failure and H_{THR} for security. We use them to refine the obstacle node as the sub-obstacle node. Then we can select hazard events after getting the sub-obstacle nodes. For example, a sentence applying "OTHER THAN" to "obtain information on a forward vehicle by communication" is "getting the false information on the forward vehicle". As for the H_{MAL}, we can get the malfunction based hazard candidate. And from the viewpoint of H_{THR}, we can get one originated by the communication tampering.

Also, we can use the static item sketch mentioned to find threats. There are various ways to find threats as the threat analysis and risk assessment (TARA), and the appendix of [2] shows several methods as a reference for TARA. But we use another approach in the field of the control system, ISA/IEC 62443 (Security for Industrial Automation and Control Systems)[3] [16]. This standard has a zone/conduit model and defines a security policy. The zone is 'grouping of logical or physical assets', and the conduit is 'logical grouping of communication assets that protect the security of the channels it contains'. The static item sketch created in the conceptual stage includes an abstract structure and data flow. So, we set the zone for resources to be protected and check the data flow through the route among zones. The infringement and unauthorized access to the data that flow through conduit and data stored in the zone is a threat. For example, in the cooperative adaptive cruise control (CACC), the other connected car information should store in a security zone because it regulates the behaviour of the own vehicle, and check authentication of the data flowing through the conduit to/from the security zone.

The safety goal uses the goal description sentence, to which we've already applied the guideword, again. For example, as a result of HARA, it is assumed that "recognizing a forward vehicle is delayed and conflicts" is recognized as a hazard event for securing safety. The safety goal is to invert the meaning and not to be delayed in recognition: "being not in collision with the vehicle ahead due to recognition delay of the forward vehicle". In the safety requirement, for example, the maximum delay time

[3] We use the SAE J3061 to analyse threats, and we think ISA/IEC 62443 is useful to find the safety relating threats.

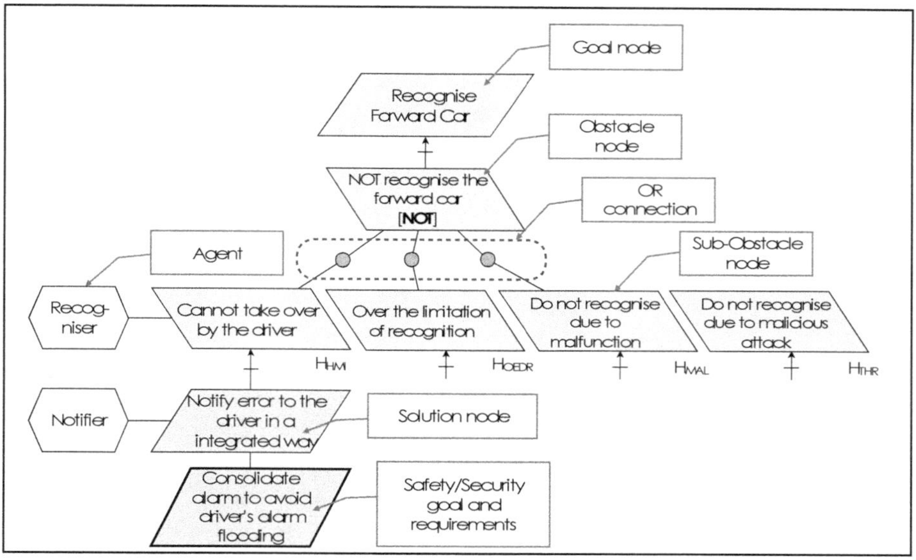

Fig. 4. Goal model and four hazard types

will be specified. It is also necessary to describe the initial architecture at this stage. We base on detailed item sketches and associate them with safety requirements.

The refinement is the top-down direction. We can traverse reversely to make sure whether the refinement is valid. In ISO 26262, we have to create the safety case to assure the validation. The GSN [20] is a candidate for writing safety case. If we can provide the arguments with evidence, we can satisfy the requirement of ISO 26262 (e.g. [21]).

Using the goal model, we can link a series of elements at the concept phase within one model diagram. The goal node indicates a function/non-functional requirement of the item, and the obstacle node is associated with a hazard belonging to any one of the four types. The refined solution nodes can show the safety and security goals. And, since the relationship between the elements in an item can be specified clearly, it is easy to judge the influence of different items.

3.2 Extension of the Approach

In this section, we extend our approach for the situation where multiple systems coexist (2.3.2). There are several points that we have to consider. And in the second half of this section, we will think about the preliminary architecture.

In a single item, it is not enough to identify hazard events, assess ASIL and consider the necessary safety mechanisms. Before defining safety and security requirements, we have to consider the influence of other items. ISO 26262 says in 3–5.4.2 that there is "interactions of the item with other items or elements" in the item definition stage, but we have the mutual influence among items during the concept phase: finding hazard events stage, risk assessment stage and the stage of setting initial architecture. And we might modify the safety/security goals of other items.

The second point is the recognition of environment. If humans mainly recognise the surroundings, the human has the responsibility. When the system is in charge of OEDR, it is necessary to confirm the degree of recognition. For ensuring safety, self-diagnosis of the system is usually carried out. If the system is in an incorrect state, the system detects the fault and moves to the safety state. There are some important time intervals, the fault reaction time and fault tolerant time interval (FTTI). This interval is for H_{MAL}. And we need the extension for other hazard types.

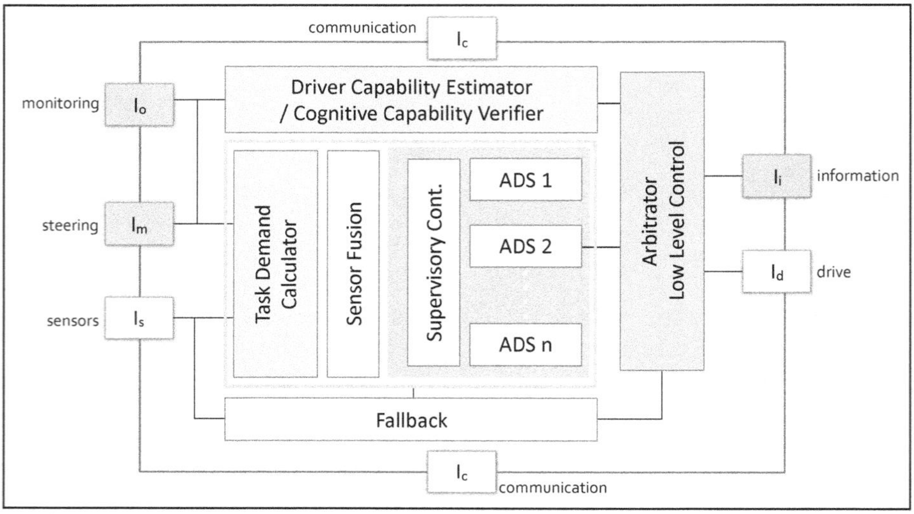

Fig. 5. A base of preliminary architecture

Next, self-diagnosis just closed in the system itself is inadequate. The system recognises the environment and makes a judgment in a stochastic way. So, we need a new type of self-diagnosis for ADS. For example, a recognition module of a system is confirmed the degree of recognition of the moving environment by other modules. When a system does same human activity as OEDR, the system needs such a new self-diagnostic function against changing the environment.

Now we can think about the preliminary architecture. We use the DESH-G (Driver, Environment, Software, Hardware and Goal) model of [14] here. DESH-G has the basic interface types is convenient when considering the control system of a vehicle. The interface types are I_o (interface monitoring a driver), I_m (driver's manoeuvring interface), I_i (interface for information display to a driver), I_s (sensor interface for environment recognition) I_d (interface controlling the actuator) and I_c (communication interface for V2 V and V2I). And also we use the item sketch that we already discussed. Figure 5 shows the base of a preliminary architecture.

We have several options for the recognition and a judgement composition. Figure 5 shows one of them. Synthesis of sensor information (Sensor Fusion) is performed first for multiple ADSs. A calculation results are passed to the Supervisory Controller (SV), and each ADS works from the information from SV. The arbitrator mediates the output of each ADS. In the automation level 3, we need a mechanism for control if a problem occurs (fallback) [1]. Though the fallback is the responsibility of the driver, ADS has to shift the system to the safe state until user ready for control.

Of course, we can consider the different structure for the higher automated level by using motion planner for finding a path and the trajectory control to control the vehicle according to the path. In this case, the item oriented approach of ISO 26262 might not be suitable.

4 Conclusion

In the ADS field, there are several hazard types besides malfunction oriented hazard: H_{THR}, H_{HMI} and H_{OEDR}. To make the vehicle safer, we have to consider those hazard types (The recent introduction of machine learning in the automobile field is another example [17]). We provided the consistent CARDION method for the concept phase. In this paper, we extended this method and finally showed the preliminary architecture. Between the automated level 2 and 3, there is a chasm. In level 3, the system is responsible for OEDR, not human (level 1,2). From the viewpoint of transition of the level, the system has to have both functionalities for OEDR, so the system becomes complicated. We believe the consistent approach is useful in this situation.

References

1. SAE: J3016: SAE international taxonomy and definitions for terms related to on-road motor vehicle automated driving systems. Levels of driving automation (2016)
2. SAE Vehicle Electrical System Security Committee, et al.: SAE J3061-Cybersecurity Guidebook for Cyber-Physical Automotive Systems. SAE-Society of Automotive Engineers (2016)
3. Knapp, A., et al.: Code of practice for the design and evaluation of ADAS. Preventive and active safety applications, eSafety for road and air transport, European Commission Project (2009)
4. DOT, HS 810 905: Integrated Vehicle-Based Safety Systems (IVBSS): Human Factors and Driver-Vehicle Interface (DVI) Summary Report (2008)
5. ISO, ISO26262: Road vehicles-functional safety. International Standard ISO (2011)
6. Yoshida, J.: Tesla's Fatal Crash: 6 Unanswered Questions:1. What did the front-camera actually see just before the crash?. https://www.eetimes.com/document.asp?doc_id=1330060&page_number=2. Accessed 1 Apr 2018
7. Spanfelner, B., et al.: Challenges in applying the ISO 26262 for driver assistance systems. Tagung Fahrerassistenz (2012)
8. Wilhelm, U., Ebel, S., Weitzel, A.: Functional safety of driver assistance systems and ISO 26262. In: Handbook of Driver Assistance Systems: Basic Information, Components and Systems for Active Safety and Comfort, pp. 109–131 (2016)

9. Ito, M.: Finding threats with hazards in the concept phase of product development. In: Barafort, B., O'Connor, R.V., Poth, A., Messnarz, R. (eds.) EuroSPI 2014. CCIS, vol. 425, pp. 277–284. Springer, Heidelberg (2014). https://doi.org/10.1007/978-3-662-43896-1_25
10. Weilkiens, T.: Systems Engineering with SysML/UML: Modeling, Analysis, Design. Elsevier, New York City (2011)
11. D'Souza, D.F., Wills, A.C.: Objects, Components, and Frameworks with UML: The Catalysis Approach. Addison-Wesley Longman Publishing Co., Inc., Boston (1998)
12. van Lamsweerde, A.: Requirements engineering: from system goals to UML models to software. Wiley, Chichester (2009)
13. IEC, B.S. 61882:2001: Hazard and operability studies (HAZOP studies). Application guide. British Standards Institute (2001)
14. Ito, M.: HMI requirements creation, as the collaboration work of human and machine in the safety-critical system. In: Stolfa, J., Stolfa, S., O'Connor, R.V., Messnarz, R. (eds.) EuroSPI 2017. CCIS, vol. 748, pp. 61–71. Springer, Cham (2017). https://doi.org/10.1007/978-3-319-64218-5_5
15. Ito, M.: Cardion.spec: an approach to improve the requirements specification written in the natural language through the formal method. In: Kreiner, C., O'Connor, R.V., Poth, A., Messnarz, R. (eds.) EuroSPI 2016. CCIS, vol. 633, pp. 58–69. Springer, Cham (2016). https://doi.org/10.1007/978-3-319-44817-6_5
16. IEC, IEC 62443-1-1: Security for industrial automation and control systems (2007)
17. Salay, R., Queiroz, R., Czarnecki, K.: An analysis of ISO 26262: machine learning and safety in automotive software, SAE Technical Paper (2018)
18. ISO, ISO/AWI PAS 21448: Road vehicles - safety of the intended functionality (under development)
19. AMASS (Architecture-driven, Multi-concern and Seamless Assurance and Certification of Cyber-Physical Systems), Standardization Survey D8.9 (2017)
20. Kelly, T.: Arguing safety-a systematic approach to managing safety cases. University of York, Department of Computer Science-Publications-YCST (1999)
21. Larrucea, X., Walker, A, Colomo-Palacios, R.: Supporting the management of reusable automotive software. In: IEEE Software, vol. 34, no. 3, pp. 40–47, May–June (2017)

A Process Framework Combining Safety and Security in Practice

Fergal McCaffery[1,2], Özden Özcan-Top[1(✉)], Ceara Treacy[1], Pangkaj Paul[1], John Loane[1], Jennifer Crilly[1], and Arthur Mc Mahon[2]

[1] RSRC&Lero, Dundalk Institute of Technology, Dundalk, Ireland
{fergal.mccaffery, ozden.ozcantop, ceara.treacy, pangkajchandra.paul, john.loane}@dkit.ie, j.crilly@statsports.com

[2] STATSports Group, Newry, UK
a.mcmahon@statsports.com

Abstract. Cyber-Physical-Systems provide huge potential for delivering highly effective solutions for multiple safety critical domains such as health, automotive, sports etc. Given the complexity of cyber physical systems, it is important to ensure the safety and security of such systems. Failure of such systems could result in potential harm to people and temporary downtime of important infrastructures with detrimental consequences for industry and society. This article describes a safety and security framework that could be implemented when building cyber physical systems for the safety critical medical device domain. We also provide details of how this framework was implemented in an organisation, STATSports Group, which develops cyber physical systems for performance monitoring of elite athletes to the specification required.

Keywords: Safety critical domain · Cyber physical systems · Security MDevSPICE · Agile software development

1 Introduction

Cyber-Physical-Systems (CPSs) “integrate physical devices, such as sensors and cameras, with cyber components to form an analytical system that responds intelligently to dynamic changes in the real-world scenarios” [1]. Some of usage areas of CPSs in healthcare are intelligent operating rooms, image-guided surgery and therapy, assisted living and fluid flow control for medicine. Given the safety critical health domain, it is important that CPSs are developed to adhere to the domains best practices standards and guidance documentation.

CPSs in the health domain routinely collect, measure and transmit sensitive Personal Health Information (PHI). This data is required to be kept secure through regulations and legislation. The impact of breaches of PHI is extensive in terms of risk to patient safety [2] and potential costs and losses in reputation for organisations [3]. This research describes a framework to address both of these aspects.

X. Larrucea et al. (Eds.): EuroSPI 2018, CCIS 896, pp. 173–180, 2018.
https://doi.org/10.1007/978-3-319-97925-0_14

2 A Safety and Security Framework for Medical Device Systems

The framework aims to assist developers to achieve regulatory compliance in safety and security through implementing safety practices and data security controls throughout the development process. It can be used for CPSs in the medical device domain as it combines regulatory process development with product centric risk assessment. Safety and security requirements for CPSs within healthcare are critical as many monitor real-world physical processes. The unique use of diverse communications technologies and mobile computing by CPSs, make safety and security for these systems different from other information systems as data is exposed to many new attack surfaces [4]. The framework promotes safety and security throughout the development process. The framework consists of two main components: (1) MDevSPICE® addresses the safety aspects of the framework [5] and (2) the Secure Data-Flow component addresses the security aspects (see Fig. 1). MDevSPICE® consists of processes, purpose statements, capability levels, process attributes, base practices and outcomes. The Secure Data Flow component includes Data Flow Security Controls (DFSCs) founded in regulatory standards, which have been categorised for developer implementation through the ITU-T X.805 Security Architecture for Systems standard [6] and mapped to the risk centric threat model Process for Attack Simulation and Threat Analysis (PASTA) [7]. The secure data flow component also presents a corresponding testing suite designed for the DFSCs to access their effectiveness.

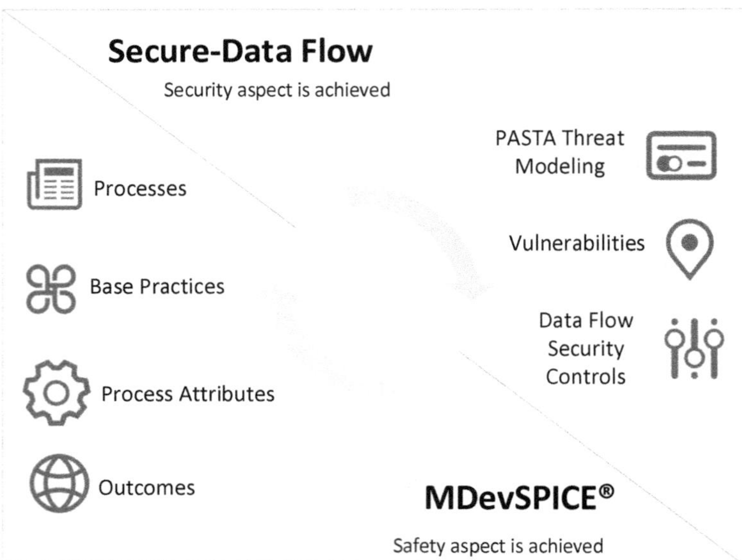

Fig. 1. Components of the safety and security framework.

2.1 MDevSPICE® Component of the Framework

MDevSPICE® is a software process assessment framework that has been designed to enable medical device software developers to produce software that will be safe and easily integrated with other sub-systems of the overall medical device [5]. Relevant medical device software standards and software engineering best practices have been integrated within MDevSPICE®. Two of the prominent regulatory standards that have been integrated into MDevSPICE® are 'IEC 62304:2006: Software life cycle processes for medical device development [8]' and 'ISO 14971:2009: Application of risk management to medical devices' [9]. MDevSPICE® consists of 23 processes grouped into system lifecycle, software lifecycle and support processes as can be seen in Fig. 2.

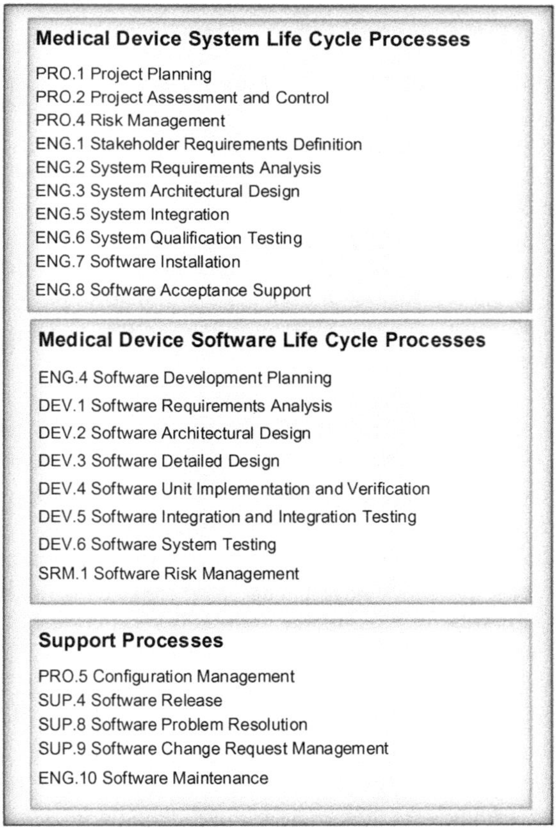

Fig. 2. MDevSPICE® processes

Software development in safety critical domains such as healthcare is typically performed in a plan-driven manner. The V-Model lifecycle is well suited to medical device software development, given that it dedicates particular attention to both verification and risk management at every stage of life cycle. Software development approaches like agile and lean are preferred industry practice, as they enable iterative and incremental development, collaboration, communication, waste elimination, fast feedback, and balance of predictive upfront work, with adaptive just-in-time work and increasing quality. However, the necessity for intense controls and risk evaluation in safety critical domains require the implementation of agile and lean approaches be performed with some limitations and adaptations. In this context, there is an ongoing process in integration of agile and lean mind-set and practices into MDevSPICE® to make it more flexible and more solution oriented. Consequently, as part of this framework, we have integrated agile practices as part of the improvement recommendations which are provided as an output of performing an MDevSPICE® assessment.

2.2 Secure-Data Flow Component of the Framework

The secure data flow component adopts a risk-centric assessment to assist developers to meet regulatory requirements and secure data in flow [10] within a CPS. CPSs operate in an environment of ever-changing threats and attacks. Security of data flow in this environment requires a risk assessment approach that considers how the evolving threats and attacks could expose the organizations assets to vulnerabilities, weakness of software, hardware, or online service that can be exploited. Threat modelling analysis and threat modelling methods deliver an important basis for the specification of security requirements of information systems and information protection. It provides a process for assessment for securing data flow within CPSs that incorporates security controls into the MDevSPICE® processes.

The developed DFSCs were based on two medical device security standards IEC/TR 80001-2-2:2012 [11] and IEC/TR 80001-2-8:2016 [12]. IEC/TR 80001-2-2:2012 provides 19 high-level security-related capabilities (functions) and risks for consideration when connecting medical devices to IT-networks. These high-level capabilities provide only an understanding of the user needs, security risks that lead to the controls. Two of these capabilities, Transmission Confidentiality (TXCF) and Transmission Integrity (TXIG), concern data transmission. IEC/TR 80001-2-8:2016 identified security controls for each of the 19 security capabilities to consider during risk management activities. The DFSCs originated from the IEC/TR 80001-2-8 controls associated to the TXCF and TXIG capabilities. However, these controls did not cover all aspects of data transmission. Further mapping of the six standards utilized in IEC/TR 80001-2-8 development was completed to address the gap. The result was 63 DFSCs for consideration when completing a PASTA assessment for data flow security. The objective of the secure data flow process is to integrate the DFSCs into a PASTA assessment. The outcome of the secure data flow process provides a set of DFSCs for implementation into the MDevSPICE® software process to address data flow security.

2.3 Implementation

We have implemented the Framework in STATSports[1], a company which develops CPSs, which include hardware sensors, firmware and software algorithms to provide performance monitoring technology to the sports industry.

A. Current Practices

STATSports aims to provide technology that meets regulatory requirements for data security and exceeds what is required in the sports domain for product safety. The company understands the requirements for compliancy with both the General Data Protection Regulation (GDPR) [13] and The Health Insurance Portability and Accountability Act (HIPAA) [14] for securing personal and health data. This understanding is due to the fact that in the future STATSports plans on releasing monitoring technology for the healthcare industry and the imminent GDPR requirements for data security. The company recognizes there are significant changes required in development to ensure that data security and product safety are a key part of the process to meet GDPR and HIPAA compliancy. Therefore, STATSports is committed to ensuring they embarked upon implementing best practice processes for both safety and security to successfully transition the development of technology for the sports domain to the medical device domain.

In order for STATSports to make this transition, the first step was to perform an MDevSPICE® assessment to observe the process gaps and challenges in relation to safety and security. This assessment provided insights on the safety and security practices prior to the implementation of the framework. Twenty-three processes were assessed and the following areas for improvement were identified below.

1. There was no single point of contact for gathering new requirements/requirement changes in the organization. The organization's Sport Scientists were directly contacting developers and demanding features to be developed. This resulted in developers' receiving different tasks from multiple sources and it was difficult to understand which new features should be prioritized.
2. A major challenge was that new requirements and features were constantly introduced throughout development.
3. Safety and security requirements were not formally defined and managed, this could give rise to potentially significant changes (i.e. architectural changes) later in the development, particularly if software was released without inclusion of these critical requirements.
4. Frequently, requirements lacked sufficient detail - this lead to instances of redevelopment as Sport Scientists were not always available to provide clarity in relation to requirements.
5. Threats to security and associated vulnerabilities of the system were unknown.
6. Which security controls to implement were unknown.
7. Continuous Risk Assessment and Risk Mitigation for both Safety and Security were not performed.

[1] www.statsports.com.

8. There was no formal traceability from system requirements to the testing and release phases.
9. Limited company experience implementing security in agile software development and how to implement the security guidelines that include security controls.

B. Implemented Solutions

The findings' number in the above list in Sect. 2.3.A will be tagged against the corresponding improvement action below. STATSports has now introduced Scrum practices in relation to the software development process issues combined with life-cycle traceability that is required to demonstrate that safety processes are in place (addresses 1–4). A Senior Sports Scientist (SSS) now works closely with the development team in a Product Owner role. Every new request or requirement change coming from different Sport Scientists and other stakeholders are delivered to the SSS, and are then prioritized by this person (1). The SSS identifies the business value of the features/user stories while the developers assess the risks involved in implementation, with associated safety, security, technical and business risks now tracked throughout development specifically, both safety and security requirements are linked with risks which are assigned to development team members (2, 3, 4). The product backlog and sprint backlog contain features/user stories that are maintained in a prioritized order in a tool, named Jira[2] (1, 3, 4). Jira is used with another tool Confluence[3] to provide traceability of requirements/features and user stories (1, 2, 8).

In addition, a security focused analyst was recruited into the development team and contributes to the architectural design to ensure emphasis on data security (3, 5, 9). The security analyst starts the PASTA process in defining the appropriate level of security requirements to support the business goals in collaboration with the SSS (1, 3). The technical scope is then defined upon receipt of the prioritized requirements from the SSS and coordinated with the architecture design (1, 6, 9). This required STATSports to list all software/hardware, the various technologies, components and services that were associated with the application (4, 6). This followed with the decomposition of the application into components, via Data Flow Diagrams (DFDs) and Use Case Diagrams, which were used to analyze the threats (5, 7). The vulnerabilities were identified for the use cases and the DFSCs required to address these vulnerabilities were presented (5, 7). The DFSCs were represented in the backlog in relation to each feature that is included for development in the sprint (1, 2, 6).

A sprint duration of one week is adopted to manage constantly changing requirements (2, 3). Sprint Review and Retrospective meetings take place at the end of the week in addition to a Daily 15-min Stand-up meeting (1–9). User stories are defined with the associated acceptance criteria, which provide the essential information for the purposes of verification and validation (3, 4). The meetings ensure all members of the development team are kept up to date with progress. It also allows the team to raise issues with the process and identify risks (1–9).

[2] https://www.atlassian.com/software/jira.

[3] https://www.atlassian.com/software/confluence.

As the system consists of hardware and firmware in addition to software, the framework is also applied to hardware/firmware development and testing. This ensures full traceability for product development from inception, to prototyping and through to final release (8). All versions of firmware and hardware are captured using confluence and all bugs, hardware/firmware faults and resolutions are logged and viewed in Jira, offering a full historic record of product evolution (1, 2, 5, 8).

We have observed that implementing the secure data flow component in a one-week sprint process was not possible due to understanding all data flow calls and identification of the controls and assessment of threats. In addition, testing requirements of the security controls need to be put in place within that sprint. These require development of a test suite against test cases which would include penetration testing. As a solution for this, we proposed running sprints in two-week intervals and running penetration testing on product release.

3 Conclusion

The Safety and Security Framework for Cyber Physical Systems is a new approach that was developed to promote safe and secure products in the safety critical healthcare domain.

The implementation of the framework in STATSports has revealed issues and opportunities for improvement in terms of both safety and security. The interoperability of the two components was our main consideration. Action items were identified and prioritized. Secure Data-Flow processes including security risk assessment and threat modelling were performed at the initial phases of the project from a higher level of abstraction. During the later stages, security of data flow and security controls were continuously revisited and repeated however not meeting every sprint. The framework has assisted the company in moving towards compliance with HIPAA and the GDPR in relation to data security. It has stimulated the development of suitable policies and procedures for data security required by the GDPR and HIPAA for regulatory compliancy, not only in development but also organization wide. Implementation of the framework has also promoted the inclusion of security in the initial stages of the development of a new product. As a result of the implementation of the framework, STATSports has overcome difficulties they have had in relation to handling changes throughout development. In addition, through introducing Agile and security practices the company has significantly improved the traceability of requirements right throughout development. The company now understands the security vulnerabilities of their system and has put appropriate controls in place.

Future work in the evolution of the framework will involve the execution of data security testing within MDevSPICE® using agile development.

Acknowledgement. This research is supported by the Science Foundation Ireland Research Centres Programme, through Lero - the Irish Software Research Centre (http://www.lero.ie) grant 10/CE/I1855 & 13/RC/2094S.

References

1. Haque, S.A., Aziz, S.M., Rahman, M.: Review of cyber-physical system in healthcare. Int. J. Distrib. Sens. Netw. **10**(4), 217415 (2014)
2. Williams, P.A., Woodward, A.J.: Cybersecurity vulnerabilities in medical devices: a complex environment and multifaceted problem. Med. Dev. **8**, 305 (2015)
3. 2016 Cost of Cyber Crime Study & the Risk of Business Innovation-Cyber Security Analysis: Ponemon Institute. https://saas.hpe.com/en-us/asset/2016-cost-cyber-crime-study-risk-business-innovation-ponemon-institute-cyber-security-analysis. Accessed 30 May 2017
4. Howser, G., McMillin, B.: Using information-flow methods to analyze the security of cyber-physical systems. Computer **50**(4), 17–26 (2017)
5. Lepmets, M., McCaffery, F., Clarke, P.: Development and benefits of MDevSPICE®, the medical device software process assessment framework. J. Softw.: Evol. Process **28**(9), 800–816 (2016)
6. International Telecommunication Union ITU-T: Recommendation X.805 Security architecture for systems providing end-to-end communications (2003)
7. UcedaVelez, T., Morana, M.M.: Risk Centric Threat Modeling: Process for Attack Simulation and Threat Analysis. Wiley, Hoboken (2015)
8. IEC 2006. IEC 62304: Medical Device Software - Software Life-Cycle Processes
9. ISO 2009. ISO 14971: Medical Devices - Application of Risk Management to Medical Devices
10. Treacy, C., McCaffery, F.: Data security overview for medical mobile apps assuring the confidentiality, integrity and availability of data in transmission. Int. J. Adv. Secur. **9**(3&4), 146–157 (2016)
11. "IEC, TR 80001-2-2:2012: Application of risk management for IT-networks incorporating medical devices Part 2-2: guidance for the disclosure and communication of medical device security needs, risks and controls (2012)
12. "IEC, TR 80001-2-8:2016: Application of risk management for IT-networks incorporating medical devices — Application guidance Part 2-8: guidance on standards for establishing the security capabilities identified in IEC TR 80001-2-2. 2016, pp. 1–56 (2016)
13. Reg (EU) 2016/679 of the European Parliament and of the Council of 27 April 2016 on the protection of natural persons with regard to the processing of personal data and on the free movement of such data, and repealing Dir 95/46/EC (General Data Protection Regulation) (2016)
14. OCR Privacy Brief: Summary of the HIPAA Privacy Rule (2003)

Validating Effectiveness of Compliance Evaluation in Safety-Critical Process Assessment

Timo Varkoi[1(✉)], Timo Mäkinen[2], Frank Cameron[2], and Risto Nevalainen[1]

[1] Finnish Software Measurement Association – FiSMA ry, Espoo, Finland
{timo.varkoi, risto.nevalainen}@fisma.fi
[2] Tampere University of Technology, Pori, Finland
{timo.makinen, frank.cameron}@tut.fi

Abstract. Safety is a growing concern in systems containing software. Process assessments are used to ensure quality of the development processes for safety-critical systems. Regulators of the nuclear power industry have increased requirements for the development processes. Now, process assessments are integrated in the qualification of the systems and are expected to provide information not only based on the assessment model but also about the domain specific requirements. Compliance evaluation utilizes assessment findings to create evidence of the relevant domain specific requirements. This study aims at validating the results of compliance evaluation by analyzing assessment findings and their use in the context of a safety-critical domain. The analysis is based on the use of binary relations. The results of this analysis indicate that process assessment findings are also relevant when evaluating compliance to other sets of requirements. The results can significantly support the trustworthiness of the process assessment method and ensure effective use of process assessments.

Keywords: Safety · Systems engineering · Process assessment

1 Introduction

Safety is a growing concern in systems containing software. Effective and reliable methods are needed to analyze both the safety-critical systems and the system development processes. Domain specific safety requirements may also imply significant requirements for systems development processes [1].

In general, process assessments are used to target the quality of the development processes. However, generic process assessment methods may not adequately cover the domain specific requirements (DSRs) and additional effort is required to evaluate e.g. compliance to domain standards [1].

The nuclear power industry is known for its strict requirements for safety. Recent updates of regulatory requirements [2–4] have increased requirements for reliable and trustworthy system development processes. From the software and systems engineering viewpoint, additional DSRs include international safety standards for instrumentation and control systems. The DSRs for the nuclear power domain are discussed in [1].

X. Larrucea et al. (Eds.): EuroSPI 2018, CCIS 896, pp. 181–192, 2018.
https://doi.org/10.1007/978-3-319-97925-0_15

One effort to address these increasing requirements is the development of the Nuclear SPICE process assessment method. This method has a special activity, *Compliance evaluation*, to use the collected process assessment findings to analyze how well the DSRs are met. However, compliance evaluation is a tedious task and the results need to be validated to ensure that the reporting is reliable and meaningful to the assessment stakeholders.

It is also important to ensure trustworthiness of the process assessment method itself. This study analyzes existing, real-life assessment data using adjacency matrices [5] to reveal relationships between DSRs and assessment findings. The key question is, how useful and efficient is process assessment in evaluating compliance to a set of DSRs?

This paper is organized as follows. Section 2 presents a domain specific process assessment method and the compliance evaluation activity as a part of it. Section 3 describes the mathematical concepts used. In Sect. 4, we present the results and discuss the conclusions related to compliance evaluation. Section 5 summarizes this study.

2 Process Assessment in Nuclear Power Domain

2.1 Nuclear SPICE Process Assessment Method

Nuclear SPICE [6] is a method to assess the development processes of instrumentation and control (I&C) systems important to safety in the nuclear power domain. The method provides evidence for safety qualification of the systems and can be used to evaluate suppliers. In the last decade, also nuclear domain regulatory requirements [2–4] have started to emphasize adequate quality of the development processes.

Nuclear SPICE relies on the most recent ISO/IEC process assessment standards and process models (also known as the SPICE models) [7, 8]. It is complemented with domain specific safety standards and regulatory requirements. The main elements of the Nuclear SPICE method are a process assessment model, an assessment process and sets of DSRS.

The process assessment model contains the reference processes and a scale to evaluate the quality characteristics of each process. Systems and software engineering processes are the core of the process model. In the latest version of Nuclear SPICE, the main reference model is the ISO/IEC 15288 standard [9] for system life cycle processes. In total, the Nuclear SPICE process reference model for systems engineering has 33 processes described with detailed assessment indicators. The processes are grouped into five categories: agreement, organizational project-enabling, technical management, technical and safety processes.

Processes to be assessed can be selected from the reference models when planning the assessment. In addition, Nuclear SPICE includes predefined process sets for *project evaluation* and *supplier selection*. These process sets are designed to satisfy common process assessment goals related to the I&C system lifecycle. The selection of processes is described in [10] and is based on an analysis of the requirements in standards and regulatory guidance, and long-time assessment experience. The process sets support repeatability of the assessments, which is a key factor for both results comparability and assessment efficiency [11].

The documented assessment process is needed to perform the assessments in a reliable and repeatable manner. The assessment process also sets requirements for the rigor of the assessment and the competency of the assessors.

The Nuclear SPICE assessment process is presented in Fig. 1 [1, 12]. The assessment process has three main phases: Planning, Data collection, and Reporting. The assessment process defines the activities and detailed tasks of the phases. Unlike a regular SPICE assessment, Nuclear SPICE defines a special activity for *Compliance evaluation*. It is needed to ensure that the I&C system development complies with the domain standards and to provide information for qualification of the systems relevant to safety. In the nuclear power domain, IEC 60880 [13] and IEC 62138 [14] are the important standards Also, the national nuclear safety authority in Finland provides requirements, which are described in the YVL guidance [3, 4]. Often these YVL requirements are also considered in the compliance evaluation. To be clear, compliance evaluation is not to be used to claim compliance to any standard. However, it may provide information or evidence related to the achievement of individual requirements [12].

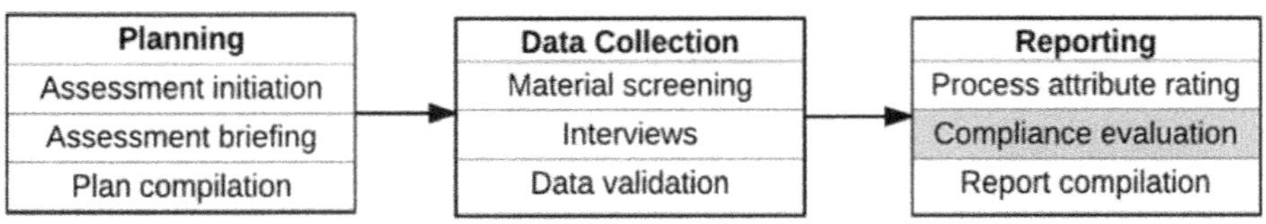

Fig. 1. Nuclear SPICE assessment process [1]

In the compliance evaluation activity, the assessment findings and ratings are analyzed and mapped to selected standards and requirements. The selection of standards and requirements is documented in the assessment plan. Any issues with the assessed processes are identified and reported based on the lead assessor's expert judgment of these processes. Compliance evaluation does not imply any compliance of the actual software product and is optional depending on the assessment goal [1].

2.2 Evaluation of Domain Specific Requirements

Compliance evaluation is used to evaluate the assessment findings to create evidence about DSRs that originate from the domain safety standards or regulatory instructions. The compliance evaluation activity is quite a laborious task [1].

Some sets of DSRs have been analyzed in [10]. The Finnish Radiation and Nuclear Safety Authority have published many guidelines and requirements. We are interested in two system engineering related sets: YVL B.1, Safety design of a nuclear power plant [3] and YVL E.7, Electrical and I&C equipment of a nuclear facility [4]. YVL B.1 and YVL E.7 have numerous requirements that are well identified by an individual ID and a short text. Some requirements are not relevant from the Nuclear SPICE viewpoint, because they are only explanatory or administrative. The key points regarding the relation between Nuclear SPICE and the YVL sets are as follows [10]:

- YVL B.1 has 372 relevant requirements, of which 43 are verifiable by Nuclear SPICE
- YVL E.7 has 185 relevant requirements, of which 118 are verifiable by Nuclear SPICE
- most of the relevant requirements apply only to the licensee (power utility).

For example, when the assessors apply the pre-defined project evaluation process set, the number of relevant YVL-requirements is further reduced to 20 for YVL B.1 and 48 for YVL E.7. This reduction is due to two features of the project evaluation type process assessment: first, it contains a limited set of processes, and second, its target is the system supplier.

In addition to the YVL sets, we use IEC 62138 as a set of DSRs. All the requirements of this standard are relevant in the process assessment scope, but some are targeted to the system, not the development process. In compliance evaluation these requirements are considered in ten groups, each with a specific sub-clause in the standard.

2.3 Available Process Assessment Data

We have a collection of data from three completed, real-life assessments performed with Nuclear SPICE. All three contain assessment findings and ratings, and compliance evaluation results. Some items in the data have been removed to ensure anonymity. The data has been cleared for research purposes by the assessed organizations and the assessment sponsors.

The data set is limited, but representative to similar assessments in the nuclear domain: the three assessed projects had strict safety requirements, they were customized and in the delivery-phase. On the other hand, the data is coherent: in each of these assessments the same process set for project evaluation was used. This set mainly addresses the need to collect system qualification material and is typically used during a delivery project. This process set consists of engineering, support and safety processes – identified using ENG, SUP and SAF abbreviations. The processes are as follows:

- ENG.1 Stakeholder requirements definition
- ENG.2 System requirements analysis
- ENG.3 System architectural design
- ENG.4 Software implementation
- ENG.5 System integration
- ENG.6 Systems qualification testing
- SUP.1 Software documentation management
- SUP.2 Software configuration management
- SUP.3 Software quality assurance
- SAF.1 Safety management

- SAF.2 Safety engineering
- SAF.3 Safety qualification.

In all three assessments, three identical DSR sets were used in the compliance evaluation: IEC 62138 [14], YVL B.1 [3], and YVL E.7 [4]. The example in Table 1 shows a portion of the compliance evaluation results together with a DSR. For YVL E.7 DSR #612, relevant assessment findings were recorded with two processes: ENG.2 and ENG.3. The actual assessment indicator is a base practice (BP). These findings cause a *hit* in the T_{YVLE7} matrix presented in Sects. 3 and 4.

Table 1. Exemplar assessment findings and a DSR

YVL E.7	Requirement	Assessment findings	Assessment indicator
612	The requirements set for software in safety class 2 or 3 shall be derivable in a traceable manner from component or system level requirements.	• Relationships in Req. Mgmt. system, traceability not complete. • Validated by an expert, requirement groups analyzed, but not individual requirements.	ENG.2.BP5 ENG.3.BP6

3 Analysis Method

3.1 The Process/DSR Relation

Suppose we are to do an assessment. Let us collect the processes in the assessment into set Ω:

$$\Omega = \{set\ containing\ assessment\ processes\}$$

Assume that in conjunction with the assessment, we are also interested in some DSRs. We collect the DSRs of interest into set Λ:

$$\Lambda = \{set\ containing\ DSR\ elements\}$$

We wish to consider the following question: how likely is it that a process x from Ω is connected with a DSR y from set Λ?

3.2 The Adjacency Matrix

A binary relation R is a set of ordered pairs (x, y). In this pair x comes from set $\Omega = \{x_1, x_2, \ldots x_n\}$ and y comes from set $\Lambda = \{y_1, y_2, \ldots y_m\}$. (We assume that set Ω has n elements and set Λ has m elements). The binary relation R can be represented by the $n \times m$ adjacency matrix M:

$$M_{ij} = \begin{cases} 1, & \textit{if pair } (x_i, y_j) \textit{ is a member of } R \\ 0, & \textit{if pair } (x_i, y_j) \textit{ is not a member of } R \end{cases}$$

For example, let $\Omega = \{x_1, x_2\}$, $\Lambda = \{y_1, y_2, y_3\}$ and $R = \{(x_1, y_2), (x_1, y_3), (x_2, y_2)\}$. The adjacency matrix M for this relation would be the following:

$$M = \begin{bmatrix} 0 & 1 & 1 \\ 0 & 1 & 0 \end{bmatrix}.$$

When a '1' occurs in M, we shall call it a *hit*.

3.3 Nuclear SPICE and Three Different DSR Sets

In our situation, R is the relation between Nuclear SPICE processes and some set of DSRs. For this relation, set Ω contains the 12 processes from Nuclear SPICE given in Sect. 2.3:

$$\begin{aligned} \Omega = \{&ENG1, ENG2, ENG3, ENG4, ENG5, ENG6, \\ &SUP1, SUP2, SUP3, SAF1, SAF2, SAF3\} \end{aligned}$$

We construct three different binary relations using the three DSR sets mentioned in Sect. 2.3 for set Λ:

(i) the binary relation R_{YVLE7} between Ω and the DSRs of YVL E.7
(ii) the binary relation R_{YVLB1} between Ω and the DSRs of YVL B.1
(iii) the binary relation R_{IEC} between Ω and the DSRs of IEC 62138.

For each relation, our question is how likely is it that some particular ordered pair (i, j) belongs to R? To answer this question, we use the three completed assessments described in Sect. 2.3. We label these assessments A, B and C. From each assessment, we have the pairs that were included in each relation, R_{YVLE7}, R_{YVLB1} and R_{IEC}. In what follows in this section, we shall simply consider a general relation R, since we applied the same techniques to all three, R_{YVLE7}, R_{YVLB1} and R_{IEC}.

Let the binary relations arising from assessments A, B and C be R^A, R^B and R^C. Let their corresponding adjacency matrices be M^A, M^B and M^C. Recall that these matrices simply contain zeros and ones. We have formed the sum of these three matrices as follows:

$$T = M^A + M^B + M^C.$$

Matrix T is not an adjacency matrix, since its elements can be greater than 1. However, the interpretation of element T_{ij} should be quite straightforward:

$$T_{ij} = \begin{cases} 0 & \text{if } M_{ij}^A, M_{ij}^B \text{ and } M_{ij}^C \text{ are all } 0 \\ 1 & \text{if exactly one of } M_{ij}^A, M_{ij}^B \text{ and } M_{ij}^C \text{ is } 1 \\ 2 & \text{if exactly two of } M_{ij}^A, M_{ij}^B \text{ and } M_{ij}^C \text{ are } 1 \\ 3 & \text{if } M_{ij}^A, M_{ij}^B \text{ and } M_{ij}^C \text{ are all } 1 \end{cases}$$

Hence, T_{ij} is simply the sum of the hits from M_{ij}^A, M_{ij}^B and M_{ij}^C. Clearly, as T_{ij} increases, the likelihood of pair (i,j) consistently occurring in the relation R increases.

For each DSR set, we computed the T matrix. We refer to these as T_{YVLE7}, T_{YVLB1} and T_{IEC}. We present these matrices in Sect. 4.

4 Results

4.1 Summary of the Analysis Results

The T_{YVLE7}, T_{YVLB1} and T_{IEC} matrices of Sect. 3.3 are shown in Tables 2, 3 and 4. In these tables the DSRs are grouped by requirement group titles and the processes are given at the table top. The related processes are listed on the horizontal axis. The results in Tables 2, 3 and 4 can be used to validate coverage of the assessment findings with respect to the DSRs. A nonzero value for some element indicates the number of hits from the three assessments. For example, in Table 2, the element at (ENG.1, 312) reveals 2 hits.

Next, the *coverage* and *accuracy* of the hits is discussed based on empirical knowledge of process assessment in the nuclear power domain. In this context, good coverage means that the vast majority of DSRs receive multiple hits. Respectively, good accuracy means that the majority of hits occur between assessment findings of a process and similar DSRs. The hits are summed in each row. The sums represent how many assessed processes provide evidence for a given DSR; the theoretical maximum with three assessments of 12 processes would be 36. The number of hits varies due to the level of detail and scope of both the DSRs and processes.

The coverage and accuracy for YVL E.7 is satisfactory: for example, requirements related to process assessment findings match well with DSRs related to specification and requirements management and the same applies to testing. Some explanation is needed for DSRs with no hits: #313 is related to hardware only; #618 is related to the whole assessment; #622 addresses all ENG-processes; and #630 is related to the actions in the operational phase of the system. Altogether, 34 DSRs have a total of at least 3 hits in the assessment findings, while 14 requirements have less than 3 hits.

The result for YVL B.1 is also plausible. For example, configuration management is precisely covered, also requirements and testing findings are easily targeted to relevant DSRs. However, findings related to design processes are spread out and somewhat scarce. This could be explained by assessment findings that are related to an entire process group (instead of an individual process) or other process capability indicators. Here, 17 requirements have a total of at least 3 hits in the assessment findings, while 3 requirements have less than 3 hits.

Table 2. The T_{YVLE7} matrix for the YVL E.7 requirements.

YVL E.7	ENG						SUP			SAF			Σ
	1	2	3	4	5	6	1	2	3	1	2	3	
3.1 General Requirements to Specify Requirements, Select and Acquire Electric and Automation Equipments													
309	1									3			4
310	1												1
312	2											1	3
313													0
3.2 Requirements Specification													
314	3												3
319	3												3
321	1	2											3
322	1	3											4
323	1	2											3
3.3 Configuration Management													
328								1					1
330							1	3					4
331				1				2					3
332							2	2					4
333	1						1	1					3
3.4 Feasibility Study													
334												3	3
339												3	3
4.2 Quality Management System													
403									3				3
410									3				3
5.3 Validation Tests													
514					2	3							5
518						1							1
5.4 Assessment of Design and Manufacturing Process of Automation Eqpt.													
525	3	3	3										9
526		1	1	1	1	1							5
527									1				1

YVL E.7	ENG						SUP			SAF			Σ
	1	2	3	4	5	6	1	2	3	1	2	3	
5.8 Validation using Analyses													
563				1								2	3
564												1	1
6.1 Special Requirements for Software based Equipments													
606												1	1
608					1							1	2
609											1	1	2
612	2	3	3										8
6.2 Validation of Base System and Application Software													
616										2		3	5
617										2	1		3
618													0
619		1								2			3
620		1								2			3
6.3 Software Design Methods and Processes													
621				1						3			4
622													0
623			1	3									4
627				2									2
628												1	1
630													0
6.5 Cyber Security and Separation of Networking													
633				1	1	2		2					6
6.7 Software Testing													
643				2	3	2							7
644				2	1								3
645					3	2							5
646				1	1	1							3
648				1	1	1			1				4
650					1	2							3
651					1	2							3

The coverage for IEC 62138 is extensive. All requirement groups have multiple hits, except *5.8, Installation of software on site*. This is to be expected, since the assessments are performed prior to the installation. In this context, the system must be qualified before installation.

When findings are missing ('empty boxes'), it means that the assessment of the process does not give information for that specific DSR (or the set of DSRs). If there are concentrated findings from a specific process to a DSR, then the result is accurate. On the other hand, if the assessment of a specific process does not yield any or only a few matching findings to DSRs, then the coverage is not good. In other words, the assessment of that process is rather useless from the compliance evaluation point of view.

The following Table 5 presents the frequency of the hits by processes and DSR sets. For example, the ENG.1 process produces a total of 4 hits for the IEC 62138 set of DSRs. As expected, the YVL E.7 set of DSRs receives high numbers of hits, because it has more DSRs than YVL B.1 or IEC 62138.

Table 3. The T_{YVLB1} matrix for the YVL B.1 requirements.

YVL	ENG						SUP			SAF			Σ
B.1	1	2	3	4	5	6	1	2	3	1	2	3	
3.1 Organizations Responsible of Design													
306	1								3				4
307										1			1
3.2 Design Processes													
311	1								1	2			4
312				1						1			2
313	1		1	1					2	1			6
314	3	1	2		2	3				1			12
316									1		1		2
3.3 Configuration Management													
324								3					3
327								3					3
328								3					3
3.4 Quality Plans													
333	1								2				3
334	1	2							1				4
3.5 Requirements Specifications													
337	3												3
339	3	3											6
341	3	3	3										9
3.8 Documentation													
361		1					2	3					6
5.2.7 Testing of Automation Systems													
5248					2	3							5
5249					1	3							4
5250					1	3							4
5253				2	1	1							4

Table 4. The T_{IEC} matrix for the IEC 62138 requirements.

IEC 62138		ENG						SUP			SAF			Σ
		1	2	3	4	5	6	1	2	3	1	2	3	
5.1	General requirements							2	3	3	3	3	3	17
5.2	Selection of pre-developed software				1								3	4
5.3	Software requirements specification	3	3		1									7
5.4	Software design			3	2									5
5.5	Implementation of new software			2	3				1					6
5.6	Software aspects of system integration				1	3	1							5
5.7	Software aspects of system validation				1		3			3				7
5.8	Installation of software on site						2							2
5.9	Anomaly reports					1	2			2	1	1		7
5.10	Software modification	1			1	1		1	2			2		8

Based on Table 5, all processes of the project evaluation process set provide useful information for compliance evaluation. SAF.2 has the lowest total number, but it seems to be important for the IEC 62138 set of DSRs. The numbers only illustrate the frequency of the assessment findings by process in providing evidence for the DSR sets, but comparison between DSR sets or processes is not meaningful.

Table 5. Frequency of the hits by processes and DSR sets.

DSR Set	ENG						SUP			SAF		
	1	2	3	4	5	6	1	2	3	1	2	3
IEC 62138	4	3	5	10	5	8	3	6	8	4	6	6
YVL B.1	17	10	6	4	7	13	2	12	10	6	1	0
YVL E.7	19	16	8	16	16	17	4	11	8	14	2	17
Σ	40	29	19	30	28	38	9	29	26	24	9	23

4.2 Effectiveness of Compliance Evaluation

Compliance evaluation provides information on how well the DSRs are met. This information is valuable when used for qualification of the system or to identify risks related to the delivery of the system. Safety-criticality underlines that the findings need to be accurate, logical and trustworthy. This study evaluates the appropriateness of compliance evaluation as a part of the overall process assessment.

Compliance evaluation requires quite a lot of the effort in process assessment. For example, when a typical process assessment requires six working days, the effort for compliance evaluation could be two additional days. In [1] we discussed three different approaches to streamline compliance evaluation: safety oriented process line engineering; requirements mapping; and binary distance measures. The work inspired us to use binary relations to study overall effectiveness of compliance evaluation and to validate the Nuclear SPICE process assessment method. The key question in considering effectiveness of compliance evaluation is the following: Is process assessment useful and efficient in evaluating compliance to a limited set of DSRs?

The adjacency matrix proved to be an efficient and understandable approach to analyze the relationships of DSRs and assessment findings. We considered both the coverage and accuracy of the process assessment findings in relation to the DSRs. The results given in Sect. 4.1, show that assessment data is useful also in evaluating the achievement of the DSRs. The coverage is adequate for the pre-selected DSRs.

As the results show, process assessment provides findings that adequately cover the selected set of DSRs. It must be noted that the target DSRs are already pre-selected from the full set of requirements. The pre-selection should be careful and performed by domain experts. On the other hand, this study cannot determine, whether there are more DSRs that could be evaluated using the process assessment findings.

Some requirements do not have any related assessment findings. This information can be used to fine-tune the sets of DSRs. Mostly, the absence of findings is easily explainable. For example, DSR #313 in YVL E.7 deals with labeling of the equipment – this seldom comes up with software processes. Some DSRs, like YVL B.1 #334, deal with process descriptions. Such DSRs are unlikely to come up during a project evaluation assessment that focuses on performed processes.

For some processes, the relationships are quite simple. This applies to requirements management, testing and configuration management. This information is useful, because the assessor can concentrate on looking for the findings in certain processes and save some time in reporting. Similarly, it is useful to know which areas require a thorough review in the entire assessment findings. The accuracy of the assessment findings can be used to improve assessment efficiency, when there is a premise for the relationship between an assessment indicator and a DSR. All in all, this approach provides valuable information that can be used in developing the assessment methodology both for coverage of the findings and rigor of the assessment.

In general, we trust that the results validate the use of Nuclear SPICE in compliance evaluation. The process assessment findings can be efficiently used to evaluate compliance to DSRs and the results are reliable and so are meaningful to the stakeholders.

5 Summary

In this paper, we have analyzed process assessment findings and studied their relation to domain specific requirements (DSRs). The aim was to validate the usefulness of the Nuclear SPICE process assessment method in compliance evaluation. Compliance evaluation is an activity within the process assessment process that uses the assessment findings in analyzing how well the DSRs are met. The results of this study are important, because the assessment method in a safety-related domain and the assessment results must be reliable and consistent. This can be achieved when the assessment findings accurately cover the selected DSRs and the results are repeatable.

In our earlier study [1], the aim was to find solutions that can help in compliance evaluation that, by experience, is very tedious. The early results were not very promising, partly because of the process assessment approach itself. Anyway, the mathematical approach used was helpful and encouraged us to apply binary relations to study the overall effectiveness of compliance evaluation.

The results are significant. A well-defined assessment process produces findings that are relevant to DSRs. Of course, appropriate DSRs must be selected systematically. Based on this study, it is clear that Nuclear SPICE process assessments produce efficiently useful information in evaluating compliance to DSRs.

Acknowledgements. This work has been jointly funded by the Finnish national nuclear safety program SAFIR2018 (http://safir2018.vtt.fi/) and the Finnish Software Measurement Association, FiSMA (www.fisma.fi).

References

1. Varkoi, T., Mäkinen, T., Gallina, B., Cameron, F., Nevalainen, R.: Towards systematic compliance evaluation using safety-oriented process lines and evidence mapping. In: Stolfa, J., Stolfa, S., O'Connor, R.V., Messnarz, R. (eds.) EuroSPI 2017. CCIS, vol. 748, pp. 83–95. Springer, Cham (2017). https://doi.org/10.1007/978-3-319-64218-5_7
2. Common Position Revision: Licensing of safety critical software for nuclear reactors. Common position of seven European nuclear regulators and authorised technical support organisations (2013)

3. STUK: YVL B.1, Safety design of a nuclear power plant. Finnish Radiation and Nuclear Safety Authority (2013)
4. STUK: YVL E.7, Electrical and I&C equipment of a nuclear facility. Finnish Radiation and Nuclear Safety Authority (2013)
5. Grassman, W.K., Tremblay, J.-P.: Logic and Discrete Mathematics. Prentice-Hall, Upper Saddle River (1996)
6. Varkoi, T., Nevalainen, R., Mäkinen, T.: Toward nuclear SPICE – integrating IEC 61508, IEC 60880 and SPICE. J. Softw.: Evol. Process **26**, 357–365 (2013)
7. ISO/IEC 33001: Information technology – Process assessment – Concepts and terminology (2015)
8. ISO/IEC 33020: Information technology – Process assessment – Process measurement framework for assessment of process capability (2015)
9. ISO/IEC/IEEE 15288: Systems and software engineering – System life cycle processes (2015)
10. Varkoi, T., Nevalainen, R.: Compliance and rigour in process assessment for safety-critical domain. In: Barafort, B., O'Connor, R.V., Poth, A., Messnarz, R. (eds.) EuroSPI 2014. CCIS, vol. 425, pp. 296–308. Springer, Heidelberg (2014). https://doi.org/10.1007/978-3-662-43896-1_27
11. Varkoi, T., Nevalainen, R.: Process assessment in supplier selection for safety-critical systems in nuclear domain. In: Tonetta, S., Schoitsch, E., Bitsch, F. (eds.) SAFECOMP 2017. LNCS, vol. 10489, pp. 298–308. Springer, Cham (2017). https://doi.org/10.1007/978-3-319-66284-8_25
12. Varkoi, T., Nevalainen, R., Mäkinen, T.: Process assessment in a safety domain - assessment method and results as evidence in an assurance case. In: Proceedings of QUATIC 2016. IEEE Computer Society (2016)
13. IEC 60880: Nuclear power plants – Instrumentation and control systems important to safety – Software aspects for computer-based systems performing category A functions (2006)
14. IEC 62138: Nuclear power plants – I&C Systems Important to Safety – Software aspects for computer-based systems performing category B or C functions (2004)

GamifySPI

Adopting Augmented Reality for the Purpose of Software Development Process Training and Improvement: An Exploration

İpek Ohri[1,2], İrem Öge[1,2], Bora Orkun[1,2], Murat Yilmaz[1,2(✉)], Eray Tuzun[3], Paul Clarke[4,5], and Rory V. O'Connor[4,5]

[1] Department of Computer Engineering, Çankaya University, Ankara, Turkey
{c1311038, c1311040, c1311039}@student.cankaya.edu.tr, myilmaz@cankaya.edu.tr

[2] Virtual Reality Research and Development Laboratory, Çankaya University, Ankara, Turkey

[3] Department of Computer Engineering, Bilkent University, Ankara, Turkey
eraytuzun@cs.bilkent.edu.tr

[4] School of Computing, Dublin City University, Dublin, Ireland
{paul.m.clarke, rory.oconnor}@dcu.ie

[5] Lero – The Irish Software Research Centre, Limerick, Ireland

Abstract. Augmented reality (AR) is a technological field of study that bridges the physical and digital world together with a view to improving user experience. AR holds great potential to change the delivery of software services or software process improvement by utilizing a specific set of components. The purpose of this exploratory study is to propose an integration framework to support AR for improving the onboarding process, notably in introducing new hires to the development process while performing their daily tasks. In addition, it also aims to enhance the software development workflow process using AR. Similar to a GPS device that can guide you from point A to point B, our goal is to create software artifacts like navigation components where software teams may benefit from digitally enhanced working conditions provided using AR. After conducting a review in the literature, we confirmed that there is lack of studies about the combination of augmented reality with software engineering disciplines for onboarding. In this paper, we formalized our approach based on the benefits of AR. Ultimately; we propose an AR-based preliminary model for improving the software development process.

Keywords: Software development · Augmented reality · Virtual dashboard

1 Introduction

Regarded as one of the emerging technologies, *Augmented Reality* (AR) enriches the real world with digital information and media, and should reshape the ways we interact with our environment. According to Azuma [1], AR is a technology, which combines the physical world with *virtual objects* for a new kind of visualization that promises spatial interaction in real time. The studies about AR were initiated in the 1960s [2] and

X. Larrucea et al. (Eds.): EuroSPI 2018, CCIS 896, pp. 195–206, 2018.
https://doi.org/10.1007/978-3-319-97925-0_16

the interest of people for this technology increased after the success of the Pokemon GO [3] game in 2016, which is almost 40 years after AR studies are started. Within the last two years, social media conversations about AR have gone up to a rate of 33% [4]. Recently, AR has become a promising technology that is used in various fields such as education, industry, entertainment, and military. Still, the current AR market can be considered as newly growing environment, meaning that technology and market maturity are still in their early adolescence [4]. However, AR technology still continues to progress. Up to now, it has valuable contributions in the fields in which it was used. In the light of these positive feedbacks, this technology can have promising impacts on different domains as well.

The goal of the study is to provide *continuous onboarding* (i.e. organizational socialization) to software practitioners and enhance the daily workflow of software organization, which make them productive members of software development organization. Specifically, we contend that it should be possible to continually use AR infrastructure as *an interactive mechanism* to continually train and educate process actors, rendering onboarding a continuous as opposed to a discrete (or even once-off) event. While performing their daily tasks, practitioners should collect information from a variety of different sources. Here, our aim is to visualize this information using AR technology by creating a virtual war room for stakeholders. Consequently, we improve the software development process in an AR enhanced environment with the motivation of producing software artifacts in a short amount of calendar time. This approach enables clear and quick communication and collaboration among teammates by having multiple resources to consume in a meeting room, creating a multiple data-feeding environment where software development issues can be quickly identified and resolved with less distraction with personalized enhancement of the workflow. The remaining part of the paper is organized in the following way: Sect. 2 gives a brief overview of Augmented Reality in the literature. In Sect. 3, we describe the AR framework, and finally, Sect. 4 concludes with the implication of the findings for future research.

2 Augmented Reality in the Literature

Thus, far, research has been conducted to explore the benefits of AR in education. One study by Wojciechowski and Cellar [5] highlights that students tend to collaborate AR objects with real objects by using simple and cost-effective devices. Freitas and Campos [6] developed an AR application called SMART (System of Augmented Reality for Teaching) to visualize and introduce objects such as cars, airplanes, and animals to primary school students. Application was experimented upon 54 students in three different schools, and the results showed that SMART improved their ambition towards learning. AR is not only used for primary level students, but also for higher level educated students in universities and colleges to embody complicated theories and systems [6]. In biology lessons, an AR application that simulates the organs in the human body with their names and explanations is used as a demonstration for the students for a more realistic experience in classroom [6].

One of the fields in which AR can be used efficiently is tourism. Kounavis et al. [7] mention some of the AR applications for this field in their research. Tuscany+, the *first*

AR application, is a digital tourist guide in the Tuscany region. Augmented Reality for Basel which is also a special tourist guide for the city of Basel, gives its users valuable information about the city, and users can find information about museums, hotels, shopping centers, restaurants, events, etc. Urban Sleuth is another example of AR application in tourism, but it is remarkably distinctive from the others because it requires user participation/interaction in order to solve mysteries and accomplish missions while touring in the city and competing with other teams. A final application is especially designed for the demands of the Museum of London and it is called The *StreetMuseum*. It enables users to view historical places and information about them [7]. Research highlights the importance of AR technology in tourism by emphasizing that industry of tourism needs to draw the attention of people and nowadays the most efficient way to achieve this is through the usage of mobile devices, therefore tourism industry must be kept updated by new investments [8].

Carmigniani et al. [9] express that using AR in the entertainment industry may bring a breath of fresh air into it, especially for the gaming, for instance, animations can be displayed when playing a board game. With AR technology, the user experience of players can be improved. *Augmented onboarding* can be beneficial as a main component of a game, e.g. presenting how to play, showing tactics that are available, displaying ongoing characteristics of other players. Such a visual improvement makes games more attractive and interactive. As an example, Gandy et al. [10] developed AR Karaoke game. The game allows the player to play a scene from a movie. A HMD (head-mounted display) is used for getting into the environment of the scene with virtual objects. The gamer can experience the movie scene in first-person perspective. Yuen et al. [11] investigated AR technology in marketing with giving the example of automotive companies, which use real size AR virtual cars in their showrooms. With virtual buttons, customers can observe virtual model vehicles by opening doors and rotating them. They indicate that customers can gain more definite impression about the product with using the virtual models on their mobile phones. Augmented Reality is commonly used for online advertising. As an example, the car company MINI [12] developed an AR application advertised in some German magazines. In this special form of advertisement, readers show the related page to their webcams and a virtual MINI car appears on the screen [9]. Magic mirror is also an application of AR technology developed for marketing. In addition to this, Cisco's fitting room is another development for retail sales which involves AR technology. In these two applications, customers are allowed to try on virtual clothes instead of real products. With AR technology, they see how such clothing might look on them. This helps customer to make more accurate decisions during shopping [9]. Furthermore, Höllerer and Feiner [13] mention that in the future, virtual billboards may appear on the street, according to user's profile and interests to advertise a product and as a result, that would catch the attention of marketing agencies, since it would increase the customer interest in such products. In the light of these examples and tendency to using mobile technologies in every area like shopping, marketing is one of the fields that have a significant potential for AR technology investments.

In addition, AR is suitable for training military personnel. One usage of AR for military is tracking medical issues on a battlefield. The authorized commander in combat can get the information about the health status of a soldier, whether he is injured and visualize the view and conditions of the field using AR [13]. Special AR helmets that contain 360 cameras and sensors are in developing phase to help ground soldiers to experience real life combat conditions with the warnings about the battlefield conditions such as an enemy or a danger spot warning [11]. In their study, Fenier and Henderson [14] developed an AR system that provides system and equipment maintenance to bulletproof vehicle to make the repairment more quickly and securely, by a military mechanic wearing special AR glasses.

Automotive industry is one of the sectors in which AR has a potential. Many of the companies, especially car and airplane manufacturers, work with some big, costly, fast changing and time-consuming products. Consequently, producing this kind of products and training people to learn and assemble the parts of products require large amount of time and money. Reiners et al. [15] mentioned that since the products change faster and companies need to keep pace with the new technologies, AR can be used for training the service personnel in assembling and fixing the parts of a product. In their study, they worked with BMW Company in the assembly of a door lock into a car door. As a result, their work enlightened prototyping and conducting tasks in a specific part of a car. Furthermore, Azuma [1] stated that a 3D model that simulates the real components of equipment is easier and more practical rather than manuals and pictures for following instructions. Boeing, one of the largest airplane companies, uses AR technology to guide the technicians around the electrical system of an airplane. Moreover, Feiner [16] claimed that architects can use AR to visualize the installation of a building by showing the electric cables and pipe systems inside the walls. Also, it can be used to display the view from a window of a building that is in planning for the architect to see and analyze. After examining the priorities for different sectors, AR can be implemented or adapted according to the demands of that industry.

2.1 Onboarding

Onboarding is the process of incorporating new employees into an organization [17]. Onboarding, in other words adaptation process of getting used to the company culture, new colleagues, and new projects, takes some time; however, it is becoming easier with certain methods and tools [18]. Unmistakably, AR gives entrepreneurs boundless potential for putting learners in realistic situations and circumstances. Numerous representatives learn best by doing as opposed to seeing. A new approach to the onboarding process is continuous onboarding, in which the adaptation period never stops. It continues as the employee works in the company and it keeps him/her engaged in the working process. According to Leaman, the employees who have had a successful onboarding experience are more likely to stay with a company for a long period [19]. Yates [20], claimed that the onboarding process is crucial for developers, who work individually or work in a team, in order to understand the techniques, culture and the code based work in the company. It is better to get the information about co-workers, documentation, codes and code artifacts by new employees to make the onboarding process more qualified.

The business world is living and changes rapidly. Therefore, sustaining business agility and adaptability is crucial for being afloat in the sector. Taking these facts into consideration, companies work on real-time continuous training [21]. The software development industry is one of the most challenging industries in terms of employee adaptation to a job. Technology giants like Google, Apple, Microsoft are aware about this issue and are therefore investigating solutions regarding this issue. Recently, Apple created an AR application in which while walking around campus they orient their new employees by showing how each department works using AR [22].

To sum up, AR technology has a great potential in many different fields, such as education, tourism, entertainment, marketing and sales, military, and automotive industry as it can be seen in Fig. 1. It shows how the conversations in AR has changed from 2015 up until the 3rd quarter of 2017 in various fields. Regularly, technology is evolving and applications are getting more visualized and becoming more interactive.

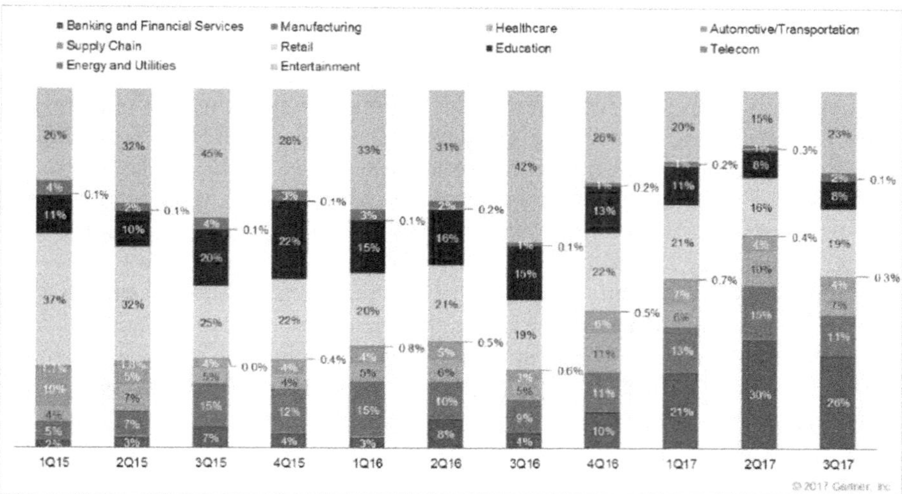

Fig. 1. Verticals driving the social media conversations in AR [23]

AR technology provides extended experiences to its users instead of flat screens, keyboards, and external components. It promises better connections to individuals with the data they want to access [24]. The ever-increasing evolution of mobile technology and the fast adaptation to these devices by people have allowed AR to become reachable to the public [25]. Recently, AR has been identified as a technology with promising advancements in application market. When all these workings about AR are taken into consideration, there is certainly, a lack of academic and scientific research on the combination of AR and Software Engineering disciplines, and also AR used for onboarding processes. The purpose of this project is to provide continuous onboarding to software practitioners, while performing their daily tasks. It would be possible by creating an enhanced version of spatial reality enriched by digital information and media. As a result, software development workflow would be improved by using this system. We believe that software developers should be interactively guided using such an AR technology. Therefore, we characterize an environment which includes AR for software development teams.

3 Augmented Reality Based Continuous Onboarding Framework

Software development is a process that has a deep background consisting of various phases. Even though, there are different methodologies used in software development, it has never been a straightforward process. Developers should always be highly motivated and continuously focused on the project. Otherwise, they can easily be disoriented during the development activities. All developers including juniors should always keep the pace of the process. By creating a combination of augmented reality (AR) and a software development workflow process, the goal of this project is to provide continuous onboarding to software practitioners, while performing their daily tasks. In addition, our plan is to visualize the profile of software practitioners, their skills, their performance and progression using AR technology. Ultimately, an aim is to collect information from a set of different sources and visualize it using AR. For the development, we have chosen Vuforia [26] integrated with Unity 3D platform [27] which is a game engine with 3D graphics and it is compatible with all different platforms and devices. Vuforia has been shown to be one of the leading augmented reality tools by developers, due to its remarkable features, such as compatibility with popular gadgets, visuals of different kinds, perception of objects. For the coding of the project, C# language is used in Visual Studio 2017 integrated with Unity 3D.

Figure 2, displays the information about the connections between system attributes. The system performs the task according to the modeID in AR Mode class. AR Mode class manages the mode that the system will work according to a user's selection. AR User class is the class that represents functions of the actor of the system. The user selects a mode and views the information about the object according to the type of the objects which are either another user or a meeting room. AR frame tracks environment in both modes. This class gets the information about scanned image and creates the augmented content. AR Anchor class is incorporated with AR Frame and according to the augmented content from AR Frame; it locates the content according to world location.

The framework consists of two main modules, which are the *user management module* and the *activity mode module*. The user management module contains the functionality of profile authorization, which controls and navigates users through system usage lifetime. The second module is the activity mode module, which comprises orientation mode and the war room mode of the system. These two submodules have their own functionalities as environment tracking, positioning and orientation of real world data and mixing virtual content. In augmented reality, we change the real world data by adding some virtual data and represent this mixed content to the user. The AR mechanism begins to work by getting the real world data through camera or sensors. After that, positioning and adaptation are done and data is ready for processing. The processing of the data is the most crucial part for developing the AR application. Changing the real world data is done in this step and mixed with virtual information. In the last step, content of mixed reality is represented to the user as video output. This part of the framework is planned to be available for company workers only. Standard users are the practitioners who are working on software development.

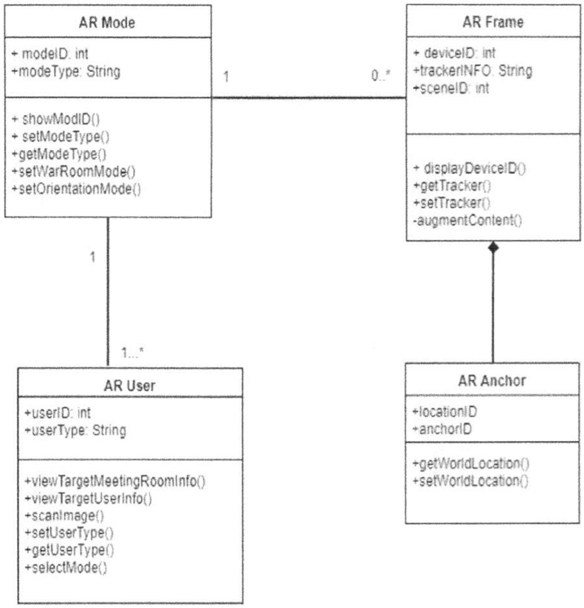

Fig. 2. Class diagram of the proposed framework

Developers can login, use orientation and war room mode, and exit from the system. First, the user should run the application and the login page is opened. The user is expected to be registered to the system by the system administrator, who manages the database of the company so that she can login to the system. By inputting a valid username and password, the user logs in to the system and is navigated to the related page according to her authorization rights. Developers can navigate to the mode selection page, from which they can continue with either orientation mode or war room mode.

3.1 Orientation Mode

In this mode, the users can access the profile information of a developer by scanning the unique image which belongs to the selected developer. The participant must be logged in and switched to the orientation mode before accessing. The camera screen is opened and the environment can be observed from the screen and application does environment tracking functionality. The user basically selects an AR target to get information about a person. After determining a target, the user scan the unique image which belongs to the target developer to get information about her/him. The user sees these information on the screen mixed with the augmented reality components. After information becomes visible, the user can scan a new image or can exit from the orientation mode by selecting exit option.

3.2 War Room Mode

In this mode, the user can access the information about the scrum board by scanning the unique image which belongs to the selected board. The user must log in and switch to the war room mode from the menu. Similar to Orientation Mode, camera screen is opened and the user sees the environment through the camera screen and the application tracks the environment. With scanning the unique image of the whiteboard in the room, the user can see the notes that are taken in the previous project meeting as "TO DO", "IN PROGRESS" and "DONE". Also, a progress bar can be seen to visualize the improvement of the development process of the project. The user can exit from the war room mode by selecting exit option.

To use the proposed *AR framework*, user chooses whether the application will be on "*Orientation Mode*" or "*War Room Mode*" by touching the screen. The user follows the office environment from the screen. If the system is on the *Orientation Mode*, the user looks for the identifier image on the employee's desk. When an image has matched from the database of the system, a virtual button will be seen to extend the information to the owner of the desk. If the user presses that button to extend, the first thing user sees is photograph, name, position, team, some personal information, specialty and current works of the person, that is the owner of the identifier image and position and department that he works in. If the system is on the *War Room Mode*, the user scans the identifier image on the scrum board to the camera. The options menu, to choose which

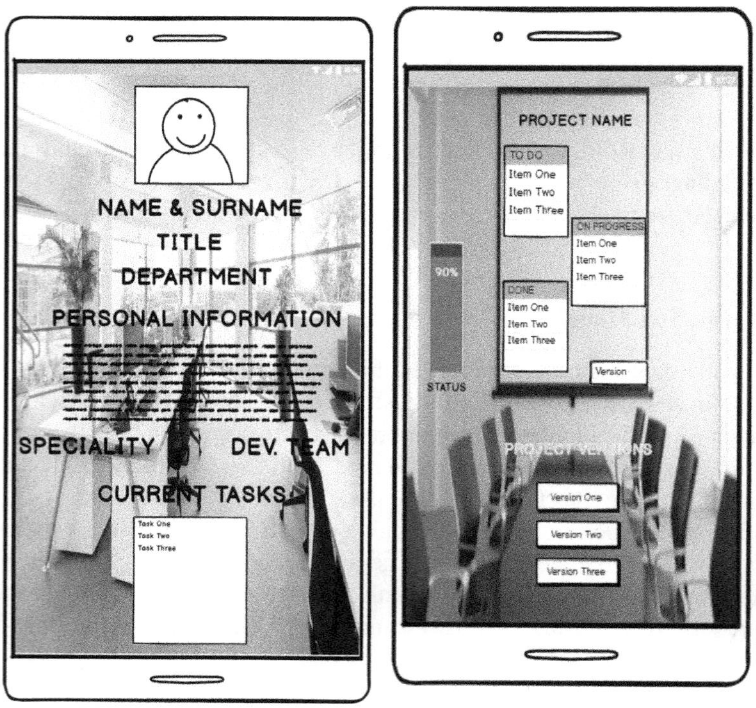

Fig. 3. Sample interface design from the orientation mode and the war room mode

meeting information to choose, is displayed on the screen. Options are shown as meeting name and meeting date. After the user chooses the meeting, meeting information is shown as project name, version of the project, and scrum board information is displayed on the whiteboard of the meeting room through the camera screen.

In the *Orientation Mode*, when the user scans the unique image of some colleague and continues with the show information button, a window like Fig. 3 (left) appears, that has entries about the selected developer's photograph, name, title, department, team, some personal information, specialty and current works of the person. Figure 3 (left) is an interface sample that we prototyped to use as the general screen design when the target image of a developer is scanned and identified in the *Orientation Mode*. In the *War Room Mode*, when the user scans the unique image of the board, a window like Fig. 3 (right), that has the entries about the project name, version of the project, and scrum board information, is displayed on the whiteboard of the meeting room through the camera screen. Figure 3 (right) is the sample interface of the War Room Mode after the whiteboard is detected in the meeting room.

4 Discussion

An initial objective of the study was to identify the potential benefits of AR in software development. This study provides a novel approach to augment software practitioners' reality. The results of this study support the view that a complementary tool is beneficial for assisting software development not only in daily task arrangement but also for onboarding novice software practitioners. To this end, a preliminary model was designed and an initial prototype was created. The prototype was tested and evaluated by software engineers who are currently working in a software company and have different years of working experiences. From the feedbacks of these users, it is observed that some design components can be improved in the system. Overall, they generally thought that the tool can be functional and beneficial for the development teams and newcomers to the company. This study suggests that technological assistance tools for software development shall emerge after continuous integration becomes a more common practice.

We believe this work to be important for the broader software engineering community as there is a growing acknowledgement, that not alone is the software process complicated [28], but also that there are a large number of factors affecting the process [29–31] with the result that the overall business of software process engineering is subject to regular change and highly complex [32]. Added to these challenges in process enactment, we must strive for appropriate levels of process focus in organizations as increased process focus has been demonstrated to be positively associated with successful business outcomes [33]. Given these various acknowledgements, and the added rich variety of individual roles in software engineering [34], steps to improve process communication and process feedback/improvement (such as is enabled by our AR proposal) are considered to offer innovative mechanisms to assist in addressing the challenging software process space. We suggest that many software developers may have an intrinsic interest in VR and AR type activities, and in the past have demonstrated the power of VR in terms of improving process-learning outcomes [35], and in assisting developers in presentation related training [36]. In this sense, the AR based research that we present herein can be considered to be a natural and important progression of our earlier work in this space [37].

Overall, this study suggests a model to assist software practitioners by using the latest technology, which also improves practitioner motivation, while performing routine activities. Consequently, the social structure of software organizations will be enhanced by emerging technologies. In future investigations, it might be possible to improve the software development process by successfully capturing the tacit knowledge in a software development organization as it is actively evolved and to feed this information into improved/adapted AR models, so that AR can become an integral part of process management for software teams, using technology that is aligned with the interest of many software developers.

References

1. Azuma, R.: A survey of augmented reality. Presence: Teleoperators Virtual Environ. **6**(4), 355–385 (1997)
2. Azuma, R., Baillot, Y., Behringer, R., Feiner, S., Julier, S., MacIntyre, B.: Recent advances in augmented reality. IEEE Comput. Graph. Appl. **21**(6), 34–47 (2001)
3. Catch Pokémon in the Real World with Pokémon GO! Pokemongo.com (2017). http://www.pokemongo.com/. Accessed 22 Oct 2017
4. Nguyen, T., Jump, A., Resnick, M.: Three Key Development Practices to Implement Effective Enterprise Augmented Reality Applications. Gartner (2017)
5. Wojciechowski, R., Walczak, K., White, M., Cellary, W.: Building virtual and augmented reality museum exhibitions. In: Proceedings of the Ninth International Conference on 3D Web Technology, 5–8 April 2004, Monterey (2004)
6. Freitas, R., Campos, P.: SMART: a SysteM of augmented reality for teaching 2nd grade students. In: Proceedings of the 22nd British HCI Group Annual Conference on People and Computers: Culture, Creativity, Interaction, vol. 2, pp. 27–30. BCS Learning & Development Ltd. (2008)
7. Kounavis, C., Kasimati, A., Zamani, E.: Enhancing the tourism experience through mobile augmented reality: challenges and prospects. Int. J. Eng. Bus. Manag. **4**, 10 (2012)
8. Xiang, Z., Tussyadiah, I. (eds.): Information and Communication Technologies in Tourism 2014, pp. 511–523. Springer, Cham (2013). https://doi.org/10.1007/978-3-319-03973-2
9. Carmigniani, J., Furht, B., Anisetti, M., Ceravolo, P., Damiani, E., Ivkovic, M.: Augmented reality technologies, systems and applications. Multimed. Tools Appl. **51**(1), 341–377 (2010)
10. Gandy, M., et al.: AR Karaoke: acting in your favorite scenes. In: Proceedings of the 4th IEEE/ACM International Symposium on Mixed and Augmented Reality, pp.114–117, 5–8 October 2005
11. Yuen, S., Yaoyuneyong, G., Johnson, E.: Augmented reality: an overview and five directions for AR in education. J. Educ. Technol. Dev. Exch. **4**(1), 11 (2011)
12. The Official MINI Website—MINI UK, The Official MINI Website—MINI UK (2017). https://www.mini.co.uk/en_GB/home.html. Accessed 22 Oct 2017
13. Höllerer, T.H., Feiner, S.K.: Mobile augmented reality. In: Karimi, H., Hammad, A. (eds.) Telegeoinformatics: Location-Based Computing and Services. CRC Press, Boca Raton (2004). ISBN 0-4153-6976-2

14. Henderson, S., Feiner, S.: Exploring the benefits of augmented reality documentation for maintenance and repair. IEEE Trans. Visual Comput. Graph. **17**(10), 1355–1368 (2011)
15. Reiners, D., Stricker, D., Klinker, G., Müller, S.: Augmented reality for construction tasks: doorlock assembly. In: Proceedings of the International Workshop Augmented Reality (IWAR 1998), pp. 31–46 (1999)
16. Feiner, S., Webster, A., Krueger, T., MacIntyre, B., Keller, E.: Architectural anatomy. Presence: Teleoperators Virtual Environ. **4**(3), 318–325 (1995)
17. What Is Onboarding? - Best Practices & Process - White Paper, Icims.com (2017). https://www.icims.com/resources/white-paper/onboarding. Accessed 8 Dec 2017
18. Kosa, M., Yilmaz, M.: Gamifying the onboarding process for novice software practitioners. In: Kreiner, C., O'Connor, R.V., Poth, A., Messnarz, R. (eds.) EuroSPI 2016. CCIS, vol. 633, pp. 242–248. Springer, Cham (2016). https://doi.org/10.1007/978-3-319-44817-6_20
19. 3 Tips to Redesign Your Onboarding Process into a Continuous Experience - eLearning Industry, eLearning Industry (2017). https://elearningindustry.com/redesign-your-onboarding-process-into-a-continuous-experience-3-tips. Accessed 8 Dec 2017
20. Yates, R.: Onboarding in Software Engineering (2014)
21. Newman, D.: Hyper-Training and the Future Augmented Reality Workplace (2017). https://www.forbes.com/sites/danielnewman/2016/09/20/hyper-training-and-the-future-augmented-reality-workplace/#33650a2728b0. Accessed 9 Dec 2017
22. Beus, B.: How Augmented Reality Can Revolutionize Employee Onboarding and Retention. Business 2 Community. https://www.business2community.com/tech-gadgets/augmented-reality-can-revolutionize-employee-onboarding-retention-01921335#shajp8sgjDJrGDKB.97. Accessed 9 Dec 2017
23. Resnick, M.: Best Practices for Using Augmented Reality in Mobile Apps. Gartner (2017)
24. Blau, B., Burke, B., Searle, S., Cearley, D.: Top 10 Strategic Technology Trends for 2017: Virtual Reality and Augmented Reality. Gartner (2017)
25. Nguyen, T., Blau, B.: Market Guide for Augmented Reality. Gartner (2017)
26. Vuforia Supported Versions, Vuforia (2017). https://library.vuforia.com/articles/Solution/Vuforia-Supported-Versions. Accessed 4 Dec 2017
27. Unity - Products, Unity (2017). https://unity3d.com/unity. Accessed 18 Nov 2017
28. Clarke, P., O'Connor, R.V., Yilmaz, M.: A hierarchy of SPI activities for software SMEs: results from ISO/IEC 12207-based SPI assessments. In: Mas, A., Mesquida, A., Rout, T., O'Connor, R.V., Dorling, A. (eds.) SPICE 2012. CCIS, vol. 290, pp. 62–74. Springer, Heidelberg (2012). https://doi.org/10.1007/978-3-642-30439-2_6. ISBN 978-3-642-30439-2
29. Clarke, P., O'Connor, R.: The situational factors that affect the software development process: towards a comprehensive reference framework. Inf. Softw. Technol. **54**(5), 433–447 (2012). ISSN 0950-5849
30. Marks, G., O'Connor, R., Clarke, P.: The impact of situational context on the software development process – a case study of a highly innovative start-up organization. In: 17th International Conference on Software Process Improvement and Capability determination (SPICE 2017), 4–5 October 2017, Palma de Mallorca (2017)
31. Clarke, P.M., et al.: Exploring software process variation arising from differences in situational context. In: Stolfa, J., Stolfa, S., O'Connor, R.V., Messnarz, R. (eds.) EuroSPI 2017. CCIS, vol. 748, pp. 29–42. Springer, Cham (2017). https://doi.org/10.1007/978-3-319-64218-5_3. ISBN 978-3-319-64218-5
32. Clarke, P., O'Connor, R., Leavy, B.: A complexity theory viewpoint on the software development process and situational context. In: International Workshop on Software and Systems Process (ICSSP 2016), 14–15 May 2016, Austin (2016). ISBN 978-1-4503-4188-2
33. Clarke, P., O'Connor, R.: The influence of SPI on business success in software SMEs: an empirical study. J. Syst. Softw. **85**(10), 2356–2367 (2012). ISSN 0164-1212

34. Yilmaz, M., O'Connor, R., Clarke, P.: Software development roles: a multi-project empirical investigation. ACM SIGSOFT Softw. Eng. Notes **40**(1), 1–5 (2015). ISSN 0163-5948
35. Aydan, U., Yilmaz, M., Clarke, P., O'Connor, R.: Teaching ISO/IEC 12207 software lifecycle processes: a serious game approach. Comput. Stand. Interfaces **54**(Part 3), 129–138 (2017)
36. Nazligul, M.D., Yilmaz, M., Gulec, U., Gozcu, M.A., O'Connor, R.V., Clarke, P.M.: Overcoming public speaking anxiety of software engineers using virtual reality exposure therapy. In: Stolfa, J., Stolfa, S., O'Connor, R.V., Messnarz, R. (eds.) EuroSPI 2017. CCIS, vol. 748, pp. 191–202. Springer, Cham (2017). https://doi.org/10.1007/978-3-319-64218-5_15. ISBN 978-3-319-64218-5
37. Yilmaz, M., Güleç, U., O'Connor, R., Clarke, P., Tüzün, E.: An industrial case study to improve the onboaring process in software management. Yazılım Yönetiminde İşe Alıştırma Süreçlerinin İyileştirilmesi İçin Düşünülmüş Bir Endüstriyel Vaka Çalışması. In: 11th Turkish National Software Engineering Symposium (UYMS 2017), 18–20 October 2017, Alanya, Turkey (2017)

Is Gamification a Way to a Softer Software Process Improvement? A Preliminary Study of Success Factors

Eduardo Herranz[1] and Ricardo Colomo-Palacios[2(✉)]

[1] Computer Science Department, Universidad Carlos III de Madrid, Av. Universidad 30, 28911 Leganés, Madrid, Spain
eduardo.herranz@uc3m.es

[2] Faculty of Computer Sciences, Østfold University College, Postboks 700, 1757 Halden, Norway
ricardo.colomo-palacios@hiof.no

Abstract. People factors and more specifically, motivational factors, are key in software initiatives given the intrinsic importance of people in knowledge intensive industries. Within software engineering knowledge areas, in software process improvement (SPI) initiatives the importance of personnel is also paramount. In this scenario gamification can increase the motivation and motivation of the workforce, and by doing so, rise productivity and performance of personnel. However, although SPI could initially benefit from gamification initiatives, it is needed to study carefully the effects of gamification in SPI arenas. Given that SPI presents its enablers and barriers, it is also true that gamification presents also its own panoply of pro and cons. In this paper, authors show some of the anti-patterns but also the enablers of a set of initiatives conducted in the joint field of SPI and gamification.

Keywords: Software process improvement · Gamification · Deployment

1 Introduction

Gamification has been proven to upsurge engagement and motivation in multiple and different non-game contexts such as education, healthcare and marketing, among others [1]. Technology and more specifically, software engineering is not out of this move. Gamification started in the marketing arena implementing mechanisms like loyalty cards, competitions, stamp books and reward memberships, yet the escalation of gamification has to do with more affordable technology solutions and the generalization of game culture in society [2]. Now gamification is a way to improve engagement in both educational and professional grounds [3].

There is a wide panoply of Gamification definitions. A generally accepted definition is as follows: gamification is the use of game elements and game-design techniques in non-gaming contexts [2].

Gamification presents several elements, although an excellent description of game design elements is available in in the works of [2, 4, 5], maybe a more succinct

X. Larrucea et al. (Eds.): EuroSPI 2018, CCIS 896, pp. 207–218, 2018.
https://doi.org/10.1007/978-3-319-97925-0_17

description is provided by [6]. In what follows these elements are listed and described with regards to their use in software environments:

- Leaderboards: are valuable to show the user progress or success compared to the evolution of other users or competitors.
- Points systems: are suitable to measure the success in realizing a task.
- Badges: are convenient to recognize personal goals and, consequently, to motivate personnel.
- Levels: are useful to provide trials, adapting difficulty to the scale of levels.
- Progress Bars: are suitable to track the advancement of a given task.
- Rewards: are convenient to make a gift to an individual in recognition of his/her performed work.
- Scores: are valuable to measure a user performance while executing an activity.
- Challenges: are useful to make users apply their knowledge and skills to achieve an activity.
- Achievements: Represent specific goals in a main activity.
- Feedback: is useful to deliver meaningful information messages as clues to develop activities.
- Unblocking content: is convenient to unblock activities when users achieve goals.

As stated before, gamification has impacted in software engineering scenarios including previous efforts in SPI [7–12], personality studies [13], lifecycle management tools [14], testing [15–17], project management [18], educational purposes [19–22] or general gamification frameworks [1, 23] naming just some of the more recent and relevant works. Following the recent trend to conduct tertiary studies devoted to several aspects in the software engineering discipline, there are also a good set of works devoted to review gamification in software engineering by means of literature studies e.g. [3, 24–26]. However, according to [24], there is a need to provide empirical evidence of the impact of gamification in activities.

In this paper, authors, after a set of implementations in software industry settings, study traditional barriers of SPI and Gamification to stablish critical success factors on the joint application of SPI and gamification.

The remainder of this paper is structured as follows: Sect. 2 outlines the proposed gamification framework intended to be implemented in organizations. In Sect. 3 main lessons learnt are presented with regards to the implementation and adoption of the framework. The final section is devoted to conclude the paper and draw main future work.

2 The Framework

In previous works, authors presented several aspects related to the gamification framework designed to introduce gamification in SPI environments and in this chapter, authors introduce main aspects of it. Namely the framework itself and the supporting tool are presented.

2.1 The Framework

The complexity of SPI and the intrinsic convolution of gamification leads to the need to develop a specific framework that must entail personnel and organizational aspects and define a set of processes to guide it. As stated before, this framework was presented in previous works [7, 27]. In the last version of the framework the lean Startup (Build-Measure-Learn) method introduced by Ries [28] was adopted. Figure 1 depicts the phases of the framework that are also explained in what follows:

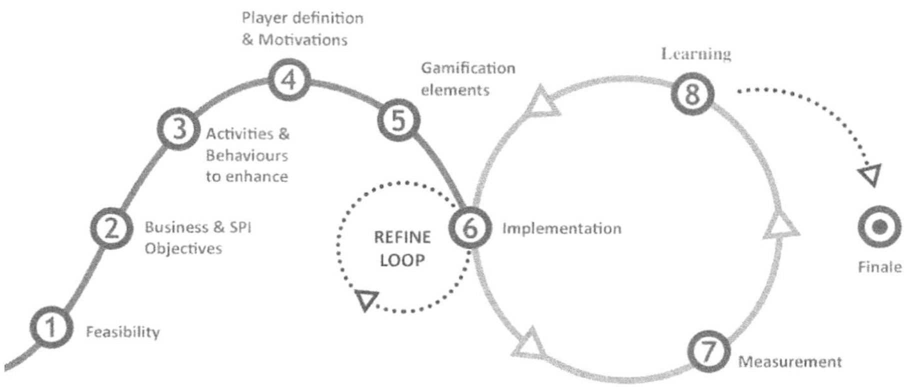

Fig. 1. SPI-Gamification framework: phases

1: FEASIBILITY: The first step is the determination of the viability of the organization in the adoption of the framework. Several aspects are assessed including: availability of necessary resources including time, commitment of top managers and SPI infrastructure.

2: BUSINESS & SPI GOALS: The next step is the definition of business objectives and their associated key performance indicators (KPIs). These aims are defined under the SMART criteria [29] meaning objectives must be Specific, Measurable, Achievable, Relevant and Time-bound. Finally, SPI objectives are defined cascading such objectives from the ones defined for business; for these objectives, metrics must be defined. GQM techniques [30] could be used in order to define metrics related to SPI.

3: ACTIVITIES & BEHAVIOURS TO ENHANCE: In this step, SPI activities and practitioners' behaviors aimed to be enhanced are identified. In order to analyze them, the level of intrinsic motivation of the SPI activity is analyzed by means of the IMI test [31]. Subsequently, Technical Customer Journey Maps [32] are employed to analyze the walk-through SPI activity from the practitioner's viewpoint. Lastly, the practitioners' behaviors and attitudes to be enhanced are identified and analyzed.

4: PLAYER DEFINITION & MOTIVATIONS: In this step, the motivational factors [33, 34] for each of the software professionals groups or SPI roles are analyzed. It is also desirable to identify each group of professionals or SPI roles with some type of players' classification (for instance by means of the taxonomy presented in [35]) for the gamification proposal.

5: GAMIFICATION ELEMENTS: For each SPI activity aimed to be improved, it is needed to sketch:

   1. Dynamics, mechanics and game elements, defined as described in [4] and refined by means of the Octalysis framework [5] as explained in previous works [8].
   2. Metrics for each of the game elements defined in the previous point.
   3. The feedback process system defined to capture and store information on practitioner's activity in real time.
   4. Aspects like resistance to change and commitment must be observed and reflected.

6: IMPLEMENTATION: In this step, the gamification proposal defined in STEP 5 is executed and implemented. Nevertheless, before implementing the gamification proposal, all stakeholders must be aware of the gamification project. The aim of this communication is to guarantee all parties understand and adopt the process as a critical aspect in SPI initiatives [36]. For this implementation, Gamiware, the tool was developed. This tool is explained in the next section.

7: MEASUREMENT: The KPIs of the SPI initiative, motivation metrics and the defined game elements are collected, measured and analyzed.

8: LEARNING: Results are assessed and the main inferences for future iterations are analyzed and documented.

REFINE LOOP: In order to introduce an improvement flavor, taking into account information obtained in the process defined above, the necessary adjustments are made in stages 2–5 in order to improve process and results.

2.2 Gamiware: The Tool

Tools are enablers of initiatives. In order to improve the acceptance of the framework, a tool was designed: Gamiware. This is a cloud tool to support the gamification process in an easy and affordable way following the process defined above. Gamiware is designed and implemented to be project and process independent. This tool is able to adapt to any organization and SPI by means of a form-oriented parametric customization. By means of this tools and enabling customization, business objectives, software objectives or SPI objectives are coded. Given the inherent nature of software process as human capital intensive activity [37, 38], the identification of software practitioners participating in the gamification process, their tasks and their associated KPIs is mandatory. Moreover, with the aim to improve the alignment of business objectives and SPI activities, it is possible to define the specific contribution of each task to the given business objective and by this mean assess the fulfilment of these objectives. The tool is presented in [9]. Figure 2 presents a screen capture of the tool. Gamiware has been developed by research team to support the gamification framework and includes support for different roles, activities and gamification elements:

Fig. 2. Gamiware: the backlog

3 Deploying the Framework

In this section, main results of the implementation of the framework are introduced. In order to do so, firstly, the sample of the three different case studies is presented, secondly, critical success factors of SPI and gamification initiatives are presented and finally, connecting the two previous points, critical success factors of the implementation of the gamification framework in the SPI settings are presented.

3.1 The Sample

Three different companies agreed to implement the framework. Companies were obtained from those who responded positively to a personal invitation sent by the authors to contacts working in Spanish, French and Latin American IT companies. In what follows the three companies are described.

ABC (fictional name) is a small company based in Madrid (Spain) devoted to develop custom-made software solutions at large. Their software development process is based by the ISO/IEC 29110 standard and some of its members hold the CSSLP (Certified Secure Software Lifecycle Professional) certification. The aim of the company in the gamification initiative is the improvement of its process of definition, execution and overall management of software testing. ABC agreed to divide the validation into two different phases: a first phase (1.5 months) in which 6 people are involved in three different types of projects. In the second phase, the gamification process is aimed to extend its works to 2 departments, but its execution would be subject to the results of the first pilot phase. Finally, the framework was deployed and a full cycle of improvement was developed as a result of the execution of the two phases. Although the improvement initiative did not achieve all its goals, it could be considered a partial success reaching some improvements.

DEF (fictional name) is a company founded back on 2012 and devoted to build and market software products mostly based on Big Data technologies. The aim of the company in the gamification initiative is the improvement of cycle times and time to market. In this case study the framework was initially deployed and some personnel embraced the initiative while others simply ignored it. The initiative was cancelled because of this lack of support, although some of the results were initially positive among adopters.

GHI (fictional name) is a Latin American company with branches in several countries like Ecuador, Panama and Peru. With around 15 years in industry, the organization is devoted to develop software solutions on web and mobile platforms, mostly by means of agile approaches and in a near-shoring scenario. The gamification project is aimed to reduce software waste and increase overall quality in the software process. The framework was defined and implemented, although the initiative was cancelled. The reasons for that are twofold: on the one hand and although there was support from company owners and CEO, middle managers were not committed enough with the initiative. On the other hand, by the time when the framework was implemented, there was a time in which a new and important customer started a project with the company and priorities changed.

In the three cases, organizations adopted the framework with the supervision of one member of the research team either on-site or by means of online communication tools. Given that, in the three cases, the research team adopted the methodology presented in previous works [7, 27], the three organizations fulfilled requisites for gamification deployment.

3.2 Critical Success Factors in SPI and Gamification Initiatives

SPI is not a new field. And the concerns of its success factors have been reported in the literature for years. According to a recent review on the topic [39], SPI success factors study is increasing interest over the years. Agreeing with [40], after a qualitative study of several success factors studies identified the following success factors:

1. senior management support
2. staff involvement
3. experience of staff
4. training
5. allocation of resources
6. communication
7. SPI goals
8. organization culture and politics

9. visibility of process and their success
10. process champions
11. reviews
12. clear vision
13. tools
14. reward schemes
15. process ownership

On the other hand, Gamification initiatives present their own critical success factors. In [7], authors define seven success factors for gamification initiatives in SPI by means of a qualitative study. Factors are listed in what follows:

1. Customized proposal
2. Priority on common motivators
3. Viability study
4. Business-users objectives alignment
5. Framework consensus
6. Previous communication
7. Monitoring and feedback

In the next chapter, the combination of these 21 factors are assessed in the three case studies provided, deriving consequences from the set of case studies.

3.3 Critical Success Factors in the Case Studies

Table 1 includes the assessment of combined critical success factors. Assessment is performed by means of the Likert scale (1: None; 2: Low; 3: Moderate; 4: High) is measuring to what extent the given factor was fulfilled in the case study. Further explanation of the values is given in the text that follows:

According to the values presented in the table, the organization that presents higher values is ABC reaching a sum of 68 points followed by GHI with 63 and finally, DEF with 57 points. These figures are aligned to the gamification results, pointing out the relative success of ABC and the failures in the other two organizations.

With regards to the factors, there are several factors reaching a sum of 12 points, including SPI goals, Tools, Reward schemes, Customized proposal, Priority on common motivators, Framework consensus and Previous communication. Overall, these aspects have to do with the framework already developed and can be controlled in an easier way by researchers. There are also other aspects presenting lower figures, being monitoring and feedback the work factor. The reason behind that could be the overall pale commitment shower by middle managers once the gamification process was started. Other aspects presenting lower values are Communication and Reviews. It is important to note the connection of these factors with Monitoring and feedback.

Table 1. Coverage of success factors by the three case studies

	ABC case	DEF case	GHI case
Senior management support	4	2	3
Staff involvement	3	2	2
Experience of staff	3	3	4
Training	3	2	2
Allocation of resources	3	2	3
Communication	2	2	2
SPI goals	4	4	4
Organization culture and politics	3	2	3
Visibility of process and their success	3	2	3
Process champions	3	2	2
Reviews	2	2	2
Clear vision	3	3	3
Tools	4	4	4
Reward schemes	4	4	4
Customized proposal	4	4	4
Priority on common motivators	4	4	4
Viability study	3	2	2
Business-users objectives	3	2	2
Framework consensus	4	4	4
Previous communication	4	4	4
Monitoring and feedback	2	1	2

4 Conclusions and Future Work

Results show that although there are factors presenting high fulfilment by organizations, lower values in other factors are spoiling overall final results. Then, the fulfilment of some factors (Tools, Reward Schemes, Priority on common motivations…), is not a guarantee for the success of the gamification initiative as a whole. Given the short sample and the preliminary approach presented in this work, we cannot provide a prioritize success factors, although this prioritization can be seen as a future work.

As stated before, some of the factors presenting higher values, are presenting these high scores because they are directly derived from the framework designed, that include them as part of its deployment. These factors are SPI goals, framework consensus, previous communication, priority on common motivators, reward scheme and customized proposal. However, this set of factors is not enough to ensure the success of the gamification initiative. Those factors that are outside the control of the framework are more complicated to comply with and have a drastic impact on the success of the proposal. In short, those factors that fall on the organization and top managers are the most sensitive and complicated to meet.

For DEF and GHI, "staff involvement" is considered a key factor. Moreover, if "senior commitment" presents moderate values, participants will ignore the initiative, especially if it is not aligned with their own personal objectives ("business-user commitment"). In this scenario, a "process champion" is a key figure to support the gamification initiative. However, this role is normally played by top managers and in the context of urgency in SMEs settings, allocating the time to play the role is not easy threatening the whole gamification process.

There are several factors hard to observe by SMEs:

1. Communication. Although the initial commitment by top managers is high their daily routine is dulling communication.
2. "Reviews" & "Monitoring and feedback". First of all, it should be noted that the feedback received by the participants presents a very low frequency. Multiple investigations indicate that, in order to obtain an adequate performance in a gamification initiative, real-time feedback is mandatory [4, 5, 27, 41]. This fact affects even more the break of the motivation loop (action - feedback - motivation), which has been considered so important to maintain motivation in gamification activities [4, 42, 43].
3. Business-users' objectives. The gamification initiative proposed by the organizations is seen by the participants as an initiative to measure their performance in the SPI tasks involved. That is, it is considered an activity for the control and evaluation of its performance

A correlation is anticipated between the success of the gamification initiative and the success of the SPI initiatives. In both cases it seems difficult to be applied in SMEs settings.

Finally, some viability factors enunciated in the gamification framework have been "relaxed". The aim of this decision is the will to implement the framework. For instance, the lack of sense of urgency is one of the factors indicated in the gamification framework [8]. This aspect is also backup by main researchers in the field as one of the main factors to be taken into account then any change management [44, 45].

As future works, apart from the previous cited initiatives, the analysis of the factors that are taken into account in the feasibility study of the gamification process and its connection with the critical success factors of the initiative is considered.

References

1. Calderón, A., Boubeta-Puig, J., Ruiz, M.: MEdit4CEP-Gam: a model-driven approach for user-friendly gamification design, monitoring and code generation in CEP-based systems. Inf. Softw. Technol. **95**, 238–264 (2018)
2. Deterding, S.: Gamification: designing for motivation. Interactions **19**, 14–17 (2012)
3. de Souza, M.R., Veado, L., Moreira, R.T., Figueiredo, E., Costa, H.: A systematic mapping study on game-related methods for software engineering education. Inf. Softw. Technol. **95**, 201–218 (2018)
4. Werbach, K., Hunter, D.: For the Win: How Game Thinking Can Revolutionize Your Business. Wharton Digital Press, Philadelphia (2012)

5. Chou, Y.K., Fuqua, J., Yuan, W.: Actionable Gamification: Beyond Points, Badges, and Leaderboards. CreateSpace Independent Publishing Platform, Scotts Valley (2015)
6. Muñoz, M., Hernández, L., Mejia, J., Gasca-Hurtado, G.P., Gómez-Alvarez, M.C.: State of the use of gamification elements in software development teams. In: Stolfa, J., Stolfa, S., O'Connor, R.V., Messnarz, R. (eds.) EuroSPI 2017. CCIS, vol. 748, pp. 249–258. Springer, Cham (2017). https://doi.org/10.1007/978-3-319-64218-5_20
7. Herranz, E., Colomo-Palacios, R., de Amescua Seco, A., Yilmaz, M.: Gamification as a disruptive factor in software process improvement initiatives. J-JUCS **20**, 885–906 (2014)
8. Herranz, E., Colomo-Palacios, R., de Amescua Seco, A., Sánchez-Gordón, M.-L.: Towards a gamification framework for software process improvement initiatives: construction and validation. J. Univers. Comput. Sci. **22**, 1509–1532 (2016)
9. Herranz, E., Colomo-Palacios, R., de Amescua Seco, A.: Gamiware: a gamification platform for software process improvement. In: O'Connor, R.V., Umay Akkaya, M., Kemaneci, K., Yilmaz, M., Poth, A., Messnarz, R. (eds.) EuroSPI 2017. CCIS, vol. 748, pp. 127–139. Springer, Cham (2015). https://doi.org/10.1007/978-3-319-24647-5_11
10. Dorling, A., McCaffery, F.: The gamification of SPICE. In: Mas, A., Mesquida, A., Rout, T., O'Connor, R.V., Dorling, A. (eds.) SPICE 2012. CCIS, vol. 290, pp. 295–301. Springer, Heidelberg (2012). https://doi.org/10.1007/978-3-642-30439-2_35
11. Yilmaz, M., O'Connor, R.: A Scrumban integrated gamification approach to guide software process improvement: a Turkish case study. Teh. Vjesn. Tech. Gaz. **23**, 237–245 (2016)
12. Gómez-Álvarez, M.C., Gasca-Hurtado, G.P., Hincapié, J.A.: Gamification as strategy for software process improvement: a systematic mapping. In: 2017 12th Iberian Conference on Information Systems and Technologies (CISTI), pp. 1–7 (2017)
13. Yilmaz, M., Yilmaz, M., O'Connor, R.V., Clarke, P.: A gamification approach to improve the software development process by exploring the personality of software practitioners. In: Clarke, P.M., O'Connor, R.V., Rout, T., Dorling, A. (eds.) SPICE 2016. CCIS, vol. 609, pp. 71–83. Springer, Cham (2016). https://doi.org/10.1007/978-3-319-38980-6_6
14. Üsfekes, Ç., Yilmaz, M., Tuzun, E., Clarke, P.M., O'Connor, R.V.: Examining reward mechanisms for effective usage of application lifecycle management tools. In: Stolfa, J., Stolfa, S., O'Connor, R.V., Messnarz, R. (eds.) EuroSPI 2017. CCIS, vol. 748, pp. 259–268. Springer, Cham (2017). https://doi.org/10.1007/978-3-319-64218-5_21
15. Fraser, G.: Gamification of software testing. In: Proceedings of the 12th International Workshop on Automation of Software Testing, pp. 2–7. IEEE Press, Piscataway (2017)
16. Rojas, J.M., Fraser, G.: Code defenders: a mutation testing game. In: 2016 IEEE Ninth International Conference on Software Testing, Verification and Validation Workshops (ICSTW), pp. 162–167 (2016)
17. Parizi, R.M.: On the gamification of human-centric traceability tasks in software testing and coding. In: 2016 IEEE 14th International Conference on Software Engineering Research, Management and Applications (SERA), pp. 193–200 (2016)
18. Calderón, A., Ruiz, M., O'Connor, R.V.: ProDecAdmin: a game scenario design tool for software project management training. In: Stolfa, J., Stolfa, S., O'Connor, R.V., Messnarz, R. (eds.) EuroSPI 2017. CCIS, vol. 748, pp. 241–248. Springer, Cham (2017). https://doi.org/10.1007/978-3-319-64218-5_19
19. Su, C.-H.: The effects of students' motivation, cognitive load and learning anxiety in gamification software engineering education: a structural equation modeling study. Multimed. Tools Appl. **75**, 10013–10036 (2016)
20. Bartel, A., Hagel, G.: Gamifying the learning of design patterns in software engineering education. In: 2016 IEEE Global Engineering Education Conference (EDUCON), pp. 74–79 (2016)

21. Palacin-Silva, M.V., Seffah, A., Porras, J.: Infusing sustainability into software engineering education: lessons learned from capstone projects. J. Clean. Prod. **172**, 4338–4347 (2018)
22. Unkelos-Shpigel, N.: Peel the onion: use of collaborative and gamified tools to enhance software engineering education. In: Krogstie, J., Mouratidis, H., Su, J. (eds.) CAiSE 2016. LNBIP, vol. 249, pp. 122–128. Springer, Cham (2016). https://doi.org/10.1007/978-3-319-39564-7_13
23. García, F., Pedreira, O., Piattini, M., Cerdeira-Pena, A., Penabad, M.: A framework for gamification in software engineering. J. Syst. Softw. **132**, 21–40 (2017)
24. Pedreira, O., García, F., Brisaboa, N., Piattini, M.: Gamification in software engineering – a systematic mapping. Inf. Softw. Technol. **57**, 157–168 (2015)
25. Hernández, L., Muñoz, M., Mejia, J., Peña, A.: Gamification in software engineering teamworks: a systematic literature review. In: 2016 International Conference on Software Process Improvement (CIMPS), pp. 1–8 (2016)
26. Kosa, M., Yilmaz, M., O'Connor, R., Clarke, P.: Software engineering education and games: a systematic literature review. J. Univers. Comput. Sci. **22**, 1558–1574 (2016)
27. Herranz, E., Colomo-Palacios, R., Amescua-Seco, A.: Towards a new approach to supporting top managers in SPI organizational change management. Procedia Technol. **9**, 129–138 (2013)
28. Ries, E.: The lean startup: how today's entrepreneurs use continuous innovation to create radically successful businesses. Crown Business (2011)
29. Doran, G.T.: There'sa SMART way to write management's goals and objectives. Manag. Rev. **70**, 35–36 (1981)
30. Basili, V.R.: Software modeling and measurement: the Goal/Question/Metric paradigm (1992)
31. Ryan, R.M., Koestner, R., Deci, E.L.: Ego-involved persistence: when free-choice behavior is not intrinsically motivated. Motiv. Emot. **15**, 185–205 (1991)
32. Richardson, A.: Using customer journey maps to improve customer experience. Harv. Bus. Rev. **15**, 2–5 (2010)
33. Baddoo, N., Hall, T.: Motivators of software process improvement: an analysis of practitioners' views. J. Syst. Softw. **62**, 85–96 (2002)
34. Baddoo, N., Hall, T.: De-motivators for software process improvement: an analysis of practitioners' views. J. Syst. Softw. **66**, 23–33 (2003)
35. Bartle, R.: Hearts, clubs, diamonds, spades: players who suit MUDs. J. MUD Res. **1**, 19 (1996)
36. Pries-Heje, J., Johansen, J., et al.: SPI manifesto. Eur. Syst. Softw. Process Improv. Innov. (2010). http://www.iscn.com/Images/SPI_Manifesto_A.1.2.2010.pdf
37. Casado-Lumbreras, C., Colomo-Palacios, R., Gomez-Berbis, J.M., Garcia-Crespo, A.: Mentoring programmes: a study of the Spanish software industry. Int. J. Learn. Intellect. Cap. **6**, 293–302 (2009)
38. Colomo-Palacios, R., Casado-Lumbreras, C., Misra, S., Soto-Acosta, P.: Career abandonment intentions among software workers. Hum. Factors Ergon. Manuf. Serv. Ind. **24**, 641–655 (2014)
39. Kuhrmann, M., Diebold, P., Münch, J.: Software process improvement: a systematic mapping study on the state of the art. PeerJ Comput. Sci. **2**, e62 (2016)
40. Sulayman, M., Urquhart, C., Mendes, E., Seidel, S.: Software process improvement success factors for small and medium web companies: a qualitative study. Inf. Softw. Technol. **54**, 479–500 (2012)
41. Hamari, J., Koivisto, J., Sarsa, H.: Does gamification work? – a literature review of empirical studies on gamification. In: 2014 47th Hawaii International Conference on System Sciences (HICSS), pp. 3025–3034 (2014)

42. Zichermann, G., Linder, J.: The Gamification Revolution: How Leaders Leverage Game Mechanics to Crush the Competition. McGraw Hill Professional, New York (2013)
43. Marczewski, A.: Even Ninja Monkeys Like to Play. Gamified UK, New Haw (2015)
44. Pries-Heje, J., Christiansen, M., Johansen, J., Korsaa, M.: The ImprovAbility TM model. Proj. Profits **7**, 20–29 (2007)
45. Kotter, J.P.: Leading change: why transformation efforts fail. IEEE Eng. Manag. Rev. **25**, 34–40 (1997)

Gamification to Identify Software Development Team Members' Profiles

Mirna Muñoz[1(✉)], Adriana Peña[2], Jezreel Mejia[1], Gloria Piedad Gasca-Hurtado[3], Maria Clara Gómez-Álvarez[3], and Luis Hernández[1]

[1] Unidad Zacatecas, Centro de Investigación en Matemáticas, Parque Quantum, Ciudad del Conocimiento. Av. Lassec, andador Galileo Galilei, Manzana 3, Lote 7, 98160 Zacatecas, México
{mirna.munoz, jmejia, luis.hernandez}@cimat.mx

[2] CUCEI, Universidad de Guadalajara, Blvd. Marcelino García Barragán 1421, 44430 Guadalajara, Jalisco, Mexico
adriana.pena@cucei.udg.mx

[3] Maestría en Ingeniería de Software, Facultad de Ingeniería, Universidad de Medellín, Carrera 87 No. 30-65, Medellín, Colombia
{gpgasca, mcgomez}@udem.edu.co

Abstract. Nowadays, the software development means teamwork, in both industry and academia. Because of the soft skills and knowledge that each team member brings to the team, for high performance teams, the human factor turns out to be a key element. Therefore, building a well-structured team implies to consider its members' individualities, which will compose the coexistence that will directly impact the team. In order to observe collaboration in a similar to real life situation, in this paper we propose the use of a contraption based on the Rube Goldberg machine to gamify the identification of software development team roles focusing on knowledge, skills and interactive styles toward the integration of high performance teams. A virtual reality tool was developed to provide an attractive way to support the integration of high performance teams for software engineering. This paper includes both the description of the virtual environment and the first results of implementing it. The first results show that after using the virtual environment the teams obtained better performance.

Keywords: Gamification · Software engineering · Teamwork
Collaborative work

1 Introduction

Nowadays, software development has become a teamwork job; a task that does not imply just the system programming. Diverse factors impact the team failure or success, among them, the denominated soft skills competencies [1]. For the team members to get a good coupling could take a long time, which might interfere in the project goals. In this context, significant characteristics such as personality, knowledge and skills of the members affect the team performance [2, 3].

X. Larrucea et al. (Eds.): EuroSPI 2018, CCIS 896, pp. 219–228, 2018.
https://doi.org/10.1007/978-3-319-97925-0_18

It is fundamental for the software development team members to have the soft skills that favor teamwork such as communication skills, interpersonal relations or solving problems capacity, in order to correctly achieve the assigned tasks and perform them in time for the benefit of the project goals.

Up to now, questionnaires and/or experience are typically the followed approaches for role assignment in software development teams, sometimes with not optimal results. There are few tools to build software development teams, particularly tools aimed to create a highly effective team for software engineering where gamification presents some advantages.

The term gamification is applied to the use of game elements in a not game environment, obtaining a better experience and commitment from the participants [4]. In software engineering, gamification has been applied to support certain activities' achievement and to reinforce communication for software development [5, 6]. However, there are few gamification approaches that consider the team integration. Likewise, there are few tools to support the proper role assignment for the team members of a software development team.

In this paper, we present a virtual environment as software tool proposal for properly assigning work roles in a software development team using gamification, the Rube Goldberg machine idea [7], and the Introduction Team Software Process (TSPi^{SM}) methodology [8].

The Rube Goldberg machine was designed to motivate teamwork and the problem solving among students of all ages [7]. It consists of starting with a simple action that a person launches and carries out a set of chain reactions until achieving the objective. Some examples of challenges are to cook a hamburger, turn-on or turn-off an alarm, toast a slice of bread, open an umbrella, or water a plant. The Rube Goldberg machine was here selected because creating it covers a set of phases such as planning, designing, development (implementation) and testing, phases that can be mapped to the performed activities by a software development team.

The TSP guides engineers in the creation and maintenance of self-managed software development teams, it allows engineers to set goals and commitments as well as to plan and monitor their work [9]. TSPi methodology is the academic version of TSP. It provides a set of practices and roles to be performed during the development of software in teams. TSPi provides a well-defined process that can be tailored according to the organization needs, providing a set of resources such as guidelines, templates and metrics [8]. TSP has been used in order works as base for characterize software development team roles such as in [10, 11].

Gamification elements were implemented in a virtual environment, where the profile evaluation can be conducted based on the team members' performance, knowledge, skills and interactive styles observed during the session.

The rest of the paper is organized as follows: Sect. 2 describes the related works; Sect. 3 describes the development of a tool based on the concept of the Rube Goldberg Machine; Sect. 4 shows the case study that allows the validation of the development software tool; and Sect. 5 presents the discussion, conclusions and future work.

2 Related Works

This section shows selected papers that present relevant knowledge regarding the use of gamification in teamwork.

In *a serious game to develop and assess teamwork competency* [12], the authors present a framework for the development of a serious game to evaluate team competencies. The problem addressed demonstrates to the students the consequences of the decision making within teamwork. The serious game aims to improve communication. This proposal is a fundamental theoretical approach, still not evaluated in a real situation.

In *gamiware a gamification platform for software process improvement* [13], the authors present how through a web platform the gamification concept can be applied to the development of software. The use of the platform improves the employees' participation in the software improvement processes. They aim to study the impact of this tool on motivation. They present a case study which results show an increment in the employees' participation in the software improvement processes. In *Building a virtual world for team work improvement* [14], the authors present a virtual environment design to improve soft skills. Their main goal is to explore the use of serious games to support activities such as: communication, effective cooperation, decision-making, interpretation and processing of information. The virtual environment has three scenarios with security topics. Two scenarios are used to evaluate the leadership capacity, and the third one evaluates the team self-direction. Their results show that virtual environments improve teamwork abilities, especially communication skills.

In *designing a collaborative serious game for team building using minecraft* [15], the authors design a serious game to improve soft skills such as communication, collaboration, motivation and teamwork. The proposed game consists in solving a set of puzzles, each with a higher degree of difficulty. Their results show that participants collaborate during the game, furthermore, that digital multiuser videogames motivate the trust among team members as well as the cooperative behavior.

In *games for virtual team building* [16], the authors create a set of games for construction activities in distributed virtual teams. A great number of communications does not mean a good communication; it might be an indicative of the absence of clarity in the ideas interchange. They use three types of activities: a puzzle, a tower construction, and a castle design and construction. They conclude a not proper role assignation in teams entails a negative effect in both work coordination and team development.

In *multiplayer 3D game in supporting team-building activities in a work organization* [17], the authors explore how to improve communication in the building of a team. With the purpose to support the team building in enterprises; they create the eSpace game to solve puzzles with levels to gradually integrate the team improving its communication skills. Preliminary results show that the game can be useful to build teams and evaluate leadership in enterprises, as well as to support human resources when hiring people.

Finally, *in virtual team networks: how group social capital affects team success in a massively multiplayer online game* [18], the authors create a number of models to predict team effectiveness. Their models include: variables to control the team, intergroup closures, intergroup remunerations, and leadership. According to them, a team performance is based on three factors: (1) standards to get quality instead of quantity; (2) social norms to support team members' interdependence; and (3) create learning positive experiences.

Table 1 presents a comparison of these related works focused on gamification elements, teamwork analysis and team building.

Table 1. Comparison of the related works regarding gamification elements application

Study	Gamification elements application	TWA	TB
[8]	◒ Yes (leaderboard, points system, levels, challenges)	●	○
[9]	● Yes (leaderboard, points system, badges, levels, progress bar, achievements)	◒	◔
[10]	◔ Yes (immediate feedback)	●	○
[11]	◒ Yes (points, levels)	◒	●
[12]	◔ Yes (score)	◒	◔
[13]	○ No	◒	○
[14]	○ No	●	◒

TWA = Team Work Analysis; TB = Team Building.
● = Totally addressed criterion / ◒ = Partially addressed criterion / ◔ = Eventually addressed criterion / ○ = Not addressed criterion in the study

3 Tool Development: Virtual Environment Based on the Rube Goldberg Machine

To develop the software tool based on the Rube Goldberg machine, the prototype from Valdez Gómez and Peña [19] was used following the steps of: modeling the objects; creating the scenario and associating the physics to the 3D objects; defining the gamification elements to include; constructing the virtual environment; and testing and validating of the tool.

The objects for the scenario were modeled in Blender™, and then in Unity 3D™ the scenario was created associating physics to the 3D models. Based on the results of a systematic literature review [20] and the analysis of the use of gamification elements [21], four gamification elements were selected for the tool. In Table 2 are presented in detail the four elements and how they were implemented.

Table 2. Selected gamification elements for the tool

Gamification element	Functionality	Function
Points	To show the accumulated points according to the acceptance criteria to built the Rube Goldberg machine. For example: 10 points if the team uses all the objects to construct the machine.	The accumulated points are shown in the screen with a start figure. 
Levels	The actual level is indicated. The game has three levels with different objects to construct the Rube Goldberg machine.	A label in the screen shows the game level. 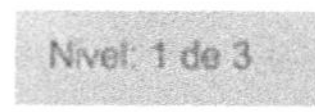
Rewards	A reward of five extra minutes is given to the participants in case they achieve the next level.	A message with the cumulated time is presented in a label on the screen. **4:15.31**
Immediate feedback	Messages with information regarding the objects are presented, and some ideas on how to construct the machine.	A message in the center of the screen is presented. In the example the message in Spanish says: "Dominoes can cause a nice chain reaction. Use them carefully" 

A game scenario of the constructed virtual environment is presented in Fig. 1.

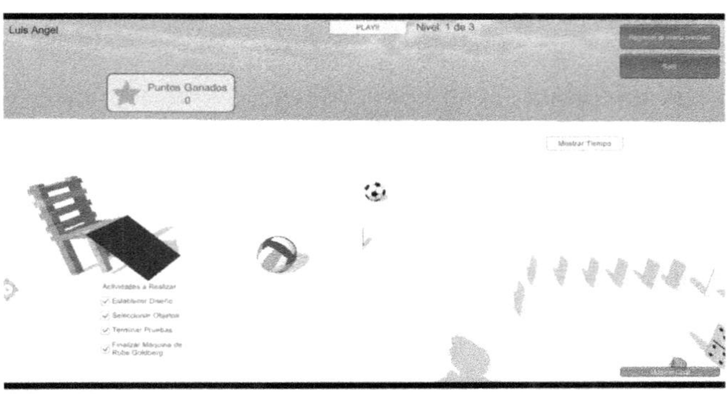

Fig. 1. Game scenario in the virtual environment

To validate the virtual environment, a case study was conducted in order to understand its performance in a real situation [22]. In the next section is presented the case study, designed accordingly to the recommended steps by Yin [22] and Runenson and Höst [23].

4 Case Study

4.1 Case Study Design

(a) *Objective:* to evaluate the virtual environment's viability for the identification of roles for development software teams, using the main five roles in TSPi [8]: (1) leader team, (2) development manager, (3) implementation manager, (4) quality and process manager, and (5) test manager.
(b) *Participants:* eight students participated, forming two teams of four members. All the participants are graduate students of the Software Engineering Master, and they had experience working in teams and with team roles.
(c) Research questions are the following 4: Q1. Are the methods to assign roles in a team appropriate?; Q2. Does this tool facilitate the role identification of the members of a development team?; Q3. Is the assignation method to assign roles using the designed tool adequate?; and Q4 Is the usability level of the tool acceptable for the user?
(d) *Data collection:* The data was collected through a Google forms questionnaire. It was collected in a three step process.

   - Step 1: Collect data of quantity and quality, in an initial common activity performed by teams in which the team members assign the roles by themselves.
   - Step 2: Collect data of the behavior of each team member focused on a set of interactive styles such as making decisions, ambiguity tolerance, frustration tolerance, achievement or persistency, dependence on signals, impulsivity, curiosity, tendency to risk, and conflict resolution.
   - Step 3: Collect data of quantity and quality, in a second common activity performed by teams in which team roles were assigned according to the results of the role analysis in Step 2.

4.2 Case Study Execution

The next five activities followed in the case study:

1. Tool presentation: the virtual environment was presented to the two teams as well as the goal of the case study.
2. First common activity: the team was asked to assemble as much paper-ships as they could, following the instruction as in [24]. For this activity, the team members assigned roles by themselves. The quality and quantity of the paper-ships developed by the team was registered.

3. Tool interaction: the team uses the virtual environment to generate a Rube Goldberg machine.
4. Role analysis: During this session with the tool, two experts in the topic analyze the team members' interactive styles. It is important to mention that there is a previous mapping of the interactive styles and the TSPi roles (see insert name of authors [24] for details). According to the analysis, the experts assigned a role for each member, in such a way, that some of the team members' roles were changed.
5. Second common activity: similar to the first common activity, the team was asked to assemble paper-ships with the new role assignment. The quality and quantity of the paper-ships developed by the team was also registered.

4.3 Results

The results were analyzed based on teams' performance regarding on how much paper-ships they could make and the paper-ships quality in four phases as follows:

- In phase 1 and 2, they had 5 min to assemble as much paper-ships as they could by following a set of instructions.
- In phase 3 and 4, they had 15 min to assemble as much paper-ships as they could by following a set of instructions, but they should include more details to the paper-ships such as draws and colors.

Results of the first team (01) are shown in Table 3. In this table the results of the first activity (without role assignment) can be compared with the results of the second activity (with assigned roles). In activity one, it can be observed that the greater number of errors was in phase 3 and the less number of errors was in phase 4, the total number of errors was 83 for the first activity.

In the second activity, the higher number of errors was in phase 3, same as in the first activity, and the phase with fewer errors was in phase 1. However, when the second activity was finished the number of errors was 23, a smaller amount of errors compared with the first activity with a difference of 60 errors.

Table 3. Team 01 results

Team 01	First activity (without role assignation)	Second activity (after role assignment)	Errors differences	Elapsed time
Phase	Errors by phase	Errors by phase		
Phase 1	13	2	11	5 min
Phase 2	25	7	18	5 min
Phase 3	34	10	24	15 min
Phase 4	11	4	7	15 min
Total of errors by activity	83	23	60	–

In Table 4 the second team (02) results are presented. A comparison between the first activity (without role assignation) and the second activity (with role assignment) is shown. Results show the phase 3 as the one with more errors and phase 4 with fewer errors. The total of errors in the first activity is 72. However, at the end of the second activity the number of errors is 33, a difference of 39 errors between the first and the second activity.

Table 4. Team 02 results

Team 02	First activity (without role assignation)	Second activity (after role assignment)	Errors differences	Elapsed time
Phase	Errors by phase	Errors by phase		
Phase 1	10	7	3	5 min
Phase 2	25	12	13	5 min
Phase 3	33	12	21	15 min
Phase 4	4	2	2	15 min
Total of errors by activity	72	33	39	–

5 Discussion and Conclusions

Nowadays, the application of gamification in diverse areas is increasing and the software engineering area is not the exception. However, there are a number of factors to consider when selecting gamification elements like the implementation environment, how to apply them and the target users, because of that the gamification element can vary based on the established goals.

In this paper we proposed a software tool to identify the roles for a software development team based on gamification using an attractive way such as a virtual environment, in which a combination of two or more elements were used to achieve the expected results.

It is worth to mention that the proposed tool facilitates the role identification in a manual way, that is to say, a person that analyses the team members' behavior during the game session is required to assign a proper role. However, these activities are easy to recognize through the traceability to the software development activities to the activities in the tool.

With the support of a comparative of the related works, it can be concluded that there are very few studies to determine the suitable role for a person supported by a gamification approach like the one here presented.

References

1. Matturro, G., Raschetti, F., Fontán, C.: Soft skills in software development teams: a survey of the points of view of team leaders and team members. In: Proceedings - 8th International Workshop on Cooperative and Human Aspects of Software Engineering, CHASE 2015, pp. 101–104 (2015). https://doi.org/10.1109/CHASE.2015.30
2. Dorling, A., McCaffery, F.: The gamification of SPICE. In: Mas, A., Mesquida, A., Rout, T., O'Connor, R.V., Dorling, A. (eds.) SPICE 2012. CCIS, vol. 290. Springer, Heidelberg (2012). https://doi.org/10.1007/978-3-642-30439-2_35
3. Yilmaz, M., O'Connor, R.V., Colomo-Palacios, R., Clarke, P.: An examination of personality traits and how they impact on software development teams. Inf. Soft. Tech. **86**, 101–122 (2017)
4. Korn, O., Funk, M., Schmidt, A.: Towards a gamification of industrial production. A comparative study in sheltered work environments. In: Present at 7th ACM SIGCHI Symposium on Engineering Interactive Computing Systems (2015). http://dx.doi.org/10.1145/2774225.2774834
5. Berkling, K.: Gamification behind the scenes. In: Zvacek, S., Restivo, M.T., Uhomoibhi, J., Helfert, M. (eds.) CSEDU 2015. CCIS, vol. 583, pp. 274–292. Springer, Cham (2016). https://doi.org/10.1007/978-3-319-29585-5_16
6. Akpolat, B.S., Slany, W.: Enhancing software engineering student team engagement in a high-intensity extreme programming course using gamification. Presented at Conference on Software Engineering Education and Training (CSEE&T) (2014). http://dx.doi.org/10.1109/CSEET.2014.6816792
7. Rube Goldberg, I.: Rube Goldberg Machine Contest ® 2016 Official Rule Book, July 2015, pp. 1–19 (2016)
8. Humphrey, W.S.: Introduction to the Team Software Process. Addison-Wesley, Reading (2006)
9. Hernández-López, A., Colomo-Palacios, R., García-Crespo, A., Soto-Acosta, P.: Team software process in GSD teams: a study of new work practices and models. Int. J. Hum. Cap. Inf. Tech. Prof. **1**(3), 32–53 (2010)
10. Colomo-Palacios, R., González-Carrasco, I., López-Cuadrado, J.L., Trigo Ribeiro, A., Varajao, J.: I-COMPETERE: using applied intelligence in search of competency gaps in software project managers. Inf. Syst. Front. **16**(4), 607–625 (2014)
11. Ruano-Mayoral, M., Colomo-Palacios, R., García-Crespo, A., Gómez-Berbís, J.M.: Software project managers under the team software process: a study of competences based on literature. Int. J. Inf. Tech. Proj. Manag. **1**(1), 42–53 (2010)
12. Guenaga, M., Eguiluz, A., Rayon, A., Nunez, A., Quevedo, E.: A serious game to develop and assess teamwork competency. In: 2014 International Symposium on Computers in Education, SIIE 2014, pp. 183–188 (2014). https://doi.org/10.1109/SIIE.2014.7017727
13. Herranz, E., Colomo-Palacios, R., de Amescua Seco, A.: Gamiware: a gamification platform for software process improvement. In: O'Connor, R., Umay Akkaya, M., Kemaneci, K., Yilmaz, M., Poth, A., Messnarz, R. (eds.) EuroSPI 2015. CCIS, vol. 543. Springer, Cham (2015). https://doi.org/10.1007/978-3-319-24647-5_11
14. Lukosch, H., van Nuland, B., van Ruijven, T., van Veen, L., Verbraeck, A.: Building a virtual world for team work improvement. In: Meijer, S.A., Smeds, R. (eds.) ISAGA 2013. LNCS, vol. 8264, pp. 60–68. Springer, Cham (2014). https://doi.org/10.1007/978-3-319-04954-0_8

15. Wendel, V., Gutjahr, M., Battenberg, P.: Designing a collaborative serious game for Team building using minecraft, pp. 569–578, October, 2013. Retrieved from http://search.proquest.com/openview/f11c9d6e0d896ca4a090c285fc678ce7/1?pq-origsite=gscholar
16. Ellis, J.B., Luther, K., Bessiere, K., Kellogg, W. A.: Games for virtual team building. In: Proceedings of the 7th ACM Conference on Designing Interactive Systems - DIS 2008, pp. 295–304 (2008). https://doi.org/10.1145/1394445.1394477
17. Häkkinen, P., Bluemink, J., Juntunen, M., Laakkonen, I.: Multiplayer 3D game in supporting team-building activities in a work organization. In: Proceedings of the 12th IEEE International Conference on Advanced Learning Technologies, ICALT 2012, pp. 430–432 (2012). https://doi.org/10.1109/ICALT.2012.242
18. Benefield, G.A., Shen, C., Leavitt, A.: Virtual team networks: how group social capital affects team success in a massively multiplayer online game. In: Proceedings of the 19th ACM Conference on Computer-Supported Cooperative Work & Social Computing - CSCW 2016, pp. 677–688 (2016). https://doi.org/10.1145/2818048.2819935
19. Valdez Gómez, E., Peña, A.: Development of a virtual prototype of 3D collaborative virtual environment for analyzing the users interaction/Desarrollo de un prototipo de entorno virtual colaborativo 3D para el estudio de la interacción entre usuarios. Universidad de Guadalajara (2014)
20. Hernández, L., Muñoz, M., Mejía, J., Peña, A., Rangel, N., Torres, C.: A systematic literature review focused on the use of gamification in software engineering teamworks. Revista Ibérica de Sistemas y Tecnologías de Información, RISTI, No. 21, pp. 33–50, March 2017. https://doi.org/10.17013/risti.21.33-50
21. Muñoz, M., Hernández, L., Mejia, J., Gasca-Hurtado, G.P., Gómez-Alvarez, M.C.: State of the use of gamification elements in software development teams. In: Stolfa, J., Stolfa, S., O'Connor, R.V., Messnarz, R. (eds.) EuroSPI 2017. CCIS, vol. 748, pp. 249–258. Springer, Cham (2017). https://doi.org/10.1007/978-3-319-64218-5_20
22. Yin, R.K.: Case Study Research. Design and Methods. SAGE Publications, Beverley Hills (2003). https://doi.org/10.1097/FCH.0b013e31822dda9e
23. Runeson, P., Höst, M.: Guidelines for conducting and reporting case study research in software engineering. Empir. Soft. Eng. **14**(2), 131–164 (2009). https://doi.org/10.1007/s10664-008-9102-8
24. Gasca-Hurtado, G.P., Gómez-Alvarez, M.C., Muñoz, M., Mejía, J.: Gamification proposal for defect tracking in software development process. In: Kreiner, C., O'Connor, R.V., Poth, A., Messnarz, R. (eds.) EuroSPI 2016. CCIS, vol. 633, pp. 212–224. Springer, Cham (2016). https://doi.org/10.1007/978-3-319-44817-6_17

Towards a Standard to Describe and Classify Serious Games as Learning Resources for Software Project Management

Alejandro Calderón[1(✉)], Manuel Trinidad[1], Mercedes Ruiz[1], and Rory V. O'Connor[2]

[1] University of Cádiz, Cádiz, Spain
{alejandro.calderon,manuel.trinidad,mercedes.ruiz}@uca.es
[2] Dublin City University, Dublin, Ireland
rory.oconnor@dcu.ie

Abstract. In recent years, there have been an increasing number of new serious games in many fields such as health, science, government and education. It is desirable to describe and classify these new serious games as learning resources with the aim to facilitate its use in education and integration in the learning process. The goal of this work is to analyze a commonly used evaluation method to describe, classify and assess the suitability of serious games for use in software project management education. As a proof of concept, we have applied the proposed evaluation method to assess and analyze the strengths and weaknesses of a serious game regarding its pedagogical, playful and technical features. The outcomes of the evaluation have allowed us to identify the main features needed to design an evaluation method to describe, classify and assess the ability of serious games to be used in software project management education.

Keywords: Assessment · Serious game · Learning tool · Education Software engineering · Software project management · Classification

1 Introduction

The motivation of providing more effective learning resources for supporting Software Project Management (SPM), software process standards, software process, and, generally, Software Engineering education have led to a significant increase in the design and use of Serious Games (SGs) [1, 2]. SGs are learning tools designed for purposes other than mere fun or entertainment that allow participants to experiment, learn from their own mistakes and acquire experience, in a safe way within risk environments [3]. Advances in technology have allowed the development of SGs on several platforms that provide access and give a meaningful and educational value to the use of mobile phones, game consoles, media players and other devices which are devices that have become an important part of our daily life. Therefore, more specific evaluation methods for assessing the educational effectiveness of SGs are needed.

By focusing on the software engineering domain, many new learning resources with different features and objectives can be identified. This causes university and

X. Larrucea et al. (Eds.): EuroSPI 2018, CCIS 896, pp. 229–239, 2018.
https://doi.org/10.1007/978-3-319-97925-0_19

industrial trainers to search, analyze, use and evaluate different scenarios to be applied in their courses. As a result, trainers need to invest a significant amount of time during the process of selecting the best learning resource to satisfy their objectives. In addition, they may not be able to perform the decision making when information is missing or insufficient. Therefore, there are possibilities that they will ignore learning tools that could be the best option to supporting their teaching.

As Hendrix stated [4], there is a need of a standard to describe and classify SGs as learning resources, with the aim to facilitate their location, evaluation and use in education. This would contribute to support the integration of SGs in the learning process, as [5, 6] show in their proposals. Moreover, the creation of tools for describing and classifying SGs as learning resources allows trainers to identify and reuse the best SGs to be used in their subjects, to reduce time consuming in their selection and to take advantages of all the features of SGs [7, 8].

Based on the foregoing motivation, we can identify a number of studies in the literature whose aim is to provide an evaluation method to assess and classify SGs for use in the educational field [5, 7]. However, the evaluation methods currently available based their evaluation on a set of features that none of them allow to evaluate the particularities of the SPM field, where the majority of SGs are based on simulation techniques and teach specific concepts, practices or processes of SPM. Hence, it is also important to have an evaluation method in the field of SPM in particular, to support the evaluation and classification of SGs. For that reason, in this work, we analyze an existing evaluation method to assess SGs for use in the educational field [5] and show an example of its application to the evaluation of a SG, called ProDec [9]. Our proposal is to discuss the suitability of the evaluation method to assess the quality of SGs intended to be used in software engineering education with the aim of providing a procedure to classify the SGs within this scope, according to their complexity and capability to teach in the different processes of the SPM.

The structure of the paper is as follows: Sect. 2 shows the works related to our proposal; Sect. 3 briefly describes the evaluation method of SGs for education; in Sect. 4, we provide the results of applying the evaluation method to ProDec, a simulation-based SG to teach SPM; Sect. 5 discusses the suitability of the evaluation method to assess the quality of SGs for SPM education. Finally, Sect. 6 summarizes the paper and presents our conclusions.

2 Related Works

Even though, the number of contributions of SGs for software engineering, in general, and SPM, in particular, is growing, there is a lack of proposals to classify SGs and assess their suitability as learning resources. Indeed, recent systematic literature reviews related to SGs evaluation in the scope of software engineering or SPM describe proposals focused on assessing mainly the SGs educational effectiveness and enjoyability [10–13]. The analysis of the related works of SGs evaluation for SPM education shows that there is not a formal evaluation proposal that allows to describe SGs and to assess their suitability as a learning resource within SPM education.

During the searches performed for one of our previous work on SGs evaluation [13], we identified an evaluation method proposed by El Borji and Khaldi, which evaluates the quality of SGs intended to be used in the educational field [5]. This evaluation method is based on SG-LOM, a method for describing SGs as learning resources that takes into account the specification of the LOM (Learning Object Metadata) standards [7]. This method is designed as an evaluation and analysis GRID to assess the educational, technical and playful features of SGs in order to define the items for their selection and integration in education (see Sect. 3). However, the features evaluated by this method do not allow the evaluation and classification of SGs for education according to the particularities of SPM field such as the concepts, practices or processes of SPM that the SGs are able to teach. Hence, this is a general evaluation method that establishes a common core of features to describe any SG but does not focus on SPM education.

We can conclude that not only is the educational effectiveness evaluation of SGs needed, but also a deeper analysis of their features to promote and facilitate their integration and use in SPM education as learning resources, should be explored. For these reasons, we have analyzed the evaluation method proposed by [5] to assess and classify SGs as learning resources for use in education, with the goal of providing an initial set of features that allow to describe SPM SGs and, therefore, extend this evaluation method to describe and classify SGs as learning resources for SPM.

3 Evaluation Method

The evaluation method proposed by El Borji and Khaldi in [5] was developed as an evaluation and analysis GRID. This GRID evaluates the educational, technical and playful features of SGs in order to define the items for their selection and integration in education. The GRID is divided into 4 sections that, at the same time, each section is defined by a set of items. It is composed of 36 items in order to identify the relevance information and evaluate the educational, technical and playful features of SGs. Each item of the GRID is evaluated through a scoring system based on 5-point Likert Scale [14], where a value of 0 means total disagreement with the statement and a value of 5 means total agreement with the statement, that allows to make two types of evaluation at the same time: an overall and specific evaluation.

In the overall evaluation, the GRID allows to analyze and evaluate the suitability of a SG in an educational context. The SG evaluated with the GRID can achieve a score ranging from 0 to 130 that helps to classify it into one of the following quality levels: Substandard, Average, Superior, or Very Superior [5]. Figure 1 shows the information about the analysis of the score rating obtained and the quality level that a SG can be accomplished when is evaluated with the GRID. On the other hand, the evaluation and analysis of each section provide a specific evaluation of the features of the SGs that allows to find and observe the strengths and weaknesses of the SG. For assessing each section, we only need to divide the sum of the scores achieved on the total score of the section. The total score of a section is calculated by multiplying the number of items of the section by the highest Likert Scale value, that is, 5 (see Fig. 2). Based on the score obtained in each section, we can analyze the pedagogical, playful and technical sections independently of the overall evaluation.

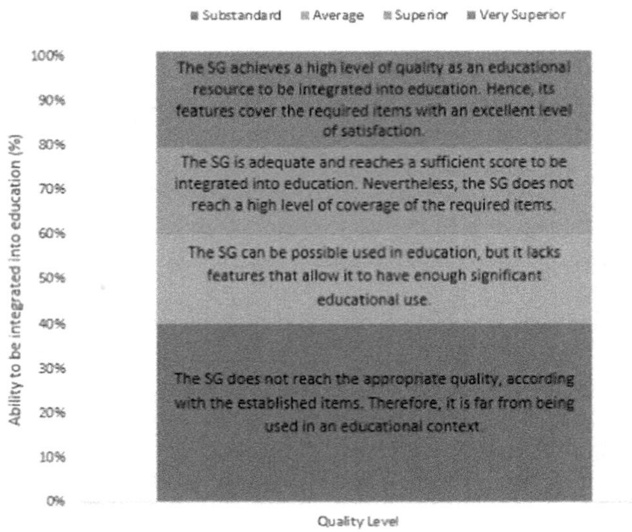

Fig. 1. Relation between the score rating obtained and the quality level reached.

4 ProDec's Evaluation

This section shows an example of applying the GRID to assess a SG intended to be used in SPM education called ProDec [9]. ProDec is a simulation-based SG that helps learners to acquire practical experience in a virtual organization where they can manage software projects and solve real-life problems in a risk-free environment, and trainers in the tracking and assessing the knowledge and skills that learners must acquire by playing the game. This evaluation has been performed by the authors of the SG who are experts in the features and design of the SG. Nevertheless, in order to address possible threats to this evaluation, the outcomes of the evaluation have been exposed to three university professors (n = 3) that had experience in the use of ProDec as learning resource within SPM courses.

4.1 Serious Game Identification

The first step when using GRID is to perform the SG Identification. Thus, in this section, we identify the general features of ProDec. As we have commented above, ProDec is a simulation-based SG to teach SPM. Table 1 shows the information required by the GRID [5].

Table 1. Serious game identification (ProDec).

Serious game identification	
Name of the game	ProDec
Game developer	Alejandro Calderón & Mercedes Ruiz (University of Cádiz)
Game Type	Software Project Management game
Game genre	Simulation
Age group Or ESRB rating	No age
Game experience required	Beginner
Game license	Proprietary software
Description	ProDec (Project Decision), simulation-based serious game for SPM education, where the goal is to successfully manage a software project
Language	English
Keywords	Software project management, simulation, decision-making

Regarding age group, ProDec is a game suitable for all ages, as it has no adult themes or strong language. ProDec is a game intended to be used in advanced stages of an SPM course, it does not teach learners the basic principles of SPM, so, before playing, the players need to acquire these principles in lectures. For this reason, ProDec requires that players have at least a basic knowledge about SPM concepts and techniques.

4.2 Evaluation of the Specific Sections

Once we have identified the general features of the SG, the second step is to evaluate the pedagogical, playful and technical specifications of the SG. As an example of applying the assessment GRID to ProDec, Tables 2, 3 and 4 show the items related to the pedagogical, playful and technical specifications sections and the score achieved by ProDec in each item. In addition, Table 4 presents a brief summary of the SG features that support the rating.

Table 2. Results of the evaluation of the pedagogical specifications of ProDec

Pedagogical specifications		
Items		Rating (score/5)
Strategies	Specification of objectives	4
	Existing knowledge and representations	4
	Pedagogical Approach	5
	Ability to adapt to each learner profile	4
Assessment method	Assessment procedure	4
	Progress indicator	5
	Player Tracking	4
	Presence of tutor	3
	Assessment Type	3

Table 3. Results of the evaluation of the playful specifications of ProDec

Playful specifications		
Items		Rating (score/5)
Attractiveness (fun)	Motivation	4
	Immersion	3
	Interactivity	4
	Emotion	3
	Gameplay	5
Playability aspects	Replayability	5
	Multiplayer value	3

Table 4. Evaluation of the technical specifications of ProDec

Technical specifications			
Items		Rating (score/5)	Evaluation factors
Technical efficiency	Graphics	3	The graphics of the SG, although fictitious, are suitable for the scope of the game. The graphical aspects are consistent and immerse players in the game environment with no abrupt changes along the three applications that make up the game. However, its simplicity is limited by the constraints of the simulation software
	Dialogues and sound	2	The game only incorporates sounds when an alert or mistake message occurs, because it is not a game where music has special relevance to immerse players in the playing environment. Dialogues are scarce but concise and they are shown to players by text, informing and warning of events that occur along the execution of the gameplay
	Browsing and design	4	The game design facilitates players to browse the different screens of the SG, thus, allowing players to progress in an easy way through the different stages of the game. At the same time, the browsing and design of the game help players to find all the needed information at any time and offer ease of use
Requirements	Install requirements	5	The game provides a software for install/uninstall and installation/setup tutorial that specifies, in detail, all the steps to carry out the correct installation and start-up of the game
	System Requirements	2	ProDec runs on Anylogic®, therefore, it is necessary to count with a license. Thus, the system requirements of ProDec are basically limited by the requirements of AnyLogic®
	Guide and Instructions	3	The game provides several tutorials for learners and trainers that can be consulted in any time. At the same time, the game offers information to facilitate its correct use and helps players in some scenarios during the progress of the gameplay

4.3 Results

After applying the GRID on ProDec, the results of the evaluation show an overall score of 100 out of 130, which means that ProDec has achieved 77% of items. According to the quality levels of the assessment GRID (see Fig. 1), the obtained percentage reflects a superior quality level of the SG, this means that the game is adequate and sufficient for educational use, however, there are still glitches that need to be improved where there are less coverage of items for obtaining a higher level of quality.

Considering the evaluation of each section, ProDec reaches more than 60% in all the sections (see Fig. 2). Therefore, we can conclude ProDec takes into account all the elements needed to be a learning tool for education, being the pedagogical and playful specifications its main strengths and the technical specifications, the section where it has more weaknesses.

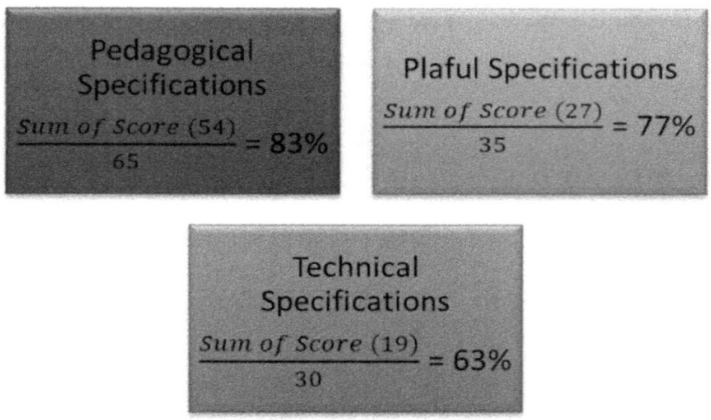

Fig. 2. Results per section of the GRID application

Taking into account the results of the overall and the specific evaluation of the SG, ProDec presents an adequate level of features related to the pedagogical specifications such as the content and the evaluation method, and offers a sufficient coverage of playful items to keep learner's attention. Therefore, potential users can observe that ProDec can be an adequate learning resource to be used in an educational context, although they need to pay attention to the SG technical aspects, in order to use it properly.

On the other hand, from the point of view of the SG's authors, the results of the evaluation help them to analyze the strengths and weaknesses of ProDec as a learning resource regarding the pedagogical, playful and technical specifications.

5 Discussion

The GRID proposed by El Borji and Khaldi [5] establishes the basis for evaluating the suitability of the SGs to be used in education. However, for this to be applied in teaching SPM, information provided in the GRID is insufficient for selecting the most suitable SG to be integrated into a specific SPM course. Hence, we decided to analyze the GRID in order to identify their weaknesses for collecting useful information about SGs for teaching SPM. This is with the intention of facilitating the selection process of a SG intended to be used in teaching SPM.

The analysis of the features of SGs for SPM education by [15] and analysis of other SPM-related SGs such as DELIVER! [16], or Go for it! [17], helped us to collect an overall view of the main features highlighted by the authors of these games when they introduced their SGs and compared their proposals with others. Moreover, in a previous work [18], we analyzed and compared the main features of SGs for teaching SPM with the goal of observing the advantages and disadvantages of this kind of education resources intended to be used in SPM education field, as part of a process to design a new SG that will be able to overcome the deficiencies discovered. The results of these studies allows us to discuss the quality of the GRID in an SPM educational context in order to provide ideas for the identification of a set of specific features to extend it. These features are based on the main features that authors use to identify, define, design and compare their SGs for teaching SPM and are commented in the following sub-sections.

5.1 Computational Simulation

In SPM, where bringing real-life to the course is a challenge, the use of simulation-based SGs can be adequate to add realism to the game scenarios. Besides, it allows learners to acquire knowledge in real-life scenarios, in a risk-free environment. There are two ways to use simulation in a learning environment: role-play simulations and computational simulations.

In the case that the SG is based on role-play simulations, the analyzed GRID provides the Game Genre item in the SG identification section. Nevertheless, the GRID does not provide any item to describe computational-simulation SG, a type of resource frequently uses in SPM education. For example, ProDec uses discrete-event simulation models to simulate the execution of a project plan scenario. This information is not directly collected by the GRID. For this reason, we consider that a new field to identify the computational simulations features of a SG is needed.

5.2 Automatic Evaluation

In SPM, learners need to take into account an extensive amount of information during the whole project lifecycle and they need to analyze the information on the project and make decisions continuously. A SG that allows automatic evaluation helps trainers to analyze and assess all the actions performed by learners during the game play, and also helps learners to get instant feedback on their performance, helping them, at the same time, to improve their knowledge during the game play.

Considering the pedagogical specifications related to the evaluation features, the analyzed GRID provides several items to evaluate the features of the SGs related to the process of gathering and analyzing information from multiple sources to assess learners. However, the GRID does not include any item to evaluate the level to which the game helps trainers to assess the learners automatically.

For instance, ProDec is able to perform the learners' assessment by analyzing the information recorded during the game play and applying the evaluation items set by the instructor in an automatic way, generating, as a result, a detailed assessment report that describes the skills acquired by the learners. Through the GRID we can assess the evaluation procedure that ProDec follows but not if the SG performs the evaluation in an automatic way.

5.3 SPM Specifications

Regarding the SPM specifications, the GRID provides some items to reflect the scope of the SGs and their objectives, but it does not include items to identify indeed the practices, concepts and processes that the SG is able to teach, as well as the covered learning objectives.

For example, ProDec is a simulation-based SG for SPM education that allows learning along the whole project lifecycle, helping to understand the group of processes of a project lifecycle from the initiation stage to the closing stage. Moreover, ProDec is able to cover at least six out of ten of the knowledge areas defined by the PMBOK, takes contact with seven of the ten subject groups of the ISO 21500 standard, covers 19 tasks of the 26 tasks that the ISO/IEC 29110 standard defines for the Project Management process of the Basic profile, and covers 33 out of 43 processes of the ISO/IEC 12207 software lifecycle process standard. Through the GRID, we can collect the general training purposes but there are not items to gather the specific information regarding each of the practices, concepts and processes that the SG is able to teach.

In an evaluation method for assessing and analyzing SGs to be used in SPM education, it is crucial that the method provides items to evaluate thoroughly the level of knowledge that an SG covers in relation to SPM knowledge areas, as well as, the level of coverage of the different processes and techniques proposed by well-known standards and guidelines such as ISO 21500 standard, PMBOK guidelines, or ISO/IEC 12207 standard.

5.4 Game Elements, Mechanics & Dynamics

Finally, in recent years, the design and use of gamification strategies has turned into an emerging phenomenon that has attracted the attention of trainers in order to provide a more interesting education in SPM, software process and software engineering [2, 19]. Gamification "seeks for improvement of the user's engagement, motivation, and performance when carrying out a certain task, by means of incorporating game mechanics and elements, thus making the task more attractive" [19]. One of the common practice for the application of gamification in education is the use of games as a component of the gamification strategy [20]. In that sense, it will be helpful that the evaluation method provides the necessary items to assess and identify the game elements, mechanics and dynamics that SGs implemented with the goal to facilitate trainers their integration into their learning process based on gamification strategies. For example, ProDec includes game dynamics such as emotions, narrative, or constraints, game mechanics such as challenges, chance or feedback, and game component such as teams or achievements. This information that could be useful to integrate ProDec within a gamification strategy, although it is not collected by the current features of the GRID.

6 Conclusions

Our previous research, aimed at finding an evaluation method for the educational effectiveness of SGs [13], led us to identify not only an empirical method for the educational effectiveness evaluation of SGs, but also beginning a new research line on the road to designing an evaluation method to describe, classify and evaluate the suitability of SGs as learning resources for SPM education.

The growth of new SGs for use as learning resources requires the creation of new systems to evaluate their suitability to be used in education and facilitate potential users to find them. In this paper, we analyzed an assessment GRID to evaluate the quality level of the SGs intended to be used in education [5]. For that, we have provided an example of how to apply the GRID to evaluate the suitability of a SG, ProDec, to be used as a learning resource for SPM education. Through this example, we identified several weaknesses such as the inability of El Borji's proposal [15] to describe the specific learning concepts and practices that a SPM SG is able to train, to collect specific information related to the computational techniques, and to identify the game elements, mechanics and dynamics involved in a SG. The identified weaknesses need to take into consideration in order to extend the analyzed GRID or design a new evaluation method for describing, classifying and evaluating the suitability of SGs as learning resources for SPM education.

Our intention with this work is to provide an initial platform from which the design of an evaluation tool which helps trainers in the selection process of a SG for their SPM courses and to promote the necessity of tools and standards, which allow describing, classifying and evaluating the learning resources for education, specifically for SPM education. This is to facilitate their use, reuse and integration within the learning syllabus. The next step, in this research scope, is to consider the outcomes of the analysis of the assessment GRID with the goal of defining new items to extend the analyzed GRID to the scope of SPM education or creating from scratch a new evaluation method that deals with this issue, at the same time, designing the basis and guidelines to provide a standard to evaluate SGs in this scope. Therefore, research effort should be aimed at the evaluation of SGs not only in terms of their educational effectiveness but also as learning resources is relevant and challenging.

Acknowledgments. This work has been carried out during a post-doctoral contract, funded by the Program of Promotion and Impulse of Research and Transfer at the University of Cádiz 2018–2019 and a pre-doctoral contract for the training of research personnel, funded by the University of Cádiz through the University Research and Transfer Plan (UCA/REC01VI/2017). This work was funded by the Spanish National Research Agency (AEI) with ERDF funds under projects BadgePeople (TIN2016-76956-C3-3-R) and the Andalusian Plan for Research, Development and Innovation (grant TIC-195).

References

1. Djaouti, D., Alvarez, J., Jessel, J.-P.: Classifying serious games: the G/P/S model. In: Felicia, P. (ed.) Handbook of Research on Improving Learning and Motivation through Educational Games: Multidisciplinary Approaches, pp. 118–136. Hershey, Derry Township (2011)
2. Kosa, M., Yilmaz, M., O'Connor, R., Clarke, P.: Software engineering education and games: a systematic literature review. J. Univ. Comput. Sci. **22**(12), 1558–1574 (2016)
3. Abt, C.: Serious Games. University Press of America, Lanham (2002)
4. Hendrix, M., et al.: Defining a metadata schema for serious games as learning objects. In: eLmL 2012 - The 4th International Conference on Mobile, Hybrid, and On-line Learning, Valencia, Spain (2012)
5. El Borji, Y., Khaldi, M.: Comparative study to develop a tool for the quality assessment of serious games intended to be used in education. Int. J. Emerg. Technol. Learn. (iJET) **9**(9), 50–55 (2014)
6. Aouadi, N., Pernelle, P., Marty, J.-C., Carron, T.: A model driven architecture MDA approach to facilitate the serious game integration in an e-learning environment. In: European Conference on Games Based Learning (2015)
7. El Borji, Y., Khaldi, M.: An IEEE LOM application profile to describe serious games <<SG-LOM >>. Int. J. Comput. Appl. **86**(13), 1–8 (2014)
8. Aouadi, N., Pernelle, P., Amar, C.B., Carron, T.: MDA approach for reusability in serious game and e-learning design. In: International Conference on Web-Based Learning (2016)
9. Calderón, A., Ruiz, M.: ProDec: a serious game for software project management training. In: ICSEA 2013 - Proceedings of the 8th International Conference on Software Engineering Advances, Venice, Spain (2013)
10. Calderón, A., Ruiz, M., O'Connor, R.V.: A multivocal literature review on serious games for software process standards education. Comput. Stand. Interfaces **57**, 36–48 (2018)
11. Petri, G., von Wangenheim, C.G.: How games for computing education are evaluated? A systematic literature review. Comput. Educ. **107**, 68–90 (2017). http://dx.doi.org/10.1016/j.compedu.2017.01.004 (in Press, Accepted Manuscript)
12. Petri, G., von Wangenheim, C.G.: How to evaluate educational games: a systematic literature review. J. Univ. Comput. Sci. **22**(7), 992–1021 (2016)
13. Calderón, A., Ruiz, M.: A systematic literature review on serious games evaluation: an application to software project management. Comput. Educ. **87**, 396–422 (2015)
14. Likert, R.: A technique for the measurement of attitudes. Arch. Psychol. **22**(140), 55 (1932)
15. Caulfield, C., Xia, J., Veal, D., Maj, S.P.: A systematic survey of games used for software engineering education. Mod. Appl. Sci. **5**(6), 28–43 (2011)
16. Von Wangenheim, C.G., Savi, R., Borgatto, A.F.: DELIVER! – an educational game for teaching earned value management in computing courses. Inf. Softw. Technol. **54**(3), 286–298 (2012)
17. Sánchez-Gordón, M.-L., O'Connor, R.V., Colomo-Palacios, R., Sanchez-Gordon, S.: A learning tool for the ISO/IEC 29110 standard: understanding the project management of basic profile. In: International Conference on Software Process Improvement and Capability Determination (2016)
18. Calderón, A., Ruiz, M.: Bringing real-life practice in software project management training through a simulation-based serious game. In: CSEDU 2014 - Proceedings of the 6th International Conference on Computer Supported Education, Barcelona, Spain (2014a)
19. Pedreira, O., García, F., Brisaboa, N., Piattini, M.: Gamification in software engineering - a systematic mapping. Inf. Softw. Technol. **57**, 157–168 (2015)
20. Yildirim, I.: The effects of gamification-based teaching practices on student achievement and students' attitudes toward lessons. Internet High. Educ. **33**, 86–92 (2017)

Assessment Framework for Gamified Environments: A Gamification Assessment Model for Implementing the Framework

Gloria Piedad Gasca-Hurtado[1], María Clara Gómez-Alvarez[1(✉)], Mirna Muñoz[2], and Jezreel Mejía[2]

[1] Maestría en Ingeniería de Software, Facultad de Ingeniería, Universidad de Medellín, Carrera 87 No. 30-65, Medellín, Colombia
{gpgasca, mcgomez}@udem.edu.co

[2] Centro de Investigación en Matemáticas, Av. Universidad no 222, 98068 Zacatecas, Mexico
{mirna.munoz, jmejia}@cimat.mx

Abstract. Gamification is a recent strategy used in several contexts like marketing, education and public health. We implement gamification as a strategy to promote a dynamic environment in Software Process Improvement initiatives. However, there are insufficient well-established theoretical guidelines for design and assess gamified experiences. Our research is oriented to the use of a framework for assessing gamified environments, which comprises the identification and adoption of gamification principles, as well as a design method for gamified activities. This framework is a proposal for the assessment of gamified environments looking for assure that gamified experiences meet the purposes, goals, principles and elements that are defined as gamification fundamental components. In this paper, we present a gamification assessment model for implement the framework that allows to calculate the level of gamification of a gamified environment. Such model is applied in an environment called Video Scrum and allows to verify gamification level from measurement rules.

Keywords: Gamification · Software process improvement · Framework Assessment model

1 Introduction

Gamification is a recent strategy used in several contexts where the human factor is a key for the success of the different initiatives. In particular, gamification is an alternative to increase the motivation and commitment levels in work teams.

The propose of use gamification in software process improvement initiatives is achieve high levels of motivation to work with team members, integrate participants to increase technical knowledge and increase progress indicators of project teams [1]. However, the procedures and methods for creating gamified environments are useful tools but is important have mechanisms to verify the incorporation of the principles, fundamentals and gamification elements in new gamified environments. Such

X. Larrucea et al. (Eds.): EuroSPI 2018, CCIS 896, pp. 240–253, 2018.
https://doi.org/10.1007/978-3-319-97925-0_20

verification is fundamental for assure the transformation from a traditional environment to a gamified environment.

Therefore, we develop a proposal for the assessment of gamified environments for assure to meet the purposes, goals, principles and elements that are defined as gamification fundamental components [1]. Our proposal is oriented towards the definition of an assessment framework for gamified environments that comprises the identification and adoption of gamification principles, as well as a design method for gamified activities [1].

In this paper, we present a gamification assessment model for implement the framework looks for calculate the level of gamification of an environment as an indicator of the level of incorporation of gamification fundamentals in such environment. The proposed model is applied in an environment called Video Scrum.

Video Scrum is a simulation of the Scrum framework. This simulation is considered a game very effective for teaching and demonstrating main Scrum concepts.

The structure of the paper is as follows: Sect. 2 presents the main concepts which fundaments the proposal. Section 3 contains a brief description of the assessment framework proposal. Section 4 presents the gamification assessment model. Section 5 describes the application of the gamification assessment model in the case study Video Scrum and the conclusions and future work are presented in Sect. 6.

2 Background

2.1 Gamification

Gamification is a growing trend where the human factor is fundamental in terms of motivation and engagement of the work teams [2–4]. Such trend can promote in individuals' social interaction, quality and productivity of his actions [5].

Gamification can be defined as: (i) an approach that involves the same psychological experiences of the games [4]; (ii) the application of the same principles and environments of the games, regardless of expected results [2] and (iii) a process implementing motivational affordances for obtain psychological and behavioral outcomes in individuals [6–8].

The growing interest in gamification as a strategy for process improvement in organization is evident because: (i) the growth of computer game industry over the last two decades motivating individuals to play; (ii) the pervasiveness of social media and mobile and web-based technologies is changing the way how individuals interact inside organizations [9]; and (iii) organizations are continually looking new ways for influence the behavior of employees and clients.

However, there are a few well-established theoretical guidelines for design gamified experiences. This problem is the main motivation of this work oriented to propose a framework like a set of tools for: (i) create gamification environments guaranteeing the application of gamification principles and the achievement of the specific goals and, (ii) verify the accomplishment of gamification fundamentals in an existing gamified environment.

2.2 The MDE Framework

MDE Framework is an approach to design games emphasizing the need to understand games mechanics, dynamics and emotions for obtain an improvement in commitment levels from team members, employees and customers [10].

The elements of MDE framework are:

Mechanics. Are related with the designers' decisions for gamify a non-game context such as goals, rules and the guidelines that stablish the boundaries of the gamified environment. Game mechanics are known before the gamified experience begins and are the same for all game participants.
Dynamics. Is a result of how the players follow the game mechanics. In other words, game dynamics emerge during play [11]. In the case of gamified environments, the interaction of team members can lead to dynamics like cooperation, competition or conspiracy.
Emotions. Refers to the mental affective state and reactions promoted in players when they participate in a gamified environment. In this sense, the main goal for gamification is create the player enjoyment for guaranteeing the continuity of the gamified experience. Some positive emotions promoted by games are excitement, surprise, wonder and amazement.

2.3 Gamification Principles

Oprescu *et al.* propose ten principles for implement gamification experiences [12]. Table 1 presents the description of each principle.

Table 1. Gamification principles proposal by Oprescu *et al.* [12]

ID	Principle name	Description
1	Orientation	Gamified processes place the user (employee) at the center of the experience
2	Persuasive elements	Gamified processes include persuasive elements based on sound, psychological and behavioral theories
3	Learning orientation	Focus on knowledge acquisition, skill development, motivational outcomes or behavior change
4	Achievement based rewards	Focus on a justifiable and predictable return on investment
5	Y Generation adaptable	Generation Y is the fastest growing segment of the workforce and they are looking for work experiences that are supportive, fun and engaging
6	Amusement factors	Inclusion of humor, play and fun elements as part of the work processes
7	Transformative	Use of a balanced and attractive combination of competition and collaboration in order to transform existing work processes within an organization
8	Wellbeing oriented	Focus on personal and organizational wellbeing
9	Research generating	Collaborative research efforts must be encouraged to justify future investments in the area
10	Knowledge-based	Based on knowledge, either as an outcome or as feedback

2.4 Assessment Proposal

Gamification is a trend that receives increasing attention from researchers as well as practitioners. For this reason, exists different approaches to faces gamification projects [13] including the phases business modelling, design, implementation and monitoring, and adaptation [15]. However, the activity less mature is the monitoring of the gamification designs. For this reason, Heilburnn *et al.* [14] suggest the use of gamification analytics tools to measure the success of gamification designs allowing to quantify and understand user behavior improvements [14]. Moreover, they propose the use of semi-structured interviews as a mechanism for obtain a direct feedback of user satisfaction and additional requirements for the gamified experiences.

In [15] the authors identify relevant software solutions for measure the fulfillment of user requirements in gamification projects.

In such proposals, the assessment is centered in collecting data for software applications about user behavior using gamification analytics. However, our proposal is oriented to a generic gamification environment, supported of not by software artefacts. For this reason, the data of participants' behavior will be collected directly for users through neuroscience equipment. This alternative will allow discover at first-hand how participants react to the different elements of the gamified environment.

3 Assessment Framework Proposal

Software process improvement is an approach used by software industries for increase the productivity and quality of their processes and products. One important issue is the social interaction among the team members for improve motivation and engagement levels in such team members. This situation could be address using gamification like a strategy to improve the social factors related to the software development process. In this sense is necessary to define methods, guidelines and frameworks to assurance the proper implementation of the gamification strategy.

Our framework is a layered structure and is the result of the analysis of different studies, cited in the previous section, which describes gamification elements, components and principles. Such framework is composed by layers containing basic components (fundamentals, methods, procedures) looking for obtain the expected results with the incorporation of gamified environments in SPI initiatives (Fig. 1).

This framework is designed with two purposes:

(1) Inductive: the creation of gamified environments starting from the identification and adoption of gamification elements to the assessment of the gamified environment.
(2) Deductive: the verification of the accomplishment of gamification fundamentals in an existing gamified environment.

The framework begins with a principles identification layer as a conceptual support of the principles adoption layer. The first layer allows to reflect the elements necessary to guarantee that gamification is using adequately as a strategy to improve the participants' behavior. Starting with the gamified environment design, the validated

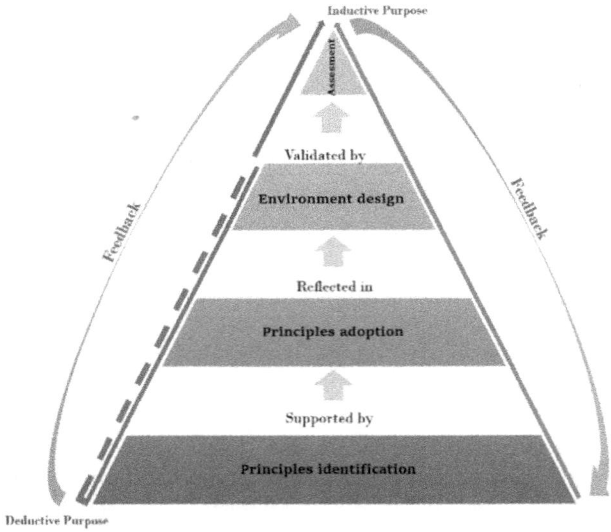

Fig. 1. Assessment framework for gamified environments (Color figure online)

assessment is carried out based on principles identified, adopted and reflected in the design.

Finally, the framework improves through constant feedback including the four-layer conforming it. Moreover, Fig. 1 shows the way of framework is used according with the purposes mentioned above. The yellow arrow shows the sequence for the inductive purpose, in other words, when the goal is create a gamified environment from scratch.

The orange arrow shows the descending sequence for use the framework (deductive purpose). In this purpose is necessary begins with the environment design layer looking for identifying the game elements in the existing gamified environment. As indicate the orange dotted line we should continue with the procedure indicated in the assessment layer.

The four-layer conforming the framework are: (1) principles identification that will contextualized the gamified environment; (2) principles adoption identified at the previous layer; (3) gamified environment design and (4) assessment of gamified environment validating its design from the principles adopted at previous layers.

The framework layered-structure is defined identifying for each layer three key elements: (a) base component, (b) procedural component and (c) results component.

Base component of a layer includes the fundamental aspects for the use of the framework. Each layer will have a basic starting point, so that the framework user can establish the application basis of each layer.

Procedural component of a layer is equivalent to methods, procedures and guidelines allowing obtain each layer goals and expected results.

Results component of a layer includes templates for indicating to framework user the structure of expected results in each layer.

The results component is a unique template that will be built layer by layer. The construction of such template is the result of the applications of the instructions of the procedural component of each layer, so in each results component the template is improved with respect to the previous layer [17].

4 Gamification Assessment Model for Implementing Framework

The framework includes an assessment gamification model with the purpose of determine the level of gamification of an environment. The goal of this model is implements each framework layer providing variables and a set of equations for obtain gamification level indicators.

The model has the following components: (a) terms and variables definitions, (b) equation set, (c) measurement rules and (d) results reports template. The relationship between components is shown in Fig. 2.

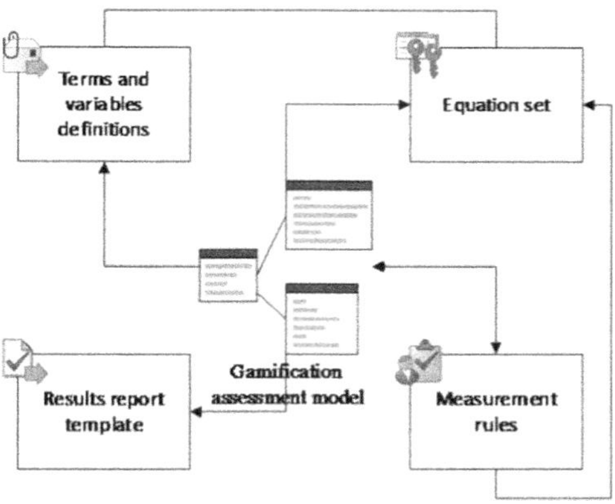

Fig. 2. Model components

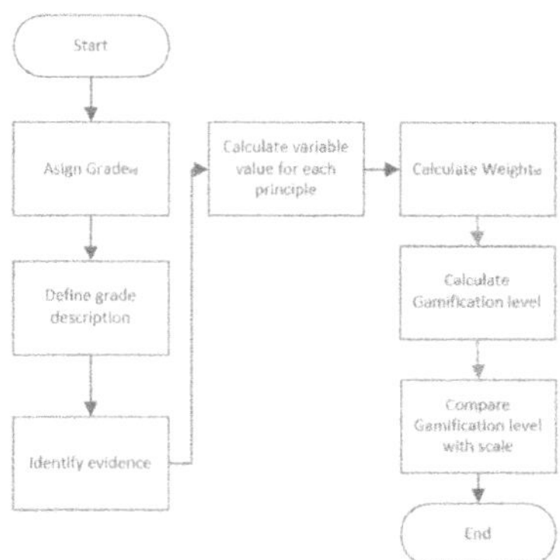

Fig. 3. Model procedure

4.1 Terms and Variables Definitions

This component describes the terms associated with the model as well as the procedure for calculate the model variables (Fig. 3). Besides, such component include the definition of variables and constants (Table 2) and the Likert Scale used for determine the evidence grade value (Gr_{id}) necessary to measure Principle Weight.

Table 2. Variables and constants definitions

Symbol	Variable name	Description
Gr_{id}	Grade	Identification of evidence of the level of incorporation of each principle in environment under assessment. For achieving this grade, a qualitative assessment scale was defined according to a Likert scale. See Table 3
W_{id}	Principle Weight	Sum of the assessment of each evidence multiplied by the grade of incorporation of each gamification principle identified. See Eq. (1)
LW_{id}	Gamification level	Percentage of incorporation of gamification of the environment under assessment. See Eq. (2)
Tlg	Total learning goals	Number of learning goals identified in the game elements that are described in the framework design layer [17]
Tru	Total rules	Number of game rules in the game elements that are described in the framework design layer [17]
Symbol	Constant name	Description
r	Roles	Indicate the roles identified in the game elements that are described in the framework design layer [17]
m	Materials	Indicate the materials identified in the game elements that are described in the framework design layer [17]
s	Steps	Indicate the steps identified in the game elements that are described in the framework design layer [17]

Table 3. Likert scale for grade value evidence (Gr_{id})

Likert scale	Name	Description
1	Null	There is no evidence that the principle is fulfilled or is present in the gamified environment
2	Medium	There is some evidence that the principle is fulfilled or is present in the gamified environment and it is possible to identify at least one element associated with this principle with some difficulty
3	Significant	There is some evidence that the principle is fulfilled or is present in the gamified environment and it is possible to identify at least one element associated with this principle
4	High	There is evidence that the principle is fulfilled or is present in the gamified environment and it is possible to identify the elements associated with this principle easily
5	Very high	There is evidence that the principle is fulfilled or is present in the gamified environment and it is easily identifiable

4.2 Equations Set

This component presents the equations of the model. Each variable represents a measure necessary for obtain the value of the variable Principle Weight (W_{id}) required for apply the established measurement rules. Table 4 presents the equations of the model.

Table 4. Equations set

Symbol	Variable name	Equations	
W_{id}	Principle Weight	$W_{\mathrm{id}}=(\sum Tlg + r + m + Tru + s) * Gr_{id}$, $where\ id = principle\ identifier$	(1)
LW_{id}	Gamification level	$LW_{id} = \frac{W_{id}*100}{5000}$	(2)
Tlg	Total learning goals	$Tlg = \left(\frac{40}{n}\right) * x, where\ n = quantity\ of\ learning\ goals\ and,$ $x = quantity\ of\ leargning\ goals\ for\ each\ principle$	(3)
Tru	Total rules	$Tru = \left(\frac{30}{m}\right) * y, where\ m = quantity\ of\ rules\ and,$ $y = quantity\ of\ rules\ for\ each\ principle$	(4)
r	Roles	$r = 10$	(5)
m	Materials	$m = 5$	(6)
s	Steps	$s = 5$	(7)

4.3 Measurement Rules

This component describes three rules for determine the gamification level. Such rules are defined from the variable LW_{id} which corresponds to the percentage value of Principle Weight (See Table 5).

Table 5. Measurement rules

Rule number	Rule description
1	If, LW_{id} is between 100% and 76%, then the environment is a totally gamified environment
2	If, LW_{id} is between 75% and 11%, then the environment is a partially gamified environment
3	If LW_{id} is between 10% and 0%, then the environment is a non-gamified environment

4.4 Results Report Template

This component shows the suggested template for report the results of all framework layers. This template shows gamification principles and evidence identified, and the calculation of gamification level for the environment under assessment (See Table 6).

Table 6. Template for result component of gamification assessment model

1	2	3	4	5	6	7	8
ID	Principle	Gr_{id}	Definition	MDE	Environment justification	Environment evidence	W_{id}

- Column 1 refers to the principle identifier (ID) when the principles of framework identification layer are used [16]. According to the procedure of this layer, if exist more principles identified its suggested use the same consecutive.
- Column 2 corresponds with the principle name included in framework identification layer [16].
- Column 3 refers to the variable Gr_{id} defined according to a Likert scale. See Table 3.
- Column 4 is an initial identification of the presence of the principle in the gamified environment.
- Colum 5 refers of the MDE Framework element related with each principle.
- Column 6 includes a brief description of each principle in the environment under assessment.
- Column 7 presents the identification of environment elements related with each principle.
- In Column 8, the Principle Weight W_{id} is registered (See Eq. (1)).

The procedure of the gamification assessment model ends with the calculation of gamification level for determinate if the environment incorporate the gamification fundamentals totally, partially or not at all according to the measurement rules.

5 A Case Study Video Scrum

In this section, we present a case study of the framework application using Video Scrum as a gamified environment. The goal of this case study is apply the assessment framework for gamified environments in a deductive way. In other words, use the framework for verify and stablish if such environment can be considered as a gamified environment. This goal is obtained thanks to the application of the assessment gamification model in such environment.

Table 7 shows the resultant template for the assessment layer for this model. Such table include the results of the execution of the procedural components of each framework layer.

According to the procedure defined for the gamification assessment model (See Fig. 3) the next step is calculate the level of gamification with the data obtained in Table 7, for obtain the comparison data and determine the gamification level according to the measurement rules.

The application of Eq. (1) for Video Scrum results in (1) $W_{\text{id}} = 668.75$ and according to Eq. (2) $LW_{id} = 13.375$. The comparison of LW_{id} with the rules previously presented indicates that Video Scrum is a partially gamified environment.

Table 7. Template for gamification assessment model

ID	Gr_{id}	Definition	MDE	Environment justification	Environment evidence	W_{id}
1	5	Scrum team is the center of the experience	Mechanics	Collaborative work in teams is a rule game	**Learning goal 4** related with self-learning, self-organization and self-management. Such goal are essential in the Scrum Framework	40
2	4	Scrum simulation through Video Scrum facilitates the adoption of new way of work	Dynamics	This framework component is oriented to the participants' behavior and in Video Scrum the persuasive elements are: free topic selection and use of technology for video edition and mobile devices	**Rule 1.** Scrum team can select free topic when facilitator presents a legend **Step 5**. Sprints execution for develop video film. This is a persuasive element for IT professionals because is no software but is a technological product **Materials**. Use the smartphones or mobile device in academic environment **Materials**. Use an editor video is a new challenge for IT professionals who do not use this technology frequently	55
3	5	Video Scrum is a game created for teaching Scrum framework	Dynamics, Emotions	Video Scrum is an educational game and promotes learning during game execution	**Learning goal 1.** To teach professionals out of IT industry (marketing, sales etc.) the fundamentals framework Scrum	200

(continued)

Table 7. (*continued*)

ID	Gr_{id}	Definition	MDE	Environment justification	Environment evidence	W_{id}
					Learning goal 2. To demonstrate the philosophy of iterative-incremental development software method **Learning goal 3.** To use framework Scrum to create a real, not a "toy" product simulating a software development process **Learning goal 4.** The team is able to generate skills associated to self-organization and self-management **Learning goal 5.** The participants are able to work in teams for generate the requested product	
5	4	Scrum team is the center of the experience	Emotions	Video Scrum has features interesting for Y Generation: free topic selection and the use of mobile devices	**Rule 1.** Scrum team can select free topic when facilitator presents a legend **Materials**. **Step 5.** Sprints execution for develop video film (include Sprint planning, Sprint review and retrospective). Sprint Review when each team show their film and get feedback from their	55

(*continued*)

Table 7. (*continued*)

ID	Gr_{id}	Definition	MDE	Environment justification	Environment evidence	W_{id}
					peers. This is a funny step in the game	
6	2	Scrum simulation through Video Scrum facilitates the adoption of new way of work	Dynamics	In Video Scrum the amusement factors are: (1) have a space for collective product presentation in each sprint (2) Increase team satisfaction when obtain better results in the retrospective meeting	**Step 5.** Sprints execution for develop video film (Include Sprint planning, Sprint review and retrospective)	10
7	5	Video Scrum is a game created for teaching Scrum framework	Dynamics	In Video Scrum, the product is developed in a collaborative way and with competition among teams	**Learning goal 5. Roles and Responsibilities** defined by Scrum framework requires team members interaction, therefore collaboration is evidenced **Rule 1.**	108.75
10	5	Video Scrum is an educational environment created for develop skills and capabilities for use Scrum framework in an organizational context	Mechanics	Video Scrum is an educational game that simulate the Scrum framework with all his rules, meetings, roles and work products	**Learning goal 1** **Learning goal 2** **Learning goal 3** **Learning goal 4** **Learning goal 5**	200

According to our proposal and model results, Video Scrum simulation applies basic principles gamification and use gamification elements established in framework MDE. It is possible to demonstrate that Video Scrum is a simulation that responds to principles such as those defined by Oprescu and gamification elements established in frameworks like MDE. In fact, Video Scrum structure facilitates identification of components of a gamified instrument defined in framework design layer [17].

6 Conclusions and Future Work

This work proposes an assessment framework for gamified environments aims to facilitate the verification of principles and gamification elements identified and adopted as a part of the design of gamified activities included in a gamified environment for software process improvement.

In this work, we present a gamification assessment model for implement the framework with the following characteristics: (1) a set of variables and constants, (2) a set of equations for calculate each variable value, (3) measurement rules for determine if the environment incorporate gamification partially, totally or not at all, and (4) a results report template that is the result of the execution of the procedural component of all framework layers. The value of the variables is determined for evidences of the incorporation of gamification principles and the existence of game elements associated with each principle. This model is a first approximation for calculate the gamification level of an environment existent.

As a future work, we suggest: (1) apply the gamification assessment model of an environment built from the scratch using the framework, (2) refine the framework assessment layer including not only the gamification assessment model but also HCI measures and approaches for assessing the users' behavior and (3) evaluate results obtained for Video Scrum case study respect to other gamification proposals.

References

1. Dorling, A., McCaffery, F.: The gamification of SPICE. In: Mas, A., Mesquida, A., Rout, T., O'Connor, Rory V., Dorling, A. (eds.) SPICE 2012. CCIS, vol. 290, pp. 295–301. Springer, Heidelberg (2012). https://doi.org/10.1007/978-3-642-30439-2_35
2. Deterding, S., Dixon, D., Khaled, R., Nacke, L.: From game design elements to gamefulness: defining gamification. In: Proceedings of 15th International Academic MindTrek Conference: Envisioning Future Media Environments, pp. 9–15. ACM, Finland (2011)
3. Hamari, J., Lehdonvirta, V.: Game design as marketing: how game mechanics create demand for virtual goods. Int. J. Bus. Sci. Appl. Manag. **5**(1), 14–29 (2010)
4. Huotari, K., Hamari, J.: Defining gamification: a service marketing perspective. In: Proceedings of 16th International Academic MindTrek Conference, pp. 17–22. ACM, Finland (2012)
5. Hamari, J.: Transforming homo economicus into homo ludens: a field experiment on gamification in a utilitarian peer-to-peer trading service. Electron. Commer. Res. Appl. **12** (4), 236–245 (2013)
6. Hamari, J., Kovisto, J., Sarsa, H.: Does gamification work?–a literature review of empirical studies on gamification. In: 47th Hawaii International Conference on System Sciences, pp. 3025–3034. IEEE, Waikoloa (2014)
7. Robson, K.: Is it all a game? Understanding the principles of gamification. Bus. Horiz. **58**(4), 411–420 (2015)
8. Hernández, L., Muñoz, M., et al.: Gamification in software engineering teamworks: a systematic literature review. In: International Conference on Software Process Improvement (CIMPS), pp. 1–8. IEEE (2016)

9. Kietzmann, J., et al.: Social media? Get serious! understanding the functional building blocks of social media. Bus. Horiz. **54**(3), 241–251 (2011)
10. Hunicke, R., LeBlanc, M., Zubek, R.: MDA: a formal approach to game design and game research. In: Proceedings of the AAAI Workshop on Challenges in Game, San Jose, CA, pp. 1–5 (2014)
11. Camerer, C.: Behavioral Game Theory: Experiments in Strategic Interaction. Princeton University Press, Princeton (2003)
12. Oprescu, F., et al.: I PLAY AT WORK—ten principles for transforming work processes through gamification. Front. Psychol. **5**, 14–17 (2014)
13. Herzig, P., Ameling, M., Wolf, B., Schill, A.: Implementing gamification: requirements and gamification platforms. In: Reiners, T., Wood, L.C. (eds.) Gamification in Education and Business, pp. 431–450. Springer, Cham (2015). https://doi.org/10.1007/978-3-319-10208-5_22
14. Heilbrunn, B., Herzig, P., et al.: Towards gamification analytics-requirements for monitoring and adapting gamification designs. In: GI-Jahrestagung, pp. 333–344 (2014)
15. Kumar, J.: Gamification at work: designing engaging business software. In: Marcus, A. (ed.) DUXU 2013. LNCS, vol. 8013, pp. 528–537. Springer, Heidelberg (2013). https://doi.org/10.1007/978-3-642-39241-2_58
16. Heilbrunn, B., Herzig, P., et al.: Tools for gamification analytics: a survey. In: 7th International Conference on Utility and Cloud Computing Proceedings, pp. 603–608. IEEE, Washington, USA (2014)
17. Gasca-Hurtado, G.P., Gómez-Alvarez, M.C., Muñoz, M., Mejía, J.: Toward an assessment framework for gamified environments. In: Stolfa, J., Stolfa, S., O'Connor, R.V., Messnarz, R. (eds.) EuroSPI 2017. CCIS, vol. 748, pp. 281–293. Springer, Cham (2017). https://doi.org/10.1007/978-3-319-64218-5_23

Towards a Role Playing Game for Exploring the Roles in Scrum to Improve Collaboration Problems

Zulal Akarsu[1(✉)], Özgün Onat Metin[1], Deniz Gungor[1], and Murat Yilmaz[2]

[1] Research and Development Center, Huawei Technologies, Istanbul, Turkey
{zulal.akarsu, ozgun.onat.metin, deniz.gungor}@huawei.com

[2] Computer Engineering, Çankaya University, Ankara, Turkey
myilmaz@cankaya.edu.tr

Abstract. Scrum is the most popular, useful and lightweight framework based on agile software development philosophy. In particular, software development organizations are willing to transform their software development culture to benefit from its fruitful practices. In addition, it is almost inevitable for the organizations with historical development practices to face many dysfunctions during transformation phase, which is normal and expected. It is important to uncover, analyze and solve these dysfunctions, which may take some time. One of the problems organizations may encounter is the confusion and misapplication of the roles in Scrum. This dysfunction creates problems from task creation, follow-up, taking responsibility to collaboration problems in the project. The goal of this study is to address such situations using an interactive role playing game-based approach among team members to improve collaboration.

Keywords: Software development · Agile · Scrum · Gamification Role play · Roles

1 Introduction

Software development is a complex process. While trying to cope with technical challenges, changes done in the processes may increase the complexity and human factor may even add more complexity to these processes. Habits, learning difficulties, adaptation problems, inability to change organizational culture that is not familiar with core agile values may be encountered when new techniques are introduced. There is also the possible issue of trying to fit agile elements into a non-agile framework. Change is inherently difficult, uncomfortable and people may fear it. For established organizations, Scrum may prove challenging to install. Moving from long period releases to weekly iterations is very hard. Switching an organization to start using Scrum requires a fundamental mindset shift that will shake up old habits and transform them into more effective ones. The journey of the transformation is not easy, especially

X. Larrucea et al. (Eds.): EuroSPI 2018, CCIS 896, pp. 254–264, 2018.
https://doi.org/10.1007/978-3-319-97925-0_21

for the organizations that have historical and successful development practices. The first step is to understand exactly why individuals are resistant to change and what their true feelings are about adopting new practices like Scrum. By digging to the root cause of people's resistance and from our observation, understanding responsibilities of Scrum roles is one of the main problems.There are several software development roles that are defined by traditional development approaches. Beside this, Scrum is a lightweight framework with mainly three defined roles. It is important to have open-minded individuals who are able to create the right organizational attitude for embracing the change. To ensure that everybody understands the Scrum roles in the proper way, help with specific practices through training and coaching is important. In the recent years, researchers have been working on the game theories in a variety of areas including learning methodologies in software engineering. Gamification is a new learning methodology that responds to a reality: new generations need to learn in a different style [1].

Historically, HUAWEI started its R&D presence in Turkey with a strong Component Development & Testing under the framework Capability Maturity Model (CMM) and subsequently over a period of years spreading its business capability and ownership through handling independent Analysis, Design, SW & info development, as well as Maintenance of the Components. Today, with its decade long experience and expertise in SW Engineering and effective Business Management, it spreads its wings to include several associated capabilities, which include Market Technical Support, E2E Component Development, SW Product Development, Baseline Solution Development, Customization Solution Development, and Service Operation & Delivery. Within a couple of years, our organization has improved its software development process maturity and was certified with CMMI L3 and CMMI L5 short time after. Primarily, Quality Management System was almost completely designed for V-Model and the organization exercised a few practices using agile methods. Beside this, the necessity of agile transformation is inevitable to get its technical and commercial benefits to strengthen the E2E Business ownership capability. This aims to give an advantage for HUAWEI Turkey R&D Center to reach and continuously provide a value-driven approach both for the customer and for the organization.

The primary aim of this paper is to investigate an interactive game-like approach to teach roles, responsibilities, and accountabilities clearly in software development, particularly in Agile Software Development, while the player is acting each role in Scrum in many possible cases. The remaining part of the paper proceeds as follows: Sect. 2 gives the role definitions in traditional and theAgile Software Development process and the possible root causes of the role based conflicts. In Sect. 3, gamification in software engineering will be analyzed. Section 4 will give details of the role playing game to teach the roles. In Sect. 5, Role Play Game Based Framework will be introduced and in Sect. 6 we discuss the role playing game and its effects.

2 Roles in Traditional Software Development Lifecycle and Agile Software Development Lifecycle

There are many different types of software development life cycles (SDLC) to develop high quality, within budget, within scope, and on-time software in the software world. In this section, the roles involved in Traditional SDLC and Agile SDLC, their definitions, and the difference between them are explained.

Scrum is one of the frameworks that embraces the Agile SDLC understanding and vales. In the roles in Agile SDLC section, roles are explained based on the roles defined in the Scrum framework. In addition, possible reasons of role based conflicts are mentioned in this section.

2.1 Roles in Traditional SDLC

Traditional SDLC separates the software development process into a number of explicitly defined steps, and each next step is commenced when the previous one is finished. Due to the fact that these are sequential steps, the output of the previous phase will be the input for the next phase. This structure is generally called the Waterfall model, since process flow resembles a Waterfall.

To solve complex problems in software development, roles are used for sharing tasks among the team members. Arole includes the scope of that role's responsibility, assignments, and the capability to accomplish particular tasks for development. In the essay, *The Cathedral and the Bazaar*, Raymond states that because of the strict roles defined in traditional software development, the traditional approach is similar to building a cathedral, where a small team of people works in an isolated environment [2]. For this reason, working with the strict roles can be seen as a disadvantage, since a lot of the artifacts are visible, and reviewed by only limited or allowed roles.

Below, each role in the Table 1 is explained in sequence:

Table 1. Roles in traditional software development lifecycle

Acronym	Role	Main value
PM	Project manager	Allocates resources, assigns tasks, plans the project
DES	Software designer	Finds solution for the requirements
DEV	Software developer	Develops the requirements
TST	Software tester	Ensures quality of the developed requirements
BA	Business analyst	Manages stakeholders
SP	Sponsor	Funds for the project

- In the traditional approach, the project manager (PM) is responsible for resource allocation, project planning, task distribution, progress review and, achieving objectives of the project. S/he is also responsible for taking care of addressing any major team related issues. Moreover, the PM is accountable for project success and failure.

- A software designer is responsible for turning the requirements into the design by finding the most appropriate one among alternatives.
- A software developer is responsible for designing, and coding software programs while a software tester is responsible for creating test plans and testing the developed programs according to written test cases.
- A business analyst is responsible for analyzing the business needs to help identify the problems and business solutions, eliciting requirements by acting as a bridge between the business and the technical stakeholders, documenting requirements of a software project.
- A sponsor is responsible for providing budget and fund for the project.

In addition to these roles, others can also be seen in order to compensate the requirements; e.g. requirements engineer, systems analyst, etc.

2.2 Roles in Agile SDLC/Scrum

Agile SDLC model is an integration of iterative and incremental processes by focusing on customer satisfaction with the rapid delivery of highest value. In this model, product development process is broken into small incremental parts. These parts are given in iterations, and at the end of each iteration, cross-functional teams develop required functionalities of the product, and show them to the customer.

One of the popular agile frameworks is Scrum which is the concern for explaining the roles of Agile SDLCin this part, which focuses specifically on how to manage tasks within a self-organized, cross-functional team, and turn the product requirements into the releasable functionalities in time-boxed events.

Below, each role in Table 2 is explained in sequence:

Table 2. Roles in scrum framework

Acronym	Role	Main value
SM	Scrum master	Teaches scrum framework
PO	Product owner	Optimizes value for product
DEV	Development team	Turns requirements into releasable functionalities
MNGT	Management	Assesses the decisions and funds for the project
CUS	Customer	Assesses backlog items

- The Scrum Master (SM) is a role specific to Scrum, who is responsible for the ensuring the compliance of practices of the Scrum framework. SM maximizes the productivity of the development team by removing impediments and practicing the Scrum values. SM also works with the Product Owner, and Organization to spread the agile culture.
- The Product Owner (PO) is responsible for ordering, optimizing the product backlog,which contains items to be developed, and making visible, clear whole requirements to the development team.

- The Development Team is self-organizing, cross-functional and has the capability and maturity to turn product backlog items into working functionalities. There is no tester, analyst titles or sub-teams in the group; all members are called `developers`. The Development Team is also responsible for reviewing the progress of the sprint according to the sprint backlog.
- The management role is responsible for assessing the decisions and providing funds for the project, and also covering decision making activities.
- The customer role is to evaluate the product backlog items, give feedback and help the Scrum team for selecting which items to include to the next sprints primarily[3].

Possible Root Causes of the Role Based Conflicts

As the types of software development processes increase, some problems have occurred in people's minds about understanding roles in SDLC; such as the Scrum Master role in Agile SDLC. SM can be misunderstood as the project manager. Therefore, it is important to clear the role concept with the examples in organization.

Below, possible root causes of the role-based conflicts in some organizations were listed:

- Overlapping responsibilities: Same responsibilities been own by multiple people for example Scrum Master or lead or technical lead or manager etc.
- Confusion about responsibilities and accountabilities of roles.
- Role ortitle confusion: Such as; a developer's title in the Scrum team can be asenior developer.
- Disappearance of traditional roles: There seems to be confusion about sudden disappearance of some roles such as Project Manager, Business Analyst, and Functional Manager rolesetc.
- Old habits from traditional roles: For instance; a Project Manager's role has been turned to SM, but SM still acts like a PM by allocating tasks to the team members [4].
- Role of Managers: For instance senior management still expect one person (typically, the Manager) to be accountable for delivery and do not understand 'ownership by team'.

3 Gamification in Software Engineering

Creating a lively visual metaphor or analogy helps permanent learning [5]. Also, the body puts out chemicals such as cortisol when it is under stress. Researches shows that it is how you interpret these symptoms. During the game, positive thinking and locking onto the target generates cortisol's positive effect in long term learning [6]. Game history is so old and fundamental in human civilization. Based on the story of Heredot 440 BC, it goes up to dice and ball which was invented in the kingdom of Lydia [7]. Game Theory is a set of analytical tools, which can be used to model the interactions between participants in a game form [8]. The concept, gamification was defined as "turning something not a game into a game" by Bartle, the inventor of the first MUD (Multi-User Dungeon) game [9].

There are a variety of different areas that could benefit from gamification, such as software development. The main purpose of the game theory and gamification in the field of software development is to provide higher motivation in software engineers to adopt or improve the best programming practices while working on software projects. Gamification has a strong relationship with behaviorism, as it is built on the concept of rewards (points, badges, etc.) for specific actions [7]. There are successful gamification examples in software engineering such as Stackoverflow which gives badges for the best answers, encourages the software engineers to be specialized on their areas. Also there are some useful online tools to improve the coding skills by using gamification practices such as Codeacademy, Code School, Khan Academy, CodeClub. It is important to keep software engineers' motivation high since the software development process, especially in complex products brings stressful working environment while trying to comply with rapid changes of the technology, requirements and processes. Motivation is a key factor to successfully implement best practices of agile methodologies into development teams.

As software development is a continuously improving, evolving process, it is an inevitable need to learn something new in a short period of time. The question is how we can keep the high motivation, qualified output and also teach/learn something new and adapt as soon as possible? And, since it is a collaborative work, how can we handle the problems caused by interpersonal conflicts? Games will help to resolve these issues. Several methods are suggested by researchers to reveal such problems. For example "Prisoner's dilemma" is a basic framework that is often used by researchers to observe interpersonal conflicts suggested by Hazzan and Dubinsky [10]. The "Prisoner's dilemma" is useful to highlight the problems in software development. Not to cause confusion, gaming is not about rewarding people with badges and tokens, its aim is to enrich the activities and gain maximum benefit with "game full" aspects [7].

4 Role Playing Game to Teach Software Development Roles

One of the techniques that can be used by software development practitioners is Role-Play game activity. This activity gives opportunity to team members to practice different roles in different business cases. In addition, it also allows team members to build empathy by putting themselves in another role for a while, and it may allow the members to adapt to new roles faster and smoothly.

Definition of Role Play

Role play is a technique that allows people to experience and explore realistic situations by interacting with other people. Role play activity is held in a managed way in order to develop experience and trial different scenarios in a supported environment. Depending on the aim of the activity, participants might be playing a role similar to their real-life roles or could play an imaginary role where they can put themselves into somebody else's shoes. Both options provide the possibility of better learning.

Participants are given particular roles to play in a case or an interaction. In our context imaginary people will be the Scrum roles and the roles in traditional software development processes. Participants can be given specific instructions on how to act or what to say. For example, an aggressive product owner or commanding Scrum Master is required to act and react in their own way depending on the requirements of the activity. Imaginary cases can be any given scenario that can be practiced. In the software development context, imaginary cases can range between any situation from "attending a daily Scrum meeting" to "constantly commanding and assigning tasks to members". The participants will then act out the situation, reflect and discuss the interactions afterwards. The scenario can then be adapted or repeated with changes based on the outcome of the discussion.

Terms used in literature; simulation, games, role-play, simulation-game, role play simulation and role playing game are often used interchangeably [11]. While simulations are more complex and relatively inflexible activity, role play, on the other hand, may be an easier technique to organize and more flexible. Role play activity leaves room for initiative and imagination. Byrne comments that role play is a part of drama activity. He defined three terms to address the drama activities. The terms are mime (mimicry - memorization), role play and simulation. He described mime as the participants perform actions without using words. Secondly, role play is the interaction between participants in imaginary situations. Lastly, he described simulation as it involves role playing. However, the participants normally discuss a problem with some pre-defined setting for them [11].

5 Role Play Game Based Framework for Software Development Project Team Members Learning Different Roles

Software development processes do not suggest the most efficient methods to teach software practitioners about the roles especially if they are subject to a transition to a new development methodology that brings different definition of roles and responsibilities. The goal of this model is to use a role play game based approach that fosters empathy between members through individual interactions to improve learning efficiency while employees are learning about or transitioning to new roles.

The game layout is given as in the Fig. 1. The game elements consists of three elements; Game board, Role Cards and Case Cards. The game board shows the progress of the participants on a path where they can move their avatars. Role cards are the possible roles in the SDLC and piled in a random order. Case cards are the given imaginary or possible business scenario that are piled in a random order.

The game flow is as given in the Fig. 2. The game is played in turns. Participants can select one card randomly selected from each piles of "role card" and "case card" when it is their turn. The imaginary context of the role play is then settled and the participant shall role-play the given role in the given business case. After that the facilitator or another member will read the correct answer and the role play performance and reactions are evaluated by the group by comparing with the "should-be reaction". If the action is found correct, the player will receive points to move their avatar on the path given on a board. If the action is found not proper, the player does

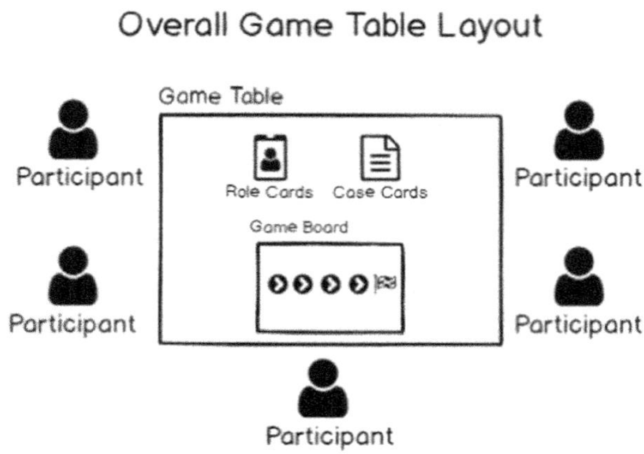

Fig. 1. Overall game table layout

not get any points and cannot move on the game board. In both cases, the turn goes to the next participant in a decided manner.

To better explain the model an example is given as in the following. For example, a development team member has the turn and picks a card from role and case card piles. She gets the role of "Scrum Master" and the situation: "A Development Team decides that the frequency of Daily Scrum should be reduced to once a week.". The development team member tries to give correct reaction to this situation thinking in the Scrum Master's shoes. After his role play in a time boxed period, the correct answer is given to participants as "The Scrum Master should coach the team on the essentials of conducting Daily Scrums." Answer can be elaborated, if further explanation is needed: "Though individuals may report to some management authority on the "people aspects" there is no exclusive manager for a Scrum Team". In Scrum, there is no role called Agile Coach. Self-organization is about the empowerment of the Development Team to decide how to get the development work done to meet the Sprint Goal. So, it is only limited choices they make about how to perform the development work. They are still subject to following other rules included in Scrum. As a guardian of the Scrum implementation, the Scrum Master should coach the team on Scrum essentials." [12]. If the development team member gave a correct answer s/he gets point and moves his/her avatar on the game board. The turn moves to the next participant.

Users can experience multiple roles in multiple situations that are identified in software development world. Business cases can be related to anything regarding software development such as requirement analysis, software testing, event and ceremonies etc. Therefore, users can experience arole, which they are already in, will be doing or an opposite role. This model is proposed as a resource management framework to teach Scrum roles based on role-playing. This method aims to make the transitions to Scrum smoother and more efficient.

The main aim of using role play and game based activity is to improve the software development activities in a resource economy model where software practitioners are selected based on their capabilities and necessary skill set for the defined roles which

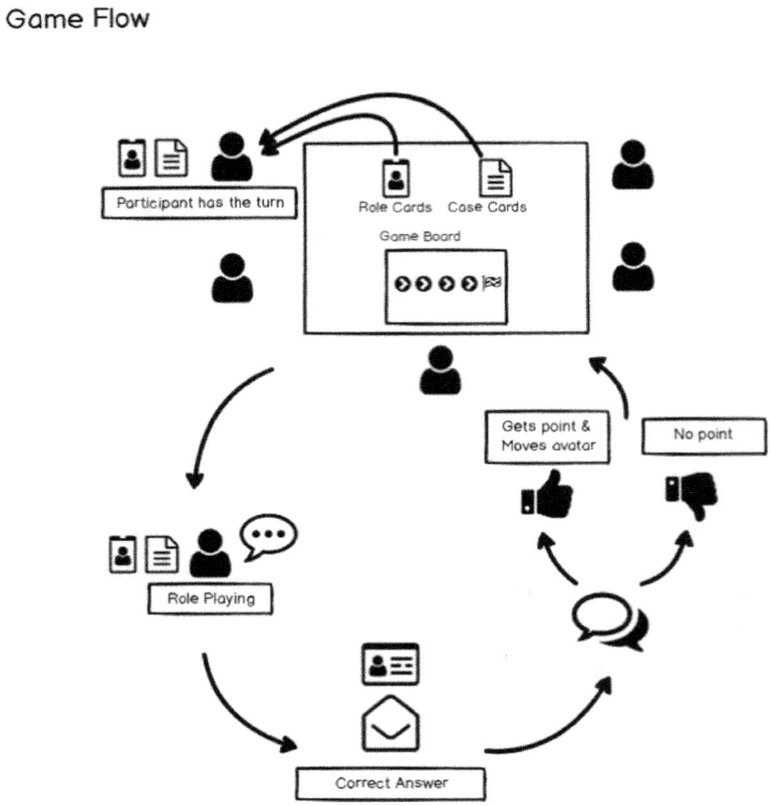

Fig. 2. Game flow

enable them to better understand the roles and possible situations they might face in advance. Based on the proposed model, we aim to teach the roles in software development methodologies to practitioners in a safe environment. A practitioner experiences a set of possible business scenarios of specific roles by using role play activity. In this way, a gamification based role experience becomes possible. A set of game elements to motivate its users such as badges, motivational titles for levels on the board (i.e. Knowledgeable, Superb etc.) might be used as well. Consequently, participants who acts the given role in a given situation correctly are rewarded by progressing on the board path. The first participant to reach the highest level first is rewarded by the system. This reward mechanism is available to all system participants to foster their motivation.

Individuals in a team can experience different roles by interactions and empathy by using this technique. We believe that this practice may have further links for knowledge diversity among individuals in software development teams. This could be a useful tool for risk reduction that might be caused by unclear understanding of roles in software companies, since everyone has the chance to experience different roles from different perspectives in the context of various business scenarios.

6 Discussion

This preliminary training model explains the possibility of using role play game based approach in training about software development processes. The goal is to propose role play activity based on gaming concepts and to explore potential ways for application game elements in software development activities and ultimately improve software development practices. Consequently, this study strengthens the idea that software practitioners should be able to understand what the Scrum roles and responsibilities are through a role playing teaching method. Games may potentially create a positive impact on practitioners' performance and foster motivational factors. In order to take advantage of the power of game elements roles are presented in a game like structure. This preliminary study claims that playing a role play game based training activity provides participants an activity that is more effective and also less boring. In addition, it would guide individuals to learn to develop empathy during all phases of a project. An eventuality of this approach is the possibility to improve the social structure of a software organization. A further benefit of this practice is to improve overall project awareness and knowledge.

Our initial proposal was submitted to the quality and operations management board of HUAWEI Turkey R&D Center. HUAWEI Turkey R&D Center is a large software development company which works in Turkey with around 500 engineers. Various technologies and software development methodologies (e.g. Agile, Waterfall) are used in projects and departments as their focus and products are different. Our initial proposal received positive feedbacks and this study has revealed many questions in need of further investigation. Future research should therefore concentrate on the implementation of the proposed method and more assessments are primary to determine its effectiveness.

Acknowledgement. This research work was conducted at the Huawei Turkey Research and Development Center, Quality and Operations Department. During the research, we have received help and generous support from many people, to all of whom we would like to express our gratitude.

References

1. Quinton, S.: The learning preferences of current generational groups. In: Koul, R., Fisher, D., Zandvliet, D., Gaynor, I. (eds.) Fourth International Conference on Science, Mathematics and Technology Education, 25 August 2005, pp. 478–489. Curtin University of Technology, Victoria (2005)
2. Raymond, E.S.: The Cathedral and the Bazaar: Musings on Linux and Open Source by an Accidental Revolutionary. O'Reilly & Associates, Inc., Sebastopol (2001)
3. Schwaber, K., Beedle, M.: Agile Software Development with SCRUM. PrenticeHall, Upper Saddle River (2002)
4. Jain, A.: How to resolve Agile roles conflicts, confusions and doubts at workplace? (2016). https://www.linkedin.com/pulse/how-resolve-agile-roles-conflicts-confusions-doubts-ajay/. Accessed May–June 2018

5. Oakley, B.A.: A mind for Numbers: How to Excel at Math and Science (Even if you Flunked Algebra). Jeremy P. Tarcher/Penguin, New York (2014)
6. Schwabe, L., Bohringer, A., Chatterjee, M., Schachinger, H.: Effects of pre-learning stress on memory for neutral, positive and negative words: different roles of cortisol and autonomic arousal. Neurobiol. Learn. Memory **90**(1), 44–53 (2008)
7. Sasso, T.D., Mocci, A., Lanza, M., Mastrodicasa, E.: How to gamify software engineering. In: 2017 IEEE 24th International Conference on Software Analysis, Evolution and Reengineering (SANER) (2017)
8. Üsfekes, Ç., Yilmaz, M., Tuzun, E., Clarke, P.M., O'Connor, R.V.: Examining reward mechanisms for effective usage of application lifecycle management tools. In: Stolfa, J., Stolfa, S., O'Connor, R.V., Messnarz, R. (eds.) EuroSPI 2017. CCIS, vol. 748, pp. 259–268. Springer, Cham (2017). https://doi.org/10.1007/978-3-319-64218-5_21
9. Bartle, R.A.: Designing Virtual Worlds. New Riders, Berkeley (2006)
10. Hazzan, O., Dubinsky, Y.: Social perspective of software development methods: the case of the prisoner dilemma and extreme programming. In: Baumeister, H., Marchesi, M., Holcombe, M. (eds.) XP 2005. LNCS, vol. 3556, pp. 74–81. Springer, Heidelberg (2005). https://doi.org/10.1007/11499053_9
11. Byrne, D.: Teaching Oral English: Longman Handbooks for English Teacher, p. 115. Longman Group, Singapore (1986)
12. Ali, M.M.S.: Scrum Narrative and PSM™ Exam Guide: Comprehensive Guide for Professional Scrum Master™ (PSM™ 1) Assessment. Smashwords, Los Gatos (2016)

A Classification of Roles for Gamification in Business – a CHANGCE-Thinking Approach

Sebastian Janocha[1], Peter Witzgall[2(✉)], Adrian Indefrey[2], and Peter Kapfhammer[2]

[1] Technical University of Munich (TUM), Arcisstraße 21, 80333 Munich, Germany
sebastian.janocha@tum.de
[2] pi.con – Pulse of Innovation Consulting, Lindberghstr. 11, 82178 Puchheim, Germany
peter.witzgall@picon.services

Abstract. The CHANGCE-thinking mindset focuses on the identification and exploration of chances. As a part of this concept the CHANGCE-Game provides a systematic framework and ludic approach to discover an organization's potential for improvement within a workshop setting. This method exploits the benefits of gamification to successfully initialize a change process within an enterprise. The case study within this research paper shows the advantages of incorporating roles as a game design element. The roles foster a change of perspective, thereby increasing creativity of workshop participants. This specific game element furthermore helps to break down hierarchies within teams and organizations, providing a criticism-free environment in which every opinion has equal value.

Keywords: Gamification · Role play · Change process · Innovation

1 Introduction

Gamification is no longer a mere trend with individual appearances in business. Usage ranges from physical recreational applications and platforms for software development to workshop methods and educational tools. Nike uses their tracking bracelet and their NikeFuel application in order to track athletes' activities and let these compete with others or themselves [1]. Educational, gamified systems aid by intrinsically motivating students in a learning process [2]. The role classification of a gamified workshop method to systematically discover chances within an organization or team (CHANGCE-thinking) will be presented in this paper.

Gamification can be effective in many contexts, if designed properly. Because of its broad application, existing research and literature suggest frameworks for a successful gamification design. Some frameworks present typical required elements, others phases of developing successful gamification [3].

The focal point of analysis in this paper is the use of roles in a gamified method within the concept of CHANGCE-thinking. The "CHANGCE-Game" aims to discover

X. Larrucea et al. (Eds.): EuroSPI 2018, CCIS 896, pp. 265–276, 2018.
https://doi.org/10.1007/978-3-319-97925-0_22

chances within an organization to initiate a change process. The benefit towards team dynamics and breaking of hierarchies of the incorporated role perspectives will be analyzed by the case of a real-life industry application.

The paper is structured as follows: Sect. 2 refers to related research on gamification in the business context specifically the roleplay component, as well as hierarchies in organizations. In Sect. 3 the research design and context of this study is presented. Section 4 will explain in detail the categorization of the CHANGCE role types and its origin. Observations made in an industrial application of the CHANGCE-Game with regards to this specific game component will be presented. In Sect. 5 these observations will be discussed and evaluated based on previous findings in research. Finally, conclusions, including limitations and prospects, will be drawn.

2 Theoretical Background

2.1 Gamification

Gamification has become a widely recognized term in business vocabulary. In literature, the most commonly used definition is by Deterding et al. stating that, “gamification is the use of game design elements in non-game contexts.” [4]. Among other prominent definition proposals, researchers have focused on the development of gamification frameworks, design and various fields of application. Apart from the evident business application, gamification also shows utility for educational purposes [5].

Several of the available models on gamification have obtained general prominence. Hunicke et al. in 2004 provide the MDA framework which distinguishes mechanics, dynamics and aesthetics as the three central components of game design [6]. In their game element hierarchy Werbach and Hunter propose a game design element categorization into components, mechanics and dynamics [7]. Deterding et al. provide a similar framework with five levels of game design elements and corresponding levels of abstraction [4]. These approaches differentiate between the level of interaction between a game component and its user. This means, some elements are not directly perceived by the user, however have an impact and a need to be incorporated by the game designer.

Keeping in mind the different levels of abstraction of game design elements, in 2016 Sailer suggests a list of game design elements, which are directly visible to the user. These elements are: points, badges or achievements, leaderboards or high-score lists, as well as team leaderboards, performance graphs, stories and avatars [8]. In literature, the clear definition of components may vary but revolve around these core elements. As gamification originates in computer science and gaming background, terminology such as “avatars” still carries an industry typical connotation. As we see from Thomas Voit in a business example, these avatars can also be called roles and can have a more universal application. This distinction is essential for the game design element of role types in CHANGCE-thinking, which will be analyzed in this paper [9].

2.2 Roles and Change of Perspectives (Diversity)

In modern day a team with multifaceted characters is known to exhibit a higher performance than one that composes of like-minded people. Thomas Voit builds upon this aspect of diversity to further extend the benefits of gamification. Using roles in a gamified context can provide a wider spectrum of perspectives [9].

In literature not specifically addressing the topic of gamification, a multitude of role models exist. Belbin proposes a model for 9 team roles typically found in management teams [10]. Kelley and Littman provide several characters that employees can take, known as the "Ten Faces of Innovation" [11]. The infamous "Six Thinking Hats" by Bono also exploit the advantages of the variety of perspectives to foster innovation and creativity. His method encourages workshop participants to adopt roles which they do not normally embody to inspire a change in thought processes and lateral thinking [12]. Minati et al. state that cognitive diversity, in other words assuming different roles, is a success factor for creativity [13].

2.3 Hierarchy in Organizations

In the past decades organizational structures have developed from bureaucratic conglomerates, to enterprises with flat hierarchies and agile, multidisciplinary teams. Researchers claim that incorporating flat management improves efficiency due to shorter lines of communication and simultaneously increases agility. Even still, different organizations may need individually tailored structures. Certain managerial skills are a prerequisite in order to successfully introduce flat management [14].

Regardless of the needed organizational design, if creativity is required, flat hierarchies (also known as self-organization) are more beneficial. According to Minati et al., it allows the development of bottom-up innovation processes. This means, if creativity is needed, a delayering of hierarchy levels must take place. [13] To extend this thought, if creativity is not required permanently, applying methods to temporarily neutralize hierarchy within a group and thereby foster a creative environment can be advantageous.

Additionally, creating an environment for open-mindedness, researchers address the arising generation Y ("Millennials"). The previous generation was accustomed to long-lasting and steady employment. With the turn of the century, globalization through digitalization dictates more flexible employer-employee-relationships. Advancing one more step we arrive at the generation Z ("iGeneration"), providing employees who demand agile work environments and flat hierarchies. This again shows the development and need for delayering in organizational structures [15].

3 Methodology

To analyze a certain element of gamification a proper research methodology is applied. Considering the prematurity of the field of gamification compared to other fields of study a qualitative approach is taken. The case study helps magnify the benefit of a key aspect of a gamification example. In this chapter, first the examined method is introduced, then the applied research design, the sampling, data collection and data analysis methods and approach are presented.

3.1 Research Context Case-Study CHANGCE-Thinking

The context of this analysis is the gamification example underlying CHANGCE-thinking. The CHANGCE-thinking mindset provides an approach combining the systematic identification and realization of chances, turning risk aversion into chance affinity. In this context, chances are generally understood as an organization's opportunities for improvement of any given nature (e.g. increase in revenue by the means of product diversification). CHANGCE-thinking is a framework that provides guidance and a toolset throughout a change process of an organization. The initial impulse is set in a ludic manner, creating intrinsic motivation for change and a lasting momentum. During the CHANGCE-Game the players expand their views by exploring eight chance-rooms while representing eight different roles. The game results deliver a strategic orientation for the enterprise. Many of the gamified elements stimulate creativity and "out of the box thinking" by the participants, thereby resulting in a thorough examination of chances and potential.

The roleplay and respective change of perspective is a key component of the gamified method. In this paper, the classification scheme of these role types and the effect of this game component will be analyzed based on existing research as well as observations and experience made with this method in practice. A more detailed description and origin of CHANGCE-thinking is provided by Witzgall et al. [16].

The CHANGCE-Game encompasses three playing phases: the preparation phase, the game phase and the debriefing phase. Prior to the game each player chooses a role which they would like to represent during the game. The roles are embodied by playing pieces and belong to eight corresponding perspectives which will be explained in detail in Sect. 4.1.

The next element of the first phase is the development of an enterprise portrayal in the present as well as for the future. For this step the players rank a deck of cards by importance and relevance. These cards are labeled with phrases or adjectives describing possible issues or changes within and outside of the organization (e.g. increased competition). The chosen ones are then laid down onto a ranking pyramid as shown in Fig. 1.

The second phase is the actual playing phase. The game board contains fields which encircle a balanced platform on which "houses" containing the chance-rooms stand. Puzzle segments of the chance-rooms are spread around the playing field (see Fig. 2). The composition of houses with different rooms on a balancing platform is used to visualize the need for the team to consider the different perspectives to get a comprehensive view on the different issues. The aim of the game as a team is to balance the central platform by filling the chance-rooms with the appropriate puzzle segments.

The playing pieces are moved around the platform on fields by the players, who take turns rolling a dice. The fields are assigned to the eight chance-rooms or event

Fig. 1. Example of a ranking pyramid

cards. On each field a corresponding card is drawn. Those pertaining to chance-rooms, contain statements which are discussed within the group. The group determines to which degree within a given range it agrees with the statement and delivers a justification as well as a suggestion for potential improvement. Once all the playing cards of a chance-room segment are answered, the players may put the respective puzzle piece into its designated space on the CHANGCE-Platform. Thereby, all the houses are filled during gameplay, visualizing the progress throughout the game. The game ends once all the cards of the eight chance-rooms have been discussed equally and the balance within the CHANGCE-Platform is restored.

In the final debriefing phase each player fills in a prepared web-diagram to estimate the actual potentials of the eight chance-rooms within the company according to one's own assessment. Meanwhile, the CHANGCE-thinking moderator analyzes the numerical ratings of the playing-cards and creates a web-chart with the average results (see Fig. 2).

It is from this numerical result that an analysis of the chances and potentials is derived to serve as the basis for strategic orientation. Keeping in mind the initially developed future self-image and this new orientation, the embarkment into the CHANGCE-thinking process can take place. Notably, the team of employees produce the input for these results by themselves during the CHANGCE-Game.

Fig. 2. The playing field of the CHANGCE-thinking game

3.2 Research Design

The CHANGCE-Game is a consulting method that uses gamification in business. Although gamification is presently applied in various fields such as education, marketing, employee motivation, from a research and development perspective it is still at an early stage. Therefore, this research takes a qualitative perspective, using a descriptive single case study in the shape of a real-world context example to gain insight on the benefits of role distribution within gamification. The purposeful sampling, using the CHANGCE-Game as the unit of analysis, is suitable for analyzing the impact of a framework of roles in gamification in business.

Most of the data collected and observed in this study is of observational nature. The two moderators of the CHANGCE-Game took on the role of researchers during the industrial implementation of the method, focusing on the role component. To lessen the influence of subjectivity, other researchers took upon themselves the analysis of the field observations. The data analysis is done abductively to lead to a general theory on the impact of using roles in gamification for business.

4 Results

4.1 Roles in CHANGCE-thinking

To fully comprehend the logic behind the role types introduced in CHANGCE-thinking, the fundamental framework which underlies the roles must be explained. The eight chance-rooms represent the first dimension of the entire method. The first four of the eight rooms, which can be seen in Table 1, represent concepts which are crucial for an organization's success. The latter four rooms consist of the main stakeholder groups. It is by this logic, that this concept aims to include all areas of a company, including its surrounding environment (Fig. 3).

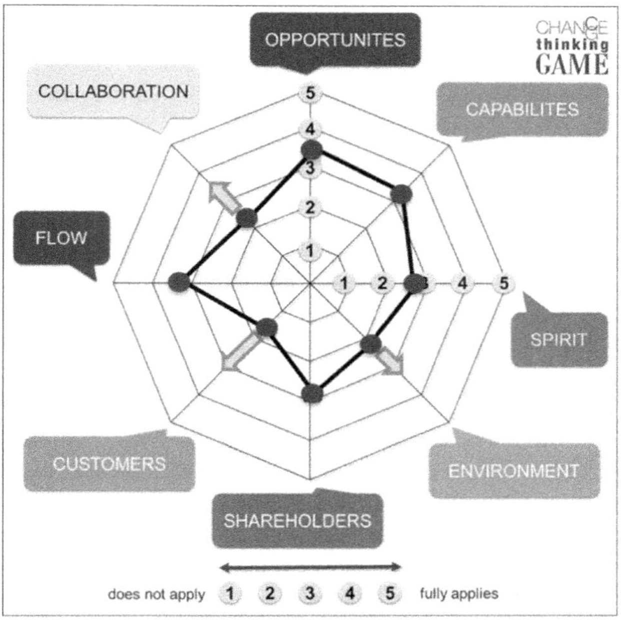

Fig. 3. Example result of the web-chart evaluation

Table 1. The CHANGCE-thinking chance-rooms and the respective roles

Chance-room	Role type	Description of role
Spirit	Spirit	Creator, reformer initiative, intuitive, lively
Opportunities	Space	Leader, manager defining, aware, fact oriented, controlling
Capabilities	Skill	Worker process and result oriented, constant
Collaboration	Collaboration	Team player, connector, motivating, open, communicative, cooperative
Shareholders	Shareholder	Business man, director, goal oriented, motivating, visionary, dominant
Flow	Flow	Bridge builder caring, calm, supportive, balanced, cautious
Customers	Customer	Buyer, user confident, demanding, selective, critical
Environment	Social Minder	Observer, protector social, just, preserving, sensible

A key concept of this categorization is the notion of balance, which is a key ingredient in using this approach. The eight chance rooms do not have a ranking or individual weights but are of equal value. When investigating the chance rooms of an enterprise during the CHANGCE-Game, the framework of rules, as previously touched upon, ensures an equal examination of each.

It is taken into consideration that a definite boundary between two chance rooms does not exist, especially not during play and discussion. Components of the chance-room Collaboration can at times be found in the Flow chance-room. Interests of Customers can share similarity with those of Shareholders. However, this overlap does not pose a disadvantage but rather ensures the analysis of all chances. The necessary balance is furthermore ensured by the CHANGCE-Game moderators.

The advantage and benefit of the division into chance-rooms lies in providing a logical framework for dividing any given organization into eight areas. These areas are the basis for in-depth analysis and balanced discussion of the enterprise.

Congruent and based on the chance-rooms the role typology was developed (**Error! Reference source not found.**). Each role type and its assigned participant is seen as the advocate for the respective chance-room. It is the player's responsibility to take on the role and argue from its perspective. The aim is not to present an exaggerated interpretation of this role type. Rather the player should represent the interest of actual employees of this position in his/her organization. An important aspect in the distribution of the role types is letting the participants choose the role they wish to embody. At the same time, to foster new perspectives the moderator should pay attention that no participant takes on the same perspective he or she has in the daily work routine.

4.2 Observations from the Field

The impact of previously described role types of CHANGCE-thinking will now be displayed in a real-life industry example. The CHANGCE-Game was applied with a workshop team of an international service and hardware provider of event and media technology headquartered in Germany. The workshop served as a kick-off for a change process to develop and establish an efficient supplier network.

Over the course of one and a half days the participants consisted of nine employees of different rank and position. To anonymize and at the same time distinguish between the participants, the acronyms P1 to P9 will be used.

The nine employees can be categorized into three levels of hierarchy: P1 is from the highest corporate level, P2–P6 are in the second managerial level and the remaining P7–P9 participants belong to the third level. P1 can be described as the entire division leader. P2–P6 are group managers each responsible for their own team within the organization. P7 is a lower level employee with P2 as the team leader. P8 is of the first-level corporate unit, however compared to the employees participating is also in the third and lowest level of hierarchy. P9 belongs to the third level of hierarchy because it is an external worker, not directly employed by the organization.

Due to previously held interviews by the two moderators, each participant can be thoroughly described with respect to their role and position in the company. Once the CHANGCE-Game is initialized, the participants choose the role they wish to represent during the workshop. The allocation of the role types is displayed in Table 2. The work environment of the group as described by the employees and observers is perceived as friendly and collegial. Nevertheless, a hierarchy and its implications (see Sect. 2.3) exist. The result of the application of the CHANGCE-thinking method is that this strict hierarchy seems to crumble (Note: We have made similar observations in other industrial applications of the method). The criticism-free environment, which is needed to accomplish the goals of the CHANGCE-Game, is provided by the role play element of this method. Since participants defend unordinary perspectives, especially in hierarchical terms (e.g. manager to worker), the hierarchy and chain of command is no longer of importance. The central concept of balance in CHANGCE-thinking allows every voice to be considered. Giving equal value to each perspective creates a 'level playing field'.

Table 2. Participants and their roles during gameplay

Participant	Role during CHANGCE-Game	Level of hierarchy
P1	Skill Type	1
P2	Space Type	2
P3	Shareholder Type	2
P4	Spirit Type	2
P5	Customer Type	2
P6	Flow Type	2
P7	Collaboration Type	3
P8	Social Minder Type	3
P9	Collaboration Type	3

The first result of this field observation is that during the workshop participants take on new perspectives than the ones they are commonly do. P1 is ordinarily the superior of all employees participating and takes on the Skill Type or worker perspective during gameplay. P3 is generally a team manager and must take on the perspective of the company's shareholders. P7 can be described as a representative worker and embodies the Collaboration Type, which is responsible for the successful collaboration of all employees (compare the Description of Roles in Table 1).

Furthermore, the spectrum provided by the eight different role types of CHANGCE-thinking is greater than the one that can be observed in the workshop team. Without neglecting the individuality of each participant as a person, the role classification of this method provides complementary perspectives. In the original team constellation, a majority holds a similar team leader position. In this context, the variety of the eight role types adds perspectives such as the Social Minder, the Flow Type and the Collaboration type.

These two findings lead to a more thorough examination of the enterprise by its employees during the workshop. Participants generally represent a new and unfamiliar point of view, leading to a greater team dynamic during discussion. A greater number of standpoints are considered, again fueling a productive and diverse analysis of the organization's chance-rooms.

The hierarchical constellation of the participants who took part in this gamified workshop is complex compared to the relatively small size of the group. The work environment of the group as described by the employees and observers is perceived as friendly and collegial. Nevertheless, a hierarchy and its implications (see Sect. 2.3) exist. The result of the application of the CHANGCE-thinking method is that this strict hierarchy seems to crumble (Note: We have made similar observations in other industrial applications of the method). The criticism-free environment, which is needed to accomplish the goals of the CHANGCE-Game, is provided by the role play element of this method. Since participants defend unordinary perspectives, especially in hierarchical terms (e.g. manager to worker), the hierarchy and chain of command is no longer of importance. The central concept of balance in CHANGCE-thinking allows every voice to be considered. Giving equal value to each perspective creates a 'level playing field'.

5 Discussion

The aim of the CHANGCE-Game is for the participants to systematically identify and discuss chances within their organization in a playful manner. The results observed in the industrial application concerning the benefits of the roles in CHANGCE-thinking are apparent.

As Sailer and Voit describe in their list of game elements, roles can be a component within gamification [8, 9]. The roles assigned in this industry study lead to a change of perspective for the participating employees. Researchers argue that a change of perspective provokes new thought processes and lateral thinking [10–12]. The variety of roles within the CHANGCE-Game, therefore allows the participants to efficiently discover chances within their organization. The productivity is furthermore increased through the additional creativity this method fosters in its participants. As Minati et al. argue, cognitive diversity is a key success factor for creativity [13]. The variety of roles and the change of perspective incite creative ideas on new discussion points for the group.

To further increase the productive identification of the organization's chances, the role schematic breaks down the existing hierarchy. As Minati et al. states, flat hierarchies produce a more creative environment [13]. This creative surrounding, also provided by the CHANGCE-Game, allows for a criticism-free and diverse discussion of an organization's chances. According to Klaffke, the modern day employee seeks self-organizing enterprises with flat hierarchies, further increasing the benefit of the role schematic of CHANGCE-thinking [15]. This breakdown of a hierarchy can be observed during the implementation of the CHANGCE-Game. The hierarchy within a team or organization will typically dissolve in both the vertical and horizontal dimension. The method serves as an initialization of a change process. It should therefore be analyzed, whether hierarchy rebuilds over time or the deconstruction of hierarchy within a ludic method is sufficient for long-term endeavors.

6 Conclusion

Gamification has proven to be an effective tool in the context of education and business. A wide variety of applications can be found for example in the form of training methods, learning applications and customer engagement.

In this study, the benefits of incorporating roles as a game design element are displayed in an industrial application and supported by existing literature. Utilizing a framework of various roles, which participants take on within a workshop, provides diverse perspectives when searching for an organization's chances. Employees leave the role they embody on a day-to-day basis and take on a new one, analyzing and interpreting matters through a fresh pair of eyes. This role component within the CHANGCE-Game helps to dissolve hierarchies, giving equality to every employee's opinion. It is through this element and the gamified framework in its entity that a change process can be initialized successfully.

This study exemplifies a gamified method that has found application in various fields of industry. It is solely one of many existing methodologies of incorporating roles in a gamification setting. To increase the validity of the theory on benefits of this game element, future analysis should incorporate the empirical analysis of numerous methods. Moreover, this study lays focus on a single element of gamification and others may well be target of further analysis. Apart from research on the elementary level, general effects of gamification on its users in different environments and contexts should continue to be subject of investigation.

References

1. Hipp-Gruner, M.: Gamification in der marketingkommunikation. Brand Evolution, pp. 441–462. Springer, Wiesbaden (2017). https://doi.org/10.1007/978-3-658-15816-3_24
2. Witte, J., Westbrook, R., Witte, M.M.: Gamification and training. In: Global Conference on Education and Research (GLOCER 2017) CONFERENCE PROCEEDINGS, pp. 157–159 (2017)
3. Mora, A., Riera, D., Gonzalez, C., Arnedo-Moreno, J.: A literature review of gamification design frameworks. In: IEEE (ed.) 2015 7th International Conference on Games and Virtual Worlds for Serious Applications (VS-Games), Skövde, Sweden, 16–18 Sep 2015, pp. 1–8. IEEE (2015). https://doi.org/10.1109/vs-games.2015.7295760
4. Deterding, S., Khaled, R., Nacke, L.E., Dixon, D.: Gamification: toward a definition. In: Tan, D. (ed.) Proceedings of the 2011 Annual Conference Extended Abstracts on Human Factors in Computing Systems, pp. 12–15. ACM, New York (2011)
5. Ferreira, A.T., Araújo, A.M., Fernandes, S., Miguel, I.C.: Gamification in the workplace: a systematic literature review. In: Rocha, Á., Correia, A.M., Adeli, H., Reis, L.P., Costanzo, S. (eds.) WorldCIST 2017. AISC, vol. 571, pp. 283–292. Springer, Cham (2017). https://doi.org/10.1007/978-3-319-56541-5_29
6. Hunicke, R., Leblanc, M., Zubek, R.: MDA: a formal approach to game design and game research (2004)
7. Werbach, K., Hunter, D.: For the Win: How Game Thinking Can Revolutionize Your Business. Wharton Digital Press, New York (2012)

8. Sailer, M.: Die Wirkung von Gamification auf Motivation und Leistung. Springer, Wiesbaden (2016). https://doi.org/10.1007/978-3-658-14309-1
9. Voit, T.: Gamification als change-management-methode im prozessmanagement. In: Strahringer, S., Leyh, C. (eds.) Gamification und Serious Games. EH, pp. 43–54. Springer, Wiesbaden (2017). https://doi.org/10.1007/978-3-658-16742-4_4
10. Belbin, R.M.: Management Teams: Why They Succeed or Fail, 3rd edn. Elsevier/Butterworth-Heinemann, Amsterdam (2011)
11. Kelley, T., Littman, J.: The Ten Faces of Innovation: IDEO's Strategies for Beating the Devil's Advocate and Driving Creativity Throughout Your Organization. Currency/Doubleday, New York (2005)
12. Bono, E.D.: Das Sechsfarben-Denken. Ein neues Trainingsmodell. ETB Econ-Lebenshorizonte, vol. 23013. Econ-Taschenbuch-Verlag, Düsseldorf (1989)
13. Minati, G., de Toni, A.F., Biotto, G., Battistella, C.: Organizational design drivers to enable emergent creativity in web-based communities. Learn. Organ. **19**, 335–349 (2012). https://doi.org/10.1108/09696471211226699
14. Lemons, J.F.: Established companies flatten structures. In: SAGE Business Researcher. SAGE Publishing (2015)
15. Klaffke, M.: Millennials und generation Z – charakteristika der nachrückenden arbeitnehmer-generationen. In: Klaffke, M. (ed.) Generationen-Management, pp. 57–82. Springer, Wiesbaden (2014). https://doi.org/10.1007/978-3-658-02325-6_3
16. Witzgall, P., Kapfhammer, P., Trenz, E.-M., Kiechle, T., Gebler, T., Indefrey, A.: CHANGCE-thinking – a ludic kick-off to chance orientation. In: Stolfa, J., Stolfa, S., O'Connor, R.V., Messnarz, R. (eds.) EuroSPI 2017. CCIS, vol. 748, pp. 269–280. Springer, Cham (2017). https://doi.org/10.1007/978-3-319-64218-5_22

SPI in Industry 4.0

Developing and Testing of a Virtual and Augmented Reality Maturity Model

Sonja Hammerschmid(✉)

IMC University of Applied Sciences, Piaristengasse 1, 3500 Krems, Austria
sonja.hammerschmid@imc-krems.eu

Abstract. The aim of this article is to develop a virtual and augmented reality maturity model and test it in selected companies. First, the terms were defined and a literature search was carried out on existing and established maturity models. In the second part of the work, the model was built and tested in four companies with the help of focus group discussions. The next step was to analyze the maturity of these companies. The results of the focus groups show that three of the four companies are already involved in VR and/or AR. Furthermore, the analysis also shows that these four companies would like to deal more intensively with the technologies in the next few years. Three of the four companies have already an application in the field of marketing and sales. Furthermore, all four companies see high potential in the field of customer service and human resources. The potential in the corporate sector is increasingly seen in the AR area, whereas VR is seen as an entry into the technology. All four companies believe that VR and/or AR will be very important tools in the business world to keep up to date. After the maturity model was tested, it seems that every company needs slightly changes of the levels to fit their needs.

Keywords: Virtual reality · Augmented reality · Maturity model

1 Definition Virtual Reality and Augmented Reality

1.1 Virtual Reality

In computer science the term "virtual" has been used for a long time, e.g. virtual drives. The virtual drive is the opposite of the physical drive, the virtual drive is only simulated via the main memory [1].

Simulation can be named as the basis of virtual. In contrast to a simulation, the virtual world should give the impression that it is reality. In other words, a simulation tries to illustrate reality, using virtual content to tend to replace reality. Thus Bühl describes VR as a technology that integrates people directly into a computer-generated development environment and implements all movements in real time, in contrast to pure computer simulation in which no immersion occurs [2].

Immersion describes the degree of involvement in VR through objective, quantifiable stimulation of human perceptions. Due to a higher degree of immersion, the probability of presence is greater [3]. If it feels to the user as if he or she were in the

X. Larrucea et al. (Eds.): EuroSPI 2018, CCIS 896, pp. 279–288, 2018.
https://doi.org/10.1007/978-3-319-97925-0_23

virtual environment, then this feeling can be described as presence. This environment is represented by an immersive VR system [4].

According to the Gabler Wirtschaftslexikon, VR is a computer-generated reality in 3D, often with sound. It can be used either in large-screen formats, in special rooms or via VR glasses. Another special feature of VR is the interaction in this simulated reality, e.g. by movement and/or by handling input devices [5].

However, there is still no uniform definition of VR, as this field of science is relatively new. Nevertheless, there are several ways to define VR. One approach is the technology-oriented view, in which the input and output devices used are considered in order to distinguish it from 3D content in computer graphics. The creation of a human-machine interface for a particularly natural or intuitive interaction in an apparent reality can be seen as a further characterization and goal of VR. A perfect virtual world would address all sensory impressions of the user through the computer and thus lead to presence [4].

A purely technology-based approach probably does not make sense, since technologies change relatively quickly and the definitions would therefore no longer be appropriate in the event of technological development or change. The most frequent definition attempts, according to which this article is oriented, include the degree of immersion or presence in a computer-generated world, in which it is usually possible to trade interactively and in real time.

1.2 Augmented Reality

As described in the previous chapter, the goal of VR is to present and simultaneously perceive a virtual reality without further perceiving the real environment. AR, on the other hand, is about enriching the real world with computer-generated additional objects. This means that no completely new worlds are created, but that the real environment is supplemented with a virtual environment [6, 7].

The definition of Azuma has largely established itself: AR is a combination of reality and virtuality, which is interactive, in which the representation takes place in real time and in which 3D objects are registered [8].

In the popular science environment, AR is often limited to the aspect of adding virtual content to reality, while ignoring the other characteristics. Another definition approach from the perspective of perception is that AR is a (direct, interactive and real-time capable) extension of the perception of the real environment by virtual content. The expression and impression is oriented as far as possible to reality, so that in extreme cases a distinction between real and virtual (sensory) impressions is no longer possible [9].

Mixed Reality (MR) is often used as a synonym for AR, but MR represents a continuum in contrast to AR. This continuum extends between reality and virtuality, with the proportion of reality continuously decreasing while virtuality increases accordingly. If virtuality predominates without the environment being exclusively virtual, augmented virtuality is used. If, on the other hand, the proportion of reality is greater, it is AR [10].

Important terms that are important for the understanding of AR are tracking and rendering. Tracking refers to the detection and following of objects. Rendering is defined as a technique of visual output, new scenes are created by combining real and virtual objects [11].

The definition of AR according to Azuma is widely accepted in the literature and is also used as a basis in this article. Furthermore, the terms AR, Augmented Virtuality and MR are used synonymously, since a demarcation of the individual cases would exceed the scope of this paper and the existing or already established technologies make a distinction almost impossible.

2 VR and AR Maturity Model

Maturity models can be used to describe the quality of processes. By analyzing the processes, they can be made more comprehensible and, above all, more efficient [12]. An appropriate maturity model can be a helpful tool for determining the actual situation of processes. An anticipated, desired or typical development path of an object is to be described with consecutive and predefined rankings. These objects can be the entire organization or individual processes, for example. Most maturity models have a level system with five different ranks, while five represents the highest maturity. By 2015 there were already more than 150 different maturity models for different areas [13].

The aim of the VR and AR maturity model is to offer companies support in deciding for or against VR and/or AR. In an initial workshop, the possible applications in the company were presented. After a short discussion or a more detailed explanation of the areas of application of VR and AR a decision should be made as to in which area(s) the use of VR and AR offers the greatest potential. After this workshop, the corresponding actual and target level can be entered into the maturity model.

A scale of one to five is used to evaluate the individual fields, since this method has already proven to be useful for existing models and a further subdivision of the technologies does not make much sense at present. Most of the established maturity models have a scale of five levels, because of this the author decided to include five levels. If the technology has progressed further, then an adaptation of the maturity levels and a possible expansion can be considered (Fig. 1).

Nevertheless, an individual maturity level should be defined for each stage of the value chain, since the programming and handling of the individual application areas can be very different. Even with minimal deviations between the applications, the user should have the opportunity to prepare for the application area in as much detail as possible.

This initial classification can help companies to decide on a technology. The detailed maturity levels of the individual applications can be used for a more in-depth analysis of company conditions (Tables 1 and 2).

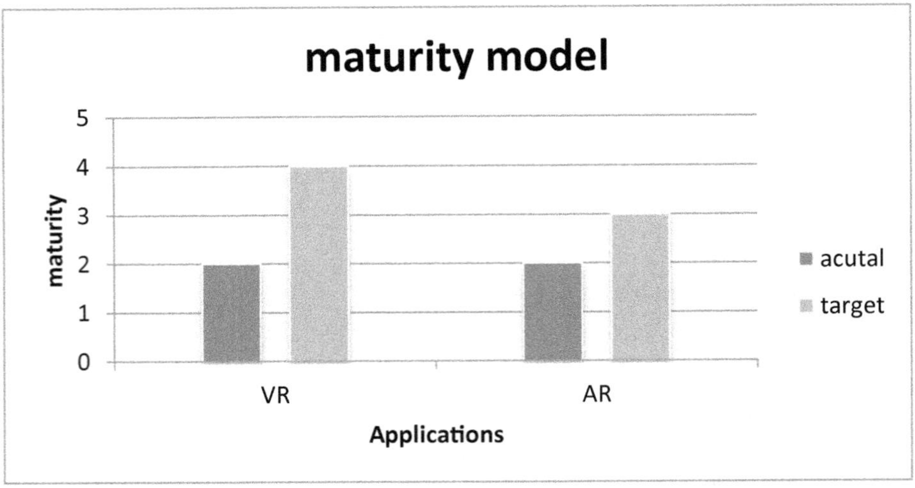

Fig. 1. VR and AR maturity model (own representation) (The values given are the average of the analyzed companies; they serve purely to clarify the illustration.)

Table 1. VR maturity levels (own representation)

Level 5	Total immersion (e.g. physical laws, detailed environment, etc.)
Level 4	Configuration of the 3D models
Level 3	Interaction in the virtual world
Level 2	Adjust background to 3D model
Level 1	View 3D model in virtual world

Table 2. AR maturity levels (own representation)

Level 5	Problem areas are automatically recognized and suitable solution suggestions are displayed
Level 4	Connecting other people to share information and presentations
Level 3	Objects and information can be configured
Level 2	Objects and information are displayed
Level 1	Products or environment are tracked (e.g. QR codes) and recognized by AR devices, e.g. smartphones, data glasses

3 Methodology

A focus group discussion is a method of qualitative social research and is one of the explorative studies in which a small group is stimulated to discuss a specific topic through an information input. Qualitative research is more open and flexible than quantitative research and is suitable for describing, interpreting and understanding interrelationships. Due to this open design, the possible answers of the discussion partners are unrestricted and deeper information content can be achieved. Nevertheless, the statements are usually not representative, which is why they are more suitable for obtaining detailed descriptions of impressions and individual opinions. Therefore, the goal of qualitative research is to represent reality with the help of subjective views of the interviewees and thus to understand causes and behavior as comprehensibly as possible. One advantage of qualitative research is the investigation of new, unknown facts [14].

The input can be provided, for example, by a short film, a picture, a homepage or a lecture. The discussion process can be structured with the help of a guide, as in individual interviews, thereby ensuring that all relevant aspects are addressed. Furthermore, the comparability of the results is increased if several focus group discussions are conducted. Normally, several focus group discussions are held either with the same participants on different topics or with different participants on the same topic. As a rule, three to five focus groups with six to twelve participants are conducted. For larger groups, control can be more difficult, while for smaller groups it can be difficult to keep the discussion going [15, 16].

The biggest advantage of the group discussion in comparison to other types of survey is to work out collective orientations in the development process. While opinions can change during the discussion with other participants, they become clearer and more thoughtful. Nevertheless, opinions can be prevented due to the group dynamics; individual participants can monopolize the discussion [16].

The focus group discussion is used because this work is an exploratory topic that is still relatively unexplored; especially the maturity model is a new development that must be tested before it can be used on the market and possibly also commercially.

The design of exploratory studies is very flexible, whereby openness does not stand for arbitrariness. Several points need to be decided in order for a high-quality group discussion to take place [16].

It must be decided which groups will participate in the discussion and how they will be recruited. Furthermore, the technical and local conditions, moderation and motivation of participants, as well as the degree of structuring, group size and number of groups must be decided. Important for the implementation is the intention to learn, as well as the transcription and analysis of the discussion. Finally, it must be determined how the results are to be presented and presented [16].

The composition of the group is decisively related to the quality of the group discussion. There are two different groups, the "real groups" and the "ad hoc groups". A real group consists of people who also form a group beyond the round of talks, e.g. a department of a company. In ad hoc groups, people are recruited who have not yet come together in this composition [17].

The use of a guideline in qualitative research is controversially discussed, and some researchers find that the guideline narrows the discussion too much and thus impairs openness. However, there should be a guide in which at least the topics should be listed and discussed in the discussion. Respondents should be encouraged to discuss with the help of the guide, so a guide for group discussion should be smaller in scope than that of qualitative individual interviews [17].

In this work real groups are preferred, as it is to be tested whether the developed maturity model can be used in companies and to find out in which stage the companies are. Therefore, colleagues at work are interviewed, although not all of them have to work directly with each other. There is also only one rough guideline, i.e. there is only an overview of the topics to be discussed in order to keep the discussion as open as possible.

A possible evaluation of group discussions can be divided into three steps, the thematic course, the formulating interpretation and the reflective interpretation. In the first phase, the recordings are listened to again and the topics addressed are summarized by headings. This first protocol also defines the relevance of the individual topics. In the next step, the selected passages are transcribed and subjected to a formulating interpretation. Headings (topics) are identified again in this process. This is already an interpretation, because something is possibly mentioned in the paraphrasing that cannot be found in the transcription. In the last step of the reflective interpretation, the focus is on the motivation of what is said. In other words, it is analyzed and interpreted as something was said [18].

In this paper, this form of evaluation is used because the group discussions are not necessarily comparable and therefore one interpretation per group is better. It is not possible to establish general rules, but rather to research the current and target situation of companies and their individual maturity in the field of VR and AR.

4 Maturity Levels of Different Companies

All four focus groups come from companies that are internationally active and have their origins in German-speaking countries. All companies have already dealt more or less in advance with the subject of VR and/or AR. Three of the four companies already have their own VR and/or AR applications. All companies agree that the costs should not exceed the benefits.

In the area of marketing and sales, the participants in the focus groups see the greatest potential, at least in the product presentation. Three of the four companies already have existing applications in this area, both in VR and in AR. In the coming years, these applications will be expanded even further, but more into the broad, i.e. that more products are available for users. The investment in interaction and configuration is currently considered too uneconomical. As soon as cheaper software of good quality is available, more money will probably be invested in immersion. On the other hand, virtual meetings are viewed with skepticism and participants are relatively satisfied with their current systems in the companies. All companies use either Skype for Business or Lync, many also video transmission. Only one company has problems with the video application because the works council is against it and is skeptical about data protection.

An application in customer service is rated as very interesting by one focus group in particular, whereby it must be emphasized that all participants work in this area and can therefore imagine the application very well. One of the focus groups sees no need in this area because its products can be set up so easily that no further help is needed. The other two focus groups can well imagine investing in this area. All participants have the opinion that an application in this area is quite efficient.

Investments will be made in employee training in all four companies. Due to the shortage of skilled workers, it is becoming increasingly important to train the employees in the companies. These measures are also conceivable with the VR and AR for the participants. Above all because investments are to be made in the area of product presentation and these applications can also be used for training. This synergy effect was recognized by all companies.

Product development is seen even more skeptically, especially because the software is not yet as mature. Nevertheless, it is conceivable that developers worldwide could consult on a product even before it is produced at high cost. When it comes to virtual development or configuration, there are the same problems as with product presentation. Although the potential is seen, there is the opinion that such an application cannot be used cost-effectively in the near future.

A smooth target/actual comparison is always positive, especially in production. The earlier deviations are detected, the lower the costs incurred. The participants are of the opinion that the manufacturer of the production machine should also be responsible for the AR application. One of the companies has already bought the first machine with AR technology, but the reason for the purchase was, presumably, not the technology. It is also not yet clear whether this application will be used at all.

Navigation systems are already regarded as very good, and it is also suspected that a functional application will only be possible in several years' time. The Pick-by-Vision area is better rated. Nevertheless, two of the four focus groups see this area as dying out. More and more storage activities are already carried out exclusively by robots.

In general, the basic mood towards the technologies is very positive. As a result, the companies surveyed see the greatest potential in marketing and sales for the time being. After that, however, the boundaries will become somewhat blurred, with customer service and human resources also playing a major role.

Another interesting aspect is that more money will probably be invested in the AR area. One of the focus groups stressed that AR would probably offer more advantages than VR. The aspect of hygiene in connection with VR was addressed by two focus groups.

Figure 2 shows that two of the four groups have already reached their target maturity. However, this does not mean that these companies do not want to develop further. For example, focus group 3 and 4 aim to broaden further, i.e. to add more products with same maturity. In other words, the possibilities of the technologies are not yet to be deepened in the near future. Since the costs are not yet related to the benefits for a more in-depth development, these companies are consciously opting for a lower maturity and are waiting for the further development of the technologies and thus for a cost reduction of the software as well as the hardware. Companies see somewhat more potential in the use of AR, as primarily more customers can be addressed, since most already have at least one AR-capable terminal at home. Nevertheless, VR is seen as a kind of entry point for the technologies.

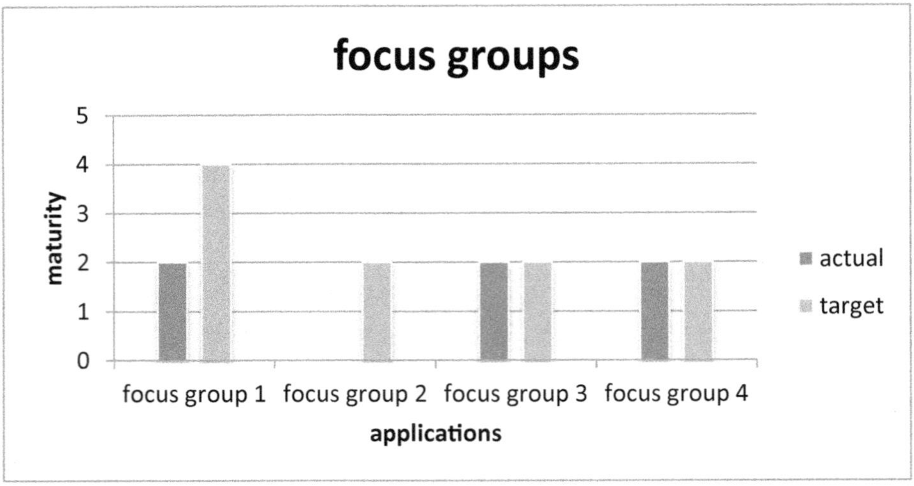

Fig. 2. Analysis of focus groups (own representation)

5 Conclusion

After the first draft of the VR and AR maturity model was tested in four companies the result is, that it is very different to find one appropriate model for every company. But all four companies were able to handle the model they would need just simply changes. In the next years when companies use the technologies daily the definition of individual levels would be easier. Furthermore, at this stage of the technologies the companies want to concentrate on the width of the applications and not on the depth of them. In other words, if a company has an AR application to show products they concentrate on showing more products before enhancing the application.

The VR and AR maturity model is a first step but it should be tested with even more companies to get an model which is appropriate for all companies.

6 SPI Manifesto

The SPI Manifesto can also help if a company wants to implement VR and/or AR. It is very important that people get involved in the implementation phase. Most of the people are skeptical about change but if they are working on the project from the beginning they accept the change easier. As not everybody can work on a project, it is very important to explain the value of the change. The culture of an organization is very important while implementing new software and/or technologies. In an agile company it would be easier to change something than in a conservative organization. Another important subject is the real value for the company. From time to time companies just implement new technologies or software because their competitors work with it, without analyzing their own need. A maturity model can help you visualize the value for a process, project or the whole company. Also, the VR and AR maturity model can help to explain the extra value of these technologies [18–21].

As the SPI Manifesto states there is not one model that fits for everyone, like the VR and AR maturity model. Every company must identify their challenges and objectives before using a special model or parts of it. As every implementation could go wrong it is very important to have a risk management and think about the worst case [18–21].

The SPI Manifesto is a good start before implementing new software. But not only for software, it can help to get an overview about change management.

References

1. Hennig, A.: Die andere Wirklichkeit. Virtual Reality - Konzepte, Standards, Lösungen. Addison-Wesley, Bonn (1997)
2. Bühl, A.: Die virutelle Geschellschaft. Ökonomie, Politik und Kultur im Zeichen des Cyberspace. Springer Fachmedien, Wiesbaden (1997). https://doi.org/10.1007/978-3-322-93548-9
3. Dörner, R., Steinicke, F.: Wahrnehmungsaspekte von VR. In: Dörner, R., Broll, W., Grimm, P., Jung, B. (eds.) Virtual und Augmented Reality (VR/AR). Grundlagen und Methoden der Virtuellen und Augmentierten Realität, pp. 33–64. Springer, Heidelberg (2013). https://doi.org/10.1007/978-3-642-28903-3_2
4. Dörner, R., Jung, B., Grimm, P., Broll, W., Göbel, M.: Einleitung. In: Dörner, R., Broll, W., Grimm, P., Jung, B. (eds.) Virtual und Augmented Reality (VR/AR). Grundlagen und Methoden der Virtuellen und Augmentierten Realität, pp. 1–32. Springer, Heidelberg (2013). https://doi.org/10.1007/978-3-642-28903-3_1
5. Bendel, O.: Gabler Wirtschaftslexikon. (S. G. Verlag, Herausgeber) Called up on 05. March 2017 von Virtuelle Realtiät (n.a.). http://wirtschaftslexikon.gabler.de/Archiv/-2045879784/virtuelle-realitaet-v1.html
6. Klein, G.: Visual tracking for augmented reality. Edge-based tracking techniques for AR applications. VDM Verlag, Saarbrücken (2009)
7. Azuma, R.M.: A survey of augmented reality. In: Teleoperators and Virtual Environments, vol. 6, pp. 335–385 (1997)
8. Broll, W.: Augmentiere realität. In: Dörner, R., Broll, W., Grimm, P., Jung, B. (eds.) Virtual und Augmented Reality (VR/AR). Grundlagen und Mehtoden der Virtuellen und Augmentierten Realität, pp. 237–290. Springer, Heidelberg (2013). https://doi.org/10.1007/978-3-642-28903-3_8
9. Milgram, P., Takemura, H., Utsumi, A., Kishino, F.: Augmented reality: a class of display on the reality-virtuality continuum. In: Telemanipulator and Telepresence Technologies, vol. 2351, pp. 282–292, December 1995
10. Mehler-Bichler, A., Steiger, L.: Augemented Reality - Theorie und Praxis. Oldenbourg Wissenschaftsvertrag, München (2014)
11. Grande, M.: 100 Minuten für Anforderungsmanagement. Kompaktes Wissen nicht nur für Projektleiter und Entwickler. Vieweg + Teubner Verlag, Wiesbaden (2011). https://doi.org/10.1007/978-3-8348-8135-9
12. De Bruin, T., Rosemann, M., Freeze, R., Kulkarni, U.: Understanding the main phase of developing a maturity assessment model. In: 16th Australian Conference on Information Systems, Queensland University of Technology, Brisbane, Australia, p. 11 (2005)

13. Berger-Grabner, D.: Wissenschaftliches Arbeiten in den Wirtschafts- und Sozialwissenschaften. Springer Gabler, Wiesbaden (2016). https://doi.org/10.1007/978-3-658-13078-7
14. Schulz, M.: Quick and easy!? Fokusgruppen in der angewandten Sozialwissenschaft. In: Schulz, M., Mack, B., Renn, O. (eds.) Fokusgruppen in der empirischen Sozialwissnschaft. Von der Konzeption bis zur Auswertung, pp. 9–22. Springer VS, Stuttgart (2012). https://doi.org/10.1007/978-3-531-19397-7_1
15. Vogl, S.: Gruppendiskussion. In: Baur, N., Blasius, J. (eds.) Handbuch Methoden der empirischen Sozialforschung, pp. 581–586. Springer VS, Deutschland (2014). https://doi.org/10.1007/978-3-531-18939-0_41
16. Kühn, T., Koschel, K.-V.: Gruppendiskussionen. Ein Praxis-Handbuch, 2nd edn. Springer VS, Wiesbaden (2018). https://doi.org/10.1007/978-3-531-93243-9
17. Loos, P., Schäffer, B.: Das gruppendiskussionsverfahren. In: Bohnsack, R., Lüders, C., Reichertz, J. (eds.) Qualitative Sozialforschung, pp. 7–105. Leske + Budrich, Opladen, Deutschland (2001)
18. Korsaa, M., et al.: The SPI Manifesto and the ECQA SPI manager certification scheme. J. Softw. Evol. Process **24**(5), 525–540 (2012)
19. Korsaa, M., et al.: The people aspects in modern process improvement management approaches. J. Soft. Evol. Process **25**(4), 381–391 (2013)
20. Larrucea, X., O'Connor, R.V., Colomo-Palacios, R., Laporte, C.Y.: Software process improvement in very small organizations. IEEE Softw. **33**(2), 85–89 (2016)
21. Sanchez-Gordon, M.L., Colomo-Palacios, R., Amescua, A.: Towards measuring the impact of the SPI manifesto: a systematic review. In: Proceedings of European System and Software Process Improvement and Innovation Conference, pp. 100–110 (2013)

Best Practices in Implementing Traceability

ALM Tool Infrastructure with a Focus on DevOps Culture

Suha Akman(✉), Elif Berru Aksuyek, and Onur Kaynak

iNNOVA IT Solutions, METU Technopolis, Ankara 06800, Turkey
{sakman, eaksuyek, okaynak}@innova.com.tr

Abstract. At iNNOVA IT Solutions, with our team of more than 1300 IT professionals, we tailor platform-independent customized software and systems solutions. The ALM tool infrastructure has been continuously improved over the several years in order to maintain the work item traceability, define a single source of truth and increase communication and collaboration which is one of the key cultural aspects of DevOps. This paper describes how the tool infrastructure is set up and used in order to manage traceability between work items such as change requests, configuration items, technical documents, test cases, technical tasks and code; make use of the knowledge base and history during impact analysis; track the real time status of releases, change requests, sprints, test plans and all the related work items; generate formatted customer documentation in long term maintenance projects.

Keywords: Application Lifecycle Management · Requirement traceability
Software process improvement
Software development life cycle tool infrastructure · DevOps

1 iNNOVA IT Solutions

iNNOVA is a leading software developer and integrator in Turkey, which provides innovative software solutions and services, covering the entire project lifecycle from consulting, design, application development and integration to support. Established in September 1999, iNNOVA serves its client base from main offices in İstanbul and Ankara, a manufacturing facility for kiosks in Istanbul, as well as support offices in 12 cities in Turkey. Areas of business include Operations Support System/Business Support System for Telco operators, Financial Transaction Applications, Enterprise Resource Planning, Customer Relationship Management and Business Intelligence systems, portals, custom software development Information Technology (IT) systems management and infrastructure, IT security and kiosk systems. As of 2018 Q1 with a team of more than 1300 IT Professionals serving its clients, iNNOVA has delivered solutions and services to customers in 37 countries to date [1].

X. Larrucea et al. (Eds.): EuroSPI 2018, CCIS 896, pp. 291–303, 2018.
https://doi.org/10.1007/978-3-319-97925-0_24

2 iNNOVA Configuration Management Team

Configuration Management Team was established in 2015 with the goal of having an independent support staff in projects to make sure configuration management practices are applied. The team currently works on exploring the current technologies in Application Lifecycle Management (ALM) tool infrastructure, deploying, configuring, integrating and maintaining the tool infrastructure in order to support the ALM processes' tool needs. The team also gives trainings regarding the infrastructure tools, leads the determination of the department configuration management process considering the needs of the project teams & quality requirements, and fulfills the service requests regarding the managed tools.

3 Motivation and Goals

As one of the largest departments in iNNOVA, Telco Department has over 350 employees and 30+ ongoing projects at a given time. These projects can be categorized in two, namely maintenance and new projects. Almost all of the new projects turn in to maintenance projects after the UAT phase is successfully completed and the system is deployed in the production environment. In the maintenance projects all of the work is done through Change Requests (CR).

In the ongoing projects, many different tools were being used during the ALM, depending on the project dynamics, project members and habits. In 2016, an ALM process & infrastructure improvement has been started in order to unify the best practices between different teams and make a tool infrastructure available for all project teams to use. The infrastructure improvement project had to go through several versions because of usage and maintenance difficulties, and most importantly for the lack of support from all of the stakeholders.

The first version had four main tools that were used in different phases of the lifecycle. For project, requirements and test management-Microsoft TFS, for Design-Enterprise Architect (EA), for development task planning-Atlassian Jira, for source code management-Apache SVN were used. With this setup, linking requirements on TFS with design items on EA had to go through Jira, as there were no plugins available to integrate TFS with EA. Along with the complex setup, difficulty of use and steep learning curve negatively affected the support of some stakeholders.

The second version had three main tools. For requirements and test management-HP ALM, for project management, development task planning, design decision management- Jira, for source code management-Visual SVN were used. Because of the extra maintenance effort in Jira-HP ALM integration and lack of linked bulk issue import in HP ALM, this setup was also not supported by some stakeholders. Thus, both solutions had to be abandoned as not all of the expectations we have set out below were met. Some of the needs were discovered after the implementation. This was an example that SPI must involve people actively and affect their daily activities [6].

- Ease of Use
- Change Management

- Development Planning
- Meeting Notes
- Task Planning
- Test Management
- Source Code Management
- Impact Analysis
- Release Management
- Design Documents
- Custom Reports
- Collaboration
- Seamless tool Integration
- Ease of maintenance

Since the outputs of the processes become inputs of other processes, it's important to have a seamless information flow between the people and teams involved in these processes. We believe that the way to accomplish this goal is through DevOps. DevOps is the combination of cultural philosophies, practices, and tools that increases an organization's ability to deliver quality applications and services at high velocity. One of the key cultural aspects of DevOps is increased communication and collaboration. With the use of DevOps tooling and automation of the software delivery process, teams set strong cultural norms around information sharing and facilitating communication through the use of chat applications, issue or project tracking systems, and wikis. Which in turn speed up communication across project managers, business analysts, developers, testers, operations support teams, allowing all of the stakeholders to align more closely on the project goals [2].

4 Current Infrastructure

Current infrastructure being used is made of six tools (see Fig. 1).

(1) Atlassian Jira, for project, requirements, test management and development task planning
(2) Atlassian Confluence, for design and project wiki documentation
(3) Atlassian Bitbucket, for source code management
(4) Jenkins, for Continuous Integration and orchestration
(5) SonarSource SonarQube, for code quality control
(6) JFrog Artifactory, for binary artifacts management.

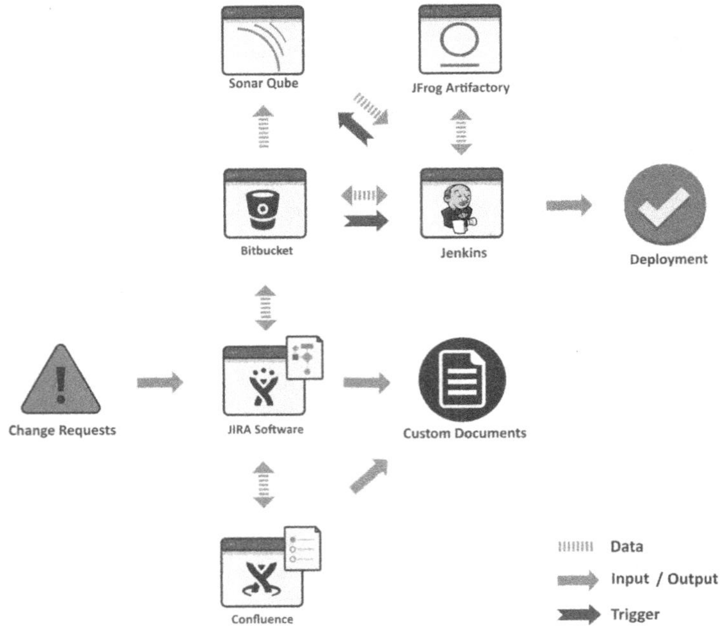

Fig. 1. The integrations and interactions between the tools

5 ALM Issue Relationships

"Traceability" is used in many industries where the transparency of processes, and the ability to accurately track changes is essential. In the software development lifecycle (SDLC), traceability primarily points to the traceability of requirements through application development. This helps to ensure that the delivered software fulfills all of the requirements and increases quality. As the SDLC involves human processes, software contains bugs that need to be fixed. Traceability supports to localize and fix these bugs, thus reducing production failures [3].

In the new projects, traceability starts with Business Requirements (BR). After a baseline is taken, Change Requests (CR (Epic)) are added to the project traceability links. Each CR is linked with the derived BR, which are in turn linked with the derived Functional (FR) and Non Functional Requirements (NFR). Documentation stored in Confluence pages, are used during the creation of the FR/NFRs. New pages are also derived from these requirements. Both the derived pages and pages that were made use of during requirement specification, are linked to the FR/NRFs. These links can be to the customer meeting notes, requirement specification documents, design specification documents such as high level design and interface specification documents. In the development phase, stories and sub-tasks are created with regards to the FR/NFRs. With the use of hooks in Bitbucket, code commits are required to have a valid Jira issue in the commit message. This enforcement together with the Jira - Bitbucket integration enables the traceability from the CR all the way to the source code.

Test cases (TC) are created and linked with the verified requirement(s). When needed test runs (TRun) are generated from the previously created TCs and grouped in test plans (TPlan). Through this setup coverage reports such as requirement - test case coverage, or requirement - test run can be taken (see Fig. 2).

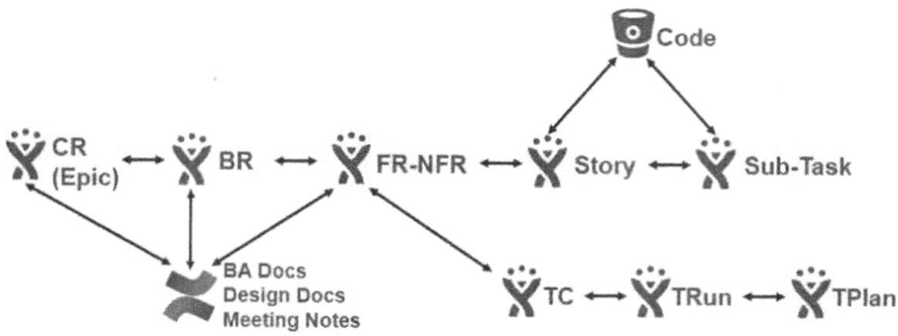

Fig. 2. Work item traceability

6 Impact Analysis

After a CR has been generated internally or through the customer request, the obsolete BRs are marked by linking them with a "is cancelled by" link to the Epic and these BR's statuses are also changed to "Cancelled" in Jira. After just marking the affected BRs, advanced queries can be used to help understand which related work items would have an impact on. Following the traceability, these items can be FR/NFRs, stories, development tasks, test runs, test cases and all the subtasks derived from them. Each items' related Configuration Item can be seen in through the Component field. Also the related code sections can be reached through the commits linked to each development task or subtask.

In order to simplify the readability and increase the user experience, filters in filters are used, where users can just change the sub filter called "CRs" by entering the CR (Epic) key and query the main filter "Impacted Work Items" afterwards. If necessary several CRs that needs to be delivered together can be queried together.

CRs: issuekey in (SIP-63)

Impacted Work Items: issueFunction in subtasksOf("issueFunction in linkedIssuesOfAllRecursive(\"issueFunction in linkedIssuesOf('filter = CRs', cancelled)\", 'is related with')") OR issueFunction in linkedIssuesOfAllRecursive("issueFunction in linkedIssuesOf('filter = CRs', cancelled)", "is related with") ORDER BY "Test Case" ASC

Impact on Specific Work Items: issueFunction in linkedIssuesOfAllRecursive("issueFunction in linkedIssuesOf('filter = CRs', cancelled)", "is related with") and issuetype in ("Solution Requirement")

With the information gathered through the supporting queries, a better estimation regarding the change cost and risk can be made (see Fig. 3).

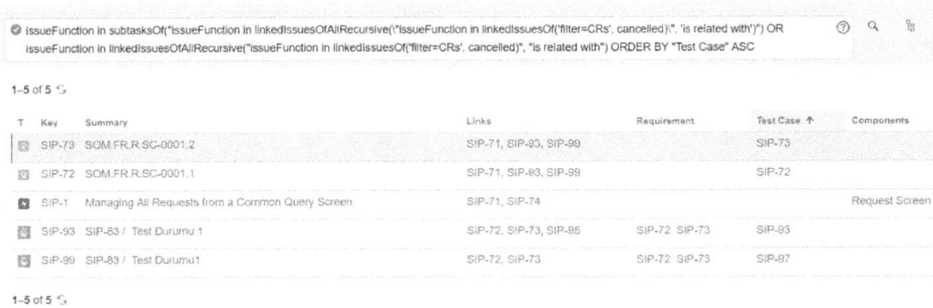

Fig. 3. Impacted work items

7 Day to Day Work

7.1 Change Requests and Requirement Management

In the maintenance projects, customer CRs are periodically received, implemented and deployed, usually in one major and two minor releases every month. In order to plan and track the change requests Epic issue types are used in Jira as a grouping mechanism. Customers submit their CRs with a Business Analysis Document which are imported in Confluence as a page and linked with an Epic in Jira. This Epic summarizes the CR and acts as a place holder for every related item regarding this CR. The Business Analysis Document is also split up in to Business Requirements (BR) and imported in Jira with a "relates to" link to the Epic. The obsolete BRs from the original analysis or previous CRs are investigated and marked as cancelled in their status fields. The related work items linked to the cancelled BRs are also cancelled in the status fields. These items can be reused to create updated versions of the work items by making a copy without their previous links or history.

Analysis team further break down the BR's in to Functional (FR) and Non-Functional Requirements (NFR) with internal and external analysis meetings. The meeting notes held in Confluence are also linked with the related Epic and BR's. The FR and NFR items that are stored in Jira, can be created in bulk from within the meeting notes with the use of excel like tables in the meeting notes template in Confluence. These FR/NFRs are also manually linked with the related BRs. In order to link multiple FR/NFRs to a BR, links are added through the BR's user interface as in Jira bulk linking is not possible from an FR/NFR list to a single BR.

7.2 Design

After the FR and NFRs are derived the design pages are updated or new pages are created and linked with the requirements as wiki pages in Confluence (see Fig. 4).

Fig. 4. Confluence wiki page link seen on Jira issue

7.3 Code Traceability and Quality

Through the Bitbucket – Jira integration "Yet Another Commit Checker" plugin was used in pre-receive hooks in order to force a valid Jira issue in code commit messages. With the Jira issues entered in the code commit messages, Bitbucket-Jira integration automatically recognizes the link, and each development task in Jira is linked with the commits in Bitbucket. Commit links in the "Development" panel of Jira issue view screen, allow investigation of file and line based code changes (see Fig. 5).

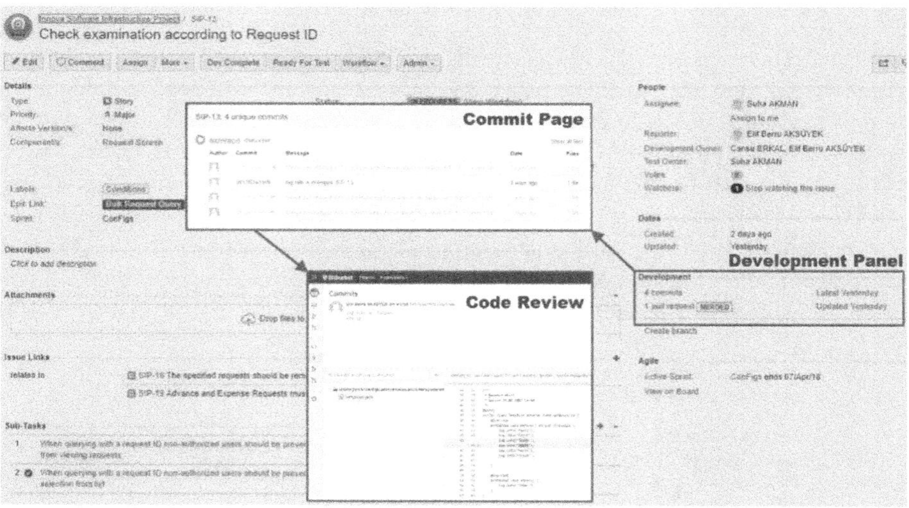

Fig. 5. Bitbucket Jira integration

Jenkins-Bitbucket integration was also implemented in order to trigger Jenkins jobs and observe the status of the code build statuses through Bitbucket (see Fig. 6).

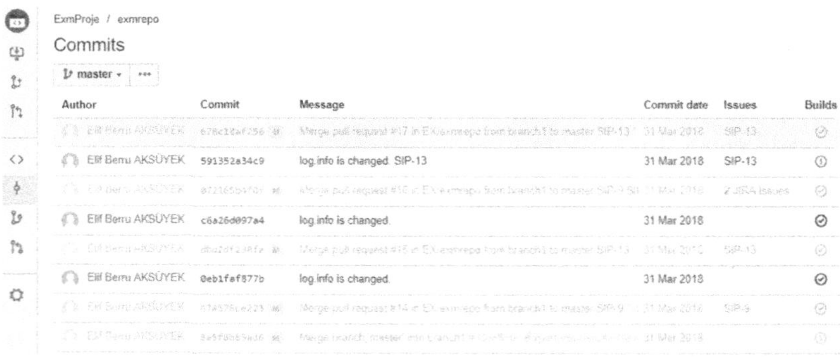

Fig. 6. Build status of commits on Bitbucket page

In the Jenkins jobs code quality inspections are triggered on SonarQube and the built artifacts are stored in the Artifactory for further use such as automatic deployments.

7.4 Test Case (TC) Development and FR/NFR Traceability

Software testing as a part of SDLC, is a very diverse topic—or even seen as a milestone of software development [4]. For managing test activities in Jira "TestFlo" plugin was used. There are two was to enter TCs in to Jira. They can be written directly in Jira, which should be preferred in order to promote DevOps culture and increase collaboration. Or they can be imported via excel. Each FR/NFR should be linked to at least one TC and tested successfully. FR/NFR-TC linking is done through "Test Case" issue type screen during TC development process. The TCs mapped to the FR/NFR (Coverage) and the statuses of the test runs (Tests Under Execution) can be monitored on each FR/NFR (see Fig. 7).

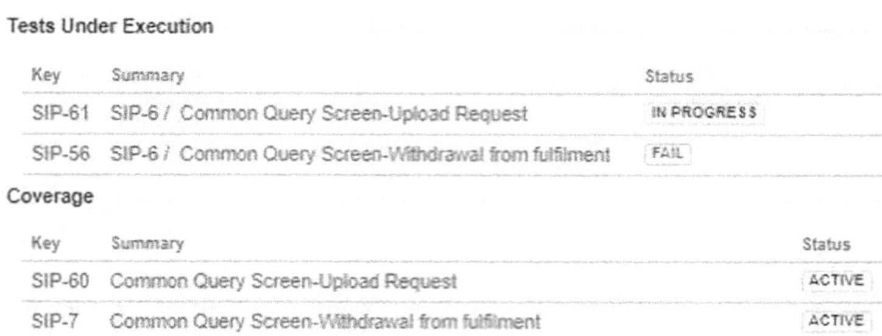

Fig. 7. Test case execution and coverage on FR/NFR

With Requirement Coverage reports, requirements that are not mapped to any of the test cases can be quickly identified during quality assurance activities (see Fig. 8).

Fig. 8. Requirement test coverage report

7.5 Test Planning

"Test plan" issue type is used to group TCs on Jira. It is used for software test cycles and scenarios. Test runs' step progress and pass/fail status can be monitored from the test plan (see Fig. 9).

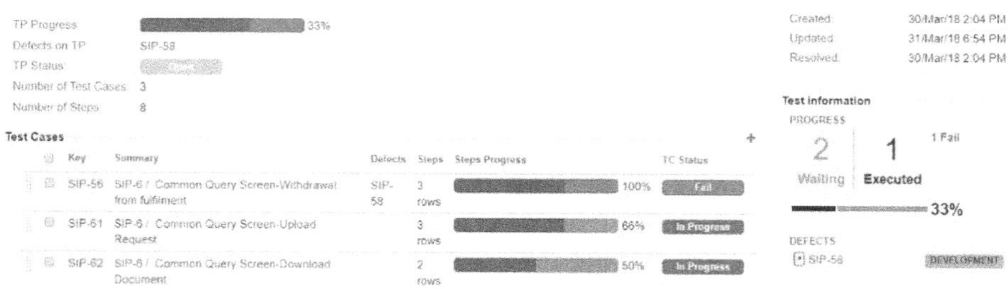

Fig. 9. Test plan page

7.6 Test Runs - Defects Traceability

Multiple test runs can be generated from one TC on different test plans. Each step of the test run can be granularly passed or failed. When a test run's step fails, a new "bug" can be created from the same test run window. Test runs can also be re-run.

7.7 Custom Report Creation Aligned with Customer QA Formats

In order to fulfill customer QA needs Requirement Traceability Matrix (RTM) and Test Report Document (TRD) are generated complying with the customer QA formats. In order to generate the documents in the required format groovy scripts utilizing Jira API, JQL and SQL were coded, "Better Excel for Jira" plugin was used (see Fig. 10).

	Solution Requirement	Test Case Name	Test Type	Linked Test Cases/Dependency
1	Solution Requirement	Test Case Name	Test Type	Linked Test Cases/Dependency
2	SIP-3, SIP-4	Common Query Screen-Withdrawal from fulfilment	UAT	Common Query Screen-Upload Request
3	SIP-4	Common Query Screen-Upload Request	UAT	
4	SIP-3, SIP-18	Common Query Screen-Download Document	UAT	

	Step No	System	Actions	Expected Result	Test Step Data	Explanation	Step Statu
1	Step No	System	Actions	Expected Result	Test Step Data	Explanation	Step Statu
2	1	Production	Enter the user name and password to log ir	Session open successfully	Username/Password	Users can be login witho	Pass
3	2	Production	Subscriber inquiry is selected.	The Subscriber inquiry screen opens	Custom Query	Screen should be open w	Pass
4	3	Production	The system to be queried is selected. The c	The detail screen opens. The default is the abone tab.	Detail Screen	Result should be opend (	Pass
5	1	Production	Enter the user name and password to log ir	Session open successfully	Username/Password	Users can be login witho	Pass
6	2	Production	Upload button is clicked.	File Explorer screen opens	N/A	File Explorer should be o	Pass
7	3	Production	The upload button is pressed.	Request should be uploaded.	Detail Screen	Request should be uploa	Pass
8	1	Proton Product	Enter the user name and password to log ir	Session open successfully	Username/Password	Users can be login witho	Pass
9	2	Proton Product	Dowload button is pressed.	The Download screen opens. The default is the abone tab	The Download screen opens. The default is the abone tab.		Pass

Fig. 10. Test report document

7.8 Release Management

Release management is done by creating Versions in Jira. Although there is no limit on what can be used in the version names, version numbers are used as the naming convention. These versions are containers for all of the related work items in that release such as change requests, bugs, stories and sub-tasks. Through this setup overview of all of the work items in each container can be monitored via Backlog and Releases pages, as well as Version Report and Release Burndown Reports.

7.9 Change Management

CRs are created as Epics in Jira. These Epics are containers for all the work items related to the CR. Through the epic links overview of the CRs can be monitored via Backlog and Active Sprints pages (scrum board), as well as Epic Reports. Epics being used as swim lane can be seen in scrum boards.

7.10 Development Task Management

Development planning is done through sprints created in Jira. Story and sub-task issue types are used for development task planning. Each story is assigned a story point depending on the work and with the use of team sprint velocity and capacity next sprint in line is planned. The status and health of the sprint can be monitored via Active Sprints page (scrum board), Sprint Report and Burn Down Chart (see Fig. 11).

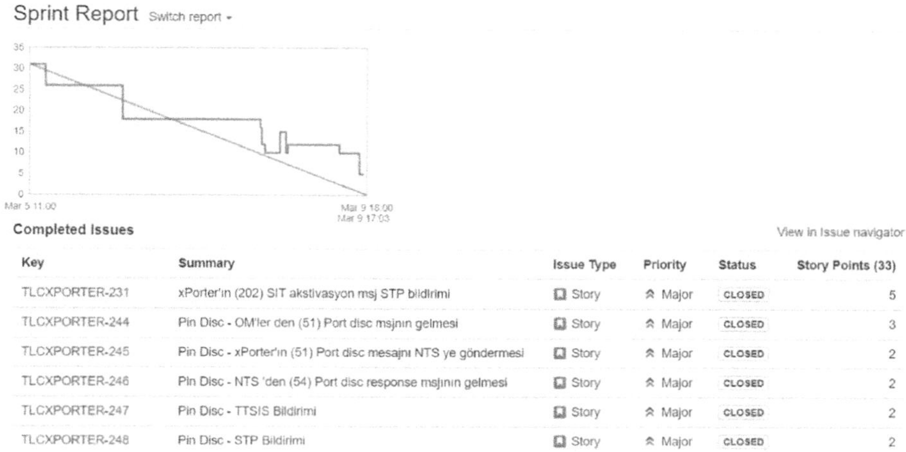

Key	Summary	Issue Type	Priority	Status	Story Points (33)
TLCXPORTER-231	xPorter'ın (202) SIT akstivasyon msj STP bildirimi	Story	Major	CLOSED	5
TLCXPORTER-244	Pin Disc - OM'ler den (51) Port disc msjnın gelmesi	Story	Major	CLOSED	3
TLCXPORTER-245	Pin Disc - xPorter'ın (51) Port disc mesajnı NTS ye göndermesi	Story	Major	CLOSED	2
TLCXPORTER-246	Pin Disc - NTS 'den (54) Port disc response msjının gelmesi	Story	Major	CLOSED	2
TLCXPORTER-247	Pin Disc - TTSIS Bildirimi	Story	Major	CLOSED	2
TLCXPORTER-248	Pin Disc - STP Bildirimi	Story	Major	CLOSED	2

Fig. 11. Sprint report

7.11 Test Monitoring via Custom Dashboards

In addition to the panels in the TCs and Test Plans, custom Jira dashboards are created to further track test process. This allows other stakeholders such as the Quality Assurance Team, Test Process Management and Upper Management to monitor test process and KPIs in real time at a higher level than each test plan.

Defect counts and mapping, requirement coverage and Pass/Fail Rates are some of the reports that can be visualized. The dashboard data can be customized to project or multiple projects level with the use of JQL queries.

8 Changing the Culture

One of the main reasons why the first two implementations of the tool infrastructure improvement have failed was the lack of Devops culture. Social engineering and changing the way each role sees the big picture, which is the business everybody is a part of, is critical for success. Every role in the business must be a part of the culture, listen to each roles' concerns and build a trust based environment [7]. When a problem occurs, such as a bug from the production, the goal is not to blame a role, but identify the root cause. If the problem is people related, provide constructive feedback and plan additional training if necessary. If it is tool related continuously improve the infrastructure.

In order to unite the different roles, common goals must be established. During the process and tool improvement project, common KPIs were determined, such as lowering the production defect counts and improving the customer satisfaction survey results. The KPIs were assigned to all project members regardless of their roles. Also process audit findings were exempt from the KPIs in the first year. Instead when there was a finding, the focus was on process and tool trainings, as well as filing the rough edges in the process and tools in order to align the real life implementation with the process. Change requests for processes and infrastructure are encouraged and clearly stated that nothing is set on stone and everything can be changed if it supports the Devops culture and deemed necessary by the process teams.

9 Lessons Learned and Conclusion

Throughout the tool infrastructure and process improvement project, we have learned in first-hand that key elements for a successful organizational change are top management sponsorship, employee involvement at a large scale and honest & timely communication. Most importantly, soft, people-related factors formed greater challenges than hard, technology related factors which are easier to identify and measure [5]. In order to overcome this difficulty, benefits of the new infrastructure was emphasized during design and training activities so that the users could see what is in it for themselves. Management support was also given in order to motivate all people involved. It's important to realize improvement requires real people to really change behaviors [6].

The main advantage of the current tool infrastructure setup is: for the teams to have a familiar user interface in most of the ALM phases, closer integration with out of the box application links, community supported market place add-ons, flexible system that can be customized via scripts according to the user's needs and lastly minimal additional cost to the already existing licenses. Our experience is that these advantages promote a better user experience, which in turn increases the support of the change and usage of the tool infrastructure by the employees.

The tool infrastructure is also aligned with the internal processes defined by Project Management, Requirement Management, Design, Test Management, Quality Assurance, and Configuration Management process teams. The teams were made up of domain specialists from several project teams in order to maximize the involvement of the entire department. Thus, 'process' was not seen as 'somebody else's process description'. Requirement gathering and training via live use case demonstrations were done to the users. As mentioned in the SPI Manifesto, active involvement of the people working in an organization who have sufficient information and training ensures the success of an SPI initiative [6]. With this approach we were able to better align People, Process and Tools which are the 3 main areas to focus for a successful organization.

References

1. iNNOVA Company information. https://www.innova.com.tr/download/files/innova_genel_brosur_eng_6178857467.pdf. Accessed 18 Apr 2018
2. Amazon Web Services - What is DevOps? https://aws.amazon.com/devops/what-is-devops/. Accessed 18 Apr 2018
3. Intland Web Services: Benefits of requirements traceability in application development. https://content.intland.com/blog/alm/benefits-of-requirements-traceability-in-application-development. Accessed 18 Apr 2018
4. Myers, G.J., Sandler, C.: The Art of Software Testing, 2nd edn. Wiley, Chichester (2004)

5. Jørgensen, H.H., Owen, L., Neus, A.: Making change work. http://www-935.ibm.com/services/us/gbs/bus/pdf/gbe03100-usen-03-making-change-work.pdf. Accessed 18 Apr 2018
6. SPI Manifesto. http://www.iscn.com/Images/SPI_Manifesto_A.1.2.2010.pdf. Accessed 11 June 2018
7. Walls, M.: Building a DevOps Culture-DevOps is as much about culture as it is about tools, 1st edn. 2nd release. O'Reilly Media, Sebastopol (2015)

Good and Bad Practices in Improvement

Development of "SPI Strategy Framework" and Its Application

So Norimatsu(✉), Toshiyuki Kishi, and Noriko Wada

Japan Software Process Improvement Consortium (JASPIC), Toshima-ku, Tokyo, Japan
contact@jaspic.org

Abstract. The authors have been working on developing a framework for SPI strategy in one of the working groups at "Japan SPI Consortium (JASPIC)". Our objective is to identify important (i.e. influential) strategic factors when promoting SPI, and to understand how they are evaluated and determined, so that the SPI efforts become more successful. Based on the "SPI Strategy Model" we presented in 2012, we expanded it to "SPI Strategy Framework" by adding more strategic factors to the model, establishing evaluation methods for the factors, and devising a diagnostic method to analyze the weaknesses in the strategy using the relationships among the factors. This paper describes the contents of the current Framework, reports the results of its application to SPI efforts, and discusses the applicability and usefulness of the Framework.

Keywords: Software process improvement · SPI strategy
Strategic factors · Strategy architecture · Evaluation of strategy
Diagnostics for strategy adjustment

1 Introduction

Degree of success in SPI efforts seems to depend on various factors and conditions. Using the same improvement methods and models may not lead to the same level of success in different organizations. The objective of our efforts is to identify what is causing such differences, and to understand how we can control these factors in a given set of conditions where the SPI activities are situated.

To achieve this objective, we believe the following set of capabilities is needed.

- Identifying and understanding success factors at a strategic level.
- Establishing and evaluating strategic factors at the start of SPI efforts.
- Diagnosing problems in SPI efforts to identify weaknesses among the factors and to identify corrective actions during the performance of SPI activities.

In 2012, we presented the "SPI Strategy Model" [1] that covers the first capability, as a result of various SPI case studies. We also proposed the future directions to address other capabilities. Section 2 explains the overview of the model and our findings.

Since 2012, we have continued our efforts to improve the framework through a group work at JASPIC [2]. Section 3 explains how we expanded the model into a framework, by adding more factors from other sources, by conducting architectural

X. Larrucea et al. (Eds.): EuroSPI 2018, CCIS 896, pp. 307–317, 2018.
https://doi.org/10.1007/978-3-319-97925-0_25

analysis of the factors, and by establishing an evaluation tool kit. Section 4 discusses two case studies at JASPIC to explain how the framework was applied in real SPI efforts to improve their performance. Section 5 discusses future directions based on lessons learned in the case studies and our current ideas to improve the framework. Section 6 explains the relevance of this study with the SPI Manifesto, and shows that the SPI Strategy Framework will ensure the overall implementation of the concepts in the manifesto.

2 SPI Strategy Framework 2012

In our 2012 paper, we conducted case studies in the historical SPI efforts among various organizations, and extracted critical success factors that are considered to have influenced the decisions made in conducting such efforts. Combined with contextual factors and outcome indicators, we developed a model as a basis of the framework.

These factors include the following three types

a. Promotion: Promotional factors are identified by analyzing what stakeholders considered most carefully in planning and conducting SPI activities.
b. Context: Contextual factors are identified by analyzing why the specific promotional factor was chosen. Causal analysis may reveal a hidden contextual factor when two similar sets of promotional factors lead to different outcomes.
c. Outcome: Outcome indicators are identified during the evaluation of SPI activities in terms of business values, performance indicators, and other measures.

Each factor is assigned a "variable" (i.e. "keyword"), and these variables have been expanded as we observed more SPI efforts. Many factors are currently characterized by nominal data, and a few can be characterized by some quantitative data.

We also found that the overall integrity of these factors is a very important attribute to be maintained. Under a given context (e.g. organizational culture, business and project environment, desired performance), appropriate set of promotional factors would lead to a better achievement of outcome indicators.

3 SPI Strategy Framework 2018

In this section, we describe the new concepts introduced in the current framework.

3.1 Adding More Strategic Factors

To expand the applicability of our Strategy Model, we referred to a collection of general strategy theories. One of such sources [3] lists 30 military and business strategies. For each strategy, its historical backgrounds and critical success factors are explained along with their applicability to contemporary business cases.

We analyzed these strategy theories, and mapped each success story to our SPI strategic factors. We usually identified several key factors from the existing factors in our original model, but also found additional factors. We also found new variables in the existing factors. Eventually, we found 15 new factors added to the 2012 version, as shown in Table 1. Table 2 in Appendix A shows a comprehensive list of factors in our current Framework along with a brief description of the factors.

Table 1. Added strategic factors

Type	Factors
Contextual	- External competitive environment - Internal competitive environment - Situational recognition - Historical cases - Improvement target - Trigger
Promotional	- Evaluation method - Leadership - Interaction - Capability enhancement - Innovation - Process change mechanism - Grouping
Outcome	- Business performance - Improvement capability

3.2 Understanding Strategy Architecture

To understand the integrity of as many as 30+ factors, we need to discuss at the "Architecture" level. Architecture of a strategy can be discussed through the following perspectives:

- overall patterns of factors (i.e. typical sets of factors)
- structure of factors (i.e. relational view of factors)
- dynamic behaviors (i.e. temporal view of factors)

Pattern Analysis of Strategic Factors

"Strategy" is usually labeled by its characteristic attributes. For example, ISO 33014 lists ten families of change strategies [4]. In our 2012 paper, strategy for each SPI efforts was named by a combination of the organizational structure (e.g. scope of the SPI activity) and its leadership style (e.g. top-down or bottom-up).

In our current Strategy Framework, a strategy for specific SPI efforts is defined by a set of values (i.e. variables) for the model factors, which collectively characterizes the nature of the strategy. In other words, a pattern of strategic factors would comprise a "strategy family". Through a pattern analysis of sets of factors among multiple SPI efforts, we can identify a new strategy family or describe a strategic similarity in a quantitative term among two different SPI efforts.

Another use of Strategy Pattern is to set the initial strategy for the SPI efforts by selecting from the known patterns. Two SPI efforts with similar contextual factors may select their strategies from the same strategy family, but they should tailor the individual factors differently due to the specific nature of such efforts.

Structure Analysis of Strategic Factors

Based on seven components defined in the "process improvement knowledge model" [5], we categorized our strategic factors. Since these seven components are structured to describe the SPI case, the factors can be grouped using the same structure. Not only this structure facilitates the analysis of SPI efforts from a strategic viewpoint, it also made it easier to further group the factors and analyze the relationships among them. The overall structure is described in Fig. 1.

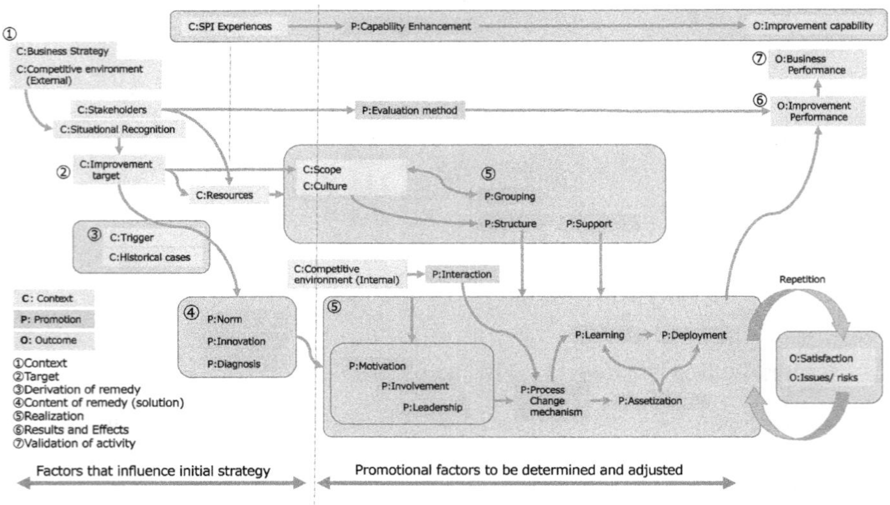

Fig. 1. Structure of strategic factors

In Fig. 1, following structural views are described.

- Strategic factors are first mapped to one of the seven components introduced in the SPI case template [5]. These components include the following:
  - 1. Context
  - 2. Target
  - 3. Derivation of remedy
  - 4. Content of remedy (solution)
  - 5. Realization
  - 6. Results and Effects
  - 7. Validation of activity
- Factors are further grouped by relevance, and ordered by dependencies. Logical dependencies and temporal flows are described by arrows.

Dynamic Behavior Analysis of Strategic Factors

Figure 1 shows some dynamic natures of the SPI strategy.

- Factors on the left side are mostly contextual factors that are set in the early stage of the SPI efforts. Factors that correspond to the "Solution" (i.e. technologies and concepts to solve the Target issues) will also serve as inputs to determine other promotional factors.
- Vertical relationships also show temporal layers among factors. Upper factors are long term factors that may not change in the short run.
- Most promotional factors will influence the "Realization" part of the SPI case. These factors will be evaluated and revised more frequently as issues arise.

Figure 1 also helps sensitivity analysis of the factors, which will guide establishing and updating the strategy during the SPI efforts. At this time our capability is limited by a lack of quantitative baseline model to conduct fully quantitative analysis.

3.3 Establishing Strategy Evaluation Kit

To evaluate the actual strategy which is planned and/or enacted in specific SPI efforts, we developed a "Strategy Evaluation Kit". The kit is used in the following steps.

a. Describing SPI efforts as "SPI case"
b. Characterizing strategic factors of the SPI case.
c. Evaluating existence and relevance of strategic factors.
d. Diagnosing issues for strategy adjustment.

Describing SPI Efforts as "SPI Case"
First, the "SPI case template" [5] is used to describe the SPI efforts being evaluated. This has been a big improvement from a free form interview in 2012. We usually ask the interviewees to cover the overall "story" even in the early stage of the SPI efforts. Even before conducting the next step of evaluation, we tend to identify many issues, risks and "To Be Determined", which will clarify the overall planning of the SPI activities.

Characterizing Strategic Factors of the SPI Case
After the SPI case is described (at least at high level), we clarify the intended strategy (both conscious and unconscious). For each strategic factor specified in the Framework, variables (i.e. value of strategic factors) that represent the nature of SPI efforts are determined. At this step, we use a standard questionnaire that includes the factors, typical variables, and their descriptions.

This step can be done as self-evaluation by the stakeholders, but we usually use an interview/dialogue with a third party, which tends to identify more "hidden" or "unconscious" strategic considerations.

As shown in Fig. 1, strategic factors are mapped to the seven components of the SPI case, so the discussion can be facilitated by a logical flow of the SPI case. It can also be described in the form of "SPI Strategy Map".

Evaluating Existence and Relevance of Strategic Factors
This step can be performed simultaneously starting at the first step (at least informally). Through the characterization of factors, we quickly start to identify the following findings in the strategy.

- Holes: missing factors or factors that have not been carefully considered.
- Inconsistency: inappropriate or invalid combination of factors where logical relationships should be satisfied.
- Weakness: ineffective selection of variables, which can be monitored as a risk.
- Strength: leverage point for greater outcome.

These findings will lead to either re-planning of the strategy or the identification of risks to be monitored carefully along with possible mitigations.

Diagnosing Issues for Strategy Adjustment
As the SPI activities are performed, issues and problems arise. Some of these can be solved in short time, without changing strategic factors. However, major issues (e.g. total suspension of activities) tend to suggest a misalignment of factors, which requires adjustments of the current strategy. Strategy Diagnosis can be performed at such an event.

If a "Strategy Map" had been developed during the previous evaluation, it is easy to identify a factor as a "Direct Cause" which is causing the outstanding issue. The remediation can be as little as changing the variable of such a factor. For a bigger issue, there may be a more fundamental misalignment. Multiple factors could have been set inappropriately, or some deeper weakness is causing the issue. Causal analysis is required to identify such a "Real Cause" or "Root Cause".

A structured Strategy Map becomes especially useful here, since it shows the relationships among the factors. We can trace from the "Direct" factor back to the "Root" factor on a diagram. When multiple factors are involved in the issue, we need to consider the controllability of these factors. Lower level factors (see Fig. 1) tend to have a quicker response within a narrow scope, while upper level factors tend to have a greater impact in the long run. Changing one factor will create ripple effects on other factors both in the short run and long run, so we need to understand the dynamic behavior of the overall structure to select and change the appropriate factor.

4 Application of Strategy Framework

We have applied the current (or earlier) version of Strategy Framework to several SPI efforts within JASPIC. Five instances were internally reported from our 2017 efforts. In this paper, we report two case studies briefly to highlight the "strategy adjustment" capability of the framework. Only the Framework-relevant information are reported here, and specific "Target and Solution" and organization's specific information are not reported to protect the confidentiality.

4.1 Case Study 1: Strategy Evaluation

Case Description: The organization has identified a "(good) practice" that should have been enforced at the organizational level, but not followed as desired. It had been performed quite effectively in one part of the organization, but not well implemented in another part. Improving the operational adherence became the "Target" of this SPI case. The scope of this case included about 160 people, and the duration was set to be 4 months as an initial cycle. Due to the improvement history in the organization, this effort was not considered as a major challenge.

Application of Strategy Framework: Strategy evaluation was performed at the planning stage using the strategy evaluation kit described in Sect. 3.3. The effort was described as "SPI case" first using the template, and variables are assigned for the factors by the manager who has been responsible for the effort. Evaluation of these factors revealed that most traditional factors have been already set properly, and one of the new factors, the "internal competitive environment" was suggested as an opportunity to raise the "motivation" factor. The case used the "grouping" factor and compare the actual "improvement performance" of subgroups to establish an internal competitive environment. Motivation was expected to be enhanced through the competition as expected in the gamification of SPI. The case was performed successfully. Percentages of practice adherence improved from 73% to 99%, and stakeholders started realizing the effectiveness of the practice. Stakeholder "Satisfaction", one of the outcome factors was evaluated high, including that of the managers in the organization. The introduction of the internal competition was considered effective as it showed rapid improvement in the performance.

Lessons Learned: Success of SPI efforts can be accelerated by utilizing only a few strategic factors. A newly found strategic factor was useful, so adding new factors from a general strategy theory can be beneficial in the future.

4.2 Case Study 2: Strategy Diagnosis

Case Description: The organization had identified a new technology (development methodology) to be introduced. Pilot projects were performed along with additional steps to document the new processes in the organization's standard processes before the deployment.

Application of Strategy Framework

First Increment:

This effort was also described in the form of SPI case by one of the facilitator of the effort, and factors were characterized at the initial planning phase. Strategy diagnosis was conducted at one of the early milestones when the efforts faced a major issue after piloting the new technology. Two factors (Factor A and Factor B) were identified as major causes. Structural analysis using relationships among factors (see Fig. 1) suggested Factor B as a direct cause, while Factor A is a root cause for B. Remediation was enacted only for B at this time, since B had a better controllability and a shorter response time. The remediation was effective and the case seemed to have resolved the issue.

Second Increment: After a while, the efforts reported another kind of issue, and a short strategy diagnosis was conducted again. This time, Factor A was determined to be the direct cause. The case implemented remediation for A, which again worked effectively.

Lessons Learned: Strategy diagnosis can be performed when SPI efforts faces a major issue. It can identify strategic factor(s) that is causing the problem using a Strategy

Map. Then an effective remediation can be suggested. When multiple weaknesses/risks exist, problems may be realized incrementally as the activities are performed. The strategy map can reveal the structure of such weaknesses, and multiple adjustments can be enacted either simultaneously or incrementally. Remediating more fundamental weakness will work more effectively in the long run, but probably at a higher cost, so the balance should be considered carefully.

5 Future Directions and Discussions

5.1 Expanding Strategy Framework

We plan to expand the framework to improve our overall capabilities to manage the SPI strategy. For the first capability of "Identifying and understanding success factors at a strategic level", we plan to continue adding more factors from other strategy theories, both from SPI related studies and from other domains. Current framework has been established based on our experiences plus some literature research, so other inputs would be beneficial to explore other factors.

For the second capability of "Establishing and evaluating strategic factors at the start of SPI efforts", we need more methodical approach. Selecting a base strategy from known strategy family (patterns) seems to be usual at this time. We're currently exploring a method using a technology diffusion model. Rule based setting of strategic factors is also planned.

For the third capability of "Diagnosing problems in SPI efforts to identify weaknesses among the factors and to identify corrective actions during the performance of SPI efforts", we plan to formalize our current approach of using the architecture of factors. Current set of diagnosis rules worked in our case studies, but it needs to be further validated in other SPI cases.

5.2 Applying Strategy Framework

Another plan for future direction is to apply the framework to more SPI efforts. We plan to validate its usefulness through more case studies.

6 SPI Manifesto Revisited

We believe that an effective mechanism for establishing an appropriate SPI strategy will enhance the possibility and degree of success of SPI efforts. This belief is in alignment with the concepts found in the SPI Manifesto [6]. The following components of the manifesto are most relevant with our findings.

- Value C "Change": SPI is inherently linked with change.
- Principle 8 "Manage the organizational change in your improvement effort".

Establishing a strategy will enhance the overall management capability. Also, the factors in our framework are categorized by the process change structure, so they are more tailorable for the specific organizational change, and more frequent adjustments become feasible.

We also found that every principle in the SPI Manifesto can be mapped to one or more of the strategic factors in the framework, either directly or in combination. Therefore, we believe that a use of the framework will ensure an effective implementation of the SPI Manifesto as a whole. We suggest that the Manifesto refers to the strategy concept at least in Principle 8, or at a global level to ensure a balanced implementation of the Manifesto.

7 Conclusions

We found the following as current understandings with regard to the applicability and usefulness of the SPI Strategy Framework.

- As a measure to evaluate and discuss the strategy of SPI efforts, current set of strategic factors is adequately expanded and comprehensive within the cases we have experienced. Newly added factors from strategy theories in other domains were found to be useful. However, we still need to consider existing researches to evaluate and improve applicability of the framework.
- Strategy Evaluation tools are developed to be used for ongoing SPI efforts. Evaluations at planning phases and milestones can be conducted to identify weaknesses or risks to be mitigated or monitored. More formal method for evaluation needs to be developed for greater effectiveness.
- Strategy Diagnosis can be conducted to identify the problematic factors that are causing the major issues. Strategy adjustment can be made incrementally and flexibly as problems become recognized. More formal method for diagnosis needs to be developed for consistent application.

Acknowledgements. This paper was written as a result of activities performed by a working group for "process improvement strategy" in Japan SPI consortium (JASPIC). We are thankful to the JASPIC steering committee and staff for supporting our activities.

Appendix A: Comprehensive List of Strategic Factors

Table 2. Comprehensive list of strategic factors

Type	Factors	Descriptions
C	Business strategy	Needs, expectations, constraints given by the business strategy
C	External competitive environment	Competitive environment at the business level
C	Stakeholders	Important stakeholders and their expectations and needs
C	Situational recognition	Current situations including causes/principle/constraints that are creating the current issues to be solved
C	Improvement target	Issues and challenges that are specified as the target for the improvement efforts

(*continued*)

Table 2. (*continued*)

Type	Factors	Descriptions
C	Resources	Resources provided for the SPI activities
C	Trigger	Events that triggered the initiation of improvement efforts
C	Historical cases	Historical improvement cases that provided information as references
C	Scope	Scope, structure and scale of the target organization or activities
C	Culture	Organizational paradigm (e.g. behavior in response to changes, communication mechanisms, team vs. individual behavior)
C	Internal competitive environment	Competitive environment within the organization, including collaborative environment
C	SPI experiences	Historical SPI experiences and accumulated process assets
P	Norm	Criteria to determine the validity of SPI (e.g. process model, quality attributes)
P	Innovation	Approach to manage the innovation
P	Diagnosis method	Method to evaluate the validity of SPI based on criteria
P	Evaluation method	Method to evaluate the actual performance as a result of improvement efforts
P	Grouping	Approach to group sub-organizations, and establish priorities among them
P	Structure	Organizational structure for SPI promotion (e.g. hierarchical, horizontal, vertical)
P	Support	Support from external entities
P	Interaction	Competitive interaction with other internal efforts and groups. This could be a mixture of competition and collaboration
P	Motivation	How to motivate stakeholders
P	Involvement	Mechanism to involve stakeholders
P	Leadership	Leadership of changes introduced in the improvement efforts
P	Learning	Mechanism to communicate norms and new processes
P	Process change mechanism	Mechanisms to propose, evaluate and determine the process changes due to the improvement efforts
P	Deployment	Mechanism to deploy the outcome of SPI and expand the scope of activities
P	Assetization	Mechanism to make the outcome of SPI (i.e. process assets) available for reuse
P	Capability enhancement	Approach to enhance organizational capability in terms of conducting and managing improvement efforts
O	Improvement performance	Degree of achievement measured against the norm, including secondary effects if any
O	Business performance	Actual business performance achieved as a result of improvement efforts
O	Satisfaction	Degree of satisfaction of the stakeholders
O	Issues/risks	Problems, issues, and risks arising from improvement efforts
O	Improvement capability	Actual organizational capability enhanced or damaged as a result of improvement efforts

References

1. Wada, N.: Analysis of SPI strategies and their modeling – exploring the art of SPI promotion. In: Industrial Proceedings, European Systems Software and Service Process Improvement & Innovation. EuroSPI2012 (2012)
2. Ogasawara, H.: Status of SPI activities in Japanese software – a view from JASPIC. In: Industrial Proceedings, European Systems Software and Service Process Improvement and Innovation. EuroSPI2013, pp. 8.21–8.30 (2013)
3. Suzuki, H.: Strategy Classroom. Diamond Inc., Tokyo (2014)
4. ISO, ISO/IEC/TR 33014: Information technology – process assessment – guide for process improvement, Geneva, Switzerland (2013)
5. Norimatsu, S.: Formulation of process improvement knowledge – 7 components of a good PI story. In: Industrial Proceedings, EuroAsiaSPI 2017 (2017)
6. SPI Manifesto. http://2018.eurospi.net/images/eurospi/spi_manifesto.pdf. Accessed 1 Apr 2018

ISO 33020 Cornerstone or Pitfall of Process Improvement

Tomas Schweigert(✉) and Michael Phillipp

SQS Software Quality Systems AG, Cologne, Germany
Tomas.schweigert@sqs.com

Abstract. Since the beginning of CMMI the underlying ideas of process capability and the roadmap to process improvement did not face substantial changes. This fact is documented in the ISO 33020 Standard that except of some minor changes reflects the mainstream of process capability thinking. The paper presents some critical remarks regarding this standard. They are Inspired on the work of Michael Hammer, practical experiences with SPICE Assessments in Dutch PPP programs and several special capability models. The paper also develops a first idea of an alternative that might also fit to the requirements of the ISO 33003 standard.

Keywords: Measurement framework · ISO/IEC 33020 · ISO/IEC 33003 PEMM · Process and enterprise maturity model · Process capability Capability model · Process improvement · SPI Manifesto Global software development · Process integration · ImprovAbility ISO/IEC 15504 part 4 · ISO/IEC TR 33014 · Bootstrap

1 Introduction

2010 the SPI Manifesto [1] was launched. It contains the PI knowledge of many leading experts of PI. Everybody being in Alcala that year thought that this paper would have great impact on the evolution of PI (Fig. 1).

The SPI Manifesto at a glance:

Fig. 1. Values and principles of the SPI Manifesto

X. Larrucea et al. (Eds.): EuroSPI 2018, CCIS 896, pp. 318–328, 2018.
https://doi.org/10.1007/978-3-319-97925-0_26

2 A Review of the ISO 33020 Standard

The basic capability model of the ISO 33020 Standard [2] was developed 1994 with the Version 1 of the Bootstrap approach [3]. Today, 20 years later, this approach is still in use and did not receive a fundamental reengineering. But since this date lots of capability and maturity aspects were discovered examples see [4–11] that were not integrated in the model.

It can be seen as a part of the PI journey that -according to the typical industrialisation cycle- an organisation has to produce running software first, then gain experience mostly related to work products and their quality, later also related to planning issues. Achieving this, organisations were happy to deliver in a reliable quality, timeframe and budget. In the next steps organisation struggled with experience exchange, adoption of external expert knowledge and streamlining of work. Standardisation became a big issue. And in a later stage, organisations tried to reduce variance and tackle common and specific causes of variance. At the end, this was the journey to the current capability model finished by the publication of the Bootstrap model.

But published once and used in the SPICE and Automotive SPICE Model this capability model showed its weak points. Its monolithic architecture did neither support the integration of additional capability aspects nor did it support alternative roadmaps of process improvement.

The problem is condensed in clauses 5.2 and 5.6 of ISO/IEC 33020.

In the following sections, some examples of this pitfall are discussed.

2.1 A Belief Valid in the Past Is Wrong in the Present - the PA 3.1 Dilemma

The first pitfall of the ISO 33020 Standard is to make the capability to define a standard a level 3 issue. This might have been correct in the 1990th. But hampers the creation of customer driven roadmaps. This was especially a challenging issue for the Dutch construction industry when executing PPP projects [12]. In these projects standardized processes and their tailoring to the given project were in place long before the standard was implemented by doing the real work [12]. Assessor teams and the customer were in a dilemma as the customer wanted a reliable organisation ready to execute expressed by capability level 3 but only being ready and not executing causes a level 0 in a SPICE Assessment [12]. As a result, it becomes plausible that process definition is a starting point equal to process performance. ISO 33020 has no answer for this.

2.2 Practical Experience: Gaining Success by Turning Improvement Roadmap by 180°

From a top management perspective, all aspects of Level 1 to three are not interesting. Management representatives are more interested in quantitative process control (Number of projects in time and budget, number of quality issues..) [13]. From this perspective, the generic practices of PA 4.1 and PA 4.2 are the starting point of PI. By doing so it becomes evident that a KPI driven roadmap is not supported by the ISO

33020 Standard. Process capability is in risk to be rated 0 even if in the back-ground lots of work is performed:

To deliver reliable data for the calculation of the KPI lots of activities must use a standard process (PA 3.1 and 3.2) [13] and by knowing that a standard process includes all practices of PA 1.1, 2.1 and 2.2, the process deployment creates a managed process execution producing high quality artefacts [13].

But this work is not visible when it comes to process assessment. Even if lots of invest is spent progress is not reported adequately b assessment results.

2.3 Michael Hammers PEMM as a Challenge for Traditional Capability Models

2007 Michael Hammer published the Process Enterprise Maturity Model (PEMM) [14]. It was not only a fundamental attack against CMMI and all related capability and maturity models, arguing that organisational maturity is not build on the capability of processes but that the organisational maturity provides frame and limitation for process capability [14]. This part of Hammers argument is not challenging process capability metrics. Evaluating process capability with SPICE or CMMI can focus on the capability of the process without any rating influence of the organisational framework.

The real challenge for the traditional understanding of process capability is Hammers understanding of high process capability: the capability to integrate processes across several legal entities, e.g. customer and supplier.

This capability is not part of the measurement framework of ISO 33020 and it wasn't a part of the frameworks of ISO/IEC 15504 Part 1 or CMMI.

2.4 The Software Process Improvement Implementation Maturity Model (SPIIMM)

2017 Khan et al. published a paper presenting a maturity model dealing with global software development [15].

In this paper the authors explicitly analysed if CMMI or SPICE are capable to support an assessment dealing with the special challenges of global software development [15]. The analysis ended up with the construction of a new maturity model and a related assessment model [15]. The authors did not try to integrate their view into the existing measurement framework of SPICE but created an own Maturity Model [15].

2.5 Agile Development Approaches

2001 the agile manifesto was published [16]. Since this date lots of agile maturity models were developed [17, 18]. The driver behind these models is the poor support of agility given by CMMI or SPICE. There are several case studies showing that you can high maturity level using agile practices [19]. But up to now no case study was published showing that agility is supported by SPICE or CMMI.

2.6 The Architectural Problem and Restrictions of ISO/IEC 33020

The ISO 33020 contains 2 key constructs: levels and process attributes [2]. Both constructs are combined as shown in clauses 5.2 and 5.6.

The strength of this model is that it is easy to understand and that it contains characteristics that apply to every organisation even if in the software business or in other fields of business e.g. infra-structure [12].

Another strength is that the model fosters comparable ratings which are capable to support internal or external benchmarks.

Even if the architecture as such can be discussed as shown in Sects. 2.1 and 2.2 the main weakness is that the architecture can't integrate new aspects of process capability. The following tests will provide evidence for this thesis:

2.6.1 Test 1: PEMM

Given that is possible to describe a "Cross organisational border process integration attribute" and its outcomes. Which level will be the right level to add this process attribute?

It could be assumed that Level 3 would be the right level as it requires a capability of standardisation to run cross border processes. Integrating the "Cross organisational border process integration attribute" as a new PA of Level 3 seems to be possible for clause 5.2. This has the consequence that - according to clause 5.6 the new PA must be fully implemented if the organisation wants an assessment result that level 4 or 5 is achieved. But this will exclude every organisation from achieving level 4 or 5 that does not need to run cross organisational border processes. This problem can be solved by adding this attribute to level 5 instead of level 3. But this does not really help an organisation that needs a roadmap.

2.6.2 Test 2: Global Software Development

Given that is possible to describe a "Global software development attribute" and its outcomes. Which level will be the right level to add this process attribute?

It could be assumed that Level 3 would be the right level as it requires a capability of standardisation to run efficient global software development. Integrating the "Global software development Attribute" as a new PA of Level 3 seems to be possible for clause 5.2. This has the consequence that-according to clause 5.6 the new PA must be fully implemented if the organisation wants an assessment result that level 4 or 5 is achieved. But this will exclude every organisation from achieving level 4 or 5 that does not need to run cross organisational border processes. This problem can be solved by adding this attribute to level 5 instead of level 3. But this does not really help an organisation that needs a roadmap for global software development.

2.6.3 Test 3: Agile

Given that is possible to describe an "Agile development attribute" and its outcomes. Which level will be the right level to add this process attribute?

It could be assumed that Level 2 would be the right level agile is mostly seen as a method to man-age software development teams. Integrating the "Agile development attribute" as a new PA of Level 2 seems to be possible for clause 5.2. Level 2 will as a consequence have a process management, a work product management and an agile management attribute. Now the decision must be made if this new attribute will also be integrated in clause 5.6. If not, the new attribute is nice to have but not a real part of the measurement framework if yes, the complete mechanism of Clause 5.6 applies. That means that now three attributes must be found at minimum largely implemented in order to achieve level 2 and fully implemented in order to achieve higher levels. This problem can be solved by adding this attribute to level 5 instead of level 2. But this does not really help an organisation that needs a roadmap for agile software development. Another solution could be to replace PA 2.1 the "Performance management attribute" by the "Agile development Attribute" when assessing agile organisations. In this case an additional requirement for the development of the "Agile development attribute" will be to cover also the key essentials of PA 2.1.

As a result, it can be assumed that fitting the ISO/IEC 33020 for agile development could be possible with slight adaptions, but these adaptions must be compliant with the guidelines of ISO/IEC 33003 [20].

2.6.4 Summary

It has proven that the measurement framework of ISO/IEC 33020 has limited adaptability. Even valuing its undoubtable strength to be valid for all organisations and fields of business and its support for benchmarking, it contradicts the SPI Manifesto principle "Use dynamic and adaptable models as needed".

2.7 Complications

One of the worst complications of the limited adaptability of ISO/IEC 33020 is the need to define a singular maturity model for each aspect of service, systems and software development and delivery. These models are often driven by research teams or results of PhD studies but are not integrated in bigger communities e.g. assessor qualification schemes. Even if most of these models use a structure like CMMI these maturity models cause confusion as it becomes more and more challenging to explain all the dimensions of understanding of maturity and they degrade the value of PI from a management perspective.

3 Solution Options?

3.1 Are Levels Relevant for Process Improvement?

Looking at clause 5.6 of ISO 33020 it seems that it contains somewhat a learning ladder containing ratings and levels and it seems that it describes a way of process improvement. It also implies that levels are somewhat important for process improvement. If this is true levels must play an important role in PI models. In the following sections the role of levels in typical PI models will be analysed.

3.1.1 The Bootstrap Model

The Bootstrap model was published in 1994 as a result of the ESPIT II project of the European union. The Model contains an assessment and an improvement approach. Improvement planning is linked to levels. The reason is the numerical nature of this recommendation provides a powerful psychological aspect as people are committed to achieving a clearly defined goal [3].

The idea is based on the Humphries cycle [21]

(1) Understand current status
(2) Develop a vision of the desired process
(3) List required process improvement actions in priority order
(4) Produce a plan to accomplish the required actions
(5) Commit the resources to execute the plan
(6) Start over at step 1.

3.1.2 The Ideal Model

The Ideal model -published 1996- was developed as an open guideline on how to perform SPI initiatives. In the core description of SPI capability or maturity levels are neither set mandatory or urgently required. The CMM model is frequently used as example but it is considered that other than the CMM can be considered. In section C0 it requires to develop a baseline and goals. The expression in CMM Maturity levels is meant more as a potential example then as a recommendation.

The IDEAL model differs from the Humphries cycle as it requires "Critical business needs to improve software development processes exist and are fully understood" [22]. So the current capability is no longer the starting and driving force, it is replaced by business needs.

3.1.3 ISO/IEC 15504 Part 4

The former standard for process improvement was issued in 2004. In clause 5.3 the standard opened 2 ways of target setting.

1. Describe a target capability profile and decide if a process attribute is not required or must be implemented largely or fully.
2. Describe the target in capability levels.

This model also opens a way to set improvement targets that are not linked to capability levels. It sets an exemplar improvement life cycle always based on the analysis of business goals (Fig. 2).

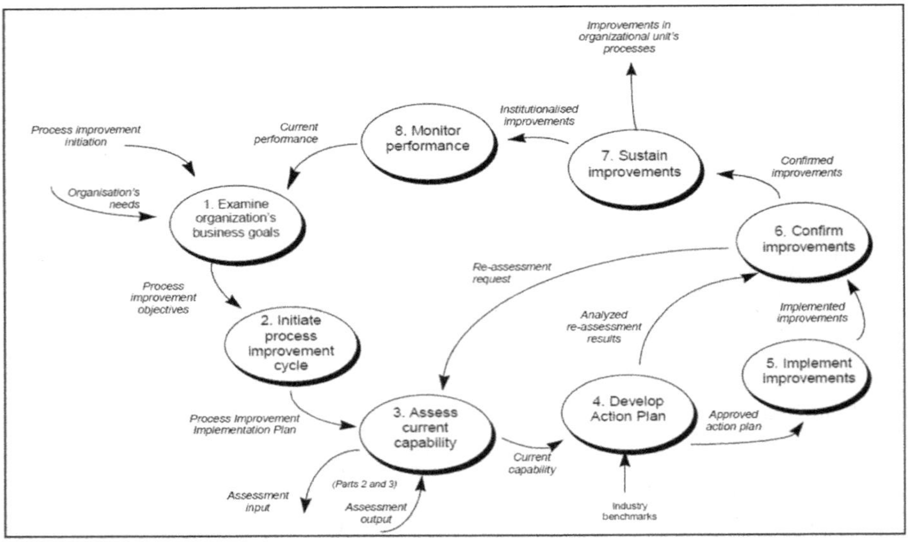

Fig. 2. The improvement life cycle of ISO/IEC 15504 Part 4 (2004)

Also here organisations needs and business goals are the key drivers for process improvement [23].

3.1.4 Improvability

The ImprovAbility Model of process improvement was mainly developed by IT-University, Copenhagen, Denmark, DELTA and 4 companies in a 3-year project. It created a view on organisations and projects ability to improve (Fig. 3).

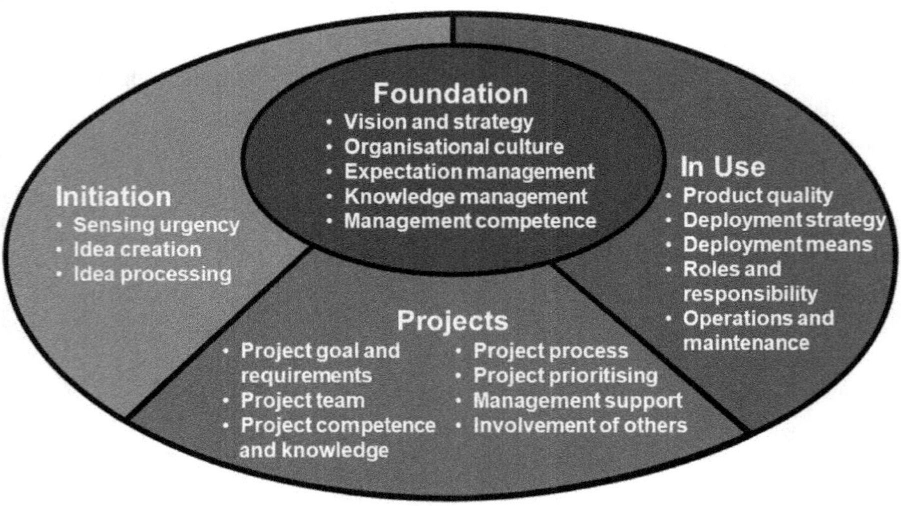

Fig. 3. The ImprovAbility Model

The whole approach does neither recommend a process reference model nor does it recommend an external measurement framework like ISO/IEC 15504 Part 2 or ISO/IEC 33020 [24].

3.1.5 ISO/IEC TR 33014

In 2013 the ISO/IEC TR 33014 [25] standard was published as a successor for ISO/IEC 15504 Part 4.

The standard also describes an improvement approach that -according to clause 5.2.1- starts with the analysis of business goals the selection of a process reference model (PRM) and a target profile. In this clause no mandatory level requirement is stated.

Levels are mentioned in clause 5.2.4.2: Process strength are expressed in levels. In the same clause process weaknesses are expressed in process attribute ratings.

Clause 5.2.4.3 recommends giving priority to the processes with the lowest process level. Clause 5.2.4.6 states that “it is generally unrealistic to seek to increase by more than one process level in a single cycle of improvement, since each level builds on the process level below.” Clause 5.2.5.4 recommends to “evaluate the impacts of the implemented improvement actions on the process attribute ratings and process level ratings”.

Clause 5.2.8 states

“Further process assessments can be an important component of the continual improvement programme, for instance in the following circumstances:

- where a long-term goal to achieve higher process levels is to be approached by stages;
- when changing organizational business goals indicate a requirement to achieve higher process levels”.

Another more implicit view in process levels is given in clause 6.4 where SCRUM is mentioned as a model to be used as a basis of success in process improvement projects. It is obvious that SCRUM does not deal with process levels [25].

Summarizing the findings, the relevance of levels in the ISO/IEC TR 33014 is unclear. By referring to alternative models as SCRUM it becomes likely that the concept of process levels is dispensable.

3.1.6 Improvement Model Summary

Process capability levels have diverging relevance in process improvement models. While at the one hand Levels are indispensable in the BOOTSTRAP approach they are recommended but not mandatory in modern approaches like ImprovAbility. Based on this finding the conclusion is that ISO/IEC 33020 is not the only way to describe process capabilities.

3.2 Consequences for Measurement Frameworks

If -as analysed above- capability levels are not necessary for improvement planning and implementation why continue to use a framework that is not adaptable?

Looking at the potential benefits of capability levels, benchmarking and psychological support, there is no evidence that a valid benchmarking database exists and no study from the last 5 years that top management is motivated by capability and/or maturity levels.

4 Overall Result and Need for Action

Despite of some more technical issues as described in Sects. 2.1 and 2.2 it was analyzed in Sect. 2.6 that the monolithic architecture of ISO/IEC 33020 is not capable to integrate new aspects of process capability. The analysis in Sect. 3 also showed that the capability level construct is dispensable when it comes to planning and implementing PI.

An alternative is needed to avoid the damage of fluently invented capability or maturity models with limited ability to apply and/or maintain the model in the market.

An alternative concept of process capability should be based on

- a set of industrial proven capabilities expressed in process attributes
- a guideline how to develop new process attribute proposals
- a procedure to accept and integrate new process attribute proposals
- a guideline for target setting and target validation
- a guideline for the measurement of target fulfillment
- a basic idea how to align this new approach with ISO/IEC 33003

Having such a concept would be a substantial fulfillment of the SPI Manifesto principle use dynamic and adaptable models as needed.

References

1. Pries-Heje, J., Johansen, J., (eds.): MANIFESTO Software Process Improvement. eurospi.net, Alcala, Spain (2010). http://www.iscn.com/Images/SPI_Manifesto_A.1.2.2010.pdf
2. ISO/IEC 33020: 2014 - Information technology—Process assessment—Process measurement framework for assessment of process capability (2014)
3. Kuvaja, P., Similä, J., Krzanik, L., Bicego, A., Saukkonen, S., Koch, G.: Software Process Assessment & Improvement: The Bootstrap Approach. Blackwell, Oxford (1994). ISBN 0-631-19663-3
4. von Wangenheim, C.G., Hauck, J.C.R., Salviano, C.F., von Wangenehim, A.: Systematic literature review of software capability/maturity models. In: Rout, T., Lami, G., Fabbrini, F. (eds.) 2010 Proceedings of 10th International SPICE Conference, Pisa (2010). ISBN 978-884672663-6
5. Stallinger, F., Neumann, R., Vollmer, J., Plösch, R.: Assessing reuse maturity in complex system engineering contexts, experiences and results from the industrial engineering domain. In: Rout, T., Lami, G., Fabbrini, F. (eds.) 2010 Proceedings of 10th International SPICE Conference, Pisa (2010). ISBN 978-884672663-6
6. Alves, A.M., Pessoa, M., Salviano, C.F.: Towards a systemic maturity model for public software ecosystems. In: O'Connor, R.V., Rout, T., McCaffery, F., Dorling, A. (eds.) SPICE 2011. CCIS, vol. 155, pp. 145–156. Springer, Heidelberg (2011). https://doi.org/10.1007/978-3-642-21233-8_13. ISBN 978-3-642-21232-1

7. Besson, J., Woronowicz, T., Mitasiunas, A., Boronowsky, M.: Innovation, knowledge- and technology transfer process capability model – innoSPICE™. In: Mas, A., Mesquida, A., Rout, T., O'Connor, R.V., Dorling, A. (eds.) SPICE 2012. CCIS, vol. 290, pp. 75–84. Springer, Heidelberg (2012). https://doi.org/10.1007/978-3-642-30439-2_7. ISBN 978-3-642-30438-5
8. Boronowsky, M., Mitasiunas, A., Ragaisis, J., Woronowicz, T.: An approach to development of an application dependent SPICE conformant process capability model. In: Woronowicz, T., Rout, T., O'Connor, R.V., Dorling, A. (eds.) SPICE 2013. CCIS, vol. 349, pp. 61–72. Springer, Heidelberg (2013). https://doi.org/10.1007/978-3-642-38833-0_6. ISBN 978-3-642-38832-3
9. Mayer, N., Barafort, B., Picard, M., Cortina, S.: An ISO compliant and integrated model for IT GRC (governance, risk management and compliance). In: O'Connor, R., Umay Akkaya, M., Kemaneci, K., Yilmaz, M., Poth, A., Messnarz, R. (eds.) Systems, Software and Services Process Improvement. CCIS, vol. 543, pp. 87–99. Springer, Cham (2015). https://doi.org/10.1007/978-3-319-24647-5_8. ISBN 978-3-319-24646-8
10. Rea-Guaman, A.M., San Feliu, T., Calvo-Manzano, J.A., Sanchez-Garcia, I.D.: Comparative study of cybersecurity capability maturity models. In: Mas, A., Mesquida, A., O'Connor, R. V., Rout, T., Dorling, A. (eds.) SPICE 2017. CCIS, vol. 770, pp. 100–113. Springer, Cham (2017). https://doi.org/10.1007/978-3-319-67383-7_8. ISBN 978-3-319-67382-0
11. Patón-Romero, J.D., Rodríguez, M., Piattini, M.: A SPICE-based maturity model for the governance and management of green IT. In: Mas, A., Mesquida, A., O'Connor, R.V., Rout, T., Dorling, A. (eds.) SPICE 2017. CCIS, vol. 770, pp. 143–155. Springer, Cham (2017). https://doi.org/10.1007/978-3-319-67383-7_11. ISBN 978-3-319-67382-0
12. Pfauder, D., Schweigert, T., Hendriks, P.: Using SPICE in the real world: a large infrastructural project example, vol. 20, no. 2, p 27. Software Quality Professional, March 2018
13. Schweigert, T., Philipp, M.: SPI consulting in a level 1 company: an experience report. In: Münch, J., Abrahamsson, P. (eds.) PROFES 2007. LNCS, vol. 4589, pp. 201–206. Springer, Heidelberg (2007). https://doi.org/10.1007/978-3-540-73460-4_19. ISBN 978-3-540-73459-8
14. Hammer, M.: The process audit - a new framework, as comprehensive as it is easy to apply, is helping companies plan and execute process-based transformations, p. 111. Harvard Business Review, April 2007. http://class.svuca.edu/~laurauden/class/Session-11-materials/11-03%20Handouts%20on%20assessment/11-03b-Process%20capability-PEMM/1-Hammer-Process%20Audit.pdf
15. Khan, A.A., Hussein, S., Keung, J., Niazi, M., Zhang, H.: A proposed model for software process assessment and improvement in the domain of Global Software Development. In: Selected Papers of the 24 th EuroSPI Conference. Graz 2017, Ostrava (2017). ISBN 978-3-9504505-0-7
16. Beck, K., et al.: Manifesto for agile software development, Snowbird Ski Resort (2001). http://agilemanifesto.org/
17. Schweigert, T., Vohwinkel, D., Korsaa, M., Nevalainen, R., Biro, M.: Agile maturity model: analysing agile maturity characteristics from the SPICE perspective. J. Softw. Evol. Process (2013). Published online in Wiley Online Library (wileyonlinelibrary.com). https://doi.org/10.1002/smr.1617
18. Ozcan-Top, O., Demirörs, O.: A reference model for software agility assessment: AgilityMod. In: Rout, T., O'Connor, R.V., Dorling, A. (eds.) SPICE 2015. CCIS, vol. 526, pp. 145–158. Springer, Cham (2015). https://doi.org/10.1007/978-3-319-19860-6_12. ISBN 978-3-319-19859-0

19. Glazer, H., Dalton, J., Anderson, D., Konrad, M.D., Shrum, S.: CMMI or Agile: Why Not Embrace Both! SEI 2008, CMU/SEI-2008-TN-003 (2008)
20. ISO/IEC 33020:2015 Information technology – Process assessment – Process measurement framework for assessment of process capability (2015)
21. Humphrey, W.: Managing the Software Process. SEI Series in Software Engineering. Addison-Wesley Longman Publishing Co., Inc., Boston (1989)
22. McFeeley, B.: IDEAL(SM): A User's Guide for Software Process Improvement, SEI (1996)
23. ISO IEC 15504-4:2004 Guidance on use for process improvement and process capability determination (2004)
24. Pries-Heje, J., Johansen, J. (eds.): ImprovAbility™ - Success with Process Improvement. Delta, Horsholm (2013). ISBN 978-87-7398-139-9
25. ISO/IEC TR 33014:2013 Information technology – Process assessment – Guide for process improvement (2013)

Safety and Security

Qualifying Dependent Failure Analysis Within ISO26262: Applicability to Semiconductors

Alison Young and Alastair Walker(✉)

Lorit Consultancy, Edinburgh, Scotland
{r.alison.young, alastair.walker}@lorit-consultancy.com

Abstract. In early 2018, the second edition of ISO 26262:2018 [1] functional safety standard for road vehicles, was released. One of the main challenges in safety analysis is the decision on suitability of dependent failures. Many discussions ensue on the suitability and the potential impact of any common cause or dependent failures. ISO 26262 parts 9 and 11 give guidance of the categories of dependent failures initiators, but how to gauge acceptability is not so easily quantified. There is a lot of excellent literature on calculating failure rates for common causes, but this information may not easily support design teams in assessing the dependency of the 7 groups of dependent failure initiators listed in ISO 26262-9:2018. IEC 61508 uses a grading system based on a series of questions, however it relates any score gained to the beta factors used in calculating failure rates. Ultimately it is desirable for dependent failures analysis to produce a quantitative result, but not one that feeds into failure rates, as many decisions based on failure rates involve software or system level considerations and are systematic rather than random. One other significant factor in the dependent failures analysis is that many products being assessed against ISO 26262 were not originally designed to meet the standard and are being adapted to comply. In this case an assessment of additional safety mechanisms and the quality of them is key. This paper proposes a quantitative approach to grade dependent failures analyses such that an acceptability criterion can be defined for different ASILs.

Keywords: Functional safety · Dependent failures analysis (DFA)
Common cause failures

1 Introduction

Many design teams in the automotive industry working to ISO 26262 implement the requirements of parts 4, 5 and 6 of the standard to the letter of the law. The activities defined in part 9 such as DFA however are both trickier to define down to the limited amount of available information. The DFA like the dependent failures initiator (DFI) identification in ISO 26262 is good, but how to actually define what is or is not acceptable is a trickier question. In ISO 26262 there are two defined goals for the DFA activities:

X. Larrucea et al. (Eds.): EuroSPI 2018, CCIS 896, pp. 331–340, 2018.
https://doi.org/10.1007/978-3-319-97925-0_27

- Identify single events, single causes & failure modes
- Identify safety measures to mitigate dependent failures

For point a. above identifying the events is typically a straight forward activity but deciding that the impact is or is not acceptable is more difficult.

By defining a weighting system based on the type of dependence between the components permits a grading system of acceptability to be defined and hence whether the dependency is permissible in the given project.

Equally for point b. a weighting system can be used for any safety measure to define the necessary effectiveness and quality of the mechanism.

Techniques can be equally applicable to discrete or semiconductor components. Dependent failure analysis on a single silicon die looks for interdependencies between hardware elements on the same die, or between hardware and software elements. Typically, analysis focuses on hardware elements performing a safety function and their safety mechanisms.

2 Dependent Failure Analysis

2.1 Dependent Failure Initiators

Dependent failure analysis typically begins with identification of pairs – usually a hardware element and its safety mechanism. The scope of the analysis should be defined at the outset, and may include safety mechanisms implemented in hardware, software, or both. Following the methodology recommended by Faller [2], each of the pairs in this list are then examined to determine if:

- A potential dependent failure would impact the safety function
- No test exists for the potential dependent failure of the hardware element and safety mechanism
- No safety measures exist to control or mitigate the effects of the dependent failure.

If the answer for these three questions is positive then the pair should be included in dependent failure analysis. The next step is to examine potential root causes of a dependent failure, these are termed Dependent Failure Initiators (DFI) in ISO26262-9:2018.

ISO26262-9: Annex C describes 7 groups of dependent failures initiators (DFI), these are represented in Fig. 1 below. This annex also lists typical examples of DFI for each of the 7 categories, and maps the categories to the topics in ISO26262-9:2018 clause 7.4.4 and those described along with related mitigation measures in the Guideline on application of ISO26262 to semiconductors in ISO26262-11:2018 clause 4.7.5.

When analysing dependent failures within a semiconductor device there will be some dependent failure initiators that can influence a large portion of the device, for example shared resources such as common clocks and shared power supplies. It is often possible to address these dependencies within standard safety analysis. Dependent failure analysis focuses on the dependent failure initiators that cannot be addressed in standard safety analysis.

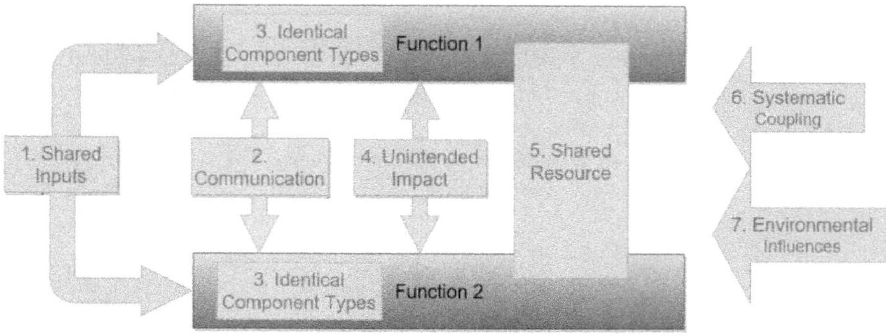

Fig. 1. ISO26262-9:2018 dependent failure initiators

One particular challenge when performing analysis on semiconductors is choosing pairs of components and initiators that have the greatest potential impact, and having confidence that the breadth of the analysis is sufficient. A weighting system that helps prioritise the key functions and initiators that can influence them is therefore very useful.

2.2 Common Cause Failure Analysis

IEC61508 Strategy for Common Cause Failure Analysis

To enable the calculation of beta factors for common cause analysis in IEC 61508 [3] a series of 37 questions are used to estimate the common cause frailties of the system in question. These questions are split into the following categories:

- Separation
- Diversity/Redundancy
- Complexity/Design/Use/experience
- Judgment/analysis of data
- Procedures/usage
- Competence/Training/Safety culture
- Monitoring the surrounding conditions
- Test and environment.

From the results of these 37 questions a weighted value results, this result determines the beta factor used in scaling the failure in time rates.

Controller Strategy

There are many different controller architectures [4] available to support functional safety relevant projects – symmetric, asymmetric and multicore processers. The pros and cons of the different types in relation to common cause failures is also well documented (Fig. 2).

Heading level	Example	Font size and style
Title (centered)	**Lecture Notes**	14 point, bold
1st-level heading	**1 Introduction**	12 point, bold
2nd-level heading	**2.1 Printing Area**	10 point, bold
3rd-level heading	**Run-in Heading in Bold.** Text follows	10 point, bold
4th-level heading	*Lowest Level Heading.* Text follows	10 point, italic

DFI group	DFI type	Detail	Score
Shared resources	Clock	Same clock source for both channels no checks	10
		Test only for stuck at faults	7
		Test for stuck at, jitter, DC, drift	4
		Full independent clock monitoring	1
	Power supply	Identical Power Supply	10
		Same technology but different PSU implementation	7
		Different power supply technology	4
		Different power supply technology, with independent monitoring, level, transient and oscillation	1
	Common software	Identical software component	10
		Different provider same functionality	7
		Different provider similar functionality different hardware	4
		Different SW implementation	1
	Same silicon package	Intended function and safety measure in the same silicon package – no monitoring	10
		Intended function and safety measure in the same silicon package – single level of internal monitoring	7
		Intended function and safety measure in the same silicon package – single level of external monitoring	4
		Intended function and safety measure in the same silicon package – multiple levels of external monitoring	1

(*continued*)

(*continued*)

DFI group	DFI type	Detail	Score
Shared information inputs	System or HW - external physical signals	Identical data handling of the signals	10
		Diverse handling through the same interface	7
		Diverse handling through different interface	4
		Diverse handling through a different interface with independent monitoring	1
	Software global variables	High number of global variables	10
		Minimal number of global variables	7
		Minimal number of global variables EDC-ECC	4
		Minimal number of global variables EDC-ECC, full static analysis, control and data flow	1

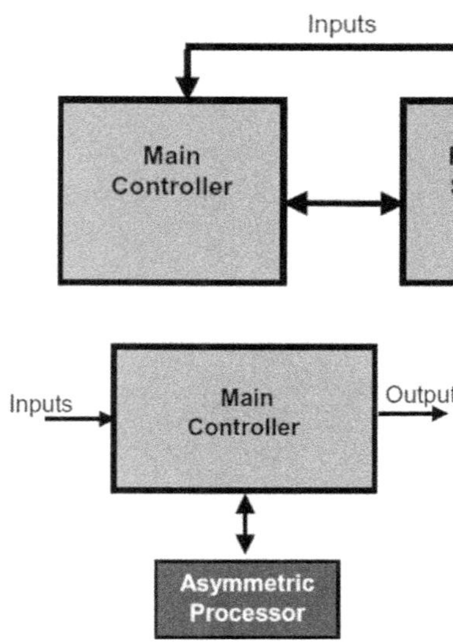

Fig. 2. Symmetrical and asymmetrical controller strategies

2.3 Inherent Good Design Against Safety Mechanism

In the cases where an existing product is being assessed for suitability to comply with ISO 26262 the architecture may not have been designed in accordance with ISO 26262. In these cases risk control measures may need to be added to the architecture.

The risk management standard ISO 14971 [5] for medical devices recommends 3 techniques for reducing risk. The first is inherent good design, the second risk control measures and lastly the use of accompanying documents. The last option would not be applicable for the automotive industry, however if we use scaling factors for safety mechanisms these risk control mechanisms can be graded for the reduction they can make to the DFA grading score.

3 Proposed Strategy

3.1 Dependent Failure Initiator Grading

A scoring system for acceptance of DFI impacting a new design could be typically defined as below. The categories are those listed in ISO 26262-9:2018 Annex C, but this is not an exhaustive list, there are others that will be applicable for any given project.

DFI group	DFI type	Detail	Score
Environmental influences	Mechanical shock	Designed to meet the mechanical requirements	10
		Designed and tested to meet all mechanical requirements (one sample)	7
		Designed and tested to meet all mechanical requirements (multiple samples)	4
		Designed and tested to exceed all mechanical requirements (multiple samples)	1
	Water ingress	Not designed to specified IP rating	10
		Designed to meet IP rating requirements	7
		Designed tested to meet IP rating requirements and expected servicing and service life	4
		Designed tested to exceed IP rating requirements and expected servicing and service life	1
	EMC	Designed to meet all emission and immunity levels (not tested in all scenarios)	10
		Designed and tested to meet all emission and immunity levels (one sample)	7
		Designed and tested to meet all emission and immunity levels (multiple samples)	4
		Designed and tested to exceed all emission and immunity levels (multiple samples)	1

(*continued*)

(*continued*)

DFI group	DFI type	Detail	Score
	Transient upsets	No testing of transient immunity	10
		Design principles to minimise transient impact	7
		Transient testing of devices e.g. JEDEC 89	4
		Full confirmation of devices to ISO 26262 for transient metrics. ECC for memory	1
Systematic coupling	Same algorithms	Identical	10
		Same function different processor	7
		Same function different implementation	4
		Different function different implementation	1
	Connection technology	Designed to meet the requirements	10
		Designed and tested to meet all requirements (one sample)	7
		Designed and tested to meet all requirements (multiple samples)	4
		Designed and tested to exceed all requirements (multiple samples)	1
Components of identical type	Identical hardware	Identical	10
		Same function different software control	7
		Similar functional different software control	4
		Independent monitoring of results	1
	Identical software libraries	Identical	10
		Same function different hardware platform	7
		Similar functional different hardware platform	4
		Independent monitoring of results	1
Communication	Failure of the physical layer of the communication SW Exchange of information Failure of the application or protocol layer of the communications	Minimal checks on data integrity	10
		Time-outs, message counters, CRC checks	7
		Full end to end ECC	4
		Full end to end ECC with external confirmation	1

DFI group	DFI type	Detail	Score
Unintended impact	HW crosstalk	No consideration connection impedance	10
		Basic matching of impedances	7
		Full evaluation of impedance and termination	4
		Full evaluation of impedance, termination and physical location	1
	Thermal impact	Basic design analysis	10
		Design analysis and test per requirements	7
		Design and analysis of overstressed levels, thermal analysis (one sample)	4
		Design and analysis of overstressed levels, thermal analysis (multiple samples)	1
	SW Timing and execution e.g. Repetition of information Loss of information Delay of information Insertion of information Masquerade or incorrect addressing of information Incorrect sequence of information Corruption of information Asymmetric information sent to multiple receivers Information from a sender received by only a subset of receivers Blocking access to a communications channel	Minimal checks on data integrity	10
		Time-outs, message counters, CRC checks	7
		Full end to end ECC	4
		Full end to end ECC with external confirmation	1
	SW Memory e.g. Corruption of content Inconsistent data Stack overflow or underflow Read or write access to memory allocated to another software element	Basic defensive design	10
		Full static analysis	7
		Full static analysis data & control flow	4
		Full static analysis data & control flow. ECC	1

(*continued*)

(*continued*)

DFI group	DFI type	Detail	Score
	Training of development and QA personnel	Basic design training	10
		All training by certified bodies	7
		All personnel at least 5 years functional safety experience trained by certified bodies	4
		All personnel at least 5 years functional safety experience trained by certified bodies. All hold functional safety qualifications and similar e.g. AutomotiveSPICE	1
	Training of service personnel	Basic or no training	10
		All personnel trained on the specific project	7
		All personnel trained to certified qualifications and on multiple projects	4
		All personnel trained to certified qualifications and on multiple projects. Servicing inspected by colleagues	1

3.2 Additional Safety Mechanism Grading

If we take the example of a lack of inherent good design or a device developed prior to consideration of ISO 26262 requirements, then the addition of a safety mechanism can also be given a weighting factor to determine quantitatively the acceptability of the functionality combined with safety mechanism. The guidelines would follow those of Sect. 3.1 above again comparing the safety mechanism to the intended functionality to determine the independence.

4 Acceptable Outcomes

The acceptable outcomes from the grading system can be applied based on the ASIL of the safety goal. e.g. for ASIL D the total score must be lower than 40 with the caveat that no single category score can exceed 4. ASIL C should be less than 80 and ASIL B should be lower than 120. Again, the categories in Sect. 3.1 are not exhaustive and if additional categories are added, then the acceptance limits can be scaled up accordingly.

5 Conclusions

ISO 26262:2018 provides a good framework for design teams to develop compliant products and those that offer satisfactory levels of functional safety. However, the analysis of dependent failures and that of common cause failures often leaves more questions that it provides answers. The lack of guidance to design teams on what is an acceptable level for DFA is an issue that many organisations find difficult to answer.

Much of the theory on common cause failures focuses on hardware failures, but considering the competence of service personnel is a far harder question to judge.

In this paper we propose a solution based on the ideals of IEC 61508, but not aligning the outcomes with beta factors, in this case giving criterion on how one can accept or reject a given level of dependent failure. Lorit Consultancy is working to enhance this approach to DFA and further document the strategy in order to support customers in ISO 26262 DFA activities, in both semiconductor devices and discrete component design.

References

1. ISO DIS 26262:2018 Road vehicles – Functional safety
2. Faller, R.: Specification of a software common cause analysis method. In: Saglietti, F., Oster, N. (eds.) SAFECOMP 2007. LNCS, vol. 4680, pp. 162–171. Springer, Heidelberg (2007). https://doi.org/10.1007/978-3-540-75101-4_16
3. IEC 61508:2010 Functional safety of electrical/electronic/programmable electronic safety-related systems
4. Sundaram, P., D'Ambrosio, J.G.: Controller Integrity in Automotive Failsafe System Architectures. Delphi Corporation. SAE Technical Paper Series 2006-010840
5. ISO 14971 Medical Devices - Application of risk management to Medical Devices

Towards Executable Dependability Properties

Jürgen Dobaj(✉), Johannes Iber(✉), Michael Krisper(✉), and Christian Kreiner

Graz University of Technology, 8010 Graz, Austria
{juergen.dobaj,johannes.iber,michael.krisper}@tugraz.at

Abstract. Cyber-Physical Systems (CPSs) provide enormous potential for innovation. Examples are modern road vehicles (assisted and autonomous driving), CPS road networks (car2x), power plants, smart grids and healthcare devices. However, due to the dynamic interconnection and the largely unpredictable number of possible system configurations the dependable cooperation of CPS can not be fully assured at design time. The malfunction of a CPS could threaten human life, cause environmental damage and major financial loss. In order to address these challenges, this paper presents an early excerpt of an ongoing holistic approach and toolchain architecture that supports the design, development, implementation, operation and maintenance of dependable CPS. The proposed approach uses the dependability information accumulated during the system specification process as an input configuration for self-adaptive systems. These self-adaptive systems then test and assure the dependability properties of the CPS throughout the whole system life cycle.

Keywords: Executable Dependability Property · Dependability
Safety · Security · Risk assessment · Self-adaptive system
Model based development · Digital Dependability Identity

1 Introduction

Today's software and hardware technologies enable the expansion of CPS into the realms of mobility (car2x, autonomous driving), energy (power plants, smart grid) and healthcare (health monitoring), paving the way into a highly interlaced world. However, this also dramatically broadens the threat landscape for potential attacks on such CPS. The Threat Horizon 2017 report lists "death from disruption to digital services" [5] as one of these threats, especially in the medical and mobility domain. Additionally, the newest Threat Horizon 2019 report claims that the cause of service disruption may come "from an over reliance on fragile connectivity" [9]. This situation is further sharpened by the lack of comprehensive methods for the development of dependable CPS that can also assure dependability at runtime [2–4,21]. The malfunction of such CPS could, however, threaten human life and other assets, which encourages the development of methods and tools that assure the dependable cooperation of CPS throughout the

X. Larrucea et al. (Eds.): EuroSPI 2018, CCIS 896, pp. 341–353, 2018.
https://doi.org/10.1007/978-3-319-97925-0_28

whole system life cycle. In the course of this paper, we present an early excerpt of ongoing work that addresses these unsolved challenges. We propose a holistic method and toolchain architecture that supports the design, development, implementation, operation and maintenance of dependable CPS. The proposed method can be tailored to address the assurance of various dependability properties. In this paper, we explicitly focus on CPS, where security and safety are a critical aspect that requires an in-depth risk assessment.

The paper is organized as follows: Sect. 2 presents an overview of related work. Section 3 introduces the INtegrating Security Into Risk Assessment (INSpIRA) approach and explains how the INSpIRA workflow can be tailored to assure the dependable operation of automotive systems. Section 4 proposes the software architecture to implement the INSpIRA workflow and discusses the seamless development and integration of systems in a collaborative manner, even across companies and industries, as well as cooperative operation of dependable systems across multiple domains. Finally, Sect. 5 concludes with an outline of potential challenges and future work.

2 Related Work

Cherdantseva et al. [2] reviewed twenty-four security risk assessment methods for the development of Supervisory Control and Data Acquisition (SCADA) systems. They pointed out that tool support would be especially beneficial to automatically generate and analyze risk models, recommend countermeasures, or even trigger them as a response to undesired events. Additionally, these tools could ease the evaluation of different methods on real and more complex use cases in a less tedious way, if the risk assessment processes was at least partially automated. However, out of the twenty-four evaluated papers only seven discussed tool support and neither tool architectures nor user interfaces were demonstrated. Cherdantseva et al. also concluded that future risk assessment tools may consider the capturing and formalization of expert opinion and the evaluation and validation of the risk assessment process.

Chockalingam et al. [3] conducted a survey to identify the key characteristics and applications of integrated safety and security risk assessment methods to provide a base for future investigations and the development of more effective risk assessment methods and tools. Based on their inclusion criteria they evaluated seven methods and identified the issue that none of these methods take into account runtime system information to perform dynamic risk assessment.

Schneider et al. [21] also discussed the importance of runtime system information to assure the dynamic and dependable cooperation of CPS. Due to the dynamic interconnection and the largely unpredictable number of possible system configurations, the dependability of CPS can not be fully assured at design time. Thus they proposed the concept of a Digital Dependability Identity (DDI). DDIs are analyzable and potentially executable models of information about the dependability of a component or system. This information must be maintained over the whole life time of a component and can then be used at runtime to check whether systems can dependably cooperate or not. In their work,

Schneider et al. showed how safety properties can be used at runtime to optimize the trade-off between availability and safety of a round baler. Macher et al. [14] proposed an initial framework using DDIs to support functional safety levels for, and validation of, fully automated vehicles.

In summary it is established that despite the fact that a large number of methods and tools for dependable system design and development is available, there is still room for further research and tool improvements. In this paper we propose a holistic approach that supports the design, development, operation and maintenance of dependable CPS. We propose a toolchain architecture that enables the provisioning of runtime information in a central repository. This runtime information is used during both, system development and operation, to automatically assure the dependable cooperation of the System under Development (SuD).

3 The INSpIRA Approach: INtegrating Security Into Risk Assessment

As pinpointed in the previous section, there is a need for comprehensive methods and tools that support the inter-domain development of dependable systems throughout the whole system life cycle. The INSpIRA approach proposed by Dobaj [4] depicts such a holistic approach that also offers tool support to efficiently design, develop, implement, operate and maintain dependable CPS across multiple domains. The INSpIRA workflow is separated into two main phases, the system specification phase and the runtime phase as shown in Fig. 1. In the system specification phase various tools and methods can be combined to construct a human readable knowledge base. The human readable knowledge base accumulates the system requirements, structure, functionality, potential failures and

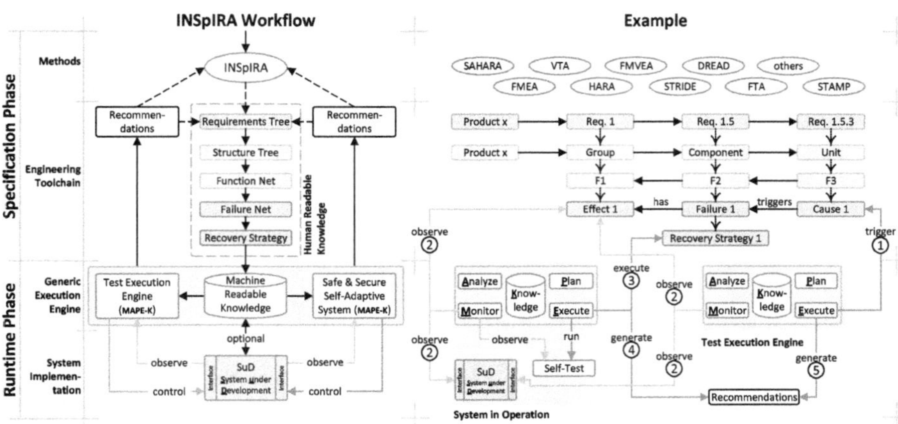

Fig. 1. The left-hand side shows the INSpIRA Workflow with its development and operation phases, and the right-hand-side shows the interaction between the system in operation and the test execution engine. (Color figure online)

vulnerabilities, as well as strategies to recover from failures. In the runtime phase this knowledge base is as an input configuration for self-adaptive systems to test and assure the dependability properties of the SuD. In this section we describe the INSpIRA approach and workflow based on these two phases.

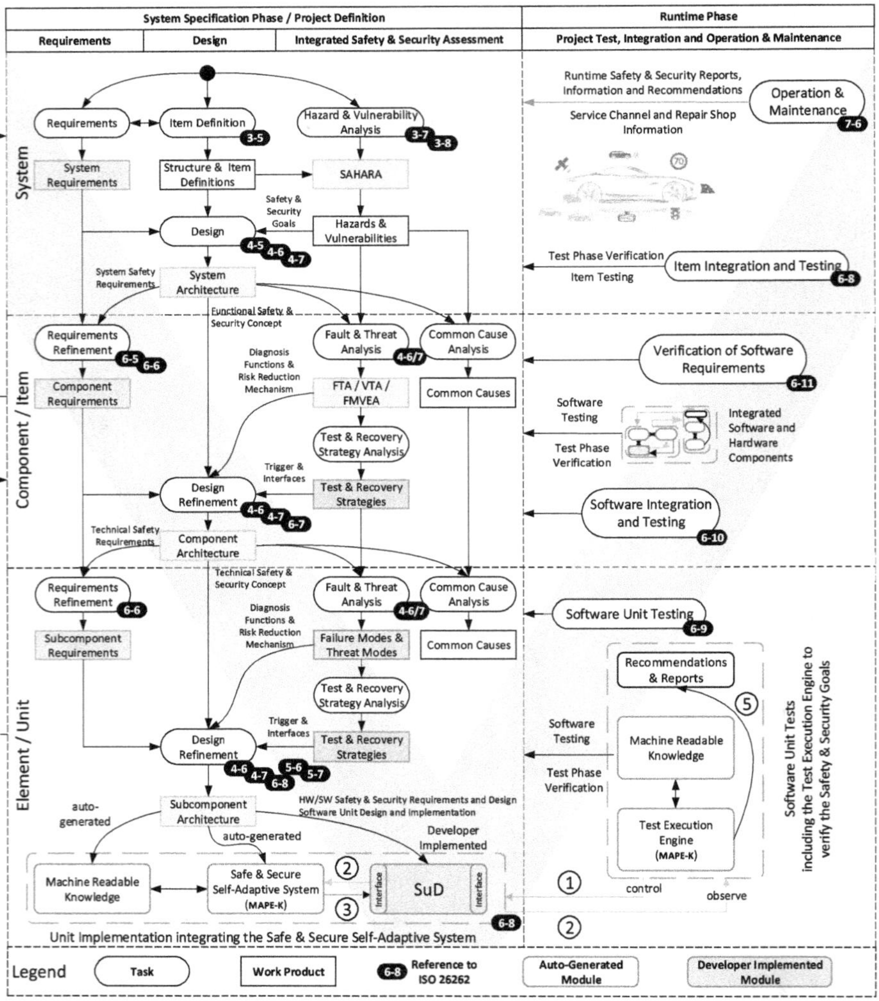

Fig. 2. Unfolded integrated safety and security assessment workflow with hierarchical systems adapted from [13]. The workflow shows how the INSpIRA approach can be tailored to support the development of dependable automotive systems, wherever security and safety are critical aspects requiring an in-depth risk assessment. (Color figure online)

3.1 System Specification Phase - Project Definition

Set of Safety and Security Analysis Methods: The INSpIRA approach allows to combine different risk and security analyses methods to identify the safety and security requirements of the SuD. Depending on the given use case and established development processes users (generally a group of experts) can define which workflow and set of analysis methods the engineering toolchain should use. An overview of the INSpIRA workflow and toolchain including a general example is shown in Fig. 1. A concrete configuration showing an integrated safety and security assessment workflow tailored towards the development and operation of dependable automotive systems is exemplified in Fig. 2. This workflow definition is based on best practices in engineering of systems exhibiting functional safety [13] and extended by methods proposed by the INSpIRA approach. The tasks that are related to functional safety reference the corresponding parts in the ISO 26262 standard [10].

The Engineering Toolchain supports the user by applying the previously defined workflow. The knowledge generated during the workflow execution should be human and machine readable. The toolchain thus organizes the knowledge in tree and net structures, similar to the APIS risk analysis tool [11]. The tree and net structures are divided into five main groups: (1) Requirements Tree, (2) Structure Tree, (3) Function Net, (4) Failure Net, and (5) Recovery Strategies. The groups and structures are interconnected, as exemplarily shown in Fig. 1, which allows (to force) full traceability between requirements, design decision, HW/SW implementations, tests and components operating in the field throughout the whole product life cycle. The toolchain even allows full traceability between components developed by subcontractors by still protecting the intellectual property of all involved parties, which is further elaborated in Sect. 4. Depending on the applied method, different groups in the knowledge base are affected and modified, as highlighted in Fig. 2 by coloring the work products of each task in the corresponding group color introduced in Fig. 1. The following steps explain the workflow implemented by the engineering toolchain and the relationship between the five main groups:

1. The development of a system generally starts with the concept phase where the system requirements are defined mainly in a textual manner. This information is stored in the **Requirements Tree**. In the concept phase it is also important to identify potential hazards and vulnerabilities (e.g. Hazard Analysis and Risk Assessment (HARA), Security-Aware Hazard And Risk Analysis (SAHARA) [16]), and to implement countermeasures early in the development phase. As changes later in the development process are increasingly expensive and disruptive as development proceeds.
2. After the concept phase, a systematic approach based on the Failure Mode, Vulnerability and Effect Analyzes (FMVEA) [20] is applied to obtain a more technical specification. The FMVEA requires that the system's structure, functions, potential failures, vulnerabilities and countermeasures must be identified. The FMVEA's first step is the division of the system into groups,

components and units, which are stored in the **Structure Tree**. The structure tree might already contain information obtained by methods applied in the previous step like block diagrams, network models or threat models. All elements in the structure tree are linked to their describing element in the requirements tree.
3. As each element of the structure tree implements one or more specific functions, a structure tree element is linked to at least one element in the **Function Net**. The elements in the function net describe the functionality or service provided and contain a technical description of the structure tree element (e.g., flowchart, interface definition, (link to) implementation).
4. A function could fail or be the target of an attack by definition. The FMVEA thus requires the analysis of potential failures and vulnerabilities by constructing cause-mode-effect and vulnerability-thread-effect relations that are stored in the **Failure Net**.
5. The INSpIRA method extends the FMVEA and additionally requires the definition of **Recovery Strategies** that are linked to the failure and thread modes stored in the failure net. A recovery strategy describes the necessary actions to either enter a safe state or recover from a failure whenever possible.

Generic Execution Engine: The Human Readable Knowledge constructed in the previous steps is used to generate the Machine Readable Knowledge for the *Generic Execution Engine (GEE)*. The GEE is implemented as a self-adaptive system and uses MAPE-K loops [12] to integrate the security and safety knowledge for testing the SuD, and to assure that the defined safety and security goals are met during operation. The test results should provide evidence about the SuD's safety and security properties. If discrepancies are detected, the GEE generates a notification and attempts to recommend potential fixes. The properties of the generic execution engine are further discussed in Sect. 3.2.

Implementation: The SuD must, of course, be implemented based on the previously engineered requirements specification. This is shown in Fig. 2 where all design decision influence the subcomponent architecture and hence the implementation of the SuD. The INSpIRA method requires the implementation of an interface for the interaction between the GEE and the SuD, which imposes an additional development effort. However, the GEE is planned to already implement relevant parts of the required testing mechanisms and system functionality and this significantly reduces the overall development effort. The interface also encapsulates implementation specifics, which allows the use of a SuD digital twin [7] during development. This digital twin could be an arbitrary implementation enabling the support for simulation-based development and verification.

3.2 Runtime Phase

In its runtime phase INSpIRA uses the knowledge accumulated during the system specification phase to auto-generate mechanisms for testing and system operation. During system development and integration the test execution engine verifies that the SuD meets the desired safety and security goals, while during system operation and maintenance the knowledge is used to configure a self-adaptive system that assures the SuD's safety and security properties in the field. Both scenarios use the generic execution engine to test and assure the safety and security properties engineered during the system specification, hence making these dependability properties executable. These scenarios are explained in the following two paragraphs and exemplified in Figs. 1 and 3 (functional view), as well as in Fig. 2 (life cycle integration view).

Development Phase - System Testing and Integration: In the *development phase* the FMVEA requires the definition of cause-mode-effect and thread-mode-effect relations for all identified failure modes and vulnerabilities. The GEE uses this information to generate test cases and to run its test execution engine. An example of the testing data flow is shown in Fig. 3, where the test execution engine (1) triggers a cause that results in a subsequent failure. If the system in operation is designed and implemented correctly, then it must be able to both (2) detect this failure and (3) react accordingly. The test execution engine also (2) observes the reactions of the SuD and based on these observations, the test execution engine may decide if the SuD is working correctly. If after the cause triggering no failure can be detected, this is a hint pointing to a potential design or implementation failure. The test execution engine then (5) generates a report and notifies a development engineer to reevaluate the SuD. This approach encourages constant evaluation and improvement of the SuD and its requirements.

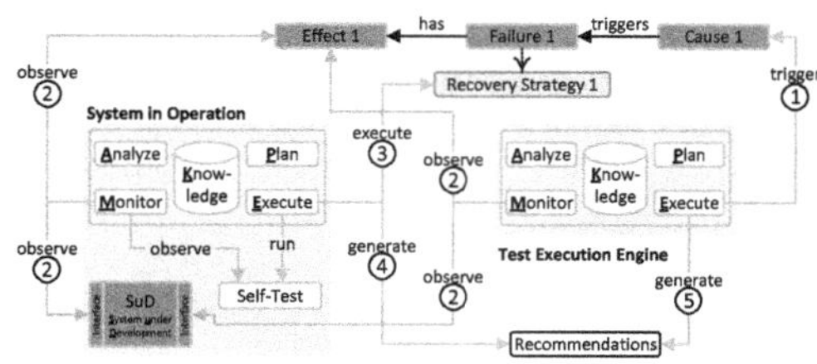

Fig. 3. Interaction between system in operation and test execution engine (from Fig. 1).

Operation and Maintenance Phase: In the *operation and maintenance phase* the triggering of failures is deactivated, because forcing the system into a failure mode would provide a serious attack vector and safety issue. Instead of this, the GEE runs auto-generated self-tests at system startup and during operation the GEE acts as a self-adaptive system executing safety and security mechanisms. The GEE thus continuously observes the SuD behavior. Once the GEE observes effects that indicate a failure mode or security attack, the GEE can execute a corresponding Recovery Strategy. If the GEE detects an undesired behavior that is not documented by a mode-effect relation, the GEE should also notify the engineering team to request improvement or maintenance. If the detection of failures and the recovery can be established within an acceptable timespan or even in real-time, then the GEE can replace parts or the entire safety and security mechanisms, otherwise implemented in the SuD. If the real-time reaction is not possible, the GEE can still be used to implement resilience mechanisms, such as re-routing, hot standby device management, fault recovery and maintenance cycle planing [8].

Self-evaluation: If the GEE can be used to establish both, the generation of test cases and the implementation of safety, security and resilience mechanisms for the SuD, then the GEE would be able to test itself. In order to test itself, two instances of the GEE must be launched as shown in Fig. 3. One instance runs the test execution engine and the other instance runs the safe & secure self-adaptive system that is integrated into the system in operation. The test execution engine (1) triggers a cause, which should result in a failure mode and (2) observable effects. (2) The safe & secure Self-adaptive system observes these effects and (3) executes a recovery strategy after detection. If the safe & secure Self-adaptive system observes unexpected behavior that is not document in the knowledge base, then (4) a report is generated and forwarded to the development engineers. The test execution engine again observes the SuD's reactions and finally (5) generates a report and recommendations.

4 The INSpIRA Software Architecture

Figure 4 shows the proposed INSpIRA software architecture that is structured into three main layers: the data layer, the development layer, and the runtime layer. The software architecture and the toolchain must facilitate the integration and operation of (embedded) devices that operate in different domains, under different environmental conditions and technical or legislative constraints. Thus, the architecture must be extensible and adaptable to support diverse development processes and tools. The INSpIRA software architecture attempts to address this diversity by enabling seamless development and integration of systems in a collaborative manner, as well as cooperative operation of dependable systems.

Data Layer: The data layer accumulates all the information created during the system development process. This includes all design decisions, work products, system models, safety and security assessment data, SW/HW source code, and more. To make this information traceable everything is connected via relationships. The data layer uses graph data bases to express this relationships in a graph data model. Graph data bases natively implement the storing of data as graphs. Common use cases of graph data bases are (a) fraud detection & analytics solution, (b) digital asset management (knowledge graphs), (c) network & IT operations, (d) real-time recommendation engines, (e) master data management, (f) social networks, (g) identity & access management, and (h) privacy, risk and compliance management [1]. Because of this broad field of supported applications, we think that graphs and graph data bases are well suited for the modeling of complex large scale socio-technical systems such as the upcoming CPS and the Internet of Things (IoT). However, it is very unlikely to feasibly integrate all available information into graph data bases. Thus linking to external data bases, source code repositories and other storage entities must be supported. The communication with the data layer and the integration of such external entities is managed by the development layer.

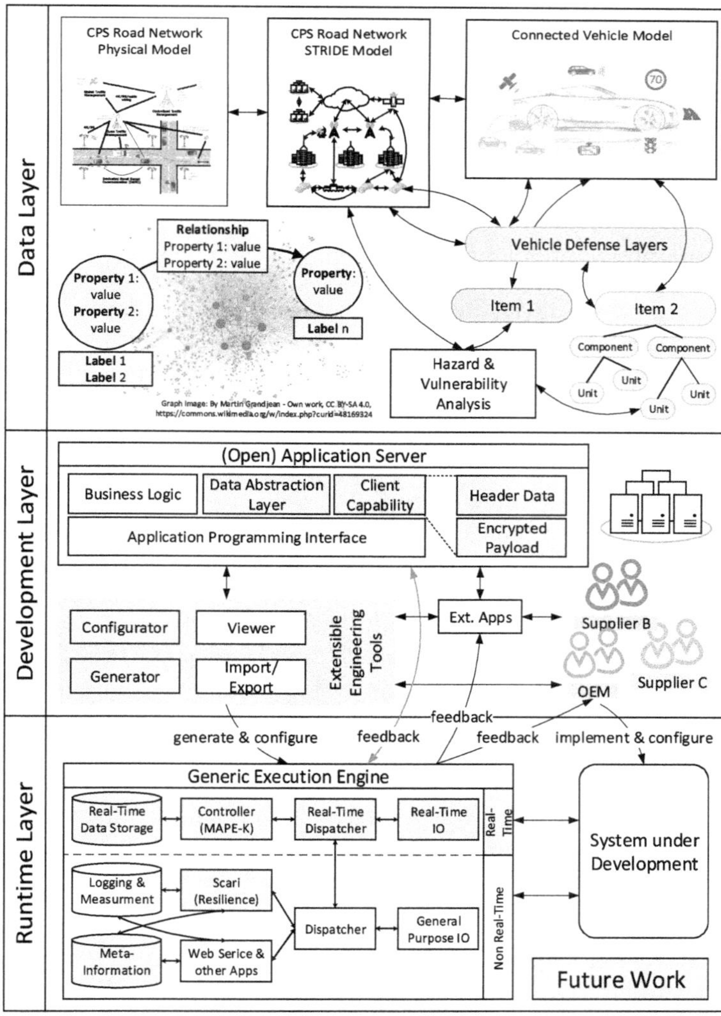

Fig. 4. Toolchain Architecture. The INSpIRA toolchain is separated into three layers. The data layer accumulates the information created during the system development. The System development is supported and managed by the engineering tools in the system development layer. These tools are extensible to be adaptable for various development processes, and are used to generate and configure the components of the runtime layer.

Development Layer: The core component of the development layer is the application server. Multiple instances of the application server manage the access to the data layer and ensure that everything is scaling well. As stated before, there exist diverse approaches and methods that are tailored towards dependable system development in a specific domain. This diversity is addressed in the development layer by providing an extensible engineering toolchain and an open Application Programming Interface (API) that allows multiple clients to access the application server. This enables companies to integrate and adapt different sets of methods and tools for system development and operation. Furthermore, this encourages experts from different domains, departments and even companies to collaboratively design and develop safe and secure cooperative CPS. To protect the intellectual property of all involved parties, the system must be capable of securely managing multiple clients. Protecting the entire data, however, hinders System of Systems (SoS) and CPS from operating cooperatively. Thus at least a subset of the data must be made publicly available to allow the dependable cooperation of systems. Schneider et al. claimed necessary properties of such a subset and proposed the concept of Digital Dependability Identitys (DDIs) [21]. In this work we propose a software architecture that uses the concept of DDIs to allow both the collaborative development and the cooperative operation of systems by still protecting the intellectual property of all involved parties. The Data worth being protected is split into two portions: header and payload data. The header data is publicly accessible and contains the information described by the DDI concept. The portion containing intellectual property is stored as encrypted payload and hence is inaccessible without knowing the private key. In order to guaranty privacy, the involved parties are responsible for the storage and management of the private key themselves. If the header data is made publicly available in a central repository, the proposed concept enables the evidence based analysis of dependable large scale systems during both, system development and operation. This enables companies early in the development process to check whether their systems dependably integrate into an existing system or not. Furthermore, systems operating in the field can use this information to dynamically adapt to changes and unforeseen events, and they can also distribute observed changes and events via the central repository.

Runtime Layer: All systems operating in the field are part of the runtime layer. Traditionally, the configuration of these systems did not significantly change during operation. However, it is in the nature of the upcoming CPS to be loosely connected and come together as temporary configurations of smaller systems that again dissolve and give place for new configurations, making the number of configurations over the system life time unknown and potentially infinite. State of the art approaches are currently applied at design time and require a-priori knowledge of the final system configuration. These approaches are, however, infeasible for assuring the dependability of CPS at runtime. The traditional safety life cycle of automotive vehicles, for example, usually ends with the release for production. The security of a system can, however, never be guaranteed at design time over the complete life cycle. Thus security updates after release for production are necessary. Cyber-attacks on vehicles and ongoing research [15,17–19] showed that cyber-security has a critical impact on system safety. This drives the need to design future systems that can dynamically adapt to unforeseen changes, which further requires the development of novel approaches for safety engineering. As stated before, DDIs provide a promising approach to enable collaborative and cooperative engineering and operation of dependable CPS. The Generic Execution Engine (GEE) proposed by the INSpIRA approach uses the information created during system engineering to assure the safety and security properties of the System under Development (SuD). If changes of the environment are detected or unforeseen events happen, the GEE can dynamically adapt to the new situation and provide feedback to the development engineers and publish the observed changes also in a central data base to make it available to other systems operating in the field.

5 Conclusion and Discussion

The INSpIRA approach is intended to be used as a holistic approach that supports the efficient cross-domain design, development, implementation, operation and maintenance of dependable CPS. Examples of such systems are modern road vehicles (assisted and autonomous driving), CPS road networks (car2x), power plants, smart grids or healthcare devices. These systems operate in different domains, under different environmental conditions and technical or legislative constraints. INSpIRA addresses this diversity by enabling the seamless development, integration and operation of systems in a collaborative manner across companies, industries and domains. The proposed toolchain also attempts to combine the benefits of model based design, development and testing into a single workflow, and the encapsulation of the SuD via interfaces allows the use of a SuD digital twin during the product development. This enables the simulation of dependability properties early in the development phase, which reduces the management overheads and makes the development process more efficient, less tedious and less error-prone.

To argue about the safety and security properties of a system is often a serious problem companies are faced with [6]. Companies must convince their customers or the legislative authorities that the systems developed achieve the required safety and security goals, which may also include the certification of the entire development process. The use of different environments during product development, testing and operation complicates this certification process. The envisioned INSpIRA toolchain is not only suitable for testing and implementing safety and security requirements, it also establishes traceable links between the requirements and the implementation, testing and operation of the system. This allows both tracking and evidence based argumentation about the fulfillment of the desired safety and security goals. Once the establishment of the links is certified, the INSpIRA method can be used as a holistic method for developing products, all of which will benefit from a strong safety and security argument. The toolchain uses the same information source and technology for testing, operation and self-validation. This reduces the development and integration effort, but might result in systems having the same limitations regarding error detection and controllability. This could be addressed by adding additional test cases, or by using different information sources or technologies.

The proposed INSpIRA method addresses several open research questions including: (i) a comprehensive tool support for the dependable development of

CPS, (ii) the collaborative capturing of domain expert's opinion, (iii) the automatic analysis of risk models during system development and operation, (iv) the automatic generation of test cases, (v) the automatic recommendation of potential improvements, (vi) the triggering of recovery strategies on undesired and unforeseen events, (vii) the incorporation of runtime system information to enable dynamic risk assessment, (viii) the dependable and dynamic adaption to changes at runtime. If these questions are answered in future research, INSpIRA will provide a starting point for building comprehensive and sustainable methods and tools to efficiently design, develop, implement, operate and maintain dependable systems, all of which will benefit from a strong safety and security argument.

References

1. Graph Database Use Cases and Solutions. https://neo4j.com/use-cases/
2. Cherdantseva, Y., et al.: A review of cyber security risk assessment methods for SCADA systems. Comput. Secur. **56**, 1–27 (2016)
3. Chockalingam, S., Hadžiosmanović, D., Pieters, W., Teixeira, A., van Gelder, P.: Integrated safety and security risk assessment methods: a survey of key characteristics and applications. In: Havarneanu, G., Setola, R., Nassopoulos, H., Wolthusen, S. (eds.) CRITIS 2016. LNCS, vol. 10242, pp. 50–62. Springer, Cham (2017). https://doi.org/10.1007/978-3-319-71368-7_5
4. Dobaj, J.: INSpIRA: INtegrating Security Into Risk Assessment. In: 2018 IEEE/ACM 13th International Symposium on Software Engineering for Adaptive and Self-Managing Systems (SEAMS 2018), Gothenburg, Sweden, p. 5 (2018)
5. Information Security Forum: Threat Horizon 2017: Dangers accelerate (2015)
6. Gall, H.: Functional safety IEC 61508/IEC 61511 the impact to certification and the user (2008)
7. Glaessgen, E.H., Stargel, D.S.: The digital twin paradigm for future NASA and U.S. air force vehicles (2012)
8. Iber, J., Rauter, T., Krisper, M., Kreiner, C.: The potential of self-adaptive software systems in industrial control systems. In: Stolfa, J., Stolfa, S., O'Connor, R.V., Messnarz, R. (eds.) EuroSPI 2017. CCIS, vol. 748, pp. 150–161. Springer, Cham (2017). https://doi.org/10.1007/978-3-319-64218-5_12
9. Information Security Forum: Threat Horizon 2019: Disruption, Distortion, Deterioration (2017)
10. International Organization for Standardization: ISO 26262 Road vehicles - Functional safety (2011)
11. APIS IQ-Software: Funktionale Sicherheit (2017). https://www.apis.de/
12. Kephart, J.O.J., Chess, D.D.M.: The vision of autonomic computing. Computer **1**, 41–50 (2003)
13. Kreiner, C.: Trident architectural views - a pattern for dependable systems design (2015)
14. Macher, G., Armengaud, E., Schneider, D., Brenner, E., Kreiner, C.: Towards dependability engineering of cooperative automotive cyber-physical systems. In: Stolfa, J., Stolfa, S., O'Connor, R.V., Messnarz, R. (eds.) EuroSPI 2017. CCIS, vol. 748, pp. 205–215. Springer, Cham (2017). https://doi.org/10.1007/978-3-319-64218-5_16

15. Macher, G., Much, A., Riel, A., Messnarz, R., Kreiner, C.: Automotive SPICE, safety and cybersecurity integration. In: Tonetta, S., Schoitsch, E., Bitsch, F. (eds.) SAFECOMP 2017. LNCS, vol. 10489, pp. 273–285. Springer, Cham (2017). https://doi.org/10.1007/978-3-319-66284-8_23
16. Macher, G., Höller, A., Sporer, H., Armengaud, E., Kreiner, C.: Service Deterioration Analysis (SDA): an early development phase dependability analysis method. In: Proceedings - 2015 45th Annual IEEE/IFIP International Conference on Dependable Systems and Networks Workshops, DSN-W 2015, pp. 27–32 (2015). https://doi.org/10.1109/DSN-W.2015.13. ISBN 9781467380447
17. Messnarz, R., Kreiner, C., Macher, G., Walker, A.: Extending Automotive SPICE 3.0 for the use in ADAS and future self-driving service architectures. J. Softw.: Evol. Process **30**(5), e1948 (2018). https://doi.org/10.1002/smr.1948
18. Messnarz, R., Kreiner, C.J., Riel, A.: Integrating Automotive SPICE, functional safety, and cybersecurity concepts: a cybersecurity layer model. Softw. Qual. Prof. **18**(4), 13–23 (2016)
19. Much, A.: Automotive security: challenges, standards, and solutions. Softw. Qual. Prof. **18**(4), 4–12 (2016)
20. Schmittner, C., Gruber, T., Puschner, P., Schoitsch, E.: Security application of failure mode and effect analysis (FMEA). In: Bondavalli, A., Di Giandomenico, F. (eds.) SAFECOMP 2014. LNCS, vol. 8666, pp. 310–325. Springer, Cham (2014). https://doi.org/10.1007/978-3-319-10506-2_21
21. Schneider, D., Trapp, M., Papadopoulos, Y., Armengaud, E., Zeller, M., Hofig, K.: WAP: Digital dependability identities (2015)

Approach for Enabling Security Across PLC Phases: An Industrial Use Case

Xabier Larrucea[1(✉)], Félix Nanclares[1], Izaskun Santamaria[1], and Ricardo Ruiz Nolasco[2]

[1] TECNALIA, Derio, Bizkaia, Spain
{xabier.larrucea, felix.nanclares, izaskun.santamaria}@tecnalia.com
[2] RGB Medical Devices, Madrid, Spain
rruiznolasco@rgb-medical.com

Abstract. Security and safety aspects are tightly related between them, and they are two major issues to be tackle during the development of any system, especially safety critical systems. In fact, these systems are framed in highly regulated domains and they involve a huge set of standards which have been focused on safety related issues. However, security issues have been playing a key role until now. In the context of medical devices, the U.S. Food and Drug Administration and The National Institute of Standards and Technology have published special considerations in this sense. This paper extends the assurance cases approach and integrates security aspects. A tool chain is outlined for linking assurance cases and a source code vulnerability analysis tool. This approach is illustrated with an industrial use case.

Keywords: Safety · Security · FDA · Assurance case · Life cycle

1 Introduction

A seminal paper on product life cycle (PLC) [1] discusses the main life cycle phases of a product, and it highlights the nature of the systemic approach to the PLC. A product development must include, not only product development activities, but also other relationships such as customers and providers interactions. In this sense, approaches have been applied in order to develop a wide set of products such as [2] where electronic design automation is used along a PLC. There are several PLC methods/approaches, and depending on the industry the specific terminology and activities are different. Traditionally "ISO/IEC 12207:2008, Systems and software engineering — Software life cycle processes" indicates and establishes a common framework for software life cycle processes without explicitly taking special considerations about security and safety. These two aspects are becoming critical for safety-critical domains.

Assurance cases are product-related data and they have a clear role during development of safety critical systems [3] including certification [4], and even within the flow of safety critical requirements related to PLC [5], for example. Several usages can

X. Larrucea et al. (Eds.): EuroSPI 2018, CCIS 896, pp. 354–367, 2018.
https://doi.org/10.1007/978-3-319-97925-0_29

be identified within different contexts such as product integrity [6]. Concerning PLC, it has been used in several industries such aerospace [7] and nowadays, the development of engineering products are becoming more complex and difficult due to the increase of requirements [8]. In this sense, development processes are interconnected with several aspects of a project management area such as risks management [9]. In fact, the quality management of the products during their life cycles at design stage is still a challenge [8].

A PLC phases effective management is to the reduction of requirements changes [10]. Tests are considered one of the largest costs [11]. Therefore model based techniques are suggested to manage, for example, test requirements throughout the PLC [12]. Product's data management throughout the entire life cycle [13] is also a key element in complex product developments, and they use to be widespread among different places. The information flow across the product lifecycle [14] is essential, and most of the articles in the area of PLC are related with the exchange of product-related data [15]. Assurance cases play a key role for eliciting requirements and arguments along the PLC.

From safety point of view, system engineers are widely using the IEC 61508 [16]. This standard provides guidance on safety engineering using electric and electronic process control systems. The IEC 61508-3 [17] specifies informative software security requirements. From security point of view, there are several standards which are relevant such as ISO/IEC 15408-1 [18] which provides a basis for evaluation of security properties of information technology products and systems. The ISO/IEC 7498-2 [19] provides open systems interconnection and basic reference model for security architecture. However, none of the above standards provides an integrated approach for dealing with safety and security at the same time during the whole system life cycle.

Recently, several cybersecurity efforts have been devoted to relating safety and security from different perspectives. In this sense, the National Institute of Standards and Technology (NIST) has just issued (March 2018) a special publication related to systems security engineering guidance document [20]. This document is the basis of our approach because it combines International Standards such as ISO, IEC and IEEE, and it identifies the most relevant security practices. Another relevant document is the NASA framework appeared within the NASA System Safety Handbook, Version 2.0 [21]. Here NASA describes the Risk-Informed Safety Case framework where safety cases are used for describing arguments.

This paper provides a methodology for considering (enabling) security aspects along the system life cycle, and a tool chain for supporting the approach which is illustrated with an industrial use case. This methodology includes some relevant practices of the Software Process Improvement (SPI) manifesto [22]. The industrial use case is provided by the RGB medical company. RGB aims to include within their product development life cycle safety and security considerations.

This paper is structured as follows. First section provides a background on safety life cycle and medical devices. Second, we introduce ISO/IEC/IEEE 152888, and the cybersecurity framework. Third, we provide our methodology approach with a tool support. Four, a use case scenario is described and where it has been used our approach. Finally, we provide a conclusion and we outline future works.

2 Background

2.1 System Life Cycle Processes

The ISO/IEC/IEEE 15288 "Systems and software engineering — System life cycle processes" [23] defines 4 groups of processes related to the product life cycle such as agreement processes, organisational project-enabling processes, project processes and technical processes. These kinds of standards and guides do not prescribe any approach to tackle safety and security considerations at the same time in a coherent system lifecycle approach. This is a reference framework for any system life cycle process including big data projects [24], and it has been the basis for frameworks related to safety critical software developments [25].

In the context of safety critical systems, the IEC61508 [16] (Fig. 1) which consists of seven parts, defines an overall safety lifecycle which includes safety requirements management, risk management, design, integration and so forth. This standard has been widely used by several industries including automotive and aerospace.

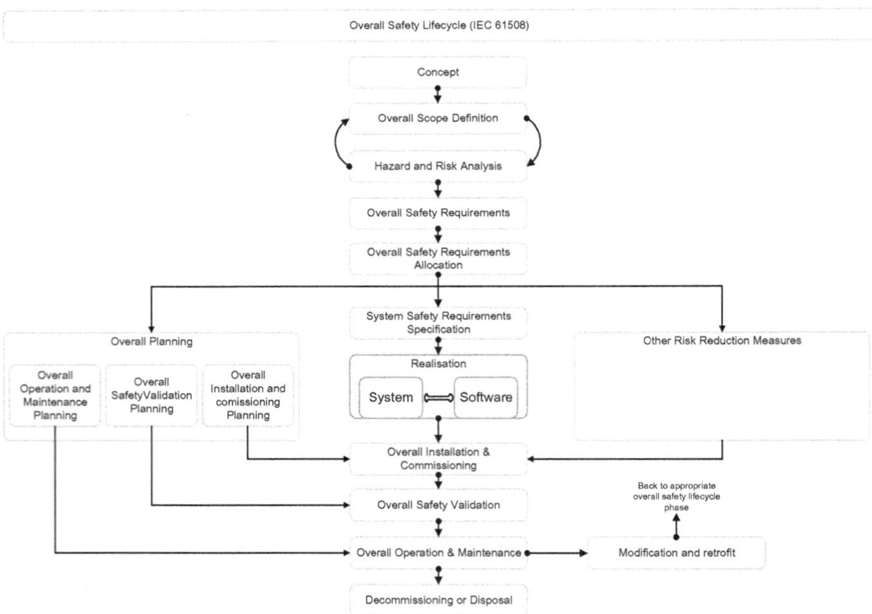

Fig. 1. Overview of the IEC61508 [16]

Recently, a NIST document (NIST SP 800-160) [26] recognizes the importance of incorporating security and safety engineering throughout a system's lifecycle, and therefore they specify additional security practices to considered during the following system life cycle processes: agreement processes, organizational project enabling processes, technical management processes and technical processes. In fact, they use as the ISO/IEC/IEEE 15288 as lifecycle reference and for aligning the concepts with the international community.

2.2 Cybersecurity Framework – Medical Devices

The National Institute of Standards and Technology (NIST) published a Framework for Improving Critical Infrastructure Cybersecurity [27] which activities are identify, protect, detect, respond and recover.

Medical devices domain is a regulatory environment with a huge set of standards and regulations. In fact, The Food and Drug Administration (FDA) published in 2016 a "Postmarket Management of Cybersecurity in Medical Devices" [28] where they state that "the manufacturer should establish, document, and maintain throughout the medical device lifecycle an ongoing process for identifying hazards associated with the cybersecurity of a medical device". In this sense, all manufacturers are required to be consistent with the NIST cybersecurity framework, and they need to identify the appropriate mechanisms for setting a cybersecurity risk management program. Medical devices are considered part of the critical infrastructure in several countries such as the United States [29] that are promoting the use of cybersecurity programs for managing threats. These Cybersecurity Frameworks include a set of standards, methodologies, procedures, and processes that align policy, business, and technological approaches to address cyber threats (risks).

2.3 Safety Cases

Safety Cases have been used in a wide set of environments and especially in safety critical domains [30]. A safety case can be defined as "A structured argument, supported by a body of evidence, that provides a compelling, comprehensible and valid case that a system is safe for a given application in a given environment" [31]. Argumentation is a key part for developing assurance case, and it has been use in critical domains [30, 32]. There are different notations such as GSN (Goal Structuring Notation) [33] or CAE (Claim Arguments and Evidence) [34]. Both graphical notations facilitate the understanding of argumentations performed by the reviewer or assessor during an assurance case assessment.

The NASA System Safety Handbook, Version 2.0, November 2014 [21] describes a framework which is based on assurance cases for arguing acceptable security. In this sense, they define The Risk-Informed Safety Case (RISC) which evolves over the course of the system life cycle, and it is based on assurance cases. This approach supports decision making at system life-cycle reviews and other major decision points. Basically, the use of assurance cases confers a trustworthy environment and they are used to demonstrate an acceptable security based on risk appetite. This handbook states "system safety activities are organized around the accomplishment of clearly stated safety objectives that collectively define adequate safety for the system, and are communicated to decision makers via a risk-informed safety case that provides a compelling, comprehensible and valid argument, supported by evidence, that the system is or will be adequately safe for a given application in a given environment." [21]

2.4 SPI Manifesto as Enabler

The SPI Manifesto identifies and highlights some values and principles applied by successful organisations adopting process improvement initiatives. In fact, these values are not just for SPI organisations, but also for organisations adopting a new way of thinking. This manifesto states that "*SPI is a tool to improve the competitiveness of organisations*", and "*active involvement of the people working in an organisation ensures the success of an SPI initiative from the business perspective*!". In fact, this manifesto has been applied in several situations such as [35] for a certification schema. In addition, this manifesto has been extended with social responsibility aspects [36], or even with people aspects in modern process improvement management approaches [37]. In general, each SPI manifesto principle supports our approach, and vice-versa. In fact, principle 3 is related to the definition of a base improvement on experience and measurements, and principle 7 is related to apply risk management. These elements are key aspects for our approach.

3 Safety and Security Life-Cycle Approach

3.1 Methodology

Our proposal is to consider assurance cases (safety cases) as enablers for gathering safety and security requirements in a common place where these aspects are discussed during PLC. We are considering assurance cases (safety cases) as a cornerstone element of the PLC phases.

Our approach (Figs. 2 and 3) is a blend approach mixing the ISO/IEC/IEEE 15288, NIST cybersecurity framework and the NIST guidance [27]. In addition, we add specific milestones to be reached during each stage of the life cycle. These milestones are essentials in order to meet and agree upon safety and security aspects. On the one hand, the ISO/IEC/IEEE15288 does not include specific practices for security aspects, but it is a framework for system life cycle. On the other hand, the IEC61508 does not prescribe any specific practice for security assurance. In addition, we have mapped each phase of the ISO/IEC/IEEE15288 with each phase of the IEC61508. Our approach wants stay domain agnostic but considering IEC61508 as a generic approach for all safety lifecycle activities [38].

When we are introducing security practices within each phase, we need to identify how security and safety practices can coexist. These interactions are between these two worlds and are represented by milestones where both types of requirements are discussed in order to identify constraints and dependencies among others.

While NASA and NIST approaches are considering milestones such as Key Decision Points (KDP) by NASA, and check points by NIST, our proposal provides a step forward considering several milestones. At the end of system life cycle stage (e.g. Concept) we need to have fulfilled 5 internal milestones. Therefore, for each stage, we need to carry out the following activities stemming from NIST cybersecurity framework:

- Identify (ID): security requirements are considered and added to the resulting assurance case. All these security requirements can be related to safety requirements. A first trade off process between them are considered. Each relationship shall be included as a risk.
- Protect (PR): specific actions are considered and argued for each requirement.
- Detect (DE): based on potential scenarios there is a detection of potential threats.
- Respond (RS): the resulting assurance case contains measures on how respond to each potential threat. This is part of the risk management process.
- Recover (RC): the assurance case should contain how to recover the system from an unforeseen event. Traditionally this aspect is not included as part of the assurance cases.

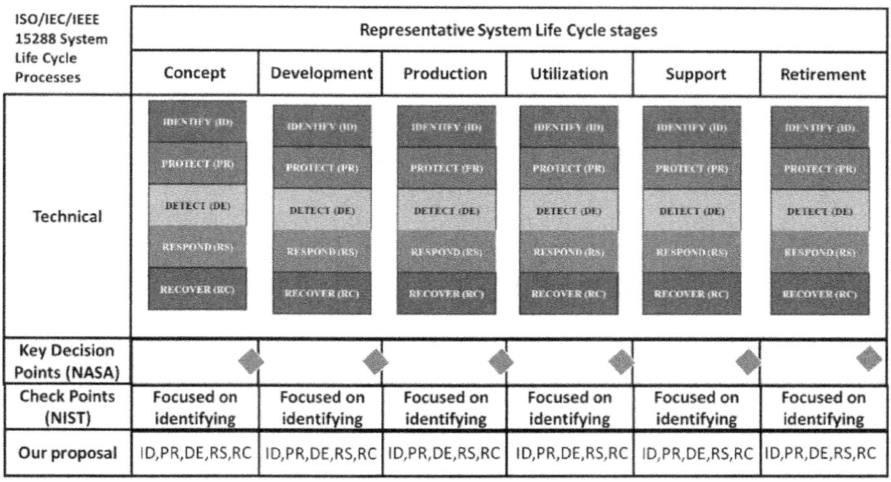

Fig. 2. Methodological approach for safety and security using assurance cases

The following table represents a chunk of cybersecurity activities to be carried out. All of them are considered as requirements in every system, so they should be considered when analyzing a system. For example, the activity described as "Identify the security aspects of the problem or question that requires system analysis" is an activity which requires as an evidence the identification of the problem. This is an integral part of the assurance cases developments. Another activity such as "Apply the selected security analysis methods to perform the security aspects of required system analysis" requires the support of a tool for analyzing security aspects such as source code vulnerabilities (Table 1).

Table 1. Extract from the cybersecurity activities to be carried out

System analysis process	Prepare for the security aspects of system analysis	Identify the security aspects of the problem or question that requires system analysis
		Identify the stakeholders of the security aspects of system analysis
		Define the objectives, scope, level of fidelity, and level of assurance of the security aspects of system analysis
		Select the methods associated with the security aspects of system analysis.
		Define the security aspects of the system analysis strategy.
		Identify, plan for, and obtain access to enabling systems or services to support the security aspects of the system analysis process.
		Collect the data and inputs needed for the security aspects of system analysis
	Perform the security aspects of system analysis	Identify and validate the assumptions associated with the security aspects of system analysis
		Apply the selected security analysis methods to perform the security aspects of required system analysis
		Review the security aspects of the system analysis results for quality and validity
		Establish conclusions, recommendations, and rationale based on the results of the security aspects of system analysis.
		Record the results of the security aspects of system analysis.
	Manage the security aspects of system analysis	Maintain traceability of the security aspects of the system analysis results
		Provide security-relevant system analysis information items that have been selected for baselines

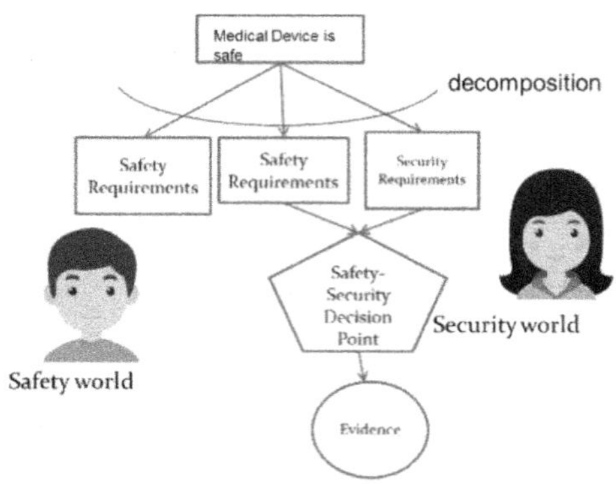

Fig. 3. Assurance cases schema and how objectives are decomposed until evidence

Figure 3 introduces a new concept in assurance cases which is "Safety Security decision point" (Table 2). This element is used during the trade-off process between safety and security aspects which are analyzed and balanced between them. A similar concept is included by NASA and NIST, but their approaches do not include an exhaustive set of cybersecurity related activities. Some cybersecurity measures are related to the analysis of source code vulnerabilities. Therefore, our approach is enhanced with a toolchain which is explained in the following section.

Table 2. Safety security decision point, key decision point and checkpoints

Concept	Source	Explanation
Key Decision Point	NASA handbook version 2	The event at which the Decision Authority determines the readiness of a program/project to progress to the next phase of the life cycle (or to the next KDP)
Checkpoints	NIST	Identify any unspecified emergent behavior that occurs, regardless if that behavior is desirable or undesirable
Safety-security decision point	Our proposal	The event at which a Decision Authority identifies, protects, detects, responds and recovers safety and security events

4 Tooling

Assurance cases are the key elements to be managed and enriched during the whole PLC. Therefore, we need a support tool for modelling all the arguments to be described during the lifecycle. In this sense, security and safety constraints stemming from ID, PR, DE, RS, RC are taken into account. Figure 4 illustrates how our assurance cases tool is linked to a source code analyzer based on Sonarqube. This tool is essential for demonstrating the evidence related to source code analysis, especially those related to security aspects.

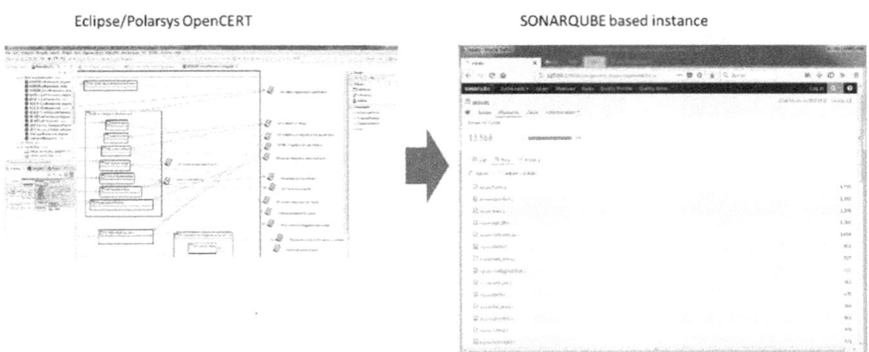

Fig. 4. Toolchain based on eclipse/polarsys opencert and sonarqube instance

5 RGB Case Study

RGB is a medical company, and it has developed a neuromuscular transmission (NMT) device for Hospital Operating Room critical care performance. This device is using a very innovative technology to support the anaesthesiologist in controlling muscle relaxation during an operating room intervention. RGB's current engineering methodology includes the following regulatory aspects related to safety:

- UNE-EN60601 (European Medical Devices Directive 93/42/EEC of 14 June 1993) safety norm as the main requirements during the development stage as part of the patient safety requirements.
- The development process shall consider requirements of applicable safety standards (IEC 61508, DIN EN 62304, DIN EN 60601-1/2)
- The ISO 11073 standard for Medical Devices interoperability.

Their PLC is based on the following generic product lifecycle phases:

- **Requirements**: at this phase a requirement engineering approach enhanced with safety/security/performance requirements should be defined and carried out
- **Modelling**: modelling is relevant for managing PLC, and several contributions are aligned with modelling data and resources [13, 39, 40]. However we need a common place where safety/security requirements are modelled.
- **Simulation**: some papers such as [41] which outlines a structure for a so-called Product Life Cycle Simulation System.
- **Implementation:** safety/security/performance requirements are implemented in the resulting product.
- **Validation:** validation is an integral part of the PLC
- **Operation:** during the operation we need to manage the value [42] generated among PLC phases. This means that reuse strategies should be set up, among others. Standards such as ISO/IEC/IEEE 26531 [43] also highlights the value of PLC, reuse strategies, and metadata and workflows concepts. Therefore PLC management is an integral part of total quality management system [8], and therefore it should take into account quality aspects such as safety, security and performance.
- **Retirement:** an impact analysis is required in order to identify which elements are affected by a specific change.

There is a matching among these RGB's product lifecycle phases, and our approach based on ISO/EC/IEEE15288. Due to space limitations we include in the following table a summary of the relationships between them (Table 3).

Table 3. Mapping between RGB method and our reference framework

RGB method \ISO/IEC/IEEE15288	Concept	Development	Production	Utilization	Support	Retirement
Requirements	X					
Modelling	X	X				
Simulation	X	X	X			
Implementation			X			
Validation				X		
Operation				X	X	
Retirement						X

RGB has identified the following security requirements which requires a specific requirement support tool to be taken into account along the whole life cycle:

- Risk Analysis tools will be applied: Risk evaluation and assessment shall be defined and used during the whole life cycle.
- Recommended use of a requirements modelling tool that enables tabular viewing and editing of safety requirements and the definition of dependencies between requirements: Different requirements tools are used such as DOORS, but in this case assurance cases can be used for gathering the safety and security related requirements.
- Security requirements should be modelled in tabular form with the possibility of defining dependencies: Assurance cases can be used in this sense.
- Security requirements shall be linkable to system design artefacts: we can easily link Opencert tool with other Eclipse based tools.
- Security requirements shall be linkable to implementation components: our current proposal links assurance cases with chunks of source code.
- It shall be feasible to perform a combined analysis of security and safety requirements: the analysis of the assurance cases containing the most parts of the system.
- Security-related requirements shall be linkable to applicable clauses from security standards.
- It shall be possible to propagate requirements co-engineering assumptions at least to the design, simulation and validation phases: As stated previously our approach assumes the use of assurance cases along the different phases of the PLC.

From a PLC generic point of view, the assurances cases include all the above requirements, and they are carried out through the different PLC phases (Fig. 5).

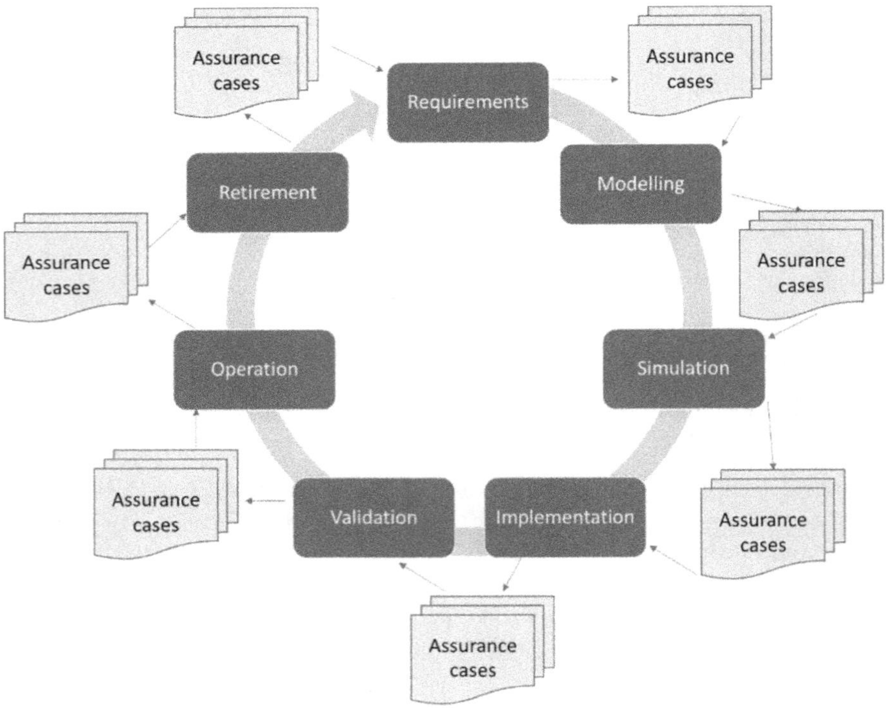

Fig. 5. Assurance cases carried through PLC phases

6 Conclusion

This paper provides a methodology for considering security aspects along the system life cycle. Our approach is based on the ISO/IEC/IEEE 152888 which is a well-known standard. However, it has been enhanced with a cybersecurity framework for considering security aspects when analysing and developing a system. The complete definition of the approach has been carried out within the AQUAS project which is a European project. This approach is just used as a framework supporting the PLC with security aspects. Real scenarios such RGB include much more requirements and standards fulfilment. This paper is not explaining how to extend or apply specific standards, nor how to describe and use assurance cases. This last aspect can be considered for future publications.

A tool chain for supporting the approach is illustrated with an industrial use case. This use case is provided by the RGB medical company. RGB aims to include within their product development life cycle safety and security considerations. Some of them are listed within this paper, but it is hard to described them completely due to their complexity. This toolchain is going to be enhanced with additional tools for simulation analysis for example.

Assurance cases can be used as a mechanism and tool for gathering safety and security aspects in the same place. This is really relevant because it helps us to balance safety and security aspects. In fact, when we are defining an argument within an assurance case, we need to consider the following activities: identify, protect, detect, respond and recover. All these activities force the identification and mitigation of safety and security risks. Therefore, we include all these activities in order to reduce or mitigate the inherent risks of every system in any conditions. Safety and security requirements are considered along the PLC, but a trade-off process must be described. This paper does not include the description of this trade-off process.

As a future work we will describe this process, and we will apply this approach to other domains different from the medical domain.

References

1. Finkelstein, L., Finkelstein, A.C.W.: The life cycle of engineering products–and analysis of concepts. Eng. Manag. J. **1**(3), 115 (1991)
2. Stallard, B., Silverman, M.: Using electronic design automation throughout the product life cycle, pp. 1–5 (2010)
3. Larrucea, X., Combelles, A., Favaro, J.: Safety-critical software [guest editors' introduction]. IEEE Softw. **30**(3), 25–27 (2013)
4. Linling, S., Wenjin, Z., Kelly, T.: Do safety cases have a role in aircraft certification? Procedia Eng. **17**, 358–368 (2011)
5. Kumari, S., Kondeti, G., Pakki, S., Chandrasekhar, T., Balu, S.: Method of safety critical requirements flow in product life cycle processes 2011, pp. N2-1-N2-4
6. Merchant, S.: Role of safety and product integrity. Procedia Comput. Sci. **8**, 443–451 (2012)
7. Rupp, T.M., Surth, W.: Product lifecycle management for collaborative engineering and manufacturing in the aerospace industry, pp. 1–8 (2006)
8. Nguyen, D.S.: Total quality management in product life cycle. In: 2014 IEEE International Conference on Industrial Engineering and Engineering Management (IEEM), pp. 754–758 (2014)
9. Larrucea, X., Gonzalez-Perez, C., McBride, T., Henderson-Sellers, B.: Standards-based metamodel for the management of goals, risks and evidences in critical systems development. Comput. Stand. Interfaces **48**, 71–79 (2016)
10. Ebert, C.: Understanding the product life cycle: four key requirements engineering techniques. IEEE Softw. **23**(3), 19–25 (2006)
11. Sutton, B.: Board test and the product life cycle. Get wise to board test strategies. IEEE Des. Test Comput. **16**(3), 28–33 (1999)
12. Bukata, E., Davis, D.C., Shombert, L.: The use of model-based test requirements throughout the product life cycle. IEEE Aerosp. Electron. Syst. Mag. **15**(2), 39–44 (2000)
13. Chen, G., Su, S., Gong, Y., Zhu, M.: The product life cycle-oriented modeling method, pp. 373–378 (2010)
14. Clermont, P., Kamsu-Foguem, B.: Experience feedback in product lifecycle management. Comput. Ind. **95**, 1–14 (2018)
15. Madenas, N., Tiwari, A., Turner, C.J., Woodward, J.: Information flow in supply chain management: a review across the product lifecycle. CIRP J. Manuf. Sci. Technol. **7**(4), 335–346 (2014)
16. IEC 61508 - Functional safety of electrical/electronic/programmable electronic safety-related systems (2010)

17. IEC: IEC 61508 - 3 - Functional safety of electrical/electronic/programmable electronic safety-related systems – Part 3: Software requirements, 06 April 2011
18. ISO/IEC 15408-1:2009 Information technology – Security techniques – Evaluation criteria for IT security – Part 1: Introduction and general model (2009)
19. ISO 7498-2:1989 Information processing systems – Open Systems Interconnection – Basic Reference Model – Part 2: Security Architecture (1989)
20. Ross, R., McEvilley, M., Oren, J.C.: Systems security engineering: considerations for a multidisciplinary approach in the engineering of trustworthy secure systems, vol. 1. National Institute of Standards and Technology, Gaithersburg, MD, NIST SP 800-160v1, March 2018
21. NASA System Safety Handbook, Volume 2: System Safety Concepts, Guidelines, and Implementation Examples, November 2014
22. Pries-Heje, J., Johansen, J.: SPI Manifesto (2010)
23. International Standard Organisation: ISO/IEC/IEEE 15288:2015 Systems and software engineering – System life cycle processes (2015)
24. Lin, Y.-T., Huang, S.-J.: The design of a software engineering lifecycle process for big data projects. IT Prof. **20**(1), 45–52 (2018)
25. Bujok, A.B., MacMahon, S.T., Grant, P., Whelan, D., Rickard, W.J., McCaffery, F.: Approach to the development of a unified framework for safety critical software development. Comput. Stand. Interfaces **54**, 152–161 (2017)
26. Zemrowski, K.M.: NIST bases flagship security engineering publication on ISO/IEC/IEEE 15288:2015. Computer **49**(12), 86–88 (2016)
27. National Institute of Standards and Technology: Framework for improving critical infrastructure cybersecurity, Version 1.1, 05 December 2017
28. Postmarket Management of Cybersecurity in Medical Devices - Guidance for Industry and Food and Drug Administration Staff, 22 January 2016
29. The White House and Office of the Press Secretary: Presidential Policy Directive – Critical Infrastructure Security and Resilience (2013)
30. Larrucea, X., Walker, A., Colomo-Palacios, R.: Supporting the management of reusable automotive software. IEEE Softw. **34**(3), 40–47 (2017)
31. Defence Standard 00-56 and Ministry of Defence: Safety Management Requirements for Defence Systems, Issue 4, Part 1: Requirements. Ministry of Defence, Glasgow, UK (2007)
32. Larrucea, X., Mergen, S., Walker, A.: A GSN approach to SEooC for an automotive hall sensor. In: Kreiner, C., O'Connor, R.V., Poth, A., Messnarz, R. (eds.) EuroSPI 2016. CCIS, vol. 633, pp. 269–280. Springer, Cham (2016). https://doi.org/10.1007/978-3-319-44817-6_23
33. Spriggs, J.: GSN—The Goal Structuring Notation. Springer, London (2012). https://doi.org/10.1007/978-1-4471-2312-5
34. Adelard: Claims, Arguments and Evidence (CAE) (2013). http://www.adelard.com/asce/choosingasce/cae.html
35. Korsaa, M., et al.: The SPI manifesto and the ECQA SPI manager certification scheme. J. Softw.: Evol. Process **24**(5), 525–540 (2012)
36. Messnarz, R., et al.: Social responsibility aspects supporting the success of SPI. J. Softw.: Evol. Process **26**(3), 284–294 (2014)
37. Korsaa, M., et al.: The people aspects in modern process improvement management approaches. J. Softw.: Evol. Process **25**(4), 381–391 (2013)
38. Münch, J., Armbrust, O., Kowalczyk, M., Soto, M.: Software Process Definition and Management. Springer, Heidelberg (2012). https://doi.org/10.1007/978-3-642-24291-5
39. Hong-Bae, J., Kiritsis, D., Xirouchakis, P.: Product life-cycle metadata modeling and its application with RDF. IEEE Trans. Knowl. Data Eng. **19**(12), 1680–1693 (2007)

40. Nagorny, K., Colombo, A.W., Barata, J.: A survey of service-based systems-of-systems manufacturing systems related to product life-cycle support and energy efficiency, pp. 582–587 (2014)
41. Sakita, K., Mori, T.: Product life cycle simulation system for ecodesigners, pp. 527–528 (2005)
42. Kovacs, G.L.: Evaluation of value changes between different phases of the product life-cycle, pp. 101–106 (2013)
43. ISO/IEC/IEEE 26531:2015 (E): ISO/IEC/IEEE International Standard for Systems and software engineering – Content management for product life-cycle, user, and service management documentation (2015)

Use-Cases for Uncertainty Propagation in Distributed Control Systems

Michael Krisper[(✉)], Johannes Iber, and Jürgen Dobaj

Institute for Technical Informatics, Graz University of Technology,
Inffeldgasse 16/I, 8010 Graz, Austria
office@iti.tugraz.at
http://www.iti.tugraz.at

Abstract. This paper describes how data quality can be used to gain trust between components in distributed control systems by adding information about quality to data values. Especially numeric uncertainty is a helpful tool for making highly informed decisions. To illustrate the benefits and challenges, several use-cases are discussed in the context of industrial and automotive settings. The target audience are architects and developers of cyber-physical systems in industrial and automotive domains, researchers in such domains and software developers who are writing software for embedded or distributed control systems which also use uncertain sensor measurements.

Keywords: Quality · Uncertainty · Measurement
Error propagation · Tolerance · Predictive maintenance
Sensor-fusion · Approximate computing

1 Introduction

In the past, control systems were isolated and closed systems which have been under control of one manufacturer or closed and protected environments. This paradigm changed with the recent upcoming of ubiquitous and distributed devices, the Internet of Things (IoT), and Cyber-Physical Systems (CPS). Control systems now are often distributed and may be highly dependent on other systems which are developed by other companies. This leads to many exciting kinds of problems. In order to cope with many of those problem fields, standards were established to harmonize technical compatibility (e.g. communication, data formats, and protocols) as well as warranty, safety and contracting issues (safety and quality standards like ISO61508, ISO26262, ISO25012, AUTOSAR, ASPICE, Functional Safety, 6σ). While safety and quality standards cover the whole development and production process until delivery, the newest trend shifts the actual binding time of decisions far beyond delivery to the actual usage and runtime of a product [24,26]. Amorim et al. describe in their papers [1,2] how to do this by using contracts consisting of demands and

X. Larrucea et al. (Eds.): EuroSPI 2018, CCIS 896, pp. 368–379, 2018.
https://doi.org/10.1007/978-3-319-97925-0_30

guarantees between components and evaluating them at runtime. In their contracts they depend on using attributes which can be evaluated during runtime. The challenge is now to evaluate information about the environment during runtime. In order to do this, the notion of data quality comes into play. The ISO 25012 [15] defines characteristics of data quality and in this paper, we especially look at accuracy, precision, consistency and credibility. We illustrate this in use-cases which use the measurement uncertainty of sensors as an attribute for data quality. These use-cases concern not only safety but also other dependability attributes like availability and reliability. The main idea is to evaluate the quality of a sensor via its uncertainties of measured values. This data quality attribute should be used and propagated over the whole signal path of a system in order to make informed decisions and to have more information about a systems' state available at runtime. If the sensor has small measurement errors and is not biased, the measured data has high quality and can be trusted. In such a way a consumer of a value can decide dynamically at runtime if the values are trustworthy and react based on changes of data quality e.g. when a sensor gets dirty or faulty.

We want to encourage and motivate developers and architects to be involved in this culture of quality based thinking in order to increase business value in changing environments and contexts. This corresponds to the main values and principles of the Software Process Improvement Manifesto (SPI Manifesto) [23], which is a guide for exchanging wisdom and experiences in all areas of software process improvement.

The remaining paper is structured as follows: Sect. 2 gives an overview over the related work and background. The main part of the paper focuses on the use-cases for uncertainties beginning from Sect. 3 to Sect. 9. The paper closes with a conclusion in Sect. 10.

2 Background and Related Work

Uncertainty in Measurements. According to the ISO GUM Standard *"Error is an idealized concept and errors cannot be known exactly."* [17]. Measuring the reality is a task which always involves some kind of uncertainty. Measurement devices cannot be infinitely precise or measured objects may change, and it may even be impossible to measure everything exactly. In lack of infinitely precise measurements, we try to tackle uncertainty by equipping our sensors and values with tolerance ranges or limits. Such tolerances tell us how precise our values can be. The ISO GUM (JCGM 100:2008) standard and all additions define how to express uncertainty in measurements [17–21].

Uncertainty in Distributed Control Systems. Distributed control systems cover many areas like control systems, embedded systems, or cyber-physical systems (CPS) as they are called nowadays. They all involve some kind of uncertainty. Classic literature about this topic is e.g. "Distributed Systems" by Tannenbaum et al. [29], or "Distributed Systems Architecture" by Puder et al. [28]. According to Amorim et al. "CPS usually operate in uncertain environments and are often safety-critical" [1]. This dangerous combination of uncertainty and safety-critical devices could lead to threatening situations causing harm, injuries and the death of humans as well as substantial damage of properties and financial losses. According to the HAZOP model, data errors in control systems are categorized as *Provision Errors*, *Timing Errors*, and *Value Errors* [4,11,12]. To handle these kinds of errors, contracts with requirement definitions can be used [3]. For example, in the ConSerts M model [1,2], every component provides guarantees to the consuming component, while requesting demands to the serving components. In such a way it is possible to define safety contacts at design time which are evaluated at runtime and acted upon via safety mechanism through self-adaptive systems [14].

Uncertainty in Probabilistic Programming. Basically every measured value can be represented as random variable, which is done in probabilistic programming. Such random variables have continuous or discrete probability distributions which are used for inference, arithmetic and conditionals in a program. They have some generic mechanisms in common [25]: (i) *a probabilistic model*, (ii) *propagation rules*, and (iii) *inference techniques*. Andy Gordon wrote a survey about the current state of probabilistic programming [13]. Bornholt et al. published several papers about their implementation approach of such mechanisms [5–7]. Another aspect of this is approximate computing, which creates software with just enough precision as needed. Darulova et al. investigated many aspects of approximate computing and created a framework for compiling programs with uncertainties, to be faster and use less memory [8–10,16].

3 Use-Case 1: Quality Evaluation Based on Uncertainty

"*Researchers in computer systems either do not know about measurement bias or do not realize how severe it can be.*" [27].

Using uncertainty for measured values allows for informed decisions, better evaluation of the environment and sophisticated safety arguments, which can contain lower and upper bounds for safety margins (Fig. 1).

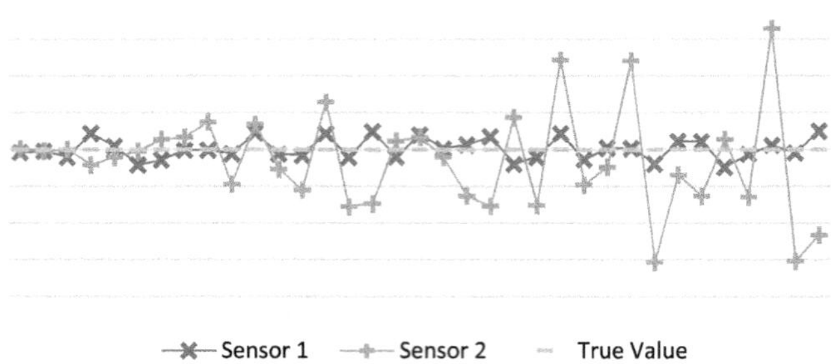

Fig. 1. Quality evaluation based on uncertainty in Sensor Data: which of the two sensors is more trustworthy?

Very often decisions and calculations are done with data directly coming from a sensor or other systems, and are trusted to be 100% correct. Contracts and design arguments protect us from getting biased or uncertain data, but do we really know for sure even during runtime? Mytkowicz et al. [27] showed that experimental measurements of computer systems regarding performance are always flawed by not using diverse environments and could potentially lead to wrong claims by not considering measurement bias. That is why they proclaim a call to action to consider measurement bias in computer systems. While this mainly applies to experimental measurements, it is also important for sensors, which exhibit even more uncertainty, which can't be reproduced as easily as in experimental environments. In safety, redundancy and diversification are key concepts for reducing failure rates and common cause failures. We propose to expand these concepts to allow better informed decisions about systems.

Wrong decisions potentially could lead to endangering human life, harm and injuries, but also enormous financial damage. For example, autonomous self-driving cars constantly monitor the environment and decide in adaptive control-loops which action is the most appropriate. Such decisions are guided by data from multiple sensors in order to drive safely and avoid accidents.

This use-case exhibits following forces or challenges:

- Sensor Data is always uncertain (as is every measurement). Therefore, it could be inaccurate, and without modeling these uncertainties this could lead to wrong assumptions and decisions.
- Exact tolerances are often unknown. Of course, you could assume the worst-case tolerances from the data sheet of a sensor, but oftentimes they are way overrated, and still one cannot guarantee during runtime that they are still satisfied.
- Decisions based on inaccurate or oversimplified data could lead to wrong results (injuries, fatalities, ...). Assuming a measured value is infinite precise is very dangerous and careless.

The goal in the context of this use-case is to make safe and informed decisions with the help of error-margins and safety assumptions to avoid and mitigate injuries and erroneous behavior. For this, we need systems which have mechanisms for defining uncertainties, for propagating them, and finally for decision-making with known guarantees and confidence.

4 Use-Case 2: Predictive Maintenance

The evaluation of uncertainty and measurement tolerances could potentially increase the prediction accuracy for predictive maintenance. By establishing degradation models which reason about how failure and quality of a component are related, a manufacturer can predict how long the product lifetime will be based on the current state of quality in the product evaluated during runtime. In such a way it would be possible to avoid unnecessary maintenance efforts, but

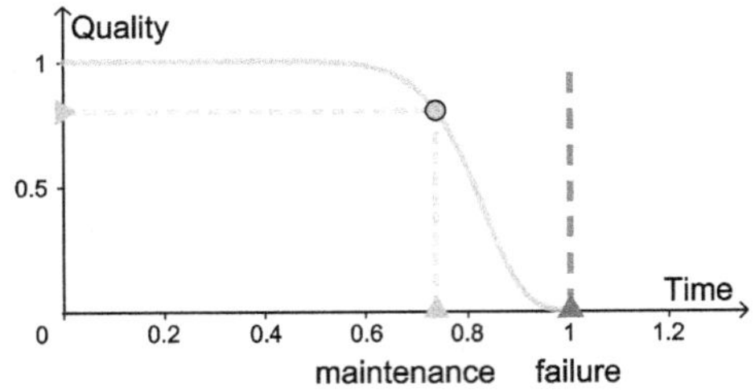

Fig. 2. Usage of quality information for predictive maintenance: as soon as the quality of the sensor is under a predefined limit, maintenance actions should be done before the component fails.

just replacing or reconditioning those parts where and when the attention really is needed (Fig. 2).

Think of the trivial example of motor oil. We have long periodic maintenance intervals because modern engines are working much cleaner as ever before. Nevertheless, motor oil is still replaced in regular intervals (either time span or driven distance) although it may not be necessary in many cases. A sensor which measures the viscosity or contamination of the oil could give feedback about its state and inform the driver when it is time to be changed.

The challenges in this context are:

- Sensors may get damaged, polluted and fail over time. The precision and quality of the produced data also decreases with such decay processes.
- Periodically scheduled maintenance may be inefficient, because parts could still be fully functional even after some time and would be replaced prematurely.
- The other side of periodic maintenance is when parts fail or decay earlier than the cycle has foreseen this may go unnoticed until the maintenance time. In such cases maintenance should have been earlier to ensure correct functionality of the components.

The goal in this use-case is to safe costs for unnecessary maintenance while ensuring that all safety goals are met and the functionality of all components is ensured. Just doing maintenance when it is really needed has many advantages to the whole ecosystem of products. The predictive maintenance model and its evaluation during runtime also has another very beneficial side effect: By continuously monitoring the health state of the components we can detect early or unexpected failures during runtime. By knowing and monitoring the quality level (especially the sensor tolerances) one can predict the failure rate more accurately during runtime. By using a model for failure-rates based on the runtime tolerances we can predict the point in time when the sensor will fail. Based on that, maintenance should be planned.

5 Use-Case 3: Sensor Fusion

Use data quality, e.g. uncertainty, to combine several input values in order to get results with even higher quality, accuracy and less uncertainty. Also, use it to give the most accurate data more weight than the inaccurate (Fig. 3).

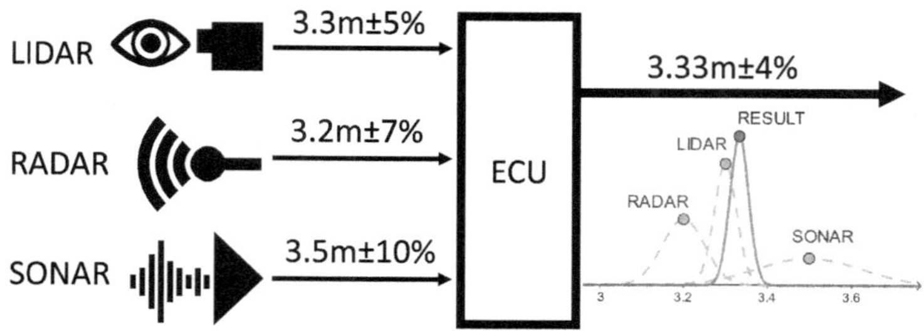

Fig. 3. Sensor fusion by combining the individual sensor value and their according probability distributions. The result has higher quality and lower uncertainty than every single sensor.

Sensor fusion is a huge area in control systems which is researched for many decades now but still makes huge advancements when it comes to new technologies and how to combine them. For more information about Sensor Fusion we propose the book by Klein: "Sensor and data fusion: a tool for information assessment and decision-making" [22]. In this use-case we concentrate on the fusion of data signals which are semantically similar (measuring the same information), e.g. distance, energy consumption, or signal strength. The only things which differ for similar measurements are the actual measured value, and the uncertainties exhibited by the sensor and the measurement. This makes it easier to combine the values by just combining their respective measurements seen as random variables with uncertainties. Equations for combining multiple independent input values with normal distributions (μ is the expected value or mean, σ is the standard deviation):

$$X_0, \ldots, X_n \sim \mathcal{N}(\mu_i, \sigma_i^2) : \hat{X} = \frac{1}{n} \sum X_i \sim \mathcal{N}\left(\frac{1}{n} \sum \mu_i, \frac{1}{n^2} \sum \sigma_i^2\right)$$

It is noteworthy, that for the above equations we assumed independent random variables. This is not the case all the time, because the sensors try to measure the same "true" value, and are therefore correlated to each other. If the "true" value changed, all sensor values are expected to change accordingly – therefore, they are dependent and for sensor fusion also the covariances of the sensors should be considered. Another assumption here is that all sensor uncertainty is described using normal distributions for their measurements. When they have different distributions, this should be considered accordingly in order to maintain their probability properties.

The challenges in this context are:

- A single sensor may be inaccurate and its quality may change during usage over time.
- Computing simple averages amongst multiple sensor hides the uncertainty coming from the sensors and therefore gives a wrong image of certainty.
- Better and worse data are mixed together, which should be accounted accordingly.

The goal is to use data from multiple sensors to get more accurate information about the environment. The combined value should exhibit lower uncertainty than any single sensor value. Therefore, it is needed to evaluate the quality of the sensors during runtime and use this quality information for the sensor-fusion.

We propose to weight the sensors according to their uncertainty, in order to prefer more accurate sensors over the ones which are imprecise. This has two highly beneficial consequences:

1. **Environmental Adaption:** When one sensor is better for near distance measurements (e.g. in low-speed situations) and another is better at far distance measurements (e.g. high-speed situations), weighting them according to their precision would result in an automatic adaption to the current environment and always using the best source of data for a given situation.
2. **Failover:** In cases where a sensor fails completely, it can be completely overruled by the still functional working sensors, because its uncertainties would get very high and therefore its value would be weighted very low. This would result in failover situation where the system still continues to function, despite a sensor failing. Of course, this only is possible for systems which are designed to have redundant signal paths or even diverse sensors, in order to avoid common cause errors. Amorim et al. described an architecture which makes use of alternative data sources in case of failures [2].

6 Use-Case 4: Approximate Computing

Perform calculations only with the needed precision to increase performance and save memory.

Figure 4 shows the time needed for calculating pi with a variant of the Gregory-Leibniz Series ($\pi = 4\sum_{k=0}^{\infty} \frac{(-1)^k}{2k+1}$). The figure shows that for increasing the accuracy (decreasing the error) much more time is needed. For example, if we need the value to have a precision of 10^{-3}, the algorithm only needs about 0.5 ms, but if we need a precision of 10^{-4}, we would have to let it run for 5 ms (10 times longer). Of course, in this case, there are much faster methods available, but it shows how beneficial approximate computing could be for algorithms which do not have a fast alternative. By aborting the calculation as soon as the needed precision is reached one can save much computing time [8].

In addition to performance also memory could be saved by using approximations. Many applications use double or float as data types for their floating-point variables, but only need precision of a few decimal places. These could be replaced by fixed point arithmetic which perform much faster while still supplying the needed precision [8–10, 16]. The challenges in this context are:

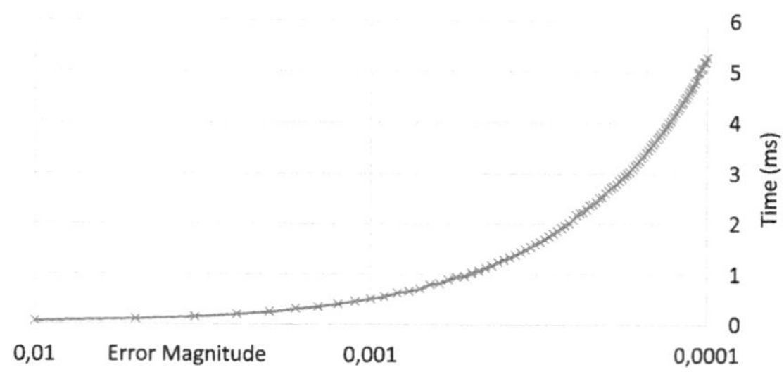

Fig. 4. Performance benchmarks for calculating π with the Gregory-Leibniz Series. To increase the accuracy of the solution, much more computing time is needed.

- Exact calculations often take unnecessary long time.
- Approximate calculations may be faster, but you need to balance the precision to your needs.

For this use-case the goal is to speed up calculations and save memory by using approximations which only use as much preciseness as is needed. In order to do that, uncertainty information comes in handy because it could be applied in two ways: Firstly, the maximum precision depends upon the precision of the input values, respectively the input sensors. It does not make sense to apply more exact algorithms when the uncertainty of the input data is already very high. Secondly, the needed precision in calculations depends upon the ultimately required precision of the output value. For example, it would be futile to numerically optimize some algorithms to the 10^{-6} decimal place, while the calculated output value is then rounded to whole integer numbers.

7 Use-Case 5: Fault Detection

Use quality information (e.g. uncertainty or standard deviation), to detect additional faults in components which would go unnoticed otherwise.

Using quality information like accuracy or uncertainty gives the possibility to define additional checks for fault detection. Thresholds on the *quality* of a signal can be defined in addition to the range-checks which are defined at design time according to the data-sheet or interface description of a component (e.g. the HSI: Hardware-Software-Interface-Specification) (Fig. 5).

The challenges are:

- Sensor Quality (e.g. tolerances) may change over time.
- Safety functions rely on good quality information to e.g. apply boundary or threshold checking.
- Tolerances coming from data sheets may be exaggerated and represent maximum values, which leads to very conservative assumptions.

The goal of this use-case is to have tolerance information available during runtime in order to be used for safety functionality and to detect faulty and

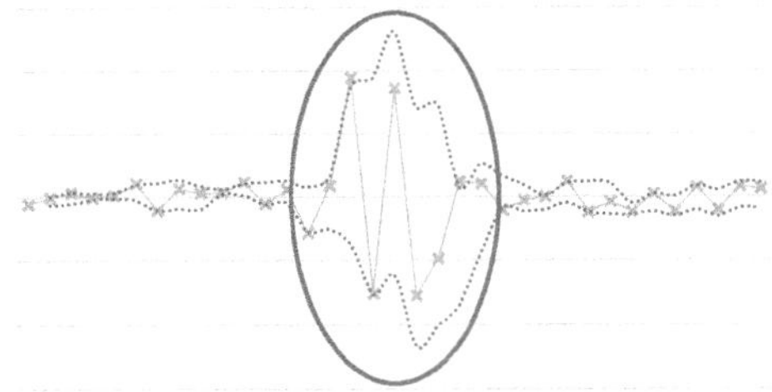

Fig. 5. Detect faults by evaluating the uncertainty of a value series.

maybe even harmful situations. When a system would know the tolerances and uncertainties of the used signals and sensors at runtime, it could easily detect when something goes out of bounds, or when tolerances of a value suddenly increase without any reason. This demands that the sensor quality is measured periodically in order to have recent information available to guarantee the liveness and correctness of the error margins.

8 Use-Case 6: Fingerprinting

Use quality information as fingerprints to identify individual components (Fig. 6).

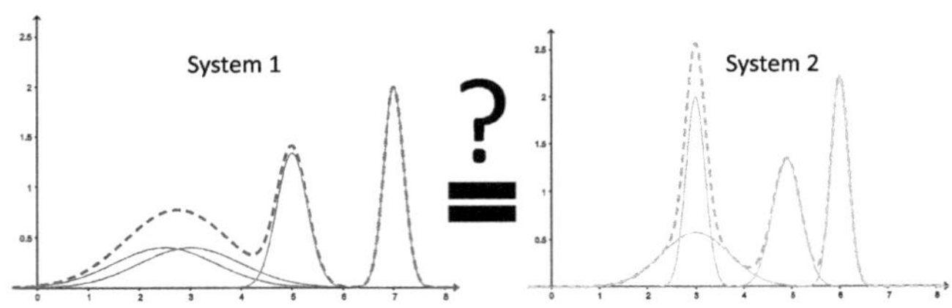

Fig. 6. Identify systems based on their individual calibration or uncertainty profile.

During production the uncertainties of sensors are measured and their calibration is set. This configuration of calibration data is a set unique to each system. By utilizing the initial calibration and uncertainty information one can calculate a unique fingerprint for the identification of a system and use this as an identification later on. The challenges of such a use case are:

- Devices and Sensors cannot be trusted a priori.
- Devices and Sensors in combination have a pretty unique configuration of calibration data, uncertainties and tolerances.
- Authentication mechanism need additional functionality (TPM, certificates, identities, key-exchange) which may be too expensive.

The goal is to identify sensors and devices according to their fingerprints without having to implement additional security features or hardware. This can be done by utilizing the uncertainty and calibration data of the systems' sensors during production and storing this profile information as fingerprint. During runtime measure the system again and compare to the stored fingerprint. If the profile is mostly the same, this is a strong indicator that the measured system actually is the same.

9 Use-Case 7: Graceful Degradation

Degrade functionality of a system based on the quality of the sensors and sophisticated safety assumptions (Fig. 7).

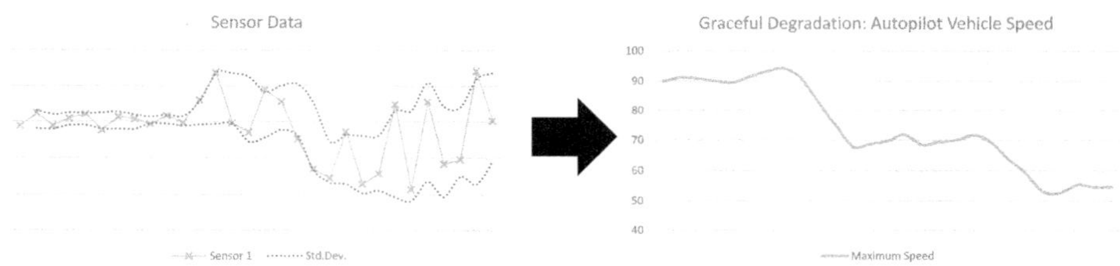

Fig. 7. Depending on the quality of the sensor input data, an autopilot can regulate the maximum speed for a degraded state.

Graceful degradation is a technique which is applied as safety measure if a system's functionality must be ensured but cannot be fully supplied. There can be two reasons why a degraded system is valuable: Firstly, when the system has to go into a safe-state, this oftentimes cannot be done immediately, but has to degrade gracefully over time, so that the driver or user can accustom to the new situation. Secondly, it is often preferred to have at least a degraded functionality than no functionality at all. Amorim et al. wrote about graceful degradation and how it can be applied to situations when the contracts are not fulfilled at runtime [2]. They depicted the situation where a sensor fails to operate and their solution was to search for other data sources which can be used despite the possibility that they may be more inaccurate. If the other inputs can't provide the needed ASIL level, the car should still be controllable, but in degraded mode in order to minimize possible hazards (the maximum speed is reduced).

Despite graceful degradation, also graceful improvement would be possible: if the uncertainty and data quality gets better, a system could adaptively increase the functionality. If the constraints are still met due to better sensors with smaller measurement tolerances, the maximum speed could even be increased while maintaining the same safety level.

10 Conclusion

In this paper we showed seven use-cases where the use of uncertainty as indicator for data quality is very beneficial for the dependability of a system. Trust in the sensors, the data, and the whole signal path can be increased by evaluating data quality of the numerical values. Especially using numerical uncertainty is helpful in making highly informed decisions which could potentially safe lives. In the future, we plan to investigate each use-case in detail and find appropriate techniques and integration possibilities for existing systems in real life projects and scenarios. In the spirit of the SPI manifesto [23] we want to motivate and encourage manufacturers, developers and software as well as system architects to apply uncertainty and quality considerations in their systems to change their daily business for the better.

References

1. Amorim, T., et al.: Runtime safety assurance for adaptive cyber- physical systems: ConSerts M and ontology-based runtime reconfiguration applied to an automotive case study. In: Solutions for Cyber-Physical Systems Ubiquity, pp. 137–168. IGI Global (2018). https://doi.org/10.4018/978-1-5225-2845-6
2. Amorim, T., Ruiz, A., Dropmann, C., Schneider, D.: Multidirectional modular conditional safety certificates. In: Koornneef, F., van Gulijk, C. (eds.) SAFECOMP 2015. LNCS, vol. 9338, pp. 357–368. Springer, Cham (2015). https://doi.org/10.1007/978-3-319-24249-1_31
3. Beugnard, A., Jézéquel, J.M., Plouzeau, N.: Contract aware components, 10 years after. Electron. Proc. Theor. Comput. Sci. **37**, 1–11 (2010). https://doi.org/10.4204/EPTCS.37.1
4. Bondavalli, A., Simoncini, L.: Failure classification with respect to detection. In: Proceedings of the Second IEEE Workshop on Future Trends of Distributed Computing Systems, pp. 47–53, September 1990. https://doi.org/10.1109/FTDCS.1990.138293
5. Bornholt, J., Meng, N., Mytkowicz, T., McKinley, K.S.: Programming the internet of uncertain <T>hings, pp. 1–7 (2015)
6. Bornholt, J., Mytkowicz, T., McKinley, K.S.: Uncertain<T>: a first-order type for uncertain data, p. 21 (2013)
7. Bornholt, J., Mytkowicz, T., McKinley, K.S.: Uncertain<T>: a first-order type for uncertain data, pp. 51–66. ACM Press (2014). https://doi.org/10.1145/2541940.2541958
8. Darulova, E.: Programming with numerical uncertainties, p. 172 (2014)
9. Darulova, E., Kuncak, V.: Sound compilation of reals, pp. 235–248. ACM Press (2014). https://doi.org/10.1145/2535838.2535874
10. Darulova, E., Kuncak, V., Majumdar, R., Saha, I.: Synthesis of fixed-point programs, pp. 1–10. IEEE, September 2013. https://doi.org/10.1109/EMSOFT.2013.6658600
11. Ezhilchelvan, P.D., Shrivastava, S.K., Elphick, M.J.: A characterisation of faults in systems. University of Newcastle upon Tyne, Computing Laboratory (1985)
12. Fenelon, P., Hebbron, B.: Applying HAZOP to software engineering models. In: Risk Management and Critical Protective Systems: Proceedings of SARSS 1994 (1994)

13. Gordon, A.D., Henzinger, T.A., Nori, A.V., Rajamani, S.K.: Probabilistic programming. In: Proceedings of the on Future of Software Engineering, FOSE 2014, pp. 167–181. ACM, New York (2014). https://doi.org/10.1145/2593882.2593900
14. Iber, J., Rauter, T., Kreiner, C.: A self-adaptive software system for increasing the reliability and security of cyber-physical systems. In: Solutions for Cyber-Physical Systems Ubiquity, pp. 223–246 (2018). https://doi.org/10.4018/978-1-5225-2845-6.ch009
15. ISO, IEC: ISO/IEC 25012:2008 data quality model (2008)
16. Izycheva, A., Darulova, E.: On sound relative error bounds for floating-point arithmetic, pp. 15–22. IEEE, October 2017. https://doi.org/10.23919/FMCAD.2017.8102236
17. JCGM: JCGM 100:2008 evaluation of measurement data Guide to the expression of uncertainty in measurement, September 2008
18. JGCM: JCGM-WG1-SC1-N10 guide to the expression of uncertainty in measurement (GUM) - supplement 1: numerical methods for the propagation of distributions (2004)
19. JGCM: JCGM 104:2009 evaluation of measurement data - an introduction to the "guide to the expression of uncertainty in measurement" (2009)
20. JGCM: JCGM 102:2011 evaluation of measurement data - supplement 2 to the "guide to the expression of the uncertainty in measurement" - extension to any number of output quantities (2011)
21. JGCM: JCGM 106:2012 evaluation of measurement data - the role of measurement uncertainty in conformity assessment. Chem. Int. - Newsmagazine IUPAC **35**(2) (2013). https://doi.org/10.1515/ci.2013.35.2.22
22. Klein, L.A.: Sensor and data fusion: a tool for information assessment and decision making. SPIE Press, Bellingham (2004)
23. Korsaa, M., et al.: The SPI manifesto and the ECQA SPI manager certification scheme. J. Softw.: Evol. Process **24**(5), 525–540 (2012). https://doi.org/10.1002/smr.502
24. Kreiner, C.: A binding time guide to creational patterns, pp. 1–10. ACM Press (2015). https://doi.org/10.1145/2739011.2739025
25. Krisper, M., Iber, J., Dobaj, J., Kreiner, C.: Uncertain values, error-propagation, and decision confidence, p. 5. ACM, Irsee (2018, unpublished)
26. Krisper, M., Kreiner, C.: Describing binding time in software design patterns, pp. 1–15. ACM Press (2016). https://doi.org/10.1145/3011784.3011811
27. Mytkowicz, T., Diwan, A., Hauswirth, M., Sweeney, P.F.: Producing wrong data without doing anything obviously wrong! p. 12 (2009)
28. Puder, A., Römer, K., Pilhofer, F.: Distributed Systems Architecture: A Middleware Approach. Elsevier, Amsterdam/Boston (2006)
29. Tanenbaum, A.S., van Steen, M.: Distributed Systems: Principles and Paradigms, 2nd edn. Pearson Education, Harlow/Essex (2014)

Verification of the Effectiveness of Risk Management in the Medical Device Industry

Armin Riess[1], Marion Lepmets[2], Sharon McKechnie[3], and Alastair Walker[3(✉)]

[1] B. Braun, Melsungen, Germany
armin.riess@bbraun.com
[2] SoftComply, Dublin, Ireland
marion@softcomply.com
[3] Lorit Consultancy, Edinburgh, Scotland
alastair.walker@lorit-consultancy.com

Abstract. The Risk Management standard ISO 14971 has been used in the medical device sector for many years, and offers or suggests many techniques, for evaluating, analysing and reducing risks, but how effective is each of these techniques and at which stage of the life cycle should one choose a given technique. There is now in the medical device sector a much greater emphasis on risk management driven by recent standards updates and the appearance on the EU Medical Device Regulation [1]. The MDR has placed a much greater emphasis on post market surveillance, however post-market surveillance in itself is often a rather long-term activity and many problems may arise long before sufficient metrics can be gathered to identify the issues through a post market approach. ISO 14971:2007 [2] does advocate eight sources of assessing risks and by using a wider set of techniques organisations can gain a better estimate of risk and additionally a more accurate output from the risk management process.

In this paper, we discuss the aspects in which the risk management techniques used in medical device industry could be improved based on what are industries are doing to manage risks and decrease possible failures.

Keywords: Functional safety · Risk management · Post-market surveillance Medical Device Regulation

1 Introduction

ISO 14971 is at the core of medical device development as it drives most of the risk-based decisions in the industry and is used to assess a very varied set of different requirements in medical device development e.g. hardware design, software design, electromagnetic compatibility and biocompatibility. Being able to take all the different medical device development aspects and technology areas into account when assessing risks, shown on Fig. 1, is no easy task nor is it a simple activity to know that all the risk assessment outcomes are adequate.

X. Larrucea et al. (Eds.): EuroSPI 2018, CCIS 896, pp. 380–386, 2018.
https://doi.org/10.1007/978-3-319-97925-0_31

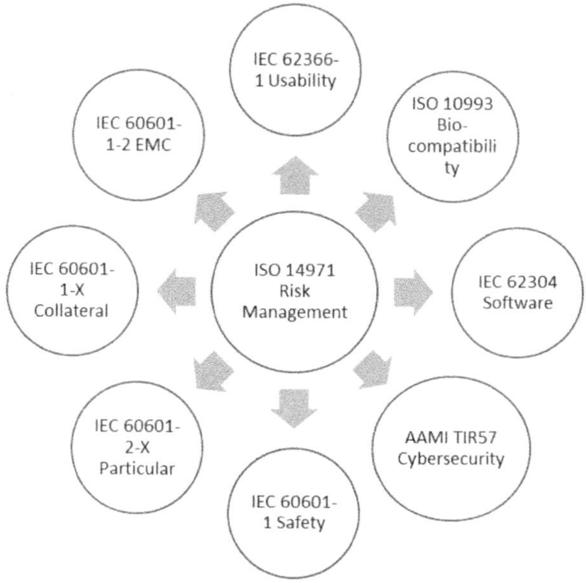

Fig. 1. ISO 14971 relation to other medical device standards

2 ISO 14971 Approach to Risk Management

The well-known risk management process flowchart based on ISO 14971 is illustrated on Fig. 2

Section 4.4 of ISO 14971 encourages the use of 8 different sources when estimating the risk of each hazardous situation:

- (a) published standards;
- (b) scientific technical data;
- (c) field data from similar medical devices already in use, including published reported incidents;
- (d) usability tests employing typical users;
- (e) clinical evidence;
- (f) results of appropriate investigations;
- (g) expert opinion;
- (h) external quality assessment schemes.

From the above list, expert opinion is very often the route declared by many companies, in such cases the quality of the risk management process is likely to be fairly variable if not less effective.

Databases exist for medical device failure publication e.g. the FDA MAUDE database [3], however these databases tend to be more effective in naming and shaming companies into finding quick fixes for problems rather than sources of well-defined failure statistics.

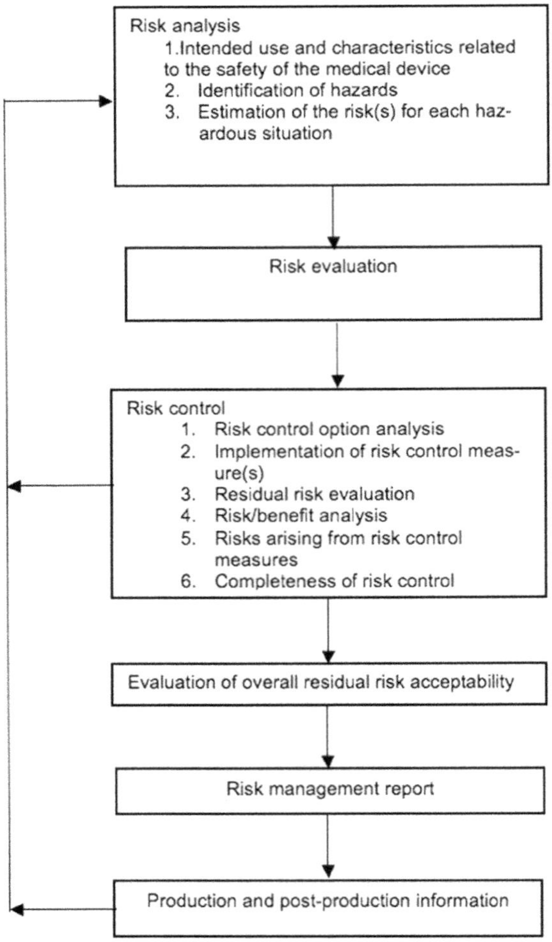

Fig. 2. ISO 14971 risk management process

For electronic hardware there are many good sources available such as reliability standards IEC TR 62380 [4] or Siemens SN 29500 [5] likewise for mechanical components there is e.g. Handbook of Reliability Prediction Procedures for Mechanical Equipment NSWC-11 [6]. However, the assessment of the reliability of software is more difficult. Software can only fail in a systematic fashion in comparison to hardware, which can fail both randomly and systematically.

IEC 62304:2006 + Amd1:2015 [7] the medical device life-cycle model for software development does address some of the potential concerns. Encouraging the assessment of Software of Unknown Provenance (SOUP) usually referred to in other industry sectors as commercial of the shelf software (COTS) and also assessing legacy software developed prior to the introduction of the first version of IEC 62304 in 2006.

ISO 13485:2016 also includes the requirement for verification of computer software that may affect the ability of the product to comply with regulations, e.g. software that could affect the quality of the product or the configuration of the quality management system.

2.1 Software Tool Failure

Unlike other industries such as automotive ISO 26262 [8] and aviation DO-330 [9] the requirement to assess the quality of software tools and the negative impact they could have on the reliability and safety of medical devices. Figure 3 indicates the software tool qualification process defined in ISO 26262. Both the impact and ability to detect software tool failure are utilised to provide a confidence level for the software tool, the rigour then required to assess the tool is then defined based on the automotive safety integrity level (ASIL) which defines the level of risk for the given product.

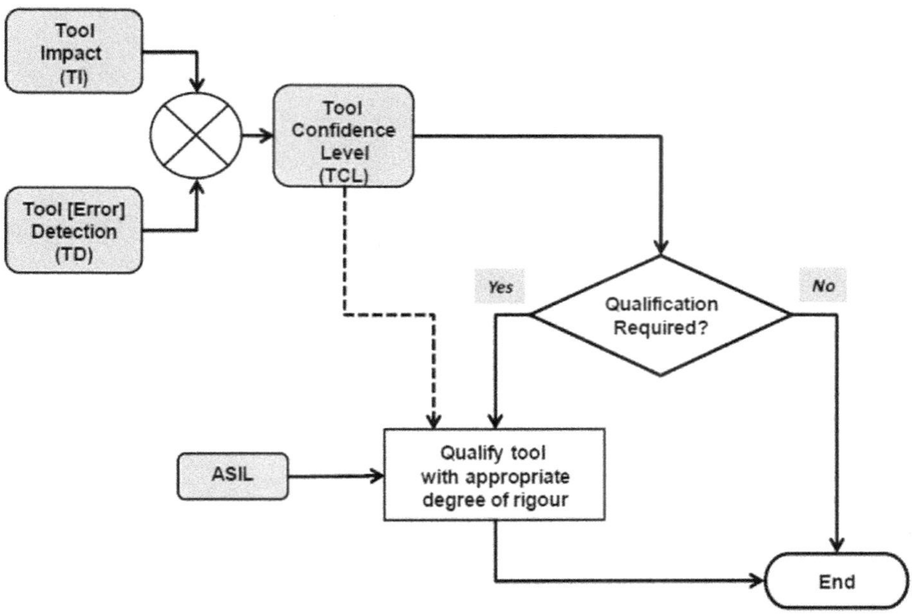

Fig. 3. ISO 26262 tool confidence flowchart

ISO 13485 requires the verification of software applications that support the design, development, and maintenance of a medical device. The latest version of the standard extends the validation requirement also to software systems that support the QMS.

The level of software verification required can be determined by adopting a risk-based approach: the higher and more critical the impact and effect of the software, the more intense the verification required. Complex systems such as enterprise resource planning (ERP), electronic quality management systems (eQMS), and laboratory information management systems (LIMS) would require an extensive verification approach.

2.2 Software Classification and Interference

Compared to ISO 26262, medical device software standards like IEC 62304 do not discuss the impact of interference and dependent failure analysis. Although there is a section in IEC 62304 on classifying software at 3 different levels of criticality (Sect. 4.3), the impact of interference between these elements is not well handled and IEC 62304 only calls for the assessment of segregation between software items if one of these is the highest classification C. This leaves medical device software developed in line with IEC 62304 rather vulnerable to interference problems between software items.

ISO 26262 calls for a dependent failures analysis where seven different types of interference based on the ability of two functions to have either common cause or interference related concerns. Examples of 3. Identical Component Types are middleware, communications stacks and standard library components (Fig. 4).

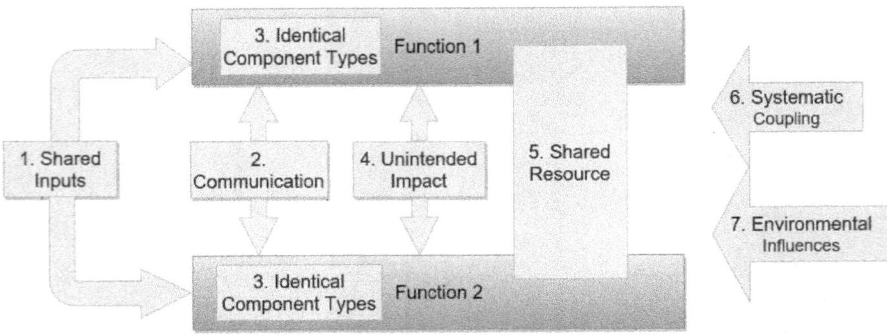

Fig. 4. ISO 26262 sources of dependent failures

3 Methods for Improving Risk Reduction and Verification

Based on Sect. 1 a technique that could benefit the quality of risk assessment for medical devices is a defined set of the 8 points dependent on the medical device classification i.e. type III highest class in the EU or US. This could be a stipulation such as Table 1.

Using the more rigorous techniques listed above in Sect. 1 in addition to more thorough post-market surveillance techniques defined in the MDR companies can improve both the prelaunch and post-production risk assessment. As defined in ISO 13485:2016[10] Sect. 8.4 companies shall analysis data including identifying trends to improve the quality management system, likewise identifying trends will improve post-market risk analysis.

Table 1. Typical risk evaluation techniques based on medical device classification

Medical device class (EU)	Device technology	Risk evaluation techniques
III	Electronic hardware	Published standards Scientific technical data Field test data from similar designs Results of appropriate investigations
	Software	Use of best practice software techniques e.g. from ISO 26262 or IEC 61508 in addition to IEC 62304 Field test data from similar designs Results of appropriate investigations Usability tests
	Implanted applied part	Field test data from similar designs Results of appropriate investigations Usability tests
IIb	Electronic hardware	Published standards Scientific technical data
	Software	Use of best practice software techniques e.g. from ISO 26262 or IEC 61508 in addition to IEC 62304
	ECG electrodes	Field test data from similar designs
I	Electronic hardware	Published standards
	Software	Use of best practice software techniques from IEC 62304

4 Conclusion

Risk management and the importance of it is widely documented in the medical device sector and increasingly so in the last 10 years. How effective the risk management has been once a product has been launched is however a far more difficult question to answer. The drive to improve post market surveillance in the medical device sector defined in the new EU Medical Device Regulation, is welcomed with open arms, as this definitely helps improve post-launch data analysis.

Post-market surveillance is however not sufficient alone and by improving the rigour of techniques used during the development phase the quality of the product and the confidence that it will improve the risk assessment outcomes can be raised significantly. Increased rigour in development may come at additional cost, but the benefits of this additional cost may only be a fraction of the cost of failure once a device has been shipped to customers and the failure is identified.

The authors of this paper are working on techniques that could further enhance the verification of risk management processes in ISO 14971. The work is this paper will be extended in coming months.

References

1. Regulation (EU) 2017/… of the European parliament and of the Council on medical devices, amending Directive 2001/83/EC, Regulation (EC) No. 178/2002 and Regulation (EC) No. 1223/2009 and repealing Council Directives 90/385/EEC and 93/42/EEC
2. ISO 14971:2007 Medical devices - Application of risk management to medical devices
3. FDA – Manufacturer and User Facility Device Experience database. www.accessdata.fda.gov
4. IEC TR 62380:2004 Reliability data handbook – Universal model for reliability prediction of electronics components, PCBs and equipment
5. Siemens SN 29500 Failure rates of components
6. Handbook of Reliability Prediction Procedures for Mechanical Equipment NSWC-11
7. IEC 62304:2015 (Ed 1.1) Medical device software – Software life cycle processes
8. ISO 26262:2018 Road Vehicles - Functional safety
9. DO-330/ED-215 Software Tools Qualification Considerations

Functional Safety Case with FTA and FMEDA Consistency Approach

Richard Messnarz(✉) and Harald Sporer

ISCN GesmbH, Graz, Austria
rmess@iscn.com

Abstract. Based on the hazard and risk analysis of ISO 26262 possible malfunctions are analysed for different situations and rated by Severity, Exposure, and Controllability which leads to a QM, or ASIL A-D ranking. For each ASIL A-D case a safety goals is formatted. And for each safety goal with a rating of ASIL C or ASIL D an FTA (Fault Tree Analysis) and FMEDA (Failure Modes Effects and Diagnostics Analysis) are methods which are highly recommended. Both methods calculate an overall FIT (Failure in Time) and both consider a diagnostic coverage. In this paper an approach is described of how to assure in FTA (top down analysis) and FMEDA the same overall FIT calculated (bottom up analysis). The paper creates a use case scenario for the example "Function 2" in ISO 26262:2011 part 5 Annex E. The example used in the ISO 26262:2011 part 5 Annex E. [1] does not contain background information on system level. This paper adds the missing background information and shows how the system safety concept decisions are mapped onto hardware architecture decisions.

Keywords: Automotive SPICE 3.1 · Functional safety · ISO 26262 FTA · FMEDA · Use case of an ABS brake system

1 Scenario Background - The H&R and Safety Goals

Figure 1 illustrates the item definition of the ABS brake system [1, 2, 6, 13].

A typical item drawing shows the input layer, the calculation layer, and the actuation and output layer. Also the interfaces to the vehicle are included. Additionally the functional concept of the item is considered.

Functional Concept:
Name: Anti-lock braking system (ABS)

Allows the driver to maintain steering control in situations like heavy braking or on slippery surfaces by preventing significant wheel slip. The system constantly monitors the rotational speed of each wheel. When it detects a wheel rotating significantly slower than the others (a condition indicative of impending wheel lock) it actuates the valves within the brake hydraulics to reduce hydraulic pressure to the brake at the affected wheel, thus reducing the braking force on that wheel. The wheel then turns faster; when the wheel is turning significantly faster than the others, brake hydraulic pressure is increased so the braking force is reapplied and the wheel slows. This process is repeated continuously, and can be detected by the driver via brake pedal pulsation.

X. Larrucea et al. (Eds.): EuroSPI 2018, CCIS 896, pp. 387–397, 2018.
https://doi.org/10.1007/978-3-319-97925-0_32

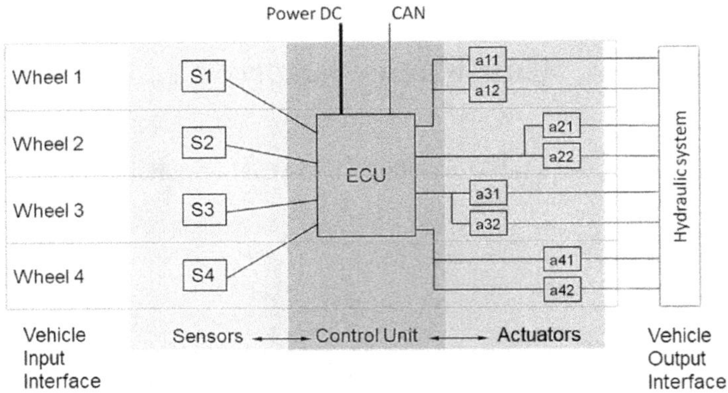

Fig. 1. Item definition ABS brake system - electrohydraulic

In the Hazard and Risk Analysis malfunctions are rated for different driving situations using categories, such as severity, exposure and controllability. Tables from the norm help to identify the proper ratings.

Severity is S3 when a rear, front or side crash is possible a medium speed (which includes the high speed as well), on a scale of S1–S3.

Exposure E4 is given when the system that can cause the hazardous malfunction is active at every drive, or is used at more than 10% of the operating hours in the car. Therefore braking is listed as E4, on a scale of E1–E4.

And a car is seen as being uncontrollable if steering or braking does not work. So also here the ABS brake would be rated usually at C3 (on a scale of C1 – C3). In case of the highest ratings S3, E4, C3 the risk graph of the norm delivers the highest ASIL (Automotive Safety Integrity Level) ASIL – D (on a scale of A-D).

Figure 2 shows a typical line of the H&R (Hazard and Risk Analysis) with ratings for severity, exposure and controllability, the derived ASIL level and a safety goal. In fact the safety goal with the ASIL rating is then the input to the system safety concept design [1–12, 17, 18].

	B) Hazard identification (EXAMPLE)		A) Situation (EXAMPLE)	C) Classification (EXAMPLE)			D) Determination of ASIL and safety goals (EXAMPLE)	
Fkt	Failure	Conseq.		S	E	C	ASIL	Safety Goal
ABS	p_min	No braking force at the wheels	...	S3 ...	E4 ...	C3 ...	ASIL D	The ABS-system must not limit the reliability of the braking system. Reducing the braking pressure more and/or longer than necessary must be avoided.
	p_max	wheels can block (destabi-lizing possible)	...					
	p<	Inadequate braking -> stopping distance too long / longer than expected by driver	...					

Fig. 2. Hazard and risk analysis – ASIL rating – safety goals

2 Scenario Background - the System Safety Concept and Design Decisions

The brake pedal is pressed and the brake pedal input is input to an ECU (Electronic Control Unit). The ECU has a connection to an electric motor of a pump that then produces the corresponding pressure in the hydraulic system to create a brake force at the wheel. A traditional hydraulic brake with no electronic would produce only some 40–50% of the pressure (measured in Pounds per square inch) than electronic supported brakes can do (up to ca. 2000 PSI).

The ABS (Anti-Lock Braking System) includes valves in the hydraulic system that allow to decrease the pressure on single wheel. An inlet valve can close and a further outlet valve can decrease the pressure by releasing the hydraulic fluid and redirect it back to the hydraulic tank.

Figure 3 shows the system concept of an electro-hydraulic brake system. The brake pedal signal is used as an input to calculate a demanded brake force which is converted to a demanded pressure in PSI. The brake ECU then actuates an electric pump (electric motor of the pump) to create the demanded PSI pressure in the 2 hydraulic channel systems (braking at front wheel, braking at rear wheels). Two separated brake channels are needed so that in case of failure at least either the front wheel or the rear wheel will brake. For the control cycle in the ECU PTS (Pressure and Temperature Sensors) are needed to measure the achieved pressure. Temperature is needed as well because the fluid changes the viscosity depending on the temperate. The system also is based on characteristic curves where brake pressure is translated to brake force at the wheels in the calculation models of the software.

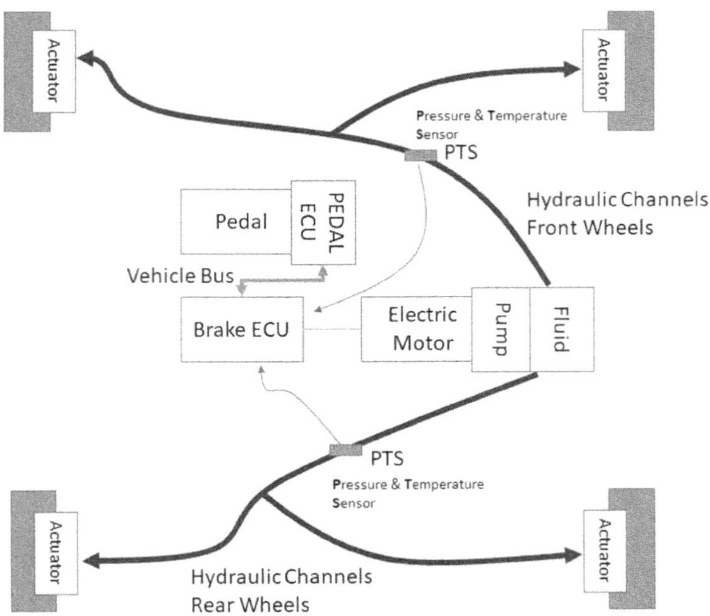

Fig. 3. System concept electro – hydraulic brake system

Figure 4 shows the integration of the ABS brake system concept where by closing an inlet valve the brake pressure built up can be stopped and additionally by using an outlet valve the pressure can be reduced by redirecting the hydraulic fluid back to the brake fluid cycle/container. Figure 4 only shows the concept for one wheel, the same is operating on all 4 wheels. The ABS pump includes 4 separate hydraulic channels and the valves per channel.

Safety Concept and Decomposition Assumptions
The hazard and risk analysis led to an ASIL – D rating. This ASIL – D is then inherited for the functional signal flow that has to assure functional safety of the system [5, 7, 8]. The hazardous fault (malfunction) is that the inlet valve incorrectly closes and the outlet valve incorrectly opens. In this case no brake pressure could be built up on a wheel. Moreover, if one wheel for a longer time has no brake force while the other wheels are braking the car will steer in an uncontrollable way.

The safety critical path is that incorrect position of the valves will be recognised by the ABS ECU with ASIL D. Therefore the control valves, the read back of valves, the ECU inherit an ASIL D rating.

Fail Safe Concept
The ABS system has to be developed in a fail safe mode where if no electric power is supplied any more by the ABS (ABS is deactivated) the inlet valve is fail safe open and the outlet valve is fail safe closed. This means that a deactivation of the ABS system leads to a normal electro-hydraulic brake like in Fig. 3.

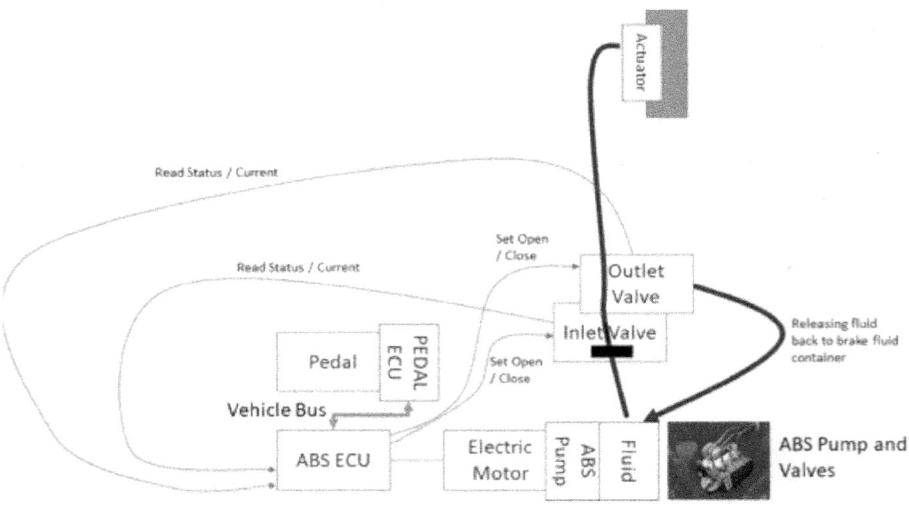

Fig. 4. System concept ABS brake system

Diagnostic Coverage
The actuation of the valves must be read back by an ADC. To reach a higher diagnostic coverage of 99% (as it is used in the example for FMEDA and FTA below) the underlying electro-hydraulic brake system can provide pressure and temperature sensor

values, plus a mathematical model demanded brake force versus achieved PSI value in the hydraulic system. This means that if the inlet valve incorrectly closes and the output valve incorrectly opens the PTS sensors (see Fig. 1) would see a sudden decrease in the pressure for a period longer than a threshold ms time.

Additionally the mathematical model of expected brake force (deceleration of wheel speed) can be compared with the real deceleration as a second independent path. Both parallel independent diagnose functions allow a plausibility check and a 99% diagnostic coverage assumption.

Decomposition Assumptions

In the functional safety norm a high ASIL rated system can be decomposed into 2 parallel independent ASIL B channels. An ASIL B could further be decomposed into two ASIL A. The brake pedal position must be provided at ASIL D. Usually this is provided over CAN by two independent brake pedal position signals, both being rated ASIL B.

The ABS ECU contains 2 cores, one controls the valves and one is measuring the PTS sensors. Both can compare (expected pressure by PTS versus valves position) and both can deactivate the ABS function. This usage of a mathematical model for plausibility check would allow a decomposition of the μCs but in the example below we just assume to reach ASIL D with no decomposition of the cores.

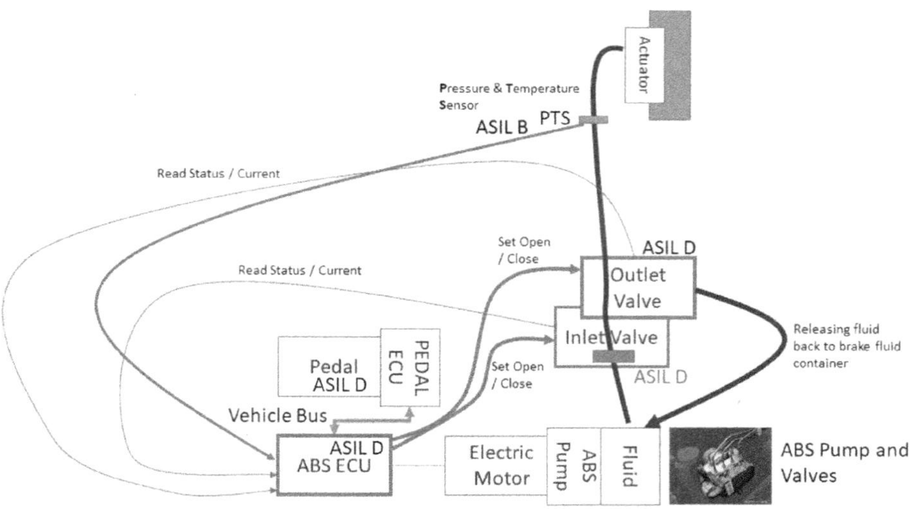

Fig. 5. System concept ABS brake system with an ASIL assignment

3 Application of Consistent FTA and FMEDA

Figure 5 shows the ASIL D rated parts of the system which are impacted by the safety goal described in Fig. 2 above. Each ASIL rating of a safety goal defines a hardware architecture metric for single point faults to be achieved. ASIL D relates to 10^{-8} which means 1 hazardous fault not detected and avoided in 10^{8} operating hours in the fleet.

Figure 6 below shows the example schematic used in ISO 26262:2011 part 5 [1] to explain hardware architecture metrics calculation. In the chapters before we added the ABS background system concept considerations which were not published in the norm but are required to fully understand the use case.

In Sect. 1 the hazard analysis and risk assessment (HARA) is shown. The safety goal "The ABS-system must not limit the reliability of the braking system. Reducing the braking pressure more and/or longer than necessary must be avoided." was classified with ASIL D. According to the hardware design safety analysis methods defined in [1] a deductive and an inductive analysis is highly recommended. Within automotive industry projects this is usually carried through by the application of a fault tree analysis (FTA) and a failure modes, effects and diagnostic analysis (FMEDA).

To showcase the correlation between the inductive design analysis FMEDA and the deductive design analysis FTA one channel out of a four channel ABS has been extracted. The main parts (see Fig. 6) considered in the following ABS use case are

- inductive sensor I1, measuring the front left wheel speed
- coils of inlet valve I61 and outlet valve I71, integrated into the hydraulic circuit of the front left wheel brake
- ABS warning lamp L1
- microcontroller µC
  - reading wheel speed via In1
  - controlling inlet and outlet valves via Out 1 and Out 2
  - reading valve's status via InADC1 respectively InADC2
  - switching on/off ABS warning lamp via Out 3
- watchdog WD, introduced as system monitoring device for the microcontroller

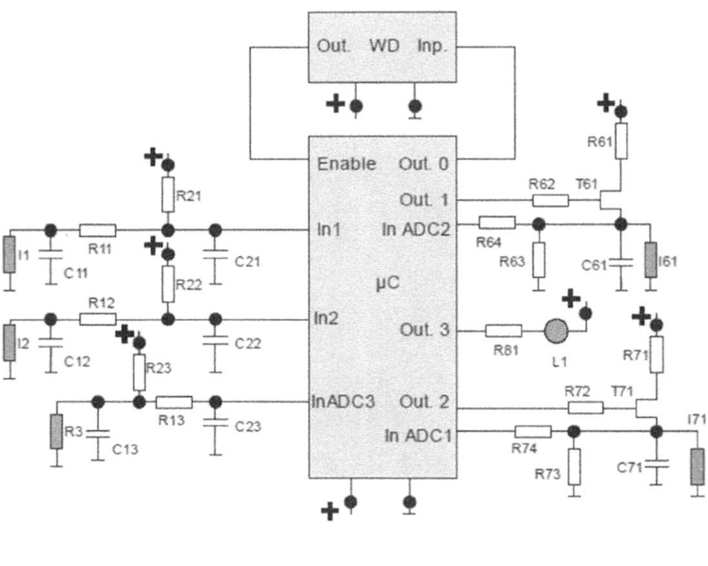

Figure E.1 — Example diagram

Fig. 6. Example HW schematic ABS brake system valve control [1]

As mentioned above the described use case is based on "Function 2" from ISO26262 Annex E [1]. To meet the requirements for the selected vehicle function ABS the description can be restated as following.

The function has one input (wheel speed measured via sensor I1 generating pulses) and two outputs (inlet valve controlled by I61 and outlet valve controlled by I71) and its behaviour is to decrease hydraulic pressure at the brake calliper in case of a potential brake lock/wheel lock.

Low pressure has been identified as a possible hazard during the (HARA) that can lead to a missing break force at the wheels. Due to a failure within the hard- or software the inlet and outlet valves could be controlled in a way that arouses the described hazard. More details about the hazard analysis and risk assessment can be found in Sects. 1 and 2 above.

From an electro-mechanical point of view the inlet and outlet valves are designed to enable a fall back scenario in case of an ABS failure. That is, when no current is supplied at the coils, the inlet valve remains open and the outlet valve remains closed.

Figure 8 shows the typical FMEDA done for single point fault metrics for the hardware parts effected. Each part has FIT (failure in time measured in faults per 10^9 operating hours in the fleet), failure modes which can be a hazard (with percentage of occurrence), and a diagnostic coverage. The single point fault FIT is calculated with the formula:

$$\begin{aligned} &\mathit{Fit\ of\ part} * \mathit{Percent\ Occurrence\ of\ hazardous\ failure\ mode} \\ &\quad * (1 - \mathit{Diagnostic\ Coverage}). \end{aligned}$$

The calculation in line for T61 short cut in Fig. 8 is therefore $5 \times 0{,}5 \times (1-0{,}9) = 0{,}25$. The 5,86 is the sum of the single point FIT of the affected parts.

Component Name	Failure rate/FIT [10^{-9}]	Safety-related component to be considered in the calculations?	Failure Mode	Failure rate distribution	Failure mode that has the potential to violate the safety goal in absence of safety mechanisms?	Safety mechanism(s) allowing to prevent the failure mode from violating the safety goal?	Failure mode coverage wrt. violation of safety goal	Residual or Single-Point Fault failure rate/FIT
T61	5	YES	open	50%				
			short	50%	x	SM3	90%	0,25
T71	5	YES	open	50%				
			short	50%	x	SM5	90%	0,25
R62	2	YES	open	90%	x	SM3	90%	0,18
			closed	10%				
R72	2	YES	open	90%	x	SM5	90%	0,18
			closed	10%				
uC	100	YES	All	50%	x	SM4	90%	5
			All	50%				
								5,86 FIT

Fig. 7. Example extract from the HW FMEDA

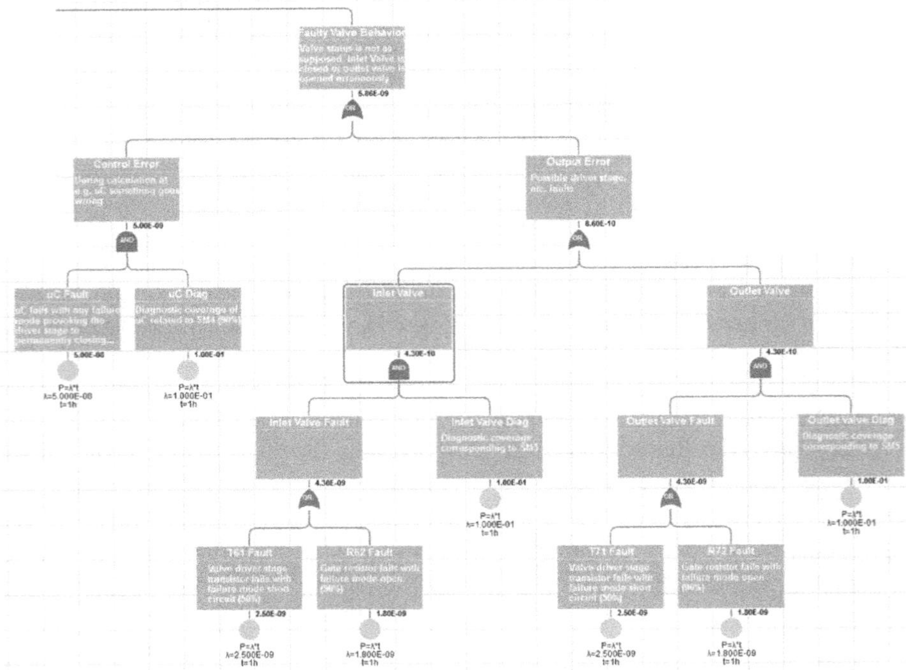

Fig. 8. Example fault tree consistent with the example shown in the HW FMEDA

Note: While for ASIL D a diagnostic coverage of 99% must be achieved the example "Function 2" in ISO 26262:2011 part 5 Annex E only used 90% diagnostic coverage. To stay consistent with the norm example we used 90% for the below calculations, although in the real case 99% should be applied (as described in section 2).

The diagnostic coverage of 90% used in Figs. 7 and 8 has been used in the norm example for wrong closing of the inlet valve can be detected by a decrease of pressure by the PTS sensor over a threshold of ms time.

Figure 9 shows a selected part of Fig. 8 (see the square in Fig. 8) which shows the necessary FTA design pattern to come up with same FIT for the safety goal in the calculation. Looking at Fig. 9 you see that the faults of the hardware are events connected by OR since if one fails the hazard will appear. The diagnose function is added to the FTA with an AND gate because the fault only becomes a hazard if the system diagnostic coverage of 90% (therefore multiplication with 1-09 = 0,1 = 10^{-1}) does not detect it.

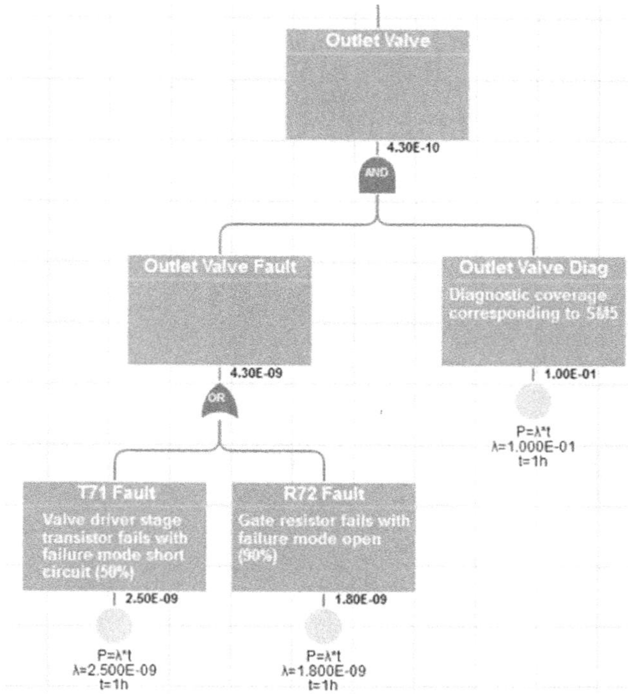

Fig. 9. Example fault tree – pattern combining diagnose coverage with FIT

FMEDA and FTA deliver same FIT results only if such design patterns are used and consistently compared. So if a further diagnostic coverage is considered in the FNEDA the FTA has to be updated correspondingly. FMEDA (bottom up) and FTA (top down) are different approaches, and still both should stay consistent and reach the FIT goals.

4 Expected Impact and Outlook

The example used in the ISO 26262:2011 part 5 Annex E. [1] does not contain background information on system level. This paper adds the missing background information and shows how the system safety concept decisions are mapped onto hardware architecture decisions. This can help readers of the ISO 26262:2011 and also the 2nd norm edition in 2018 to better understand the example of hardware architecture metrics in the context of a system use case.

Also the norm just mentions that FMEDA and FTA need to be done in ASIL – C and ASIL – D case but there is no example of how to achieve in both approaches the dame FIT goal. The paper adds such a consistency criteria.

This consistency approach is also explained in the SafEUr project materials and training developed together with the SOQRATES working party [5–8].

5 The SPI Manifesto Revisited

The SPI manifesto [14–16] describes values and principles which need to be considered to make improvements work in an organisation. One of the approaches is to start with an assessment and to derive an improvement list. This is then used to set up an improvement program.

The principle "**Use dynamic and adaptable models as needed**" means that depending on the need of organisations specific models can be adapted. The safety norm is such a new model which is needed in the Automotive domain.

The principle "**Base improvement on experience and measurements**" means that best practice experiences need to be shared and the usage must be tracked and measured. Since the model was developed in a group of Tier 1 in the SOQRATES working group the model development was based on such an experience and best practice sharing approach.

Also the measurement of FIT (Failure in Time) allows to design systems where the probability of a hazard decreases $< 10^8$ operating hours in cars. This is an important improvement concept for systems that can provide hazards, such as cars, planes, trains, etc.

An additional principle proposed for the SPI manifesto is: "**Observe new trends and state of the art practices on the market and adopt**". The product liability law and the RAPEX (www.rapex.com) database changed the market because hazardous faults as well as legal violations in cars lead to a mandatory recall action and all cars must be repaired. This creates huge cost and thus new state of the art standards like functional safety, cybersecurity etc. became an important issue.

Acknowledgements. We are grateful to the members of the SOQRATES [4] working group who have contributed: Alastair Walker (LORIT), Alexander Much (Elektrobit), Frank König, Martin Dallinger, Thomas Wegner (ZF Friedrichshafen AG), Armin Riess (BBraun), Dietmar Kinalzyk (HELLA), Ralf Mayer (BOSCH Engineering), Gerhard Griessnig (AVL), Andreas Gruber (ZKW), Rainer Dreves, Ivan Sokic, Stephan Habel (Continental), Christian Schlager, Thomas Stiglhuber (Magna Powertrain ECS), Andreas Riel (ISCN/Grenoble INP), Helmut Zauchner, Christoph Karner (KTM), Andreas Gruber (ZKW), Georg Macher (AVL), Bernhard Sechser (Methodpark), Lutz Haunert (G&D), Damjan Ekert (ISCN), Richard Messnarz (ISCN).

We are also grateful to the European Commission which has funded some of the initiatives that funded the development of skills in the Automotive sector. ISCN is a member of AQUA (Knowledge Alliance for Quality in Automotive Engineering, 2013–2015) [17, 18], and AQU (Automotive Quality Universities, 2015–2017), and the BLUEPRINT project DRIVES (2018–2021).

References

1. ISO - International Organization for Standardization: ISO 26262 Road vehicles Functional Safety Part 1-10 (2011)
2. Haken, K.L.: Grundlagen der Kraftfahrzeugtechnik. Carl Hanser Verlag, München (2013). ISBN 978-3-446-43527-8

3. ISO – International Organization for Standardization: ISO CD 26262-2018 2nd Edition Road vehicles Functional Safety (to appear)
4. SOQRATES: Task Forces Developing Integration of Automotive SPICE, ISO 26262 and SAE J3061. http://soqrates.eurospi.net/
5. Messnarz, R., Kreiner, C., Riel, A.: Integrating automotive SPICE, functional safety, and cybersecurity concepts: a cybersecurity layer model. Softw. Qual. Prof. **18**, 13 (2016)
6. Messnarz, R., Kreiner, C., Riel, A., et al.: Implementing functional safety standards has an impact on system and sw design - required knowledge and competencies (SafEUr). In: Software Quality Professional (2015)
7. Macher, G., Sporer, H., Brenner, E., Kreiner, C.: Supporting cyber-security based on hardware-software interface definition. In: Kreiner, C., O'Connor, R.V., Poth, A., Messnarz, R. (eds.) EuroSPI 2016. CCIS, vol. 633, pp. 148–159. Springer, Cham (2016). https://doi.org/10.1007/978-3-319-44817-6_12
8. Macher, G., Messnarz, R., Kreiner, C., et al.: Integrated safety and security development in the automotive domain, Working Group 17AE-0252/2017-01-1661. SAE International, June 2017
9. Redmill, F.: Understanding the use, misuse and abuse of safety integrity levels. In: Proceedings of the Eighth Safety-critical Systems Symposium, Southampton, UK, 8–10 February 2000
10. Much, A.: Automotive security: challenges, standards and solutions. Softw. Qual. Prof. **18** (4) (2016)
11. Messnarz, R., et al.: Integrating functional safety, automotive SPICE and six sigma – the AQUA knowledge base and integration examples. In: Barafort, B., O'Connor, R.V., Poth, A., Messnarz, R. (eds.) EuroSPI 2014. CCIS, vol. 425, pp. 285–295. Springer, Heidelberg (2014). https://doi.org/10.1007/978-3-662-43896-1_26
12. Kreiner, C., et al.: Automotive knowledge alliance AQUA – integrating automotive SPICE, six sigma, and functional safety. In: McCaffery, F., O'Connor, R.V., Messnarz, R. (eds.) EuroSPI 2013. CCIS, vol. 364, pp. 333–344. Springer, Heidelberg (2013). https://doi.org/10.1007/978-3-642-39179-8_30
13. ABS Brake System, wikipedia. https://en.wikipedia.org/wiki/Anti-lock_braking_system
14. Korsaa, M., et al.: The SPI manifesto and the ECQA SPI manager certification scheme. J. Softw.: Evol. Process **24**(5), 525–540 (2012)
15. Korsaa, M., et al.: The people aspects in modern process improvement management approaches. J. Softw.: Evol. Process **25**(4), 381–391 (2013)
16. Messnarz, R., et al.: Social responsibility aspects supporting the success of SPI. J. Softw.: Evol. Process **26**(3), 284–294 (2014)
17. Larrucea, X., Mergen, S., Walker, A.: A GSN approach to SEooC for an automotive hall sensor. In: Kreiner, C., O'Connor, R.V., Poth, A., Messnarz, R. (eds.) EuroSPI 2016. CCIS, vol. 633, pp. 269–280. Springer, Cham (2016). https://doi.org/10.1007/978-3-319-44817-6_23
18. Larrucea, X., Walker, A., Colomo-Palacios, R.: Supporting the management of reusable automotive software. IEEE Softw. **34**(3), 40–47 (2017). https://doi.org/10.1109/MS.2017.68

Experiences with Agile and Lean

How to Deliver Faster with CI/CD Integrated Testing Services?

Alexander Poth(✉), Mark Werner(✉), and Xinyan Lei(✉)

Volkswagen AG, Berliner Ring 2, 38436 Wolfsburg, Germany
{alexander.poth,mark.werner,xinyan.lei}@volkswagen.de

Abstract. After Volkswagen AG has setup its hybrid cloud products and services are expected to have a significant shorter time-to-market and a high quality level. To satisfy these expectations, the existing testing procedures should have to speed up, so that it won'tbe the bottle neck for new features that have to be shipped fast. In order to realize a faster delivery of products and services Testing as a Service is developed with lean/agile methods [1, 2] and integrated into the CI/CD pipeline of the Volkwagen Group IT Cloud.

Keywords: Agile software development · Quality assurance (QA)
Cloud · Testing · CI/CD

1 Motivation and Context for the Demand of Testing as a Service

To meet the needs for testing in a cloud native fashion, Testing as a Service (TaaS) is setup as one of the Volkswagen Group IT cloud (GITC) services. The focus is to offer a testing service that is able to scale natively based on cloud technologies. The service focuses on offering state of the art testing capability for both functional and non-functional testing in the cloud environment. The motivation for developing TaaS was a missing link in existing cloud native tools, which could also be run on premise in a private or hybrid cloud. For a public cloud approach there exists different tools like BrowserStack, BlazeMeter, etc. But these tools did not offer any possibility to run on premise in a private cloud and therefore could not be used for testing sensitive data/applications. As a matter of fact filling a gap like this leads mostly to create a tool or to change workflows in IT context. As a result of that TaaS has to make a choice of creating tools or workflows to achieve the goal. Furthermore nowadays companies have a cloud-first/cloud-only strategy for development of applications. The new approach leads to a change in thinking and designing new IT applications. The existing well-proofed development concepts must be reconsidered if we want to make the best out of the new found possibilities of developing cloud native applications. Based on the experiences that were gathered during the development of TaaS, it was recognized that both an API for machine usage and a self-service portal (SSP) for human interaction are a must for TaaS to be implemented. If we want to make the most out of TaaS for our company, we have to take the integration concept of the new service into existing processes into consideration. Most of the benefits from TaaS could be achieved only if

X. Larrucea et al. (Eds.): EuroSPI 2018, CCIS 896, pp. 401–409, 2018.
https://doi.org/10.1007/978-3-319-97925-0_33

the TaaS can be integrated smoothly in the existing processes in the organization. In the following chapters it will be described, how the TaaS team improved itself during the development and achieved success step by step by motivating others and keeping the focus on the needs of customers.

2 Rapid Development of a Product or a Service

This section describes the implementation of TaaS. To implement TaaS quickly and to make it customer (user) centric, the GITC implements an intrapreneurship [3] friendly environment. This environment focuses on selling a "product vision" for the service and applying for an initial financial support. This basic financial setup is used to implement a proof of concept (PoC). The 1st venture capital was given in the fourth quarter of 2016 to develop a PoC for the GITC exhibition in December. After delivering a successful PoC, the GITC council offers further venture capital for product increments. The product owner has to apply for the next increment of the service. Each increment is called a minimal viable product (MVP). This approach is used to analyze the customer's feedback and acceptance of the growing service. Furthermore, the financial support can be stopped quickly in case of not fulfilling the expectations of performance or business perspectives. Depending on the speed of revenue generation by the service, the amount of financial support can be adjusted easily to service "incomes" and support other services with the money "saved".

This intrapreneurship-based environment encourages the TaaS team to develop more than MVPs. Because MVPs are not "attractive" enough for the customer and have sometimes many constraints. The TaaS team decides to develop SLCs [4]. SLC is the abbreviation for simple, lovable and complete. This gives the option to run TaaS every time as a stable product in case the venture capital flow stops and the income is not enough to cover finance complex stabilization tasks and enhancements to make the service "user-acceptable".

Based on the described environment, the TaaS DevOps team focuses on a strategic view to optimize TaaS for:

- Making testing faster
- Making it more comfortable and easier to use
- Reducing service resources and costs

This motivates the TaaS team to work more in a feedback driven fashion rather than specification driven. Also it forces the TaaS team to fix bugs as fast as possible and have a low technical debt in TaaS for fast and nimble reactions to feedbacks.

The formal 4 MVPs in 2017 focused on shipping non-functional load testing, performance testing, functional testing for responsive web design (RWD) and multi-browser testing on a user perspective. On a cloud perspective the rollout to GITC was focused. The MVP roadmap in 2018 focuses on more rollout and enhancement of existing functions based on user feedback. To get user feedback for every new key feature, at least one pilot customer has to act as a development partner of TaaS. Furthermore, after a new feature was released into production, the customers would be asked for feedback about these particular features..These feedback sessions were based on the starfish retro approach [5].

The TaaS team started with Scrum, but realized later on, that there were dependencies (for example database), that often blocked the implementation of TaaS. This observation led to a change in Kanban. In 2018 the TaaS team is practicing a Scrumban approach. The Kanban component is used for operational issues of the DevOps teams.

This agile and lean development method can also have negative impacts to the DevOps TaaS team. TaaS started in 2018 with no budget. These days were difficult for the team because it was unclear how long it needs to convince the GITC council for the next MVP/SLC and how much venture capital will be offered for the rollout to AWS and feature development for the upcoming MVP/SLC.

A strategic decision was to integrate TaaS into the Volkswagen Group IT devstack of the Volkswagen AG. Devstack is a project-customizable CI/CD (continuous integration/continuous deployment) toolchain for Volkswagen AG. Devstack is not only available for GITC users but offers cross-selling options to a much bigger market for TaaS. This integration idea TaaS@devstack was born in 2017 but will need some time for management commitment. Furthermore, the TaaS DevOps team can reduce ops activities by the delegation of support tasks to the 24 * 7 devstack operation team in the third quarter of 2018. This will give the TaaS team more flexibility to focus on user demands and a more stable “financial basis”.

3 Deep Dive into TaaS

TaaS is designed to support all kinds of tests from the commonly known test automation pyramid [6]. In a classic test pyramid approach there are the following kinds of tests: unit tests; integration tests; and acceptance tests. The focus is a little bit different for TaaS because TaaS uses a cloud native approach and therefore from TaaS point of view the pyramid would be like this:

- unit tests for micro-services on the base layer
- integration tests in the mid-section
- system or business related tests on top

So at the end, several abstraction levels are covered. TaaS is designed to write tests once and run often – in best case integrated into a CI/CD toolchain. This enables the user to build a broad base of automated tests, which are executed on each triggered build. This can ensure a high level of quality of the product built, because the execution of tests are automated and will become native to the development team. Providing automated tested applications will also reduce the time-to-market because it ensures that the developed features of the application will be tested on each build. Using iterative sprints and a set of regressions tests to build up an application ensures correct functionalities of the developed application.

Developers focus on developing new features and using an agile approach but the tests have to be automated and integrated into the build/deployment process. This approach ensures that the tests are still in the focus of developers and that they are responsible to deliver new features. A benefit of this setup is that all shipped/delivered applications are also tested automatically using regression tests and therefore ensure an objective quality of the delivered application.

By using a Definition of Done (DoD) concept, the development team ensures that every micro-service is tested automatically. This is a strong basis to build more complex integration tests to cover the interaction between micro-services. It would be possible to verify a whole system of business workflows through these kind of tests.

Because TaaS supports different testing tools, a wide range of testing is possible, from API (application programming interface) tests for example REST-based to GUI (graphical user interface) tests using different browsers. Depending on the testing tools, TaaS supports not only functional testing but also non-functional testing.

Depending on the processed data (sensitive or private) it is not an option for testing these applications in a public cloud. Using standard already existing testing tools will miss the capabilities/benefits, that cloud native approach offers. TaaS is designed to be cloud native and therefore benefit from the different advantages that a cloud native application will offer. TaaS makes use of well-known open source software such as Selenium [7], JMeter [8], Docker [9], Kubernetes [10] etc.

TaaS does not use any proprietary tools and interfaces and can be easily integrated into different CI/CD-toolchains without a complex setup. This open design prevents also any tool constraints, which could lead to a tool lock-in later on.

TaaS does not limit the development team to follow either a top-down approach or a bottom-up approach because it supports both ways of testing an application. Following the top-down approach, the tests have to follow defined business processes and cover the acceptance criteria of customer journeys. Using this approach, we are starting from the top of the test pyramid to cover relevant customer journey and features.

In a bottom-up approach, tests are designed and developed for micro-services, which will be deployed. This ensures that all the developed micro-services are covered with automated tests. These could be integrated with integration tests covering basic steps.

3.1 The API and the Self-service-Portal

As already noted before, TaaS is designed to write a test once and run it often (see Fig. 1). In the first step, the tests which should be executed later are designed and written in the IDE (integrated developer environment) of the tester. This also helps to reduce the time-to-market because the development team can use all the well-known tools to write necessary tests.

The registration in TaaS and the execution of tests via TaaS is implemented using a two-step process. Senior user/administrator double checks and therefore limits the valid URLs (unified resource locator) or IP (internet protocol)-addresses/endpoints which could be used for the tests to prevent DoS (denial of service) attacks using the provided cloud resources. The endpoints for the test object are fixed and cannot be changed by the provided test cases. After a valid configuration of the tests, that includes which test cases to run and how often, the configuration of the test is completed.

Depending on the project requirements the tests can be triggered manually using the self-service-portal or can be integrated into an already existing CI/CD-tool chain.

After executing the tests and finishing the test runs, the logs of the test execution are collected and stored for analyzation. Depending on the test results, the development team has to decide how to process it further:

- fixing the bug, that was found during the execution
- adjusting the tests according to the acceptance criteria of the feature

In both cases, the quality of the developed application is raised and enables a faster time-to-market. In the first case, a fixed bug means one error less in the developed application. The second case raises the quality because a test, which tests the wrong use case/feature does not affect the overall quality of the application. Tests have to be handled like code, which means that test cases have to be refactored from time to time.

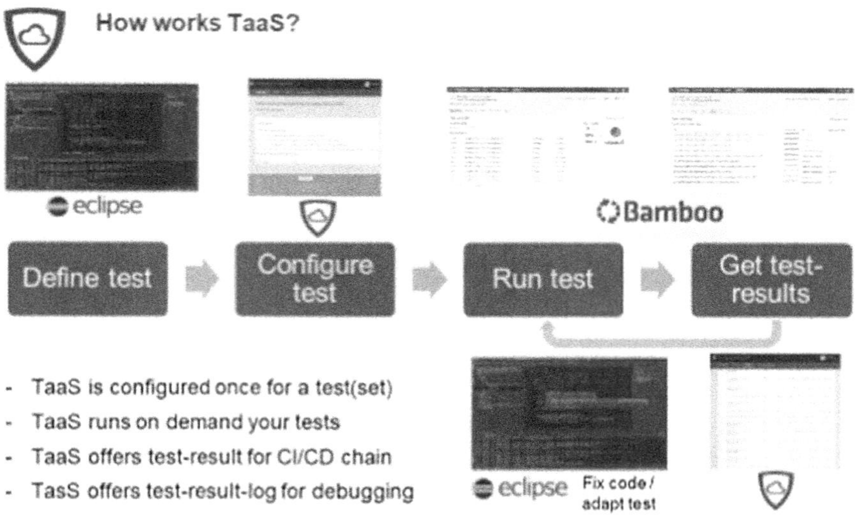

Fig. 1. An overview of the workflows with TaaS

3.2 Load and Performance Testing

The kind of tests which cover load and performance testing is also possible to be executed using TaaS. Performance testing is used to determine the performance of a test objective in terms of responsiveness under a defined work load. In general the minimum, maximum and average response times are measured. A load test is a specific form of performance testing because it tests the system behaviour under a defined work load. The work load could be a number of users/sessions performing specific number of actions within a defined duration. These tests are used to identify bottlenecks in the application. To support these kinds of testing, the open source tool JMeter is supported by TaaS and can be found in the self-service portal.

To cover several scenarios different versions of JMeter are offered from which the customer could use the desired version. JMeter was designed to simulate test behaviour and measure performance. By design, JMeter is capable to test the performance on static and also dynamic web applications. It provides a simulator for heavy load to check the overall performance of the test objective under different load scenarios. The most commonly used protocols are web protocols (http, https) and REST based web services.

JMeter's built-in multi-threading framework offers the possibility to run concurrent tests by many threads and could scale natively on a cloud platform. The customer is able to select the desired amount of JMeter workers using the self-service portal. To offer the customer horizontal scaling options, a cluster is set up with one master and depending on the customer needs several slaves. The master controls the slaves and manages the distribution of tests to be executed. The slaves for the heavy work are testing the defined test objects with the desired load as defined in the test configuration.

3.3 Functional Testing

To offer responsive web design and multi-browser testing, dynamic grids with required settings are dynamically allocated. To quickly offer the required and specific settings, different Docker containers with the demanded browsers, like Firefox [11] or Chrome [12] and desired versions are setup in the grid. Selenium is used as the test engine.

To support this kind of testing TaaS supports the usage of Selenium to enable the testing of different browsers and versions. Selenium is an automated testing framework for web applications and provides features like playback of formerly recorded business processes. Using this approach no specific knowledge is needed to be able to build test steps.

For each test run, a preconfigured Docker image is used in which the target browser, version and the tests to be executed are prepared. So the customer can decide which web browser and which version he needs to use for testing his business processes. In the self-service portal, the customer is able to configure relevant meta data for his test execution including the size. Using the provided WebDrivers from Selenium, most web browsers are supported and can be controlled by several programming languages (Java, C#, JS, …). This enables the development team to write tests in the preferred programming language, which reduces the time for writing tests and setting up testing tools etc. An agile development team could focus on delivering new features, which are covered by tests written in the preferred programming language.

For enabling the testing of web browsers running on remote machines Selenium offers the Selenium Grid. Since the Selenium Grid has a scalable design, it allows executing tests in parallel on different machines. This approach matches perfectly with the cloud-native approach of TaaS. In the end, a highly scalable and flexible infrastructure could be offered to the customer to support the testing of different web browsers. Without the need to setup an instance of Selenium or Selenium Grid, TaaS enables the customer to execute tests for different web browsers at a fingertip. After the test execution, TaaS enables downloading the test results for analyzation of the test runs.

TaaS supports the whole testing life cycle of software testing starting from providing the necessary testing infrastructure (JMeter, Selenium), offering a highly scalable and flexible architecture to scaling horizontally.

To offer maximum flexibility to the customers of TaaS the application specific setups and configurations are shipped with the customers Docker container.

To minimize the overhead of managing the different configurations of testing setup, the TaaS design uses Docker containers. These containers are prepared in advance with the different versions of the offered testing tools. The customized test configuration including the tests to execute are mounted onto the prepared Docker containers, which are started according to the customer setup.

Depending on the setup, several nodes are spun up in the existing Kubernetes cluster which starts the desired number of pods to support the customer specific test configuration. This lean architecture allows a fast and flexible way to manage several different customer setups.

Important to notice is that each customer uses his/her own network, which is generated on demand for each test run. This limits the potential (negative) side effects of running instances in parallel or shared resources etc.

From the customer point of view, the whole setup of testing tool is already done and he can focus on the design and preparation of his specific tests. He does not need to know how to setup and maintain an architecture on a cloud but can benefit from the offered TaaS solution.

He is an expert in his domain of the test objective and can now use the saved time to invest in more and better tests. Using the possibility to integrate TaaS in an already existing CI/CD toolchain could improve the overall quality of the developed application, because all defined tests run automatically after each application deployment. This helps the customer of TaaS to get a fast feedback of the quality of the build and the delivered application.

Using TaaS enables the customer to control the development process very tightly to ensure that the development team focuses on delivering new and tested business values. The development team is still aware of the new developed features and is therefore very quick in fixing defects that are found and also in adjusting new business features. In the past there was a large time gap between developing new business features and getting feedback of the testing on the productive environment. The development team may have been changed in the meantime or they are working on different projects. In either way, it costs time to recall the past activities and to focus again on the new task.

This container contains technology specific things for example for an Angular application the protractor [13] test-stack and the specific tests for execution. The figure below (Fig. 2) shows a setup with cucumber [14].

3.4 Outlook

The next functionality on the roadmap of TaaS is mobile testing integration. The SLC approach leads the TaaS team to focus on 80% of the solution with Appium [15].

The goal is to test an Android app to ensure a good scalable approach. This will enhance the feature set provided by TaaS to support the wide range of mobile development and therefore testing.

Consumer-driven contract testing is another candidate on the roadmap of TaaS. With this feature TaaS would cover all the levels of the testing pyramid that was

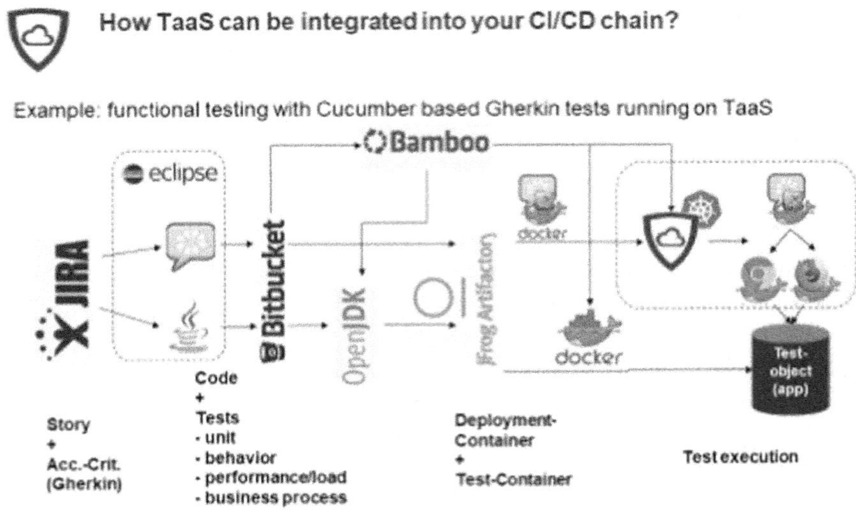

Fig. 2. An example setup of CI/CD integrated functional test

introduced in Sect. 3. The ultimate goal of TaaS is to be an open testing platform with extensible capabilities.

4 Conclusion

In this paper, we have presented the history and details about TaaS in Volkswagen AG. The product enables developers to enjoy the benefits of rapid development velocity in the cloud native age. TaaS supports different kinds of tests. With the help of TaaS, tests can be easily integrated into a CI/CD toolchain and can be implemented with different frameworks. TaaS hides the complexity of setting up and managing the test-environment away from software developers, so that software developers can focus more on developing business values. In order to ensure all the benefits and the ongoing agility, the TaaS team developed the service in a more feedback driven way rather than a specification driven way. The TaaS team has worked closely with pilot users in order to keep the feedback loop shorter for all the core functionalities. It also helps to focus on implementing the SLCs.

This paper shows our effort to ensure quality even with a high development velocity and our experiences about agile/lean product development in large and sometimes bureaucratic corporations. It also shows a possible way to improve the innovative nature in a large corporation with the help of an intrapreneurship friendly environment.

From a software process improvement view, the summary should be that in the future the process and method authority is not enough to deliver added value without understanding the involved technological principals, which are the drivers for an operative excellence in a fast changing and scaling environment.

5 SPI Manifesto Reflection

The presented TaaS approach also follows the values and principles that are described in the SPI Manifesto [16, 17, 18]. The TaaS team has tried to motivate all the people involved, for example the venture capital and the customers. As a part of the motivation, the TaaS team has improved the development process based on the experiences gained with customers from MVP to SLC. It is a dynamic and adaptable way to satisfy customer needs with an agile/lean mindset. The SPI Manifesto's values and principles are a guide for the TaaS team to make the best choice for the team and its customers.

References

1. Sutherland, et al.: http://www.agilemanifesto.org
2. Sutherland, et al.: http://agilemanifesto.org/principles.html
3. Pinchot, G.: Intrapreneuring: Why You Don't Have to Leave the Corporation to Become an Entrepreneur. Berrett-Koehler Publishers, 2. Auflage (1985). ISBN 1-57675-082-5
4. https://blog.asmartbear.com/slc.html
5. Schwaber, K.: Agile Project Management with Scrum. Microsoft Press, Redmond (2004)
6. Cohn, M.: Succeeding with Agile: Software Development Using Scrum. Pearson Education (2010)
7. https://www.seleniumhq.org/
8. https://jmeter.apache.org/
9. https://www.docker.com/
10. https://kubernetes.io/
11. https://www.mozilla.org/de/firefox/
12. https://www.google.com/chrome/
13. https://www.protractortest.org/
14. https://cucumber.io/
15. http://appium.io/
16. Korsaa, M., et al.: The SPI Manifesto and the ECQA SPI manager certification scheme. J. Softw.: Evol. Process **24**(5), 525–540 (2012)
17. Messnarz, R., et al.: Social responsibility aspects supporting the success of SPI. J. Softw.: Evol. Process **26**(3), 284–294 (2014)
18. Sanchez-Gordon, M.L., Colomo-Palacios, R., Amescua, A.: Towards measuring the impact of the SPI Manifesto: a systematic review. In: Proceedings of European System and Software Process Improvement and Innovation Conference, pp. 100–110 (2013)

Experiences with a Compliance-Assuring Framework for Decentralized Process Management in a Large Agile Organization

Markus Meichau(✉)

Bosch Software Innovations GmbH, Ullsteinstraße 128, 12109 Berlin, Germany
markus.meichau@bosch-si.com

Abstract. The tayloristic approach of applying centralized processes falls short in volatile and agile environments. In hastily diverting and changing environments, it's foremost biggest asset – the unified optimization – turns into an unbearable burden. This paper illustrates a more agile approach to process management applicable to both small and large organizations at the example of an existing solution for software development processes. Instead of a centralized one-size-fits-all process itself, a risk based framework of process requirements is provided centrally whilst the valid processes themselves are defined and maintained at the most local level. This approach enables both flexibility and compliance even in highly volatile environments as organizations in the midst of an agile transformation.

Keywords: Agile process management · Local process ownership
Process maturity · Process requirement framework · Agile transformation

1 Introduction

Large organizations, large corporations in particular, tend to stack huge piles of internal standards, regulations and somehow obligatory processes over the years. This pile of regulations tends to be frightening when encountered for the first time. Especially when an agile startup is merged into a cooperation after a successful acquisition. The agile, pragmatic habits of a startup necessarily conflict with the elaborated and optimized regulation of a huge cooperation. The clash of cultures seems to be inevitable. For the one culture to persist, the other has to vanish. But has it?

The essence of these internal standards and regulations are quite often not the issue. Years, decades and even centuries of valuable experience are cast into these regulations. A value that can be clearly seen and easily adopted by agile teams as well once it has been explained properly. Unlike the traditional habits of large corporations, uncovering and utilizing this value in an agile environment needs a different set of skills and proceedings of which we will present our solution to in this paper.

We will show how a centrally maintained framework of processual requirements can enable a team local development process ownership that is agile, compliant and cutting edge. We will furthermore illustrate how this approach can embrace the agility of the agile methodologies and unite it with more sophisticated high-level process improvements.

X. Larrucea et al. (Eds.): EuroSPI 2018, CCIS 896, pp. 410–420, 2018.
https://doi.org/10.1007/978-3-319-97925-0_34

2 Challenges of Agile Methods

2.1 How Agile Organizations Differ from Hierarchical Ones

Agile organizations are, in their core, highly focused on the customer and the value stream. All functions not directly assigned to the value stream itself are to be aligned to support it. All of them - up to the top management – have to serve the process to create customer value and those who perform it. In our case as a software company, this clearly means supporting the software development process and the software developers who perform it [6]. As one might easily assume transforming a hierarchically structured organization into an agile company is a complex and painful process. Lastly, it requires nothing less than turning the hierarchical pyramid upside down to let it face directly to the customer rather than to the will of the upper management [1].

One of the key roles in this agile transformation lies in the sometimes-misunderstood concept of "servant leadership" [1]. "Servant leadership" does not subject the leaders under the will of their former subordinates but has to be perceived as a supportive leadership to enable them to get the best out of their abilities. Enhancing the role of the developers does not naturally come with a degradation of the leadership roles but shifts their focus from a more commanding to a more consulting and exemplary role [6]. Due to this role shift, persuasion, motivation and the ability to elucidate, become key skills for all kinds of leaders in agile organizations. Traditional command and control functions vanish and are to be replaced by supportive and consulting roles.

2.2 Process and Quality Management in an Agile Environment

As with all roles that are not directly contributing to the value stream, Process and Quality Management has to revise its role in an agile organization. Although it might be mainly seen as a burden to the development by some developers, it actually still plays a vital role in ensuring the adherence to essential standards and regulations. One of its core remaining roles is to make the valuable experiences cast into the regulations and standards clear and accessible to those working directly on the value stream.

To fit into its role in the agile organization, its way of communicating and introducing its legal, regulatory and processual requirements (process requirements) has to adapt to a more supportive and empowering way rather than just setting rules. Any regulation in an agile organization has at least to try to convince those involved. Making both the intention of a regulation and the effect of not following it transparent is key to success. Process and Quality Management in an agile organization has to revise all its regulation under the proposition of the following questions:

- Why does this regulation exist? What is its basic intention?
- How does it affect the value stream?
- Does the intention justify the effects to value generation (e.g. extra efforts)?
- Could the negative effects on the value stream be minimized or better aligned with the agile methodology while still upholding the requirements?

Following these questions, the widespread methodology of defining and optimizing software development processes centrally has been revised and found no longer to be sufficient. In ever diverse and volatile environment, any attempt to optimize through a – however elaborated - one-size-fits-all approach is doomed.

3 Process Management in an Agile Environment

3.1 The Agile Methodology and the SPI Manifesto

Although sometimes perceived differently, the often quoted first point of the agile manifesto

INDIVIDUALS AND INTERACTION over processes and tools [3]

does not condemn processes or process optimization. The opposite is true. Constant short running inspect and adapt cycles are the core essence of the agile methodology. What it most certainly does is prioritizing. So does the SPI manifesto. If 'only the active involvement of the people working in an organization ensures the success' [2] and 'what you do [is] to make business successful NOT to live to deploy a standard' [2] both the agile and SPI manifesto are aligned. The priority is not and cannot be optimizing or following a process for the sake of the process.

The SPI as given in the SPI manifesto can broadly contribute to process management in an agile environment if it acts as a partner to the agile methodology rather than an opponent. Accepting and embracing the diversity and volatility of the implementations of agile methodologies rather than attempting to 'domesticate' and unify them is key. The agile methodology already provides all fundamentals needed for a successful software process improvement. It in fact inherently contains SPI mechanisms with its embracement of change, its constant drive for improvement, its broad commitment and its clear focus on business and customer value. All it needs to thrive is room to evolve and support to align.

3.2 Why Centralized Processes Do not Work for Agile Software Development

The main idea behind centralizing value stream processes is a tayloristic one. This approach had its biggest success in assembly lines where simply taking a stopwatch and optimizing every single movement could reduce efforts in large magnitudes [4]. It is ideal for simple manual tasks but inappropriate for any creative work [5]. Unfortunately, writing software is exactly that – a creative work. Experience shows, that stopwatch optimized processes are not applicable to software development.

If this kind of optimization has never been working for software development, there had to be another reason for applying centralized processes to it. We found this reason to lie plainly in the assurance to fulfill all applying process requirements throughout the development process. If every step to be taken is predefined, it is quite unlikely to forget any. Therefore, the core essence of defining centralized processes in software development lies in its ability to ensure all given process requirements are fulfilled.

The biggest advantage of agile methods on the other hand lies in its ability to adapt almost immediately to any kind of change. To be successful in volatile markets, agile methods rely heavily on immediate inspect and adapt cycles applied on the most local level. In environments like this, the minimal optimization effect of centralized processes completely diminishes and turns itself into a disadvantage for processes cannot be adapted at a reasonable speed. Therefore, other methods have to be found to ensure all process requirements to be fulfilled. We consider the INST Software Development Policy to be such a method.

3.3 Process Management on the Most Local Level

If the strength of the agile methodology lies in its ability to adapt to changes even on the most local level, the management of the software development processes has to be transferred there in order to profit from this strength. This transfer should not only include the management, but the ownership of the according software development processes as well. This is not only fully aligned with the basic principles of agile software development but fundamental in an ever diverse and volatile environment.

With having the software development process definition and ownership on a very local level, a huge variety of different implementations might come up. Every team itself might follow a slightly different approach for their software development. However, this is not necessarily bad. Applying a variety of different solutions to a variety of different challenges seems to be more fitting than any - however elaborated - one-size-fits-all approach.

Nonetheless, all of these different software development processes should ensure the fulfilment of all applying process requirements. Moreover, it should be clear which process requirements are actually applying. To be able to do so, all process requirements and their degree of application have to be both known and understood on the local level as well. Therefore, following a likewise approach requires well-edited and processed process requirements and a clear set of applicability rules. How such a set of process requirements and rules might look like and how their adequate application can be effectively assured is illustrated in the INST Software Development Policy presented this paper.

3.4 Alignment of Local Level SPIs

Once the definition and ownership of the software development process is done at the most local level, its improvement should be executed there as well. The constantly run inspect and adapt cycles are hereby the core element of the local SPI while adaptions to the framework of process requirements can be used to guide the improvement throughout the whole organization.

4 INST Software Development Policy

4.1 Historical Background

As most business units within Bosch, Bosch Software Innovations (INST) used to have a centrally defined product development process (PEP) – our software development process. Due to differences in the proceedings, a second software development process was added while entering the new business area of cloud services. Therefore, in early 2017 there were two centrally defined software development processes in place intended to cover the full variety of projects at INST.

Although these two processes were quite broadly defined, brief interviews conducted in almost half of our 30+ developing teams of four to ten developers found more than a dozen different flavors of software development processes in the field. Although most of them where quite similar, they were scarcely covered by our two centrally defined processes. Additionally internal audits found that a few other – particularly very small – projects did not follow any defined process at all.

At this point action had to be taken. Given these all these insights and the broad application of agile software development methods throughout the teams, the old proceeding of maintaining centralized software development processes seemed no longer to be helpful. Redefining our centralized software development processes or adding new ones would barely relieve some of the symptoms but could not cure the underlying affliction. As argued in Chap. 3, the further application of centralized software development processes has found to be insufficient in the given volatile and agile business environment. Change was inevitable.

4.2 Placement in the Process Landscape

The centralized software development processes - and hence the INST Software Development Policy that replaces them - cover all process requirements regarding the process of software development itself. This includes all activities performed to transform functional and nonfunctional requirements into software artefacts as well as according validation, verification and documentation tasks. Any other preceding (e.g. customer acquisition and project setup), adjacent (e.g. project and resource management) or subsequent (e.g. market launch and operation) activities are not covered by the INST Software Development Policy but other processes and therefore not discussed here.

4.3 Basic Rules for the INST Software Development Policy

For the INST Software Development to succeed, it had to follow and set a basic set of rules we consider elementary for it and any likewise regulations. The core essence of these rules is to improve the acceptability of the policy through maximum transparency, commitment and fairness. This chapter outlines these rules accordingly.

- **Equitable rules for everyone.** Although a variety of topics and fields will lead to a variety of well-fitting solutions, the basic framework of process requirements applies for everyone developing software – no matter how small or big the project.
- **No software development outside of this policy.** Projects running fully off record bear an incalculable risk and can therefore not be tolerated at any time.
- **Single source of process requirements.** All internal and external regulations regarding software development have to be incorporated into the policy. The policy will only be found the useful first contact source for process requirements if it provides all necessary information at once.
- **Evident and transparent process requirements.** All process requirements defined in the policy have to be clear and comprehensible. They have to be worded with regard to their target audience.
- **Risk based tailoring.** Although the convention of equitable rules for everyone is elementary for this policy, this does not imply a one-size-fits-all approach. The applicable process requirements are to be tailored with regard to both the economical and reputational impact of the project. The policy defines according tailoring rules.
- **Local ownership.** The responsibility for defining and maintaining the software development process lies with the instance that sets the rules and restrictions for a developing team. In some cases, this refers to the according project manager, in others to the team itself. This so-called process owner can adapt the software development process at any time.
- **Supportive agile assessment.** To preserve the important four-eyes principle and guarantee the fulfilment of all applying process requirements, the central Quality and Process Management assesses the locally defined software development process and changes to it in a supportive and agile manner.

4.4 Software Development Process Maturity

As mentioned earlier, the set of applying process requirements differs due to the economical and reputational risks imposed by the project. Accordingly, five successive classes of projects have been defined based on the project size and economical and reputational impact. This approach enables to apply a gradually improving set of process requirements on projects of these classes. Since we consider following a certain set of process requirements to be a grade of maturity, the according classes have been named 'maturity level'. With regard to project size and economical and reputational impact, minimum maturity levels have been defined for the processes these projects follow. Table 1 shows how different project specifics require different minimal maturity in the software development processes it follows.

The according process requirements for every maturity level are defined comprehensively within the INST Software Development Policy and the Quality and Process Management assesses their fulfilment on a regular base.

Table 1. Minimum maturity levels.

Minimum maturity level required	Project specifics
Maturity level 0	Only for rapid prototyping or proof of concept. *A productive use* of any outcome of a maturity level 0 process *is prohibited*
Maturity level 1	Only for small projects or projects of minor economic impact and reputation risks
Maturity level 2	Minimum set of process requirements for regular software development of all type except of high economic and reputation risks and projects with continuous delivery
Maturity level 3	Minimum set of process requirements for any software development with continuous delivery or of high economic and reputation risks
Maturity level 3+	Process requirements for extraordinary high development standards

4.5 Local Software Development Process Maturity

The software development processes are both defined and owned at the most local level with regard to who defines the rules and restrictions for the development. This might be the project lead or even the developing team itself. The habits defined in the software development process constitutes its maturity. According maturity levels are awarded to the teams with regard to their processes. These awarded maturity levels come in the form of something like ‘The processes team x follows awards them the allowance to perform projects up to minimally required maturity level y’ and are revoked if the team no longer follows their process or changed their process in a way that no longer justifies the awarded maturity level.

Given that the maturity levels are successive, a team following a more mature process can easily work on projects of lower minimum maturity process requirements. A team with less mature software development processes than required will on the other hand have to adapt their processes to be able to take on projects of higher minimum maturity process requirements.

Since following a more mature process includes additional efforts, some teams might require being able to switch between different processes for different projects they are engaged in. Since all process requirements are transparent, such teams might define a set of steps to be easily skipped at smaller projects within their process description and therefore maintain one process instead of a set of processes.

Teams that do not intend to define or adapt their own software development processes are provided with several exemplary processes as templates. These exemplary processes are fit to distinctive maturity levels and can be used out of the box. They can be as well used as starting points for the definition or adaption of more team specific processes.

4.6 Software Development Process Requirements

To be able to use the definitions in the INST Software Development Policy as the primary, let alone, single source of process requirements for software development processes, the process requirements of a set of different internal and external regulations and standards had to be collected and aggregated into the policy. This included international standards like ISO 20000 as well as several Bosch internal standards. We unified, grouped and listed their collective process requirements in a list of 49 potentially applicable process requirements. In the rephrasing and unification of the process requirements, we found the following three rules to be very useful:

Intelligibility Is Key
Each of the process requirements has to be summarized and rephrased in a manner that deemes appropriate for both managers and developers. This not just includes the rephrasing itself but the provision of the underlying rationale and indicators for the approval as well.

Each process requirement in the listing contains

- a punchy headline
- a more detailed description
- a rationale (including links to the underlying source of the requirement) and
- a set of applicable indicators or quantifications for the approval.

All of these sections are primarily phrased with a clear focus on the targeted users. Its main goal is to enable the managers and developers to understand and fulfil the intention of the applying regulations rather than following them word by word.

Clearly Recognizable Applicability
The minimum maturity level requiring the particular process requirement is clearly marked in the list of process requirements (see Fig. 1). To ensure best usability, the detailed descriptions are collapsed by default leaving only the headlines and the applicability for a certain maturity level visible.

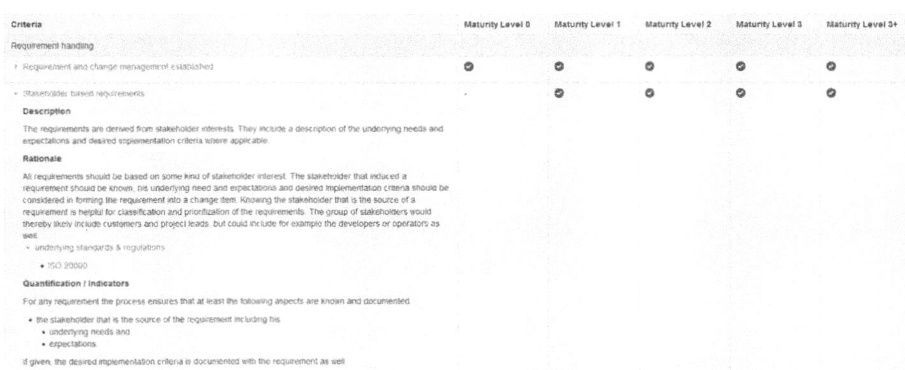

Fig. 1. Display of collapsed and expanded process requirements in the List of software development process requirements.

This ensures easy access to the most important information of what process requirement is applicable for the according maturity level but still keeps detailed information instantly at hand.

Sequential Grouping

As the total number of 49 process requirements might be obfuscating, a clear grouping has been added to improve the locating of single process requirements. The grouping hereby is derived from the most common sequential steps in software development leaving the groups at process requirements regarding

- Requirement handling
- Technical and information security risk management
- Review and acceptance
- Software architecture
- Software analysis
- Software filing, packaging and deployment
- Feedback and stakeholder involvement
- Software operation and support
- Skill management and knowledge transfer.

4.7 Software Development Process Assessments

Handing over the ownership of the software developing processes to the most local level results in both bigger levels of freedom and the necessity for approvals to avoid unintended misuse. As the four-eyes principle is a widely spread technique throughout the agile community motivating the need for these approvals has proven to be easy. To keep its acceptance at these high levels, a supportive approach for the process assessments is vital.

The assessments are conducted through evidence based inspective interviews with the according process owner. Hereby the process owner is free to apply for any maturity level and his process is evaluated against all applying process requirements. The assessments are based on the given process requirements and on their indicators and quantifications in particular. While major findings prevent the awarding of a maturity level, maturity levels can be conditionally awarded for three months if minor findings occur. Within the period of conditional awarding, the identified findings have to be fixed to gain a regular maturity level. If the assessment is successful, it both approves and awards the requested maturity level. The resulting assessment documents have proven to be useful evidences in both internal and external audits.

Assessments were defined to be obligatory at the initial setup of a process, any major changes to the process and a recurrent interval of two years. It has to be emphasized that while bigger changes make an assessment obligatory, these changes only trigger a so-called ‘delta assessment’ that focusses solely on the recent changes to avoid unnecessary efforts. The full-blown regular assessments only take place on request or every two years.

5 Experiences

Before putting the INST Software Development Policy into regulation, the processes actually in place have been reviewed in more than the half of our 30+ developing teams. As stated earlier, we found the most of them being barely aligned with our old centralized processes. Nonetheless, an exemplary application of the Software Development Policy has shown a great level of compliance to the underlying process requirements. We did not just found the processes of all teams assessed to be compliant with the applicable process requirements of their regarding minimum maturity level, but we found the majority of them to be more, sometimes even much more, mature than minimally required.

We indeed did found some areas of non-compliance every now and then, but none of these where severe. We could easily and successfully point them out and initiate team based process adoptions that removed them. The newly gained empowering and degrees of freedom showed to be highly motivating for everyone involved. Not only did the teams more lightly agree on improving their processes where necessary, but also some of them even targeted for processes of higher levels of maturity than required. Being shown the opportunities for improvement motivated them to find even better and more fitting solutions.

Given the different approach of focusing on specific process requirements rather than the obedient execution of a centrally given process, we experienced a huge shift in the communication. It proved to be much more successful to discuss and defend given process requirements than to persist in processual accuracy with regard to a centrally defined process. The discussion totally shifted from the 'how to do it' to the 'what to do and why'. This shift in communication patterns has proven to provide much higher levels of acceptance for the applying regulations. 'Translating' the process requirements to the common wording of the audience has proven to be a big plus for this as well.

Given the already high level of compliance on the level of the single process requirement, we figured out, that shifting from the old centralized development processes to the INST Software Development Policy seemed much easier than originally expected. The very most of the agile teams did not have to apply bigger changes to their already existing processes, but could just keep them and improve from where they were. The main, but manageable, work lied in documenting the existing state of the art so it could be used as evidence for both the assessment and internal and external audits.

The most of the smaller projects, that tried to exist 'below radar' to avoid the application of the full-blown centralized software development process beforehand, now have an opportunity to define lean and fitting processes themselves. They can get out of the 'grey zone' they tried to exist in and no longer have to worry about 'getting caught'. Some of them already applied fitting processes while others are on their way. The now more clear communication that everyone who produces software for someone else to use – no matter how big or small the project - has to follow the INST Software Development Policy and that this policy is no one-size-fits-all approach spread words. As result, we already came out more compliant although we are still in the midst of the rollout process of the policy. For the most of the bigger teams their formerly often undocumented and unapproved deviations to the old centralized processes disappeared. Their now more clearly and transparently defined processes fit well into the INST Software Development Policy and reflect their real working habits. Several smaller projects on the other hand used the opportunity and assistance offered to define fitting light-weighted processes to reflect and improve their work. This even included team in areas uncommon to follow software development processes as the quality assurance or operations department. Therefore and throughout all projects, process definitions and reality match much better and aberrations to the underlying process requirements are detected early on and usually dissolved by the teams themselves.

6 Expectations and Outlook

We are currently rolling out the INST Software Developing Policy right now and will finally remove the last centralized software development processes by end of 2018. We expect to see further adaptations of the policy and its process requirements throughout the rollout process and in the upcoming years as its definition is a living and agile process as well. We expect to see even further improvements in both the alignment and compliance throughout the whole company.

With the growing application of the policy, we expect to see a growing set of best practices and pre-existing processes that can be used as examples for other teams. We do not expect to experience an ever-growing variety of processes in our process landscape but a rather converging landscape of a hand full of well working processes.

With the growing application agile principles throughout the company and Bosch as a whole, we expect to see a spread of the underlying principle of agile process management both horizontally and vertically. The process of spreading this Software Development Policy throughout and beyond the Bosch already started. We do expect to see and provide similar principles for other processes that might profit from greater agility and diversity. Beyond others, this might include adjacent processes as the project management or sales and acquisition process.

References

1. Greenleaf, R.K., Spears, L.C., Vaill, P.B.: The Power of Servant-Leadership. Berrett-Koehler Publishers, Oakland (1998)
2. Pries-Heje, J., Johansen, et al. (eds.) SPI Manifesto. Alcala 2010. http://2018.eurospi.net/images/eusospi/spi_manifesto.pdf. Accessed 8 Jun 2018
3. Manifesto for Agile Software Development. http://www.agilemanifesto.org. Accessed 8 Jun 2018
4. Taylor, F.W.: The Principles of Scientific Management. Harper & Brothers, London (1911)
5. Pink, D.H.: Drive: The Surprising Truth About What Motivates Us. Riverhead Books, New York (2009)
6. Appelo, J.: Management 3.0: Leading Agile Developers, Developing Agile Leaders. Addison-Wesley Professional, Boston (2011)

How to Assure Agile Method and Process Alignment in an Organization?

Alexander Poth(✉) and Mario Kottke(✉)

Volkswagen AG, Berliner Ring 2, 38436 Wolfsburg, Germany
{alexander.poth,mario.kottke}@volkswagen.de

Abstract. After rollout agile methods to an organization with many teams the question is how aligned are these agile teams to the organizational process framework and the team specific internal agile procedures. To address this question and fullfill requirements of the ISO 9000 context the Agile Center of Excellence of Volkswagen AG introduced in 2017 the agile project review. This review is applied to random samples of projects and make the results transparent in a gamification fashion.

Keywords: Agile software development · Agile transition
Quality management · Quality assurance (QA) · Qualification
Integrated quality approach · Gamification of quality metrics/indicators

1 Motivation and Context for the Demand of an Agile Project Reviews

Agile methods and procedures are only one kind of process implementation from the perspective of the ISO 9000 and other standards. An organization, which have to fit to quality standards like the ISO 9000 have to demonstrate its continuous improvement procedure and an internal quality check procedure. After the rollout of lean [KANBAN] and agile methods and procedures [AGPI] by the Agile Center of Excellence (ACE) to many projects [POTH15] over the past years the "pilot" status of the few early adopters has gone. To fulfill the expectations to be compliant to established standard the ACE has to setup a procedure for cyclic checks about the current implementation of relevant quality management (QM) procedures. Furthermore, the governance responsibility of the ACE as owner of the agile change in the Volkswagen Group IT requires an establishment of a continuous improvement procedure.

Both formal procedures, the QM and the continuous improvement procedure, will described here. To have a lean and effective implementation of both formal procedures the ACE developed them in one operational procedure. This operational procedure is called agile project review. The agile project review is applied to randomized samples, which are "drawn" by a public tombola in the monthly agile community of the Volkswagen Group IT. The "winners" have the chance to get professional feedback from the agile project reviewer team. The top 3 projects are listed on the "champions league" to show the benchmark to all projects and motivate with this gamification approach the projects to improve their results for future agile project reviews.

X. Larrucea et al. (Eds.): EuroSPI 2018, CCIS 896, pp. 421–425, 2018.
https://doi.org/10.1007/978-3-319-97925-0_35

2 Development of the Agile Project Review Procedure

The ACE decides to develop the procedure in an open fashion, which invites all agile project review "candidates" to design the review. To realize this in an agile community, which happens monthly, the working group was setup. Over months, the working group developed the agile project review in an iterative fashion and got feedback from the agile community in which milestones were presented and discussed. The focus was not to develop a formal assessment model like or oriented on the ISO/IEC 33000. The focus was to define a lightweight review model for a quick deep dive into agile projects and give feedback about the status quo of the established agile mindset [AGMA], the procedures of the project and the alignment of agile teams to the organizational process framework. The documentation and expected outcomes are not as formalized like in the Automotive SPICE because the reviewer team is nominated of a pool of agile guides or coaches of the Volkswagen Group IT. These coaches are working have their communities of practice to align their values and mindset. This makes it easier to conduct the reviews with only a short introduction (training on the job) into the agile project review approach. A complex training like the intacs certifications is not needed.

3 Deep Dive into the Agile Project Review

After presentation of the demand and the development procedure, this chapter presents the agile project review more detailed. This chapter is like a how to derive an own agile project review which fits the demands of your environment.

3.1 The Categories

The working group defined after some discussions and feedbacks the categories of the agile project review. The working group defined the categories generic to address teams at different levels of the spiral dynamics model [BEC05]. The categories are:

(a) The customer satisfaction: check if and how often customer feedbacks are collected and evaluate the adequateness of tasks, which are derived from the feedbacks
(b) The artefacts: looks about the agile artefacts like Definition of Done (DoD), backlog structure, story format and structure and so on
(c) The events: checks the establishment of agile procedures like for scrum [SCRUM] about at least the backlog refinement, sprint planning, daily and the retrospective but also it look for cycle time and other processual aspects
(d) The process: looks about the establishment of agile rituals like feedback culture, realize continuous improvement and so on
(e) The product safeguarding: check the application of the DoD, evidences for acceptance criteria and CI/CD capability of test-automation or defects in production

(f) The alignment to the standard development process: checks some of the important process outcomes of the Volkswagen Group IT development process for a minimum alignment

To answer the question how aligned are agile teams to the organizational process framework, therfore part (f) is relevant. To inspect the team specific internal agile procedures, than part (a)–(e) is relevant.

For rating, four levels are defined. Higher is better. The zero, as neutral element, is applied to categories, which are not applicable in an agile projected review due to specific restrictions.

Figure 1 shows an example of rated categories and one category is not rated and set to zero.

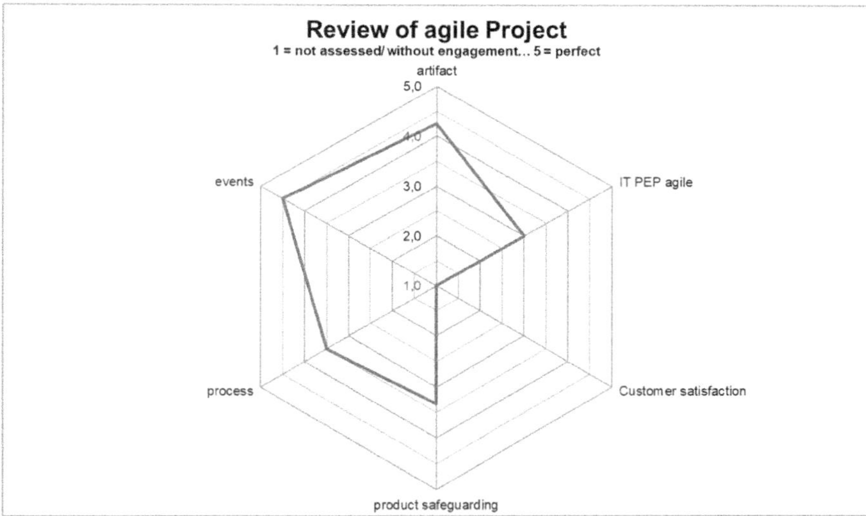

Fig. 1. An example of a rating of the categories

During model development, the working group specialists reflected the definitions with their real life experience to assure that the right focus is set.

3.2 Examples from the Questionnaire and the Review Procedure

The amount of check aspects differs between the categories. The amount is depending on the complexity of the categories and the aspects, which are focused for the agile project, review during model specification. To support the evaluation of the review team during an agile project review each aspect has some rating criteria's. For more help some examples are given in the additional evaluation help field. The working group defined the aspects and especially the evaluation help comments to address teams at different levels of the spiral dynamics model. The "maturity" of the project team leads to different approaches to address issues that should be have positive effects to the rating. Furthermore, the agile project review have to check the minimum requirements of standards like the formal approval of a release.

The Fig. 2 shows an example of the "check list" from the reviews perspective.

Category of Review	Purpose	Rating criteria	Rating information
IT-PEP-Agil	Documents from IT PEP agile are used and for all Stakeholder accessable	https://group-wiki.wob.vw.vwg/wikis/display/ITPEPAGIL/Dokumente+und+Tools	e.g. Projecthandbook, User Guide, Stakeholderanalysis, SHB, Project briefing ...

Fig. 2. An example of reviewer's evaluation sheet

3.3 The Gamification Approach

To make the agile project review results for benchmarking available the top 3 projects are listed on group level and region level. Region level mostly are locations like plants of the Volkswagen AG. Figure 3 shows a part of this champion's league table. The position depends on the average of the rating for the 6 categories, described in Sect. 3.1.

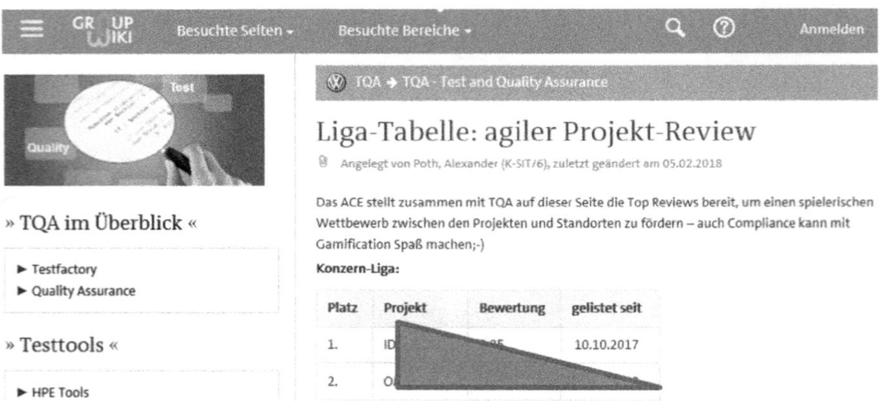

Fig. 3. Part of the champion's league page (in German)

3.4 Sampling of Projects

During the agile community, a tombola is celebrated/drawn to realize a transparent selection of the randomized agile project review samples. The tombola is filled up with lots of all as agile defined projects. As agile defined projects are projects with a positive agile readiness approval at the end of the ACE coaching phase. The amount of drowned lots is the workload of agile project reviews up to the next tombola.

Projects are for the time of implementing improvement actions not in the tombola. This period is approximately 6 months. After this time, the project can be volunteer or lucky winner of the tombola.

In addition, volunteer projects can request for an agile project review on top of the tombola winners to get an expert feedback about their current state of their agile journey.

3.5 The Agile Project Review and Its Next Steps

The review is announced to all project team members in the kick-off. The review itself is done on another day. Each review starts with the same question: How comes you and your team from the customer demand to customer satisfaction? During review the project team members show and tell their outcomes about the categories and aspects. The reviewer team logs the relevant comments and outcomes. In addition, the reviewer team ask for open or missing aspects. After the review the reviewer team, which consists of at least two experts, adjust their individual views to common and harmonized rating. The harmonized rating is communicated to the project team at the end of the agile project review. The project team defines based on the feedbacks by their own improvement actions to "fix findings" or to "rise potentials". The project driven improvement actions should be discussed about adequateness with the reviewer team before implementation. The reviewer team also analyse the agile project review results for structural deficits in the organization to trigger improvement actions on the organization level if needed. Furthermore, the agile community have always the right to initiate a working group to enhance or adjust the agile project review approach.

4 Conclusion

The ACE and the agile community have found a way to realize their governance responsibility. The setup and improvement of the agile project review is steered by the agile community. The selection of the samples is done completely transparent. The results of the agile project review is used for "local" project improvement and for "global" organization reflection and improvement. The feedback character of the agile project review approach gives a high acceptance by the projects, which have "won" the tombola up to now. The presented agile review approach also fits to the three believes of software process improvement (SPI) from [KOR12].

References

[AGMA] Sutherland et al. http://www.agilemanifesto.org

[AGPI] Sutherland et al. http://agilemanifesto.org/principles.html

[BEC05] Beck, D.E., Cowan, C.: Spiral Dynamics: Mastering Values. Leadership and Change. Wiley-Blackwell, Hoboken (2005). ISBN 978-1-4051-3356-2

[KANBAN] Anderson, C.: Essential KANBAN condensed. http://leankanban.com/guide/

[POTH15] Poth, A.: Effectivity and economical aspects for agile quality assurance in large enterprises. In: 22nd European Asia Systems & Software Process Improvement and Innovation Conference 2015 (EuroAsiaSPI 2015), Ankara, Turkey (2015)

[KOR12] Korsaa, M., et al.: The SPI manifesto and the ECQA SPI manager certification scheme. J. Softw. Evol. Process **24**(5), 525–540 (2012)

[SCRUM] Sutherland, S.: The official Scrum Guide. http://www.scrumguides.org/scrum-guide.html

Being Agile While Coaching Teams Using Their Own Data

Marcos Pacheco[1], Antoni-Lluís Mesquida[2(✉)], and Antònia Mas[2]

[1] Agile Coach & Trainer, Mallorca, Spain
mpacheco1988@gmail.com
[2] Department of Mathematics and Computer Science, University of the Balearic Islands, Cra. de Valldemossa, Km 7.5, 07122 Palma de Mallorca, Spain
{antoni.mesquida, antonia.mas}@uib.es

Abstract. This paper presents a case study of a Scrum team that decided to establish metrics to be aware of its way of working. Visual Agile, is a software tool to support Agile coaching, which has been developed to monitor and control the values for the metrics established by the team. The interpretation of these metrics can be helpful to build team awareness and facilitate constant delivery of value. The tool is considered by the case study team as a basic asset to have objective inputs to find improvement opportunities.

Keywords: Agile coaching · Metrics · Software tool
Software process improvement

1 Introduction

Agile teams and, specially, Scrum teams use to give great importance to the collaboration between the members of the team and to the constant delivery of value [1]. In a Scrum team, there should not be silos which does not mean there are no specializations [2].

It should be avoided that team members have the perception that when they finish "their" work, they should do the "work of others". All members are responsible for the team's work, from the beginning of a task until it is finished [3, 4]. It is really a complicated challenge to make the team understand that all members must feel responsible for the software the team creates and, also, for its quality [5].

In a software development team that works by sprints, each task usually goes through two phases: development and testing. It usually happens that the team assigns to Quality Assurance (QA) the responsibility of guaranteeing the quality of the deliverable, as if the rest of the team did not have any competence on the testing phase. This view is wrong because the value chain is not completed until the testing has been carried out [6]. Therefore, the entire team should be responsible for the task from the start of its development until the testing phase is completed [7]. The previous situation, very common in many teams and projects, occurs due to a misinterpretation of the role of QA. Actually, the responsibility of QA is to provide the adequate infrastructure so that the team can guarantee the quality of the product developed and tested throughout the value chain [8].

X. Larrucea et al. (Eds.): EuroSPI 2018, CCIS 896, pp. 426–436, 2018.
https://doi.org/10.1007/978-3-319-97925-0_36

Teams do not tend to be aware of the impact that can be generated by the way they work [9]. One of the impacts that should be thoroughly analysed is the creation of queues. Queues can take place in different parts of a Scrum team. They usually occur when a link in the value chain finishes the work, assuming that the next steps are no longer his/her concern [10]. This approach is undesirable; the team must be a whole. Although team members have different specializations and responsibilities, they must work in the same direction, avoiding silos and feeling responsible for all aspects that may affect the final quality of the product [11, 12].

It could be very useful to be able to represent in some way the economic impact that queues cause in the organization [13]. One of the most accepted terms to evaluate what is left to win due to the existence of queues is Cost of Delay. Cost of Delay has the power to transform the mind-set of organisations. It evaluates the cost of queues, the value of excess capacity, the benefit of smaller batch sizes and the value of variability reduction. Reinertsen reports than $\sim$85% of product managers do not know the Cost of Delay [14].

In addition to the Cost of Delay, there are other metrics that can be established in a team to let it know the way it works and to facilitate decision making. Some of these metrics are Cycle time, Lead time, Flow efficiency, Cumulative flow diagram, Burndown Chart, Throughput, among others [14].

This paper presents a case study of the metrics defined by a Scrum team to be aware of its way of working. Visual Agile, is an internal software tool which has been developed to collect data and graphically represent the values for the metrics established in the team. These metrics are used, on the one hand, to build team awareness and, on the other, to constantly deliver value.

The case study team is composed by a group of six developers, one Product Owner, one QA engineer and one Scrum Master. The team focuses its efforts on the development of an internal CRM. The roles in the team are the traditional roles of Scrum, development team, Product Owner and Scrum Master. Nevertheless, within the team there are different specialities: Front-End, Back-End developers and one QA Engineer. The average age of the team is 29 and most of the team members have been working together for already 2 years.

This paper is organized as follows. Section 2 presents the metrics established in the case study team. Section 3 shows how Visual Agile can be used by a team to get metrics and to interpret the results. Finally, Sect. 4 opens discussion about the vision of the case study team and concludes the paper.

2 Metrics Established in the Case Study Team

The definition and use of metrics can be helpful to demonstrate the progress of the team. It is true that the need for metrics will depend on each particular organization and work team. The case study team was willing to define and use metrics, as their members agreed that it is better to be driven by the power of proof than by assumptions. This reasoning is aligned with the principle "Base improvement on experience and measurements" of the SPI Manifesto [15].

The first step of the team for defining the metrics was to identify the factors that contribute to valuable metrics. Four factors were considered:

- Raise Warnings: metrics should warn when certain number is reached, in a good way or in a bad way but they should help to see that something happened.
- Drive Behaviour: metrics should have an impact in the people behaviour, should make members feel willing for a change.
- Teach: metrics should help to understand what's going on. They should help to learn and to understand how the system works.
- Expire or Recycle: metrics should be replaced when they are old, or at least, they should be recycled. They have to be checked periodically to find out if they still make sense.

In the case study team the following metrics were defined, all of them considering the four factors above:

- *Flow efficiency*: Given a work item or a process, the efficiency is calculated based in the amount of time used in "working" and the amount of time in "waiting". Formula is Work Time/(Work Time + Waiting Time).
- *Cycle time*: It describes how long it takes to complete a specific task from the beginning to the end.
- *Lead time*: the time from the moment the customer places an order to the moment it is ready for delivery.
- *Tasks finished flow comparison*: Given the number of tasks finished, this metric shows how many of them were stopped or blocked at some point during the development and how many were not.
- *Reopens*: This metric shows how many tasks were reopened during the cycle time period. Reopens can come from other developers during code reviews or from the QA during the testing.
- *Time in status*: Each task can go through different statuses such as "In Progress", "In Code Review", "Blocked", "Stopped Progress", etc. This metric shows the average time spent in each of these statuses.
- *Time spent extremes*: It shows the tasks with most time spent in status where there is an active work being done (like "In Progress") and most time spent in status where there is no active work being done (like "Stopped Progress").

3 Visual Agile: A Tool for Agile Coaching

Even if the team uses a task management software such as Jira, all the information is not commonly available for free. Therefore, there comes the need to buy add-ons, such as eazyBi, in order to get all the information needed for a complete team management. Moreover, in Jira, workflows can get complicated. Users can have different workflows for different types of tasks in the same project. This fact adds complexity to the system and makes it harder for the team to be efficient.

In the case study team, with the main goal of making the members aware of the way how they were working, the Scrum Master designed and developed an ad-hoc software tool. Visual Agile is the name of this tool, which was built for gathering the data to calculate team efficiency metrics, and representing them in visual charts to facilitate further analysis and decision-making. Visual Agile is developed in Symfony 3.5 and uses MySql 5.6. The vendor used to connect to Jira API is madmis/jira-api.

The first action to be done in order to start using Visual Agile is to specify the project key. Based on the selected project key, a list of the different types of tasks will appear for the user to select. Examples of types of tasks are: "Bug", "Story", "Spike", etc. Next, a list of statuses in which can be a task are displayed. Examples of possible statuses are: "Ready for Development", "In Progress", "Stopped Progress", "In Code Review", "Pending for QA", "In QA". Once the statuses to be considered for checking have been selected, the next step is to start clustering them. The possible clusters are:

- Statuses that imply an active work being done, that produce value, like the status "In Progress".
- Statuses that not imply work being done and, therefore, no value is being generated, like the status "Blocked".
- Statuses that for the team mean that the task is finished, like "Released", "Resolved" or "Closed".
- Statuses used when a task is not able to continue moving forward through the system like "Stopped Progress".
- Statuses used to reopen tasks, like "Reopened".
- A cluster for the statuses that are used to get the Cycle time and the Lead time. Some possible statuses to calculate the Cycle time could be: "In Progress", "In QA", "Blocked" or "Done". And for the Lead time: "In Backlog", "Ready For Development", "In Progress", "In QA", "Blocked", "Done", among others.

The work hours range must be also specified. There are options to exclude non-working hours, weekends and bank holidays.

Finally, the tool has a field where a query, in Jira Query Language (JQL), indicating the project key needs to be introduced. Visual Agile will analyse all the tasks returned by the JQL.

Visual Agile works the same for two different scenarios: Scrum and Kanban teams. The difference is that for Scrum teams there is no need to introduce the periods of time. In this case, the tool automatically takes the start and end date of the sprint. For Kanban teams, the date ranges to compare should be specified. If, for example, the user want to check the whole year of a Kanban team, 12 date ranges, one per month, could be created.

The following subsections show the different metrics and associated charts that Visual Agile can generate.

3.1 Flow Efficiency

Figure 1 shows an example of the *Flow efficiency* diagram during four different periods (four sprints).

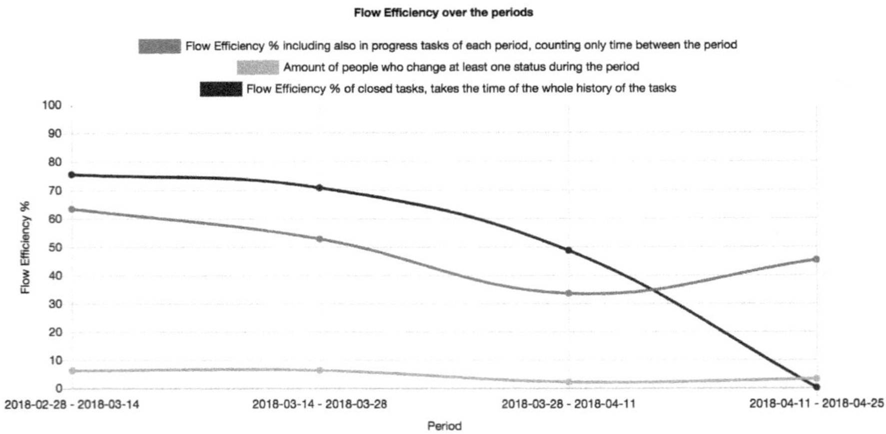

Fig. 1. Flow efficiency (Color figure online)

In Fig. 1, three data sets can be observed:

- Blue line shows the flow efficiency (Work Time/[Work Time + Waiting Time]) given the time spent in the statuses set as work being done and the statuses where there is not work being done. The blue line only counts the time spent during the period. This means that if a task was forgotten in "In Progress" during one month, it will count only the time that was "In Progress" during the sprint.
- Black line shows the flow efficiency of the tasks finished in each period, and it counts the whole life cycle of the task. In this case, if the task that was forgotten in "In Progress" it is finished in the third sprint, it will count all the time. The reason why in the last period is 0 is because no tasks were finished during that period.
- Orange line shows the amount of people that worked together during the period. It can be seen that in the third period there were less people working together. This sometimes could explain a drop in the flow efficiency.

This metric can be useful to measure how efficient is the team and how harmful can be certain problems we have in our system. Normally a good flow efficiency starts from 40%.

3.2 Cycle Time and Lead Time

Figure 2 presents the *Cycle and Lead times* of the tasks finished in each period. *Cycle time* is the amount of time spent since the team started to work on the item, that is since the task was moved to "In Progress". *Lead time* is since the team got the request, that is since the task was introduced into the system.

The example presented seems quite healthy, except the last period. The reason of why we have this gap between both lines is probably because the tasks finished were in the system for a long time before the team started to work on these tasks.

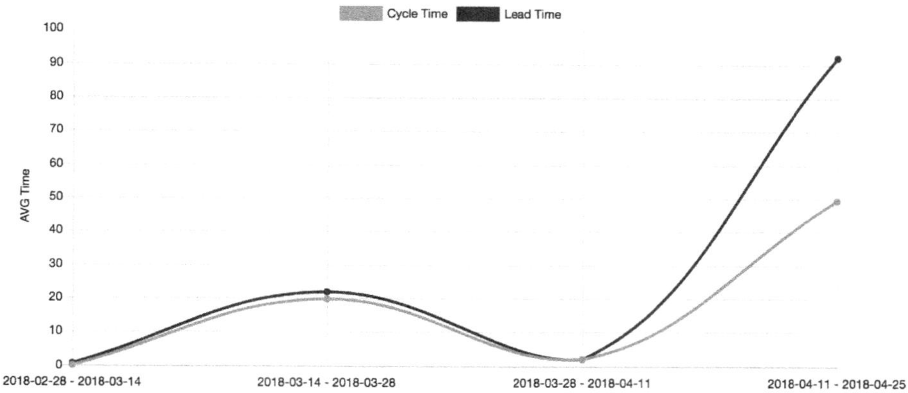

Fig. 2. Cycle time and lead time

The job of the Product Owner can be more visible here, because normally is the one who creates the tasks. This metric is very useful to see if the Product Owner is creating tasks too in advance, with the consequence of oversizing the backlog.

3.3 Tasks Finished Flow Comparison

Figure 3 shows the *Tasks finished flow comparison* during the four periods.

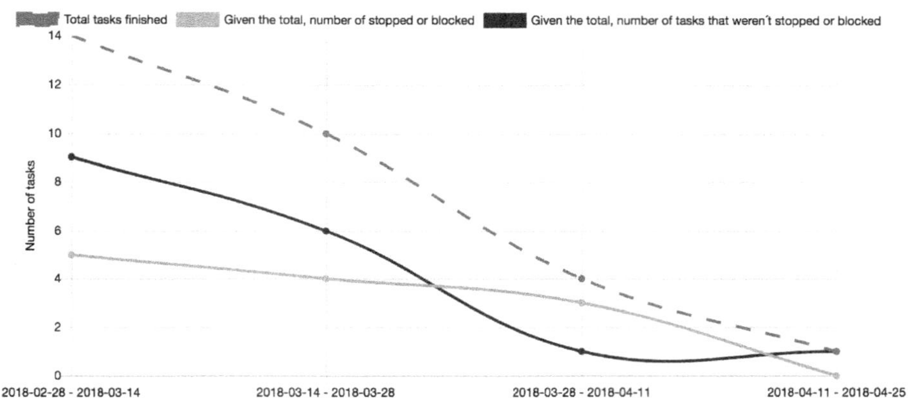

Fig. 3. Tasks finished flow comparison (Color figure online)

The chart contains three data sets:

- Blue line shows the number of tasks finished during each period.
- Orange line shows that given the total number of tasks finished, how many of them were stopped or blocked at some point during the period.

- Black line shows how many went "clean" through the system without being stopped or blocked.

Two important issues can be read from the chart:

- The team has been finishing less tasks over the last sprints.
- In the third sprint something happened that made almost all the tasks to be stopped or blocked.

Aspects like context switching can be reflected here, as the more context switching the team has, more times the team has to stop tasks already started in order to start others.

3.4 Reopens

Figure 4 shows how many *reopens* the team had during each period.

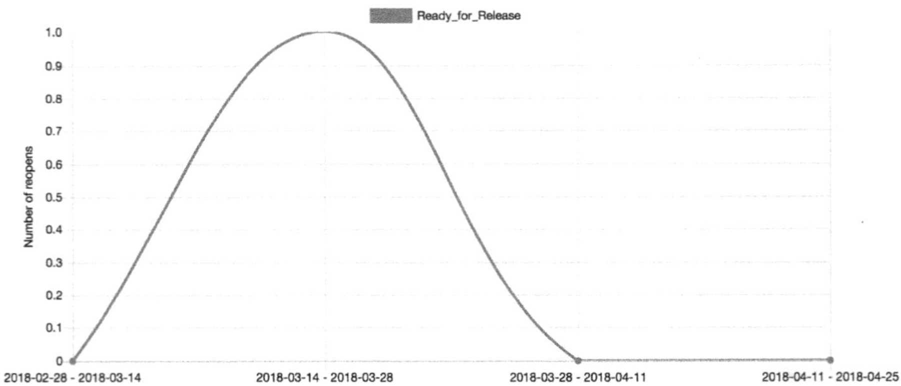

Fig. 4. Reopens

In this example, tasks are not being reopened, at least during the last four periods, except in the second where one task was reopened. The reopen came from the status "Ready For Release". Probably a bug was found or something important happened and blocked the release, so the task had to be reopened.

Reopens can come from different sources, from a code review, from a QA, etc. It can be quite useful for a team to see the reopens over the periods. For example, when a team is rushing to deliver a result without paying too much attention on the development, it could happen that the QA needs to reopen tasks to correct detected problems that are breaking the application.

3.5 Time in Status

Figure 5 shows the average *time spent in each status* of the tasks.

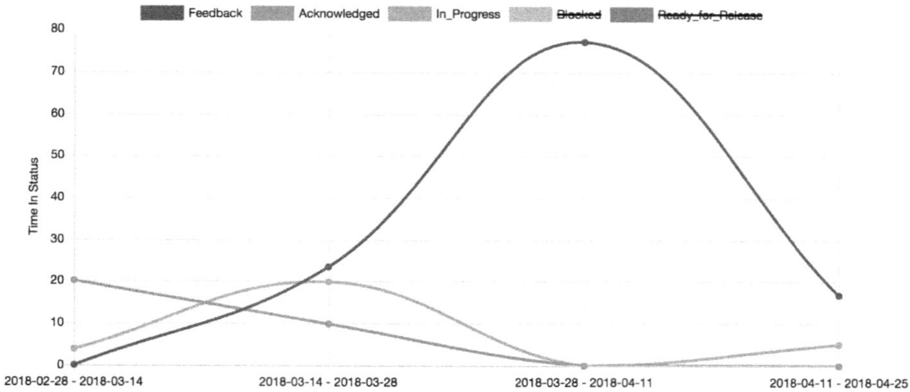

Fig. 5. Time in status

In this example, it can be seen that in the third period the team had a task in "Feedback" for a long time (75 h in average in this status; 9 working days). This fact, in consequence, would also affect to the flow efficiency.

With this metric, the team can detect patterns over the time. It is useful when the team has statuses that are queues in the workflow. Then, it is possible to see how harmful queues are for the system. If instead of in the status "Feedback" the task had been in the status "Ready for code review", this would mean that it takes a lot of time for the team to review each other code.

3.6 Time Spent Extremes

Figure 6 shows the tasks with most *time spent in no active work* (waiting) and most *time spent in active work*. In the charts, each colour is a task.

In order to get these two charts, the user needs to cluster in Visual Agile the statuses that represent work in progress and statuses that represent waiting time. It should be noted that it is neither good to have a task "In progress" 95% of the time of the sprint or a task "Blocked" 95% of the time of the sprint.

In the example, during the last period, two tasks were almost 80 h in one of the waiting status. This information can be useful in a retrospective meeting, where conflictive tasks could be identified.

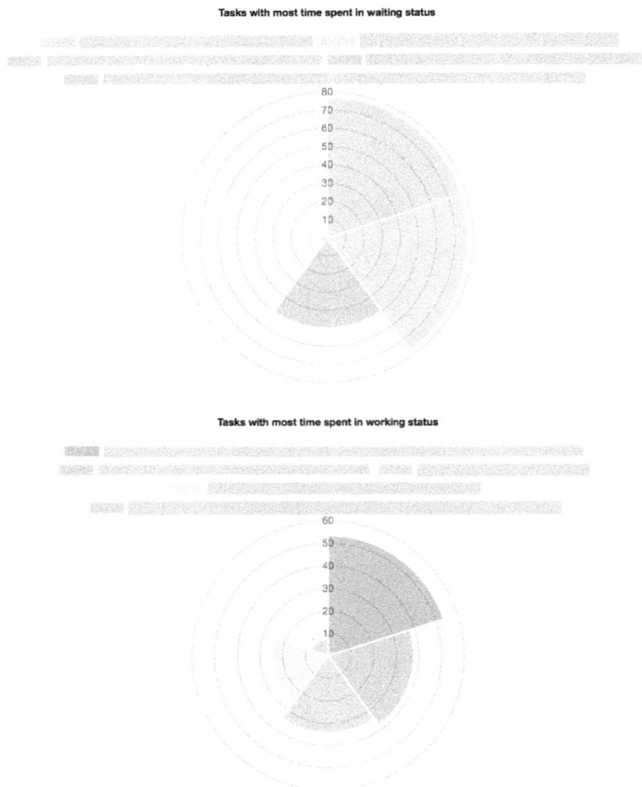

Fig. 6. Time spent extremes

4 Discussion and Conclusion

In the case study team, members liked a lot to know the values of the metrics provided by Visual Agile. The tool has become basic for them because gives the team many inputs when looking for improvement opportunities.

The main advantage for the Agile Coach of having this kind of metrics is that the impact on the team is immediate. The data is not an assumption. Data are the reality of the consequences of the team way of working, represented in figures. The team should be aware of how they are performing, because without measuring the system it is really hard to find improvement opportunities. If the team is able to measure all the wastes, queues or steps in the process that are not providing value, the team could even calculate the *cost of delay*. Calculating the cost of delay is not easy and specific skills are needed. However, it is critical for the organization to be conscious of the economic consequences of the way of working of the different teams.

One of the challenges of having metrics is to get to know how to use them. The first action to be done by the team is to try to explain itself the values obtained for the different metrics, depending on its particular context. It is not fair to compare teams, so it is neither fair to compare their data. Each team will have their own thresholds. Therefore, sprint over sprint, the team should define and refine the thresholds for each of the metrics. The whole team should be involved in the definition of the minimum acceptance criteria for certain situations. As mentioned before, a metric should drive behaviour but, at the same time, it should expire or should be recycled over the time.

It is important to be careful with the data exposed in order to handle the mood of the team in a sustainable environment. It is good that members are aware of the results of the team, but at the same time, the figures should not create stress. Let us imagine a team where all the members are conscious of that they have been struggling for the last two sprints, should metrics be exposed to even affect more the mood of the team? If all the members know that there is a problem and they are all working hard to solve it, will letting the team know that 5% of flow efficiency change the situation? The answer will depend on each particular team. In any case, Visual Agile will be very helpful to transfer the risk of the Agile Coach subjectivity to data objectivity.

Acknowledgments. This work has been supported by the Spanish Ministry of Science and Technology with ERDF funds under grants TIN2016-76956-C3-3-R.

References

1. Humble, J., Farley, D.: Continuous Delivery: Reliable Software Releases through Build, Test, and Deployment Automation. Signature Series. Addison-Wesley, Boston (2010)
2. Cohn, M.: Succeeding with Agile: Software Development Using Scrum. Signature Series. Addison-Wesley, Boston (2010)
3. Jovanovic, M., Mesquida, A.L., Mas, A.: Process improvement with retrospective gaming in agile software development. In: O'Connor, R., Umay Akkaya, M., Kemaneci, K., Yilmaz, M., Poth, A., Messnarz, R. (eds.) Systems, Software and Services Process Improvement. CCIS, vol. 543, pp. 287–294. Springer, Cham (2015). https://doi.org/10.1007/978-3-319-24647-5_23
4. Mesquida, A.L., Jovanovic, M., Mas, A.: Process improving by playing: implementing best practices through business games. In: Kreiner, C., O'Connor, R.V., Poth, A., Messnarz, R. (eds.) EuroSPI 2016. CCIS, vol. 633, pp. 225–233. Springer, Cham (2016). https://doi.org/10.1007/978-3-319-44817-6_18
5. Senge, P.: The Fifth Discipline: The Art & Practice of the Learning Organization. Currency, New York (2006)
6. Lencioni, P.: The Five Dysfunctions of a Team: A Leadership Fable. Wiley, New Jersey (2010)
7. Adkins, L.: Coaching Agile Teams: A Companion for Scrum Masters, Agile Coaches, and Project Managers in Transition. Signature Series. Addison-Wesley, Boston (2010)
8. Jovanović, M., Mas, A., Mesquida, A.L., Lalić, B.: Transition of organizational roles in agile transformation process: a grounded theory approach. J. Syst. Softw. **133**, 174–194 (2017)
9. Jovanović, M., Mesquida, A.L., Mas, A., Lalić, B.: Towards the development of a sequential framework for agile adoption. In: Mas, A., Mesquida, A., O'Connor, R.V., Rout, T., Dorling, A. (eds.) SPICE 2017. CCIS, vol. 770, pp. 30–42. Springer, Cham (2017). https://doi.org/10.1007/978-3-319-67383-7_3
10. Laloux, F.: Reinventing Organizations: A Guide to Creating Organizations Inspired by the Next Stage in Human Consciousness. Nelson Parker, Brussels (2014)

11. Jovanovic, M., Mesquida, A.L., Mas, A., Radakovic, N.: Agile retrospective games for different team development phases. J. Univ. Comput. Sci. **22**(12), 1489–1508 (2016)
12. Mesquida, A.L., Karać, J., Jovanović, M., Mas, A.: A game toolbox for process improvement in agile teams. In: Stolfa, J., Stolfa, S., O'Connor, R.V., Messnarz, R. (eds.) EuroSPI 2017. CCIS, vol. 748, pp. 302–309. Springer, Cham (2017). https://doi.org/10.1007/978-3-319-64218-5_25
13. Robertson, B.J.: Holacracy: The New Management System for a Rapidly Changing World. Henry Holt and Company, New York (2015)
14. Reinertsen, D.G.: The Principles of Product Development Flow: Second Generation Lean Product Development. Celeritas, Redondo Beach (2009)
15. Korsaa, M., et al.: The SPI manifesto and the ECQA SPI manager certification scheme. J. Softw. Evol. Process **24**(5), 525–540 (2012)

How to Innovate Software Quality Assurance and Testing in Large Enterprises?

Alexander Poth(✉) and Christian Heimann(✉)

Volkswagen AG, Berliner Ring 2, 38436 Wolfsburg, Germany
{alexander.poth, christian.heimann}@volkswagen.de

Abstract. The Test-and Quality Assurance (TQA) department of the Group IT starts in late 2016 to design an open space for ideation and innovation about software quality. The ramp up phase was in 2017 – now in 2018 its time for a making of, to reflect the outcomes and for a lessons learned of the so called Quality innovation NETwork (QiNET) of the Volkswagen AG.

Keywords: Innovation management · Software quality management (SQM) Quality assurance (QA) · Testing · Virtual organization · Self-organization

1 Motivation and Context for the Demand of QiNET

Large enterprises are historically mostly separated into hierarchical and Taylorism driven structures. These structures are not efficient in bringing up innovations like those that startups do. They are good in running, enhance and improve established things in an efficient matter. However, with the digitalization wave new technologies like cloud, artificial intelligence (AI), microservice-based architectures are demanding new QA and testing approaches. To identify, develop or customize and establish these approaches an adequate environment have to be designed and setup. This was the motivation for TQA-the Testing and QA department of the Volkswagen Group IT to build the QiNET. QiNET is an acronym for Quality Innovation Network.

The objectives of the QiNET as a space for quality innovations are:

- Enterprises need one place to discuss ideas about quality from different perspectives
- Bring togetherpeople's ideas and implementation know how
- Have the chance to work with real projects and in a safe"offline" area
- Have a network of business partners for inspirations and know-how sharing
- Bringing together long-term approaches of Universities with mid-term industrial solutions and current demands in the perspective of IT projects

These objectives leads TQA to define an adequate setting – the QiNET. In Sect. 2 the making of QiNET is presented. Section 3 makes a deep dive into the procedures and rituals of the QiNET. Section 4 concludes with the presentation of some outcomes.

X. Larrucea et al. (Eds.): EuroSPI 2018, CCIS 896, pp. 437–442, 2018.
https://doi.org/10.1007/978-3-319-97925-0_37

2 Making of QiNET

This section presents the making of QiNET, which is located in the Volkswagen Group IT and focusses on Testing and Quality issues. To define an identity of the QiNET a product vision board was setup. The short version of the product vision board is "transform quality opportunities into business value". Currently this vision leads the QiNET to focus on tree main topics:

- Methods (example: agile impact to QA approaches)
- Data (example: AI and the needed data quality)
- Software (example: QA for micro-service architecture and cloud services)

This three topics offers the evaluation for example about what chances are derived from AI for QA.

The QiNET is designed as an open space for all Volkswagen AG brands and business areas. Currently QiNET deals with IT project related topic from the:

- Digital Unit Berlin
- Agile Center of Excellence
- Group IT cloud
- and other IT department

To get new ideas and insights the QiNET established cooperation's with external entities like:

- Universities and
- External industrial partners.

To innovate complete new thinks this exchange with the external entities is crucial, because the QiNET does not have fix associated budgets or human resources (FTE). It is more a cultural cooperation than a fiscal driven approach. This approach represents a win-win situation for all partners. Real-world-problems will be discussed and solved by state-of-art solutions, whereas current technical IT challenges serve as a base for discussions with industrial partners for mid-term solutions or with the Universities for long-term approaches.

The QiNET sets up an innovation procedure within a lean [KANBAN] and agile [AGMA] fashion. The procedure in a short description: Everybody can ideate and put topics from its perspective to the QiNET backlog. Topics are ranked in the backlog [SCRUM]. Product owners are identified and apply for topics. Only topics with a product owner are realized. This "rule" is to implement the value mindset of the QiNET vision. If no product owner as driver of a topic can be found, the demand for the topic is (currently) not high enough. Via grooming the topics are refined into deliverables for one or more iterations. The cyclic show and tell events are used to update the QiNET interested persons.

The QiNET is founded as a virtual organization. This virtual organization needs a common space to interact. The QiNET uses a virtual collaboration and social media space in the Volkswagen Group Connect (basic concept similar to a "facebook group"), which is accessible for all brands of the Volkswagen AG to offer one common place for the software quality topics handled by the QiNET. This social media group can be used to discuss, share outcomes or inform the QiNET community. The QiNET community is open for everybody who is interested into the topics. This openness gives the QiNET knowledge of a wide range of skills and roles of the company. Depending on topics, the interest of individuals is also widely different – it is the self-organization of the network, which helps to find the right people. A second motivation to use the social media infrastructure is to emphasize the openness and network character of the QiNET. As initiator of the QiNET the TQA department take (currently) the role of the moderator of the QiNET virtual organization. This approach extends the existing Q-Community, which has a Volkswagen internal focus and serves as exchange platform between IT-departments and business departments on QA issues. TQAs role as moderator and facilitator of the QiNET is to guide the topics from ideation to usable outcomes – innovation ends with a real and usable outcome. Furthermore, TQAs role was to establish an initial QiNET setup, which is able to survive. Interesting aspects of the initial setup is described in the following section.

3 Deep Dive into QiNET

After the why and making of the QiNET this section gives some deeper insights into QiNETs innovation procedure.

3.1 Ideation, Grooming and Prioritization

A key for doing the right things is the ideation phase. Only identified topics can be selected and in next steps be prioritized for implementation. To get as much as possible ideas – the "quality opportunities" in QiNETs product vision wording-the ideation process is open for everybody at the Volkswagen AG. The ideas can be posted on the social media platform or presented in the ideation slot of the cyclic QiNET community meeting. In this meeting, the ideas are initial groomed to assure that the added value of the epic or story (depending on the size of the idea) is transparent. In a next step the topic is ranked in the backlog. The ranking focus on: how big is the impact and added value of the topic?

In the next step for "hot" topics the QiNETsearch's for a product owner. A topic needs a person who cares about the development and outcome delivery of the topic and assure the realization of the identified added value. This person acts as a godfather for this topic. Sometimes topics are identified and ranked high, but the QiNET cannot identify a product owner. This topics keep on the backlog and waits for a product owner. This makes at least transparent, that resources are needed or the demand is (currently) not big enough. This procedure assures that the focus is set by a pull.

3.2 Working on Backlog Items - From MVP to SLC

The product owner cares about the topic and search an implementing instance. An implementing instance is needed for the assurance of the QiNETs product vision demanded "business value". This estimated business value encourage the product owner to develop more than only a MVP (Minimum Viable Product). Because MVPs are not "attractive" from the customer perspective and have many constraints and uncomfortable things. The QiNET decides with the demand for "business value" to develop SLCs [SLC]. SLC is the abbreviation for simple, lovable and complete. This gives the option to use an outcome of a topic every time as a stable product in case that the venture capital flow stops. A product also can be a service or a method in the context of QiNET. One important step is now to get sufficient resources to implement the SLC. To get the necessary resources the product owner needs support from the QiNET partners and/or the (pilot) project, which demonstrate and realize the business value. This context requires some intrapreneur skills [INT] from the product owner, because he brings the idea through the founding phase to a SLC.

With this not trivial situation for the product owner, it is clear why not each topic is "pulled", but the QiNET use this "survival by demand" as selection criteria for ideas. However, the demand can be defined and sponsored by strategic initiatives. QiNET acts as an agent to bring together the ideas and the right people.

3.3 Show and Tell

To get feedback and the chance to adjust at least every quarter the product owners present the current state of the SLC in the QiNET meeting. By definition, a SLC is as simple as possible and this leads to short implementation time – up to now the largest topics are master thesis projects with two-quarter time span. For short running topics results or feedback demands can published every time via the QiNET social platform. This cycle time is not fixed, because the product owners are driven by the projects in which the business value have to be demonstrated. This assures that a more frequent show & tell is done in the context of the business value assurance.

3.4 Lessons Learned of Over One Year QiNET

First of all: just do it! Don't hesitate or get lost in too much questions and asking. The agile approach helps to adjust and improve in a smart way. The biggest challenge is to establish an enterprise wide network. However, it is tricky to get the relevant people in. This lead to the next lessons learned: be patient. It takes time to demonstrate benefit that convince the people to join the QiNET. All are busy and have no time for additional things, which cost additional time. The lessons learned which it keeps running: it works – the QiNET focus to its prioritized topics and assigns available capacities for delivering outcomes. Focus on quick wins helps to persuades people to play an active part.

One of the founding objectives currently is not in place: offer dedicated trainings for systematic and efficient knowledge sharing in cooperation with the Volkswagen Group Academy and AutoUni. Some ideas are send to these potential partners and are in discussion.

We hope that the right actions and topics are in the current pipe to get more impact and grow faster.

4 Conclusion

QiNET is based on a win-win approach and need an adequate culture. As described it focus on innovative topics more than stabilizing existing processes and improves established things in an effective manner. The QiNET is built to handle innovations around the software quality of the Volkswagen Group IT in a systematic manner but has in mind that innovation is people driven [INNO]. The approach of the QiNET is explicitly not based on formal innovation procedures and approaches like Design Thinking [IDEO], Value Proposition Design [OST08] or standards for innovation management like the ISO 50501. This is driven by the agile mindset of the QiNET to avoid that people are scared by complex procedures around their idea – but if a SLC team want to apply a more formal approach, they can use what is helpful. Furthermore, if the QiNET discovers a demand for more formalization in the future some aspects of these approaches and standards can selected and integrated into the QiNET procedure. The QiNET is currently established as a virtual organization in which everybody can join and participate. The following picture shows some statistics about the growing interest of the topics and discussions since the QiNET was started. The colors of the graph are defined for red are contributions, yellow are active and green are passive/reading QiNET participants. Interesting posts gets 3-digit hits of the QiNET community participants.

The QiNET develops ideas further to methods, products or services, because realizing innovations is having a usable outcome, which is at least a SLC. In addition, the QiNET is a place for testing and failing with new ideas – In this case, the lessons learned is the valuable outcome and the chance to use the knowledge about why it fails to decide next steps.

Finally are presented some outcomes from initiatives of the QiNET from the ramp up year 2017:

Methods:

- Level of Done & Product Quality Risk approach of the Digital Unit Berlin of the Volkswagen Financial Services AG [euroSPI17] confirmed as a valid approach by a compliance review.
- The agile project review approach with the ACE was rollout to the Group IT [euroSPI18a].

Data:

- A Online Failure Prediction System (OFPS) for a GITC (Group IT Cloud) service was developed in cooperation with one of the academic partners; a follow up work to transfer the results is initiated by another department
- A working group about QA of AI based systems was setup.

Software:

- TaaS (Testing as a Service) as a self-service based cloud native testing framework was developed with the GITC [euroSPI18b]

Selected outcomes of the QiNET are presented in national [http://bpt-2017.leaderscontact.com/] and international conferences (eurospi.net) and papers to share knowledge with other enterprises.

The presented QiNET approach also fits to the three believes of software process improvement (SPI) from [KOS12].

References

[AGMA] Sutherland et al.: http://www.agilemanifesto.org

[euroSPI17] Poth, A., Wolf, F.: Agile procedures of an automotive OEM – views from different business areas. In: Stolfa, J., Stolfa, S., O'Connor, R.V., Messnarz, R. (eds.) EuroSPI 2017. CCIS, vol. 748, pp. 513–522. Springer, Cham (2017). https://doi.org/10.1007/978-3-319-64218-5_42

[euroSPI18a] Poth, A., Kottke, M.: How to assure agile method and process alignment in an organization? In: Larrucea, X., Santamaria, I., O'Connor, R.V., Messnarz, R. (eds.) EuroSPI 2018, vol. 896, pp. 421–425. Springer, Cham (2018)

[euroSPI18b] Poth, A., Werner, M., Lei, X.: How to deliver faster with CI/CD integrated testing services? In: Larrucea, X., Santamaria, I., O'Connor, R.V., Messnarz, R. (eds.) EuroSPI 2018, vol. 896, pp. 401–409. Springer, Cham (2018)

[INNO] http://www.forbesindia.com/article/ie/new-trends-in-innovation-management/33905/1#ixzz2iiuuDxVq

[INT] https://mooc.house/courses/bizmooc2018

[KANBAN] Anderson, C.: Essential KANBAN Condensed. http://leankanban.com/guide/

[SCRUM] Sutherland, S.: The Official Scrum Guide. http://www.scrumguides.org/scrum-guide.html

[SLC] https://blog.asmartbear.com/slc.html

[IDEO] https://designthinking.ideo.com/?page_id=1542

[OST08] http://nonlinearthinking.typepad.com/nonlinear_thinking/2008/07/the-business-model-canvas.html

[KOS12] Korsaa, M., et al.: The SPI manifesto and the ECQA SPI manager certification scheme. J. Softw.: Evol. Process **24**(5), 525–540 (2012)

Assessing Agile in Automotive Embedded Development Projects Using Automotive SPICE 3.1

Richard Messnarz[1(✉)], Bernhard Sechser[2], Holger Höhn[2], Volker Lehmann[2], and Damjan Ekert[1]

[1] ISCN GesmbH, Graz, Austria
rmess@iscn.com
[2] Methodpark AG, Erlangen, Germany
bernhard.sechser@methodpark.de

Abstract. Automotive SPICE ® represents an assessment model which is used world-wide in mechatronic automotive projects where software is an essential part of the control system. In November 2018 a new version Automotive SPICE 3.1 has been published. This new version comes with an additional Automotive SPICE Guideline 1st Edition 2017 from VDA (available from Jan. 2018) which serves as a guideline to correctly interpret Automotive SPICE® 3.1. This Automotive SPICE Guideline for the interpretation of Automotive SPICE ® 3.1 includes rating rules and rating recommendations for agile projects. This article analyses these new rules and recommendations and illustrates how Automotive SPICE assessors will evaluate agile projects.

Keywords: Automotive SPICE 3.1 · Agile · Rating rules
Rating recommendations

1 Automotive SPICE 3.1 and Automotive SPICE Guideline Background

Figure 1 illustrates the VDA (Verband der deutschenAutomobilindustrie - German Automotive Association) scope based on Automotive SPICE® 3.1 [1] which defines a set of processes for which an assessment is planned and performed.

For each process there is a set of base practices at capability level 1. Base practices contribute to process outcomes which help to achieve a process purpose (see MAN.3 example in Fig. 3).

In an assessment of capability level 1 (process attribute "process performance" in Fig. 2) the base practices (see Fig. 3) are rated with N (Not), P (partially), L (Largely) and F (Fully). The Automotive SPICE Guideline [2] provides rating recommendations and rating rules that are to be considered when performing the N/P/L/F ratings. The Automotive SPICE Guideline [2] also describes rating rules and rating recommendations for the higher capability levels 2 and 3.

X. Larrucea et al. (Eds.): EuroSPI 2018, CCIS 896, pp. 443–455, 2018.
https://doi.org/10.1007/978-3-319-97925-0_38

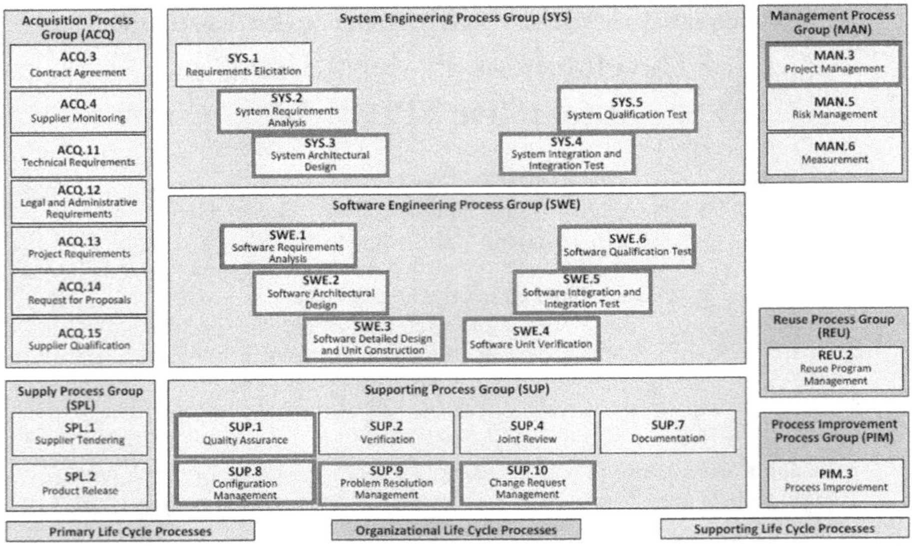

Fig. 1. Automotive SPICE 3.1 and VDA scope

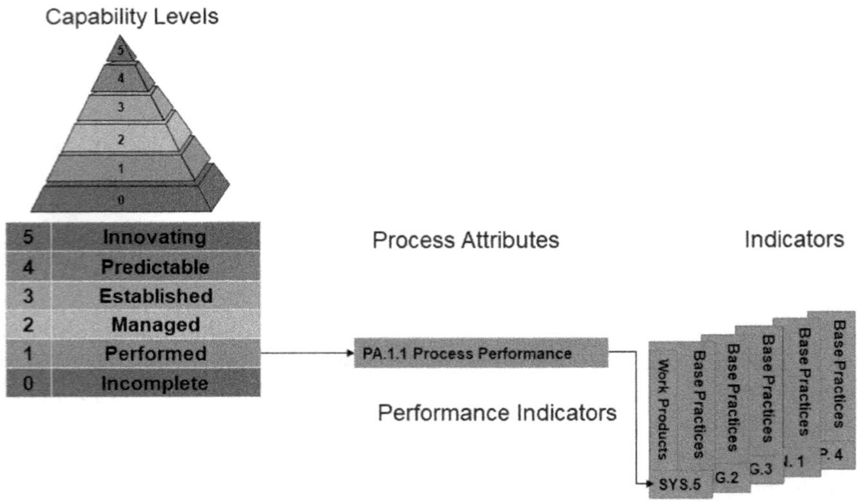

Fig. 2. Capability levels and base practices for level 1

The Automotive SPICE Guideline includes a chapter about agile developments [3, 4, 6, 17–21] and rating rules and rating recommendations in case of agile development [2].

Rating Scale: The ISO 33020 norm describes the rating scale N, P, L, F. Assessors rate at level 1 base practices and at higher levels (from level 2) generic practices and assign evidences and comments to each indicator (base practice at level 1 and generic practice at level 2).

Figure 3 below shows all base practices of the MAN.3 process because later in the paper many of the agile relevant rules and recommendations reference some of these base practices.

Process ID	**MAN.3**
Process name	**Project Management**
Process purpose	The purpose of the Project Management Process is to identify, establish, and control the activities and resources necessary for a project to produce a product, in the context of the project's requirements and constraints.
Process outcomes	As a result of successful implementation of this process: 1) the scope of the work for the project is defined; 2) the feasibility of achieving the goals of the project with available resources and constraints is evaluated; 3) the activities and resources necessary to complete the work are sized and estimated; 4) interfaces within the project, and with other projects and organizational units, are identified and monitored; 5) plans for the execution of the project are developed, implemented and maintained; 6) progress of the project is monitored and reported; and 7) corrective action is taken when project goals are not achieved, and recurrence of problems identified in the project is prevented.
Base practices	**MAN.3.BP1: Define the scope of work.** Identify the project's goals, motivation and boundaries. [OUTCOME 1] **MAN.3.BP2: Define project life cycle.** Define the life cycle for the project, which is appropriate to the scope, context, magnitude and complexity of the project. [OUTCOME 2] *NOTE 1: This typically means that the project life cycle and the customer's development process are consistent with each other.* **MAN.3.BP3: Evaluate feasibility of the project.** Evaluate the feasibility of achieving the goals of the project in terms of technical feasibility within constraints with respect to time, project estimates, and available resources. [OUTCOME 2] **MAN.3.BP4: Define, monitor and adjust project activities.** Define, monitor and adjust project activities and their dependencies according to defined project life cycle and estimations. Adjust activities and their dependencies as required. [OUTCOME 3, 5, 7] *NOTE 2: A structure and a manageable size of the activities and related work packages support an adequate progress monitoring.* *NOTE 3: Project activities typically cover engineering, management and supporting processes.* **MAN.3.BP5: Define, monitor and adjust project estimates and resources.** Define, monitor and adjust project estimates of effort and resources based on project's goals, project risks, motivation and boundaries. [OUTCOME 2, 3, 7] *NOTE 4: Appropriate estimation methods should be used.*

Fig. 3. MAN.3 process capability levels and base practices for Level 1.

	NOTE 5: Examples of necessary resources are people, infrastructure (such as tools, test equipment, communication mechanisms...) and hardware/materials. *NOTE 6: Project risks (using MAN.5) and quality criteria (using SUP.1) may be considered.* *NOTE 7: Estimations and resources typically include engineering, management and supporting processes.* **MAN.3.BP6: Ensure required skills, knowledge, and experience.** Identify the required skills, knowledge, and experience for the project in line with the estimates and make sure the selected individuals and teams either have or acquire these in time. [OUTCOME 3, 7] *NOTE 8: In the case of deviations from required skills and knowledge trainings are typically provided.* **MAN.3.BP7: Identify, monitor and adjust project interfaces and agreed commitments.** Identify and agree interfaces of the project with other (sub-) projects, organizational units and other affected stakeholders and monitor agreed commitments. [OUTCOME 4, 7] *NOTE 9: Project interfaces relate to engineering, management and supporting processes.* **MAN.3.BP8: Define, monitor and adjust project schedule.** Allocate resources to activities, and schedule each activity of the whole project. The schedule has to be kept continuously updated during lifetime of the project. [OUTCOME 3, 5, 7] *NOTE 10: This relates to all engineering, management and supporting processes.* **MAN.3.BP9: Ensure consistency.** Ensure that estimates, skills, activities, schedules, plans, interfaces, and commitments for the project are consistent across affected parties. [OUTCOME 3, 4, 5, 7] **MAN.3.BP10: Review and report progress of the project.** Regularly review and report the status of the project and the fulfillment of activities against estimated effort and duration to all affected parties. Prevent recurrence of problems identified. [OUTCOME 6, 7] *NOTE 11: Project reviews may be executed at regular intervals by the management. At the end of a project, a project review contributes to identifying e.g. best practices and lessons learned.*

Fig. 3. *(continued)*

Rating Rules: A rating rule [2] provides rating principles which are valid for the majority of assessments. This rule might be sometimes infringed, in this case the assessment report has to include an explanation of the deviation of the rating rule.

Rating Recommendation: A rating recommendation [2] provides a guidance for rating. However, if an assessor decides to not follow the recommendation there is no need to document the deviation in the assessment report.

Traceability and Consistency: Like all previous Automotive SPICE ® assessment model versions ASPICE 3.1 also highlights the importance of a traceability and consistency model. Applying the model in Fig. 4 assures that all requirements are traced throughout the entire development life cycle, e.g. tracing system requirements to system test specifications to system test results (bidirectional).

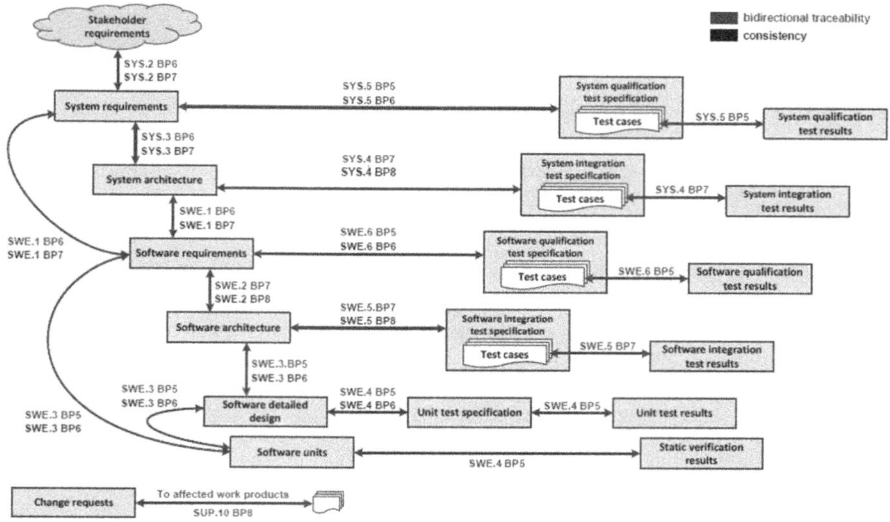

Fig. 4. Traceability and consistency

Once this framework has been set the paper discusses in the next chapter the agile specific rating recommendations in the Automotive SPICE Guideline for the interpretation of Automotive SPICE 3.1.

2 Analysis of the Agile Related Rating Recommendations in the Automotive SPICE Guideline of VDA

The following rating recommendations are described in the VDA Automotive SPICE Guideline.

Planning in Agile Environments

Recommendation AGE.RC.1: If evidences from project planning (e.g. backlog, burndown chart, and/or sprint planning) show gaps regarding release planning and this aspect is significant in the context of MAN.3.BP4, MAN.3.BP9, and SPL.2.BP1, the indicators MAN.3.BP4, MAN.3.BP9, and SPL.2.BP1 should be downrated.

Project Life Cycle

Recommendation AGE.RC.2: If the defined project life cycle does not fit to the project scope, requirements, deliveries, etc. the base practice MAN.3.BP2 should be downrated.

Interpretation of the Recommendations Above

In Automotive projects there is a feature based release plan. Features (vehicle functions) have to be mature (design, tested, released for vehicle testing etc.) at a certain functional integration release. A manufacturer agrees functional integration releases and delivery dates at project start.

Therefore the Change Requests (CR) in the backlog should be grouped into features, features are assigned to integration releases and the planning method for selecting CRs for sprints should consider the planned releases.

In practice there are risks to be managed when applying agile methods in embedded automotive projects. Risk example 1: If the average velocity of sprints (how many CRs per sprint in average are implemented?) is too low the target dates of functional integration releases will not be achieved.

Example 1: In an assessment of an agile automotive project each sprint was reported green/successful. However, in the assessment it was found out that the project was not measuring the size of the backlog. The assessor then measured the size and it contained about 800 CRs which were not considered so far. And the assessor then looked at the average speed of solving CRs in sprints and the full implementation of the backlog would then end 2 years after SOP.

Conclusion to example 1: Even if agile methods are used the release planning in automotive projects still applies.

Risk example 2: If due to the missing velocity of sprints (how many CRs per sprint in average are implemented?) issues remain in the backlog and are not delivered this will be an issue of product liability law if the project is functional safety relevant.

Example 2 additional: In the same project like in example 1 only CRs selected for sprints were analysed, so that the 800 issues in the backlog had not been analysed. A quick review showed that 200 of them were safety relevant [5, 7, 8].

Conclusion to example 2: Even if agile methods are used there must be a release strategy assuring that all relevant features are really implemented. Cars that have not all (e.g. safety relevant or cybersecurity relevant) features [9–16, 26] included are an issue for compliance and the product liability law.

In automotive projects each CR runs through certain phases of the V-model, represented by the SYS and SWE processes in Fig. 1. In Sprints CRs therefore run through the V-Cycle of requirements analysis, architectural design, detailed design, construction, unit testing etc.

Impact of Recommended Rating

If the recommendation AGE.RC.1 is not complete then

- MAN.3.BP4: Define, monitor and adjust project activities.
- MAN.3.BP9: Ensure consistency.
- SPL.2.BP1: Define the functional content of releases. Should be downrated (see Figs. 5 and 6).

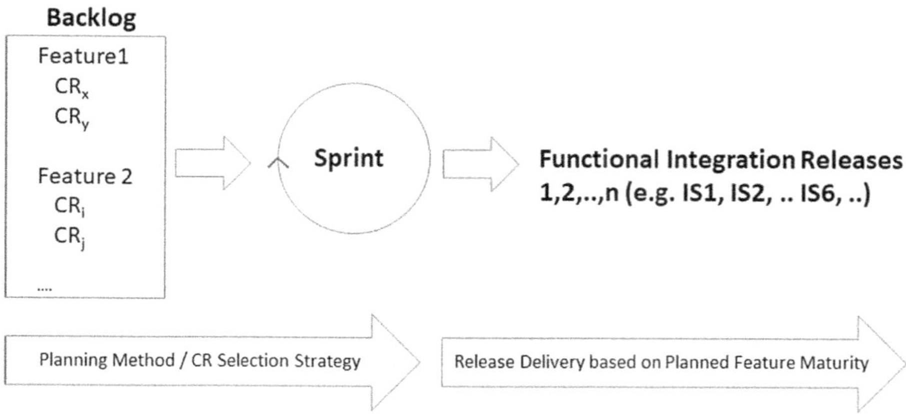

Fig. 5. Planning in agile automotive environments

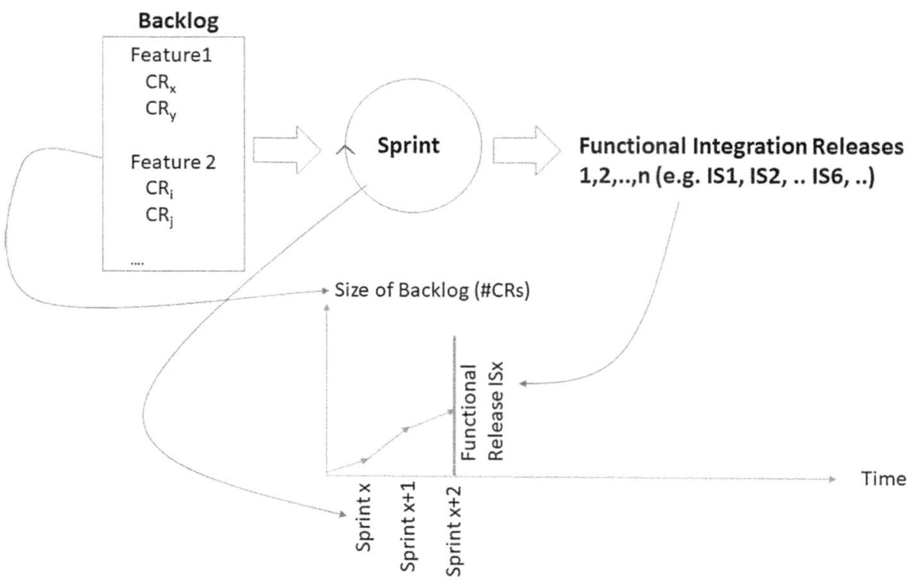

Fig. 6. Consistent sprint and functional release planning

If the recommendation AGE.RC.2 is not complete then

- MAN.3.BP2: Define project life cycle. should be downrated (see Fig. 7).

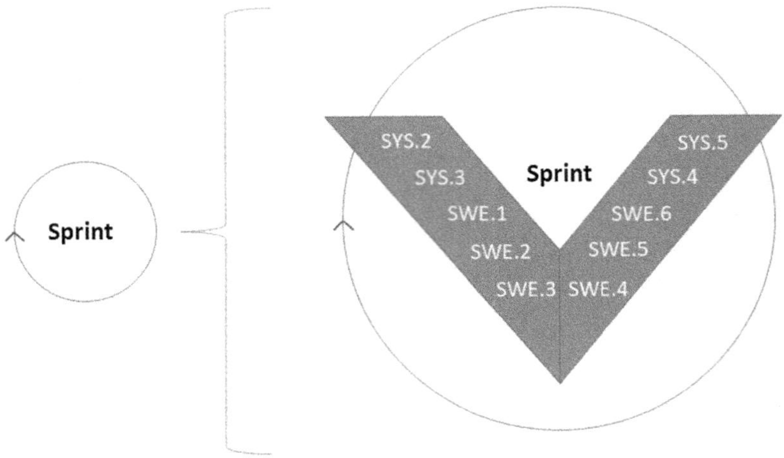

Fig. 7. Phase pattern for agile development and CR tracking

Management of Project Requirements (see Fig. 8)

Recommendation AGE.RC.3: If the project development is based on change management without a complete and consistent overview of all project requirements and this aspect is significant in the context of SWE.1.BP3 (for software) and SYS.2.BP3 (for system), then the base practices SWE.1.BP3 (for software) and SYS.2.BP3 (for system) should be downrated.

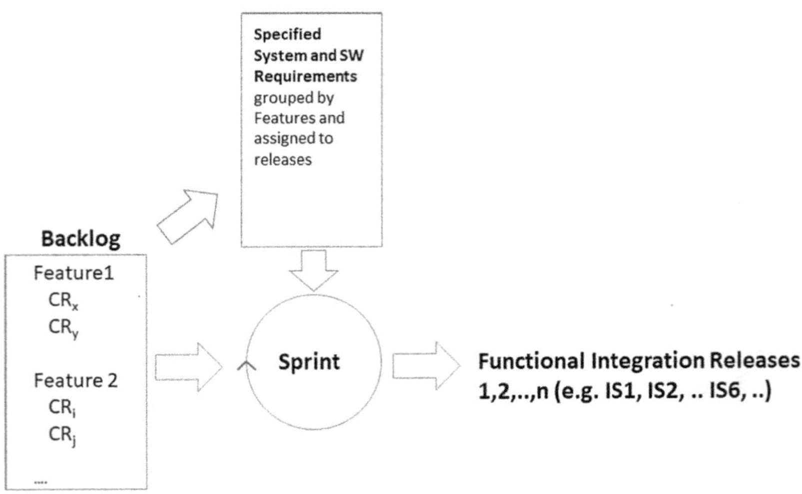

Fig. 8. Agile in automotive needs requirements and not only CRs

Impact of Recommended Rating
If the recommendation AGE.RC.3 is not complete then

- SWE.1.BP3: Analyze software requirements.
- SYS.2.BP3: Analyze system requirements should be downrated (see Fig. 7).

Risk Management

Recommendation AGE.RC.4: If risk management is required for the project but not integrated in the agile project, the base practices MAN.3.BP5 and MAN.3.BP1 should be downrated.

The risk examples 1 and 2 described below Fig. 5 above form typical risks which are observed in agile projects in the automotive embedded systems development. Especially leaving not analysed CRs which might be safety critical and legal issues not analysed in the backlog is a reason to assume that risk management is not properly done.

Testing

Recommendation AGE.RC.7: If the test level software unit verification is not consistently integrated into the agile life cycle, the base practice SWE.4.BP1 should be downrated.

Recommendation AGE.RC.8: If the test level software integration test is not consistently integrated into the agile life cycle, the base practice SWE.5.BP1 (note: there is a mistake in the Automotive SPICE Guideline, it should be SWE.5.BP2) should be downrated.

Recommendation AGE.RC.9: If the test level software qualification test is not consistently integrated into the agile life cycle, the base practice SWE.6.BP1 should be downrated. This means that (see the V inside the sprint in Fig. 7) all different test levels must still be covered.

Impact of Recommended Rating

If the recommendation AGE.RC.7 is not complete then

- SWE.4.BP1: Develop software unit verification strategy including regression strategy should be downrated (see V-Cycle in Fig. 7).

If the recommendation AGE.RC.8 is not complete then

- SWE.5.BP2: Develop software integration test strategy including regression test strategy.should be downrated (see V-Cycle in Fig. 7).

If the recommendation AGE.RC.9 is not complete then

- SWE.6.BP1: Develop software qualification test strategy including regression test strategy.should be downrated (see V-Cycle in Fig. 7).

If one of these above mentioned base practices is downrated then further process specific rating rules apply (not agile specific). For instance, if a test strategy related practice is downrated there are rating rules (not just recommendations) to downrate further practices. e.g. SWE.4.RL7: If the strategy related activities in SWE.4.BP1 are not performed according to the defined strategy, the indicators SWE.4.BP2 and SWE.4. BP4 shall be downrated.

Software Architecture

Recommendation AGE.RC.5: If no software architecture is developed and maintained, the base practice SWE.4.BP1 should be downrated.

Recommendation AGE.RC.6: If the software architecture is modified/updated incrementally including impact analysis, this should not be used to downrate the indicator SWE.2.BP1 Impact of Recommended Rating: If the recommendation AGE. RC.5 or RC6 is not complete then *SWE.2.BP1: Develop software architectural design should be downrated (see V-Cycle in* Fig. 7*)*. If the base practice SWE.2.BP1 is downrated then further process specific rating rules apply (not agile specific). For instance, if SWE.2.BP1 is doenrated the entire SWE.2 practices on level 1 shall be downrated. e.g. SWE.2.RL.8: If the development of SW architectural design is downrated PA1.1 shall be downrated as all indicators (SWE.2.BP2 to SWE.2.BP9) are affected (Fig. 9).

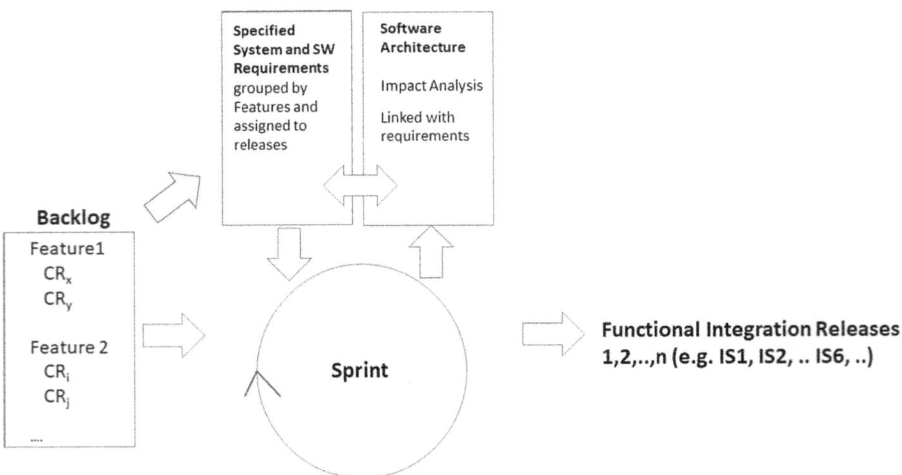

Fig. 9. Agile in automotive needs an incrementally updated SW architecture

Independent Quality Assurance

Recommendation AGE.RC.10: If the project does not ensure that work product and process quality assurance is performed at project level independently and objectively without conflicts of interest, the base practice SUP.1.BP1 should be downrated.

Experience with agile projects in Automotive shows that additional quality metrics are needed. Standard Automotive SPICE ® based metrics (customer requirements coverage, system requirements coverage, software requirements coverage, test coverage of requirements at all test levels, etc.) have to be enriched by agile based metrics [6].

- Size of the backlog
- Velocity of development (number of CRs per sprint with e.g. monthly sprints)
- Velocity of problem correction (number of CRs of type problem per sprint with e.g. monthly sprints)
- Projected time to solve the backlog
- CRs in different states based om phases (see Fig. 7).

Also the role of quality assurance has still to demonstrate an appropriate level of independence.

3 Expected Impact and Outlook

Automotive SPICE 3.1 ® together with the VDA Automotive SPICE Guideline provides a number of rating recommendations and rating rules that is to be applied by all assessors. There are above 1200 Automotive SPICE assessors active and working in the market. Major manufacturers developed and supported the guide. Therefore a large impact is expected.

The Automotive SPICE Guideline includes a section of how to assess agile development projects in the automotive area. This means on the one hand that agile is accepted but also clearly documents now the requirements and conditions under which agile projects are accepted for embedded automotive systems development.

It is interesting to note that the Automotive SPICE Guideline only considers software architecture, there are no recommendations for systems architecture. However, there are adaptations of the agile manifesto for the systems and product level [20, 21, 27]. This could be included for systems level in future versions of the Automotive SPICE Guideline.

4 The SPI Manifesto Revisited

The SPI manifesto [28–30] describes values and principles which need to be considered to make improvements work in an organisation. One of the approaches is to start with an assessment and to derive an improvement list. This is then used to set up an improvement program [22–25].

The principle "**Use dynamic and adaptable models as needed**" means that depending on the need of organisations specific models can be adapted. The agile manifesto and principles describe such a model.

The principle "**Ensure all parties understand and agree on process**" means that all stakeholders support the improvement project and established processes. An agile approach including sprints and daily stand-ups creates continuous communication in the ream and acceptance by all team members.

An additional principle proposed of the SPI manifesto is: "**Observe new trends and state of the art practices on the market and adopt**". Agile principles became popular in the automotive domain in the last years.

Acknowledgements. We are grateful to iNTACS (www.intacs.info) and VDA for the development of the Automotive SPICE ® 3.1 and the Automotive SPICE Guideline as a guideline to interpret the assessment model.

References

1. Automotive SPICE version 3.1, SPICE User Group, VDA – QMC, November 2017. www.automotivespice.com
2. Automotive SPICE – Guidelines, Process Assessment using Automotive SPICE in the development of software-based systems, 1st edn. VDA – German Automotive Association, Berlin, December 2017. ISSN 0943-9412
3. Manifesto for Agile Software Development (2001). www.agilemanifesto.org
4. Drobietz, M., Poth, A.: A new approach: not agile vs. traditional QM but applying the best of both. In: Stolfa, J., Stolfa, S., O'Connor, R.V., Messnarz, R. (eds.) EuroSPI 2017. CCIS, vol. 748, pp. 486–494. Springer, Cham (2017). https://doi.org/10.1007/978-3-319-64218-5_39
5. ISO - International Organization for Standardization: ISO 26262 Road vehicles Functional Safety Part 1-10 (2011)
6. Kösling, M., Poth, A.: Agile development offers the chance to establish automated quality procedures. In: Stolfa, J., Stolfa, S., O'Connor, R.V., Messnarz, R. (eds.) EuroSPI 2017. CCIS, vol. 748, pp. 495–503. Springer, Cham (2017). https://doi.org/10.1007/978-3-319-64218-5_40
7. SOQRATES: Task Forces Developing Integration of Automotive SPICE, ISO 26262 and SAE J3061. http://soqrates.eurospi.net/
8. Messnarz, R., Kreiner, C., Riel, A.: Integrating automotive SPICE, functional safety, and cybersecurity concepts: a cybersecurity layer model. Soft. Qual Prof. **18**, 13–23 (2016)
9. Messnarz, R., Kreiner, C., Riel, A., et al.: Implementing Functional Safety Standards has an Impact on System and SW Design - Required Knowledge and Competencies (SafEUr), Software Quality Professional (2015)
10. Messnarz, R., Spork, G., Riel, A., Tichkiewitch, S.: Dynamic learning organisations supporting knowledge creation for competitive and integrated product design. In: Proceedings of the 19th CIRP Design Conference – Competitive Design, Cranfield University, 30–31 March 2009, p. 104 (2009)
11. Macher, G., Sporer, H., Brenner, E., Kreiner, C.: Supporting cyber-security based on hardware-software interface definition systems. In: Kreiner, C., O'Connor, R., Poth, A., Messnarz, R. (eds.) EuroSPI 2016. CCIS, vol. 633, pp. 148–159. Springer, Cham (2017). https://doi.org/10.1007/978-3-319-44817-6_12
12. Macher, G., Messnarz, R., Kreiner, C., et al.: Integrated safety and security development in the automotive domain. Working Group 17AE-0252/2017-01-1661, SAE International, June 2017
13. Redmill, F.: Understanding the use, misuse and abuse of safety integrity levels. In: Proceedings of the Eighth Safety-Critical Systems Symposium, Southampton, 8–10 February 2000. Springer, Heidelberg (2000)
14. Much, A.: Automotive security: challenges, standards and solutions. Soft. Qual. Prof. **18**, 4–12 (2016)

15. Messnarz, R., et al.: Integrating functional safety, automotive SPICE and six sigma – the AQUA knowledge base and integration examples. In: Barafort, B., O'Connor, R.V., Poth, A., Messnarz, R. (eds.) EuroSPI 2014. CCIS, vol. 425, pp. 285–295. Springer, Heidelberg (2014). https://doi.org/10.1007/978-3-662-43896-1_26
16. Kreiner, C., et al.: Automotive knowledge alliance AQUA – integrating automotive SPICE, six sigma, and functional safety. In: McCaffery, F., O'Connor, R.V., Messnarz, R. (eds.) EuroSPI 2013. CCIS, vol. 364, pp. 333–344. Springer, Heidelberg (2013). https://doi.org/10.1007/978-3-642-39179-8_30
17. Poth, A., Sasabe, S., Mas, A.: Lean and agile software process improvement - an overview and outlook. In: Stolfa, J., Stolfa, S., O'Connor, R.V., Messnarz, R. (eds.) EuroSPI 2017. CCIS, vol. 748, pp. 471–485. Springer, Cham (2017). https://doi.org/10.1007/978-3-319-64218-5_38
18. Poth, A., Wolf, F.: Agile procedures of an automotive OEM – views from different business areas. In: Stolfa, J., Stolfa, S., O'Connor, R.V., Messnarz, R. (eds.) EuroSPI 2017. CCIS, vol. 748, pp. 513–522. Springer, Cham (2017). https://doi.org/10.1007/978-3-319-64218-5_42
19. Siqueira, A.A., Reinehr, S., Malucelli, A.: Using a statistical method to compare agile and waterfall processes performance. In: Stolfa, J., Stolfa, S., O'Connor, R.V., Messnarz, R. (eds.) EuroSPI 2017. CCIS, vol. 748, pp. 523–532. Springer, Cham (2017). https://doi.org/10.1007/978-3-319-64218-5_43
20. Stelzmann, E., Kreiner, C., Spork, G., Messnarz, R., Koenig, F.: Agility meets systems engineering: a catalogue of success factors from industry practice. In: Riel, A., O'Connor, R., Tichkiewitch, S., Messnarz, R. (eds.) EuroSPI 2010. CCIS, vol. 99, pp. 245–256. Springer, Heidelberg (2010). https://doi.org/10.1007/978-3-642-15666-3_22
21. Stelzmann, E.S., Spork, G., Kreiner, C.J., Messnarz, R., König, F.: Practical use of agile methods within systems engineering. International Spice Days, June 2010
22. Riel, A., O'Connor, R., Tichkiewitch, S., Messnarz, R. (eds.): EuroSPI 2010. CCIS, vol. 99. Springer, Heidelberg (2010). https://doi.org/10.1007/978-3-642-15666-3
23. Richardson, I., Runeson, P., Messnarz, R.: Software Process Improvement. LNCS, vol. 4257. Springer, Heidelberg (2006). https://doi.org/10.1007/11908562
24. Barafort, B., O'Connor, R.V., Poth, A., Messnarz, R. (eds.): EuroSPI 2014. CCIS, vol. 425. Springer, Heidelberg (2014). https://doi.org/10.1007/978-3-662-43896-1
25. Abrahamsson, P., Baddoo, N., Margaria, T., Messnarz, R. (eds.): EuroSPI 2007. LNCS, vol. 4764. Springer, Heidelberg (2007). https://doi.org/10.1007/978-3-540-75381-0
26. Riel, A., et al.: EU project SafEUr – competence requirements for functional safety managers. In: Winkler, D., O'Connor, R.V., Messnarz, R. (eds.) EuroSPI 2012. CCIS, vol. 301, pp. 253–265. Springer, Heidelberg (2012). https://doi.org/10.1007/978-3-642-31199-4_22
27. Wuest, T., Schmidt, T., WeiDavid, W., Romero, D.: Towards (pro-)active intelligent products. Int. J. Prod. Lifecycle Manag. **11**, 154–189 (2018)
28. Korsaa, M., et al.: The SPI manifesto and the ECQA SPI manager certification scheme. J. Soft.: Evol. Process **24**(5), 525–540 (2012)
29. Korsaa, M., et al.: The people aspects in modern process improvement management approaches. J. Soft.: Evol. Process **25**(4), 381–391 (2013)
30. Messnarz, R., Sicilia, M.A., Biro, M.: Social responsibility aspects supporting the success of SPI. J. Soft.: Evol. Process **26**(3), 284–294 (2014)

SPI with Retrospectives: A Case Study

Antònia Mas[1(✉)], Alexander Poth[2], and Susumu Sasabe[3]

[1] Department of Mathematics and Computer Science, University of the Balearic Islands, Ctra. de Valldemossa, km 7.5, Palma de Mallorca, Spain
antonia.mas@uib.es

[2] Volkswagen AG, Berliner Ring 2, 38436 Wolfsburg, Germany
alexander.poth@volkswagen.de

[3] Union of Japanese Scientists and Engineers (JUSE), 1-2-1 Koenji-Minami, Suginami-ku, Tokyo 166-0003, Japan
sasabe@mue.biglobe.ne.jp

Abstract. The retrospective is a common practice for continuous improvement when using Scrum. However, in many projects, retrospectives are performed in a mechanical way, with no real understanding of the goal, phases and real value of this ceremony. Some aspects about how to prepare this type of meetings should be considered by the team. This paper shows how the different phases to celebrate effective retrospectives should be deployed, using as example the retrospective celebrated at the end of the workshop "Experiences with Agile and Lean" in the EuroAsiaSPI^2 2017 conference.

Keywords: Software Process Improvement (SPI) · Agile retrospectives
Starfish · Scrum

1 Introduction

When using the Scrum method, the lifecycle of a software development project is performed in iteration cycles of up to one or more weeks called sprints. Two additional activities are performed during one sprint, usually at the end of the cycle. The first one is the *Sprint Review*, where all the stakeholders are involved. The focus of this activity is to inspect and adapt the product that is being built. The second one is the *Sprint Retrospective*, devoted to assess and improve the processes followed by the team.

Sprint retrospective meeting is the way of performing process improvement in organizations that use agile methods. Agile retrospectives help teams to learn, improve and increase business value to customers and company [1]. As a way of improvement and innovation in celebrating retrospectives, different tools and techniques, including serious games, are used with the main objective of promoting creativity, motivation and cohesion of the team [2, 3].

The use of gamification in agile software development is recent. Several researchers have proposed game thinking approaches in software development [4–8]. According to them, games help participants to focus on development tasks and to define better objectives. Games used in agile retrospectives are made of basic game elements, but they support teams to improve and be motivated, have an important impact on social

X. Larrucea et al. (Eds.): EuroSPI 2018, CCIS 896, pp. 456–466, 2018.
https://doi.org/10.1007/978-3-319-97925-0_39

behaviour, team building and help organizations to become more lean and agile. In [9, 10] authors present a research related on collecting, analysing and classifying games to increase the success of Agile retrospective meetings. They propose a set of games that can be used in Scrum retrospectives, to reflect and analyse the past and to prepare for the future.

Before organizing a retrospective it is important to investigate the history and environment of team [1, 3]. Even though the facilitator most probably would have been selected from the team members, assumptions of the moral and environment of the project team should be reviewed. It is important to gather background information in order to be capable to tailor the retrospective meeting to the needs of the team.

The paper is structured as follows. Section 2 presents retrospective meetings and details how should be deployed. Section 3 presents a case study of the retrospective meeting celebrated during the first edition of the "Experiences with Agile and Lean" in the EuroAsiaSPI[2] 2017 conference. Section 4 concludes the paper and brings up future research initiatives to be undertaken.

2 Retrospective Meetings

The main purpose of a retrospective meeting is to review what happened during the last sprint and to propose actions to be carried out in the following iterations. All participants can give feedback about the sprint in the defined timeframe. Anything that affects how the team creates the product is to be discussed in the retrospective meeting [11–13].

Sprint retrospective would involve Scrum Master and the development team. Product Owner should be also present if needed and has gained trust from the development team.

The facilitator and the rest of project team members should plan and prepare the retrospective meeting in advance. Depending on social and situational factors, the retrospective meeting agenda should be set and dynamics should be selected. Feedback is collected, grouped and prioritized, depending on the selected methods and tools. It is important that the facilitator do not act as a decision maker, in order to involve all team members and to contribute and influence the decision-making process.

The celebration of a retrospective can be divided into four different phases: Planning the retrospective, Deployment of the retrospective, Analysis of the retrospective outcomes and Proposal of improvement actions. Next subsections detail each one of these four phases.

2.1 Planning the Retrospective

Holding retrospective meetings according to the same pattern and using the same method and tools week after week can cause a certain monotony and lack of motivation. Topics like: what worked well, what did not work and innovative ideas should be discussed, but varying the method.

In order to prepare an effective retrospective, the following parameters should be established before the beginning of the meeting [2, 14]:

1. Learning about history and environment: team's history, general assumptions about current state and team moral should be taken into account.
2. Retrospective goal: what are the expected outcomes from the meeting.
3. Duration of the retrospective: four different parameters may be used to set duration: sprint iteration length, complexity (technological or organizational), team size and level of conflicts and controversy.
4. People: all the people who have to participate in the retrospective. The invitation/announcement to the retrospective meeting will give all the participants the chance to be prepared for the retrospective.
5. Method, tools and techniques. Once the goals of the retrospective are defined and the list of participants is known, activities, dynamics and games to be conducted in the retrospective meeting may be selected. Based on the retrospective focus and participant list, activities should be chosen to help participants to engage, explore and think collectively. Proper selection of activities should foster equal participation, focus the conversation and encourage new perspectives.
6. Agenda. A retrospective meeting has to be structured in order to be effective. Exact day, time and meeting venue should be defined.
7. Infrastructure. Materials to be used during the meeting.

The main responsibility of the retrospective facilitator is to support the retrospective meeting as a whole, and to create an environment in the team to reach the expected outcomes. He also should respect the planned retrospective agenda. If the facilitator is coming from the team it is easy to get caught up in discussion. Main obligations of the facilitator are to manage activities, group dynamics, time and himself [3].

2.2 Deployment of the Retrospective

To carry out the retrospective itself, Derby and Larsen [3] propose five different stages in a retrospective meeting:

- Set the stage. Involves welcoming and explaining the aim of the retrospective meeting.
- Gather data. Involves agile teams sharing their review and feedback, reporting on what happened during the previous sprint and briefly discussing with other team members.
- Generate insight. Agile teams participate in a further discussion and making agreements about what issues to focus on.
- Decide what to do. Participants decide how to solve those issues and what areas need to improve.
- Close the retrospective. Involves summarizing the retrospective meeting and appreciating all team members' efforts.

Gray et al. [15] propose three different stages: Open, Explore and Close. In [16], authors propose three different time phases for a meeting: Warming up, Playing and Wrapping up. In any case and regardless of the selected phases, during the celebration of the retrospective, data should be gathered objectively, in time and in the established manner. In [17] fifty quick ideas to improve retrospectives are presented.

2.3 Analysis of the Retrospective Outcomes

Depending on the size of the team, the time estimated to run the retrospective and the established goals of the meeting, the analysis of the retrospective outcomes can be done in the timeslot for the retrospective or later on.

The benefits of an integrated approach are that assistants can interpret and give feedback about “short phrases” and can help to group the statements. However, it could be not trivial to find a good grouping for the feedbacks; this needs time and often cannot be done instantly. Moreover, it is not useful to make the time-consuming analysis with the entire team if not all of them are responsible for the change or improvement actions.

The prioritization of the topics before its analysis is needed because, often, not all suggestions can be considered and implemented in an easy way and immediately. Depending on the scope of the improvement phase, some topics could have more or less priority.

2.4 Proposal of Improvement Actions

In this last phase, it is time to identify the improvement actions to be performed during the next sprints. These actions are obtained and derived from the analysis of the retrospective outcomes. The defined actions can have a wide range of effort and time to be implemented, so they have to be scheduled to assure their implementation.

In a Scrum environment, these actions will be stories or tasks, depending on their size. These stories or tasks are ranked into the product backlog and implemented during the next sprints. As performance facilitator of the team, the Scrum Master’s job is to assure that actions become implemented. It is useful to remind all team members about the goal for the next sprint, who will be responsible, and what are the associated deadlines.

Sometimes the effort for implementing new actions from the retrospective allocate team resources and reduce the sprint performance from the Product Owner’s perspective. In this case, the Scrum Master and the Product Owner have to find a solution to solve the resource conflict.

For improvements beyond the team boarders stakeholders outside the team have to be contacted and involved into the improvement demand. Often, it is more difficult and slower to establish improvement actions outside the team boarders, but with an adequate change culture and a stakeholder management, the improvement actions can berealized because everything which improves the company’s overall performance is welcomed.

3 Case Study

This section describes how a retrospective celebrated during the workshop "Experiences with Agile and Lean" in the EuroAsiaSPI^2 2017 Conference was carried out. The workshop moderators (authors of this paper) followed the four different phases described in Sect. 2, which matches with the first four stages of a retrospective meeting proposed by Derby and Larsen [3] (in brackets):

- Planning of the retrospective (Set the stage).
- Deployment of the retrospective (Gather data).
- Analysis of the retrospective outcomes (Generate insights).
- Proposal of improvement actions (Decide what to do).

In this case study the stages are not done with the same team. Only the deployment of the retrospective was done with all the workshop participants.

The presented retrospective approach also fits to the three believes of the SPI Manifesto [18].

3.1 Planning of the Retrospective (Set the Stage)

To set the stage of the retrospective, the factors mentioned in Sect. 2.1 were taken in to account.

1. Any kind of possibility of learning about the history (it was the first edition of the workshop) nor about the team (the exact composition was unknown).
2. Retrospective goal: to get feedback of the first workshop edition to improve next editions.
3. Duration: We did not use the four different parameters to set the duration. We decided to plan 45 min for the retrospective.
4. People: All the workshop attendants (around 20 participants) and the workshop program chairs & moderators.
5. Method, tools and techniques. Starfish diagram on the wall. Smartphone pictures.
6. Agenda. Ostrava, September 6, 2017. Duration of the retrospective: 15:45–16:30 (45 min), during the Panel discussion. Room of the workshop.
7. Infrastructure. Sticky tape, sticky notes and pens.

3.2 Deployment of the Retrospective (Gather Data)

To foster the thinking around what happened during the workshop, to collect feedback of all the workshop participants and help them to understand each other's perceived value, a Starfish diagram [14] was drawn on the wall. Starfish is a great data gathering technique from which the team can get good value.

In order to run the Starfish, the next five activities were performed:

1. A 5-pointed star with five different areas was drawn:
    a. **Keep doing.** Contains the tasks to which devote the same effort.
    b. **Do more.** Tasks to which efforts should be increased.

   c. **Do less.** Tasks to which efforts should be reduced.
   d. **Stop.** Tasks to stop doing. Something that is not adding value.
   e. **Start.** Tasks to start doing. New ideas or actions to be undertaken.
2. Participants were asked to write on sticky notes the tasks, ideas or feedback that could be assigned to each area. Each participant placed the notes in the corresponding area.
3. A discussion among all workshop participants was initiated. Once the diagram was completed, the sticky notes where discussed within the group. Some participants did clarifications or gave additional information to assure a common understanding of the shot terms on the sticky notes. Different suggestions made by all the participants were commented out alive.
4. Ideally, the participants should have been asked to write on sticky notes of a different colour, the actions to be taken to boost or to slow down the proposals in each area. However, this activity was not performed.
5. Many pictures of the resulting Starfish were taken (Fig. 1). Then, they were shared with all the workshop participants. This was the recommended method to store the collected data.

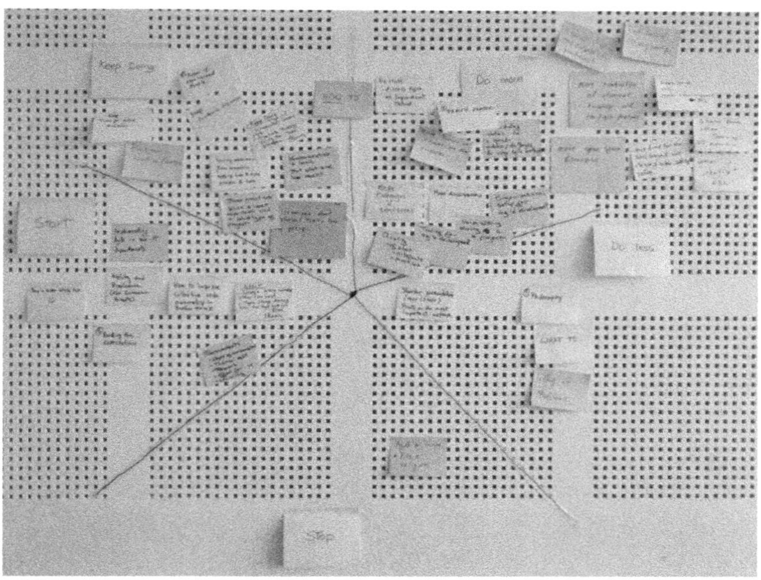

Fig. 1. Starfish diagram of the workshop "Experiences with Agile and Lean" in the EuroAsiaSPI^2 2017.

3.3 Analysis of the Retrospective Outcomes (Generate Insights)

After the execution of the retrospective, the workshop moderators started the analysis by generating two categories, where all the suggestions collected in the five areas of the Starfish diagram were grouped:

- Category 1: Topics to be discussed in the next editions of the workshop (Table 1). These topics can be prioritized if needed to focus on the most important actions first.
- Category 2: Organization of the new edition of the workshop (Table 2).

Table 1. Topics to be discussed in the next editions of the workshop.

Starfish areas	Suggestions made by workshop participants
Keep doing	1-1 Papers of experienced people 1-2 Sharing experiences from companies applying lean & agile principles & tools 1-3 Base practices which is most important and in which type of project 1-4 Best practice based on experience 1-5 How to … 1-6 Academic discussion
Do more	2-1 Discuss Agile as Improvement method 2-2 More combination of classical knowledge and lean/agile principles 2-3 Defining factors of Success and failure 2-4 What is really NEW 2-5 Stories how to solve practically 2-6 Demonstrating solutions for a specific problem 2-7 Challenges for using agile methods 2-8 Experience with teams greater than theory (team size 7 plus/minus 2?) 2-9 Organizational setup for agile development 2-10 Value setting during an agile project 2-11 Tooling for agile development 2-12 Quality of artefacts/practices 2-13 Fact-based SW engineering 2-14 Exchanges of experiences 2-15 Chairs from other domains: IT, Automotive, etc. 2-16 Practical examples
Do less	3-1 Telling of problems
Stop	4-1 “Agile” or “Scrum” like a religion
Start	5-1 Implementing Agile in non-IT departments 5-2 Agility and Resilience (the unknown threats) 5-3 How to improve collective code ownership in Scrum teams 5-4 Measurements: Degree of communication, Technical debt, Rework 5-5 Reading the expectations

Table 2. Organization of the new edition of the workshop

Starfish areas	Suggestions made by workshop participants
Keep doing	6-1 Introduction session style 6-2 Timetable tracking 6-3 Voting for topic storage 6-4 Discussions about different topics from the group 6-5 Keep time for active discussions 6-6 Communication is basic, But what and how much?
Do more	7-1 More time for the Panel subject with a subject to be identify before 7-2 More open space discussions 7-3 More discussions
Do less	8-1 Shorter presentation (max, 10 min) Focus in the most important message 8-2 Philosophy 8-3 What to …
Stop	9-1 None
Start	10-1 Surveys before workshop session or via email 10-2 Topic storage voting from few days ago or via email 10-3 Buy a better sticky tape :)

3.4 Proposal of Improvement Actions (Decide What to Do)

Our next step for making decisions regarding the topics to be discussed in the next workshop edition was to classify the suggestions from the three areas *Keep doing*, *Do more* and *Start* into two groups: "Theoretical topics" and "Experiences". Theoretical topics where classified into three categories:

- Evolution. To refer to those aspects related to the trends and challenges for using Agile methods.
- Indicators. Those aspects related to the establishment of indicators to measure in agile environments.
- Deployment. Referring to aspects that can help or influence the agile deployment.

Experiences were also divided into three categories:

- Real experiences. Indicating that the topics related to real experiences are very interesting for the workshop.
- Application domains. Papers dealing with issues regarding implementing agile in non-IT departments.
- Technical issues. Demanding papers related to agile technical issues.

Figure 2 shows the proposed topics to be discussed in the next workshop edition. Left side shows the theoretical topics and right side shows the experiences.

From Fig. 2, the specific improvement action consists of including this list of topics in the Call for papers of a forthcoming edition of the workshop.

Regarding the organization of the next workshop edition, the suggestions collected in Table 2 were used to define the concrete actions to be undertaken. Figure 3 shows these actions.

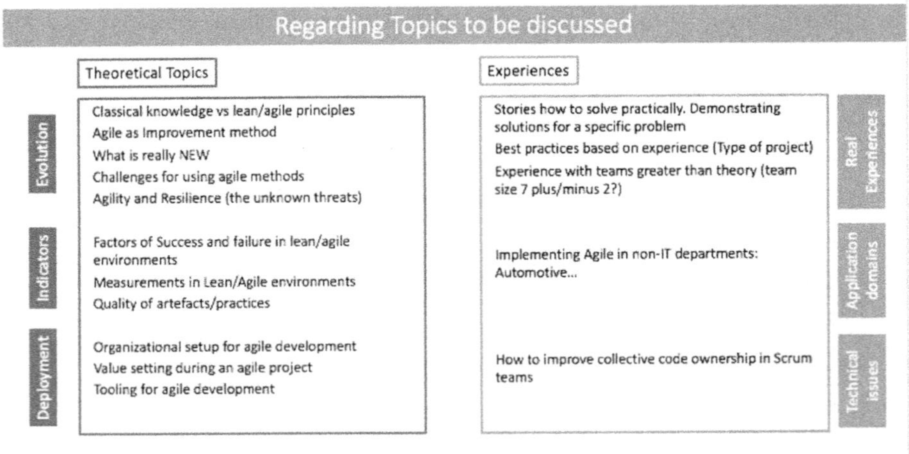

Fig. 2. Topics to be discussed in the next workshop edition.

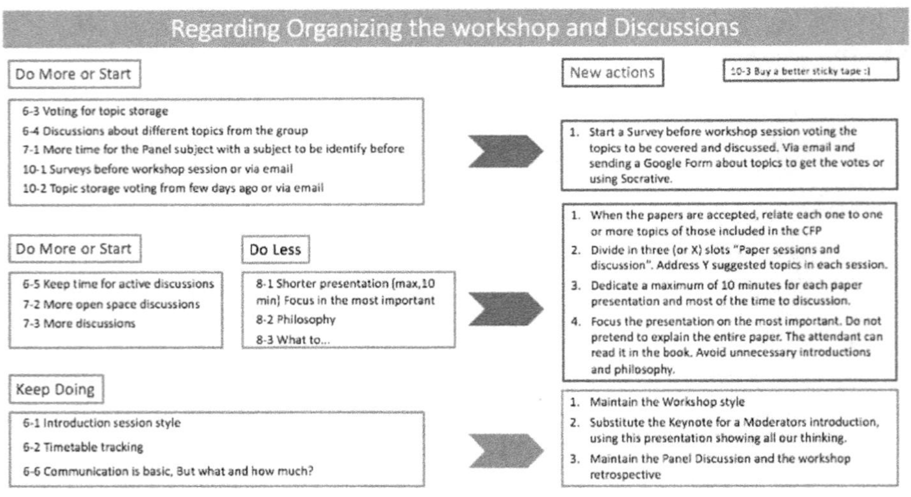

Fig. 3. New actions to be taken in the next workshop edition.

4 Conclusion

In this paper, we explain how we conducted a retrospective meeting, a common practice applied in organizations using Scrum, in order to get feedback from the participants to the workshop "Experiences with Agile and Lean workshop" in the EuroAsiaSPI^2 2017 Conference and also, to improve future editions. Workshop moderators followed a four-phase retrospective. Not the same people participated in each phase.

Moderators performed the planning, analysis and proposal of improvement actions. All the workshop attendants participated in the gathering data phase.

Using the resulting starfish, the moderators summarized to the workshop participants the contents of each of the five sections of the diagram. This ensured that the diagram reflected well the feedbacks and all participants were satisfied with the retrospective results.

Incorporating the retrospective meeting at the last period of the workshop was effective and efficient. The feedback from the participants was accurate and full of inspirations when their memories were fresh, just after the workshop discussions. It was a good way to close the workshop involving all the participants and motivating them to customize new editions of the workshop. It is very important to get commitment to perform the actions derived from a retrospective and to transmit this commitment to the attendants. This could be a way to retain the attendance of participants to new editions of the workshop.

Acknowledgments. Contributions from the University of the Balearic Islands to this work have been supported by the Spanish Ministry of Science and Technology with ERDF funds under grants TIN2016-76956-C3-3-R.

References

1. Kua, P.: The Retrospective Handbook. Leanpub, Vancouver (2013)
2. Gonçalves, L., Linders, B.: Getting Value Out of Agile Retrospectives. A Toolbox of Retrospective Exercises. Leanpub, Vancouver (2013)
3. Derby, E., Larsen, D.: Agile Retrospectives - Making Good Teams Great. The Pragmatic Bookshelf, Dallas (2006)
4. Yilmaz, M., O'Connor, R.V.: A scrumban integrated gamification approach to guide software process improvement: a Turkish case study. Tehnički vjesnik **23**(1), 237–245 (2016)
5. Cockburn, A.: The end of software engineering and the start of economic-cooperative gaming. Comput. Sci. Inf. Syst. **1**, 1–32 (2004)
6. Ogland, P.: The game of software process improvement: some reflections on players, strategies and payoff. In: Norsk konferanse for organisasjoners bruk av informasjonsteknologi (NOKOBIT 2016), Trodenheim, pp. 23–25 (2009)
7. Yilmaz, M., Yilmaz, M., O'Connor, R.V., Clarke, P.: A gamification approach to improve the software development process by exploring the personality of software practitioners. In: Clarke, P.M., O'Connor, R.V., Rout, T., Dorling, A. (eds.) SPICE 2016. CCIS, vol. 609, pp. 71–83. Springer, Cham (2016). https://doi.org/10.1007/978-3-319-38980-6_6
8. Herranz, E., Colomo-Palacios, R., Amescua, A., Yilmaz, M.: Gamification as a disruptive factor in software process improvement initiatives. J. Univ. Comput. Sci. **20**(6), 885–906 (2014)
9. Jovanovic, M., Mesquida, A.L., Mas, A.: Process improvement with retrospective gaming in agile software development. In: O'Connor, R., Umay Akkaya, M., Kemaneci, K., Yilmaz, M., Poth, A., Messnarz, R. (eds.) Systems, Software and Services Process Improvement. CCIS, vol. 543, pp. 287–294. Springer, Cham (2015). https://doi.org/10.1007/978-3-319-24647-5_23

10. Jovanovic, M., Mesquida, A.-L., Radakovic, N., Mas, A.: Agile retrospective games for different team development phases. J. Univ. Comput. Sci. **22**(12), 1489–1508 (2016)
11. Kerth, N.: Project Retrospectives - A Handbook for Team Reviews. Dorset House Publishing, New York (2013)
12. Eckstein, J.: Retrospectives for Organizational Change - An Agile Approach. Leanpub, Vancouver (2015)
13. Krivitsky, A.: Agile Retrospective Kickstarter. Leanpub, Vancouver (2015)
14. Caroli, P., Caetano, T.: Fun Retrospectives - Activities and Ideas for Making Agile Retrospectives More Engaging. Leanpub, Vancouver (2015)
15. Gray, D., Brown, S., Macanufo, J.: Game Storming - A Playbook for Innovators, Rulebreakers, and Changemakers. O'Reilly Media, Sebastopol (2010)
16. Mesquida, A.-L., Karać, J., Jovanović, M., Mas, A.: A game toolbox for process improvement in agile teams. In: Stolfa, J., Stolfa, S., O'Connor, R.V., Messnarz, R. (eds.) EuroSPI 2017. CCIS, vol. 748, pp. 302–309. Springer, Cham (2017). https://doi.org/10.1007/978-3-319-64218-5_25
17. Roden, T., Williams, B.: Fifty Quick Ideas to Improve Your Retrospectives. Leanpub, Vancouver (2015)
18. Korsaa, M., et al.: The SPI manifesto and the ECQA SPI manager certification scheme. J. Softw. Evol. Process **24**(5), 525–540 (2012)

Standards and Assessment Models

Towards Quantitative Evaluation of Reuse Within Safety-Oriented Process Lines

Barbara Gallina(✉) and Shankar Iyer

IDT, Mälardalen University, Box 883, 721 23 Västerås, Sweden
{barbara.gallina,shankar.iyer}@mdh.se

Abstract. Recently, Safety-oriented Process Line Engineering (SoPLE) has been proposed as a sound solution to systematize reuse in the context of safety-oriented processes described within safety-related standards. Currently, however, no metrics have been used to measure the actual gain in terms of reuse that the application of this engineering method entails. To overcome this lack of quantitative evidence, we adopt the GQM$^+$ Strategies model, an extension of the Goal/Question/Metric (GQM) paradigm, for measurements. After having defined our specific measurement goals, we build on top of existing metrics, defined for measuring product-related reuse, and we translate them in our semantic space to evaluate our goals. We then apply our GQM$^+$ Strategies model on a ECSS-compliant SoPL to illustrate and assess its usefulness.

Keywords: SoPLs · Process improvement · Change management GQM$^+$ Strategies · GQM · ECSS-E-ST-40C

1 Introduction

In the context of (safety) life-cycles mandated by standards, process improvement via Safety-oriented Process Line Engineering (SoPLE) seems to be feasible. SoPLE represents a solution to manage change in the context of safety-critical systems development processes. Change management is a key component in process improvement infrastructures [24]. Implementation of SoPLs in an organization, however, needs to be planned and justified. Metrics to measure their effectiveness have been so far neglected. A lack of metrics can impede their adoption. Organizations considering adoption of SoPLs are faced with the upfront questions regarding the selection of the right processes for conversion to derive the maximum benefits in the shortest time frame. Measurement of SoPLs starts at the design phase of software development and also covers all verification and validation activities.

Resources can be allocated to an endeavor only in the presence of objective justification of the economic benefits. To provide such justification, we need an appropriate measurement methodology. In this paper, we build on top of the GQM$^+$ Strategies model [9] (shortened GQMPS), extension of the

X. Larrucea et al. (Eds.): EuroSPI 2018, CCIS 896, pp. 469–479, 2018.
https://doi.org/10.1007/978-3-319-97925-0_40

Goal/Question/Metric (GQM) paradigm [10], a goal-based software implementation and measurement paradigm. More specifically, we customize it to offer a SoPLE-targeted GQMPS, which we apply on a space domain-related SoPL. Finally, we discuss our findings and sketch future research directions.

The rest of this paper is organized as follows. In Sect. 2, we provide background information. In Sect. 3, we present our GQM$^+$ model for SoPL evaluation. In Sect. 4, we evaluate the benefits of an ECSS-compliant SoPL. In Sect. 5, we discuss the synergies between the SPI Manifesto and SoPLE-targeted GQMPS. In Sect. 6, we discuss the related work. Finally, in Sect. 7, we conclude the paper and sketch future research directions.

2 Background

2.1 ECSS Standards: Focus on Software Development

ECSS-E-ST-40C is a space standard that covers all aspects of space system software engineering including requirements definition, design, production, verification and validation, transfer, operations and maintenance [3,20]. Tailoring rules are provided in a specific annex, *Annex R (normative)*, to enable manufacturers as well as suppliers to customize their engineering processes. The tailoring is conducted based on the software criticality, which ranges from A to D. Different customizations, performed by the different customers, can be seen as different single processes within a family of processes.

In this section, we limit our attention to a very small portion of ECSS-E-ST-40C, Section 5.6.2 (validation process implementation). We recall that this process is constituted of a series of activities. Each of these activities consists of various tasks, which in turn contain various steps.

Establishment of a software validation process (5.6.2.1)
- Establish validation process to validate the software (5.6.2.1a)
- Select associated methods, techniques, and tools for performing the validation tasks (5.6.2.1b)
- Determine the validation effort and the degree of organizational independence of the effort (5.6.2.1c).

Selection of an independent software verification and validation (ISVV) organization (5.6.2.2)
- Select a qualified organization if the project warrants an independent validation effort (5.6.2.2a)
- Assure the independence and authority of the conductor to perform the validation tasks (5.6.2.2b).

The activity *5.6.2.2* is composed of two tasks, *5.6.2.2a* and *5.6.2.2b*. According to Annex R, for instance, the tasks *5.6.2.2a* and *5.6.2.2b* are applicable for criticality levels A and B only. This limited process portion exemplifies what is typically required in terms of process engineering, i.e., complying with the requirements while tailoring.

2.2 SoPLE

SoPLE was introduced by Gallina et al. [14,17] and applied in various domains (see for instance [15] for its usage in the context of tool qualification re-certification and [25] for its usage in the nuclear domain). SoPLE consists of a two-phase method. The first phase is aimed at engineering the domain from a process perspective i.e., identifying and systematizing process-related commonalities and variabilities in order to concurrently engineer a set of processes (SoPL). The second phase is aimed at deriving single safety-oriented processes via selection and composition of commonalities and variabilities. From a tooling perspective, SoPLE can be supported by the integration of Eclipse Process Framework (EPF) Composer [2] and Base Variability Resolution (BVR) Tool [1], where EPF Composer is used to model the base process and its related library, while BVR Tool is used to model (VSpec), resolve (Resolution) and realize (Realization) the variability. More precisely, VSpec permits users to model the variability in a feature diagram-like fashion. Resolution permits users to configure (make choices at variation points, where desired variants can be selected) their process. Finally, Realization permits users to bind the conceptual representation of the variable elements with the concrete elements in the base model. The integration of EPF Composer and BVR Tool is described in more details in [19].

2.3 Reuse-Related Metrics

In [12], Berger et al. define several metrics which provide different perspectives for assessing the suitability for setting up product lines. Among such metrics, in this section, we recall Size of Commonality (SoC) and Product-related Reusability (PrR).

(a) *SoC* measures the number of reusable/identical components in a product line. For evaluating a given set of similar products constituted of n products, each product pi with $1 \leq i \leq n, n \geq 2$ is decomposed into a set Cpi of m so called reasonable atomic pieces, where each piece is denoted cj with $1 \leq j \leq m, m \geq 1$. To perform a decomposition, all components/atomic pieces must be identified and formally specified. An annotated, directed graph is specified for each product which reflects the dependencies (called signatures) between all components. These dependencies can be logical or communicative. SoC is determined by comparing the component signatures. A syntactic comparison of signatures is made based on the names of the components while a semantic comparison is made from the behavioral profiles of the components which capture behavioral constraints. If the signatures are identical, the components are identical. *SoC* is computed as shown in Eq. 1(a), where pi represents the products of the product line, i ranges from *1* to n and C_{pi} represents the set of components of the product i.

(b) *PrR* measures the extent of reusability of the common components for a specific product. *PrR* is computed as shown in Eq. 1(b).

$$(a)\ SoC = \left| \bigcap_{1}^{n} C_{pi} \right| \quad (b)\ PrRi = \frac{SoC}{|Cpi|} \tag{1}$$

2.4 GQM$^+$ Strategies

The GQMPS model links measurement programs to higher level organization goals and strategies [9]. GQMPS is built as an extension of the GQM paradigm, a top down approach, in which measurements are based on measurement goals [10]. The GQM paradigm consists of three levels: the conceptual level (Measurement Goal) where the objectives are defined, the operational level (Question) where the questions are made and the quantitative level where the metrics are defined. These levels are also hierarchically organized in a pyramid structure. The apex of the pyramid is represented by a measurement goal, which specifies the purpose of measurement, the object which is being measured, the issue to be measured and the viewpoint from which the measurement is taken. This measurement goal is refined by a set of questions which breaks down the goal into its significant elements. Each question is further refined into one or more metrics. These metrics may either be objective or subjective in nature. Further, a particular metric may be used to answer more than one question.

The GQMPS model helps organizations to align multi-level organization goals and strategies to the measurement goals. It consists of two perspectives, the Organizational and Planning Perspective (OPP) and the Control Perspective (CP). The OPP and CP structures help incorporate dependencies among different levels of the organization. The OPP is concerned with the organizational goals and strategies while the CP is concerned with the measurements. The structure of the OPP resembles a pyramid with the top goal of the organization at the apex. The top goal is broken down into one or more strategies. Each strategy can be further split into one or more goals and associated strategies until the strategies cannot be further split into lower goals. The CP structure is built using the GQM paradigm. Each organizational goal is linked to a GQM structure in the CP via a measurement goal. These links enable alignment of organizational goals and strategies with measurement goals. This ensures that organizations invest resources only in meaningful and essential data collection and analysis activities.

3 GQM$^+$ Strategies Model for SoPLE Evaluation

In this section we develop our GQMPS model for a SoPL with a focus on reusability of safety-oriented processes. A consolidated view of the GQMPS model is shown in Fig. 1. The SoPLE organization may be concerned with goals related to the feasibility of establishing SoPLs (pre-SoPL) or goals related to assessing the effectiveness of the established SoPLs (post-SoPL). In this paper, we limit our discussion to pre-SoPL goals, established SoPLs are not in place yet.

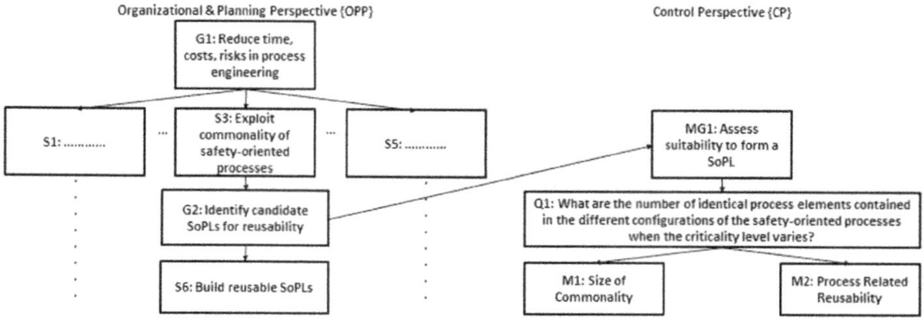

Fig. 1. SoPLE-targeted GQM$^+$ Strategies model

The OPP structure reflects the organizational goals and strategies starting with the overall organization goal at the top and the related strategies broken down below, reflecting the SoPLE organization goals and their related strategies. We show the association of the top organizational goal (*G1*) to the strategy (*S3*) of 'Exploit commonality of safety-oriented processes'. The strategy *S3* is further reduced to the software development organization (SDO) goal *G2*, that of 'identify candidate SoPLs for reusability' supporting the strategy *S6*, 'Build reusable SoPLs'. Strategy *S3* is reduced to a single SDO goal for illustration purposes, though, it may be reduced to additional goals, such as productivity and quality related goals. The CP part of the model links the goal *G2* to the measurement goal *MG1*, 'Assess suitability to form a SoPL'. The viewpoint is that of the SoPL manager who belongs to the SDO and has overall organizational responsibility for software development with formation of SoPLs as the object. *MG1* is progressively refined to questions *Q1* and *Q2* and the metrics *M1* and *M2* addressing the extent of commonality.

4 Evaluating the Benefits of an ECSS-compliant SoPL

4.1 ECSS-compliant SoPL

Based on the information recalled in Sects. 2.1 and 2.2, in this section, we model the ECSS-compliant SoPL related to the *Validation Process Implementation.* To model it, we use BVR/VSpec Editor. Figure 2 presents our SoPL for *Validation Process Implementation (5.6.2).* As mentioned in Sect. 2.1, the activity 5.6.2.2 is composed of two tasks. The variants of this activity depend on the associated process criticality. This results in a certain number of reusable elements and zero or more variable elements of the validation process implementation (5.6.2) depending on the associated criticality. The choices in our SoPL are the activities and tasks described in Sect. 2.1 and the criticality levels. One and only one of the four criticality levels are valid for any SoPL variant. The constraints are enforced when resolving a particular SoPL variant. For instance, in our SoPL, constraint c1 enforces the requirement that f7 is required only when the criticality level is either A or B.

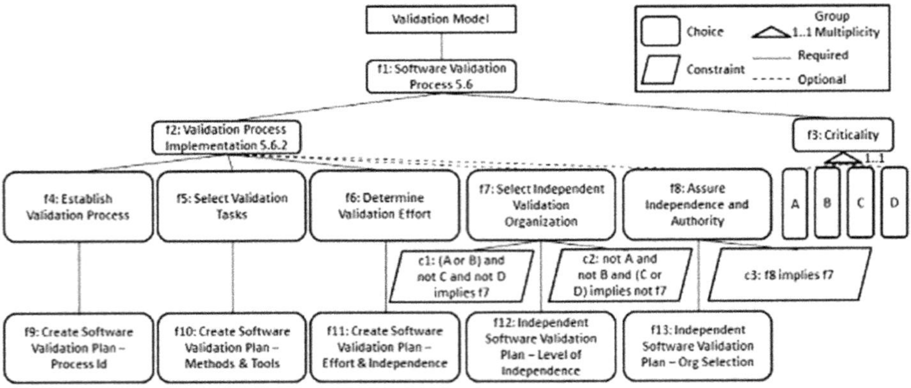

Fig. 2. ECSS-compliant SoPL

4.2 Applying GQM$^+$ Strategies

An application of our SoPLE-targeted GQMPS model is shown in Fig. 3. Goals *G1* and *G2* are the AMASS consortium organization goals [8] while *G7* is a SoPLE organization goal, namely that of the Software Development Organization (SDO) of the space-related partner [5]. The pre-SoPL implementation goal of the SDO is *Identify candidate SoPLs for reusability.* The SDO goal *G7* links to the measurement goal *MG1*, *Assess suitability to form a SoPL.* Question *Q1* refines *MG1* and addresses process element counting based on the semantic signature of the processes subject to constraints imposed by criticality levels of the processes. *Q1* pertains to the commonality of the process elements. We can logically infer that, higher the commonality, the more likely is the suitability for adopting a process line approach. We define two metrics (*M1* and *M2*), regarding the question *Q1*, which are *SoC* and *PrR* respectively interpreted for processes i.e., *SoC* measures the number of reusable/identical components in a (safety-oriented) process line and *PrR* measures the extent of reusability of the common components for a specific process.

Validation Process Implementation constitutes our SoPL and is treated in a similar manner to the product line referred to in Sect. 2.3. The activities which make up our SoPL constitute the elements and are similar to the components in the product line. The single processes can be configured based on the applicable criticality level and the associated constraints. As we have 6 common elements (see features f4, f5, f6, f9, f10 and f11), *SoC* computes to 6. The metric *PrR* is computed for each single process. As our SoPL consists of 4 criticality levels, we have at least 4 single processes. The number of elements in the single processes for criticality levels A, B, C and D are 10 (f4 through f13), 10 (f4 through f13), 6 (f4, f5, f6, f9, f10 and f11) and 6 (f4, f5, f6, f9, f10 and f11) respectively. Thus, *PrR's* for single processes A, B, C and D are computed as 0.6, 0.6, 1 and 1 respectively.

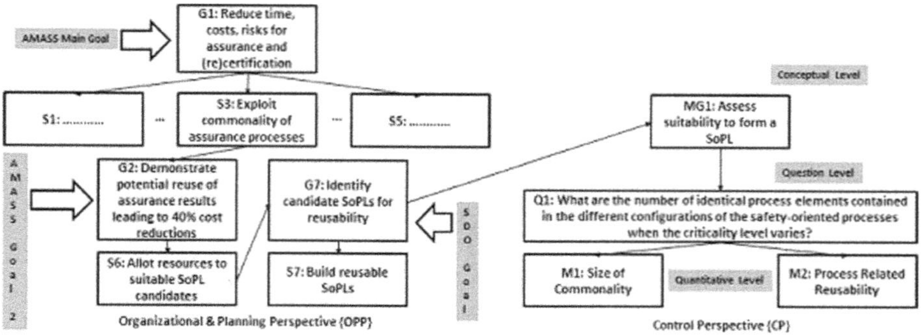

Fig. 3. Application of our SoPLE-targeted GQM$^+$ Strategies model

4.3 Discussion

In this section we discuss the findings related to the application of SoPLE-targeted GQMPS. The discussion covers the following three main bolded aspects.

General Soundness. Despite the simplicity of the considered example, we can state that the application of SoPLE-targeted GQMPS for measuring SoPLE effectiveness is sound since it has the potential to generate objective justifications for its adoption. We have employed our SoPLE-targeted GQMPS model to measure SoPL effectiveness with reference to the AMASS consortium organization and the space-related partner. Our rather small SoPL and the computed metrics establish a case for the adoption of SoPLE to the ECSS software development process. The *SoC* determined for our SoPL indicates a high degree of commonality despite the variability introduced by the criticality levels. We observe from the computed *PrRs*, the extent of reusability of the common elements for SoPLs related to criticality levels C and D are higher than that for levels A and B.

Maturity. SoPLE-targeted GQMPS's maturity varies with respect to the examination's angle. In terms of motivation and definition, SoPLE-targeted GQMPS is fairly mature. However, in terms of validation, it is still in its embryo stage. A true in-depth validation in industrial settings has not yet been carried out. We need to further examine our findings and the impact of the other process elements, which have a bearing on the safety-oriented process line such roles, tools employed, input/output work products. With respect to roles, as known, processes are nothing if not performed by people [22] and people skills are recognized to be crucial and need to be audited. According to ECSS-M-ST-10C [4], 5.2.1.2.e, for instance, the supplier shall demonstrate that the key personnel have the necessary qualification, skills and experience to perform the task for which they are allocated. Clearly, the necessary skills may vary based on the criticality of the tasks to be performed. With respect to tools employed, their reusability will be constrained by the existence of evidence in favour of their usage to automate a specific critical task. A tool qualified for a certain level will need to be re-qualified to be used to automate a task of a higher criticality level. With respect to input/output work products, in the context of SoPLE, only their syntactical reusability is expected to be considered. Their semantic content is instead expected to be addressed via product line engineering. In addition to the space domain, other domains could/should be explored. Within the AMASS project, SoPLE-targeted GQMPS has been included as part of the AMASS measurement framework [6] and thus additional validation data should be developed as part of the last iteration of the project, after application of the measurement framework.

Tool Support. SoPLE-targeted GQMPS is not yet tool-supported. The computation of Size of Commonality and Product-related Reusability could be easily implemented as additional functionalities of BVR Tool. Similarly, an Eclipse-based editor could be developed to be able to edit SoPLE-targeted GQMPS applications.

5 SPI Manifesto and SoPLE-Targeted GQMPS: Synergies

SoPLE-targeted GQMPS enables the measurement of SoPLE effectiveness and thus permits process engineers to achieve an objective justification regarding the economic benefits related to the application of SoPLE as software process improvement strategy. SoPLE represents a solution to manage change in the context of safety-critical systems development processes. Change management is a key component in process improvement infrastructures [24].

As discussed in Sect. 4.3, when applying SoPLE, not only the breaking down of the work should be considered but all other relevant process elements, which may have an impact on SoPLE evaluation as well as on Software Process Improvement. Concerning roles, in addition to the technical skills (as per standards used in safety-critical software engineering), management skills [21,22] as well as social responsibility-related skills [23] should also be considered in order to ensure SPI-readiness attitude. Moreover, as observed by Gallina et al. [16] in the Swedish context, culture may also influence the SPI-readiness. Thus, technical skills alone are not sufficient and thus they cannot be analysed in isolation when reasoning about the reusability of a role from one process to a different one since cultural, managerial, and social responsibility-related (lack of) skills may (hinder/) foster his/her successful deployment. Existing dependencies between skills and other process elements should be specified. To this purpose, the integration between EPF Composer and BVR Tool offers an adequate tool support for SoPLE. Via EPF Composer, process engineers have the possibility to model a single process of the SoPL and then make it vary via BVR Tool (more specifically, via the VSpec, Resolution, and Realization editors). As shown in Fig. 2, process engineers have also the possibility to specify constraints that limit the selection and composition of reusable process elements. Skill-related constraints could/should be specified in order to properly constrain the role-reusability based on contextual information.

6 Related Work

In the literature, other works have tackled the necessity of measuring reuse. In [18], Her et al. define a framework for evaluating reusability of core assets in a product line. The authors model the measures based on various characteristics of core assets. A key limitation of the defined metrics is their subjective nature. Our GQMPS model also considers metrics based on core asset characteristics but the characteristics can be judged objectively. Moreover, we also relate measurement objectives to organization goals and strategies. In [13], Dijkman et al. propose similarity measures for comparison of process models held in a repository to enable reuse, based on node matching, structural and behavioral similarity with similar results. We also make use of similarity-based measures but we build on top of different metrics. Becker et al. [11] present a survey of methods to define and calculate 23 similarity measures for business processes and compare these when applied to a same set of models to study the differences in similarity and observe differences based on process characteristics. Our work focuses on safety-oriented processes and not on business processes. Moreover, our primary goal in this paper is to shape a methodological framework for measurement.

7 Conclusion and Future Work

In the context of safety life-cycles mandated by standards, process improvement via SoPLE seems to be feasible. Implementation of SoPLs in an organization, however, needs to be planned and justified. This requires the ability to measure the effectiveness of the implementation at all stages of the development effort. In this paper, we have proposed a SoPL-targeted GQMPS model to enable the measurement of SoPLE effectiveness. Then, we have applied it and demonstrated the effectiveness of SoPLE in the context of ECSS standards. We may logically infer that because we measured and have the evidence for appropriateness of SoPLE, implementation should enable process improvement. Our SoPL is built on a very small part of the ECSS specifications and adopts an organization goal/strategy linked measurement model. Though our study has been performed in relation to an organization's specific processes and the associated standards, we examined only pre-SoPL implementation metrics.

In the near term future, the proposed SoPL-targeted GQMPS model requires to be validated by assessing several SoPLs. Moreover, further work is required to extend our SoPLE-targeted GQMPS model to incorporate post-SoPL implementation metrics and link the related measurement goal to goal *G2* in our SoPLE-targeted GQMPS model. Finally, in a long-term future, tool-support will be developed.

Acknowledgments. This work is supported by EU and VINNOVA via the ECSEL JU under grant agreement No 692474, AMASS project [7].

References

1. BVR Tool. http://modelbased.net/tools/bvr-tool/. Accessed 9 July 2018
2. Eclipse Process Framework Project. http://www.eclipse.org/epf/. Accessed 9 July 2018
3. ECSS, ECSS-E-ST-40C: Space Engineering-Software. http://wwwis.win.tue.nl/2R690/doc/ECSS-E-ST-40C(6March2009).pdf. Accessed 9 July 2018
4. ECSS, ECSS-M-ST-10C: Space project management - Project planning and implementation. http://everyspec.com/ESA/download.php?spec=ECSS-M-ST-10C.048180.pdf. Accessed 9 July 2018
5. AMASS. Deliverable D1.1: Case Studies Description and Business Impact (2017). Accessed 9 July 2018
6. AMASS. Deliverable D1.3: Evaluation framework and quality metrics (2017). Accessed 9 July 2018
7. AMASS: Architecture-driven, Multi-concern and Seamless Assurance and Certification of Cyber-Physical Systems. http://www.amass-ecsel.eu. Accessed 9 July 2018
8. AMASS Consortium: Objectives. AMASS. http://www.amass-ecsel.eu/content/objectives. Accessed 9 July 2018
9. Basili, V., et al.: GQM^{+}strategies in a nutshell. Aligning Organizations Through Measurement. TFISSSE, pp. 9–17. Springer, Cham (2014). https://doi.org/10.1007/978-3-319-05047-8_2
10. Basili, V.R., Caldiera, G., Rombach, H.D.: The goal question metric approach, 1994. Citado **3**, 11 (2012)
11. Becker, M., Laue, R.: A comparative survey of business process similarity measures. Comput. Ind. **63**(2), 148–167 (2012)
12. Berger, C., Rendel, H., Rumpe, B.: Measuring the ability to form a product line from existing products. arXiv preprint arXiv:1409.6583 (2014)
13. Dijkman, R., Dumas, M., Van Dongen, B., Käärik, R., Mendling, J.: Similarity of business process models: metrics and evaluation. Inf. Syst. **36**, 498–516 (2011)
14. Gallina, B., Kashiyarandi, S., Martin, H., Bramberger, R.: Modeling a safety-and automotive-oriented process line to enable reuse and flexible process derivation. In: IEEE 38th International Computer Software and Applications Conference Workshops (COMPSACW), pp. 504–509 (2014)
15. Gallina, B., Kashiyarandi, S., Zugsbratl, K., Geven, A.: Enabling cross-domain reuse of tool qualification certification artefacts. In: Bondavalli, A., Ceccarelli, A., Ortmeier, F. (eds.) SAFECOMP 2014. LNCS, vol. 8696, pp. 255–266. Springer, Cham (2014). https://doi.org/10.1007/978-3-319-10557-4_28
16. Gallina, B., Nyberg, M.: Reconciling the ISO 26262-compliant and the agile documentation management in the swedish context. In: Critical Automotive applications: Robustness and Safety (CARS), Matthieu Roy. HAL, Paris, September 2015
17. Gallina, B., Sljivo, I., Jaradat, O.: Towards a safety-oriented process line for enabling reuse in safety critical systems development and certification. In: 35th Annual IEEE Software Engineering Workshop (SEW), pp. 148–157 (2012)
18. Her, J.S., Kim, J.H., Oh, S.H., Rhew, S.Y., Kim, S.D.: A framework for evaluating reusability of core asset in product line engineering. Inf. Softw. Technol. **49**(7), 740–760 (2007)

19. Javed, M.A., Gallina, B.: Safety-oriented process line engineering via seamless integration between EPF composer and BVR tool. In: 22nd International Systems and Software Product Line Conference (SPLC), 10–14 September, Gothenburg, Sweden. ACM Digital Library (2018, in press)
20. Jones, M., Gomez, E., Mantineo, A., Mortensen, U.K.: Introducing ECSS software-engineering standards within ESA, August 2002. http://www.esa.int/esapub/bulletin/bullet111/chapter21_bul111.pdf
21. Korsaa, M., et al.: The SPI manifesto and the ECQA SPI manager certification scheme. J. Softw.: Evol. Process **25**(5), 525–540 (2012)
22. Korsaa, M., et al.: The people aspects in modern process improvement management approaches. J. Softw.: Evol. Process **25**(4), 381–391 (2013)
23. Messnarz, R., et al.: Social responsibility aspects supporting the success of SPI. J. Softw.: Evol. Process **26**(3), 284–294 (2014)
24. Pries-Heje, J., Johansen, J. (eds.) MANIFESTO Software Process Improvement eurospi.net, Alcala, Spain (2010). http://www.iscn.com/Images/SPI_Manifesto_A.1.2.2010.pdf. Accessed 9 July 2018
25. Varkoi, T., Mäkinen, T., Gallina, B., Cameron, F., Nevalainen, R.: Towards systematic compliance evaluation using safety-oriented process lines and evidence mapping. In: Stolfa, J., Stolfa, S., O'Connor, R.V., Messnarz, R. (eds.) EuroSPI 2017. CCIS, vol. 748, pp. 83–95. Springer, Cham (2017). https://doi.org/10.1007/978-3-319-64218-5_7

Hardware SPICE Extension for Automotive SPICE 3.1

Christian Schlager[3], Richard Messnarz[1(✉)], Harald Sporer[1], Armin Riess[2], Ralf Mayer[4], and Steffen Bernhardt[4]

[1] ISCN GesmbH, Graz, Austria
rmess@iscn.com
[2] BBraun, Melsungen, Germany
Armin.Riess@bbraun.com
[3] Magna ECS, St. Valentin, Austria
Christian.Schlager@magna.com
[4] BOSCH Engineering Gmbh, Gerlingen, Germany
ralf.mayer@de.bosch.com

Abstract. Automotive SPICE is an assessment model which is published and maintained by the VDA and the SPICE User Group (www.automotivespice.com). Version 3.1 has been published in Nov. 2017 and in Jan. 2018 a guideline for interpreting (Blue-Gold Book) ASPICE 3.1 has been published by the VDA. Also Automotive SPICE 3.1 in Annex D outlines that the plugin concept will foresee that a hardware and a mechanics SPICE assessment model will be integrated in the future. The SOQRATES working group (www.soqrates.de) which includes a group of leading Automotive suppliers developed a hardware SPICE model in 2016 – 2017 which can be plugged into Automotive SPICE 3.1 and used for hardware assessment. Also in the working party the ISO 26262 norm has been reviewed since product safety assessments according to the ISO 26262 functional safety norm include hardware assessment. All base practices of the hardware SPICE assessment model therefore have been extended with further checklists to include a functional safety scope. The paper describes the main elements of the hardware SPICE assessment model, how it can be plugged into Automotive SPICE 3.1, and where it is mainly used in the first trial projects.

Keywords: Automotive SPICE 3.1 · Functional safety · ISO 26262
Hardware assessment · Hardware SPICE

1 The Plug in Concept of Automotive SPICE 3.1

Figure 1 below illustrates the plugin concept in Automotive SPICE 3.1 [1]. The system V-model includes the processes SYS.1 Requirements Elicitation, SYS.2 System Requirements Analysis, SYS.3 System Architectural Design, SYS.4 System Integration and Integration Test, and SYS.5 System Qualification Test.

The software V-model includes the processes SWE.1 software requirements analysis, SWE.2 SW architectural design, SWE.3 SW detailed design and unit construction, SWE.4 software unit verification, SWE.4 software integration and integration test, SWE.5 SW qualification test.

X. Larrucea et al. (Eds.): EuroSPI 2018, CCIS 896, pp. 480–491, 2018.
https://doi.org/10.1007/978-3-319-97925-0_41

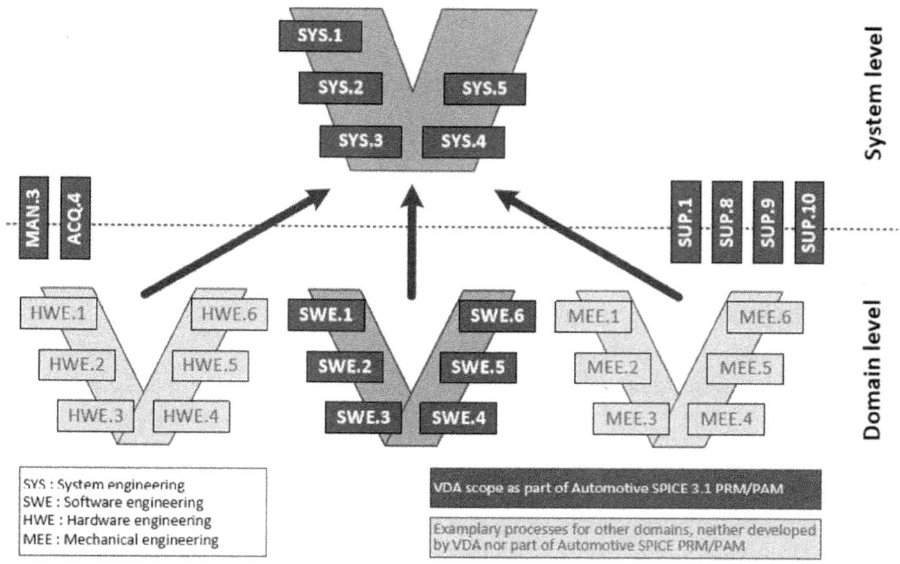

Fig. 1. The plugin concept of Automotive SPICE 3.1

Figure 2 below shows the traceability concept of Automotive SPICE which in Annex D describes the traceability concept for system and software level but still not for the hardware or mechanics level.

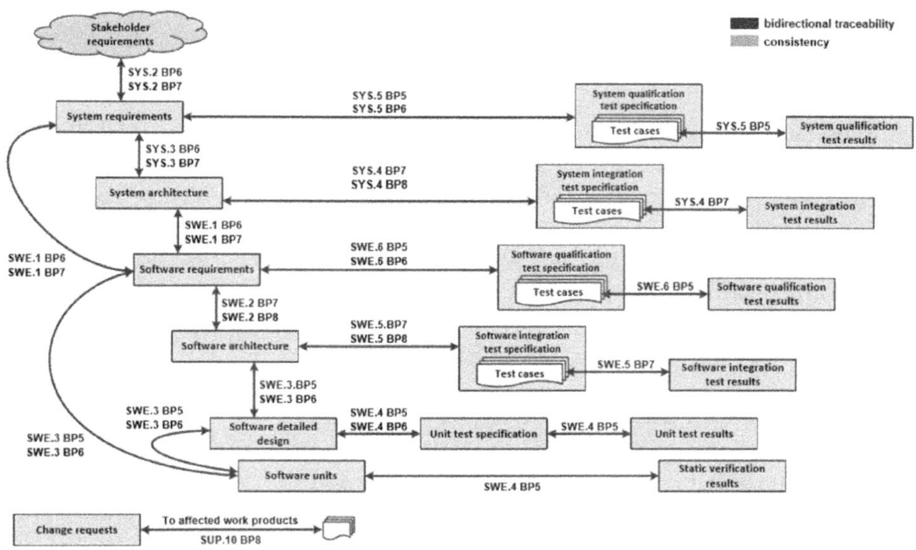

Fig. 2. Bidirectional traceability and consistency concept of ASPICE 3.1

Automotive SPICE 3.1 (see Fig. 1) does not contain a description and base practices for the HWE.1 to HWE.6 processes. However, Automotive SPICE 3.1 foresees a plug in model that can be used for an extended assessment including hardware. The SOQRATES working group developed a first version of this HWE.1 – HWE.6 processes and base practices.

HWE Spice includes the following processes

- HWE.1 Hardware Requirements Analysis
- HWE.2 Hardware Architectural Design
- HWE.3 Hardware Detailed Design
- HWE.4 Hardware Unit Verification
- HWE.5 Hardware Integration and Integration Test
- HWE.6 Hardware Qualification Test.

2 Research Method

The European Commission directive 2001/95/EC on General Product Safety and the decision 768/2008 of the European Parliament forced the Automotive industry -

- to report any safety critical issue to a publicly available database. These news are also used by journalists to report about large recall actions of Automotive manufacturers.
- to either solve the safety critical issue or to withdraw the products from the market.

Automotive manufacturers are not liable if they apply the state of the art in their developments and consider the safety norms appropriately. However, there is no clear definition of what a state of the art really is. Research papers might be used but they are not strong enough to withstand in court because you always find papers with contradictory views.

Therefore task forces like SOQRATES [7] (www.soqrates.de, formed in 2003 and with a large group of leading suppliers in Automotive) agreed a research method to define a state of the art. Best practices for analysis methods, design approaches, assessment model understanding etc. are compared among the group of the largest suppliers and joint best practices are agreed and published. This way these best practices are declared as a state of the art. This paper publishes such a consensus of a group of experts from leading suppliers in Automotive industry.

3 Extended Hardware SPICE Terminology

In Automotive SPICE the smallest part into which a software is decomposed is called SW unit. One of the research questions was: What is a hardware unit and the smallest part we will look at in an assessment?

The functional safety (ISO 26262) norm already included a hardware assessment and therefore the terminology of the ISO 26262 norm has been re-used. However, also the ISO 26262 norm did not define hardware unit, but hardware element and hardware part. Below you find the terminology from the ISO 26262 as well as the hardware unit definition which was agreed in the SOQRATES working party.

HW Element (ISO 26262):

- ISO 26262: "system (1.129) or part of a system including components (1.15), hardware, software, hardware parts (1.55), and software units (1.125)" NOTE A component is a part of a system." The numbers 1.xx in this paragraph refer to definitions in part 1 of ISO 26262:2011.
- The top level of HWE in this scope
- HWE.1 requirements are related to this level
- HWE.2 describes the architecture of the element

HW Unit (New Definition):

- "A hardware unit is the smallest block of hardware to which a specific hardware sub-function can be assigned."
- HWE.2 describes an architecture, where the HW units of the HW element are defined
- HWE.3 describes the detailed design of these HW units, that consist of HW parts
- Example: Electrical power supply

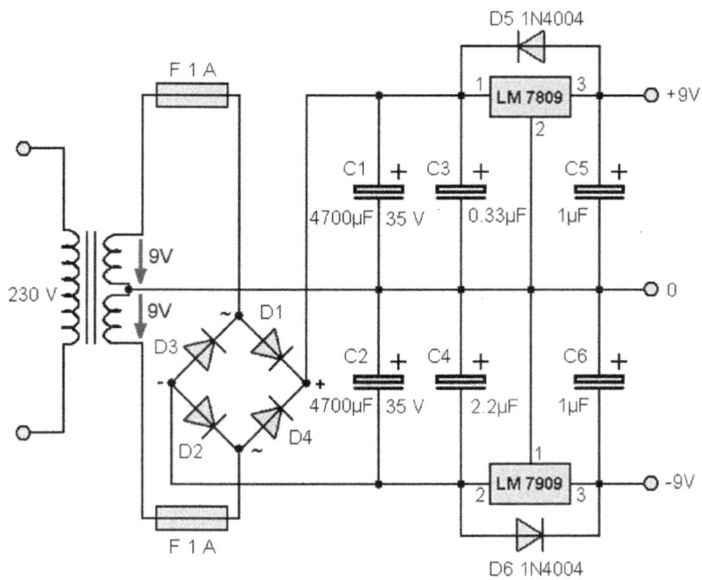

Fig. 3. Example of a hardware unit – electric power supply

In Fig. 3. Above the function of this module is to convert the 230 V to a circuit supply of 9 V. This includes different hardware parts and integrates them to a hardware unit. The hardware unit has a function which can be mapped onto unit testing including e.g. equivalence class test:

- Testing above 240 V, the fuses F1 shall fire, no voltage output
- Testing in 230 ± 10 V range, the system operates and delivers 9v

Hardware units can also include diagnose outputs such as a connection to an ADC that then writes the measured voltage to a register.

HW part (ISO 26262):

- Lowest level of HW
- Parts that are considered not to be sub-divided in this application scope
- E.g. a resistor or an IC.

4 Integrating Functional Safety Aspects in the Hardware Assessment Model

In ISO 26262 [2–4, 6, 8–13] two forms of assessment are done, a safety audit and a safety assessment. While the safety audit is a process assessment like Automotive SPICE the safety assessment is an assessment and evaluation of the product. Also the safety audit includes further aspects which need to be considered when assessing hardware.

Because ISO 26262:2011 assessments are used since years the members of the SOQRATES group expected an integration of both approaches. Therefore in the assessment model in chapter 5 of the paper safety related clauses are listed per Hardware SPICE base practice.

Below you find some specific work products which are additionally needed. The below is just an overview, more details have been described in previous safety related publications.

Safety Selects Parts that are Affected by a Safety Goal: All hardware parts that are affected by a safety goal inherit the ASIL (Automotive Safety integrity level, ASIL A – D) from the safety goal. E.g. In a steering system to not create more torque then demanded by the driver. The driver steering torque is measured by a torque sensor, and this torque is calculated by an ECU (Electronic Control Unit) and used to control an e-motor to provide this torque on the steering rack/system. Every hardware part in this functional chain and which is affected by the safety goal is marked with the proper ASIL A-D level. In steering the above mentioned safety goals is rated as ASIL – D. This includes e.g.

- The controller
- The torque sensor
- The connector from the torque sensor to the ASIC
- The ASIC/IC to convert the torque sensor
- The connection/bus between the ASIC and the controller
- The memory on the ECU
- The bridge to actuate the motor
- the bridge to connect to the motor and the IC to provide the phase currents.

Safety Looks at a FIT Rate: FIT stands for Failure in Time which is measured in hazardous errors occurring in 10^9 operating hours. 1 Fit is 10^{-9}, so one hazardous error in 10^9 operating hours. The higher the ASIL the higher the reliability of a hardware part has to become. And a safety goal rated ASIL D e.g. needs to achieve 10 FIT, which is 10^{-8}. 10^9 h observation time can easily be reached nowadays because cars are nowadays estimated with 10^4 h life time and a fleet of cars might by more than one million (10^6) using that component, making a total of $10^4 * 10^6 = 10^{10}$ h. When looking at single hardware units which are affected by the safety goal the ISO 26262 norm assumes around 100 such components in average and each having 10^{-10} h, so that $100 * 10^{-10} = 10^{-8}$ (meeting 10^{-8} ASIL – D goal).

Safety Uses Diagnostic Coverage to Reduce the FIT: The annex D of part 5 of the safety norm ISO 26262 includes guidance material to address 60%, 90%, or 99% diagnostic coverage. A simplified understanding is the following for signals:

- 60% - only values within range are accepted, so that the system only calculates with valid values.
- 90% - drift can be identified, so if the sensor starts to drift, the deviation can be detected. This usually requires a second separate channel and sensor to compare with.
- 99% - spiked and impact of oscillation is detected.
- 99.9% - together with the hardware manufacturer all known field issues are tested and the faults are detected.

The diagnostic coverage is then used to reduce the fit. E.g. if a controller has 400 FIT but in the architecture a second diverse controller is used to compare with the diagnostic coverage increases to 99%. If all known controller errors are detected (e.g. that both diverse controllers have not the same faults) the diagnostif coverage increases to 99.9%. The probability that the hazardous error is not detected is then decreasing to only $1 - 0.999 = 0.001$. The 400 FIT are then reduced to $400 * 0.001 = 0.4$ FIT.

Safety Looks at Single Point Faults and Latent Faults: The FIT rate is to be considered for single point and latent faults. A single point fault means that if a single hardware part is failing the hazardous error will appear. The latent fault means that the hardware part fails, the diagnose does detect the fault, and then the latent fault appears. The single point fault metric uses the FIT and the diagnose coverage as outlined above.

Safety Uses Decomposition Strategy: If you assign an ASIL – D to a hardware unit a design decision needs to be taken because

- mostly the hardware units/parts cannot be acquired at ASIL-D quality
- by using two different independent and diverse channels helps to increase the diagnostic coverage to 99.9% to get rid of the FIT.

Therefore in most ASIL ranked systems a decomposition into parallel independent parts/channels takes place.

Safety Uses an HSI – Hardware Software Interface: The HSI specifies safety critical hardware interfaces and assigns raw software variables (base software, physical values, registers) and functional software variables. This allows to monitor and test safety critical physical and software parameters influencing the safe system behaviour.

Safety Expects an FMEDA - Failure Modes, Effects, and Diagnostic Analysis, and an FTA [5]: For each safety goal the affected hardware parts and their related diagnostic coverage are used to calculate a total FIT for single point faults. For each safety goal the affected hardware parts and their related diagnostic coverage are used to calculate a total FIT for latent point faults. There are many more such design strategies and they were integrated (using clauses from part 5 of ISO 26262) into the hardware SPICE assessment model.

5 The Hardware SPICE Assessment Model

Below you find an example HWE process as it is defined in the hardware SPICE assessment model. The whole model can be provided by the SOQRATES working party, under the condition that the materials are properly referenced and review input is provided back to the model developers in the SOQRATES group. This model then includes all 6 HWE processes with all base practices and ISO 26262 additional checklists. See example parts of the HWE.3 process below (the complete HWE.3 process is in the appendix (Table 1):

Table 1. Selected example of the HWE.3 Hardware Detailed Design Process

Process ID	HWE.3
Process name	Hardware Detailed Design
Process purpose	The purpose of the Hardware Detailed Design Process is to establish a detailed design for the hardware units
Process outcomes	As a result of successful implementation of this process: 1. A detailed design is developed that describes the composition of all hardware units into hardware parts and interfaces; 2. A detailed description of each hardware component and its interface is available; 3. The dynamic behaviour and resource consumption objectives of the hardware unit and software units related to the particular hardware unit are analysed; and 4. Consistency and bidirectional traceability are established between hardware requirements and hardware detailed design and consistency and bidirectional traceability are established between hardware architecture and the detailed hardware design 5. Hardware detailed design and the relationship to the hardware architectural design is agreed and communicated to all affected parties *Note: Definition of component detailed design includes development of verification criteria*

(*continued*)

Table 1. (*continued*)

Process ID	HWE.3
Base practices	**HWE.3.BP1: Develop hardware detailed design** Develop a hardware design, typically established through schematics, PCB design, layout, integrated circuit design, and similar artefacts, that represents a composition of all required hardware components, and that enables the fulfilment of the established functional and non-functional hardware requirements Develop criteria for verification of the detailed design. [Process Outcome 1] **HWE.3.BP2: Define/Refine interfaces of hardware units** Identify, specify/refine and document the internal and external interface(s) of each hardware component [Process Outcome 2] **HWE.3.BP3: Describe dynamic behaviour** Evaluate and document the timing and dynamic interaction of hardware components to meet the required dynamic behaviour of the system. If applicable include also the interaction with software or mechanic elements related to the particular hardware components Develop verification criteria according to the dynamic behaviour specified above. [Process Outcome 3, 4] *Note: Dynamic behaviour is determined by operating modes (e.g. start-up, shutdown, normal mode, calibration, diagnosis) as well as signal-based (timing, power-staging, transient behaviour of filters during switch operations, EMC, phase-/frequency response, required signal dynamics of amplifiers, power supply rejection/feed-through when changing loads, etc.)*
Output work products	04-00 Design - Hardware Design [Process Outcome 1, 2, 3, 4, 5] 13-19 Review record [Process Outcome 4, 5] 13-22 Traceability record [Process Outcome 5] 17-08 Interface requirement specification [Process Outcome 2]

For each base practice the companies in the working party SOQRATES assigned content of the ISO 26262 norm. This includes assignment of ISO 26262 clauses as well as additional questions that should be asked in case of a safety relevant development project. e.g. the additional questions asked by hardware safety exerts when joining the HWE SPICE assessment for **HWE.3.BP1: Develop hardware detailed design** are (Table 2):

Table 2. Example of additional safety related questions

• Can the individual elements/functional blocks be recognized in the PCB layout? • Do style guide/checklist exist for creating schematics (no flying pins, maximum amplification, blocking capacitors, termination of wires, high speed design vs. slew rates, clarity and comprehensibility) • Layout rules (manual vs. auto routing, use of signal constraints, minimum/maximum number of layers, impedance controlled layouts, parallel routing of differential signals, isochrone routing of time-critical signals of bus lines (timed routes); isolation and creeping distances; distances between not plated vias, pins in critrical areas e.g. measurement of I, U; proximity of blocking capacitors to ICs, connecting capacitors near to VCC or GND, IO protection, EMC/EMI filtering, thermal pads for higher power dissipation, separated GND/Power planes, Signal return path vs. layers) • Have mentioned guides been used (DRC, Checklist protocol) • Are the corresponding output files present (schematics, layout, Gerber-files, programming plans, ICT, …) • Are there assembly variants? Have they been marked and documented properly? • Have part tolerance been considered in part selection and layout? • Have special measures been done to safety critical areas? (e.g. by over-provisioning of parts? see ISO 26262-5:2011, 9.4.2.4: This requirement applies to ASIL C and D of the safety goal. A single-point fault occurring in a hardware part shall only be considered acceptable if dedicated measures are taken.) • Are connectors on the PCB and the future place sufficiently accessible?
• Have designs/outputs been placed under proper version/config control • Schematics • Layout/PCB • Assembly • Configuration-/calibration data • Variants • Labels • Housing • Material ID • Are verification criteria available

For example, the assignment of clauses for **HWE.3.BP1: Develop hardware detailed design** is shown below (Table 3):

Table 3. Example of ISO 26262 clauses assigned to a base practice

7.4.2.2 Non-functional causes for failure of a safety-related hardware part shall be considered during hardware detailed design, including the following influences, if applicable: temperature, vibrations, water, dust, EMI, noise factor, cross-talk originating either from other hardware parts of the hardware component or from its environment
7.4.2.3 The operating conditions of the hardware parts used in the hardware detailed design shall comply with the specification of their environmental and operational limits
7.4.2.4 Robust design principles should be considered

6 Expected Impact and Outlook

The AQUA [18, 19] (Knowledge alliance for Quality in Automotive engineering) integrates different norms and standards related to Functional safety, Automotive SPICE, APQP, Cybersecurity to manage the complexity of the systems and to achieve quality, safety, and security in the vehicle. AQUA created a new job role of a quality engineer that can integrate these methods and standards. AQUA will integrate the hardware SPICE into their educational program.

Major Tier 1 in SOQRATES [6] have co-developed to create a first version of the hardware SPICE plugin model. It can be used as a first draft to assess not inly the system and software but also the hardware in Automotive SPICE assessments. Since functional safety (ISO 26262 [2–4, 6, 8–13]) already does hardware assessment the hardware SPICE assessment model builds the bridge between the safety and the Automotive SPICE understanding.

7 The SPI Manifesto Revisited

The SPI manifesto [14–17] describes values and principles which need to be considered to make improvements work in an organisation. One of the approaches is to start with an assessment and to derive an improvement list. This is then used to set up an improvement program.

The principle "**Use dynamic and adaptable models as needed**" means that depending on the need of organisations specific models can be adapted. The hardware SPICE assessment model is such a new model which is needed in the Automotive domain.

The principle "**Base improvement on experience and measurements**" means that best practice experiences need to be shared and the usage must be tracked and measured. Since the model was developed in a group of Tier 1 in the SOQRATES working group the model development was based on such an experience and best practice sharing approach.

An additional principle proposed for the SPI manifesto is: "**Observe new trends and state of the art practices on the market and adopt**". The product liability law and the RAPEX (www.rapex.com) database changed the market because hazardous faults as well as legal violations in cars lead to a mandatory recall action and all cars must be repaired. This creates huge cost and thus new state of the art standards like functional safety, cybersecurity etc. became an important issue.

Acknowledgements. We are grateful to the members of the SOQRATES [6] working group who have contributed: Alastair Walker (LORIT), Alexander Much (Elektrobit), Frank König, Martin Dallinger, Thomas Wegner (ZF Friedrichshafen AG), Armin Riess (BBraun), Dietmar Kinalzyk (HELLA), Ralf Mayer (BOSCH Engineering), Gerhard Griessnig (AVL), Andreas Gruber (ZKW), Rainer Dreves, Ivan Sokic, Stephan Habel (Continental), Christian Schlager, Thomas Stiglhuber (Magna Powertrain ECS), Andreas Riel (ISCN/Grenoble INP), Helmut Zauchner, Christoph Karner (KTM), Andreas Gruber (ZKW), Georg Macher (AVL), Bernhard Sechser (Methodpark), Lutz Haunert (G&D), Damjan Ekert (ISCN), Richard Messnarz (ISCN).

We are also grateful to the European Commission which has funded some of the initiatives that funded the development of skills in the Automotive sector. ISCN is a member of AQUA (Knowledge Alliance for Quality in Automotive Engineering, 2013–2015) [18, 19], and AQU (Automotive Quality Universities, 2015–2017), and the BLUEPRINT project DRIVES (2018–2021).

References

1. Automotive SPICE 3.1, November 2017. www.automotivespice.com
2. ISO - International Organization for Standardization. ISO 26262 Road vehicles Functional Safety Part 1–10 (2011)
3. ISO - International Organization for Standardization. IEC 61508 Functional safety of electrical/electronic/programmable electronic safety-related systems
4. ISO - International Organization for Standardization. IEC 60812 Analysis techniques for system reliability - Procedure for failure mode and effects analysis (FMEA) (2006)
5. ISO - International Organization for Standardization. IEC 61025 Fault tree analysis (FTA), December 2006
6. ISO – International Organization for Standardization. ISO CD 26262-2018 2nd Edition Road vehicles Functional Safety (to appear)
7. SOQRATES, Task Forces Developing Integration of Automotive SPICE, ISO 26262 an d SAE J3061. http://soqrates.eurospi.net/
8. Messnarz, R., Kreiner, C., Riel, A.: Integrating automotive SPICE, functional safety, and cybersecurity concepts: a cybersecurity layer model. Softw. Qual. Prof. **18**(4), 13 (2016)
9. Messnarz, R., Kreiner, C., Riel, A., et al.: Implementing functional safety standards (SafEUr). Softw. Qual. Prof. **17**(3) (2015)
10. Macher, G., Sporer, H., Brenner, E., Kreiner, C.: Supporting cyber-security based on hardware-software interface definition. In: Kreiner, C., O'Connor, R.V., Poth, A., Messnarz, R. (eds.) EuroSPI 2016. CCIS, vol. 633, pp. 148–159. Springer, Cham (2016). https://doi.org/10.1007/978-3-319-44817-6_12
11. Macher, G., Messnarz, R., Kreiner, C., et al.: Integrated Safety and Security Development in the Automotive Domain, Working Group 17AE-0252/2017-01-1661, SAE International, June 2017
12. Redmill, F.: Understanding the use, misuse and abuse of safety integrity levels. In: Proceedings of the Eighth Safety-Critical Systems Symposium, Southampton, 8–10 February 2000. Springer, Heidelberg (2000)
13. Much, A.: Automotive security: challenges, standards and solutions. Softw. Qual. Prof. **18** (4), 4–12 (2016)
14. Korsaa, M., et al.: The SPI manifesto and the ECQA SPI manager certification scheme. J. Softw. Evol. Process **24**(5), 525–540 (2012)
15. Korsaa, M., et al.: The people aspects in modern process improvement management approaches. J. Softw. Evol. Process **25**(4), 381–391 (2013)
16. Messnarz, R., et al.: Social responsibility aspects supporting the success of SPI. J. Softw. Evol. Process **26**(3), 284–294 (2014)
17. Sanchez-Gordon, M.L., Colomo-Palacios, R., Amescua, A.: Towards measuring the impact of the SPI manifesto: a systematic review. In: Proceedings of European System and Software Process Improvement and Innovation Conference, pp. 100–110 (2013)

18. Messnarz, R., et al.: Integrating functional safety, automotive SPICE and Six Sigma – the AQUA knowledge base and integration examples. In: Barafort, B., O'Connor, R.V., Poth, A., Messnarz, R. (eds.) EuroSPI 2014. CCIS, vol. 425, pp. 285–295. Springer, Heidelberg (2014). https://doi.org/10.1007/978-3-662-43896-1_26
19. Kreiner, C., et al.: Automotive knowledge alliance AQUA – integrating automotive SPICE, Six Sigma, and functional safety. In: McCaffery, F., O'Connor, R.V., Messnarz, R. (eds.) EuroSPI 2013. CCIS, vol. 364, pp. 333–344. Springer, Heidelberg (2013). https://doi.org/10.1007/978-3-642-39179-8_30

Applying the ISO/IEC 25010 Quality Models to Software Product

John Estdale[1(✉)] and Elli Georgiadou[2]

[1] IT Architecture Specialists Ltd, Newbury, UK
john.estdale@acm.org
[2] Faculty of Science and Technology, Middlesex University, London, UK
e.georgiadou@mdx.ac.uk

Abstract. The software development process focuses on the delivery of a software implementation – its 'product', whether COTS or bespoke. However, potential acquirers are attracted by the promise of a future 'service' from that product: those aspects of the software's behavior visible outside it, particularly those that deliver value in the real world.

ISO/IEC 25010: 2011 provides the leading models for assessing software product. This is an important contribution towards establishing the delivery performance of software processes and proposed improvements. This paper explores the scope and interpretation of the ISO/IEC 25010 quality models, in the light of this broad, lifetime service-oriented view, also identifying other significant aspects of product that concern acquirers of software, and for which quality requirements and quality evaluation are potentially needed. Suggestions for refinement and extension of the standard complete the paper.

Keywords: Software product quality · Software behavior · Digital service ISO/IEC 25010 · SQuaRE · Quality models · 7Ms

1 Introduction

The value of software to users and organizations arises from its actual behavior in use, rather than from any qualities of the source code or the intended behavior as described in design documents etc. As Hofemann [1] says:

> "It requires a change in the mindset to consider software as a service rather than as a product. It is more than a change in business or delivery model, as in the case of changing to SaaS."

Furthermore, most applications of significant value will go through a series of maintenance releases, thus the simple model of software development producing software product (e.g. Sjøberg [2]) must be extended to cover post-delivery support and maintenance. In considering Software Process Improvement, we need to include post-delivery activities.

ISO/IEC 25010: 2011 *Systems and software Quality Requirements and Evaluation (SQuaRE) – System and software quality models* [3] presents the leading quality models for software products and computer systems known as 'software-intensive computer systems' [4]. This paper examines the two quality models in this standard in

X. Larrucea et al. (Eds.): EuroSPI 2018, CCIS 896, pp. 492–503, 2018.
https://doi.org/10.1007/978-3-319-97925-0_42

Sects. 4 and 5, with some additional aspects in Sect. 6. The standard mentions "secondary users who provide support" but the quality of such advice and support is not assessed in either model, so the In-life experience is considered here in Sect. 7. Section 8 draws the conclusions.

The present authors have previously applied ISO/IEC 25010 to smartphone applications destined for the Apple and Microsoft App Stores [4], and to the differences between products and prototypes [5]. These provide practical trials of the application of ISO/IEC 25010. This paper considers Digital Services from delivered software and comments on some less obvious issues with ISO/IEC 25010 interpretation.

2 ISO/IEC 250xx Series: SQuaRE

The ISO/IEC 25000 to ISO/IEC 25099 series of International Standards is entitled *Systems and software engineering – Systems and software Quality Requirements and Evaluation*, hence the acronym: 'SQuaRE'. The guide to the series, now in its 2nd edition [6] states that "the general goal … was to … [cover] two main processes: software quality requirements specification and system and software quality evaluation; supported by a system and software quality measurement process. The purpose … is to assist those developing and acquiring systems and software products with the specification and evaluation of quality requirements".

The traditional ISO 9001 position was that quality concerned "conformance to specified requirements". This has been broadened to "satisfy stated and implied needs". As the universe of such needs is not well-defined and standardized, evaluation of quality is ultimately purchaser-dependent.

2.1 The ISO/IEC 25010: 2011 Quality Model

SQuaRE has simplified the analysis from its predecessor, ISO 9126 [7], and now divides software quality characteristics into two quality models. Quality in Use is "the degree to which a product or system can be used by specific users to meet their needs to achieve specific goals… in specific contexts of use" and the catchall Product Quality is "characteristics … that relate to static properties of software and dynamic properties of the computer system". Given the previously quoted focus on needs, one might ask why include the second group at all, but ISO/IEC 25000 explains this as providing targets to drive development and verification, and to predict Quality in Use before delivery [6]. For SPI, it's helpful to have these supplier measures and exclude the impact of users and their context.

SQuaRE includes a Technical Specification: ISO/IEC TS 25011:2017 *Information technology—Systems and software Quality Requirements and Evaluation (SQuaRE)—Service quality models* [8]. This focusses on services that "make use of IT systems as tools to provide value", so includes a range of service management issues not directly relevant in this context.

Italics are used throughout this paper to denote the 13 characteristics and 40 sub-characteristics defined in ISO/IEC 25010. Definitions quoted are all taken from ISO/IEC 25010 [3].

Table 1. ISO/IEC 25010: 2011: quality models, characteristics and subcharacteristics (These are taken direct from the standard, following its English spelling, but American English is used for the remainder of this paper)

Quality in use	Product quality	Product quality (cont.)
• Effectiveness • Efficiency • Satisfaction – Usefulness – Trust – Pleasure – Comfort • Freedom from risk – Economic risk mitigation – Health and safety risk mitigation – Environmental risk mitigation • Context coverage – Context completeness – Flexibility	• Functional suitability – Functional completeness – Functional correctness – Functional appropriateness • Performance efficiency – Time behaviour – Resource utilization – Capacity • Compatibility – Co-existence – Interoperability • Usability – Appropriateness recognisability – Learnability – Operability – User error protection – User interface aesthetics – Accessibility	• Reliability – Maturity – Availability – Fault tolerance – Recoverability • Security – Confidentiality – Integrity – Non-repudiation – Accountability – Authenticity • Maintainability – Modularity – Reusability – Analysability – Modifiability – Testability • Portability – Adaptability – Installability – Replaceability

3 Applying the ISO/IEC 25010: 2011 Quality Models

Although ISO 9126 has been much used as a quality model in academic papers, many alternative quality models have been published over the years [9–11]. Oriol et al. [12] compared 47 quality models for web services from 65 papers with ISO/IEC 25010 and found little consistency. Unlike the physical world, with clearly independent dimensions and well-defined measures (length, mass, time, electric current, thermodynamic temperature, luminous intensity, etc.), software quality concepts such as compatibility are somewhat nebulous, and indeed have been redefined and reorganized as part of the ISO/IEC 25010 work [3].

Biscoglio and Marchetti [13] found similar difficulties in applying ISO/IEC 25000, which they described as “a conceptual framework and not a ready-to-use solution”.

3.1 ISO/IEC 25010 Applied to Digital Services

Behavior is what the software does as it is executed, i.e. it is the observable aspects of a computerized process. To identify all the causes of variation in the behavior of a process, one can apply the 7Ms model from quality management [14] shown in Table 2 to ensure completeness.

Table 2. Process variation across digital services

'M'	Normal interpretation in manufacturing context	Digital service equivalent
Machine	The equipment and technology required	The platform (operational environment), with the software application installed on it
Method	How the process is performed by the human element: policies, procedures etc.	Limited in this context to supporting processes in Operations and Support
Material	Raw materials and other ingredients	Requests and their parameters from the service consumer (human or app)
Man (power)	People involved in providing the service	Humans are not involved in servicing most requests, but are needed to keep the service running longer term, e.g. Operations and Support staff
Management	The organization of the manpower	The Digital Service Manager
Milieu	Environmental conditions	Existing data, infrastructure services and other apps sharing the platform
Measurement	Process measurements used to monitor and control the process	These are not further defined, so the ISO/IEC 25010 characteristics will be used

4 Quality in Use

Sections 4 and 5 follow the structure of the standard shown in Table 1, looking at each defined characteristic in turn, and commenting on how it may be interpreted, going down to subcharacteristic level where appropriate.

The definition of Quality in Use quoted in Sect. 2.1 is concerned with measuring the service to be delivered, so follows the service emphasis of this paper. In a traditional procurement, Quality in Use would be measured in the Buyer's environment as part of Acceptance Test.

4.1 Achievement of Needs

ISO/IEC 25010 does not include the evaluation of an application's specific functionality and features, as their value can only be measured in relation to the needs of the acquiring organization. The Quality in Use model therefore seeks to quantify the 'usability' (*effectiveness*, *efficiency* and *satisfaction*) of the application, when specific users attempt to meet their specified goals. ISO/IEC 25010 defines *effectiveness* as the "accuracy and completeness with which users achieve specified goals", and *efficiency* as "resources expended in relation to the accuracy and completeness with which users achieve goals".

As an example of the sort of interpretation of the standard that may be needed to apply it, much of the content of App Stores consists of games, or items for entertainment. Apple stated the need as: "If your App doesn't provide some form of lasting entertainment value, or is just plain creepy, it may not be accepted." [15] However, Apple does attempt to restrict the silly, witness their statement: "We don't need any more Fart apps" [16], (which raises the question of how they determine whether a new one provides a significant advantage over the many already in store!). This is quite a stretch from SQuaRE's solemn discussion of "stated and implied needs".

4.2 Freedom from Risk

As explained in ISO/IEC 25010, compliance was dropped in the move from ISO/IEC 9126-1:2001, as compliance with laws and regulations should be stated customer requirements, presumably 'Musts', not quantifiable qualities.

In complex industries, such as telecommunications it is known that legal and regulatory requirements, developed at different times, by different authorities, often conflict. More generally, many customers are likely to have no knowledge of the potential constraints on functionality and features of issues such as Privacy, Data Protection, the Distance Selling Regulations or the contractual rules of the five main Credit Card schemes for different industries and scenarios. Product suppliers should take responsibility for making themselves aware of all restrictions on the use of their product in the sales territory, and make explicit any usage restrictions and assumptions.

Whilst we may assume that acquirers state a need for overall legal compliance in their operating territories, it is likely that this will not be developed in detail, leaving the implications to be explored during product evaluation. We propose that Compliance be reinstated, this time as Legal Compliance under the *Freedom from risk* characteristic, to cover the product's claim for Legal, Regulatory and Contractual compliance. An associated quality measure might be "Clarity of Obligations to be met by the Customer to achieve Legal Compliance, when adopting this system", leaving the customer to decide whether the issues reported by the Supplier are acceptable under *functional suitability*.

5 Product Quality

These characteristics are primarily of interest to the supplier, and to those acquirers who wish to get more involved technically.

Functional suitability is an early view of the product's likely effectiveness, discussed in Sect. 4.1. ISO/IEC 25010 divides it into the subcharacteristics *functional completeness*, *appropriateness* and *correctness*. It is left to potential acquirers to do their own assessment and selection, based on their particular needs.

Performance efficiency includes *time behavior, resource utilization* and *capacity*. For software products, measures taken during development may not use the acquirer's exact platform/environment, so extrapolation to the delivered service may be difficult.

5.1 Compatibility

This is divided into *interoperability* between applications – the exchange and use of information, and *co-existence* – the impact on other products sharing the same platform. Note that these are concerned with how functionality is implemented, so are perhaps best thought of as 'features' not functions.

Co-existence is not a purely passive concept. Even after the arrival of properly protected multi-programming operating systems on PCs, it remains important that a product be 'well-behaved' rather than 'misbehaved' [17, 18], so should use supplied services for co-operative sharing of resources with the other (uncontrolled) applications running on the platform [5].

Interoperability is defined as "the degree to which two or more systems, products or components can exchange information and use the information that has been exchanged". Even if the product has no advertised interfaces to other products, in practice, users will assume interoperability with the native operating system capabilities, such as cut/copy/paste text between fields on a display screen, and objects between application windows [5].

5.2 Usability

Before the product is released, enabling Quality in Use to be measured as an emergent property (see Sect. 4.1), *usability* can be measured by relevant product subcharacteristics: *appropriateness recognizability*, *learnability*, *operability*, *user error protection*, *user interface aesthetics*, and *accessibility*. *Appropriateness recognizability* is described as "the degree to which users can recognize whether a product or system is appropriate for their needs", so covers the supplier's marketing literature. The availability of formal training and on-line help assist in several areas, but they are features of the supplier's solution, and it is the resulting *usability* of the product that is important.

5.3 Reliability

This includes *availability* and *recoverability*. In the real world, these are rarely pure application features, but aspects of the overall service, obliging human users and supporting staff to co-operate to handle whatever the application does not do for itself.

5.4 Security

Today's customers demand built-in mechanisms for controlling access, ensuring data *integrity* and protecting *confidentiality*. On a smartphone, much of the *security* surrounding a service is provided by the operational/usage environment, co-existing with the other applications and settings chosen by the platform owner. For example:

> "iOS is designed and built to … accept and install software that has been approved by Apple and run through the App Store. As such Apple has pretty much guaranteed that you won't encounter any malicious software on your iOS device" [19].

5.5 Maintainability

ISO/IEC 25010 defines *maintainability* as "the degree of *effectiveness* and *efficiency* with which a product … can be modified by the intended maintainers". The description of *maintainability* includes modifications carried out by "business or operational staff, or end users", so would include the deployment of supplier fixes.

Analyzability covers assessing the impact of an intended change, diagnosing deficiencies and failures, and identifying parts to be modified. *Analyzability* also covers problems noticed first in the field, requiring reliable configuration identification [5].

Testability is important, both at low-level (by allowing components to be tested independently and automatically) and at high-level, by developing and maintaining regression test suites to demonstrate that the previous service has not been downgraded. For the service, it is also useful to have post-installation and post-recovery tests, to confirm the service is working properly after human intervention.

Siakas and Georgiadou [20] proposed an extension (to ISO 9126), that Extensibility be considered as a primary level characteristic asserting that modular and object-oriented software "has become more extensible as tried and tested classes can be integrated into existing systems without the need to construct from scratch, or re-test the whole system".

5.6 Portability

Traditionally software *portability* has been a concern of developers working with the source code, involving recompilation, re-building etc. Applications are generally bought as implementations that execute only on specified platforms/computer ranges, and a customer wishing to move elsewhere has to buy the appropriate implementation for the new platform. Customers will then need to migrate their existing data, configuration, backups, users, etc. to the new environment.

Portability in ISO/IEC 25010 includes adaptation by end users and for "different … operational or usage environments", so it includes the purchased implementation's ability to run on any instance of the supported platform, including plug-compatible, virtual, outsourced or cloud-based environments.

The specification of the platform required is actually a critical matter to all commercially-minded software product vendors, as they will want to ensure that their software continues to work on any new and improved platforms added to the range in the future [4].

Replaceability focuses on the replacement of an existing product, or one version by another. Developers should also consider broader service issues such as the migration of existing data and minimizing changes to the user interface.

Established commercial practice is that any new release will at least maintain all previous functionality and features, and maintain access to existing customer data, i.e. be 'upward compatible', with no 'regression'. In some cases suppliers guarantee to meet the costs of any incompatible upgrade. Customers need surety that key product characteristics will be continued for as long as they want, so 'promises' should be backed up by contractual obligations on the supplier and any future substitute.

5.7 Supportability

The 'supportability' of a product is similar to maintainability in Sect. 5.5, contributing as one factor in the prediction of future experience, where neither the demand nor the response are known. It can be improved through the inclusion of appropriate functions and features for support activities. Most *maintainability* aids are useful contributors, although their emphasis must be changed to focus on defect reporting: the identification of defects in terms of errors in behavior and when exactly these happen. Other measures should take into account typical support scenarios from the acquirer's viewpoint, e.g. urgent calls for assistance, remote diagnosis, and support without access to source code or proprietary Intellectual Property: information or tools.

6 Other Characteristics of the Product at Delivery

6.1 Honesty and Openness

App Stores are a distinct world, with many unexpected perspectives [4]. There is an explicit requirement for open and honest communication – both for an acquirer contemplating a purchase, and for a user downloading an app. Reasons for rejection by Apple can include [15]:

- "Apps that do not perform as advertised by the developer"
- "Apps that include undocumented or hidden features inconsistent with the description"
- "Apps that are intended to provide trick or fake functionality that are not clearly marked as such".

Misleading documentation is not considered in the SQuaRE quality model.

6.2 Product Maturity

Bennett and Rajlich [21] suggested that products go through a maturity lifecycle, a staged model of initial development, active evolution, servicing and phase out. Acquirers looking for reliability might prefer a product in the third stage, whereas those hoping for growing functionality would prefer the second. In 1974 Lehman [22] emphasized that "first software systems must be continually adapted, or they become progressively less satisfactory. At the same time, software is becoming more and more complex and more expensive than before. As a software system evolves its complexity increases unless work is done to maintain or reduce it". In [23], Lehman also showed the strong effect that past product maintenance has on future quality.

7 In-life Experience, Post-deployment

This is what ultimately matters to the acquirer, but is unknown until a particular product has been bought, deployed, and a reasonable settling-in period allowed. Predictions of Quality in Use may be attempted from the supplier's Quality in Use data, from reference sites, or from previous, related work by this supplier. The ISO/IEC 25010 quality models are inevitably focused around acquisition, but could be applied to normal operation, and to mid-life or supplier reviews.

Other activities affecting the acquirer's post-deployment experience can be split in various ways, e.g. Cancian [24]. In-life administration, production, support, maintenance and their manageability should be considered before selecting a product, but SQuaRE does not currently address them. They are all Post-deployment processes, subject to the performance variability of the 7Ms (see Sect. 3.1), so further Quality in Use and Product Quality characteristics could be defined. The acquirer could request the product supplier to provide all these supporting services for an agreed price, in which case a comprehensive set of additional service level measures would be needed.

Application-specific activities that support the functionality and features provided to direct and indirect users can be split into those that satisfy the acquirer's needs as normal, and other supporting activities introduced by the developer. The former are needed by the acquirer, so are covered by the 25010 *usability* models, whereas the latter are just part of the cost of ownership of that particular product and hence overheads.

7.1 Customer Support by Supplier

Product selection will be much better informed, if the acquirer has a clear idea of the operational environment to be used, and the associated IT services it hopes to give its users (see Trinkenreich [25]). Support is sometimes confusingly included under maintenance. ISO/IEC 15504-5: 2006 [26] makes a clear distinction, with a Customer Support process (OPE-2) whose purpose is "to establish and maintain an acceptable level of service through assistance and consultation to the customer to support effective use of the product". Customer Support's objective should be to resolve issues and minimize the need for repeat or follow-up calls: Seddon's 'failure demand' [27], that is "demand caused by a failure to do something or do something right for the customer". Tourniaire [28] suggests that less than 5% of calls are actually the result of a software bug.

The QuEST Leadership Forum's TL 9000 aims to meet the "supply chain quality requirements of the worldwide telecommunications industry" [29] and has defined support metrics, which are collected from registered suppliers every month.

As support is a post-acquisition activity, with only minor influence from the product's technical implementation, ISO/IEC 25010 does not cover it. Nevertheless, the supplier's support capability is an important element in software product evaluation, and should at least be mentioned, even if it is then explicitly excluded from the scope of the ISO/IEC 250xx series.

7.2 In-life Maintenance

Most software is bought-in, so acquirers want to understand the likely work, effort and cost required to maintain the product in service for their users, depending on their management goals [30]. This will inevitably be affected by the frequency and complexity of upgrades, resulting from the policies and procedures of the supplier, in terms of commitment to fixing reported defects, quality and timeliness of new releases containing bug fixes, etc.

8 Conclusions

We have not attempted to look at all the criteria involved in acquiring software and creating and sustaining an ongoing relationship with its supplier, but restricted ourselves to the delivered software, and the product-specific implications, post-deployment.

The ISO/IEC 25000 series is a major step forward in software quality requirements specification and quality evaluation. Whilst the definitions and their notes are useful, readers may miss or dismiss many important interpretations. The acquirer's activities post-deployment are not considered, and yet must be a major part of their decision-making.

Our contribution has been to explore the scope of ISO/IEC 25010 and introduce further significant properties: legal, regulatory and contractual compliance, extensibility, supportability, honest description, product maturity, and in-life activities including Customer Support by Supplier and In-life maintenance.

Process improvement initiatives change the process, but also affect the resulting product. Management's goals may be to improve specified 'dimensions' of the product (the characteristics and subcharacteristics discussed earlier), maintain the existing levels, or disregard them (i.e. leave them unmanaged except where they appear in client requirements). ISO/IEC 25010, together with our proposed extensions, provides a comprehensive quality model which can be used as the basis for specifying whether a changed process should improve, maintain or ignore each dimension.

Future work will investigate case studies in order to assess the various impacts identified in this paper and also validate our suggestions for clarification and extension of the standard.

We thank the anonymous referees for their help in clarifying the text.

9 Relation to SPI Manifesto

This paper addresses Principle 3 of the SPI Manifesto [31]: *Base improvement on experience and measurements*. ISO/IEC 250xx series can be used to baseline the performance of existing processes in terms of the output product, and to specify any corresponding performance change intended from process improvement. ISO/IEC 25010 provides a comprehensive model to ensure all relevant dimensions are addressed.

References

1. Hofemann, S., Raatikainen, M., Myllärniemi, V., Norja, T.: Experiences in applying service design to digital services. In: Jedlitschka, A., Kuvaja, P., Kuhrmann, M., Männistö, T., Münch, J., Raatikainen, M. (eds.) PROFES 2014. LNCS, vol. 8892, pp. 134–148. Springer, Cham (2014). https://doi.org/10.1007/978-3-319-13835-0_10
2. Sjøberg, D.I.K.: The relationship between software process, context and outcome. In: Abrahamsson, P., Jedlitschka, A., Nguyen Duc, A., Felderer, M., Amasaki, S., Mikkonen, T. (eds.) PROFES 2016. LNCS, vol. 10027, pp. 3–11. Springer, Cham (2016). https://doi.org/10.1007/978-3-319-49094-6_1
3. ISO: ISO/IEC 25010:2011, Systems and software engineering – Systems and software Quality Requirements and Evaluation (SQuaRE) – System and software quality models
4. Estdale, J.: App stores & ISO/IEC 25000: product certification at last? In: Phalp, K., et al. (eds.) SQM XXIV: Systems Quality: Trends and Practices, pp. 37–48. Southampton Solent University (2016)
5. Estdale, J.: Products and prototypes: what's the difference? In: SQM XXV: Achieving Software Quality in Development and in Use, pp. 65–76. Southampton Solent University (2017)
6. ISO: ISO/IEC 25000:2014, Systems and software engineering – Systems and software Quality Requirements and Evaluation (SQuaRE) – Guide to SQuaRE
7. ISO: ISO/IEC 9126, various parts and dates. Software engineering – Product quality. Being superseded by SQuaRE [5]
8. ISO/IEC TS 25011:2017 Information technology—Systems and software Quality Requirements and Evaluation (SQuaRE)—Service quality models
9. Georgiadou, E.: Software process and product improvement: a historical perspective. Cybern. Syst. Anal. **39**(1), 125–142 (2003). https://doi.org/10.1023/A:1023833428613
10. Côté, M.A., Suryn, W., Georgiadou, E.: In search for a widely applicable and accepted software quality model for software quality engineering. Softw. Qual. J. **15**(4), 401–416 (2007)
11. Miguel, J.P., Mauricio, D., Rodriguez, G.: A review of software quality models for the evaluation of software products. Int. J. Softw. Eng. Appl. (IJSEA) **5**(6), 1–24 (2014). https://doi.org/10.5121/ijsea.2014.5603
12. Oriol, M., Marco, J., Franch, X.: Quality models for web services: a systematic mapping. Inf. Softw. Technol. **56**(10), 1167–1182 (2014). https://doi.org/10.1016/j.infsof.2014.03.012
13. Biscoglio, I., Marchetti, E.: Definition of software quality evaluation and measurement plans: a reported experience inside the audio-visual preservation context. In: Holzinger, A., Cardoso, J., Cordeiro, J., Libourel, T., Maciaszek, L.A., van Sinderen, M. (eds.) ICSOFT 2014. CCIS, vol. 555, pp. 63–80. Springer, Cham (2015). https://doi.org/10.1007/978-3-319-25579-8_4
14. Bergman, B., Klefsjö, B.: Quality from Customer Needs to Customer Satisfaction. McGraw-Hill, Maidenhead (1994)
15. App Store Review Guidelines. https://developer.apple.com/app-store/review/guidelines/. Accessed 17 Apr 2018
16. McCann, T.: The Art of the App Store. John Wiley, Indianapolis (2012)
17. Gibson, S.: 'Well-behaved' and 'misbehaved' software: past and present. InfoWorld **8**(43), 65 (1986)
18. Gibson, S.: Programs that 'behave' lend themselves to compatibility successfully. InfoWorld **8**(43), 69 (1986)

19. Haslam, K.: iOS security risks: after the XcodeGhost exploit is Apple's iOS really safer than Android? Plus: what security apps do you need for iPad & iPhone. http://www.macworld.co.uk/feature/iosapps/is-ipad-iphone-ios-safe-xcodeghost-what-security-software-need-3453938/#antivirus. Accessed 16 Apr 2018
20. Siakas, K.V., Georgiadou, E.: PERFUMES: a scent of product quality characteristics. In: International Software Quality Management Conference, pp. 211–220. BCS, London (2005)
21. Bennett, K., Rajlich, V.: Software maintenance and evolution: a roadmap. In: International Conference on Future of Software Engineering, pp. 73–90. ACM, New York (2000). https://doi.org/10.1145/336512.336534
22. Lehman, M.M.: On understanding laws, evolution, and conservation in the large-program life cycle. J. Syst. Softw. **1**(1), 213–221 (1980). https://doi.org/10.1016/0164-1212(79)90022-0
23. Lehman, M.M., Perry, D.E., Ramil, J.F.: Implication of evolution metrics on software maintenance. In: International Conference on Software Maintenance, pp. 208–217. IEEE (1998). https://doi.org/10.1109/icsm.1998.738510
24. Cancian, M.H., Hauck, J.C.R., von Wangenheim, C.G., Rabelo, R.J.: Discovering software process and product quality criteria in software as a service. In: Ali Babar, M., Vierimaa, M., Oivo, M. (eds.) PROFES 2010. LNCS, vol. 6156, pp. 234–247. Springer, Heidelberg (2010). https://doi.org/10.1007/978-3-642-13792-1_19
25. Trinkenreich, B., Santos, G., Barcellos, M.P.: SINIS: a method to select indicators for IT services. In: Abrahamsson, P., Corral, L., Oivo, M., Russo, B. (eds.) PROFES 2015. LNCS, vol. 9459, pp. 68–86. Springer, Cham (2015). https://doi.org/10.1007/978-3-319-26844-6_6
26. ISO: ISO/IEC 15504-5:2006 Process assessment – Part 5: An exemplar Process Assessment Model
27. Seddon, J.: Freedom from Command and Control: A Better Way to Make the Work Work, 2nd edn. Vanguard Education, Buckingham (2005)
28. Tourniaire, F., Jarrell, R.: The Art of Software Support: Design and Operation of Support Centers and Help Desks. Prentice Hall, London (1998)
29. TL 9000 Overview. http://www.tl9000.org/about/tl9000/overview.html. Accessed 16 Apr 2018
30. Woherem, E., Neil, M., Estdale, J.: Software process improvement through the GQM approach: a maintenance case study. In: 3rd International Conference on Software Quality, pp. 147–156. ASQC, Milwaukee (1993)
31. Pries-Heje, J., Johanson J. (eds.): SPI Manifesto. http://www.iscn.com/Images/SPI_Manifesto_A.1.2.2010.pdf. Accessed 28 May 2018

Status of the Development of ISO/SAE 21434

Christoph Schmittner[1(✉)], Gerhard Griessnig[2], and Zhendong Ma[2]

[1] AIT Austria Institute of Technology, Vienna, Austria
christoph.schmittner@ait.ac.at
[2] AVL List GmbH, Graz, Austria
{gerhard.griessnig, Zhendong.ma}@avl.com

Abstract. With the ongoing trend to incorporate new functionalities and functions based on the connectivity of vehicles, cybersecurity is becoming an important issue in the vehicle development lifecycle. While the first approaches to address this topic were based on research projects or adaptions of existing concepts of other domains, there is now a new ongoing activity to develop ISO/SAE 21434 a cybersecurity engineering standard for road vehicles. This standard addresses the complete lifecycle from development and production via operation and maintenance up to the decommissioning of the vehicles. We give an overview about the ongoing development, discuss potential contents and objectives and summarize time plan and open points.

Keywords: ISO/SAE 21434 · Cybersecurity · Standard · Automotive Road vehicles · Safety · ISO 26262 · SAE J3061

1 Introduction

The introduction of wireless connections, automated and assistive driving functionalities changed vehicles from physically isolated machines with electro-mechanical control systems into "smart phones on wheels". In the recent past with the electrification of vehicles the challenges were mainly timing, reliability and functional safety, addressed by internal guidelines and standards like ISO 26262:2011 [1]. The change towards cyber-physical automotive systems over the last years promises to improve the safety of drivers and support new applications such as monitoring system behavior or dynamically change and update configuration and software from remote. However, this also requires the consideration of cybersecurity.

Starting with activities in research projects like EVITA (E-Safety Vehicle Intrusion Protected Applications) [2], OVERSEE (Open Vehicular Secure Platform) [3] or EMC^2 (Embedded Multi-Core systems for Mixed Criticality applications in dynamic and changeable real-time environments) [4], and followed by the publication of the SAE J3061 Cybersecurity Guidebook for Cyber-Physical Vehicle Systems [5] the topic of automotive cybersecurity engineering was examined. While SAE J3061 was an important step forward it was also recognized that the guidebook could not fulfill a similar role like ISO 26262:2011 for the cybersecurity engineering of road-vehicles [6, 7]. The specific characteristic of the engineering processes for automotive systems like the distributed development made the direct application of existing cybersecurity

X. Larrucea et al. (Eds.): EuroSPI 2018, CCIS 896, pp. 504–513, 2018.
https://doi.org/10.1007/978-3-319-97925-0_43

standards like IEC 62443 [8] difficult. Differences in the risk assessments and particularities in safety engineering complicated also the direct application of existing IT-Security standards [9]. Therefore, the automotive industry decided to develop a domain-specific standard, ISO/SAE 21434 "road vehicles – cybersecurity engineering".

To give an overview about the current status and discuss the ongoing developments, this paper follows the following structure:

- Section 2 explain the motivations and gives an overview about the interaction between ISO 26262:2018 and ISO/SAE 21434
- Section 3 presents the timeline
- Section 4 and its subsections give an overview about the current content
- Section 5 gives an outlook about the ongoing development

2 Motivations for the Development of ISO/SAE 21434

There were some discussions during the development of ISO 26262:2018 [10] how to address the topic of automotive cybersecurity. Considering the history and underlying principles of these two disciplines and based on the facts that (a) not every safety-critical system is equally security-critical and (b) there are security-critical systems without immediate safety impact it was decided to restrict the cybersecurity consideration in ISO 26262:2018.

The decision was to describe only the interface from functional safety to cybersecurity in ISO 26262:2018. It was also decided to leave the interface on the cybersecurity side unspecified to not anticipate a cybersecurity standard development. In the end ISO 26262:2018 requires communication channel between safety and cybersecurity engineering. The aim is the necessity to coordinate the development of these disciplines and to exchange requirements on system, software and hardware level. An annex in Part 2 of ISO 26262:2018 gives some additional background for the interaction.

It was recognized that there is a necessity to develop an automotive cybersecurity standard. Such a domain-specific cybersecurity engineering standard is not only to collect the state of the art it should also support and ease the cooperation between partners in the automotive and its supply chain by clarifying terminology and risk management approaches and by defining clear interfaces between companies.

3 Timeline ISO/SAE 21434

The New Work Item Proposal (NWIP) was submitted in 04.2016 and the development started in 10.2016 with the definition of the overall scope and establishment of four topic groups. Of particular note is that the working group itself consists of ISO and SAE experts, one of the first active Joint Working Groups between ISO and SAE [11].

On ISO side the topic is assigned to ISO/TC 22/SC 32 [12] which is also responsible for the development of ISO 26262. At ISO the WG8 is responsible for the functional safety standard development and WG11 is responsible for the cybersecurity standard development.

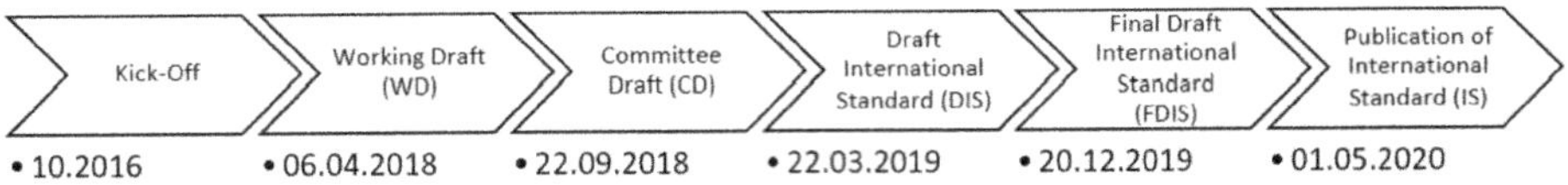

Fig. 1. ISO 21434 timeline

As seen in Fig. 1 there are different maturity stages for standard development with different expectations on the content and opportunities to contribute. We are currently at the Working Draft stage. At this stage the included contents are more or less known, but the specification of requirements and approaches is still ongoing. This means that the mentioned topics will probably be included in the final version, but detailed approaches might change.

While the WD is only shared and commented on a joint working group (JWG) level the committee draft (CD), the draft international standard (DIS) and finally the final draft international standard (FDIS) are open to additional experts from SAE and ISO national bodies. Procedures for ISO and SAE are different, but the collaborative way requires the process to satisfy both sides. In general, after each stage there will be a ballot phase with commenting. CD and DIS will receive technical and editorial comments, FDIS is restricted to editorial comments. After the balloting phase comments are discussed and resolved on JWG level. The first version of ISO/SAE 21434 is planned to be published beginning of May 2020.

4 Overview of the Contents

Due to various reasons we cannot discuss the complete draft with all ongoing developments. The goal is to give an overview of the concepts and structure and highlight and discuss a few interesting topics.

It need to be remarked that this presentation is based on our own interpretation of the current documents and discussions and we can neither claim to predict the final version nor to present all topics which are in discussion. We present a snapshot from our viewpoint of the current status at the time of the working draft which can and will change.

4.1 Generic Overview

The scope of the overall project was defined during the kick-off meeting and refined in consecutive meeting. The current wording in ISO/SAE 21434 is:

> "This document specifies requirements for cybersecurity risk management for road vehicles, their components and interfaces, throughout engineering (e.g. concept, design, development), production, operation, maintenance, and decommissioning. A framework is defined that includes requirements for cybersecurity process and a common language for communicating and managing cybersecurity risk among stakeholders. This document is applicable to road

vehicles that include electrical and electronic (E/E) systems, their interfaces and their communications. This document does not prescribe specific technology or solutions related to cybersecurity."

The work was split into four part groups, addressing all elements of cybersecurity engineering during the complete vehicle lifecycle. Below the part groups are specialized task forces preparing proposals how specific topics are addressed.

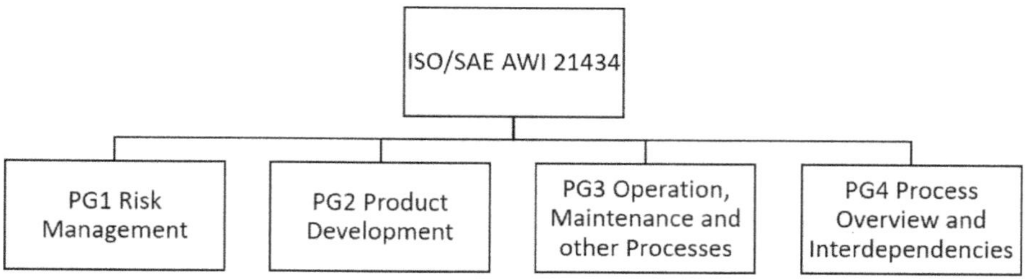

Fig. 2. ISO 21434 JWG structure

Although each group listed in Fig. 2 started with the development of a standalone document it was combined for the WD and there is still an ongoing discussion if the standard will be one combined document or multiple documents.

4.2 PG1 Risk Management

Risk Management is one of the core activity in security engineering. In the end the goal of security engineering could be summarized as ensuring that risks due to cybersecurity issues are inside acceptable parameters.

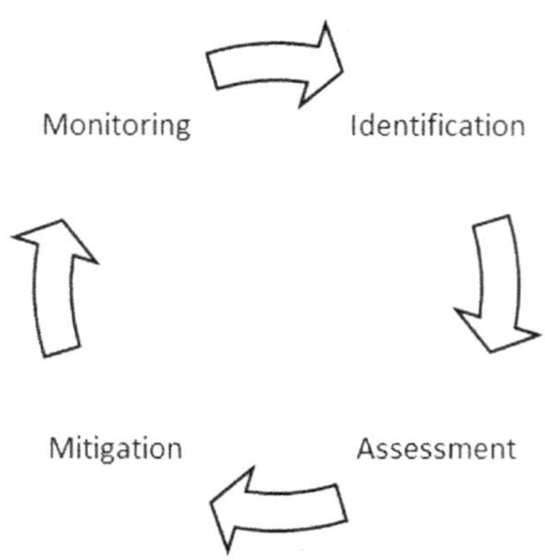

Fig. 3. PG1 risk management process

As shown in Fig. 3 there are four core activities to risk management which should follow each other. Due to the changing and evolving risk landscape in cybersecurity risk management is an ongoing process during the complete lifecycle. Therefore, the concept behind PG1 is to provide methods and approaches which can be used in other sections of the lifecycle.

One of the first methods provided is the cybersecurity relevance assessment. If one of the questions in Table 1 is answered with yes, the system is in scope of the ISO/SAE 21434. The goal of this relevance assessment was to provide a quick tool which can be used to determine if cybersecurity should be considered during the development. Due to the fact that attacks can use different attack surfaces and move through the vehicle network, the relevance assessment should ensure that no system which should be taken into account is omitted.

Table 1. Cybersecurity relevance assessment

Physical or wireless connection to any part of any internal vehicle communication network	Yes/no
Physical or wireless connection to any part of any external vehicle communication network	Yes/no
Indirect connection to any part of any vehicle communication network	Yes/no
Contains electronic or optoelectronic devices or hardware	Yes/no
Contains software	Yes/no
Contains a sensor	Yes/no

An important topic in PG1 is how to adapt existing risk management techniques for the automotive domain and distributed development. For risk management in general the ISO 2700X [13] standard series is referenced, but with adaptions to the automotive domain. An example is the concept for the division between, threat and vulnerability analysis. Threats are identified on the OEM level, with a view on the complete system. Vulnerability analysis is then the responsibility of the supplier who knows implementation details.

The risk assessment is based on parameters of ISO 15408 [14]. There was a discussion about defining a counterpart to the Automotive Safety Integrity Level (ASIL) from ISO 26262 during the risk assessment, which is then used to define rigor and applicable methods, but this is currently on hold. There was no consensus how to determine and treat such a parameter. One issue was the dynamic nature of risk parameters in cybersecurity, which could require frequent adjustments.

4.3 PG2 Product Development

The Product development sections is based on the same triple V-process as ISO 26262. System, Software and Hardware development. The strong reference to ISO 26262 was done because ISO 26262 is not only used for safety engineering but is also describing the general system engineering approach used in the automotive domain. Following roughly the same process should support the adoption (process structure and phases are easily understandable for all automotive experts) and interaction between system, safety and cybersecurity engineering. A major difference is the missing risk based tailoring. This means there is currently no tailoring based on the risk level.

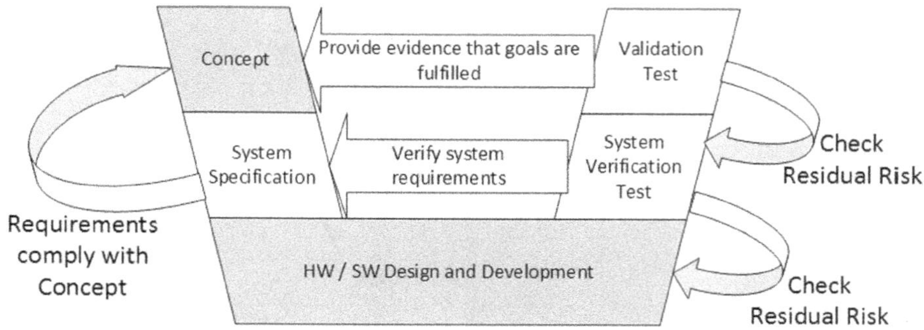

Fig. 4. System development phase

Figure 4 shows an overview of the system development phase. In the Concept Phase the Item is defined and, utilizing Threat Analysis and Risk Assessment (TARA) from PG1, Cybersecurity Goals are defined. During System Specification requirements are refined and assigned to Software and Hardware. After the System Concept is defined and during Software and Hardware Phase Vulnerability Analysis and Risk Assessment (VARA) are used to ensure that no additional threats are introduced and the residual risk is acceptable. Guidance on implementation is for Software mostly focused on secure software development and security functions and for Hardware on the usage of hardware security functions. After Software and Hardware Phases are completed Verification and Validation provide everything to release the system for production.

There is still an ongoing discussion about testing for security. Automated test methods have the advantage that they can be used earlier in the development process and their and their repeatability and comparability is better. Automated methods cannot replace manual pen-testing. Pen-testing is the best representation of a human attacker with his ingenuity, but it requires a more or less finalized system.

4.4 PG3 Operation, Maintenance and Other Processes

In cybersecurity vulnerabilities and weaknesses can be introduced throughout the complete lifecycle. It is therefore important to ensure cybersecurity during production and operation. PG3 focusses on these phases of the lifecycle.

Figure 5 gives an overview of the considered topics in PG3. The first section of PG3, gives requirements how to ensure that no unauthorized modification was introduced in the supply chain or during production. Focus is on how to protect hand-over of software and information from design to production and how to protect hardware during transport. Presented methods range from cybersecurity methods, like cryptographic hashes, to controlling and restricting the physical access. In addition, production requires relative unrestricted access in order to install and configure software and distribute cryptographic keys. During this stage the system is vulnerable and access to tools and systems need to be controlled. It is also necessary to ensure that production interfaces are deactivated and protected if they are no longer needed.

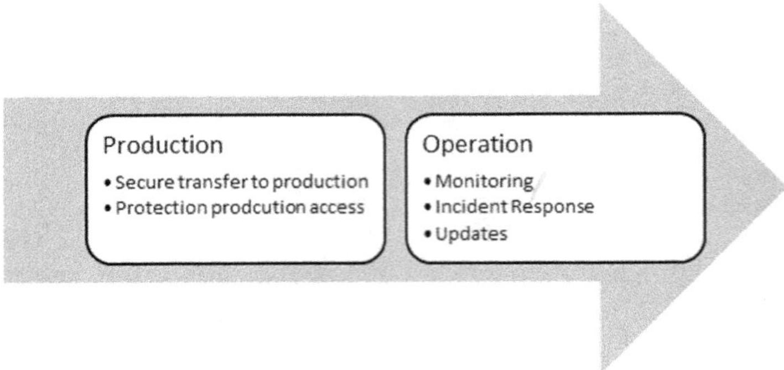

Fig. 5. Topics during production and operation

In order to ensure cybersecurity during operation it is necessary to monitor not only for incidents but also for vulnerabilities in used software and hardware components and prevent their exploitation. This section is still in development due to discussions if monitoring sources should be defined by requirements or given as informative examples. Policies and procedures on how to react on vulnerabilities and incident response programs conclude the section on cybersecurity during the operation process.

The last sections is about updating the system. The goal was here not to restrict or define technical approaches on updating, but define a state of the art about update processes. All cybersecurity related systems, meaning all system which implement cybersecurity requirements or could influence the cybersecurity of the system need to have update capabilities. In addition, the system need to be able to recover from a failed update. Failed refers here to all conditions like an interruption of the update process or a corruption during transmission which result in an unsuccessful update. It is necessary to balance here between availability, recovering back to the original state, and security. Updates for high-risk vulnerabilities can indicate that no recovery is allowed, e.g. if the update is not successful the system is no longer usable. Although there are no restrictions on the technical means by which an update is delivered, there are requirements on how to release an update, e.g. the approval process and on the protection of the update during transport.

Directly related to the update topic is the End-of-Support (EoS). After End-of-Support there are no requirements to monitor for vulnerabilities and provide updates. Each partner in the supply chain needs to inform the next partner about the EoS for the systems in his responsibility. If the support is not ensured by another partner higher-up in the supply chain the customer needs to be informed (Fig. 6).

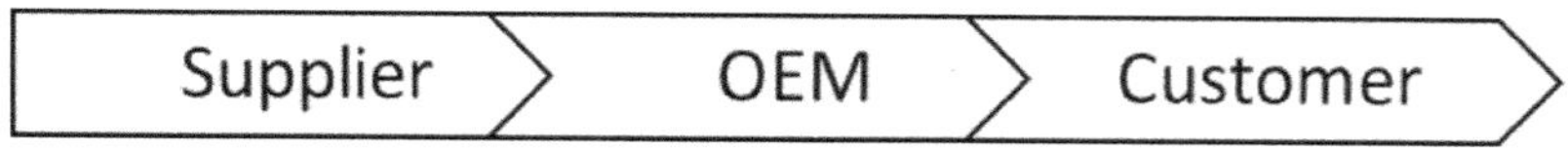

Fig. 6. End-of-Support communication

4.5 PG4 Process Overview and Interdependencies

Topics which are not directly related to a concrete cybersecurity activity, but which are nevertheless necessary for the achievement of cybersecurity are developed in PG4. An important topic addressed is the cybersecurity culture and cybersecurity management across the organization. The goal here is to define requirements and guidelines which will ensure that cybersecurity is accepted as a priority and quality attribute. It is similar in the direction and requirements to safety culture and safety management. A few examples for good and poor cybersecurity culture are given. Since cybersecurity is still a somehow new topic in the automotive domain confidence levels for cybersecurity capabilities are defined. These levels can be used to demonstrate evidence of cybersecurity in the supply chain. As an example, for incident response level 1 is reached if the responsible persons are defined. Level 2 is reached if policies are defined and accepted. Level 3 requires training and the ongoing evaluation of the policies based on training exercises.

The Development Interface Agreement (DIA) concept from ISO 26262, which is used to document responsibilities, information exchange and work share between supplier and OEM is included in an extended version. A template for the structure and the requirement to use RASIC [15] or similar models to define responsibilities tries to introduce more formalism. The concept can also be used in multiple lifecycle phase, not only during the engineering but even later during operation. For this additional Interface Agreements are introduced. Figure 7 gives an overview about described types of interface agreements. The idea was that different types can cover different stages of the lifecycle and parts, like for example the maintenance e.g. providing updates could also shifted from supplier to a third party.

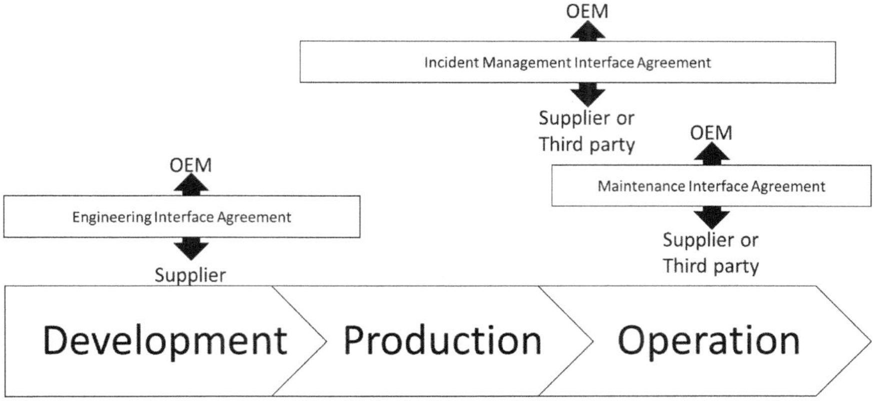

Fig. 7. Different types of interface agreements

Also similar to the ISO 26262 safety element out of context (SEooC) is the definition of a cybersecurity element out of context (CEooC). The difference between a CEooC and a component of the shelf (COTS) is that a CEooC was defined with an automotive cybersecurity context in mind. In order to use a CEooC the main focus is therefore to ensure that the assumed context and the intended usage are overlapping. For a COTS it is also necessary to check which cybersecurity activities were carried out and identify missing steps which are necessary to achieve ISO/SAE 21434 compliance.

While requirements for cybersecurity auditing and assessment are already defined, there is still an ongoing discussion about the cybersecurity case. Such a case would document and collect all evidence to show that a system was developed in accordance with ISO/SAE 21434. Some existing guidance documents [16] suggest to provide such a documentation for auditing.

Annexes in PG4 describe also the high-level interaction between functional safety, IT-security and cybersecurity.

5 Summary and Outlook

Cybersecurity is increasingly becoming an important topic and there are multiple approaches to address this topic from governmental and legislative side [17, 18]. ISO/SAE 21434 has the potential to establish a common ground within the automotive industry to address cybersecurity challenges. With the current version the collection of topics is concluded. While this was a huge step, the time plan for the development of all topics is still rather short.

Some topics, like privacy and interaction between safety and security are still in discussion due to the time pressure. The goal is to have a first edition till May 2020 which includes the core topics. There are also dependencies between cybersecurity and system quality which could be detailed in the standard if there is sufficient time.

Since: (a) Cybersecurity is still a rather new topic for the automotive domain. (b) There is no common starting point like IEC 61508 [19] was for the development of functional safety for automotive. There are some topics which are accepted as relevant but without a known state of the art. Since a standard collect and codifies state of the art there are some topics which cannot be addressed. Nevertheless, based on the current status and development speed it is likely that the first version will be published in 2020.

References

1. International Organization for Standardization: ISO 26262:2011 Road vehicles - Functional safety (2011)
2. Fraunhofer Institute for Secure Information Technology: EVITA Project Summary, Deliverable D0 (2013)
3. Project Consortium, OVERSEE Final Event and Workshop on Concepts of Open In-Vehicle Platforms takes place on 19–20 December 2012 in Brussel, 12 December 2012. https://www.oversee-project.com/index.php%3Fid=17&tx_ttnews[tt_news]=37&cHash=aa04921e19dfc4094f0e2f71c6133bce.html. Accessed 22 Mar 2018

4. Weber, W., Hoess, A.: D13.7 – Final Report Part A - Publishable Summary, 15 August 2017
5. SAE: Cybersecurity Guidebook for Cyber-Physical Vehicle Systems (2016)
6. Schmittner, C., Ma, Z., Reyes, C., Dillinger, O., Puschner, P.: Using SAE J3061 for automotive security requirement engineering. In: Skavhaug, A., Guiochet, J., Schoitsch, E., Bitsch, F. (eds.) SAFECOMP 2016. LNCS, vol. 9923, pp. 157–170. Springer, Cham (2016). https://doi.org/10.1007/978-3-319-45480-1_13
7. Macher, G., Armengaud, E., Brenner, E., Kreiner, C.: Threat and risk assessment methodologies in the automotive domain. Procedia Comput. Sci. **83**, 1288–1294 (2016)
8. International Electrotechnical Commission: IEC 62443: Industrial communication networks – Network and system security
9. Johnson, C.: Why We Cannot (Yet) Ensure the Cyber-Security of Safety-Critical Systems (2016)
10. International Organization for Standardization: ISO 26262:2018 Road vehicles - Functional safety (FDIS) (2018)
11. Attacking the cybersecurity threat - SAE International. http://articles.sae.org/15208/. Accessed 27 Mar 2018
12. ISO/SAE AWI 21434 - Road Vehicles – Cybersecurity engineering. https://www.iso.org/standard/70918.html. Accessed 27 Mar 2018
13. International Standardization Organization: ISO 27000 series, Information technology - Security Techniques
14. International Standardization Organization: ISO 15408, Information technology - Security techniques - Evaluation criteria for IT security (Common Criteria) (2009)
15. Smith, M.L., Erwin, J., Diaferio, S.: Role & Responsibility Charting (RACI), p. 14 (2005)
16. Cybersecurity Best Practices for Modern Vehicles, National Highway Traffic Safety Administration, Washington DC, USA. Report No. DOT HS 812 333, October 2016
17. Markey, E., Blumenthal, R.: Security and Privacy in Your Car Act (2015)
18. United Nations Economic Commission for Europe (UNECE): UNECE Webseite (2018). https://www.unece.org/info/ece-homepage.html. Accessed 08 Mar 2018
19. International Electrotechnical Commission: IEC 61508: Functional Safety of Electrical/Electronic/Programmable Electronic Safety-Related Systems (2010)

Self-assessment as a Path to Improvement and Recognition for Small Entities

Philippe Lohier and Patricia Rodríguez-Dapena(✉)

Softwcare SL, Avda Atlántida 100, 1-izq, 36208 Vigo, Spain
{philippelohier, rodriguezdapena}@softwcare.com

Abstract. To better understand what they can or should change to improve their ability to perform, organizations can conduct organizational assessments. Self-assessments are often the first step in an organization's journey towards effective outcomes. The goal of such assessments is to collect data that can help the organization evaluating whether or not it is making progress towards various goals. A large majority of organizations worldwide have up to 25 people and many of them develop software. Those VSEs (Very Small Entities i.e. enterprises, organizations, projects or departments with up to 25 people [1]), are interested and are aware about software process and quality standards and the potential benefits from having a quality standard, and in particular accreditation [2]. But several difficulties usually arise due to their daily operational constraints which may lean towards a no-go for the adoption of any new standard often starting with an assessment and aiming for 'earning' improvements and a certificate. The required time, the available resources, having a clear picture of the organizational goals, what to measure and which indicators to select are some of the key stoppers for VSEs engaging in necessary changes. This paper presents how to use ISO/IEC 29110 series, aimed at addressing the specific needs of VSEs, and why self-assessment is a good option for the VSEs to start improving their processes and be prepared for certification. At last it presents its contextualization against the SPI Manifesto.

Keywords: Self-assessment · Process · Process improvement
Certification · ISO/IEC 29110 · Small organizations · VSE
Software basic profile

1 Introduction

A large majority of organizations worldwide have up to 25 people and many of them develop software. Those VSEs (Very Small Entities) are interested and are aware about software processes and quality standards and the potential benefits of having a quality schema, and being certified [2].

But several difficulties usually arise due to their daily operational constraints which may lean towards a no-go for the adoption of any new standard often starting with an assessment and aiming for 'earning' improvements and a certificate. The required time, the available resources, having a clear picture of the organizational goals, what to measure and which indicators to select are some of the key stoppers for VSEs engaging in necessary changes. In addition, process models like ISO/IEC 12207 [3] or the ones

X. Larrucea et al. (Eds.): EuroSPI 2018, CCIS 896, pp. 514–526, 2018.
https://doi.org/10.1007/978-3-319-97925-0_44

contained in CMMI [6] are very big to be implemented by these VSEs in one step. Therefore these small organizations need a step by step scheme with information, guides and support to understand how to implement improvements. They also need short term actions that can quickly measure the benefits of those improvements [11]. And as a third goal, they need international recognition to open new markets and demonstrate they comply with the international buyers' requirements.

The International Organization for Standardization/International Electrotechnical Commission (ISO/IEC) in 2005 already recognized these needs and mandated to develop a set of tailored-made standards and guides to drive VSEs through a scalable, cost effective, less time consuming and manageable approach in adopting and using world class Software Engineering practices.

As a result of the ISO JTC1/SC7 working group effort, the ISO/IEC 29110 [1] was produced as a set of standards providing guidance to VSEs in the establishment of software engineering processes.

The ISO/IEC 29110 series present scalable profiles and guides (in current ISO/IEC 29110 Part 5-x-y) most of them made available at no cost by ISO, facilitating the transition towards standards like ISO/IEC 12207 [3] and/or ISO 9001 [4] through an affordable process redesign. It provides examples to encourage the standard adoption; it is adjusted to VSE needs, problems and risks, improving their performances and competitiveness in a fast and constant way.

But what VSEs really request is a specific and optimized how-to implement the processes, adapted to their particular culture and customers and including the specific tools to help them in these implementations. All these possible 'how-to's' are not provided in the ISO/IEC 29110 guides as these guides are intended to be usable by any VSE, not particularizing any how-to specific solution. In addition, when improving, VSEs want to 'easily' evaluate not only whether they follow the standard ('easy assessments') but the benefits of those improvements related to their business goals (better productivity, customer satisfaction with the first delivery, etc.).

This paper presents this new standard for small organizations and how to answer to the specific needs of the SMEs, not only thanks to the ISO/IEC 29110 standard but to extra existing detailed guides, framework and tools that facilitate its adaptation and assessment. The use and interest of self-assessment is also detailed in this paper as a perfect and affordable path for VSEs to improvement and later recognition.

2 The 29110 Standard

2.1 The Origin

Since most of the International standards and process models were made by and for bigger organization not meeting the needs of VSEs, the ISO JTC1/SC7 mandated its WG24 working group to define a set of standards focused on a step-wise approach for VSEs to increase their maturity and excellency in implementing software, systems and service provision allowing them to implement the bigger models from achieving first the initial steps contained in ISO/IEC 29110.

As a result, and after an intense survey made worldwide [10], the ISO/IEC 29110 series have been developed to define an earlier step before approaching these other bigger models like CMMI [6], ISO 15504/330xx [5] or even other domain specific requirements and standards. It provides different so-called generic VSE profiles, not specific for any domain, where each profile is grouping few processes in a scalable way. For example, the Basic profile for software contains two processes: Software Implementation and Project Management [1] based on other bigger models like ISO/IEC 12207 [3], etc.

So now, SMEs are starting to have standards, recognized internationally, focusing on their characteristics (few resources and time) and needs (without much formalism, step by step, including guides, and with easy and affordable assessment and recognition schemas).

2.2 The Basic and Organizational Profiles

Parts 5-x-y of the standard [1] are valuable for VSEs as they provide guidance for the implementation of different so-called profiles. Profiles mainly consist in a set of processes, that when performed the VSE can demonstrate certain maturity level. The main profile set for software related VSEs, is shown in Fig. 1 below and contains:

- the software Basic profile as the first generic profile to be recognized/certified with specific basic processes for software as the core processes for software companies, and
- the Organizational profile, a more mature profile intended to be implemented after the basic profile, but including the basic profile, providing management, standardization and organizational aspects to help the VSEs managing multiple projects.

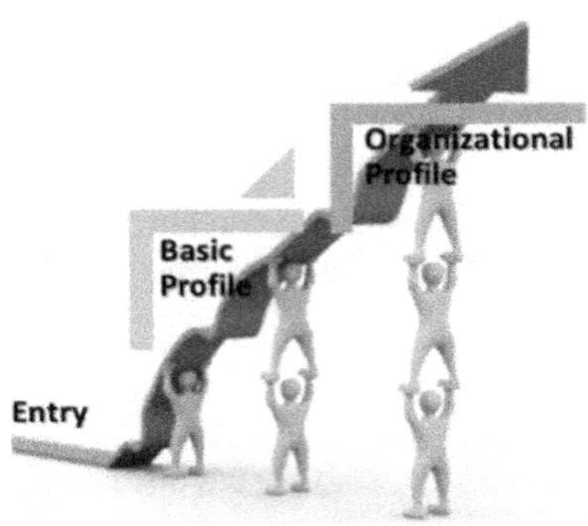

Fig. 1. Certifiable VSE generic profiles for software development [7]

The ISO/IEC 29110 standard [1] can be used for different purposes and by different types of organizations:

- For process implementation and improvement: for new or existing projects developed by the VSEs and for internal and external benefits i.e. to facilitate

communication between parties, to improve customer satisfaction, and to improve productivity and quality (less problems after delivery, control of requirements gathering and implementation, etc.).
- For process assessment: for VSEs and assessors. The results of the processes assessments can be used for process improvement, risk assessment of the existing processes or benchmarking.
- For VSEs certification: using the assessment of the processes within the published international scheme (in ISO/IEC 29110-3-3 [1]), serves to have international credibility and respect and have competitive advantage while maintaining current customers and attracting new ones. Such certification can be required by customers to their software suppliers to increase confidence in the success of a particular project.

The Basic Profile for software guide [1] details the 2 interrelated processes with their activities, and for each activity, with the tasks to be performed in each of them. Also, both the roles involved and the outputs of the processes i.e. work product, are detailed. It is composed by two processes (as shown in Fig 2):

- The Project Management (PM) process: to establish and carry out in a systematic way the tasks of the software implementation project, which will allow complying with the project's objectives in the expected quality, time and cost.
- The Software Implementation (SI) process: for the systematic performance of the analysis, design, construction, integration and testing activities for new or modified software products according to the specified input requirements (Fig. 2).

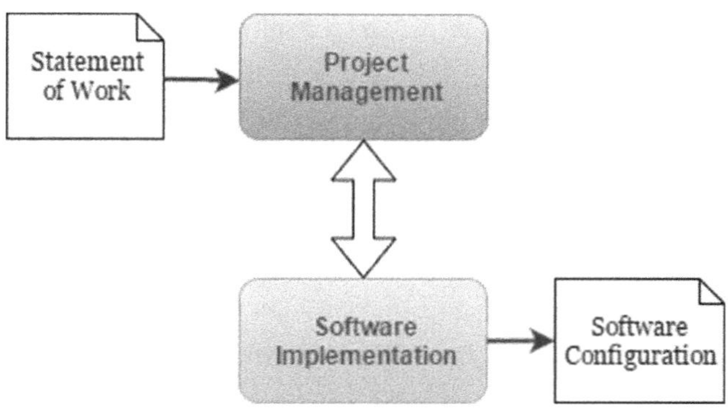

Fig. 2. The processes for the VSE generic basic profile for software [1]

As shown in next figure, the PM and SI are inter-related processes and are to be used by the VSE for any development approach, life cycle model or methodology. Each process is also defined using their purpose and scope together with the guidelines about what to do for each of their tasks and subtasks (Fig. 3).

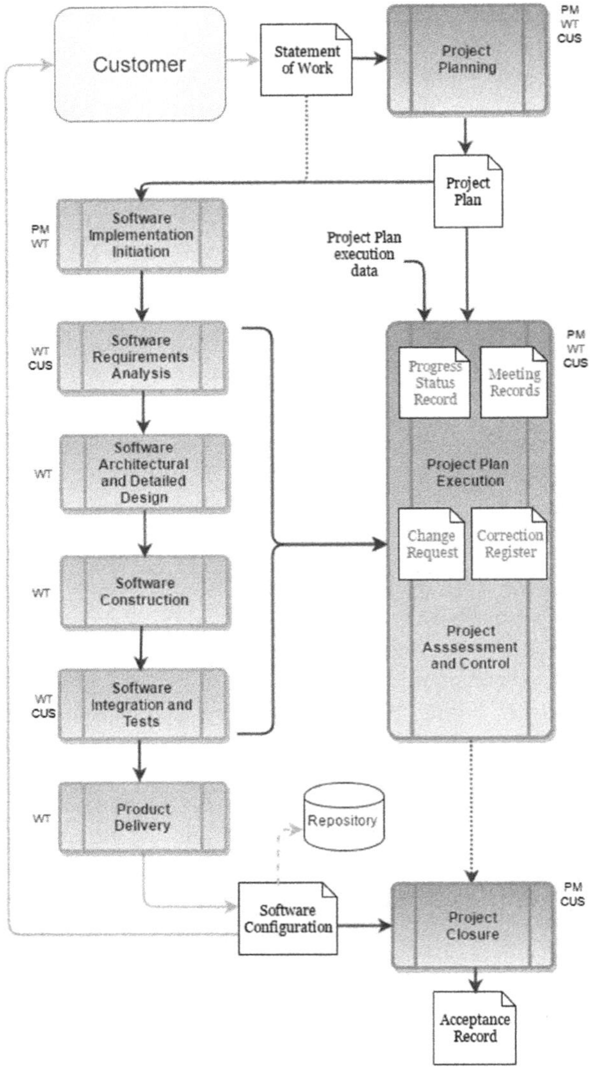

Fig. 3. Project Management (PM) and Software Implementation (SI) processes diagram [8]

The Organizational profile processes apply to VSEs which have already implemented the processes of the system engineering and/or the software engineering Basic profile. The 4 interrelated processes within this profile are presented in the following figure (Fig. 4) where:

– The purpose of the Organizational Management Process is to make sure that value is delivered by the VSE to the customer through planning, organization, monitoring and controlling organizational activities

- The purpose of the Resource Management Process is to obtain and provide the organization with the necessary resources.
- The purpose of the Process Management process is to establish and improve the organizational processes.
- The purpose of the Project Portfolio Management process is to generate projects for the organization, provide technical content to establish the projects Formal Agreement, and supervise its performance while monitoring the customer satisfaction.

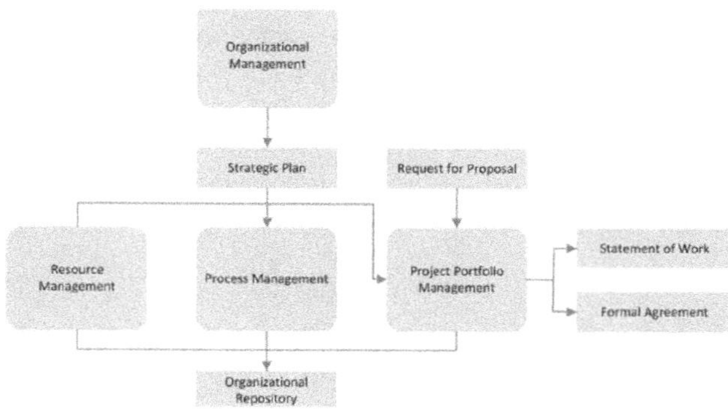

Fig. 4. Organizational profile processes diagram [1].

2.3 Improvement and Certification Needs

Improving the level of quality for an entire organization is no longer the exception but the norm, used to satisfy customers and face always more demanding challenges. Certification is a "must-have" also to meet customer requirements and get more revenue and business from new customers.

The ISO/IEC 29110 [1] standard is nationally and internationally recognized as a true mark of quality. It offers the VSE a new range of opportunities and can open doors the VSE may not be aware of. It allows, through certification, demonstrating to the customer that they use the best existing practices which will increase success in their project and relationship. Having such worldwide recognized certificate, VSEs avoid wasting time to be assessed by each one of their customers.

And more than increasing the customer satisfaction it is a perfect way to be proud, internally and externally, of how they work. Certification helps VSEs earning credibility and respect to open new markets and increasing earning potential to a significant amount, creating tangible economic benefits for VSEs business. It demonstrates commitment to the profession and acts as a determinant differentiator against the competition.

On the other side such certification is also a powerful asset for the VSE's customer which can gain in trust in their relationship with their supplier. The requirement of such certification is a perfect solution to control the right operation from start to end and to have a high level of confidence in the product to be received.

It is confirmed [9] that with the ISO/IEC 29110 [1] standard, VSEs usually require no more than 6 months preparation to be ready for certification for the first basic profile. Without the need of any expert in software quality assurance, the VSEs have the sufficient capability to adapt their processes and move from their currently often ad hoc and informal processes to a more mature methodology.

The conformity to the ISO/IEC 29110 basic profile is characterized by an assessment of a maximum of 1 day and for a maximum of 2 projects.

Once having ensured that improvements and certification are easily and rapidly achievable by VSEs, being able to reach this certification at a low cost is also needed.

For VSE profiles, these certificates are now issued by accredited certification bodies, improving the CMMI/SPICE current situation where ‘certificates’ are not issued by accredited certification bodies but by the appraiser/assessor themselves respectively with no clear/systematic validity period.

Figure below shows the relationship between all the roles and organizations involved in the certification processes, ensuring now a three years validity period with annual surveillance short assessments.

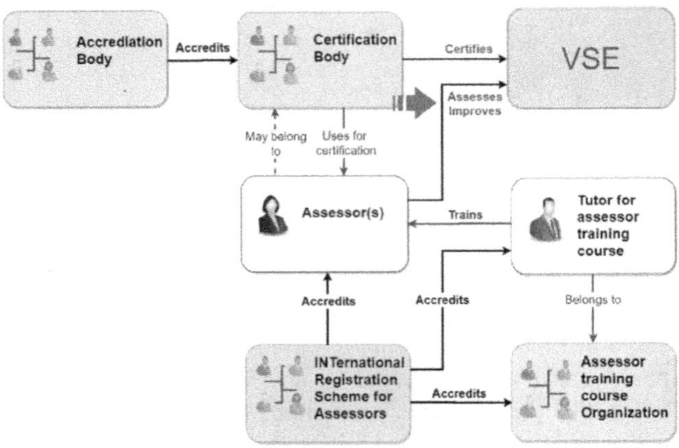

Fig. 5. Roles in an assessement/certification

As shown in the above figure, an assessor within a certification process shall be external to the VSE and with required training and accreditation for certification purpose. This is mandatory for the credibility and recognition of such international certificate (Fig. 5).

3 The Self-assessment as a Powerful Tool

3.1 Self Assessment Pros and Cons

Before any recognition or certification stage, VSEs should recognize the benefits ISO/IEC 29119 may provide them and implement its profile(s) to target their objectives (business goals). But being a VSE, it is often the case that when it commits to a process model it is usually because it helps its business goals. But it is true that to measure the effects of the improvements is not always easy as it also depends on each VSE specific goals.

But once committed to a model, e.g. ISO/IEC 29110, VSEs shall both understand and identify the gaps between how they currently perform versus the target profiles and then implement all improvements needed to achieve those target profile(s) based on the identified gaps.

To do this, VSEs, characterized by limited amount of time and money, need adapted tools and support to save external consultant's cost for improvements and also to allow affordable continuous improvements. Therefore the availability of guidelines supporting the explanation of ISO/IEC 29110 and the existence of self-assessment support are examples of important tools any VSEs may need.

Some guidance materials with what-to-do's already exist in the standard, but the how-to-do's are also needed by VSEs, although not in scope of the world-wide ISO standards. But some of them are already available outside the ISO domain, e.g. in [8]. VSEs are more willing to adapt their processes with such accompaniment in a do-it-yourself method, more flexible to the VSEs way of working. In addition, self-assessments may help VSEs to achieve the target profiles at an affordable cost. It is important to highlight some of the benefits and drawbacks self-assessment may have in general, before presenting the self-assessment support needed by VSEs.

From materials and literature about self-assessment in the education domain [13–16], one can directly apply the same principles to VSEs process self-assessment.

Some of the pros of self-assessments are:

- helping VSEs to learn directly from their previous mistakes, identify their strengths and weaknesses and learn to target their improvements accordingly.
- getting VSEs to become more active in their own improvements, helping to alter the perception of improvement as being a passive process whereby VSEs will need to listen to external assessors or consultants and then absorb the information in order to regurgitate it during the subsequent improvements (with the often risk of not really understanding well why and what to do). Self-assessments encourage the organization's ownership of the assessment, and thereby increases the latter's acceptance of feedback and commitment to the assessment for certification recommendations.
- making VSEs being participants rather than 'spectators', with the more likely consequence to engage with their own improvements, as well as this is the best way to optimize the solutions and improvements directly towards their business goals.

But self-assessments also have some difficulties in order to be 100% efficient:

- it is essential that the assessment criteria are clearly and fully described so that VSEs are able to understand exactly what is expected. The best would be to allow some degree of involvement in the development and comprehension of assessment criteria [13], but this is difficult as often the assessment indicators are standardized to get repeatable results as well as measuring the achievement of the target profiles with the same complete assessment criteria.

- In order to self-assess effectively, VSEs must have a good understanding of the criteria that they gauge their performance against. Internalizing these criteria encourages deep rather than surface learning, greater autonomy [15] and helps them to better engage with any feedback identified. In order for this to take place, the assessment criteria must be transparent and comprehensible to VSEs so that they can effectively judge how well they have met them.
- self assessment is not free and needs some time and planning. An assessment can be made at any time but needs planning and time for it and this is not always available in small VSEs. Even if a self-assessment is not required to follow a strict process, it is recommended to define an assessment plan containing the scheduled and the required resources before being shared and agreed by all the stakeholders. What process' instances to select, what to assess and be assessed, when and where the assessment will occur and which human and material resources are needed are some question to answer before executing the self-assessment
- self assessment needs specific reflective skills that provides VSEs with the ability to consider their own performance and to identify their strengths, weaknesses, and areas that require improvement. VSEs can then use this knowledge to influence their future work, directing their efforts in areas they have already recognized as needing further improvement [14].

3.2 What VSEs May Need

One could use self-assessment in the form of reflective exercises, such as logs or diaries, or in more traditional tasks such as presentations based on questionnaires that VSE staff should complete on specific Project stages, for example. This way is particularly helpful as one can compare the perception of the work performed by an external assessor with the VSEs' views on how well they have performed.

Typically a self-process assessment can be used:

- To have a first idea of how far the organization is from its target profile(s).
- During the adaptation process, on a regular basis, to visualize the progress performed and to re-design the required improvement actions. It can be used as a quick check of the implementation effectiveness of a specific improved activity or a complete profile.
- Before an official demonstration (to top management or for certification) of profile achievement recognition.

In the same way as the implementation guides (ISO/IEC 29110 Parts 5-x-y [1]), ISO WG24 has developed the process assessment model (ISO/IEC 29110 part 3-1 [1]) to facilitate and standardize the assessment of the VSE profiles. Guides and questionnaires for using this same process assessment model criteria for self-assessment are available [8].

The self-assessment questionnaire proposed by upto25.net [8] is both simple and free, allowing VSEs to answer the questions by non-experts in the process assessment field. The replies to the questions could be either 'not implemented', 'partially implemented' or 'fully implemented' (as shown in figure below). When submitting the filled in questionnaire, the VSE gets the result aligned with the standard process assessment model and also gets a detailed list of weaknesses directly implementable as improvement actions (Fig. 6).

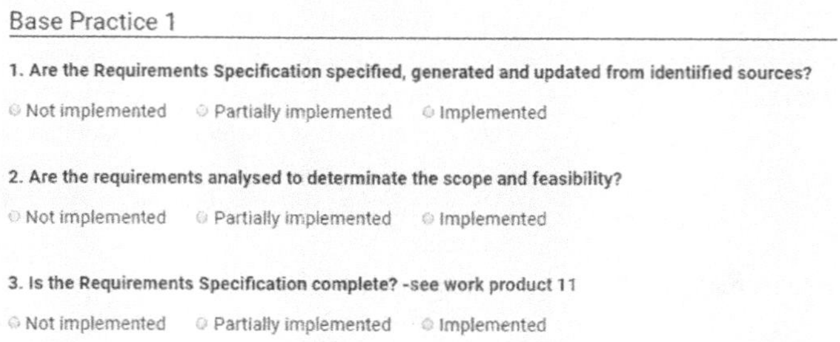
Base Practice 1

1. Are the Requirements Specification specified, generated and updated from identiified sources?

Not implemented Partially implemented Implemented

2. Are the requirements analysed to determinate the scope and feasibility?

Not implemented Partially implemented Implemented

3. Is the Requirements Specification complete? -see work product 11

Not implemented Partially implemented Implemented

Fig. 6. Example of upto25.net self-assessment questionnaire [8]

To identify improvements, VSEs' assessment does not need to be as formal as during the certification process, but can still benefit of using an established model and scheme. Such self-assessment is an efficient and easy tool to involve the complete organization in a continuous improvement process.

4 SPI Manifesto Context

Since 2009 a group of 15 specialists in Software Process Improvement (SPI) that were devoted to the EuroSPI series of conference organized in Europe, have elaborate the SPI Manifesto, published in early 2010. The manifesto includes ten principles organized around three values as key success factors for business process innovation and improvement in organizations [12]. The following table briefly lists the 3 SPI Manifesto values grouping its 10 principles and analyses them all towards the proposed self assessment schema for VSEs:

SPI Manifesto principles	Analysis
Know the culture and focus on needs	Self assessment fully supports this principle as it is the same organization who performs its own self-assessment ensuring to take the organizational culture into consideration in order to gain commitment and avoid resistance
Motivate all people involved	To be motivated for process improvement, one should be able to see what is in it for oneself. Self assessment fully supports this principle as it is the same organization who performs its own self-assessment Probably training should be provided in order to ensure all staff may be able to perform continuous

(*continued*)

(*continued*)

SPI Manifesto principles	Analysis
	self-assessments, so to widely accept the process and gain the commitment of all people and support full continuous process improvements
Base improvement on experience and measurements	Self-assessments help in optimizing the actions for improvement as the ones performing the assessment are the process performers themselves, helping in ensuring individual competences, readiness and willingness to learn and optimize the improvement actions
Create a learning organization	When self-assessment is institutionalized and all VSE staff often performs it to learn about their own work, when sharing their experiences, the VSE is becoming a learning organization
Support the organization's vision and objectives	When a VSE commits to a process model it is usually because they have ensured it helps its business goals: in the past VSEs engaged to big models, but not any more. But to measure the effects of the improvements is not always easy as often depending on each VSE specific goals, not really measured in the past to be above to compare with possible improved values
Use dynamic and adaptable models as needed	This paper is based on VSEs choosing a universally applicable model, such as ISO/IEC 29110
Apply risk management	Not really considered in this paper
Manage the organizational change in your improvement effort	Not really considered in this paper
Ensure all parties understand and agree on process	Not really considered in this paper
Do not lose focus	Not really considered in this paper although by pushing for self-assessments to all VSE staff when sharing their findings, improvements can be defined and self-assessed next time to check for effectiveness of improvements

5 Conclusions

Organizations up to 25 people have now a complete set of material for their software engineering and management projects. Indeed a dedicated ISO working group has developed the ISO/IEC 29110 series [1], specifically intended for VSEs involved in the development of systems or software, to satisfy their needs of being easy to use, support their improvements and be recognizable.

As for any ISO/IEC standard, its adaptation and certification help organizations gain market access, satisfy mandatory customer requirements, streamline processes, manage growth, drive continual improvement, and generally keep up with the competition.

This standard and some already existing websites not only propose guidelines to easily adapt VSEs own processes to the existing best practices but they also provide all the material and tools required to change toward mature and certifiable processes saving time and money: e.g. the most powerful one being the self-assessment tool.

After presenting the ISO/IEC 29110 standard and that certification is of outmost importance, this paper presented that there is an affordable and easy way small entities can effectively progress and reach key competitiveness recognitions: self-assessment, and that self-assessment tools are of first value for small organizations.

References

1. O'Connor, R., Laporte, C.: The evolution of the ISO/IEC 29110 set of standards and guides. Int. J. Inf. Technol. Syst. Approach **10**(1), 1–21 (2017)
2. O'Connor, R.V.: Evaluating management sentiment towards ISO/IEC 29110 in very small software development companies. In: Mas, A., Mesquida, A., Rout, T., O'Connor, R.V., Dorling, A. (eds.) SPICE 2012. CCIS, vol. 290, pp. 277–281. Springer, Heidelberg (2012). https://doi.org/10.1007/978-3-642-30439-2_31
3. ISO/IEC 12207:2017. Systems and software engineering - Software life cycle processes. Geneva, Switzerland: International Organization for Standardization (ISO)
4. ISO 9000:2015 - Quality management. ISO 9001 - Quality management systems Requirements - International Organization for Standardization (ISO)
5. ISO/IEC 330xx Information technology – Process assessment. International Organization for Standardization (ISO)
6. CMMI-DEV ® V1.3. CMU/SEI-2010-TR-033 ESCTR-2010-033 (November 2010)
7. Rodríguez-Dapena, P., Buitrago-Botero, M.F.: How to certify the very small entity software processes using ISO/IEC 29110. In: Rout, T., O'Connor, R.V., Dorling, A. (eds.) SPICE 2015. CCIS, vol. 526, pp. 245–252. Springer, Cham (2015). https://doi.org/10.1007/978-3-319-19860-6_20
8. http://www.upto25.net/en/improve-your-vse/tools/
9. Laporte, C.Y., O'Connor, R.V.: Systems and software engineering standards for very small entities. implementation and initial results. In: 9th International Conference on the Quality of Information and Communications Technology - QUATIC 2014, 23–26 September 2014
10. Laporte, C.Y., Alexandre, S., O'Connor, R.V.: A software engineering lifecycle standard for very small enterprises. In: O'Connor, R.V., Baddoo, N., Smolander, K., Messnarz, R. (eds.) EuroSPI 2008. CCIS, vol. 16, pp. 129–141. Springer, Heidelberg (2008). https://doi.org/10.1007/978-3-540-85936-9_12
11. Laporte, C.Y., O'Connor, R., Fanmuy, G.: International systems and software engineering standards for very small entities. CrossTalk – J. Def. Softw. Eng. **26**, 28–33 (2013)
12. SPI Manifesto (2010). http://www.iscn.com/Images/SPI_Manifesto_A.1.2.2010.pdf
13. Boud, D.: Enhancing Learning Through Self-Assessment. Routledge Falmer, London (1995)
14. Brown, S., Glasner, A.: Assessment Matters in Higher Education: Choosing and Using Diverse Approaches. The Society for Research into Higher Education & Open University Press, Buckingham (2003)

15. Brown, S., Rust, C., Gibbs, G.: Strategies for Diversifying Assessment in Higher Education. Oxonion Rewley Press, Oxford (1994). The Oxford Centre for Staff Development
16. Black, P., Wiliam, D.: Inside the Black Box: Raising standards through classroom assessment (2001). http://weaeducation.typepad.co.uk/files/blackbox-1.pdf. Accessed 9 Aug 2011

Team Skills and Diversity Strategies

How to Leverage the Potential of Diverse and Virtual Teams and Benefit from Diversity Management?

Gabriele Sauberer[1(✉)], Jolanta Maj[2], and Valery Senichev[3]

[1] Forum European Diversity Management, 1190 Vienna, Austria
gabriele@fedm.eu

[2] Faculty of Economics and Management, Opole University of Technology, Opole, Poland

[3] Faculty of Business and Management, Brno University of Technology, Brno, Czech Republic
http://www.fedm.eu/

Abstract. This paper presents the current state of managing diverse and virtual teams. The need for and success of diversity management is discussed in theory and practice. Findings from scientific research are presented and compared with good practice from industry. A new way of achieving positive performance is suggested, with positive leadership and positive communication, to make diversity management understood and successful, for the benefit of divers and virtual teams in software engineering and beyond.

Keywords: Diversity · Diversity management · Positive communication
Positive leadership · Positive performance · Industry 4.0 · Diverse teams
Virtual teams

1 Diversity in Times of Digitalization and Industry 4.0

1.1 Fear of the Unknown and Resistance to Change

Digitalization and automation are meant to help people and to take organizations and society to the next level. In reality, prognoses about 50% of jobs killed by Industry 4.0 and continued globalization could easily provoke dangerous fight-or-flight response, or a "rage against the machine" like in the beginning of industrialization. How to overcome this fear of the unknown and resistance to change with the help of diversity and diversity management? How to benefit from Industry 4.0 and the fundamental changes it will bring to our societies in Europe and all over the world?

1.2 Diverse Societies

Embracing change is embracing diversity. Is it not? At least positive change always seems to be based on an "all different, all equal" approach, as in the campaign of the Council of Europe since 1995 [1]. However, the definition of what positive change is, varies, and depends on the mindset, the values and believes of people.

X. Larrucea et al. (Eds.): EuroSPI 2018, CCIS 896, pp. 529–540, 2018.
https://doi.org/10.1007/978-3-319-97925-0_45

Some political and societal developments of the past few years seem to consider the diversity of societies, countries and the world more as part of the problem, not as possible solution. From "America First" to "Brexit", we currently see a revival of nationalism, ethno-centrism, sexism, racism, xenophobic and extreme right ideologies, in western countries, in Europe and world-wide.

On the other hand, civil society fights back the backlash: We also see powerful movements like the "#MeToo" campaign [2] which spread in October 2017 as a two-word hashtag used on social media against the widespread prevalence of sexual assault and harassment, especially in the workplace. Women stand up for their rights, for what they have achieved in the past, and for what they want to achieve in the future: equal pay and equal opportunities to make it to the top: to the boards of directors of companies, and to the government leaders of the world.

And in the European Union, we see new regulations, legislation and campaigns which foster this positive change towards equal rights and opportunities for all, at least for all EU citizens. In November 2012 the European Commission proposed legislation to increase the number of women on corporate boards by 40% in publicly listed companies [3], which at first was rejected by some Member States i.e. Germany and Poland as contradicting the principle of subsidiarity [4] yet recently is being discussed again [5].

2 Opportunities and Challenges

2.1 Teams Are Increasingly Virtual and Diverse

So, what are the opportunities and challenges of embracing and managing the diversity of people, their languages, knowledge, skills and abilities, in a globalized world driven by Industry 4.0 and increasingly working in virtual teams? What happens, when teams are "diverse"?

In general, we know since long that diversity of teams means greater creativity, innovation and flexibility. Diverse employees have a variety of point of views and share a larger amount of information [6, 7]. The challenges of diverse teams include communication problems, misunderstandings, increased probability of conflict, or reduced coherence [7–9]. These findings confirm the importance of diversity management. Without managing diverse teams in a professional and sustainable way, organizations will not get all of the advantages of diversity.

In virtual teams, results may be weaker than in face-to-face working teams, due to communication processes, and the division of responsibilities and the end result [10]. Culturally diverse teams are better off if they work virtually at the beginning of the collaboration [11]. Also, research suggests that there are differences in satisfaction with working in virtual teams due to gender [12].

Researchers have come to the conclusion that mediation of communication systems (virtual teams) minimizes the challenging effects of team diversity on a cultural background [13]. They also pointed out that efficiency was higher in heterogeneous virtual teams than in heterogeneous face-to-face teams and that the level of conflict was lower [13].

Some research supports the idea that homogenous teams are more open to communication and have a higher level of cohesion [14]. In addition, there are fewer conflicts [15]. On the other hand, diversity positively influences the results achieved by diverse teams, through a greater number of perspectives and different ideas presented in the group [16]. Furthermore, the indicated tendency for conflicts leads, on the other hand, to a more in-depth and comprehensive analysis of the problem and task [17].

Again: Diversity is not "good" or "bad", it is just a fact and characteristic of our planet. The different results in achieved effects may simply be a result of differences in understanding diversity. According to Harrison and Klein [18] diversity is not one, but three things: separation, variety and disparity. Diversity as separation refers to differences in opinions among people, primary due to values, beliefs or attitudes. In this understanding, greater diversity will lead to reduced cohesiveness, more interpersonal conflict, distrust and decreased task performance. The second understanding of diversity, as variety, refers to differences in knowledge and experience of people and leads predictably to greater creativity, innovation, higher decision quality and increase flexibility. The third understanding of diversity, as disparity refers to differences in proportion of valued assets and resources among people and leads to more competition, reduced input, withdrawal. Adopting one of these meanings by researchers but also practitioners can lead to different results.

However, biodiversity is "good" in a Darwinistic sense: The fittest plants, it is the surviving ones, are those in an environment characterized by biodiversity.

2.2 Diversity Needs to Be Managed Well

Diversity in teams, at the workplace, and in societies needs to be leveraged and managed properly. Otherwise we will always get these ambivalent research findings, with "positive" impacts and "negative" consequences of diversity. This will not bring much benefit for global developments, such as increasingly diverse and virtual teams in all spheres of work and life.

The impact of team diversification, due to the various dimensions of diversity, has been the subject of numerous studies. The most frequently analyzed diversity dimensions are gender (34% of studies) and ethnic diversity (31%) [19]. The analysis of one dimension of diversity may not provide a full spectrum of the impact of these dimensions on team functioning, yet 43% of the research focused on one dimension of diversity [19].

A comparative analysis of the functioning of face-to-face and virtual teams was made by Gera [20]. The respective studies were primarily concerned with communication issues [21–23], and with trust, coherence and efficiency.

Some research suggests that virtual teams do worse with tasks that have one solution [24]. In addition, real teams have done better in terms of decision behavior, the amount of information exchanged and discussed, discussion length, performance and unique information. Other researchers, however, have shown that while virtual teams have comparable successes to face-to-face teams, they have a lower level of satisfaction and need more time to complete the task. These analyses, however, were made without taking into account and deliberately eliminating the impact of socio-demographic variables.

Numerous studies analyzed, collected and summarized the impact of different dimensions of diversity on the functioning of teams and organizations in general. Comparative analysis of the functioning of diverse teams working face-to-face and working in virtual teams has been carried out considering the following variables:

- Gender [12, 25, 26].
- Ethnic and cultural origins [13, 27, 28]
- Functional Diversity [29]
- Cognitive Diversity [30].

The impact of different dimensions of diversity on team performance is particularly time-dependent. Because team members do not have the knowledge and information about other people, they may be inclined to make more use of visible dimensions of diversity, including age, as a cognitive basis [7]. Thus, especially in the short term, diversified teams may achieve weaker results [13], and therefore need faster and better management of diversity from the very beginning.

Review studies suggest that the occurrence of "negative" consequences of team diversity on the grounds of its members' age is more likely than "positive" consequences [31]. In industries and professions using advanced technologies, stereotypes about older workers are particularly strong [32, 33].

Research has shown that there are a number of "advantages and disadvantages" of the functioning of teams composed of age-varying workers [31]. Researchers also pointed to a number of conditions for the effective functioning of age-diverse teams, to which they included a high degree of complexity of the task, low salience and high appreciation of age diversity, low age-discrimination, the use of age differentiated leadership, ergonomic design of work places and a positive team climate.

However, the emergence of most of these factors is only possible at a later stage of group formation. In addition, the analysis of the effect of age on the functioning of the face-to-face teams indicated a negative correlation between age group differentiation and frequency of communication within the group [34], as well as a greater turnover rate [35]. In turn, other researchers found that age does not affect the quality of innovation [36].

Age belongs to the so-called "visible characteristics" [37], which have more influence in face-to-face working teams [38]. Visible characteristics can influence results and efficiency of teamwork, especially when team members have prejudice against different groups [39]. To be "different" still may be difficult for team members, as studies show: Individuals who are different from the rest of the team experience a number of negative consequences such as less trust from their peers, lower frequency of communication [34], lower involvement of the group [40], and finally an increased probability of conflicts with other members of the group [41].

3 Good Practice from Industry – Bad News from Science?

What do we learn from all this research? That diversity still needs to be managed carefully, even more in increasingly global and virtual working environments for fast changing teams. And that, in practice, the potential of a diverse workforce still is not leveraged as it could and should be, for the benefit of team performance. Furthermore the research shows that organizations may benefit from diversity if they know how to "apply" it correctly i.e. in which cases and circumstances diverse teams can flourish and what needs to be done to achieve such circumstances.

So what we can do about it? How can diversity management help people understand the benefit of managing diversity?

First of all, by sharing good practice from industry: When SAP hires autistic people for specific tasks they are very good at (controlling pieces of software and detecting errors) [42], both parties benefit: SAP finds the right people for important tasks, and the autistic people get the opportunity to have a job and live a self-determined life.

When technical universities are desperately looking for female students, and economies suffer from skilled worker shortage in technical and other subject fields, diversity management can help and does help to attract high potentials and high performers, independent from their gender, age, or ethnical background. These examples are not affirmations. They are not wishful thinking, but evidence-based. The positive impact of Diversity Management is measurable since many years - we have facts and figures from many countries, companies and industries all over the world.

3.1 Diversity as a Challenge

However, scientific research is still struggling. Diversity at the workplace is one of the biggest challenges in contemporary organizational studies. Understanding and effectively managing diverse teams deserves more and more attention in scientific literature as well as in the practice of real organizations [50]. We see high-quality solutions in implementing diversity management strategies and initiatives. However, large-scale research aiming to cover big organizations faces different challenges, as we know.

Literature review and pilot studies [43, 44] brought the following results:

- Diversity management can influence the effectiveness of organizations and teams in the long term.
- Increasing the level of team diversity does not automatically lead to higher performance and efficiency [45].
- Diversity may become a double-edged sword, by increasing both the team effectivity and the likelihood of team members dissatisfied and failing to identify with the group [46].
- Research on first-line managers is crucial for understanding diversity management.
- The number of research on diversity in organizational settings is still low [47, 48].

The positive effects of diversity on group performance have been limited to laboratory studies or experiments. Most of the research projects have not been replicated in organizational studies [48]. Large-scale diversity management research was made with university students' groups [49]. The research data and facts mentioned above was the reason to make a research on team performance and diversity in companies [43].

Senichev studied the effectiveness of diverse teams in organizations, mainly from Finance and Insurance, Information Technology and Communication, as well as Education [43]. The research group represented 98 team leaders (65% female leaders,

35% male leaders, leading a team and operate in the organization with official diversity programs or projects).

The main goal of this empirical research [43] on diversity management was to survey the impact of diversity (age, gender and informational diversity measured on Likert Scales) on the effective team performance in selected organizations in the Czech Republic, with the following results:

- a positive correlation between informational diversity and goals or specific task achievement;
- a slightly positive correlation was detected between the informational diversity and handling project or work deadlines;
- a slightly positive correlation between gender diversity and handling project or work deadlines.
- No relationship was detected between team effectiveness and team size. The same negative results were found for the organizational size and the dimensions of age, gender or informational diversity.
- The qualitative analysis of the respondents' experience with managing team diversity suggests that:
- Age diversity is linked with a situation of mixing different perspectives and experience in teams.
- Gender diversity can have a positive influence on socio-psychological dynamics in a team and can be efficient for client management.
- Informational diversity was introduced and mentioned as a factor of improving the problem-solving process and project effectiveness.

Respondents in qualitative research were asked to define the traits and factors of high performing teams. Proportions in gender were introduced in a 50:50 proportional representation of experienced and less experienced peers in teams. The role of the manager was introduced to unite the team, to support team members' potential, and to foster cooperation among them with a goal to fulfill the given tasks.

The findings of this research [43] support the results of the large-scale research made by professor Kochan in the U.S. [45], who demonstrated how difficult it was to conduct this type of field research, and how little strategic attention practitioners in various in organizations still pay to diversity issues [43]. The research of Senichev [43] showed the importance of business practice supported by data. Moreover, there is a need to stress, that quantitative data should be combined with qualitative data from the companies to bring and to highlight the meaning of data.

3.2 Critical Thinking and Negative Thinking

So, does this mean that it is still too early or too much wishful thinking to embrace diversity and integrate diversity management in our team management and in the management systems of organizations?

The findings from research do not seem to be very promising, or even convincing that the researchers themselves believe in the benefit of diversity management for organizations. Each positive research result immediately is confronted with a negative one, which leads to the impression that there is actually no proven positive effect of managing diversity at the workplace. This is simply not the case.

Do we overlook, forget or underestimate at universities, that there is so much evidence from real practice, from companies all over Europe [51, 52] and beyond [53], that diversity management is a key driver of innovation [54], positive performance and sustainability [55–57]? And, in particular in Central and Eastern European Countries, that diversity is considered to be the decisive next growth factor [58]?

Is critical thinking at academic level still misunderstood and practiced as negative thinking? Do we need a new language to describe what diversity and diversity management mean, or do we simply need to organize and conceptualize the already existing knowledge? The Austrian Standard ÖNORM S2501 [59], for instance, suggested a lot of diversity terms and definitions, providing a sound basis for the new International ISO Standard about Diversity and Inclusion (ISO/AWI 30415), which is currently under development [60].

4 Diversity Management and Positive Leadership in Teams

Yes, in science, it is all about concepts, terms and definitions. So let us have a closer look at the challenge of understanding and defining diversity management. In the first standard about Diversity Management, the Austrian standard ÖNORM S 2501:2008, diversity management is defined as: "*a strategic management approach aimed at the targeted consideration and deliberate utilization of the diversity of persons and relevant organizational environments or stakeholders in order to create structural and social conditions under which all employees can develop their abilities and reach their full performance to the benefit of all parties involved and for raising the organization's success*". Translated into accessible language, Diversity Management is a strategic management approach, using the potential of a diverse workforce for the benefits of all parties involved.

Maybe we have asked the wrong question when asking "How to foster positive performance *through* diversity and diversity management?" Maybe the wright and relevant question is "How to foster positive performance *of* diversity and diversity management?"

There are two powerful models to help us do so (see Sauberer 2017): The PERMA Model of Seligman [69], and the Positive Leadership Model of Kim Cameron, both distinguished professors and scholars in Positive Psychology, which is: "*the scientific study of human flourishing, and an applied approach to optimal functioning. It has also been defined as the study of the strengths and virtues that enable individuals, communities and organizations to thrive.*" [61].

Humans have a bias toward the negative [62]: In teams, people are more affected emotionally from a single negative piece of feedback than from a single positive piece of feedback [63]. Negative phenomena get more attention than positive phenomena. Thus, it takes conscious effort to focus on the positive, and to focus on the benefits of diversity. As a matter of fact, the positivity ratio is between 3:1 [64, 65] and 5:1 [66].

The bias towards the negative requires training in Positive Leadership and Positive Communication, since we need to "un-learn" the negative bias and learn to apply the tools of positive psychology and positive leadership. Cameron [67] gives a large amount of examples of Abundance Tools, and 4 Strategies to implement Positive Leadership:

- Foster Positive Working Climate
- Foster Positive Relationships
- Foster Positive Communication
- Give Work a Meaning.

For diversity management, we can and shall use the power of positive communication, and focus on the "abundance gaps" between the "normal state" and the "positive deviance" of Kim Cameron's powerful, proven business strategy to excel and achieve "the impossible" [63, 70].

Most Certification Criteria for Diversity Management Systems [68], based on the Diversity Standard ÖNORM S2501 [59], require a strong commitment of management and the people involved in the diversity program or project. If the goal of diversity management is to reach a "normal" level of performance through diversity, we are caught in the deficit gaps, and risk not to inspire stakeholders enough to make the diversity program sustainable. But if we focus on the abundance gaps and reach out for the extraordinary and excellent in and through diversity management, we make stakeholders part of something much bigger than themselves, which is attractive and inspiring.

5 Conclusions and Outlook

Positive Psychology and its fields of application, such as positive leadership, including positive communication and positive deviance, can help making diversity management successful, in particular the models of Martin Seligman and Kim Cameron. Diverse and virtual teams need such tools as positive leadership and positive communication, to make Diversity Management not only successful, but also sustainable in all kinds of organizations, and enjoyable for all stakeholders and key drivers of diversity management.

Embracing and managing the diversity of people, of languages and of systems, is a basic requirement of the presence and the future of a globalized world [63]. All we need to successfully manage diversity is available – all theories, studies, research results, systems and tools, as well as good practice do exist. But without our optimism, commitment and resilience, we risk failure. That is why we need the methods and tools of positive psychology, to connect diversity with positive emotions, and make diversity management successful and sustainable in diverse and virtual teams.

References

1. Europe's Human Rights Watchdog. http://www.europewatchdog.info/en/instruments/campaigns/all_different_all_equal/. Accessed 14 Apr 2018
2. Me Too (hashtag). https://metoomvmt.org/. Accessed 17 Feb 2018

3. Directive proposal for gender balance on corporate boards (2012). https://ec.europa.eu/info/strategy/justice-and-fundamental-rights/discrimination/gender-equality/gender-balance-decision-making-positions_en. Accessed 25 Jan 2018
4. Maj, J.: Gender Equality in the European Union. Nomos, Baden-Baden (2017)
5. Boffey, D.: EU to push for 40% quota for women on company boards. http://www.theguardian.com/world/2017/nov/20/eu-to-push-for-40-quota-for-women-on-company-boards. Accessed 25 Jan 2018
6. Jehn, K., Northcraft, G., Neale, M.: Why differences make a difference: a field study of diversity, conflict, and performance in workgroups. Adm. Sci. Q. **44**, 741–763 (1999)
7. Lau, D., Murninghan, J.K.: Demographic diversity and faultlines: the compositional dynamics of organizational groups. Acad. Manag. Rev. **23**(2), 325–340 (1998)
8. Hambrick, D., Canney Davison, S., Snell, S., Snow, Ch.: When groups consist of multiple nationalities: towards a new understanding of the implications. Organ. Stud. **19**(2), 181–205 (1998)
9. Williams, K., O'Reilly, Ch.: Demography and diversity in organizations: a review of 40 years of research. Res. Organ. Behav. **20**, 77–140 (1998)
10. Thompson, L.F., Coovert, M.D.: Team-work online: the effects of computer conferencing on perceived confusion, satisfaction, and post-discussion accuracy. Group Dyn. Theor. Res. Pract. **7**(2), 135–151 (2003)
11. Carte, T., Chidambaram, L.: A capabilities-based theory of technology deployment in diverse teams: leapfrogging the pitfalls of diversity and leveraging its potential with collaborative technology. J. Assoc. Inf. Syst. **5**(11–12), 448–471 (2004)
12. Lind, M.R.: The gender impact of temporary virtual work groups. IEEE Trans. Prof. Commun. **42**(4), 276–285 (1999)
13. Staples, S., Zhao, L.: The effects of cultural diversity in virtual teams versus face-to-face teams. Group Decis. Negot. **15**, 389–406 (2006)
14. O'Reilley, Ch., Caldwell, D., Barnett, W.: Work group demography, social integration, and turnover. Adm. Sci. Q. **34**, 21–37 (1989)
15. Eisenhardt, K., Kahwajy, J., Bourgeois, L.J.: Conflict and strategic choice: how top management teams disagree. Calif. Manag. Rev. **39**, 42–62 (1997)
16. Schweiger, D., Sandberg, W., Ragan, J.: Group approaches for improving strategic decision making: a comparative analysis of dialectical inquiry, devil's advocacy, and consensus approaches to strategic decision making. Acad. Manag. J. **29**, 51–71 (1986)
17. Watson, W., Kumar, K., Michaelsen, L.: Cultural diversity's impact on interaction process and performance: comparing homogeneous and diverse task groups. Acad. Manag. J. **36**, 590–602 (1993)
18. Harrison, D.A., Klein, K.J.: What's the difference? Diversity constructs as separation, variety, or disparity in organizations. Acad. Manag. Rev. **32**(4), 1199–1228 (2007)
19. Jackson, S.E., Joshi, A., Erhard, N.L.: Recent research on team and organizational diversity: SWOT analysis and implications. J. Manag. **2003**(29), 801–830 (2003)
20. Gera, S.: Virtual teams versus face to face teams: a review of literature. IOSR J. Bus. Manag. **11**(2), 1–4 (2013)
21. Warkentin, M.E., Sayeed, L., Hightower, R.: Virtual teams versus face-to-face teams: an exploratory study of a web-based conference system. Decis. Sci. **28**(4), 975–996 (1997)
22. Van Der Smagt, T.: Enhancing virtual teams: Social relations v. communication technology. Ind. Manag. Data Syst. **100**(4), 148–156 (2000)
23. Rhoads, M.: Face-to-face and computer-mediated communication: what does theory tell us and what have we learned so far? J. Plan. Lit. **25**, 2 (2010)
24. O'Neill, T.A., Hancock, S.E., Zivkov, K., Larson, N.L., Law, S.J.: Team decision making in virtual and face-to-face environments. Group Decis. Negot. **25**(5), 995–1020 (2016)

25. Furumo, K.: Differences between male and female communications and conflict management styles in virtual teams. J. Manag. Mark. **17**, 1–7 (2014)
26. Riedl, B.C., Cai, D., Ratan, R., Shen, C., Picot, A.: Champions of equality: examining gender egalitarianism in virtual teams across cultures. In: Proceedings of the Annual Hawaii International Conference on System Sciences, pp. 393–401 (2015)
27. Krawczyk-Bryłka, B.: Intercultural challenges in virtual teams. J. Intercult. Manag. **8**(3), 69–85 (2016)
28. Hung, Y.-T.C., Nguyen, M.T.T.D.: The impact of cultural diversity on global virtual team collaboration – a social identity perspective. In: Proceedings of the 4th Hawaii International Conference on Systems Science, pp. 1–10 (2008)
29. Peters, L., Karren, R.J.: An examination of the roles of trust and functional diversity on virtual team performance ratings. Group Org. Manag. **34**(4), 479–504 (2009)
30. Huang, R., Chidambaram, L., Miranda, S.M.: Understanding the salience of cognitive diversity in face-to-face and computer-mediated teams. In: Proceedings of the 12th Americas Conference on Information Systems. AMCIS 2006, pp. 4005–4013 (2006)
31. Ries, B.C., Diestel, S., Shemla, M., Liebermann, F., Jungmann, J., Wegge, J.: Age-differentiated work systems. In: Schlick, C., Frieling, E., Wegge, J. (eds.) Age Diversity and Team Effectiveness, pp. 89–118. Springer, Heidelberg (2013). https://doi.org/10.1007/978-3-642-35057-3_5
32. Perry, E., Finkelstein, L.: Toward a broader view of age discrimination in employment-related decisions: a joint consideration of organizational factors and cognitive processes. Hum. Resour. Manag. Rev. **9**(1), 21–49 (1999)
33. Schloegel, U., Stegmann, S., Maedche, A., van Dick, R.: Reducing age stereotypes in software development: the effects of awareness- and cooperation-based diversity interventions. J. Syst. Softw. **121**, 1–15 (2016)
34. Zenger, T.R., Lawrence, B.S.: Organizational demography. Acad. Manag. J. **32**, 353–376 (1989)
35. Wiersema, M., Bantel, K.: Top management team turnover as an adaptation mechanism: the role of the environment. Strateg. Manag. J. **14**, 485–504 (1993)
36. Cady, S.H., Valentine, J.: Team innovation and perceptions of consideration what difference does diversity make? Small Group Res. **30**(6), 730–750 (1999)
37. Pelled, L.H.: Demographic diversity, conflict, and work group outcomes: an intervening process theory. Organ. Sci. **7**(6), 615–631 (1996)
38. D'Souza, G.C., Colarelli, S.M.: Team member selection decisions for virtual versus face-to-face teams. Comput. Hum. Behav. **26**(4), 630–635 (2010)
39. Dovidio, J.F., Gaertner, S.L., Kawakami, K., Hodson, G.: Why can't we just get along? Interpersonal biases and interracial distrust. Cult. Divers. Ethnic Minor. Psychol. **8**, 88–102 (2002)
40. Tsui, A., Egan, T., O'Reilly, Ch.: Being different: relational demography and organizational attachment. Adm. Sci. Q. **37**, 549–579 (1992)
41. Jehn, K.A., Chadwick, C., Thatcher, S.: To agree or not to agree: diversity, conflict, and group outcomes. Int. J. Confl. Manag. **8**, 287–306 (1997)
42. Forbes. https://www.forbes.com/sites/hbsworkingknowledge/2016/07/11/the-benefits-of-recruiting-employees-with-autism-spectrum-disorder/#188d3c5440a2. Accessed 25 Jan 2018
43. Senichev, V.: Uplatnění koncepce diversity managementu v oblasti řízení lidských zdrojů. Disertační práce. Vysoké učení technické v Brně, Fakulta podnikatelská, Brno, 221 s, 2017. Vedoucí disertační práce: doc. Ing. Zdeňka Konečná, Ph.D. (2017)

44. Žizlavský, O., Senichev, V.: The role of human resource management and group factors in innovation process. In: Vision 2020: Innovation, Development Sustainability, and Economic Growth. IBIMA, Vienna, pp. 679–690 (2013)
45. Kochan, T., et al.: The effects of diversity on business performance: report of a feasibility study of the diversity research network. Hum. Resour. Manag. J. **42**(1), 3–21 (2003)
46. Milliken, F.J., Martins, L.L.: Searching for common threads. Acad. Manag. Rev. **21**, 2 (1996)
47. Watson, W.E., Johnson, L., Zgouridesz, G.: The influence of ethnic diversity on leadership, group process, and performance: an examination of learning teams. Int. J. Intercult. Relat. **26**, 1–16 (2002)
48. Podsiadlowski, A., Groschke, D., Kogler, M., Springer, C., van der Zee, K.: Managing a culturally diverse workforce: diversity Perspectives in Organizations. Int. J. Intercult. Res. **37**(2), 159–175 (2013)
49. Nederveen Pieterse, A., van Knippenberg, D., van Diererdonck, D.: Cultural diversity and team performance: the role of team member goal orientation. Acad. Manag. J. **56**, 782–804 (2013)
50. Senichev, V.: Organizational teams: linking team diversity, performance and satisfaction. Trendy Ekon. Manag. **7**(17), 139–149 (2013)
51. European Commission: The business case for diversity. Good practices in the workplace. Office for Official Publications of the European Communities, Luxembourg (2005)
52. European Commission: Continuing the Diversity Journey. Business Practices, Perspectives and Benefits. Office for Official Publications of the European Communities, Luxembourg (2008)
53. Gardenswartz, L., Rowe, A.: Diverse Teams at Work: Capitalizing on the Power of Diversity, 1st edn. Society for Human Resource Management, Alexandria (2003)
54. Forbes Insights: Global diversity and inclusion: fostering innovation through a diverse workforce (2011). http://www.forbes.com/forbesinsights/innovation_diversity/index.html. Accessed 07 July 2014
55. Sauberer, G.: An EU-wide methodology and strategy for diversity management. In: Diversity is Reality. Effective Leadership of Diverse teams in a Global Environment, pp. 46–58, Brno (2011)
56. Sauberer, G.: Der Europäische Diversity Führerschein: Neue Fähigkeiten und Strategien für Diversitäts- und Innovationsmanagement in Europa und weltweit, Masterarbeit zur Erlangung des akademischen Grades Master of Business Administration an der Fachhochschule Burgenland, Austrian Institute of Management (2014)
57. Andrlik, M., Pauser, N.: Realisierung von Diversity & Inclusion. Facultas, Wien (2015)
58. Roland Berger: Diversity in central and eastern Europe: the decisive next growth factor? http://www.rolandberger.at/media/pdf/Roland_Berger_Studie_Diversity_in_CEE_20131113.pdf. Accessed 15 July 2014
59. ÖNORM S 2501:2008 Diversity management – General guidelines on principles, systems and supporting techniques. Austrian Standards, Vienna (2008)
60. ISO Standard ISO/AWI 30415 under development: Diversity and inclusion, under development. https://www.iso.org/standard/71164.html?browse=tc. Accessed 30 Jan 2018
61. Positive Psychology Institute: What is positive psychology? (2018). http://www.positivepsychologyinstitute.com.au/what_is_positive_psychology.html. Accessed 21 Jan 2018
62. Baumeister, R.F., Bratslavsky, E., Finkenauer, C., Vohs, K.D.: Bad is stronger than good. Rev. Gen. Psychol. **5**, 323–370 (2001)

63. Sauberer, G., Riel, A., Messnarz, R.: Diversity and PERMA-nent positive leadership to benefit from industry 4.0 and kondratieff 6.0. In: Stolfa, J., Stolfa, S., O'Connor, R., Messnarz, R. (eds.) Systems, Software and Services Process Improvement. 24th European Conference. EuroSPI 2017, vol. 748, pp. 642–652 (2017). https://doi.org/10.1007/978-3-319-64218-5_53
64. Fredrickson, B.: Positivity: groundbreaking research reveals how to embrace the hidden strength of positive emotions, overcome negativity, and thrive (2009)
65. Fredrickson, B.: Positivity: top-notch research reveals the 3 to 1 ratio that will change your life (2009)
66. Carrere, S., Gottman, J.M.: Predicting divorce among newlyweds from the first three minutes of a marital. In: Family Process; Fall 1999, vol. 38, no. 3, pp 293–301 (2009). Research Library
67. Cameron, K.: Positive leadership and extraordinary organizational performance. Dean's lecture series, Melbourne graduate school of education, 26 March 2012 (2012). http://education.unimelb.edu.au/__data/assets/pdf_file/0003/628491/Kim_Cameron_pp.pdf
68. Forum European Diversity Management: Human diversity management systems. https://www.forum-european-diversity-management.eu/app/download/5801698304/AS%2BC-Zertschema_Y04-DivManV10_2013-05-01_EN.pdf. Accessed 20 Jan 2018
69. Seligman, M.: Flourish: A Visionary New Understanding of Happiness and Well-Being. William Heinemann, Random House Australia Pty Ltd, North Sydney (2011)
70. Cameron, K.S.: Practicing Positive Leadership: Tools and Techniques That Create Extraordinary Results. Berrett-Koehler Publishers, San Francisco (2013)

Imperative Ethical Behaviours in Making Systems Development and Deployment Compliant with Health & Safety and Wellbeing

Harjinder Rahanu[1](✉), Elli Georgiadou[1,2](✉), Kerstin Siakas[3](✉), and Margaret Ross[4](✉)

[1] Middlesex University, London, UK
harjinder2@mdx.ac.uk
[2] SEEQMA Ltd, Consultancy, London, UK
[3] Alexander Technological Educational Institute, Thessaloniki, Greece
[4] Southampton Solent University, Southampton, UK

Abstract. Literature on systems development has been progressively identifying the importance of social aspects in systems development, to the extent that this process has been considered a socio-technical system. More often than not there is a failure of participants in the recognition, and fulfilment, of ethical duties concerning the concepts of health and safety and wellbeing. The purpose of normative ethics is to scrutinise moral standards for the rightness and wrongness of actions, the ultimate goal being the identification of the true human good. A rational appeal can be made to normative defensible ethical rules in order to arrive at a judicious, morally justifiable judgement. In this paper our first step is to report on the findings of a literature review, which presents the current health and safety issues concerning usage of computers in organisations and the workplace. Secondly, we identify and list some basic generic Deontological and Teleological moral principles and theories that can serve as normative guidelines for addressing the issues pinpointed in the initial step. Thirdly, we prescribe a set of moral rights and duties that must be exercised and fulfilled by protagonists in systems development and software engineering in order for them to exhibit moral behaviour. Each of these suggested actions are substantiated via an appeal to one, or a number of the normative guidelines, identified in the second step. By identifying, and recommending a set of defensible moral obligations that must be fulfilled in the development and deployment of systems, protagonists such as: project managers, software engineering teams, systems analysts, clients, etc. can fulfil their ethical duties, thus increasing the likelihood a deployed system that is compliant with principles of health and safety and wellbeing of its users. Ultimately systems development and deployment must be underpinned with ethical consideration.

Keywords: Normative ethics · Health and safety · Systems development
Process improvement

X. Larrucea et al. (Eds.): EuroSPI 2018, CCIS 896, pp. 541–553, 2018.
https://doi.org/10.1007/978-3-319-97925-0_46

1 Software Process Improvement

Effective development and implementation of systems is the result of proper interplay between (1) humans-centered aspects, specifically, socio-cultural aspects; and (2) technology. Thus the study and optimisation of these should be conducted concurrently. There is a realisation in industry, commerce and government that the application of new software methodologies and technologies have failed to realise the desired gains in productivity and quality. There is recognition that the significant problem is the inability to manage the software process. There have been a significant amount of software process improvement efforts. Notable software process improvement standards and models from consulting firms include:

- The Capability Maturity Model Integration [CMMI], the replacement to the older CMM, developed at Carnegie Mellon University (CMMI 2010);
- The International Standards Organisation's 9001 Specification [ISO 9001] (ISO 2016);
- The ISO/IEC 15504 IT Process Assessment, aka Software Process Improvement and Capability Determination [SPICE] (ISO 2012);
- Six Sigma, the data driven leadership approach (Pyzdek 2003);
- The 730-2014 IEEE Standard for Software Quality Assurance Processes, which establishes the requirements for initiating, planning, controlling, and executing the Software Quality Assurance processes of a software development or maintenance project (IEEE 2014).

Central to each of these improvement models is the notion of a focused and sustained effort towards building a process infrastructure of effective software engineering and management practices. The SPI strategy aims for something that is more focused, more repeatable, and more reliable, with regards to the quality of the system developed (conformance to requirements, reliability, usability etc.), the timeliness of delivery and the expected cost. Also quality in use has implications on performance, reliability, and usability. Quality can also be understood in the context of SQuaRE (Software product Quality Requirements and Evaluation), a more extensive series of standards to replace ISO/IEC 9126 (ISO/IEC 2011). ISO 25010 has a greater number of product quality characteristics and sub characteristics, in contrast to ISO 9126, including such aspects as effectiveness, efficiency, user satisfaction and societal impacts. The overall assumption is that a sound and improving process is likely to result in high quality systems i.e. process improvement is likely to result in improved products. However, if the organisational culture and practices allow for unethical behaviour SPI efforts are likely to fail.

1.1 Professionalism and Health & Safety

When computer professionals begin work, they typically enter into relationships with one or several of the following: employers, clients, co-professionals (or the profession as a whole) and the public (Johnson 1995). Literature reviews suggest that with regards to IS development and implementation projects, more often than not, the relationship between the professional and the client is predominant, which often invokes ethical and professional issues that can determine the success or failure of such projects. Clients are heavily dependent on software and hardware suppliers for accurate, honest and open information, alongside sound and objective advice. This dependence creates special obligations for the vendor to be conscientious about advising clients.

Health and safety and the wellbeing of end users of the systems we develop as engineers are a problematic challenge for countless developers and organisations. Health and safety management is the process of identifying and minimising threats to workers and those affected by the work throughout the project, programme and portfolio life cycle. Health effects associated with the use of computer technology has important implications because of the prevalence of work with IT equipment in various forms. Special implications for developers of systems and users of the deployed solutions are invoked and these are discussed in this paper. There is UK legislation governing health and safety in the workplace.

1.2 Computer Ethics

It is generally recognised that law and morality do have in common certain key principles and obligations. Thus the law will clearly apply and lead directly to the appropriate ethical conclusion. However, to rely solely on law as a moral guideline is clearly dangerous because in certain circumstances bad laws exist (Kallman and Grillo 1996) (Spinello 1995). Inadequate laws may bind rules on society that fail to provide moral guidance. Such laws may, in some instances, excuse a society from fulfilling certain obligations and duties, or allow a society to justify their unethical behaviour. Ethical judgments simply do not have the same deductivity and objectivity as scientific ones. However, moral judgments should be based upon rational moral principles and sound, carefully reasoned arguments. Spinello (1995) states that normative claims are supported by: “An appeal to defensible moral principles, which become manifest through rational discourse”.

A normative claim can only be substantiated, and a rational discourse presented, through an appeal to such principles. Thus, with regards to the ethical issues raised by systems development and deployment, in Sect. 2 of this paper we will present a list of defensible ethical principles, which are taken from ethical theory. In Sect. 3 the authors identify the current issues concerning health and safety in the systems development and deployment process. Computerized information systems have brought with them new health and safety hazards, and these will be identified, alongside the issues pertaining to discrimination in the workplace. A number of heuristics are suggested in Sect. 4, which if followed may lead to ethical guidance concerning health and safety in the systems development and deployment lifecycle. These normative claims are substantiated via the citation of one or a number of the ethical principles from Sect. 2. Thus each heuristic is based upon rational moral and philosophical principles and sound, carefully reasoned arguments.

1.3 SPI Manifesto

The Software Process Improvement (SPI) Manifesto consists of three values and ten principles, which serves as an expression to state-of-the-art knowledge on SPI. In planning a SPI project, these values and principles can be embraced in order to better facilitate the necessary corresponding change in the organisation (EuroSPI.net 2010).

The argument put forward in this paper that we, as SPI professionals, need to fulfil ethical duties concerning the health and safety, and the wellbeing, of end users of the developed and deployed systems correlates with the values outlined in the SPI manifesto. The SPI values: must involve people actively and affect their daily activities; is what you do to make business successful; and is inherently linked with change. The corresponding principles that are fleshed out, based on these three values, serve as foundations for action. The notion of health and safety, and the wellbeing, is implicitly implied in the SPI Manifesto values and principles.

2 Defensible Ethical Principles

There are a range of ethical theories that have been developed throughout history and one or a combination of these can be selected. Fundamentally there are two basic approaches to ethics: Teleological theories (consider the consequences of an action as a measure of goodness) and Deontological theories (emphasise the rightness of an action above the goodness it produces).

Kallman and Grillo (1996) present a framework for ethical analysis. Amongst, a multitude of other details, it lists some basic moral principles and theories that can serve as normative guidelines for addressing the moral issues, cases where ethical and professional issues may have been invoked. The framework also advocates the steps that are required in order to conduct an ethical analysis. The following sub-sections enumerate these principles that have been sourced from ethical theories, including Teleological and Deontological ones.

2.1 Deontology

Kallman and Grillo (1996) state that deontological ethics, often referred to as deontology, is the normative ethical position that appraises the morality of an action based on rules. Deontology is at times described as duty or obligation or rule based ethics, because rules bind an individual to their duty.

According to Ross (1930) duty Based Ethics (Pluralism) can be viewed as seven basic moral duties, which are:

1. One ought to keep promises (fidelity)
2. One ought to right the wrongs that one has inflicted on others (reparation)
3. One ought to distribute goods justly (justice)
4. One ought to improve the lot of others with respect to virtue, intelligence, and happiness (beneficence)
5. One ought to improve oneself with respect to virtue and intelligence (self-improvement)
6. One ought to exhibit gratitude when appropriate (gratitude)
7. One ought to avoid injury to others (non-injury).

According to Kallman and Grillo in Rights-Based Ethics (Contractarianism) there are three fundamental rights. Hamelink (2000) identified, and appended, a further seven to give the following list of rights:

- The right to know
- The right to privacy
- The right to property
- The right to security
- The right to political participation
- The right to freedom of expression
- The right to freedom of association
- The right not to be discriminated against
- The right to fair access to, and development of, communication resources
- The right to protection of cultural identity

2.2 Teleology

In contrast to deontology, teleology describes an ethical perspective that asserts the rightness or wrongness of human actions is based exclusively on the goodness or badness of their consequences. Therefore, teleology views actions as being morally neutral when considered apart from their consequences. Kallman and Grillo (1996) identify three philosophies under the umbrella of teleology:

- Ethical Egoism: Moral agents ought to do what is in their own self-interest
- Utilitarianism: Operating in the public interest rather than for personal benefit; maximises benefits over costs for all involved, everyone counting equal
- Altruism: In benefit for others, even at a cost to yourself.

2.3 Further Normative Principles

- Principle of Autonomy, According to Immanuel Kant's moral philosophy, for an individual to be truly human, that person must be free to decide what is in his or her best interest.
- Principle of Informed Consent: The Kantian approach affirms that someone has given agreement freely to something (Kant 1785). For such an assent to have significance, it should be informed, that is, based on accurate information and an understanding of the issues at hand. If this information is deliberately withheld or is incomplete because of carelessness, then the consent is given under false pretences and is invalid.
- Golden Rule, "What you do not want others to do to you, do not do to them."
- The US Content Subcommittee of the ImpactCS Steering Committee (Huff 1995): Quality of life; Use of power; Risks and reliability; Property rights; Privacy; and Equity and access.

The appropriate and respective normative principles presented above will be applied to the moral dilemmas that are invoked by systems development and deployment by business process engineers, software engineering teams, process improvement managers, etc.

3 Health and Safety Considerations at Work

The principal UK legislation governing health and safety in the workplace, including the use of computers is the Management of Health and Safety at Work Regulations 1999. The Regulations were introduced to reinforce the Health and Safety at Work Act 1974. The MHSWR places duties on employers and employees including those who are clients, designers, principal contractors or other contractors (Gov.UK 2018a). Care must be taken that employees are not exposed to radiation from monitors. Provide adequate and appropriately designed equipment and furniture to minimise injury risk. Guidelines for creating and maintaining adequate working environments, including lighting and ventilation in offices, and the conditions under which computers are used, including the appropriate frequency and length of breaks for those working at computer terminals for long periods. To battle the problem of occupational injuries and diseases ISO developed the ISO 45001standard: Occupational Health and Safety (ISO 2018). It stipulates requirements, which will help organisations reduce this burden by providing a framework to improve employee safety, reduce workplace risks and create better, safer working conditions, including the software/systems engineering industries.

Under the Equality Act 2010 (Gov.UK 2018b) disability is defined concisely and succinctly as "a physical or mental impairment that has a 'substantial' and 'long-term' negative effect on your ability to do normal daily activities". The term 'substantial' is more than minor or trivial, for example it takes much longer than it usually would to complete a daily task like getting dressed; and 'long-term' means twelve months or more, for example, a breathing condition that develops as a result of a lung infection. There are a range of disabilities, including visual, auditory, physical, speech, cognitive, language, learning, and neurological disabilities.

3.1 Computers and the Workplace

Sauter and Murphy (1995) investigated the changing structure of work in our society and presents empirical research studies, which pointed to computerized information systems have brought with them new health and safety hazards. The authors argued that the computerisation of office work has resulted in increased levels of stress for workers. It was concluded that stress in the modern office, in particular where computerised monitoring and surveillance systems were implemented and utilised, could lead to, amongst other things: loss of job satisfaction; low morale; and absenteeism and poor employee-management relations.

Duquenoy et al. (2008) postulate that increased interaction with computers, instead of people, has led to a: reduced sense of personal responsibility in the modern office; resulting sense of anonymity and depersonalisation can cause a lack of respect for an organisation and its resources; and diminished sense of ethics and values on the part of its employees.

Suparna and Bellis (2001) argue that prolonged use of video display units (VDUs) can have a detrimental impact on users' health. Sustained use of computer monitors can result in a number of conditions, including eyestrain; double vision and headaches; and neck and shoulder problems. Bowey (2006) concludes, on the basis of the findings of a multitude of research studies that excessive use of a computer keyboard, and other input devices, such as a mouse, can also lead to injuries to the arms, hands and fingers. This type of physical stress is commonly known as repetitive strain injury (RSI).

3.2 Discrimination at Work

Providing equal access to information systems for disabled groups is an important element of the implementation and management of IT systems in the workplace. These rights are enshrined in the law, primarily via the Human Rights Act, 1998 and Equality Act, 2010. The former states that individuals should not be discriminated against on "any ground such as sex, race, colour, language, religion, political or other opinion, national or social origin, association with a national minority, property, birth or other status" (Gov.UK 2018c). The Equality Act places, upon an employer, the duty to make reasonable changes for disabled employees. These are known as 'reasonable adjustments'. Adjustments should be made to avoid an individual being put at a disadvantage compared to non-disabled people. The Equality Act 2010 also provides legal rights for disabled people regarding access to goods, services and facilities.

Cultural and language barriers may result in unconscious bias, misunderstandings, conflicts and project failures. Treating people unfairly at work because of their cultural, racial and sexual orientation difference may even be unlawful under equal opportunity laws. In todays' globalisation, organisations may span a variety of countries with different working cultures and different discrimination laws. Thus they must comply with national, European and international labour standards laid down by bodies such as the International Labour Organisation (ILO) (Rice-Birchall 2015).

Similarly gender discrimination continues to be an issue that is encountered by women in the workplace, such as sexual harassment and gender evaluation (the use of gender as a criterion for job-related decisions), which inevitable has negative impact on job-related outcomes (Shaffera et al. 2000). Some of the forms of discrimination discussed previously could be the result of Unconscious Bias. The BCS, The Chartered Institute for IT, has introduced an Unconscious Bias Training course, for all employees and Volunteer committee members. This includes a series of case studies to generate self-awareness (BCS UcB 2015). Case studies research carried out by Georgiadou et al. (2009) revealed that women are either not participating in It professions or when they participate they have minimal opportunities for career advancement. Such injustices are highly likely to result in process and systems failures which are detrimental to the individuals, the project, the organisation and society at large.

4 Heuristics

A number of heuristics are suggested below, which if followed may lead to ethical systems development and deployment guidance in the context of health and safety. Each rule of thumb is substantiated by citing one or a number of the ethical normative principles, listed in Sect. 2 above. Often there is a lack of relevant knowledge or inexperience of clients regarding health and safety and computers in the workplace. It is the computer professional's duty to instruct in such circumstances.

Incorporate in the Design the Utilisation of Assistive Technologies: as part of the system engineer's brief is to oversee the development and installation of new hardware and software. This must be completed within the framework of public interest. The British Computer Society Code of Conduct (BCS CoC 2018) demands that computer professionals "have due regard for public health, privacy, security and wellbeing of others and the environment"; "have due regard for the legitimate rights of Third Parties" (includes any person or organisation that might be affected by your activities in your professional capacity, irrespective of whether they are directly aware or involved in those activities); and "promote equal access to the benefits of IT and seek to promote the inclusion of all sectors in society wherever opportunities arise". This can be achieved through the incorporation of assistive technologies, for example, screen readers, refreshable braille display, eye gaze and head mouse systems, etc. In addition, the development of any web content application must be compliant with Web Content Accessibility Guidelines (WCAG) 2.1 (WC3 2017) which defines how to make Web content more accessible to people with disabilities.

- Deontology (Pluralism): Justice
- Deontology (Pluralism): Beneficence
- Deontology (Pluralism): Non-injury
- Deontology (Contractarianism): The right not to be discriminated against
- Deontology (Contractarianism): The right to fair access to, and development of, communication resources
- Teleology: Utilitarianism
- Teleology: Altruism
- The US Content Subcommittee of the ImpactCS Steering Committee: Quality of life
- The US Content Subcommittee of the ImpactCS Steering Committee: Equity and access.

Ergonomic Design: The development and installation of new systems must adhere to ergonomic design that looks to reduce strain, fatigue, and injuries by improving product design and workspace arrangement. The Health and Safety Executive (HSE 2013) advocated measures that an employer must take, in order to protect their employees from any risks associated with Display Screen Equipment (DSE). These recommendations ensured compliance with the Health and Safety (Display Screen Equipment) Regulations 1992. Guidance ranges from how to effectively arrange a workstation, through to users modifying their body mechanics and employees adjusting their work patterns. There is a moral duty on systems developers to have due regard for public health, and wellbeing of others and the environment in which their developed solutions are installed. Thus there exists an imperative on computer professionals to install solutions that comply with health and safety guidelines and instruct where there is a lack of relevant knowledge or inexperience of ergonomics (product design and workspace arrangement) in others, for example clients, for whom systems are being delivered.

- Deontology (Pluralism): Beneficence
- Deontology (Pluralism): Non-injury
- Teleology: Utilitarianism
- The US Content Subcommittee of the ImpactCS Steering Committee: Quality of life
- The US Content Subcommittee of the ImpactCS Steering Committee: Risks and Reliability

Conduct an Operational Feasibility Study: An operational feasibility study is the process of determining how a system will be accepted by people (assessing employee resistance to change, gaining managerial support for the system, providing sufficient motivation and training, and rationalising any conflicts with organisational norms and policies) and how well it will meet various system performance expectations (for example, response time for frequent online transactions, number of concurrent users it must support, reliability, and ease of use) (Stair and Reynolds 2017). There is an ethical duty for health and safety to be assessed, as an integral part of an operational feasibility study. In the first instance the study should determine how the system will be accepted by people with specific disabilities. This may imply dialogue between developers and trade union, health and safety, and disability representatives. These representatives have rights under the management regulations to be consulted by their employers and developers about anything affecting members' health and safety, including the introduction and adoption of new technology. This may result in the negotiation of a policy for working with computers, akin to HSE guides. Secondly, there is a need interweave health and safety as part of the system performance expectations. For example, for every system a non-functional requirement that should be explicitly stated, thus contractual binding, should be the compliance with the Health and Safety (Display Screen Equipment) Regulations 1992.

- Deontology (Pluralism): Beneficence
- Deontology (Pluralism): Non-injury
- Deontology (Contractarianism): The right to fair access to, and development of, communication resources
- Teleology: Utilitarianism
- The US Content Subcommittee of the ImpactCS Steering Committee: Quality of life
- The US Content Subcommittee of the ImpactCS Steering Committee: Equity and access

Formulation of a Computer-Use Policy: Organisations are continually being confronted with escalating liability with regards to employee use of electronic resources. In order to mitigate this risk of liability, companies need to develop and implement a computer-use policy, which explicitly outlines proper use of the organisations electronic resources (Cox et al. 2005). Employers that use monitoring technology face the possibility of creating an atmosphere of distrust in the workplace. An employee who feels no sense of trust from the employer lacks the incentive to be efficient and could be less productive. A balance needs to be struck between privacy needs with unrestricted control of computer usage, in other words, a point on the spectrum between the two extreme options of: do nothing or monitor everything. A computer-use policy must be formulated that explicitly states what the agreed behavior is regarding computer usage. The formulation process must commence with a consultation with their legal counsel and other relevant parties (for example, human resources, employees, and, if applicable, union representatives) to determine what type and scope of policy would be best suited for the organisation. The system engineers overseeing the installation of new hardware and software (computer resources) have an ethical duty to participate and contribute to this formulation process of a computer usage policy. Their technical expertise, understanding of the current functionality of the delivered system, will give invaluable insight into systems capabilities, thus enabling far more effective, and better, policy to be drafted for enforcement.

- Deontology (Pluralism): Beneficence
- Deontology (Pluralism): Non-injury
- Deontology (Contractarianism): The right to Privacy
- Deontology (Contractarianism): The right to Property
- Principle of Informed Consent
- The US Content Subcommittee of the ImpactCS Steering Committee: Quality of life
- The US Content Subcommittee of the ImpactCS Steering Committee: Risks and Reliability

Conduct Risk Management: In order that risks are managed effectively and efficiently, the hazards and effects associated with the implementation of computer systems have to be properly managed. At its very core risk management can be viewed as four stages: (1) Identify - Are people, environment or assets exposed to potential harm? (2) Assess - What are the causes and resulting concerns? What is the probability in the loss of control? What is the risk? (3) Control - Can the cause be eliminated? What controls are needed and how effective are they? (4) Recover - Can the potential consequences or effects be mitigated? What recovery measures are needed? Are recovery capabilities suitable and sufficient? In other words the hazards and effects should be identified; fully assessed, necessary controls provided and recover preparation measures put in place to control any hazard release (PMI 2013). Thus, a risk management plan needs to be prepared, typically as a joint effort between project manager and system engineers, in order to document foreseen risks, estimate impacts, and define responses to issues. In order that lessons are learned and Process Improvement is achieved a systematic recording and analysis of issues, errors, and failures must be carried out. In this all important process and document should be the health and safety concerns that have been identified above.

- Deontology (Pluralism): Beneficence
- Deontology (Pluralism): Non-injury
- Teleology: Utilitarianism

- The US Content Subcommittee of the ImpactCS Steering Committee: Quality of life
- The US Content Subcommittee of the ImpactCS Steering Committee: Risks and Reliability

5 Conclusions

The rationale of applying the ethical framework presented in this paper was to identify and defend ethical stances that can be taken in the concerns over health and safety regarding newly deployed and existing systems. In doing so, the authors conclude that the importance of ethical considerations in the developing and delivering health and safety compliant systems can be bought to the attention of the systems development and software engineering community: providers, project managers, developers, engineers and clients, thus help raise the visibility of ethical use.

The paper contributes to the current ethical and philosophical discourse relating to the health and safety and wellbeing in the use of computers in organisations. In particular, a set of heuristics for the ethical health and safety guidance has been proposed which will raise awareness of the moral issues and help guide developers and users of computer systems. The development of a set of heuristics presented this paper is an important one. For majority of these suggested rules UK law clearly applies and leads directly to the appropriate ethical conclusion. But to rely solely on law as a moral guideline is clearly dangerous. There are instances where the relationship between law and ethics breaks down, and the law fails to provide moral guidance. Thus to solely rely on the law for guidance, to exclusively fulfil legal duties, may lead to occasions where an individual fails to accomplish their ethical responsibility.

Additional research could include interweaving the issues of health and safety into the systems development life cycle (SDLC). Thus at each stage of the process for planning, creating, testing, and deploying an information system, systems developers will be conscious of the duty they have to incorporate health and safety into the system's specification and design. Further research in this field is needed relating to SME and micro companies where there are few if any computer professionals being employed, despite IT being a key component to the survival of the business.

The notions of health and safety, wellbeing and ethical duty need to be explicitly addressed in the SPI Manifesto. Although these are implicitly implied in the manifesto's three values and ten respective principles, there needs to be a much more unequivocal statement with regards to how these notions must govern personal behaviour in relation to Software Process Improvement work. Thus an eleventh principle could be appended to the SPI Manifesto: To Fulfil Ethical Duties

The focus of this paper has been in the delivery of new systems that must be health and safety compliant for the recipient, the client. However, it should also be noted that system developers, in turn, are, themselves, employees. Thus in their everyday working lives, they should also be entitled to work in environments that are conducive to good health and wellbeing.

References

BCS CoC: BCS Code of Conduct (2018). http://www.bcs.org/category/6030. Accessed 3 Apr 2018

BCS UcB: BCS and Unconscious Bias Training (2015). http://www.bcs.org/content/conWebDoc/55370. Accessed 3 Apr 2018

Bowey, T.C.: RSI - How to Avoid It and What to Do If You've Got It. Adlibbed Ltd (2006)

CMMI: CMMI for Development, Version 1.3, Technical report, Software Engineering Institute, Carnegie Mellon University, Pittsburgh (2010). http://resources.sei.cmu.edu/library/asset-view.cfm?assetID=9661. Accessed 10 Mar 2018

Cox, S., Goette, T., Young, D.: Workplace surveillance and employee privacy: implementing an effective computer use policy. Commun. IIMA **5**(2), Article 6 (2005). http://scholarworks.lib.csusb.edu/cgi/viewcontent.cgi?article=1263&context=ciima. Accessed 2 Apr 2018

Duquenoy, P., Jones, S., Blundell, B.G.: Ethical, Legal and Professional Issues in Computing. Cengage Learning EMEA, Boston (2008)

EuroSPI.net: SPI Manifesto (2010). http://2018.eurospi.net/images/eurospi/spi_manifesto.pdf. Accessed 10 May 2018

Georgiadou, E., Abu-Hassan, N., Siakas, K., Wang, X., Ross, M., Anand Anandan, P.: Women's ICT career choices: four cross-cultural case studies. Multicult. Educ. Technol. J. **3**(4), 279–289 (2009)

Gov.UK: The Management of Health and Safety at Work Regulations, 1999 (2018a). http://www.legislation.gov.uk/uksi/1999/3242/contents/made. Accessed 31 Mar 2018

Gov.UK: The Equality Act, 2010 (2018b). http://www.legislation.gov.uk/ukpga/2010/15/section/6. Accessed 31 Mar 2018

Gov.UK: The Human Rights Act, 1998 (2018c). https://www.legislation.gov.uk/ukpga/1998/42/contents. Accessed 31 Mar 2018

Hamelink, C.J.: The Ethics of Cyberspace. Sage Publications Limited, Thousand Oaks (2000)

HSE: Working with display screen equipment (DSE): A brief guide, Leaflet INDG36 (rev4) (2013). http://www.hse.gov.uk/pubns/indg36.pdf. Accessed 1 Apr 2018

Huff, C., Anderson, R.E., Little, J.C., et al.: Integrating the ethical and social context of computing into the CS curriculum. An interim report from the content subcommittee of the impact CS steering committee. In: Proceedings of ETHICOMP 95: An International Conference on the Ethical Issues of Using Information Technology, Leicester, 28–30 March 1995, pp. 1–19 (1995)

IEEE: 730-2014 - IEEE Standard for Software Quality Assurance Processes, IEEE (2014). http://ieeexplore.ieee.org/document/6835311/. Accessed 11 Mar 2018

ISO: ISO/IEC 15504-5:2012, International Organization for Standardization (2012). https://www.iso.org/standard/60555.html. Accessed 10 Mar 2018

ISO: Selection and use of the ISO 9000 Family of Standards. International Organization for Standardization, Geneva (2016). ISBN 978-92-67-10656-4

ISO: ISO 45001 - Occupational health and safety (2018). https://www.iso.org/iso-45001-occupational-health-and-safety.html. Accessed 10 May 2018

ISO/IEC: ISO/IEC 25010:2011: Systems and software engineering – Systems and software Quality Requirements and Evaluation (SQuaRE) - System and software quality models (2011). https://www.iso.org/standard/35733.html. Accessed 10 May 2018

Johnson, D.: Computers, Ethics and Social Values. Prentice-Hall Inc., New Jersey (1995)

Kallman, E.A., Grillo, J.P.: Ethical Decision Making and Information Technology: An Introduction with Cases. McGraw-Hill Inc., New York (1996)

Kant, I.: Grounding for the Metaphysics of Morals, 3rd edn. Hackett (1785). Translated by J.W. Ellington (1993)

PMI: A Guide to the Project Management Body of Knowledge (PMBOK Guide), 5th edn. Project Management Institute, Newtown Square (2013)

Pyzdek, T.: The Six Sigma Handbook: A Complete Guide for Green Belts, Black Belts, and Managers at All Levels. McGraw-Hill, New York (2003)

Rice-Birchall, S., Giesecke, S., Choudry, N., Vandale, J.: Dealing with diversity global workplace discrimination law and practice. Eversheds International (2015). http://www.eversheds-sutherland.com/documents/services/employment/global-discrimination-guide.pdf. Accessed 4 Apr 2018

Ross, W.D.: The Right and the Good. Clarendon Press, Oxford (1930)

Sauter, S.L., Murphy, L.R. (eds.): Organizational Risk Factors for Job Stress. American Psychological Association, Washington, D.C. (1995)

Shaffera, M.A., Joplinb, J.R.B., Bellc, M.P., Laud, T., Oguz, C.: Gender Discrimination and Job-Related Outcomes: A Cross-Cultural Comparison of Working Women in the United States and China. J. Vocat. Behav. **57**(3), 395–427 (2000)

Spinello, R.A.: Ethical Aspects of Information Technology Englewood Cliffs. Prentice-Hall Inc., New Jersey (1995)

Stair, R., Reynolds, G.: Fundamentals of Information Systems, 9th edn. Cengage Learning, Boston (2017)

Suparna, D., Bellis, J.: It's Not Carpal Tunnel Syndrome!: RSI Theory and Therapy for Computer Professionals. Simax, Philadelphia (2001)

WC3: Web Content Accessibility Guidelines (WCAG) 2.1 (2017). https://www.w3.org/TR/WCAG21/. Accessed 30 Mar 2018

Building High Effectives Teams Using a Virtual Environment

Mirna Muñoz[1(✉)], Adriana Peña[2], Jezreel Mejia[1], Nora Rangel[3], Carlos Torres[3], and Luis Hernández[1]

[1] Unidad Zacatecas, Centro de Investigación en Matemáticas, Parque Quantum, Ciudad del Conocimiento. Av. Lassec, andador Galileo Galilei, Manzana 3, Lote 7, 98160 Zacatecas, México
{mirna.munoz, jmejia, luis.hernandez}@cimat.mx

[2] CUCEI, Universidad de Guadalajara, Blvd. Marcelino García Barragán 1421, 44430 Guadalajara, Jalisco, México
adriana.pena@cucei.udg.mx

[3] Centro de Estudios e Investigaciones en Comportamiento de la Universidad de Guadalajara, Calle Francisco de Quevedo # 180, Col. Arcos Vallarta, 44130 Guadalajara, Jalisco, México
norarangel@cucba.udg.mx, jtorres@cencar.mx

Abstract. The increasing need of effective teams is a reality. And software development organizations are not the exception, because nowadays, most software is developed by teams. An important factor of a team is to achieve an adequate integration of its members, strongly linked to the team cohesion and performance. It is essential to integrate reinforced teams according to its members' abilities, knowledge and interactive styles. This paper provides a proposal for identifying team roles using a virtual environment and the idea of the Rube Goldberg machine. A first step implemented from this proposal provided goods results in the selection of adequate roles for integrating a more effective team.

Keywords: Software engineering teams · Teamwork · Collaborative work Virtual environment

1 Introduction

According to Humprey [1] a team is more that just a group of people working together, so that it takes practice and involves special skills. In this context, the activities to integrate a team are very important; they should reinforce both the personal and professional relationship among the team members. Nowadays, there is a great amount of activities focused on team's integration, aimed to improve communication, coordination and the teamwork, and supporting the improvement of the team performance, regardless the area in which the team accomplishes its activities.

However, to achieve an optimal team compliance can take a long time, that should be better invested to achieve the project goals. In this context, characteristics such as personality, knowledge and abilities of the team members are an important factor to get

X. Larrucea et al. (Eds.): EuroSPI 2018, CCIS 896, pp. 554–564, 2018.
https://doi.org/10.1007/978-3-319-97925-0_47

an adequate integration that will impact the team performance [2]. The human factor is one of the main reasons for a team to fail, mostly at the beginning of their development activities. According to the Standish Group International, within the critical factors for a project failure or success is the cohesiveness of the team members [3].

This highlights the increasing need of giving a solution to the human factor problem. Software development is not an exception; where a lot of team performance problems are other than technical ones, related to human factors [4].

So far, to assign roles in a software development team, surveys or experience are the common used paths. However, roles are not always properly assigned. Besides, there is a lack of tools to integrate software development teams, especially to help in the team training in order to gradually become a highly effective team. Considering this situation, this paper aims to present a proposal to create virtual environments (VE) using the Rube Goldberg machine idea, with the aim of providing an attractive way to guide teams' members to an adequate roles assignment.

The rest of the paper is organized as follows: Sect. 2 provides key concepts in which this research is based; Sect. 3 describes the related work; Sect. 4 describes the set of a VE; Sect. 5 shows the first results; and Sect. 6 presents discussion, conclusions and future work.

2 Background

2.1 TSPi

The Team Software Process^{SM} (TSP^{SM}) developed by Watts Humphrey, is a methodology that provides a disciplined context for software development. TSP aims to provide an operational process for guiding engineering teams that develop software, assisting them to improve quality and productivity [1].

TSP then, establishes the conditions to characterize effective teams through nine team-building principles, next briefly described [5]:

1. Establishing common goals and defined roles.
2. Developing agreed-upon strategy.
3. Defining a common process to perform their work.
4. Producing the plan with the participation of all team members knowing his/her personal role in that plan.
5. Negotiating the plan with the management.
6. Doing the job in a way they planned.
7. Communicating freely and often.
8. Forming a cohesive group.
9. The engineers know the status, they get back on their work and they have leadership for sustaining their motivation.

TSPi is and academic version of TSP for university team courses. It is composed of eight phases: (1) launch (team launch), (2) strategy (development strategy), (3) plan (development plan), (4) requirements (requirement specification), (5) design (high level design), (6) implementation (product implementation), (7) testing (integration and system testing), and (8) postmortem (analyze the process performance) [5].

It is composed by six roles: (1) team leader (he/she is the project manager in charge of building, maintaining and motivate effective teams), (2) quality/process manager (he/she ensures that the TSPi process is followed, as well as verifying the quality of teams' products), (3) planning manager (he/she produces a complete plan for the team and manages it), (4) development manager (he/she is in charge of creating the product itself based on the software architecture), (5) support manager (he/she configurates management and risk management, so that he/she is in charge that the team gets the tools and methods needed) and (6) engineer (all members participate in the development of the software product) [5].

2.2 Rube Goldberg Machine

The Rube Goldberg machine is a concept that consists on starting with a person launching a simple action and carries out a set of chain reactions until the objective or challenge is achieved. Some examples of challenges are to cook a hamburger, turn-on or turn-off an alarm, toast a slice of bread, open an umbrella, or water a plant [6].

The Rube Goldberg machine presents the next specific features [6]:

- It has to be a large structure.
- It is complicated to create it.
- It includes a set of a number of chain reactions that are usually very easy tasks.
- It encourages teamwork.
- It encourages the solution of problems.

The Rub Goldberg machine covers a set of phases such as planning, designing, development (implementation) and testing [6].

3 Related Work

Presented in Table 1, this section shows a comparison among three papers that present proposals regarding activities for team building.

Table 1. Comparative among studies focused on "team building activities"

Study	Proposal	Context	Goal	Results
[7]	Virtual environment designed to improve soft skills	Academy, security topics to assess teamwork	Explore the use of serious games to support activities such as: communication, effective cooperation, decision-making, interpretation and processing of information	Virtual environment improves teamwork abilities, especially communication skills

(continued)

Table 1. (*continued*)

Study	Proposal	Context	Goal	Results
[8]	Serious game for building distributed virtual teams	Virtual teams	Improve the communication among team members to achieve an effective communication	Roles assignation impacts in the team coordination and performance
[9]	eSpace game to solve puzzles	Teams in enterprises	Gradually integrating the team improving its communication skills	The game can be useful to built teams and evaluate leadership in enterprises

4 Virtual Environment

The proposed VE in this paper takes the Rub Goldberg machine idea with the aim to motivate teamwork and to increase problem solving in students [6]. TSPi methodology [10] was used as reference regarding a set of software development roles, as well as a set of activities to be performed along the software development cycle. The development of the environment consisted on eight steps next listed:

(1) *Identifying the activities that a software development team performs*

The TSPi methodology was selected as model to identify the activities performed by role in software development. TSPi provides a complete set of roles and the activities they perform while developing quality software. To identify the activities performed by each role, the information in the role scripts provided by the TSPi methodology was analyzed. As result were identified a total of 164 activities, which numbers are showed by role in Fig. 1.

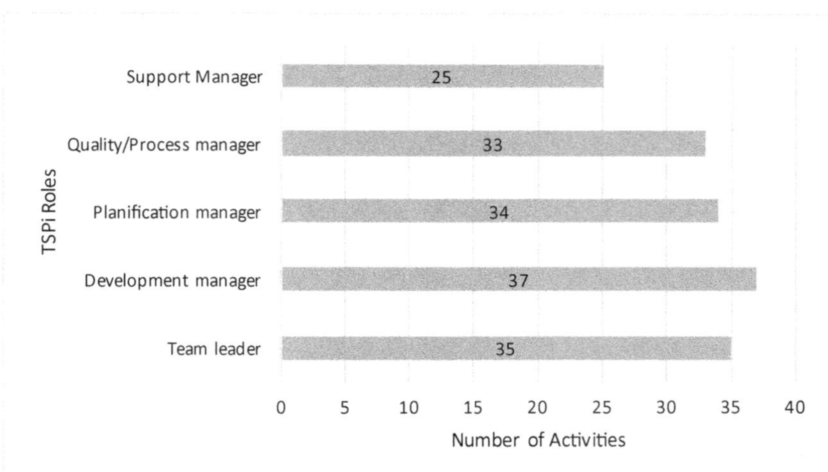

Fig. 1. Number of activities by roles according to TSPi

(2) *Selecting a set of key activities performed by a software development team*

The TSPi methodology, as mentioned, was also used to identify the activities performed through the software development cycle. TSPi provides eight phases for software development. The phase scripts provided by the TSPi methodology were analyzed to identify the activities performed in each phase information. 121 activities were identified, these numbers are by phase are shown in Fig. 2. After analyzing the activities by roles and phases, the next findings were detected:

- The role with the highest number of activities to perform is the development manager. Its main activities are those performed in the requirement, design and implementation phases.
- In second place is the team leader that performs its main activities in launch and postmortem phases.
- In third place, the quality/process manager performs its main number of activities in the implementation, strategy, planning and requirement phases.
- In fourth place, the planning manager performs its main number of activities in the planning phase.
- Finally, the support manager participates along all phases.

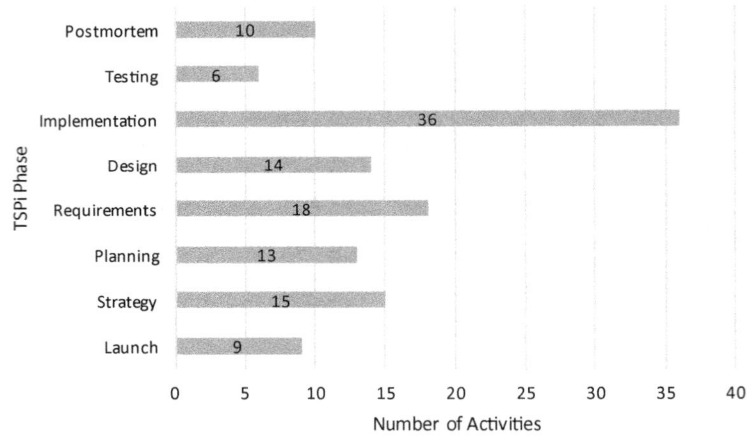

Fig. 2. Number of activities by phase according to TSPi

(3) *Analyzing, classifying and selecting the activities performed to build teams*

In this step were identified activities to build teams, to achieve it there were analyzed a set of activities proposed in [5]; first the activities focused on the identification of roles. After that, were selected those activities considered the best to build a team. The analysis performed to the activities is shown in Table 2.

It is important to highlight that most of the activities focused on building teams only specified a set of steps to achieve the integration of a team. As Table 2 shows, the analysis was performed based on: goal, time to perform the game and name of participants. The criteria to select the activity were: (1) The activity should have a goal easy to understand; (2) The activity should require no more than 12 participants; (3) The activity should be performed in a time that do not exceed the 60 min.

Table 2. Analysis of activities to build a team

Activity	Goal	Number of participants	Time to perform the game
Alignment by influence	Identify an impartial team leader	12 participants	60 min
Teamwork	Show the efficiency of working in teams	From 5 to 7 participants	30 min
Pulse	Incorporate a new member in a team	N/A	N/A
Situational space	Create relationships among members of a team	N/A	15 min
Rube Goldberg machine	Reinforce the work in teams	At least 3 participants	N/A
Cars race	Show the efficiency of working in teams	From 5 to 7 paticipants	20 min
Team building	Increment the cohesion and the identity of working in teams	8 participants	30 min

After performing the analysis, the selected activity was the Rube Goldberg machine because it is focused on reinforce the work-team, it has a requirement of at least three people, so that it could allow us to create teams for VSE and SMEs, even teams in large organizations. Finally, depending on the amount of chain reactions we can adjust the time to perform it.

(4) *Developing the virtual environment*

The Rub Goldberg machine activity was selected because it reinforces teamwork. It requires at least three participants to be performed and it does not have a specific time to be performed.

The Rub Goldberg machine also covers a set of phases such as planning, designing, development (implementation) and testing, phases that can be matched to the performed activities by a software development team [6]. Therefore, the use of the concept of building a Rube Goldberg machine is the general part of the proposal presented in this paper, which main goal is building a set of reactions in chain to achieve a goal.

Based on the above mentioned, this proposal involves three components: (1) the identification of team activities; (2) the study of iterative styles and; (3) applying gamification elements (dynamics, mechanisms and components), together the three components aim to identify the team roles in order to integrate a software development teams supported with activities performed in a play.

The development of the proposal was divided in two steps. The first step was focused on establishing the type and number of evaluation to analyze the team's members, and the second step was focused on implementing them in a VE.

For the first step, three evaluation phases were developed to be included in the VE as next described:

- First evaluation consists on establishing the team members' degree of concordance with their interactive styles in order to get their role profile.
- Second evaluation verifies if during the interaction among the participants, they keep their interactive styles while performing a role. As result of this evaluation it will be confirmed the role assignment in a teamwork situation.
- Third evaluation that is performed in case of identifying inconsistencies in the second evaluation. It consists on evaluating the new role assigned to confirm it. As result of this evaluation the role adjustments are confirmed.

Figure 3 presents a summary of the virtual environment proposal.

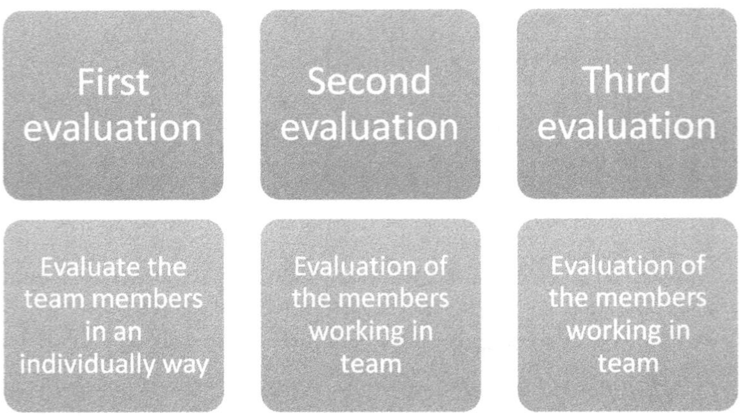

Fig. 3. Summary of the evaluations proposal

Regarding the second step, it consists on implementing the three evaluations in a VE. One of the three evaluations was actually implemented, However, we did the analysis to implement the activities that enable the three evaluations. The analysis consisted on establishing traceability among software development activities and the activities expected to be developed by a team member in the VE, and the element that will enable to evaluate the him/her. This analysis was made to each role. However, Table 3 shows an example of this traceability for the Requirement phase including one activity per role.

The resulted VE consists on four scenarios: (1) start of the application; (2) game scene; (3) objects displacement; and (4) proof of performed construction.

Table 3. Traceability of activities for evaluating each role in activities related to requirement phase

Role	Summary of TSPi activity	Activity expected by the team member	Support element for the evaluation
Team leader	Assign task among team members and get their commitment to develop the tasks	Control the activities to move the objects in the essenary	Use of the chat to give instructions
Development manager	Address the team using the SRS	Control the team in the building of the Rube Goldberg machine	Use the chat to identify the objects that will be used in building the Rube Goldberg machine
Planning manager	Produce the assigned parts of the SRS	Control the creation of the Rube Goldberg machine achieving the acceptation criteria (rules or conditions)	Movements of objects (number of objects that a team member performs for bot correct movements and without value)
Quality/process manager	Address the inspection of the SRS and the system test plan	Control the achievement of the acceptation criteria Verify that the object are located in its place and right position to achieve the goal	Checklist for evaluating the achievement of acceptation criteria Movements to the goals (number of moved objects, after evaluating the right construction of the machine)
Support manager	-	-	-

This paper focused on the game scene that is the main scenario of the VE. The elements included in this scenario are: a chair, a volleyball ball, an inclined wooden board, a set of fifteen dominoes and a bell, all these elements have physical properties of size and weigh, as in the real world. On the other hand, there are two elements, a football and a domino with an incorrect weight compared to real life.

The use of incorrect physical properties aims to encourage team members to carry out activities of planning, design and test in the game. In this way, the game activities reflect activities of software development and in consequence each member left their comfort zone, this allowed the analysis to identify the appropriate roles for each person. Figure 4 shows the virtual environment obtained. It is important to mention that this VE covers only the first evaluation.

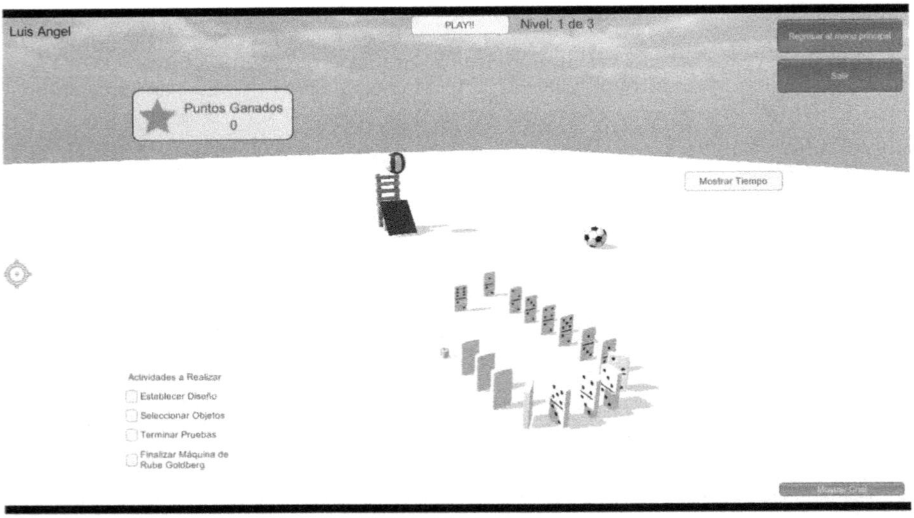

Fig. 4. Virtual environment obtained for the first evaluation

5 First Results

In order to validate a first VE in a real situation, it was performed a case. The case of study was performed accordingly to the steps recommended by Yin [11] and Runenson and Höst [12]. The objective of the case of study is to evaluate the VE viability for the identification of roles for development software teams. The participants in this case study were eight students that formed two teams of four members. The eight participants are graduate students of the Software Engineering Master with experience on working within teams. There were established four research questions:

- Q1. Is this method to assign roles in a team appropriate?;
- Q2. Does this tool facilitate the role identification of the members of a development team?;
- Q3. Does the assignation of roles method using the designed tool is adequate?; and
- Q4. Is the usability level of the tool acceptable for the user?

The data was collected through a Google form questionnaire in three stages: (1) in an initial common activity performed by teams in which the team members assigned the roles by themselves; (2) during their interaction with the VE; and (3) in a second common activity performed by teams in which team roles were assigned according to the results of the roles analysis during the stage 2.

The main results obtained from the case study are:

(a) Team performance:

  - In both teams a change in their roles was required. In team 01 four changes were made: (1) the role development manager performed by member 'C' was changed because during the interaction of the team in the VE, he showed a degree of concordance with the interactive styles and abilities related to the team leader role. (2) The leader team role performed by member 'A' changed to the development manager role. (3) The test manager role of member 'B' changed to the implementation manager role. And (4) the role implementation manager of member 'D' changed to the test manager role, he showed a degree of concordance with the interactive styles and abilities related to that role.

In team 02 three changes were made: (1) the test manager role performed by member 'B' changed to the team leader role. (2) The team leader role performed by member 'A' changed to the implementation manager role. And (3) the implementation manger role of member 'D' changed to the test manager role.

- Both teams improved their performance after the roles reassignment made accordingly to the observations done during their interaction within the VE. The team 01 decreased from 83 errors in Activity 1 to 23 errors in Activity 2. And the team 02 decreased from 72 errors in Activity 1 to 33 errors in Activity 2.

(b) Team member's perception, once the roles was assigned according to the VE:

- Six participants totally agreed that the activity achieved the goal.
- Seven participants totally agreed that their roles were adequate.
- Six participants totally agreed that the role performed by the other team members were adequate.

(c) Virtual environment:

- Six participants agreed that the VE was adequate for identifying roles for teamwork.
- Two participants totally agreed and three agreed that the roles suggested by the VE were adequate.
- Five participants totally agreed and two agreed that the role suggested by the other team members were adequate.

6 Discussion, Conclusions and Future Work

The assignation of work roles is a key activity for the success of a software development team. The proposal presented in this paper, which includes the identification of team activities, along with the study of iterative styles, and the application of gamification elements (dynamics, mechanisms and components), presents an attractive way for identifying the roles in a team using a virtual environment.

This virtual environment implemented the first evaluation of our proposal, to achieve the identification of software development roles using achievement and persistence interactive styles. Besides, the virtual environment was perceived as an attractive way for the team members.

As future work, we are implementing a second and a third evaluation in the virtual environments. Besides, due to the virtual environment needs an expert to analyze data of the team members manually, we are improving the virtual environment in order to perform the analysis in an automatic way.

References

1. Watts, H.: The team software process^{sm} (TSP^{SM}). Technical report, Carnegie Mellon, Software Engineering Institute CMU/SEI-2000-TR-023 ESC-TR-2000-023, pp. 1–51 (2000)
2. Dorling, A., McCaffery, F.: The gamification of SPICE. In: Mas, A., Mesquida, A., Rout, T., O'Connor, R.V., Dorling, A. (eds.) SPICE 2012. CCIS, vol. 290, pp. 295–301. Springer, Heidelberg (2012). https://doi.org/10.1007/978-3-642-30439-2_35
3. The Standish Group International: Chaos Report 2016, The Winning Hand (2016)
4. Muñoz, M., Mejia, J., Peña, A., Rangel, N.: Establishing effective software development teams: an exploratory model. In: Kreiner, C., O'Connor, R.V., Poth, A., Messnarz, R. (eds.) EuroSPI 2016. CCIS, vol. 633, pp. 70–80. Springer, Cham (2016). https://doi.org/10.1007/978-3-319-44817-6_6
5. Humphrey, W.S.: Introduction to the Team Software Process. Addison-Wesley, Reading (2006)
6. Rube Goldberg, I.: Rube Goldberg MACHINE CONTEST ® 2016 Official Rule Book, July 2015, pp. 1–19 (2016)
7. Lukosch, H., van Nuland, B., van Ruijven, T., van Veen, L., Verbraeck, A.: Building a virtual world for team work improvement. In: Meijer, S.A., Smeds, R. (eds.) ISAGA 2013. LNCS, vol. 8264, pp. 60–68. Springer, Cham (2014). https://doi.org/10.1007/978-3-319-04954-0_8
8. Ellis, J.B., Luther, K., Bessiere, K., Kellogg, W.A.: Games for virtual team building. In: Proceedings of the 7th ACM Conference on Designing Interactive Systems - DIS 2008, pp. 295–304 (2008). https://doi.org/10.1145/1394445.1394477
9. Häkkinen, P., Bluemink, J., Juntunen, M., Laakkonen, I.: Multiplayer 3D game in supporting team-building activities in a work organization. In: Proceedings of the 12th IEEE International Conference on Advanced Learning Technologies, ICALT 2012, pp. 430–432 (2012). https://doi.org/10.1109/ICALT.2012.242
10. Fritzen, S.J.: 70 Ejercicios prácticos de dinámicas de grupo. Sal TEARRE (eds.) (2011). ISBN 978-8429308044
11. Yin, R.K.: Case Study Research Design and Methods. SAGE Publications, Beverly Hills (2003). https://doi.org/10.1097/FCH.0b013e31822dda9e
12. Runeson, P., Höst, M.: Guidelines for conducting and reporting case study research in software engineering. Empir. Soft. Eng. **14**(2), 131–164 (2009). https://doi.org/10.1007/s10664-008-9102-8

Developing Effective Teams in Global Multidiscipline Engineering and Manufacturing Organizations

Kerstin Siakas[1(✉)], Elli Georgiadou[2,3], Dimitrios Siakas[4], and Harjinder Rahanu[2]

[1] Alexander Technological Educational Institute, Thessaloniki, Greece
siaka@it.teithe.gr
[2] Middlesex University, London, UK
[3] SEEQMA Ltd, Consultancy, London, UK
[4] Citec, Vaasa, Finland

Abstract. In today's competitive business environment most activities in global relationships (subsidiaries, outsourcing, joint ventures) are carried out by multi-cultural and multidisciplinary teams which may be collocated or distributed. The members of these teams comprise a variety of experts of diverse cultural, organizational, and professional backgrounds. Within the project lifetime they are connected together with time and money constraints for a specific period of time to accomplish certain distinct objectives. The aims of this paper are to report on findings from an extensive literature review regarding multicultural and multidiscipline team work and to provide a basis for discussion and analysis of challenges such teams experience. A case study is carried out in a global multidiscipline engineering organization to identify empirical evidence of potential challenges in projects carried out by multicultural and multidisciplinary collaborative teamwork.

Keywords: Multicultural teams · Multidiscipline teams · Process management TMP · CODE · eSCM

1 Introduction

Recent trends in the world economy, including a highly competitive and rapidly changing global environment, networking as business models and distance mode of working enabled by Information and Communication Technologies (ICTs), have increased the complexity and competition level of organizations [1]. There is a push for organizations to produce innovative products and services for survival, sustainability and growth. At the same time processes need to be innovative and to promote knowledge sharing in order to keep costs down and to improve productivity. In order to increase competitiveness in the global market place distributed teams, such as dispersed knowledge workers of multinational organizations, service providers and clients in outsourcing partnerships and partners of joint ventures need to improve their knowledge to gain competitive advantage.

X. Larrucea et al. (Eds.): EuroSPI 2018, CCIS 896, pp. 565–576, 2018.
https://doi.org/10.1007/978-3-319-97925-0_48

An increased number of organizations strive to form distributed teams in order to gain access to world class capabilities, to reduce costs and to integrate diverse perspectives [2]. Distributed teams, by their very nature, imply the presence of a group of geographically dispersed individuals often from different cultural, educational and professional backgrounds [3]. They consist of people who primarily interact electronically and collaborate from different locations using ICTs. The team members may meet face-to-face occasionally and in some projects not at all. In a distributed team the team members work interdependently across time and space and often across organizational boundaries towards a shared goal through webs of ICTs [4]. The team members solve problems and make decisions jointly; they are involved in a coordinated undertaking of interrelated activities and are mutually accountable for team results.

Teams are an important part of the functioning of an organization and most managers believe that teams are significant contributors to the effectiveness and success of organizations; they can also cause problems and restrict organizational success [5]. Due to the significance of teamwork in both business and educational environments, teamwork productivity and efficiency appraisal deal with ways to achieve effective collaboration in practice. Every team is different depending on the task the team is going to undertake, and on the social and cultural factors influencing how team members experience the team as a social unit. Team processes are generally concerned with motivation, cognition and socialisation [6].

2 Multi Cultural and Multi Discipline Teams

In the Knowledge Society skills-based work is carried out in low-cost countries, while creative, innovative, and knowledge intensive work remains in the leading organization (*Client* in outsourcing relationships and *Mother Company* in international organizations). However, high quality design requires profound experience and insight in the methodologies and tools used to implement and produce new products and services [2]. In addition, social and complementary skills are needed in today's distributed and networked engineering and production.

2.1 Compositions of Teams and Roles of Team Members

In all organizations there is a hierarchy of assigned positions, which in fact are vertical and horizontal differentiation of social systems [7]. The external and explicit part of the position is described through status symbols, such as company salary, car and office. The internal part, which is the behaviour of the position owner, is defined as the role, or role behaviour. Similarly, Hofstede [8] describes manifestations of cultures as an onion comprising practices, which are layers starting from the surface of the onion and moving inwards, including symbols (superficial and easy to copy), heroes (cultural models for behaviour) and rituals (collective activities carried out for their own sake; considered as socially essential). The core of the onion is the deepest level of values, which are qualities, principles or behaviours, considered morally or intrinsically valuable or desirable. According to Higgs et al. [7] the concept of roles includes behavioural expectations from the environment (management, colleagues etc.) as well as requirements of the team role, perceptions (dependant on the situational conditions) and attitudes of the position owner. These depend on the owner's personality and previous experiences, talents and education.

The variety in characteristics, skills and experiences of individuals within a team determine the nature and the composition of the team. The success of the individual in meeting a team role depends on how well his/her personal characteristics, skills and experience correlate with the requirements of the team role. Individual well-being in teams emerging from mutual trust and respect, a sense of appreciation and a feeling of belonging promotes an open team culture of honesty that enables team effectiveness, and provides maximum value outcome to its stakeholders (managers, customers etc.).

2.2 Culture

Hofstede's definition of culture is: 'Culture is the collective programming of the mind, which distinguishes the members of one human group from another' [8]. By this definition, Hofstede emphasises that culture is a collection of characteristics possessed by people who have been conditioned by similar socialisation practices, educational procedures and life experiences. Culture is a system of beliefs and values that shape how people think, act and behave. Hofstede calls this mental programming within people, corresponding to different levels of culture: at a national level according to one's country, at an organizational or corporate level, or at a professional level associated with a certain profession or managerial level [8]. Cultural diversity can be a competitive advantage for the company if dealt with in a proper manner. Cultural constraints determine which strategies are feasible and which are not.

2.3 National Culture

National culture is a major barrier to making global business effective [9]. Different nationalities have different expectations as to how employers and employees should act, as well as ways of expressing agreement and disagreement, different styles of management and participation in decision making, different attitudes toward hierarchy and different approaches to teamwork etc. Regarding software outsourcing there is growing awareness of cultural issues: Recognition of the fact that cross-cultural training is needed both in advance of a project and continuously [10]. Kahn et al. [17] investigated the barriers that have a negative impact on clients in their search and selection process of outsourcing providers and found 16 such factors grouped in three categories: Cultural insensitivity: Process Maturity and External factors.

2.4 Organizational Culture

Deal and Kennedy [11] propose that organizational culture plays an important role regarding the success and sustainability of an enterprise. Organizational culture involves several aspects including the structure of the organizational culture, the form, the type and the function of the organizational culture etc. [12]. In order to create effective teams there are two design factors that significantly influence the process of a project management structure, namely the level of specialisation (technical areas or development focus), and the need for coordination (required to bring unity to the various elements). Cheng and Kong [12] postulate that organizational culture has an impact on sharing of resources, which are considered to be an effective way to respond to constantly changing market conditions and to minimise market risks. With resource we can understand a source or a supply from which some kind of benefit is produced. Knowledge sharing is inevitably important for effective teamwork, and is influenced by differences in both organizational and national culture [13].

O'Neill et al. [14] propose that organizational culture and organizational structure direct the behaviour of employees. They define structure as centralisation of decision-making, formalisation of rules, authority, communication and compensation, standardisation of work processes and skills, and/or control of output by acceptance of only adequate outcomes. Research has showed that shared values guide the behaviour of the members of a cultural group, and influence the actions and judgments of the group [8]. When the values of individuals match the values of the group consensus and harmony is gained. Wellbeing of the individual participant is increased and the effectiveness of the group is improved.

2.5 Culture and Organization Leadership

Schein [15] asserts that 'cultures begin with leaders who impose their own values and assumptions on a group. If that group is successful and the assumptions come to be taken for granted, we then have a culture that will define for later generations of members what kinds of leadership are acceptable. The culture now defines leadership. But as the group runs into adaptive difficulties, as its environment changes to the point where some of its assumptions are no longer valid, leadership comes into play once more. Leadership is now the ability to step outside the culture that created the leader and to start evolutionary change processes that are more adaptive. This ability to perceive the limitations of one's own culture and to evolve the culture adaptively is the essence and ultimate challenge of leadership'.

When organizational culture is aligned to business strategy, the workforce will act and behave in ways that support the achievement of business goals. The leader will uphold the values and beliefs of the organizational culture through their actions and decisions. This, in turn, enables the implementation of the organization's strategy.

2.6 Communication and Terminology

Good communication is the most fundamental requirement for effective team work. "We are speaking the same language" is a phrase that means we understand each other well because of shared ideas and feelings. Miscommunication inexorably results in misunderstandings among team members which can lead to poor performance, hurt feelings, and lack of motivations concluded by [16] in a teaching case study. They demonstrated that due to miscommunication, different interpretations or misunderstandings, often result in productivity losses, as well as loss of trust.

In management, and in particular in team work, there are often misunderstandings because of ambiguity and subjective understanding, which cause confusion and miscommunication. Thus it is necessary to define and use terms consistently and in a standard method.

3 Acceptance of Process Improvement

3.1 Culture Change

Standard processes promise predictable outcomes. Total Quality Management (TQM) and ISO 9001 certifications rely on Process Improvement approaches, which continuously require improvements in the defined processes, hence changes in the current processes. Khan et al. [17] demonstrated a Software Process Improvement Implementation and Management Model (SPIIMM) that can assist global software organizations to successfully execute Software Process Improvement activities. Successful organizations create a strong organizational culture, but at the same time this can be a barrier to change. People tend to resist change. In global teams there may be many different cultures involved, such as different national, organizational and professional cultures. The team members need to step outside these cultures and for the duration of the project commit to a common team culture.

3.2 Process Maturity

The Software Process Improvement (SPI) manifesto [18] helps organizations to improve their process maturity. In global team work different organizations with different national and organizational cultures need to work together to maintain the basic values of people, business and change.

Cultural awareness and appreciation of a common process improvement initiative is imperative for success of global projects. Emphasis on the processes and their improvement will frame and support the common team culture. The project leader needs, through agreed upon and defined processes, to encourage vigilance and timely reports of delays, ignorance, potential misinterpretations and discrepancies in viewpoints regarding the tasks of different team members.

3.3 Knowledge Sharing

Team work within an organizational culture of knowledge sharing is likely to succeed. In a global context communication and knowledge sharing is considerably much more difficult due to language, terminology, culture, time issues and distance. Teams lacking communication and knowledge sharing will turn into detached groups of uninvolved strangers out of leadership and cooperation [13]. Georgiadou et al. [19] developed the I5P visualisation framework relates the capability maturity levels and knowledge sharing levels. The figure shows that the higher the maturity the better the knowledge sharing. This framework provides the basis, in terms of preparedness and disposition towards knowledge sharing, for estimating and measuring organizational performance. Hence the performance increases dramatically the maturity grows.

3.4 Team Effectiveness

Many previous studies have been carried out regarding teams within organizations and factors that have impact on team performance, however, according to Cacioppe and

Stace [20] these studies are considered somewhat fragmented with respect to enhancing the team effectiveness.

Adams et al. [21] found seven constructs of effective teams, namely: common purpose, quantifiable clearly defined goals, role clarity, team climate, mature communication, productive conflict resolution and accountable interdependence. The main objective of a team is to have a common purpose, which all team members agree upon. There needs to be a clear relationship between the main organizational objective and the team's objectives. In order to maintain the focus on the team's objective, clear and commonly agreed goal statements defining the tasks to be accomplished by the team, need to be described. Clearly defined and quantifiable goals help the team to manage the scope of the tasks, and thus increase the probability of team success. It is also significant that there is a common understanding of each individual's expected role in the team. Each team member's understanding of his/her own role and the roles of the other team members minimizes misunderstandings, role ambiguity and task assignment duplications. Regarding the team climate (team spirit), the team members will be comfortable being themselves in a team where there is interpersonal trust and mutual respect. In a psychologically safe context, team members are likely to affirm each other for specific contributions, thereby encouraging each other to perform effectively, creatively and innovatively. Mature communication indicates that team members are able to articulate ideas concisely and clearly as well as to express compelling reasons for their ideas. Productive conflict resolution involves procedures and actions to be taken by team members when a conflict arises. Examples of conflict resolution are exploration of alternative positions/solutions, involvement of everyone affected by the conflict, increase of cohesion among team members, enhancement of the decision-making process, as well as facilitation of the problem solution. Accountable interdependence regarding the output of the team is the responsibility of each team member. This means that each team member needs to understand the mutual dependence of all team members' responsibility for the quality and quantity of the team's work.

Yang and Choi [22] provided empirical evidence that information, autonomy, responsibility and creativity have positive and significant effects on team performance. [7] also demonstrated that there is a clear relationship between team composition (diversity), complexity of task and team performance. For complex tasks, diversity was found to be positively related to performance while for straightforward tasks negatively related. Team diversity was operationalised by using the Belbin Team Role model [23]).

4 A Case Study for Identifying Empirical Evidences of Challenges in Team Work

A case study, part of a Finnish research project [24] was designed to address different aspects of the research problem ('how' and 'why' to create effective teams in global multidiscipline engineering and manufacturing organizations), and to confirm and build on earlier findings and development of theoretical proposal from a similar study [13]. The focus of the case study was on contemporary phenomena within real life context and the aims were to explain the causal relationships between effective teams and successful outcomes. The case study reported in this paper was carried out by interviewing 10 team leaders at four different leading Finnish global multidiscipline engineering and manufacturing organizations to identify empirical evidences of potential challenges in global projects carried out by multicultural and multidisciplinary collaborative teamwork. The global companies, all four with more than 1000 experts globally, either in subsidiaries, joint ventures or outsourcing partners, provide multidiscipline products and services worldwide within the energy sector. They all work systematically with digitalisation and development by incorporating continuous learning into their daily routine. The main focus is on effective project execution in global projects and innovations. Nine of the interviews took place in 2010 and one took place in 2018 in order to validate previous findings and to verify the challenges identified.

The sub sections below are extracts from the face-to-face interviews with experts from 4 large (with over 1,000–150,000 employees), multidiscipline engineering and manufacturing Finnish firms. These extracts reveal the main issues and potential challenges in projects carried out by such teams. The most representative interview extracts are included in this paper.

4.1 Type of Project Collaboration

Currently, most Finnish companies, with a global presence, are primarily engaged in joint ventures. The reason for this is that they view joint ventures as 'an important form of collaboration for technology transfer to challenging countries. It enables the risks to be shared with a partner who already has customer and supplier network in place. Another important issue is the local knowledge and connections to authorities because in most cases all kinds of permissions are imperative for new start-ups. If we do not manage to sell in certain potential markets we may start to think about other solutions for penetrating the market. We may put up a joint venture that does a part of the production, not necessary the whole production. We prefer joint ventures over outsourcing because we want to retain, and thus have control, of certain key factors. The selection process for choosing partner companies for joint venture is a very challenging task. It depends on the level of know-how and technology they use; what kind of market we are interested in; and how willing the company is to join us. Typically a local person from the sales partner is used as surveillance in new joint ventures to minimise risk. A common quality management system is developed and frequently audited'.

4.2 Culture

'Our experience informs us that the country culture is stronger than organizational culture. If my company goes to China for example we have to adapt to the Chinese culture, we cannot expect the Chinese to adapt to the culture of our company. I see this very clearly! Particularly in China they have very strong established networks between themselves. When you arrive as a leader you cannot come with your preconceived ideas about how things have to be done. It depends of course on how strong their personalities are. At first glance it may seem that they do as you want but they do it to please you and as soon as you have left they do as they want.

If we have team members from other countries we try to invite them in the beginning to get to know each other. It takes quite a long time to understand how things work in a new culture and to get to know the people you are going to collaborate with cross-cultural training is provided to some degree, but relatively little, you primarily learn by experience. We use bridging staff (people rooted in our country and in the other country), but mostly we use local people with connections, who know English'.

4.3 Communication and Terminology

'More often than not you do not have the ability to choose the people in your team. If you are going to assemble a new team you need to specify the type of skills you need. Once you establish the team you often find that there are some technical and cultural skill gaps. You have to attempt to fill the gaps. Depending on the gap you can involve some technical experts or shadowing and support staff or send the team members to a course or ask them to read some text on e.g. cultural issues.

It does not matter if the team members are from different nationalities; what does count is the distance. In the beginning we have kick-off meetings where we discuss the objectives, team roles, obligations, milestones etc. These are usually explicitly stated by the team leader. There is not much commitment or input from the other team members. They may air their opinions, but they characteristically do not take part in decision-making. Exception occurs in circumstances where there are some specialised tasks that require addressing. It is here that the specialist will state how things should be done. In such moments a lot of belief is entrusted in the specialist. Experience reveals that distributed (virtual) teams with on-line meetings are ineffective and do not work at all. There may be teleconferencing and discussions, but everybody seems to expect somebody else does the work. Live visits are far more effective and productive, and usually work better. However, the cost involved in international teams meeting face-to-face is prohibitive.

We try to meet at least once per week, all together, in person at the commencement of a project. We have internal and interdisciplinary meetings on different hierarchical levels. The customer often participates in these meetings. The responsibility is shared in a hierarchical manner to safeguard the quality and timeliness of the project. When a new project is created with new team members, the leader is important. The team leader distributes the roles to the team members, keeps the team together and is responsible for making it going. It is quite hierarchical. People instantaneously understand and appreciate if the project leader is interested in their daily small problems and disputes. Development discussions are utilised but the problems are not usually on that level. Communication is very much dependent on the manager and the recognition that everybody is so different. Common terminology is slowly developed according to prevailing partners and customers'.

4.4 Acceptance of Process Improvement

'Process changes are very difficult to implement when the existing ones are accepted and deep rooted in the culture of the organization. The change usually is initiated by higher hierarchical levels, all the affected parties' involvement and acceptance is crucial for a successful implementation. The driver of the change needs to be fully engaged to explain, convince and motivate the affected people to recognise and adopt the change'.

4.5 Team Effectiveness

'More often than not problems exist within the teams. The Finnish idiom 'we push with a rope' concisely and neatly expresses the reality that nothing really happens. The tendency is not to really reflect much but to simply go on with daily duties and do what we have to do. Team cohesion is very difficult but good cohesion is recognised as being important. Using a sports team, as a metaphor, allows us to fully appreciate team effectiveness where everybody needs to understand their parts and know when to pass the ball to the other person. A good team leader is crucial to identify potential gaps in team effectiveness and to support team spirit. Ultimately you have to be very patient!'

5 Proposed Instruments/Tools for Developing Effective Teams

[25] created the Team Process Management (TPM) model, a management process for creating effective and successful teams. The model consists of four steps: (i) Team formation, (ii) Team building activities, (iii) Removal of obstacles and creation harmony and balance, and (iv) Creation of shared values and expectations. Such teams recognise shared ownership among the team members and work effectively towards goals in a selected timeframe. The TPM model was created for use by teams in multicultural and multidisciplinary environments. The model is likely to be particularly useful for improving impact team performance in multicultural and multidisciplinary distributed collaborative teamwork.

The effective management of cultural diversity in a global context is a challenge and a competitive advantage. Managers who are involved in cross-cultural communications and negotiations need to develop characteristics such as cultural sensitivity, flexibility and adaptability and seem to be worried about their own capabilities to be successful in an increasingly complex global context. In order to help service purchasers to search, select and collaborate with service providers we propose the use of the eSCM-SP/eSCM-CL (a capability maturity assessment model).

6 Discussion and Conclusions

Team processes are concerned with motivation, cognition and socialisation. Before articulating the role of leadership in fostering team effectiveness, it is important to understand the nature of team functioning. Teams have to reflect on their performance and adapt to the changing environment. Methods that support team members to understand their strengths and weaknesses can help in improving the performance of the team and in preventing difficulties in the functioning of the team. Motivating all people involved to work together effectively and efficiently is embodied in Principle 2 of the SPI Manifesto: Motivate all people involved.

The conceptual contemporary Team Process Management (TPM) model that aims to enhance multicultural and multidisciplinary global team performance and effectiveness was developed to support teams and increase performance in order to overcome apparent complexities and contradictions. TPM provides a structure that teams can follow to increase shared ownership and common understanding of objectives, targets, roles and responsibilities.

Limitations of the study concern the leadership style. The model was tested only within an environment of a collaborative leadership style. With other forms of leadership the outcomes may not be similar, particularly in autocratic leadership styles, where not much space is left to initiatives coming from the team members. Lessons learnt from case studies proved that in multicultural and multidisciplinary virtual collaborative teamwork, such as in projects sponsored by the EU, a certain structure is desired by the team members in order to utilise resources in an effective way and to create a team culture of trust, inspiration and high team spirit.

This paper described challenges in assembling and running multi-cultural and multidiscipline teams. A case study was carried out in four Finnish global organizations in order to identify empirical evidence of potential challenges in projects carried out by such teamwork. We proposed the integration of the Team Process Management (TPM) the eSCM-SP/CL, and the CODE assessment model as instruments and tools which can bring added value outcomes for global multidiscipline engineering and manufacturing organizations in their attempts to meet challenges influencing team effectiveness, such as maturity, technology, culture, communication, knowledge sharing and acceptance of process improvement.

Future work will concentrate on field studies for collecting more in depth evidence on effective global teams. Following that we aim to augment the SPI Manifesto with a new principle "Develop awareness of risks arising from conflicts of a multidisciplinary and multicultural nature". Once recognised risks can be mitigated through the development of customisable process models for the various types and sizes of multidiscipline, multicultural company collaborations such as mergers, acquisitions, franchises.

Acknowledgements. Many thanks are ought to the survey respondents, the anonymous reviewers for their helpful suggestions, and to Professor Rory O'Connor for his constructive editorial support.

References

1. Siakas, K., Messnarz, R., Georgiadou, E., Naaranoja, M.: Launching innovation in the market requires competences in dissemination and exploitation. In: Winkler, D., O'Connor, Rory V., Messnarz, R. (eds.) EuroSPI 2012. CCIS, vol. 301, pp. 241–252. Springer, Heidelberg (2012). https://doi.org/10.1007/978-3-642-31199-4_21

2. Siakas, K.V., Balstrup, B.: Software outsourcing quality achieved by global distributed collaboration. Softw. Process Improv. Pract. (SPIP) J. **11**(3), 319–328 (2006)
3. Järvenpää, S.L., Leidner, D.E.: Communication and trust in global distributed teams. Organ. Sci. **10**, 791–815 (1999)
4. Handy, C.: Trust and the Distributed Organization (HBR OnPoint Enhanced Edition). HBR On Point, June 2000 (2000)
5. Ross, M., Jones, E.C., Adams, S.G.: Can team effectiveness be predicted? Team Perform. Manag. **14**(5/6), 248–268 (2008)
6. Bhat, A.B., Verma, N., Rangnekar, S., Barua, M.K.: Leadership style and team processes as predictors of organizational learning. Team Perform. Manag. Int. J. **18**(7/8), 347–369 (2012)
7. Higgs, M., Plewnia, U., Ploch, G.: Influence of team composition and task complexity on team performance. Team Perform. Manag. **11**(7/8), 227–250 (2005)
8. Hofstede, G.: Culture's Consequences: Comparing Values, Behaviours, Institutions, and Organizations, 2nd edn. Sage Publications, Thousand Oaks (2001)
9. Segalla, M.: Overview: understanding values and expectations of foreign employees creates a better company. Eur. Manag. J. **19**(1), 27–31 (2001)
10. Foster, N.: Expatriates and the impact of cross-cultural training. Hum. Resour. Manag. J. **10** (3), 63–78 (2000)
11. Deal, T.E., Kennedy, A.A.: Corporate Cultures: The Rites and Rituals of Corporate Life. Perseus Books, New York City (2000)
12. Chen, X., Kong, F.: Impact of corporate culture on resources sharing between enterprises. Int. J. Netw. Virtual Organ. **12**(1), 4–13 (2013)
13. Siakas, K., Georgiadou, E.: Knowledge sharing in virtual and networked organizations in different organizational and national cultures. In: Bolisani, E. (ed.) Building the Knowledge Society on the Internet, Part 1, chap. 3, pp. 45–64. Idea Publishing (2008). ISBN 978-1-59904-816-1
14. O'Neill, J.W., Beauvai, L.L., Scholl, R.W.: Structure and culture model of organizational behaviour variability reduction. In: Annual Meeting of the Academy of Management, August 1997
15. Shein, E.H.: Organizational Culture and Leadership, 3rd edn. Jossey-Bass, a Wiley Imprint, San Francisco (2004)
16. Brewer, E.C., Holmes, T.L.: Teaching case: better communication = better teams: a communication exercise to improve team performance. IEEE Trans. Prof. Commun. **59**(3), 288–298 (2016)
17. Khan, A.A., Keung, J.W., Fazal-e-Amin, M.: SPIIMM: toward a model for software process improvement implementation and management in global software development. In: Khan, A.A., Keung, J.W., Fazal-e-Amin (eds.) IEEE Access, vol. 5 (2017)
18. Pries-Heje, J., Johansen, J.: SPI manifesto (2010). http://www.iscn.com/Images/SPI_Manifesto_A.1.2.2010.pdf. Accessed 15 May 2018
19. Georgiadou, E., Siakas, K., Balstrup, B.: The I^5P visualisation framework for performance estimation through the alignment of process maturity and knowledge sharing. Int. J. Hum. Cap. Inf. Technol. Prof. **2**(2), 37–47 (2011). ISSN 1947-3478
20. Cacioppe, R., Stace, R.: Integral team effectiveness: validity analysis of a theory-based team measure. Team Perf. Manag. **15**(5/6), 220–234 (2009)
21. Adams, S.G., Simon, L., Ruiz, B.: A pilot study of the performance of student teams in engineering education, Session 1017. In: Proceedings of the American Society for Engineering Education Annual Conference, 16–19 June, Montreal (2002)
22. Yang, S.-B., Choi, S.O.: Employee empowerment and team performance: autonomy, responsibility, information, and creativity. Team Perf. Manag. **15**(5/6), 289–301 (2009)
23. Belbin, M.: Management Teams: Why They Succeed or Fail. Heinemann, London (1981)

24. Keskonen, S., Mäenpää, T., Nyrhilä, V., Helo, P., Siakas, K., Harri, C.: Towards successful production concepts in global environment. The Final Report of Production Anticipation in Multicultural Environments Research Project, Proceedings of the University of Vaasa, Finland, (2011). ISBN 978-952-476-375-2
25. Siakas, K., Siakas, E.: A contemporary team process management model to enhance multicultural and multidisciplinary virtual team performance. Int. J. Netw. Virtual Organ. (IJNVO) **15**, 65–79 (2015)

Reflections on the Need for Disambiguation of Terminology for Software Process Improvement

Elli Georgiadou(✉)

Middlesex University, London, UK
e.georgiadou@mdx.ac.uk

Abstract. Researchers often invent new terms or borrow terms from other domains which they modify or reinterpret by attaching novel meanings to suit the context of their investigation. In established disciplines, such as traditional engineering, physics, and mathematics, there is no ambiguity in the relevant terminology as terms as well as their relationships are expressed formally, mostly using mathematical equations. In Software Engineering the fact that there is a need for a glossary or lists of definitions at the end of every book and within nearly all research papers, is evidence that the discipline is not yet mature enough even after 50 years from the coining of the term Software Engineering. Refinements and re-interpretations of existing terms, combined with new terms introduced with every innovation, every new technology or tool, by both researchers and practitioners, result in ambiguities which need to be addressed. As change is inevitable there needs to be a mechanism through which ambiguities can be identified and addressed. This paper outlines major advances in Terminology Management for Software Process Improvement and reflects on the constant need for terminology disambiguation. It proposes a bottom-up pragmatic approach for using ontologies and for integrating research and practice. It also proposes a framework based on SPI Manifesto values and principles for the disambiguation of terms for continuous process improvement and, thus, for enhancing value and for catering for change which is inevitable.

Keywords: Software measurement · Disambiguation · Terminology Communication · SPI values & principles · Framework

1 Introduction

"Speaking the same language" is a common phrase which does not necessarily refer to a natural language like English, German, Chinese… but more significantly, it means common understanding and agreeing with each other. Lack of ambiguity is a fundamental requirement for common understanding and communication. Understanding one another takes place "because there exists a code, a sort of inner competence between you and me and there exist possible messages, performed as utterances and interpretable as a set of propositions" [1].

In natural languages we use words as synonyms and thus we use them interchangeably but mostly when we intent to place particular emphasis on what we are

X. Larrucea et al. (Eds.): EuroSPI 2018, CCIS 896, pp. 577–589, 2018.
https://doi.org/10.1007/978-3-319-97925-0_49

trying to communicate. For example an item can be referred to as an object, a thing, an artefact and so on.

In pedagogy for example, the recent explosion of technology based Distance Education (DE) has resulted in the creation of new terms which, however, are often used interchangeably as synonyms. Bozkurt et al. [2] in their examination of 633 scholarly articles (covering 5 years from 2009 to 2013) they reported that at least 12 terms are being used by scholars to describe DE.

An example of erroneous use of terms as synonyms from the Information Systems and Software Engineering domains is that of method and methodology. The use of these terms as synonyms has been perpetuated for over 40 years. Evidence of this issue can be found in many articles and acclaimed textbooks such as Avison and Fitzgerald [3] and Jayaratna [4].

Howell, in her book "Introduction to the Philosophy of Methodology" [5] clarifies that "a methodology is the rationale for the research approach, and the lens through which the analysis occurs. Said another way, a methodology describes the general research strategy that outlines the way in which research is to be undertaken…A method is simply a tool used to answer your research questions—how, in short, you will go about collecting your data. Examples of research methods include: Contextual inquiry, Interview, Survey etc. The methodology should impact which method(s) for a research endeavour are selected in order to generate the compelling data."

Another term with many and varied meanings, in everyday life but also in Software Engineering and Information Systems, is the term model which can be a representation, a pattern, a prototype, a template, a blueprint, an exemplar, a framework, a paradigm and so on. Each model represents an item or a process from a specific perspective. In Software Engineering the term model could denote many different things including lifecycle development model, a process model, a reference model, a quality model, a framework, a meta-framework and so on.

According to Barn [6] "conceptual modelling provides a mechanism by which a shared understanding between business domain specialists and IT specialists positively enhances the alignment of business and IT goals leading to improved quality of IT Solutions". Thomas [7] cited in [6] argued that "no uniform grasp of the term reference model exists". This confusion partially arises out of the tendency to declare Application information models and/or enterprise Information models as "reference models". Barn et al. [8] following a review of existing reference models synthesised a definition: "A reference model is based on a small number of unifying concepts and is an abstraction of the key concepts, their relationships, and their interfaces both to each other and to the external environment. A reference model may be used as a basis for education and for explaining standards and methods to a non- specialist and can be viewed as a framework for comparing architectures and operations of existing and future systems."

In the disciplines of Software Engineering and Information Systems often many different terms are used to define the same concept. Conversely, the same term may be used to define several concepts. For example, numerous definitions of Software Quality have been proposed. Kitchenham and Pfleeger [9] identified five different perspectives of quality as follows:

- The transcendental perspective deals with the metaphysical aspect of quality;
- The user perspective is concerned with the appropriateness of the product for a given context of use;
- The manufacturing perspective represents quality as conformance to requirements;
- The product perspective implies that quality can be evaluated by measuring the inherent characteristics of the product;
- The value-based perspective of quality recognises that the different perspectives of quality may have a different importance, or value, to various stakeholders.

In Siakas et al. [10] we produced an alphabet of software quality in order to emphasise the fact that numerous terms are used by the community to describe characteristics and sub-characteristics of quality which were (and still are) being used by the community. In this paper we did not attempt to show interrelationships of the terms but produced a high level taxonomy of three classes of attributes namely those of primary interest to developers, sponsors, or users. In all 24 terms were found in the literature on the main software quality models (at the time) i.e. McCall, Boehm, Dromey, SADT, and ISO 9126 (Y proved impossible to include) and Zoticality ζ (Z was coined). In the process it was established that although there was considerable overlap between the models, many terms were used to describe the same concept and there were differences in terminology between models.

Georgiadou [11] in "Navigating the Labyrinth of Software 'Re' Words" provided definitions largely based on IEEE and differentiated between reuse, restructuring, re-engineering, retro-engineering, reverse engineering and refactoring. By identifying how these terms relate to each other, and specified what quality improvements can be gained through practicing each of these processes. In addition the benefits of the proposed disambiguation of these terms and potential problems were specified.

Kitchenham [12] encapsulated many of the issues relating to the understanding, definition, and measurement of Software Quality. She argued that "Quality is a complex concept that means different things to different individuals. It can be highly context dependent. This means that there can never be any simple measure of quality that will be accepted by everyone. If you are interested in assessing or improving quality in your organisation, you must ensure that you define what aspect of quality you are interested in and how you are going to measure it. In fact, if you define quality in a measurable way, it is usually easier for other people to understand your viewpoint".

Abran et al. [13] noted that "from the metrology perspective suggests that the field of software measurement has not yet been fully addressed by current research, and that much work remains to be done to support Software Engineering as an engineering discipline based on quantitative data and adequate measurement methods meeting the classic set of criteria for measuring instruments as described by the metrology body of knowledge in large use in the engineering disciplines".

Despite the many advances achieved by the Software Engineering community, it continues to be reported by both researchers and practitioners such as Rout [14]; Gilb [15]; Garcia et al. [16]; Navigli [17]; Prokofyev et al. [18], Clarke et al. [19]; Jacobson et al. [20]; Kirsch and Sauberer [22] Sauberer et al. [22], Clarke et al. [37] that there is a need to standardise terminology in order to facilitate communication, understanding, and team work, and thus achieve improvements in process and project management.

2 Terminology Management: Vocabularies, Taxonomies, and Ontologies

The significance of terminology management becomes evident when we look at the concerns of and debates within the Software Engineering Community (practitioners and academics) expressed in the literature. Garcia-Penalvo et al. [16] state that "Terminology is vital to the functioning of all sciences, it is concerned with designations in all other subject fields, and it is closely related to a number of specific disciplines, as already pointed out by its most distinguished modern protagonist, Eugen Wuster who called it an interdisciplinary field of study, relating linguistic, logic, ontology and information science with the various subject fields."

Taking an example from the field of Medicine, Hu et al. [24]) argue that "generalists typically attach philosophical sophistication to their approach, in supposed contrast to the narrow remit chosen by the application-bound knowledge engineers, we would like to indicate that the latter practice can often reflect a multi-faceted rationale, nuanced by the requirements of the domain." One can imagine how significant it is for doctors to speak the same language with other.

Rout [14] argues that semantic technologies are based on ontologies…Ontology formalizes knowledge meaning and facilitates the search for contents and information…The main objective of ontologies is to establish ontological agreements, which serve as the basis for communication between either human or software agents, hence, reducing language ambiguity and knowledge differences between agents, which may lead to errors, misunderstandings and inefficiencies.

Navigli [17] in a comprehensive survey concluded: "Although some contrasting works have been published on the topic, (of Word Sense Disambiguation) no conclusive result has been reported in favour or against the use of sense inventories and their granularity in applications. Unsupervised approaches might prove successful, showing that we do not need to rely on predefined lists of senses. However, it might be as well that the use of sense inventories with a certain granularity (not too fine-grained nor trivially coarse) allow knowledge-rich and supervised methods to provide a decisive contribution".

Sauberer et al. [22] in their seminal work "proposed an extension of terminology change management procedure and the development of an e-learning course which offers a user-friendly and sound introduction to basic principles and methods of terminology management."

Jacobson et al. [20, 25] believe that Software Engineering is gravely hampered today by immature practices. Specific problems include: the prevalence of fads more typical of fashion industry than of an engineering discipline, the lack of a sound, widely accepted theoretical basis, the huge number of methods and method variants, with differences little understood and artificially magnified, the lack of credible experimental evaluation and validation, the split between industry practice and academic research. The signatories and founders of SEMAT support a process to re-found software engineering based on a solid theory, proven principles and best practices that: includes a kernel of widely-agreed elements, is extensible for specific uses, address both technology and people issues which are supported by industry, academia, researchers and users, and also support extension in the face of changing requirements and technology. Table 1 presents a chronology of seminal contributions to the terminology debate, management and practice.

Table 1. The chronology of seminal contributions in the terminology debate, management and practice

Ref	Researcher (s)	Focus	Major contribution
[14]	Rout (1999)	Established that there are duplications and discrepancies in definitions of terms in various standards	Preliminary evaluation of consistency and terminology in the group of software engineering standards developed by ISO/IEC JTC1/SC7
[16]	Garcia et al. (2006)	Vocabulary conflicts and inconsistencies Between various standards	Basic software measurement ontology aligned with metrology
[15]	Gilb (2006)	Planguage	Definition of concepts – not terms
[26]	Gómez-Pérez et al. (2006)	Ontologies	Ontologies include a vocabulary of terms, and some specification of their meaning
[17]	Navigli (2007)	Word sense disambiguation	Automatic identification of correct sense for scientific literature, Formal taxonomies
[21]	Karsch and Sauberer (2011)	Terminological precision	Key Factor in Product Usability and Safety, in Design, User Experience and Usability, Theory, Methods, Tools and Practice architecture for
[27]	Henderson-Sellers (2011)	Metamodels and ontologies	Application of ISO/IEC architecture for ontology life-cycle management
[16]	Garcia-Penalvo et al. (2012)	Ontology modelling tool	Semantic technologies are based on ontologies Ontology formalizes knowledge meaning and facilitates the search for contents and information
[25]	Jacobson et al. (2013)	A thinking framework	SEMAT Kernel Software Engineering Method and Theory
[26]	Jacobson et al. (2013)	SEMAT Kernel	Practice-independent foundation for the definition of software methods, the kernel also has the power to completely transform the ways that methods are defined and practices are shared

(*continued*)

Table 1. (*continued*)

Ref	Researcher (s)	Focus	Major contribution
			SEMAT is Actionable, Extensible, Practical
[18]	Prokofyev et al. (2013)	Word sense disambiguation (WSD: the ability to identify the meaning of words in context in a computational Manner	Ontology based disambiguation
[19]	Clarke et al. (2016)	Problems with terminology diversity	Sustained effort by multiple disciplines, including terminology expertise, software development specialist, knowledge management know-how and computational linguistics Towards a canonical software development process and roles ontology
[22]	Sauberer et al. (2017)	Content development of terminology management	Extension of terminology change management procedure The development of an e-learning course which offers a user-friendly and sound introduction to basic principles and methods of terminology management

3 Communication Through Consistent Terminology and Ontologies

Misuse and polymorphism of terms hinders effective communication, resulting in miscommunication and even conflict and failure. The CHAOS Reports identify miscommunication between business and IT personnel as one of the main reasons for systems failures is [28].

The use of a common terminology among all stakeholders enables effective knowledge sharing and lays the foundation for process improvement and success of projects. One of the Principles of the SPI Manifesto is to "Ensure all parties understand and agree on process" [http://2012.eurospi.net/index.php?option=com_content&view=article&id=32&Itemid=33].

Consistent terminology minimises miscommunication and develops common understanding. Terminology involves the terms themselves, their meanings, but also and the relationships between them. The adoption of consistent terminology helps avoid each researcher inventing a language of their own from scratch. Pfitzmann and Hansen [29] asserted: "Of course, each paper will need additional vocabulary, which might be added consistently to the terms defined here". Thus by showing relationships between terms a list or glossary of terms is converted to a consistent terminology.

Quality Models such as the McCall, Boehm, Dromey, ISO9126 etc. reviewed in Côté et al. [30] are expressed in textual form but also in high level diagrammatic representations with characteristics and sub-characteristics where the decomposition of each characteristic indicates the relationship 'belongs to'. Côté et al.'s review showed commonalities across these Quality Models but also some inconsistencies and ambiguities in the classification and meaning of several terms. For example Correctness is decomposed into Traceability, Completeness and Consistency whilst in McCall Correctness is analysed into Functionality and Reliability by Dromey.

Masolo and Borgo [31] emphasize that "we need to find a common ground, as different researchers often rely on definitions of quality referring to quite different things: adherence to requirements, fitness for a particular purpose, user satisfaction etc. We believe that it can be done based on the recent efforts of establishing the notion of software quality and its usage in terms of the formal ontology".

Calero et al. [32] in an extensive review of the literature concluded that ontologies in Software Engineering and Technology aim to share knowledge of the problem domain and use a common terminology among all interested parties (not only researchers), and to filter the knowledge when defining models and metamodels.

Gómez-Pérez et al. [26] argue that "ontologies aim to capture consensual knowledge in a generic way, and that they may be reused and shared across software applications and by groups of people. Ontologies include a vocabulary of terms, and some specification of their meaning. This includes definitions and an indication of how concepts are interrelated, which collectively impose a structure on the domain and constrain the possible interpretations of terms."

Jacobson et al. [25] explain that kernel allows you to add practices, such as user stories, use cases, component-based development, architecture, pair-programming, daily stand-up meetings, self-organizing teams, and so on to build the methods you need. Mahon [36] emphasises that practitioners can use the SEMAT Kernel and particularly the pre-prepared cards to guide practitioners so that they can carry out their processes efficiently and effectively.

4 The Role of Standards in Reducing of Ambiguity

A standard is defined by Gonzalez-Perez et al. [21] as a "document, established by consensus and approved by a recognized body, that provides, for common and repeated use, rules, guidelines or characteristics for activities or their results, aimed at the achievement of the optimum degree of order in a given context". Standards are needed in order to avoid idiosyncrasy, to ensure repeatability, to reach consensus, and reassure customers. Most products have safety standards but process standards are more rare, and are also much more difficult to enforce. Standardising a process can ensure that no steps are skipped. Also a standardized process which is understood and accepted/institutionalised can improve quality (productivity and reliability).

Gonzalez-Perez et al. [33] refer to the need for various ISO International Standards to be consistent with each other in terms of terminology, structure and semantics. They propose a potential harmonization across ISO software engineering standards (within Sub-Committee 7 (SC7) of ISO/IEC within Joint Technical Committee 1 (JTC1) by creating a core set of concepts and their relationships, effectively creating an abstract domain ontology for software engineering standards creation and utilization.

Rout [14] analysed a number of SC7 standards, documenting in which standards identified terms occurred together with their (disparate) definitions, only recently has harmonization become a crucial action point (rather than a vague concern) in SC7, especially under Special Working Group 5 (SWG5). Rout provided a table of Duplicated terms in SC7 Standards and related documents. He stated that his effort at the time was "...only to establish the necessity of resolving these differences for further improvement within the standards and processes in the software-engineering domain."

The INTERNATIONAL STANDARD ISO/IEC/IEEE 24765 First edition 2010-12-15 Systems and software engineering—Vocabulary was published by ISO JTC 1/SC 7, in 2010 [23]. This International Standard was prepared to collect and standardize terminology "The scope of each concept defined has been chosen to provide a definition that is suitable for general application. In those circumstances where a restricted application is concerned, a more specific definition might be needed. Terms have been excluded (a) if they were considered to be parochial to one group or organization; (b) if they were company proprietary or trademarked; (c) if they were multi-word terms whose meaning could be inferred from the definitions of the component words; and (d) if their meaning in the information technology (IT) field could be directly inferred from their common English meaning. Approximately two- thirds of the definitions in this International Standard are new since IEEE Std 610.12 was last updated in 1990, a reflection of the continued evolution in the field".

ISO/IEC TR 14143-3:2003, [34] Information Technology—Software measurement—Functional size measurement—Part 3: Verification of functional size measurement methods (term 3.8) defines the term repeatability (of results of measurements) i.e. closeness of the agreement between the results of successive measurements of the same measurand carried out under the same conditions of measurement. Repeatability may be expressed quantitatively in terms of the dispersion characteristics of the results. [International vocabulary of basic and general terms in metrology, 1993, definition 3.6].

5 Universal Concepts, Research Ambitions and Pragmatic Customisation

Researchers often start their investigations with a top-down, wide ranging ambition spanning a large knowledge area even involving universal concepts, ideas, themes, and principles that are found and can be proven within, between, and across various subject areas and disciplines. As the researchers gradually gain insights and understanding of the enormity and complexity of their originally ambitious scope and purpose, they narrow down their investigation focussing on more specific problems. For example Software Quality Models some of which were mentioned earlier in this paper aim to provide a universal framework for all types of software systems. However, it is only when they pragmatically consider the methods and techniques used for various categories, types and complexity of a more narrow selection of systems, they gain further insights and they produce bottom-up tangible solutions.

During their journey from the general to the specific and then to the general they often generate new knowledge expressed in novel interpretations of existing terms or they even generate new terms in order to exemplify their research contribution, the originality of their work. Continuous change and continuous improvements, innovations and changes in technologies bring their own new terms (which may be synonyms to existing terms) to add to the already highly populated vocabulary of Software Engineering. This in turn generates ambiguity.

Practitioners are normally focussed on in-house projects and challenges. Their own experiential knowledge is often very useful for the theoreticians especially when they form part of the same team integrating theory and practice.

For continuous terminology improvement and process improvement too, we need to always revisit our initial research question to ensure validation and verification of our findings. As T.S. Eliot said "We shall not cease from exploration. And the end of all our exploring will be to arrive where we started and know the place for the first time". T.S. Eliot, Little Gidding (1888–1965).

Šmite et al. [35] observed that "there is no unified empirically based glossary or reference model established in the field, which contains a clear description of the various terms that are used to describe sourcing strategies, or a taxonomy that would explicitly define the relationships between the different terms. They proposed a taxonomy for Global Software Engineering by categorizing the elected terms based on generalization-specialization relationships and illustrate how the taxonomy can be used to categorize and map existing knowledge. The contribution targets future researchers, who will publish or synthesize further empirical work and practitioners, who are interested in published empirical cases. Therefore this work is expected to make a contribution to the future development of research in the GSE field, and alleviate Understandability and transferability of existing and future knowledge into practice.

6 A Framework for Achieving Disambiguation of Terms

Following this investigation, we propose a framework (depicted in Fig. 1) for launching, carrying out and implementing the terminology disambiguation process. The central node (Number 7) forms the core of the framework. It is the on-going sub-process of reviewing all the works coming from all other stages and all committees, sub-committees, standards bodies and so on. This is a continuous and cyclic monitoring and co-ordinating sub-process. The bidirectional arrows emphasise the need of change of information, updating all stakeholders and responding to external changes.

Questions to be posed and answered at this stage include:

Which terms and combinations of terms are used to characterise different elements, factors, actors, actions?

- Which terms are erroneous and Why?
- Which terms are deficient?
- Which terms are new? Are they related to existing terms?
- What are the unambiguous, correct terms, their definitions and their relationship to other terms.

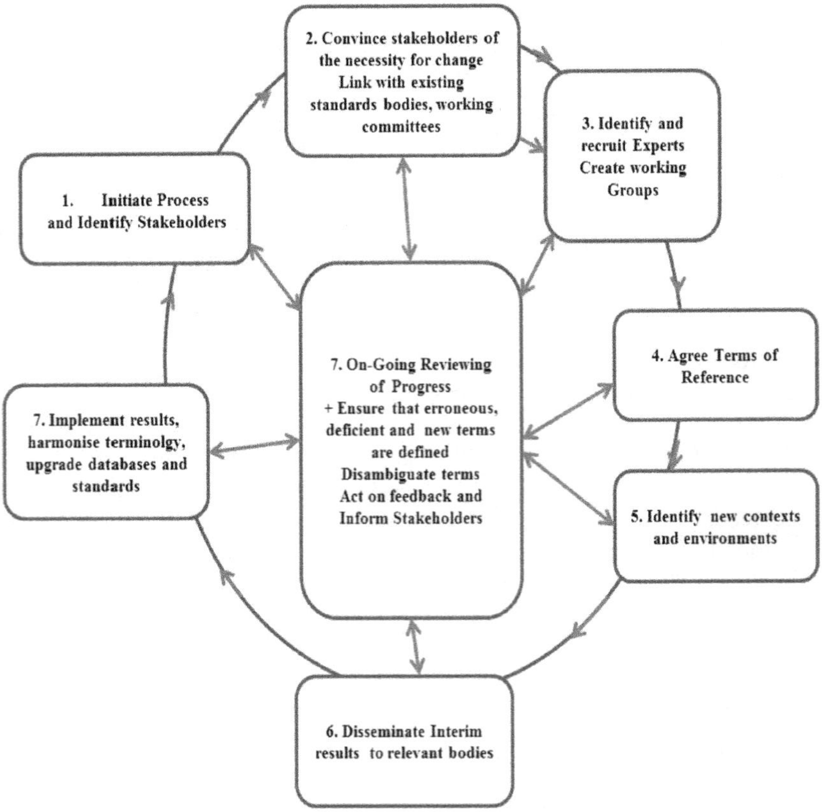

Fig. 1. A framework for the effective disambiguation of terms

Throughout the whole process pertinent questions need to be aked and answered. For example: "Who are the stakeholders? "Some of these stakeholders will be responsible for finanancing the intitiative, some will be carrying out the examination of existing terms, etc. hence at stage 2 we need to convince all stakeholders that change is necessary so the question "Why change "must be posed and answered. Terms of reference (stage 3) include questions like "What is the budget?", "What is the time-frame for the completion of the tasks", "What are the roles and responsibilities?", "Who are the people undertaking these roles".

There are distinct roles for carrying out administrative and management tasks. Domain experts are involved in the identification of inconsistencies, deficiencies, and errors in terms existing terms. Terms and their relationship to other terms may be accepted, rejected, modified, refined, and incoprorated in existing databases. If experts disagree and cannot reconcile their differences in opinion terms may be rejected or revisited for further elaboration.

7 Conclusion

7.1 Value Gains from the Elimination of Ambiguities in Terminology

Ambiguities in terminology can be addressed and minimised even eliminated through the use of ontologies which are context specific. This is the reason that there exist Ontologies for Requirements, for Risk Management, for Project Management etc. Ontologies reduce conceptual and terminological ambiguity, as they provide us with a framework for unification which in turn facilitates communication and knowledge sharing among diverse viewpoints, contexts, cultures etc.

The latest important contribution comes from Ralph [38] in his paper "Toward Methodological Guidelines for Process Theories and Taxonomies in Software Engineering". He provides an incisive analysis of the issues, "clarifies the nature and functions of process theories and taxonomies in software engineering research, and synthesizes methodological guidelines for their generation and evaluation". He is challenging us with areas of future research.

The systems and software engineering disciplines are continuing to mature while information technology advances. New technological innovations and methodological thinking reflect the rapid change. The multi-disciplinarity of Software and Systems Engineering brings immense complexity and challenges to academics and practitioners alike. New terms are being generated and new meanings are being adopted for existing terms (INTERNATIONAL STANDARD ISO/IEC/IEEE 24765).

Process improvement can be achieved and value gains can be achieved for the benefit of the organisation, the project, the individuals involved, and the whole Software Engineering community through avoiding miscommunication, confusion and even conflict. Only when agreed and accepted standards of incorporating all the revised, refined or totally new terms are systematically incorporated in a consistent and unambiguous terminology.

7.2 Future Work and Acknowledgements

Future work will involve the refinement and validation of the proposed framework, and development of technical infrastructure which will enable further automation of the process of term disambiguation.

Acknowledgements and thanks are due to the anonymous reviewers for their thorough reviews, critical comments, expert advice, and useful suggestions for improving the original submission.

References

1. Eco, U.: Social life as a sign system. In: Robey, D. (ed.), Structuralism: An Introduction, Clarendon, Oxford (1973)
2. Bozkurt, A., et al.: Trends in Distance Education Research: A Content Analysis of Journals 2009–2013 (2015)
3. Avison, D., Fitzgerald, G.: Information Systems Development: Methodologies, Techniques and Tools. Graw-Hill (2003)

4. Jayaratna, N.: Understanding and Evaluating Methodologies, NIMSAD: A Systemic Approach, McGraw-Hill (1996)
5. Howell, K.E.: An Introduction to the Philosophy of Methodology. Sage Publications, London (2013)
6. Barn, B.S.: On the evaluation of reference models for software engineering practice. In: Proceedings of the 2nd India Software Engineering Conference, ISEC 2009, pp. 111–116 (2009)
7. Thomas, O.: Understanding the term reference model in information systems research: history, literature analysis and explanation. In: Bussler, Christoph J., Haller, A. (eds.) BPM 2005. LNCS, vol. 3812, pp. 484–496. Springer, Heidelberg (2006). https://doi.org/10.1007/11678564_45
8. Barn, B.S., Dexter, H., Oussena, S., Petch, J.: An approach to creating reference models for SOA from multiple processes. In: IADIS Conference on Applied Computing, Spain (2006)
9. Kitchenham, B., Pfleeger, S.L.: Software quality: the elusive target. IEEE Softw. **13**, 12–21 (1996)
10. Siakas, K.V., Berki, E., Georgiadou, E., Sadler, C.: The complete alphabet of quality software systems: conflicts and compromises. In: 7th World Congress on Total Quality & Qualex 97, New Delhi, India, 17–19 February (1997)
11. Georgiadou, E.: Navigating the labyrinth of software 're' words. In: Dawson, R., Ross, M., Staple, G. (eds.) Proceedings of the 17th International Conference Software Quality Management (SQM), Software Quality in the 21st Century. BCS (2009)
12. Kitchenham, B.: Software Metrics, Measurement for Software Process Improvement. NCC/Blackwell, Oxford (1996)
13. Abran, A., Sellami, A., Suryn, W.: Metrology, measurement and metrics in software engineering. In: Proceedings of the 5th International Workshop on Enterprise Networking and Computing in Healthcare Industry (IEEE Cat. No. 03EX717) (2003)
14. Rout, T.P.: Consistency and conflict in terminology in software engineering standards. In: Proceeding of the Fourth IEEE International Symposium and Forum on Software Engineering Standards (ISESS 1999), pp. 67–74. IEEE Computer Society Press, Los Alamitos (1999)
15. Gilb, T.: Competitive Engineering: A Handbook For Systems Engineering, Requirements Engineering, and Software Engineering Using Planguage. Elsevier Butterworth-Heineman, Oxford (2005)
16. Garcia-Penalvo, F.J., Colomo-Palacios, R., Garcia, J.: Towards an ontology modelling tool. A validation in software engineering scenarios. Expert Syst. Appl. **39**(13), 11468–11478 (2012)
17. Navigli, R.: Word sense disambiguation: a survey. ACM Comput. Surv. **41**(2), 10:1–10:69 (2009)
18. Prokofyev, R., Demartini, G., Boyarsky, A., Ruchayskiy, O., Cudré-Mauroux, P.: Ontology-based word sense disambiguation for scientific literature. In: Serdyukov, P., et al. (eds.) ECIR 2013. LNCS, vol. 7814, pp. 594–605. Springer, Heidelberg (2013). https://doi.org/10.1007/978-3-642-36973-5_50
19. Clarke, P.M., et al.: Refactoring software development process terminology through the use of ontology. In: Kreiner, C., O'Connor, Rory V., Poth, A., Messnarz, R. (eds.) EuroSPI 2016. CCIS, vol. 633, pp. 47–57. Springer, Cham (2016). https://doi.org/10.1007/978-3-319-44817-6_4. ISBN 978-3-319-44817-6
20. Jacobson, I., Pan-Wei, N., McMahon, P., Spence, I., Lidman, S.: The Essence of Software Engineering—Applying the SEMAT Kernel. Addison-Wesley, Boston (2013). Forthcoming in January 2013 but available in a prepublication version on safaribooksonline.com

21. Karsch, B.I., Sauberer, G.: terminological precision - a key factor in product usability and safety. In: Marcus, A. (ed.) DUXU 2011. LNCS, vol. 6769, pp. 138–147. Springer, Heidelberg (2011). https://doi.org/10.1007/978-3-642-21675-6_16
22. Sauberer, G., Villar, B.N., Dreßler, J.R., Schmitz, K.-D., Clarke, P.M., O'Connor, R.V.: Do we speak the same language? Terminology strategies for (software) engineering environments based on the Elcat model - innovative terminology e-learning for the automotive industry. In: Stolfa, J., Stolfa, S., O'Connor, Rory V., Messnarz, R. (eds.) EuroSPI 2017. CCIS, vol. 748, pp. 653–666. Springer, Cham (2017). https://doi.org/10.1007/978-3-319-64218-5_54. ISBN 978-3-319-64218-5
23. ISO/IEC/ IEEE 24765, ISO International Standard ISO/IEC/ IEEE 24765 First edition 2010-12-15 Systems and software engineering—vocabulary was published by ISO JTC 1/SC 7
24. Hu, B., Dasmahapatra, S., Dupplaw, D., Lewis, P., Shadbolt, N.: Reflections on a medical ontology. Int. J. Hum.-Comput. Stud. **65**(7), 569–582 (2007)
25. Jacobson, I., Ng, P.-W., Spence, I.: Enough of process—let's do practices. J. Object Technol. **6**(6), 41–67 (2007)
26. Gómez-Pérez, A., Fernandez-Lopez, M., Corcho, O.: Ontological Engineering: With Examples from the Areas of Knowledge Management, e-Commerce and the Semantic Web. Springer, London (2006). https://doi.org/10.1007/b97353
27. Henderson-Sellers, B., Gonzalez-Perez, C., McBride, T., Low, G.: An ontology for ISO software engineering standards: 1) creating the infrastructure. Comput. Stand. Interfaces **36** (3), 563–576 (2014)
28. Standish Group: The CHAOS Report. The Standish Group International (1994). http://www.standishgroup.com/sample_research/chaos_1994_1.php
29. Pfitzmann, A., Hansen, M.: A terminology for talking about privacy by data minimization: anonymity, unlinkability, unobservability, pseudonymity, and identity management – version v0.34. Technical report, TU Dresden and ULD Kiel (2011)
30. Côté, M.-A., Suryn, W., Georgiadou, E.: In search for a widely applicable and accepted software quality model for software quality engineering. Softw. Qual. J. **15**(4), 401–416 (2007)
31. Masolo, C., Borgo, S.: Qualities in formal ontology. In: Hitzler, P., Lutz, C., Stumme, G. (eds.) Proceedings of the Workshop on Foundational Aspects of Ontologies (FOnt 2005), pp. 2–16 (2005)
32. Calero, C., Ruiz, F., Piattini, M. (eds.): Ontologies for Software Engineering and Software Technology. Springer, Heidelberg (2006). https://doi.org/10.1007/3-540-34518-3
33. Gonzalez-Perez, C., Henderson-Sellers, B., McBride, T., Low, G.C., Larrucea, X.: An ontology for ISO software engineering standards, 2) proof of concept and application. Int. J. Hum.-Comput. Stud. **65**(2007), 569–582 (2007)
34. ISO/IEC TR 14143-3:2003: [23] Information technology—Software measurement—Functional size measurement—Part 3: Verification of functional size measurement methods
35. Šmite, D.: An empirically based terminology and taxonomy for global software engineering. Empir. Softw. Eng. **19**(1), 105 (2014). ISSN 1382-3256
36. Mahon: The Essence of Software Engineering - Applying the SEMAT Kernel. With Pan Wei Ng, Paul Mc Mahon, Ian Spence and Svante Lidman. Addison-Wesley (2013)
37. Clarke, P., et al.: An Investigation of Software Development Process Terminology. In: Clarke, Paul M., O'Connor, Rory V., Rout, T., Dorling, A. (eds.) SPICE 2016. CCIS, vol. 609, pp. 351–361. Springer, Cham (2016). https://doi.org/10.1007/978-3-319-38980-6_25
38. Ralph, P.: Toward methodological guidelines for process theories and taxonomies in software engineering. IEEE Trans. Softw. Eng. (2018). https://doi.org/10.1109/TSE.2018.2796554

SPI in Medical Device Industry

A Software Process Improvement Roadmap for IEC 62304: An Expert Review

Peter Rust(✉), Derek Flood, Gilbert Regan, and Fergal McCaffery

Dundalk Institute of Technology & Lero, Dundalk, Ireland
{peter.rust, derek.flood, gilbert.regan, fergal.mccaffery}@dkit.ie

Abstract. Manufacturers of medical devices must comply with certain legislation and regulations before they can market their products in the European Union (EU). The EU has introduced this legislation and regulation to provide the frameworks by which manufacturers can produce safe and effective medical devices in a consistent manner. The EU has accomplished this by way of Medical Device Directives and harmonised standards. Manufactures, by demonstrating compliance with a harmonised standard, can be presumed to have complied with the essential requirements of the legislation. IEC 62304 Medical device software – Software lifecycle processes is a harmonised standard. However, the standard provides no clear directions for meeting the requirements of the standard. A Software Process Improvement (SPI) Roadmap for IEC 62304:2006 has been developed as a method for aiding medical device software development organizations in implementing the standard. The Roadmap is divided into two levels, the high level consists of the Activities and Tasks necessary for the implementation of the standard, while the low level contains the Design Patterns and How-to artefacts linked to the Tasks. This paper presents the findings from the expert review of the high level roadmap.

Keywords: Software process improvement · SPI · Medical device software IEC 62304 · Roadmap

1 Introduction

To market a medical device in the European Union (EU), it must be demonstrated that it has been manufactured in compliance with a very stringent set of regulations [1–3]. These regulations have been introduced to achieve a consistently high level of patient and operator safety. Medical devices increasingly rely on software for their operation and increased functionality [4]. DIRECTIVE 2007/47/EC [5] clarified that standalone software can be a medical device in its own right.

Harmonised standards are European standards developed by European Standards Organisations following a request from the European Commission [6]. Manufacturers can use harmonised standards to demonstrate that their product complies with the relevant EU legislation [7]. IEC 62304:2006 [8], is a harmonized standard that defines the life cycle requirements for medical device software [6].

X. Larrucea et al. (Eds.): EuroSPI 2018, CCIS 896, pp. 593–604, 2018.
https://doi.org/10.1007/978-3-319-97925-0_50

The implementation of standards, such as IEC 62304, is challenging as the standard sets out the requirements that must be met but does not state how to meet them. The "*how-to*" element of standards implementation is difficult. Organisations implementing standards for the first time could engage specialist consultants to aid in the implementation. Engaging consultants can be costly and Small to Medium Sized Enterprises (SME) can find the provision of these costs prohibitive.

Roadmaps are ubiquitous in the technology domain. Since their inception in the 1970's, roadmaps have been developed for numerous other sectors. More than two thousand public-domain roadmaps, organised by topic, from over fourteen different sectors have been identified and catalogued [9].

The solution proposed here is a tailorable SPI Roadmap for the implementation of IEC 62304. The Roadmap points to a series of "*How-To*" artefacts that the organisation may utilise to direct them on how-to complete certain tasks. The completion of these tasks allows the organisation to meet the requirements of the standard associated with the particular task. The definition of the SPI Roadmap in this research, based on Flood's [10] definition with minor changes, is – "*A series of Activities, comprised of Tasks that will guide an organisation through the use of specific "How-To's" towards compliance with regulatory standards.*"

The remainder of this paper is structured as follows: Sect. 2 outlines the related work while Sect. 3 outlines the proposed solution. Section 4 outlines the research method used to carry out the validation of the Roadmap. Section 5 presents the results of the expert review. Section 6 details the changes made to the Roadmap while Sect. 7 discusses the validity of the review. Section 8 outlines the future work to be carried out before Sect. 9 concludes the paper.

2 Related Work

Organisations of all sizes find difficulty in the implementation of standards. Yahya and Goh [11] reported that organisations implementing ISO 9000 encountered barriers such as: lack of understanding of the standard; constraints on resources (manpower, time, finance); lack of training and education of employees and unclear benefits of obtaining certification. As part of this research, a survey of four organisations operating in the Irish medical device software development domain was carried out to try and identify the challenges faced by organisations implementing IEC 62304. All the organisations reported that the sourcing and provision of training, incorporating traditional software development practices into an agile environment and adding new processes were among some of the challenges they faced. Additionally, the cost of implementing IEC 62304 was identified as a major challenge by 75% of the organisations surveyed. The understanding/interpretation of the requirements, sourcing template documents, production of the documentation required to demonstrate compliance, installation of a document management system, implementing overly complex processes and the rigorous planning that must be carried out at the start of the project were challenges that 25% of the respondents found difficult. Höss [12] reporting on the experience of implementing IEC 62304 in a radiotherapy unit stated that the "*initial effort is significant and a learning curve must be overcome*", which can be costly.

One solution to overcome the challenge posed by these costs could be the use of Roadmaps. Road mapping is a process that has developed from its inception in the 1970's to an internationally accepted practice today. Bob Galvin the then CEO of Motorola is credited with the development of the first technology roadmap [13]. Roadmapping is used companywide by Motorola and they state that it is responsible for adding over two billion dollars of value to the company since the 1970's [14]. Technology roadmaps are accepted as the correct way of planning the way forward to achieve a desired goal by describing what has to be done to reach it [15]. The power of a roadmap lies in its ability to clearly show the route that is planned [16]. Cooper and Edgett reported that 38% of the best performing businesses used product development roadmaps [17]. The provision of a guide on how to implement IEC 62304 would be one method of aiding medical device software development organisations in meeting the challenges of implementing the standard.

3 Proposed Solution

The proposed solution is an SPI Roadmap, detailed in Fig. 1, consisting of two levels, the high level contains the Activities and Tasks necessary for implementing IEC 62304 and the low level contains the Design Patterns and How-to artefacts that guide the organisation in how-to complete the Tasks.

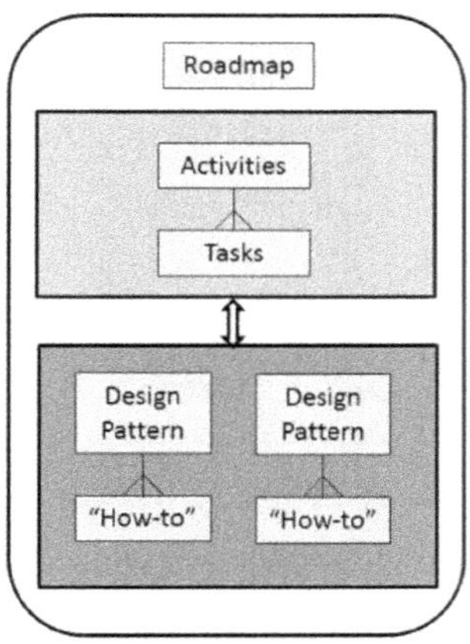

Fig. 1. Roadmap structure

The high level Roadmap comprises sixteen Activities, grouped in four bands that allow for their introduction to the organisation in a timely manner. The bands are: 1-Foundational, 2-Production, 3-Post Production and 4-Change/Problem Management. It is important to note that the Roadmap is constructed using a spreadsheet. The graphic is included in one worksheet and each Activity has its own linked worksheet containing all the associated Tasks. The graphic for the SPI Roadmap developed as part of this research is presented in Fig. 2.

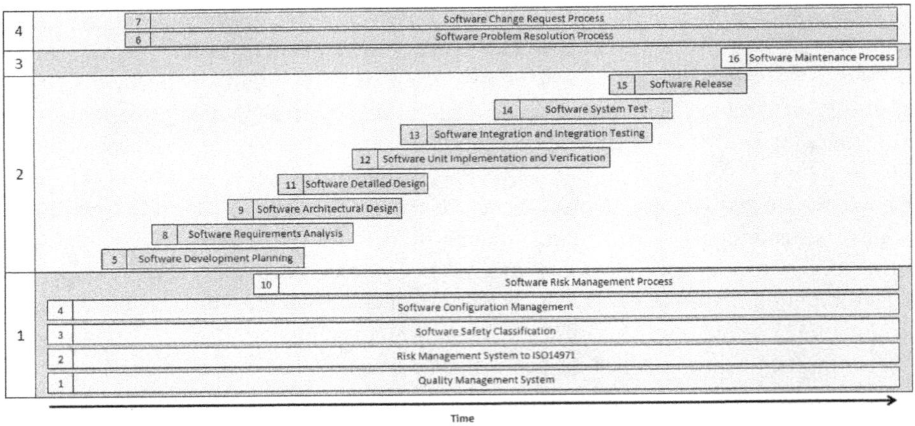

Fig. 2. Roadmap graphic before expert review

The Roadmap has been developed in accordance with well-established practice [18]. The aim of the expert review was to determine if the Activities and Tasks in the high level Roadmap are correct.

4 Research Method

The research method consists of five stages as detailed in Fig. 3.

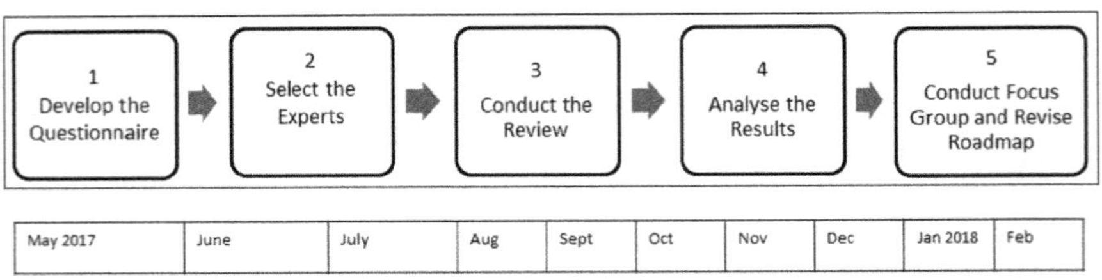

Fig. 3. Steps in research method

1 Develop the Questionnaire

The design of the questionnaire was developed in line with Burgess's findings [19]. Three questions were developed to determine if the high level Roadmap contains all the Activities necessary for the implementation of IEC 62304, if the order of the Activities is correct and if their grouping is appropriate. A further three questions were developed to review each of the Activities, to determine if the Tasks are suitable for the Activities, if their order within each Activity is correct and will the Tasks, once completed, fulfil the objectives of each of the Activities. A Likert scale was used in association with each of the six questions to allow the reviewer to rate the answers to the questions posed. One corresponded to "*strongly disagree*" and five with "*strongly agree*".

A comment box was also included with each question to allow the expert explain their answer in more detail if they wished.

2 Select the Experts

Experts from the medical device standards community with specialized knowledge of IEC 62304 were contacted and invited to participate in the review. These same experts were also asked to nominate other experts with the same type of experience with medical device standards. Six experts agreed to participate in the review.

- Expert 1 has eleven years working with the implementation of IEC 62304 and six years actively involved in developing the standard.
- Expert 2 has worked for over thirty years with a major international medical device and systems manufacturer, in positions ranging from project manager, through to group manager. They have also served as a medical device software expert to the IEC and ISO joint working groups developing the standard.
- Expert 3 has twenty six years' experience in medical device software, sixteen of which as an active member of the ISO/IEC working group responsible for the development of IEC 62304.
- Expert 4 Commenced as a software developer for IVD devices complying with IEC 62304, progressing to project manager for similar devices. Through their own consultancy firm they advise organisations on the implementation of IEC 62304.
- Expert 5 has over twenty years' experience in medical device software development and worked on the development of IEC 62304:2006.
- Expert 6 has thirty five years developing hardware and software for medical devices. They are also a co-chair of the 2nd Edition of IEC 62304.

3 Conduct the Review

The experts were forwarded a copy of the spreadsheet containing the high level Roadmap together with the questionnaires. The first two Activities refer directly to other standards, the quality and risk management systems, each consisting of single tasks. For this reason the experts were not asked questions about these Tasks. The first questionnaire related to the Roadmap and proposed three statements to which the respondent was required to rate on a five level Likert scale, a score of one represented "*Strongly disagree*" while "*Strongly agree*" was represented by a score of five. The statements were as follows: "*The Roadmap includes all the Activities that are necessary for the complete implementation of IEC 62304*", "*The order of the Activities within the Roadmap is correct*" and "*The grouping of the Activities within the Roadmap is appropriate*". The experts could add additional explanation of their answers or comments in the box provided. The second questionnaire related to the Tasks contained within each Activity and were framed similar to the first questionnaire: are they suitable for the Activity, are they in an appropriate order and are they complete. A comment box as described above was also included.

4 Analyse the Results

Two methods are utilized to analyse the results. Firstly the mean and standard deviation are calculated for the answers to each question and secondly the comments made were manually analysed using a content analysis approach.

5 Conduct Focus Group and Revise Roadmap
Following the analysis, a focus group consisting of three experts with experience of medical device software development, roadmaps and software process improvement from the Regulated Software Research Centre based in Dundalk Institute of Technology, Ireland, was convened to consider the results of the expert review. The sessions were arranged as described by Tremblay et al. [20]. The results of the Likert scale answers and the expert's comments were tabulated along with the Activities and Tasks that they referenced. The focus group discussed each comment and a consensus was reached as to whether or not a change was required.

5 Results

5.1 The Roadmap

The mean and standard deviation (SD) were calculated for the results recorded for each question. It was found that all of the Activities that are necessary (mean 4.6, SD 0.5) for the implementation of IEC 62304 are included and that the grouping of the Activities (mean 4.0, SD 1.1) is appropriate. There is no strong feeling as to whether the order of the Activities (mean 3.0, SD 0.6) is correct. The content analysis of the comments on the Roadmap resulted in the creation of four categories:

1. **Structural:** Comments concerned with the graphical representation of the Roadmap.
2. **Regrouping of Activities:** Comments with regard to the placement of the Activities within the individual bands comprising the Roadmap.
3. **Timing of Activities:** Comments about the timeline by which the Activities are introduced to the organisation.
4. **Definition of Terms used in Roadmap:** Comments referencing certain terms used in the Roadmap and where confusion might occur due to their use in the context of a medical device software improvement roadmap.

Structural: This category attracted two comments. The main concern was that the graphical representation of the roadmap implied that agile methods were not an option. To address this issue, more emphasis is being placed on the fact that the Roadmap is not a program but rather a timeline by which the Activities are introduced to the organisation. The objective of the Roadmap is to aid the implementation of the standard. It is important to note that similar to IEC 62304, the Roadmap does not prescribe any particular life cycle model. The focus group concluded that the "bars" in band 2, the production block, should be widened to emphasize that agile methods are not proscribed.

Regrouping of Activities: Two comments were made under this category. The first, that Software Risk Management is part of Software Safety Classification, was considered by the focus group, but it concluded that these activities should remain as individual Activities but that Software Risk Management should be introduced earlier in the timeline. The Activity will be moved to the left, before activity 6 and 7. The second comment, that Software Configuration Management should be placed in band 4 along with the Software Problem Resolution and the Software Change Request Activities, was considered by the focus group but was found that while there was a link between the activities, Software Configuration Management should stay in band 1.

Timing of the Activities: Four comments were made on the timing of the Activities e.g. "*All band 2 Activities should start before any one of them is complete.*" The comments will be addressed by including a new worksheet titled "*About*". This worksheet will explain the graphic in more detail and how it should be interpreted. It will explain that the Roadmap is not a programme but rather a timeline for the introduction of the Activities to the organisation implementing IEC 62304.

Definition of Terms Used in Roadmap: A total of three comments were made on the meaning of certain words used in the Roadmap, for example, the meaning of "*release*" in the roadmap was questioned. The term has a specific meaning when used in agile software development, while the term when used in the Roadmap has a different meaning. A worksheet will be inserted in the Roadmap, titled "*Definitions*" and will include definitions for the terms used in the Roadmap where concerns were raised. The terms will be capitalized in the text of the Roadmap to indicate, similar to the use of capitalization in the standard, that there is a definition for the word included in the definitions worksheet. Also, Activity fifteen will be renamed "*Software Release at a System Level*" to avoid confusion.

5.2 The Activities

Questions 4, 5 and 6 related to each Activity. The mean and standard deviation were calculated for the results recorded for each question and are presented in Table 1.

Table 1. Results of the questionnaire on the activities – anomalies highlighted

		Question 4		Question 5		Question 6	
Activity	Activity Title	Mean	SD	Mean	SD	Mean	SD
3	Software Safety Classification	4	1	5	0	4.5	0.5
4	Software Configuration Management	3	0	4	0	2	0
5	Software Development Planning	3	0	4	0	5	0
6	Software Problem Resolution Process	4	0	1	0	4	0
7	Software Change Request Process	4	0	2	0	2	0
8	Software Requirements Analysis	3	0	3	0	3	0
9	Software Architectural Design	4	1	4	1	4.5	0.5
10	Software Risk Management Process	3	0	3	0	4	0
11	Software Detailed Design	4	1	5	0	4	0
12	Software Unit Implementation and Verification	4	1	4	0	4	0
13	Software Integration and Integration Testing	3	0	3	1	4	1
14	Software System Testing	3	1	2.5	0.5	3	1
15	Software Release	1	0	4	0	3	0
16	Software Maintenance Process	3	0	5	0	5	0

Question 4 - Tasks are Suitable for the Activity: There is an overall consensus that the Tasks are suitable for each of the activities. However, Activity 15 - Software Release - was most problematic returning a mean of 1.0 and SD 0.

Question 5 - The Order of the Tasks within the Activity is Correct: There is a consensus with eleven of the Activities. However, Activities 6 (mean 1.0, SD 0), 7 (mean 2.0, SD 0) and 14 (mean 2.5, SD 0.5), are the subject of some disagreement on the order of the Tasks.

Question 6 - The Tasks Once Completed will Fulfil the Objective of the Activity: Two of the Activities 4 and 7 scored a mean value of 2.0, SD 0.0, while the remainder of the Activities achieved scores of 3.0 and above indicating that the experts agreed that the Tasks once completed will fulfil the objective of the Activity.

Forty five comments were returned with regard to the Tasks and these were categorized under seven headings, presented in Table 2.

Table 2. Categorization of activity comments

Category	Title	Number of comments
1	Coverage of Activity	5
2	Order of Tasks (Timing)	11
3	Coverage of Task	11
4	Wording of Task	6
5	Amount Detail (Intent)	7
6	Definitions	2
7	Changes to IEC 62304 in 2nd Ed	3
Total		45

Coverage of the Activity: Of the five comments made, the main concern was in regard to Activity 6 – Problem Resolution Process in that there was no reference to reproduction of the problem in any of the Tasks. This concern will be addressed by including a reference to reproducibility in the Task and in the associated Design Pattern and "*How-to*" artefact.

Order of the Tasks (Timing): Eleven comments over seven Activities were recorded. Each comment was considered by the focus group and the order of the Tasks within three of the Activities was altered. An example being Activity 7 Software Change Request Process – where the comment regarding the order of Tasks 7.6 – verify changes and 7.7 – retest after changes is acknowledged and they will be reversed in the final Roadmap, verification being executed after all changes and testing has being made.

Coverage of the Task: Eleven comments were made regarding eight Tasks in seven of the Activities in this category. An example concerns Activity 4 - Software Configuration Management which comprises four Tasks. Task 4.1 is concerned with the establishment of the configuration scheme and 4.2 with the documentation of the scheme including any SOUP items being used. The reviewer was concerned that the

Task did not identify all the elements that are used in the creation of the software, e.g. environment, tools, release manual etc. The focus group agreed that a non-exhaustive list of elements should be included in Task 4.1 and that SOUP should be referenced directly in Task 4.2 and because SOUP includes open source software which may be updated or upgraded by anybody, a note to this effect will be included in the Task.

Wording of the Task: In this category six comments were made regarding four of the Activities. For example Activity 13 - Software Integration and Integration Testing attracted a comment with regard to the use of the word "*ensure*" in Task 13.6 – *"Ensure that the integration test record contents include:"*. The standard uses the word "*shall*". The focus group concluded that the word ensure should be removed and either "*shall*" or "*must*" used in its place. The task will be reworded to include the word "*ensure*".

Amount of Detail Contained in the Task: Comments were made with regard to seven Tasks. As an example Activity 16 Software Maintenance Process comprises six Tasks and the comment was in relation to Tasks 16.4, 16.5 and 16.6 and their references to other Activities in the Roadmap. The reviewer was concerned that the tasks were duplications and this might lead to issues with the practical implementation of a Quality Management System. Following a discussion on the matter the focus group concluded that the Tasks should be maintained to preserve the completeness of the mapping of the requirements to the Roadmap, but that the comment should be addressed by cross referencing the other Activities.

Definition of Certain Terms: Comments were made with regard to the use of each of the words, "*documented*" in Activity 5 and "*ensure*" in Activity 13. The focus group agreed that a definition for "*documented*" should be included in the Roadmap and Task 13.6 will be reworded using the word "*shall*".

Changes to IEC 62304 in the 2nd Edition: Comments were made in relation to each of three changes being made in the 2nd edition of IEC 62304. For example the section on Software Safety Classification in the 2015 version of IEC 62304 has been practically rewritten, however, it does not materially change any of the Tasks in the Activity and the focus group decided that no changes were deemed necessary.

6 Revision of the Roadmap

Following the focus group all the agreed changes were made to the Roadmap and the revised graphic is presented in Fig. 4.

The first point to note is that the four bands have been maintained as in the original Roadmap. The Software Risk Management Process, Software Problem Resolution and Software Change Request Activities have all been moved to the left so that they are introduced before Software Development Planning which now becomes Activity 8. The Activities in band 2 – the production activities – are all widened to help negate the impression that agile development is not an option. Activity 15 is renamed Software Release at System Level so that there is no confusion with the use of the term "*release*" by the development team. The remaining changes are as follows:

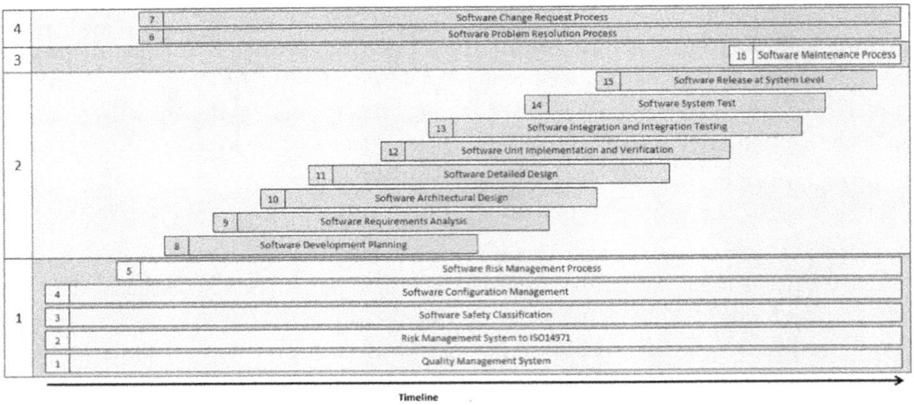

Fig. 4. Final roadmap graphic

- A worksheet titled "*About*" has been added to explain exactly what the aim of the Roadmap is.
- A worksheet titled "*Definitions*" has been added and includes all the definitions that are used in the Roadmap.
- Words that are defined for the Roadmap are capitalised within the text of the Tasks.
- A note has been included in Task 4.1 regarding SOUP.
- A note has been added to Task 6.1 regarding reproducibility.
- A note has been included in Task 6.2 referencing Task 6.8.
- The order of Tasks 7.6 and 7.7 have been reversed.
- A note has been added to Task 9.2 with regard to hardware failures.
- The order of Tasks 13.5 and 13.6 have been reversed.
- The order of Tasks 14.1 and 14.2 have been reversed.
- Task 13.5 has been reworded.
- Task 16.4, will include a reference to Activity 6, and Tasks 16.5 and 16.6 will include references to Activity 15.

7 Validity

The fourteen Activities were divided into four sub sections, each containing either three or four Activities. Each of the experts was requested to review one sub section. The result was that eight Activities were reviewed only once while the remaining six received two reviews. Five of the experts have participated in the development of the standard, while the remaining expert has fifteen years' experience in its implementation. Because of their expertise the threat to validity is considered minimal.

8 Future Work

The next phase of the validation process is industry trial, where two organisations engaged in medical device software development have been recruited to trial the roadmap. The organisations will be assessed before the implementation of the Roadmap using a tailored MDevSpice® assessment. Following the implementation of the Roadmap the organisations will be reassessed using the same assessment tool and the results analysed. Interviews will be conducted with the participant organisations to determine the usefulness and ease of use of the Roadmap within the organisation.

9 Conclusions

Medical devices increasingly rely on software for their operation and increasing functionality. Marketing of a medical device within the EU is dependent on it meeting very stringent regulations. Demonstrating compliance with these regulations can be achieved by developing the medical device in accordance with harmonized standards. Medical devices increasingly rely on software for their operation and control. The standard for medical device software life cycles, IEC 62304:2006 is a harmonized standard. However, the standard tells you what to do but not how to do it. This is a major challenge for small medical device software development organisations. The Roadmap, a guide to regulatory compliance, developed under this research is a possible solution to this problem.

Six experts reviewed the Roadmap and the Activities. The results indicated that the Roadmap did include all the Activities necessary for implementing IEC 62304 and that their grouping into the four bands is appropriate. The results also indicated that the Tasks are suitable for each Activity and that once completed will fulfil the objective of the particular Activity. A total of forty five comments were made, thirty of which suggesting changes to the Tasks and Activities. Three of these comments related to changes being made in the second edition of IEC 62304 and were not relevant to this research. Five of the seven comments relating to the amount of detail in the tasks will be addressed by inclusion of the required detail in the low level Roadmap. The sixteen changes agreed by the focus group reviewing the comments address the remaining twenty two comments. The changes have been implemented and the Roadmap will now be piloted within two medical device software development organisations.

Acknowledgement. This work was supported with the financial support of the Science Foundation Ireland grant 13/RC/2094 and co-funded under the European Regional Development Fund through the Southern & Eastern Regional Operational Programme to Lero - the Irish Software Research Centre (www.lero.ie). This work was partly funded by the DEIS H2020 project (Grant Agreement 732242).

References

1. EU: Active implantable medical devices (90/385/EEC). Off. J. Eur. Communities **L189**, 17–36 (1990)
2. EU: Council Directive 93/42/EEC of 14 June 1993 concerning medical devices. Off. J. Eur. Union **L169 36**, 1–60 (1993)
3. EU: Council Directive of 20 June 1990 on the approximation of the laws of the member states relating to active implantable medical devices (90/385/EEC). Off. J. Eur. Communities **L189**, 1–35 (1990)
4. Wallace, D.R., Kuhn, D.R.: Failure modes in medical device software: an analysis of 15 years of recall data. Int. J. Reliab. Qual. Saf. Eng. **8**(4), 351–371 (1999)
5. EU: Directive 2007/47/EC of the European Parliament and of the council of 5 September 2007. Off. J. Eur. Union **L247**, 21–55 (2007)
6. European Commission: Harmonised Standards (2016). https://ec.europa.eu/growth/single-market/european-standards/harmonised-standards_en
7. European Commission: Medical devices - European Commission (2016). https://ec.europa.eu/growth/single-market/european-standards/harmonised-standards/medical-devices_en#Note2.1
8. IEC: IEC 62304:2006 - Medical device software – software life cycle processes. ISO, Geneva, Switzerland (2006)
9. Phaal, R.: Public-Domain Roadmaps University of Cambridge. Defense, pp. 1–27, July 2009
10. Flood, D., McCaffery, F., Casey, V., McKeever, R., Rust, P.: A roadmap to ISO 14971 implementation. J. Softw. Evol. Process **27**(5), 319–336 (2015)
11. Yahya, S., Goh, W.: The implementation of an ISO 9000 quality system. Int. J. Qual. Reliab. **18**(9), 941–966 (2001)
12. Höss, A., Lampe, C., Panse, R., Ackermann, B., Naumann, J., Jäkel, O.: First experiences with the implementation of the European standard EN 62304 on medical device software for the quality assurance of a radiotherapy unit. Radiat. Oncol. **9**, 10 (2014)
13. Gindy, N.N.Z., Cerit, B., Hodgson, A.: Technology roadmapping for the next generation manufacturing enterprise. J. Manuf. Technol. Manag. **17**(4), 404–416 (2006)
14. Richey, J.M., Grinnell, M.: Evolution of roadmapping at Motorola. Res. Technol. Manag. **47** (2), 37–41 (2004)
15. Londo, H., More, E., Phaal, R., Wurtenberger, L., Cameron, L.: Background paper on technology roadmaps (TRMs). unfccc.int (2013)
16. Albright, T., Kappel, R.: Roadmapping in the corporation. Res. Technol. Manag. **46**(2), 31–41 (2003)
17. Cooper, R., Edgett, S.J.: Product innovation and technology strategy stage-gate international. Product Development Institute (2009)
18. Rust, P., Flood, D., McCaffery, F.: Software process improvement and roadmapping – a roadmap for implementing IEC 62304 in organizations developing and maintaining medical device software. In: Rout, T., O'Connor, R.V., Dorling, A. (eds.) SPICE 2015. CCIS, vol. 526, pp. 19–30. Springer, Cham (2015). https://doi.org/10.1007/978-3-319-19860-6_3
19. Burgess, T.F.: A general introduction to the design of questionnaires for survey research. Information Systems Services (2001)
20. Tremblay, M.C., Hevner, A.R., Berndt, D.J.: Focus groups for artifact refinement and evaluation in design research. Commun. Assoc. Inf. Syst. **26**, 599–618 (2010)

Empowering the Future Infrastructure

Technology Strategy Planning and Innovation Management at Rheinmetall Automotive to Face Future Mobility Challenges

Martin Neumann[1(✉)], Andreas Riel[2], and Heinrich Dismon[1]

[1] Rheinmetall Automotive AG, 74172 Neckarsulm, Germany
martin.neumann@de.rheinmetall.com
[2] Institute of Engineering, University Grenoble Alpes, G-SCOP, 38000 Grenoble, France

Abstract. In the coming decades, the radical transformation of mobility needs—mainly driven by the world's demographic changes, environmental influences, resource availability and regulation standards—call for fresh ideas in the mobility sector, leading to modified or completely new vehicle architectures and mobility solutions. In order to be prepared for these changing market conditions, global tier-one suppliers to the automotive industry like Rheinmetall Automotive AG have to operate within a selection of promising and economically interesting technology fields with the target to occupy these areas in a timely manner. This paper presents Rheinmetall Automotive's overall management approach to defining a technology strategy and to implementing it in the existing organizational environment. The Technological Direction Development Process (TDDP) is embedded in the entire innovation process of Rheinmetall Automotive and facilitates the modern paradigm of Open Innovation. Examples from the practice will show Rheinmetall Automotive's activities concerning technology strategy and innovation management to shape the future of mobility.

Keywords: Fuzzy front-end of innovations · Technology foresight
Process development · Technology strategy planning · Innovation management
Automotive supplier industry

1 Introduction

In the area of personal mobility, the most significant change is evident in new mobility ideas, especially in terms of new vehicle concepts. Besides the networking of vehicles for permanent interaction with information and control systems and the automation and autonomization of vehicles, probably the biggest change is in the transition from the current domination of the internal combustion engine to powertrains that are at least partly electric [1].

From today's perspective, it should be noted that, whilst for the foreseeable future, pure-battery powered vehicles will take an uncertain market share amongst established powertrain technologies that will very likely continue to exist for many years to come. Nevertheless for quite some time, there will be a powertrain technology mix in the marketplace, one characterized not by either internal combustion or electric powertrain

X. Larrucea et al. (Eds.): EuroSPI 2018, CCIS 896, pp. 607–618, 2018.
https://doi.org/10.1007/978-3-319-97925-0_51

but instead by both internal combustion engine and electric motor in various configurations and combinations [1].

Within these future developments, especially companies that focused on internal combustion engine technologies have to find new ways to keep pace with these upcoming challenges. The planning of technology strategies has to take into account these promising opportunities and implement innovation management activities very rapid at the forefront of the entire innovation process, the fuzzy front-end of innovations [2].

This paper outlines the steps toward the creation of a systematic approach to develop the technology strategy for Rheinmetall Automotive AG called Technological Direction Development Process (TDDP) that takes into consideration the findings of the authors' earlier publications according to ideation [3, 4]. Section 3 presents the several steps during the implementation of the technology strategy and its interdependency to innovation management. Some practical examples will also been shown. Section 4 gives an outlook about upcoming strategic and innovative actions in the company's environment.

2 Creation of the TDDP at Rheinmetall Automotive

2.1 Initial Situation and Methodology

Based on the results of our research concerning the creation of a reference stage-gate process model for ideation activities in the early fuzzy front-end of New Product Development (NPD) [5] Rheinmetall Automotive was interested in creating a similar systematic approach for defining the technological direction of the company. The definition of a technology strategy, which outlines the company's innovation focus that is aligned with the overall company's core mission and values, is essential and a major part of steering subsequent ideation activities. Therefore, the creation of the TDDP was initiated to cope with the following challenges:

1. Defining a technology strategy process that is sufficiently structured to allow assessment and improvement, yet lightweight enough to leverage the dynamics and creativity that are intrinsic to ideation.
2. Integrating this technology strategy process into existing stage-gate process landscapes in order to minimize any additional efforts and to be adoptable by a large part of the organization.

According to the experiences in implementing the ideation process at Rheinmetall Automotive the development of the technology strategy process took place in an very pragmatic way and represents a very reasonable complement to enrich the ideation process first phase of prerequisite [5].

2.2 Key Success Factors

Our extensive literature review in the principle subject areas of innovation management, fuzzy front-end research and NPD research, as well as our examination of best practice examples from the automotive industry and other worldwide recognized innovation leaders result in the identification of key success factors for an effective ideation process [6]. We recognized that some of these success factors influence as well the systematic definition of a technology strategy and should be enforced to guarantee actionable and promising next steps within the entire innovation management. Thus, we will outline the most important aspects in the following.

Ideation Starts at the Top Management

During our research on the ideation process model we interviewed external and internal experts, and one of our experts stated: "Based on my experiences, it might be important that the top management provides a statement regarding the most important innovative topics, which they really want to be realised". Top management commitment can be seen as the prerequisite for establishing the basic conditions for innovative activities to be carried out and for employees to understand their responsibility and to be encouraged to think beyond the status quo.

So, the implementation of a continuous approach to define the overall technological direction of the company supports innovation management and pushes the development of new products. One important aspect was the implementation of regular board meetings to communicate the commitment and objectives of top management.

By defining our technology strategy process we considered this very crucial process part and install a communication platform where the top management is supposed to commit to the technology and innovation strategy and innovation priorities. These regular meetings also fulfil the possibility to track innovative projects and steer the progress of further development activities. This is a very essential part for a well working technology strategy planning.

Ideation Needs a Clearly Defined Focus

This was one of the major findings from our expert interviews [6]. Idea contributors have to have a guidance in terms of which topics are considered relevant by top management. In this way, they can focus their efforts and meet the expectations of decision makers. Ideation topics shall be aligned with strategic company objectives.

Griffin and Page support this conclusion that the presence of a clear strategy has a positive influence on the success of new products [7]. Therefore the definition of the company's innovation focus that is aligned with the overall company's core mission and values is inevitable. This strategic focus helps reduce cost and time effort during the creation and realisation of ideas, and leverages the effectiveness of the ideation process [2, 8].

This finding is the confirmation that technology strategy planning is an important contribution to guarantee the focus of innovation management and proves the fact of interdependency of these two disciplines. The systematic analysis of the company's total situation and environment for the identification of areas of action increases additionally the effectiveness during the technology strategy planning and generation and selection of ideas.

Ideation Happens in Networks

On the basis of various studies on Integrated Design from Grenoble INP and several members of EMIRAcle, we have identified that the integration of stakeholders with different expertise and profession during the front-end stages of the product development process represents a key factor for sustainable development [9]. The essential consideration here is that the integration of these stakeholder groups in the innovation management process is a key step for making innovation sustainable, as it allows taking into account the requirements and constraints imposed by the different actors of the product/system life cycle [3].

Involving external stakeholders in company-wide innovation management is also the core characteristic of Open Innovation strategies, which have originally been coined by Chesbrough in 2003 [4, 10]. The move towards stakeholder-integration based ideation and innovation has become a must [11–14]. To be innovative in future, it is important that product and/or service ideas are not only the result of one core group of employees.

Throughout the creation of the TDDP we reviewed our previous findings and add new groups of external and internal stakeholders to our assumptions [4]. Figure 1 depicts the most promising stakeholder groups for the creation of the technology strategy and the implementation of innovation management within the Rheinmetall Automotive Group.

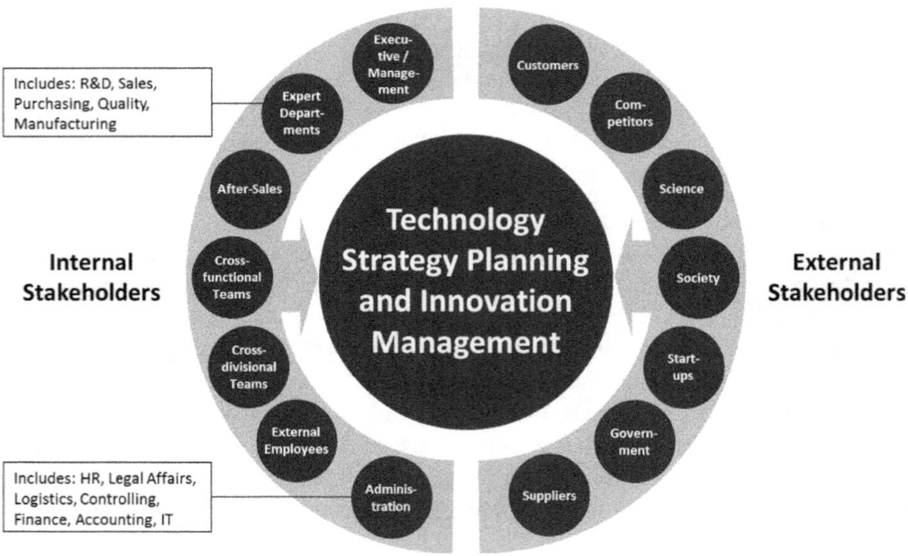

Fig. 1. Integration of stakeholders at Rheinmetall Automotive Group

All these success factors from our previous research work make a major contribution to the creation of the TDDP and reinforce an organizational culture of Open Innovation within Rheinmetall Automotive, facilitating the integration of numerous stakeholders in the ideation process. Future activities at Rheinmetall Automotive concerning technology scouting and start-up screening prove this fact.

2.3 Overview of the TDDP

With these key success factors explained in Sect. 2.2 and the determining factors of Rheinmetall Automotive's organization our design of a company-specific technology strategy process followed a systematic procedure: for each of the element of the process we analyzed the corresponding organizational and cultural elements, activities, and tools that would be concerned at Rheinmetall Automotive. We aimed at finding out which roles to assign to these entities, and where to place them in the entire process such that the key success factors and the company-specific action fields can be taken into account.

In Fig. 2 we present the resultant Rheinmetall Autmotive's specific TDDP, which is mainly developed and implemented through the commitment of the Chief Technology Officer (CTO), and accepted by the top management from Rheinmetall Automotive.

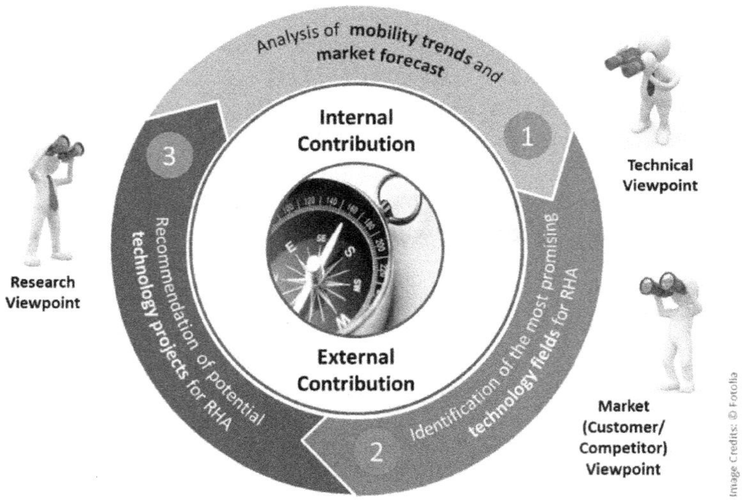

Fig. 2. Rheinmetall Automotive's Technology Direction Development Process

The TDDP represents the overall management approach to define a technology strategy for Rheinmetall Automotive and to implement it in the existing organizational environment. To define the technological direction for Rheinmetall Automotive the TDDP follows three major process phases:

1. Analysis of mobility trends and market forecast.
2. Identification of the most promising technology fields for Rheinmetall Automotive.
3. Recommendation of potential technology projects for Rheinmetall Automotive.

The TDDP runs in a structured way to guarantee sustainability through the whole product-life-cycle and is not a parallel management process or stand-alone process to the existing R&D process land-scape; the TDDP is embedded in the entire innovation process of Rheinmetall Automotive to gain acceptance within the group. The process has been continuously repeated and permanently adjusted over the years. Lessons-learned will be considered in the following runs of the process. The TDDP represents one of the core processes of Rheinmetall Automotive and has been audited against the IATF 16949.

The involvement of internal and external stakeholders during the processing of the TDDP guarantees the commitment of top management and employees as well as the establishment of an organization culture which leverages innovation by motivating employees to be creative and to actively generate and communicate ideas to shape the technology strategy and future of Rheinmetall Automotive. Thus, the results of the TDDP are a joint product of the contribution from several different external sources and the involvement of cross-divisional and cross-functional departments of the entire Rheinmetall Automotive Group as well as since last year the involvement of the parent group Rheinmetall. These diverse external and internal stakeholders provide different viewpoints from technical, market and research perspectives.

The Rheinmetall Automotive Engineering Council (REC) is the main instrument of the TDDP to assure inter-divisional activities to work proactive on a common technology strategy across the entire company and to innovate cooperatively. The REC takes place on a regular basis and headed by the CTO. It is also the communication tool to guarantee the exchange of R&D information from internal and external stakeholders. By the implementation of such a regular board meeting dedicated to the technology strategy planning, the consideration of the previously mentioned success factors is guaranteed. Our experiences in the last years have proven this fact.

The REC is prepared according to the needs of the TDDP and very flexible in its content and structure. The RECs' core team consists of the CTO, Business Unit Heads and Directors Engineering. Additionally the Executive Board attends regularly one REC per year. Different internal and external experts complete the RECs with regard to the targets of the meetings. Due to the participants of the REC, this management circle will be used particularly as a steering committee. The central fields of action are:

- identifying key know-how;
- finding first ideas as well as description and confirmation of future technology fields for Rheinmetall Automotive;
- defining "Challenges" for succeeding internal and external ideation campaigns;
- evaluation sessions to prioritize technology projects;
- pre-selection of product ideas;
- decision-making regarding responsibilities and resources;
- being the accelerator for a new innovation culture in the company;

In the first half of each year, the REC-I takes place with attendance of the Executive Board. It helps track R&D projects resulting from the TDDP. The REC-II in the second half of the year is mainly dedicated to introduce new technological trends and generate ideas how Rheinmetall Automotive can profit from these future technology fields. Thanks to its workshop character, the REC-II has a major role in ensuring the continuation and topicality of the TDDP.

3 Implementation and Results of the TDDP

Under the patronage of the CTO and his commitment in defining Rheinmetall Automotive's technological direction in future the implementation of the TDDP could be realized in a very organized way and found acceptance in the entire Rheinmetall Autmotive Group. By following the phases of the TDDP systematically, the technology strategy could be clearly defined by three major technological directions for the short-term, medium-term and long-term. In the following, the main workflow steps as well as the results will be described in detail.

3.1 The Process Phases of the TDDP

Analysis of Mobility Trends and Market Forecast: The entire TDDP starts with an impulse. Because this process is embedded in an interactive organizational environment, these impulses can come from the internal or external environment. According to the influencing factors defined by Koen et al., these impulses can be based on [15]:

- the corporation's organizational capabilities,
- customer and competitor influences,
- the outside world's influences, and
- the depth and strength of enabling sciences and technology.

To be aware of possible opportunities the internal and external analysis of these influencing factors is vital [15]. Already in the year 1964 Cochran and Thompson saw the need for sufficient market analysis to guarantee the new products' success [16]. Subsequent studies have proven this assumption [17–24]. Therefore this initial screening activities mark the start of the first phase of the TDDP.

The internal analysis has to focus on the check of core competences and capabilities first. This is crucial, because these organizational core competences and capabilities determine the following identification and analysis of internal impulses as well as the effort on using external opportunities [15]. This internal analysis has to support the identification of the company's strengths and weaknesses and the related current resource situation.

At Rheinmetall Automotive, this recommendation was realized especially at workshops with representatives from the division Hardparts. To generate ideas for new technology fields and possible products the following main questions were asked to start the discussion:

- What kinds of key know-how characterize the division Hardparts?
- What kinds of application fields will be open up by this key know-how?

This approach was very useful to get input for the TDDP.

The definition of the current market situation is the core task of the external analysis and the information of the market must be observed and explored for usable ideas. The identification of customer requirements helps to formulate customer needs and consequently starting points for the idea generation. Also the analyses of competitors' approaches may inspire and support changing previous manners in the company to solve problems. The analysis of the outside world includes government policy, environmental regulations, and laws concerning patents. Socioeconomic trends affect the ideation process as well [15].

This aspect was taken into account during the TDDP by involving sales managers in several workshop groups. By asking these colleagues it was possible to get insights about the current market situation, the needs from customer side and the competitive situation.

The stimulus for new ideas based on internal and external research with the aim to commercialize new know-how is called technology push [25]. Within the analysis phase of the TDDP it was also very important to reflect on external information to be aware of this technology push. Therefore the involvement of external consulting firms, engineering companies, etc. was also considered to complete Rheinmetall Automotive's picture of future technology trends and their consequences for the company.

Identification of the Most Promising Technology Fields: Highly technology-driven sectors like automotive, are obliged to monitor and actively influence technologies that decide about market success. Therefore the stakeholders responsible for the definition of the future technology strategy have to analyze technologies with respect to their further implementation, new arising (substituting) technologies have to be identified in time, and assessed for their commercialization and threat potential. This also implies the need for observing—and probably even participating in—fundamental research.

Technology strategy has a leading and controlling function and leverages the effectiveness of the entire innovation process. Its core is a set of future technology guidelines and promising technology and innovation search fields. These guidelines and search fields provide a framework for the innovation process concerning the following key points [26]:

- They ensure that all innovation activities are aligned with the overall technology and corporate strategy and make a supportive contribution to it.
- They channel and focus the idea generation. Thus, for example, technology and innovation search fields can be transformed directly into tasks of an ideation workshop.
- They can be used as assessment criteria for idea selection.
- They help design products or services aligned with the market needs.

In the course of this phase of the TDDP the extraction of knowledge about these future technology fields is essential. Therefore we had to deal with the procurement, storage and utilization of new technological knowledge, similar to the discipline of technology management [27]. Only through the identification of gaps in the current product portfolio of Rheinmetall Automotive and—based on these findings—clearly communicated priority fields of action, it is possible find new ideas to protect the company's competitiveness [28].

Beside the execution of workshops where the generation of product ideas and the clustering of these ideas to technology fields were done, there were several deepening workshops where the decision-making about the realization of project proposals in alignment with the defined technology and innovation search fields took place. Especially organizational enablers were discussed, like for example responsibility, resources and financing. The hereby generated knowledge is managed by Rheinmetall Automotive by an IT-based technical solution, so-called "Team Room" via intranet, to collect and to store systematically the findings throughout the whole TDDP.

Recommendation of Potential Technology Projects: This phase of the TDDP is exclusively dedicated to the confirmation of the most promising technology fields in future and the final definition of the technological direction of Rheinmetall Automotive. Within the leading management team of Rheinmetall Automotive, the CTO proposes the identified technology fields and obtains a common agreement on the defined technological direction.

In the following, several communication activities start to make the defined technology strategy transparent throughout the Rheinmetall Automotive Group. Hereby the regular RECs make a major contribution to assure communication and interaction with the business units.

Generally, an open communication and a free information flow within the company and its external networks are essential to generate ideas and achieve innovative outcomes. Communication facilitates knowledge sharing by combining the wide variety of experiences, opening dialogue, building on others ideas and exploring issues relevant to innovation. Innovative companies reward cross-functional, cross-hierarchical, cross-cultural and cross-technological exchange of information and knowledge [29]. Openness within the company's organization encourages people to be creative together [30], which is also a major trait of the SPI Manifesto [31]. Furthermore, care has been taken in order to align the TDDP with the major traits of the upcoming ISO 50501 standard on Innovation Management [32].

3.2 The Results of the TDDP

The systematic approach of the TDDP enables Rheinmetall Automotive to define comprehensively their technological direction. Based on more than 300 raw ideas and their continuous assessment and clustering, it was possible to define three essential strategic technology directions for the upcoming years. Furthermore, it was possible to create a technology roadmap with 12 major technology fields and 17 potential technology projects. And finally, the establishment of cross-divisional R&D initiatives can be seen as main results of the entire TDDP.

An example of a cross-divisional R&D initiative addresses the future electric powertrain segment. Rheinmetall Automotive has developed a Rheinmetall Automotive Demonstrator for electric mobility. The development work was targeted at a battery-powered A-segment passenger car with an integrated battery pack, electric motor, and other electrification systems [1].

This can be described as an important technology field on which Rheinmetall Automotive will expand its product portfolio, with the demonstrator vehicle being used for the integration of additional Rheinmetall Automotive components and future development efforts. Given the adaptability of the battery module, there are a variety of application opportunities in various customer scenarios. The newly developed underfloor protection and the thermal protection will play an important role in making the vehicle safe to drive. Looking to the new development of the concept for a 48-Volt electric traction module for use on very small vehicles operating in first-mile/last-mile mode, it can be seen that the available powertrain product spectrum which is based on Rheinmetall Automotive's inhouse experience, will be further extended. Together with customers and partners, Rheinmetall Automotive will continue pushing ahead with the development of both segments: components for conventional powertrains and those for battery-powered vehicles [1].

4 Outlook

The dynamic transformation in personal mobility needs and globally progressing climate change call for adjustments in mobility systems through modified or new vehicle architectures. Because of the worldwide changing legislative rules and regulations, battery and battery-only vehicles are rapidly gaining importance.

This fact makes it inevitable for automotive suppliers that obtain their competitive advantages by technologies exclusively for conventional powertrains to predict new technology strategies and innovation management measures that maintain their continuous growth in a challenging market environment.

People's mobility needs are changing at an increasing rate, with certain factors influencing this change to an over-proportional degree, such as globalization, demographic developments and urbanization. It is essential in this process of change to protect the climate, to preserve our environment and to cope with a significantly changed attitude towards experiencing, utilizing and consuming mobility. This transformation of mobility behavior, which is already underway, calls for new products and solutions that place electric mobility, connectivity, advanced driver assistance systems and mobility services in the forefront.

This means that besides electric mobility, also the very dominant trend towards digitalization in the automotive industry will influence Rheinmetall Automotive in future. Therefore, activities for the integration of more external stakeholders like start-ups, the establishment of networks and the opening of innovation to partners at Rheinmetall Automotive have started. This management of networks will positively influence the further development of Rheinmetall Automotive towards new mobility trends.

With the TDDP, Rheinmetall Automotive has established a systematic and systemic approach to be open for new technologies and to find the right balance between the freedom for creativity and its entrepreneurial and commercial objectives to support innovation and its technological leadership in the future.

References

1. Dismon H., Seggewiß, P., Hunkel, D.: Innovative Elektrifizierungstechnologien für zukünftige konventionelle und alternative Fahrzeugantriebe – Innovative technologies for the electrification of future conventional and alternative vehicle powertrains. In: Geringer, B., Lenz, H.P. (eds.) Proceedings of 39th International Vienna Motor Symposium, 26–27 April 2018, second day, Fortschritt-Berichte VDI Reihe 12, Nr. 807, vol. 2, pp. 268–290. VDI Verlag, Düsseldorf (2018)

2. Neumann, M., Riel, A., Brissaud, D.: Improvement of innovation management through the enlargement of idea sources. In: O'Connor, Rory V., Pries-Heje, J., Messnarz, R. (eds.) EuroSPI 2011. CCIS, vol. 172, pp. 121–132. Springer, Heidelberg (2011). https://doi.org/10.1007/978-3-642-22206-1_11
3. Neumann, M., Riel, A., Brissaud, D.: Innovation management system for the automotive supplier industry to drive idea generation and product innovation. In: Proceedings of the 17th EuroSPI Conference, vol. 17, pp. 7.13–7.24 (2010)
4. Neumann, M., Riel, A., Brissaud, D.: Improvement of idea generation by capitalisation on internal and external stakeholders. In: Industrial Proceedings of the 18th EuroSPI Conference, vol. 18, pp. 3.25–3.33 (2011)
5. Riel, A., Neumann, M., Tichkiewitch, S.: Structuring the early fuzzy front-end to manage ideation for new product development. In: CIRP Annals - Manufacturing Technology, 28 April 2013, vol. 62, no. 1, pp. 107–110 (2013). ISSN 0007-8506. https://doi.org/10.1016/j.cirp.2013.03.128
6. Neumann, M., Riel, A.: Success factors for ideation based on experiences in automotive industry. In: Industrial Proceedings of the 20th EuroSPI Conference, pp. 6.11–6.24 (2013)
7. Griffin, A., Page, A.L.: PDMA success measurement project: recommended measures for product development success and failure. J. Prod. Innov. Manag. **13**(6), 478–496 (1996)
8. Ili, S., Albers, A., Miller, S.: Open innovation in the automotive industry. R&D Manag. **40** (3), 246–255 (2010)
9. Zhang, Q., Doll, W.J.: The fuzzy front end and success of new product development: a casual model. Eur. J. Innov. Manag. **4**(2), 95–112 (2001)
10. Chesbrough, H.W.: Open Innovation: The New Imperative for Creating and Profiting from Technology, p. 2003. Harvard Business School Press, Boston (2003)
11. Globocnik, D.: Front End Decision Making: Das Entstehen hochgradig neuer InnovationsvoRheinmetall Automotiveben in Unternehmen. Gabler Verlag, Wiesbaden (2011)
12. Khurana, A., Rosenthal, S.R.: Integrating the fuzzy front end of new product development. Sloan Manag. Rev. **38**(2), 103–120 (1997)
13. Koen, P.A., et al.: New concept development model: providing clarity and a common language to the 'fuzzy front end' of innovation. Res. Technol. Manag. **44**(2), 46–55 (2001)
14. Herstatt, C., Verworn, B. (eds): Management der frühen Innovationsphasen: Grundlagen – Methoden – Neue Ansätze. 2nd edn. Gabler Verlag, Wiesbaden (2007)
15. Koen, P.A., et al.: Fuzzy front end: effective methods, tools and techniques. In: Belliveau, P., Griffen, A., Somermeyer, S. (eds.) The PDMA ToolBook 1 for New Product Development, pp. 5–35. Wiley, Hoboken (2002)
16. Cochran, B., Thompson, G.C.: Why new product fail. In: The Conference Board Record, October, pp. 11–18 (1964)
17. Rothwell, R., Freeman, C., Horsley, A., Jervis, V.T.P., Robertson, A.B., Townsend, J.: SAPPHO updated – project SAPPHO phase II. Res. Policy **3**(3), 258–291 (1974)
18. Cooper, R.G.: The impact of new product strategies. Ind. Mark. Manag. **12**(4), 243–256 (1983)
19. Dwyler, L., Mellor, R.: Organizational environment, new product process activities, and project outcomes. J. Prod. Innov. **8**(1), 39–48 (1991)
20. Dwyler, L., Mellor, R.: New product process activities and project outcomes. R&D Manag. **21**(1), 31–42 (1991)
21. Barczak, G.: New product strategy, structure, process, and performance in the telecommunications industry. J. Prod. Innov. Manag. **12**(3), 224–234 (1995)
22. Calantone, R.J., Schmidt, J.B., di Benedetto, C.A.: New product activities and performance: the moderating role of environmental hostility. J. Prod. Innov. Manag. **14**(3), 179–189 (1997)

23. Parry, M.E., Song, X.M.: Identifying new product successes in China. J. Prod. Innov. Manag. **11**(1), 15–30 (1994)
24. Lynn, G.S., Green, C.J.: Market forecasting for high-tech vs. low-tech industrial products. Eng. Manag. J. **10**(1), 15–18 (1998)
25. Brem, A., Voigt, K.-I.: Integration market pull and technology push in the corporate front end and innovation management – Insights from the German software industry. Technovation **29**(5), 351–367 (2009)
26. Clausen, T., Geschka, H., Krug, J.: Innovationsstrategien. In: Ili, S. (ed.) Innovation Excellence – Wie Unternehmen ihre Innovationsfähigkeit systematisch steigern, pp. 95–128. Symposion Publishing GmbH, Düsseldorf (2012)
27. Brockhoff, K.: Forschung und Entwicklung: Planung und Kontrolle, 5th edn. Oldenbourg, München (1999)
28. Cooper, R.G.: The invisible success factors in product innovation. J. Prod. Innov. Manag. **16**(2), 115–133 (1999)
29. Lawson, B., Samson, D.: Developing innovation capability in organisations: a dynamic capabilities approach. Int. J. Innov. Manag. **5**(3), 377–400 (2001)
30. Miller, P., Brankovic, A.: Building a creative culture for innovation. In: IESE Insight, Fourth Quarter 2011, no. 11, pp. 51–58 (2011)
31. Korsaa, M., et al.: The people aspects in modern process improvement management approaches. J. Softw. Evol. Process **25**(4), 381–391 (2013)
32. ISO/TC 279 Technical Committee: ISO/CD Innovation Management, WIP, publication planned for 2019 (2018)

A Project Management Decision Support Tool for Keeping Pace with the Dynamics of Corporate Innovation Projects

Karolin Gebhardt[1,2(✉)], Tom Maes[2(✉)], and Andreas Riel[1(✉)]

[1] Institute of Engineering, University Grenoble Alpes, G-SCOP, 38000 Grenoble, France
karolin.gebhardt@gmail.com, andreas.riel@grenoble-inp.fr

[2] Bayer AG, 51373 Leverkusen, Germany
tom.maes@bayer.com

Abstract. Corporate innovation projects are typically characterized by a high dynamics of needs, insights and related solution approaches. In particular, the continuously increasing need complexity of innovation projects requires an approach to identify the project methodologies that are appropriate for a particular project, sub-project and their context, as well as to apply them correctly. This article proposes a practical decision support model for innovation project managers to select the management mode and method according to the current and evolving needs of an innovation project. This model has strongly been inspired by the experiential learning model of Kolb. This model is validated within the industrial environment of a German global key player in the pharmaceutical and chemical industry based on four selected innovation projects.

Keywords: Innovation project management · Agile project management
Corporate entrepreneurship · Leadership

1 Introduction

Innovation projects in huge and complex organizations are typically challenged by a balancing act of continuously changing needs [1, 2]. In practically every industry sector, innovation projects have to deal with an increasingly complex and uncertain business environment. Embedded in their corporate context, innovation projects have to assert their position in the middle of routine processes and standards and compete with business projects for dedicated resources. Just the sheer number of innovation project management approaches (IPMA) next to the traditional project management approaches highlights that the relevance of corporate innovation for organizational competiveness is scientifically acknowledged [3, 4]. The huge number of project management methodologies shows that project needs differ. This is supported by the common understanding that there is no one fits all methodology. The Project Management Institute (2018) diagnosed that despite the existence of various methodologies, about 15% of projects fail (12% with high maturity level and 21% with low maturity level) [5]. Furthermore, the PMI emphasizes in [5] that projects are more likely to succeed when they use various different project management approaches. This leads to

X. Larrucea et al. (Eds.): EuroSPI 2018, CCIS 896, pp. 619–630, 2018.
https://doi.org/10.1007/978-3-319-97925-0_52

the assumption that either the chosen methodology does not fit to the project's needs and/or that the methodology is not used in the right way. In particular, the continuously increasing and changing innovation project and sub project need complexity requires an approach to identify the project methodologies that are appropriate for a particular project and context [6], as well as to apply them correctly [7].

This article proposes a systematic and practical model-based tool that is based on the experiential learning model [8] and the established project management concepts. This tool helps to manage innovation projects depending on their particular temporary context and maturity and to select the appropriate fitting project management approach. Section 2 introduces our hypotheses related to innovation project dynamics. Section 3 investigates related work in agile, lean and traditional project management. Section 4 proposes our model built upon the hypothesis and the findings of the state of the art. Section 5 validates this model in the specific Bayer context based on four concrete innovation projects, two of which based in the information technology (IT) domain. Section 6 points out the implications of our proposed model on the selection of relevant innovation project management methods. Section 7 concludes with a summary of the key contributions and an outlook to our future research.

2 Objectives and Methodology

The objective of this research is to elaborate a systematic and actionable approach that helps to manage innovation projects depending on their particular context and maturity and to select the project management method that fits best to the project´s current context and maturity [9]. In order to address these challenges we want to propose an approach that allows characterizing the current needs of an innovation project and is sub projects as well as to capture the evolution of these needs over time and maturity. Furthermore, the intended approach allows associating the required management approaches with these needs, as well as to derive guidelines for innovation project managers. Ultimately, our research objective is to create a basis for a measurement framework for innovation project management.

With regard to the complexity and dynamics of changes of innovation project needs, our fundamental hypothesis is that successful innovation projects in corporate organizations make flexible use of four central methodical approaches dependent on the project phase or sub-project specific context:

- Experiment: Project phases that are confronted with complex and not well-defined needs, as well as not clearly defined solution, tend to be solved by experimentation.
- Iterate: Project phases that are confronted with complicated and not well-defined needs, but a clearly defined solution, tend to be solved by iteration.
- Plan: Project phases that are confronted with complicated and well-defined needs, but a not well defined solution, tend to be solved by planning.
- Execute: Project phases that are confronted with simple and well-defined needs as well as a clearly defined solution tend to be executed directly.

Based on this hypothesis we propose a model as decision aid for innovation project managers. We derive this model from the previous research result and project experience in a grounded theory approach and validate it in four innovation projects in a corporate context.

3 State of the Art

Traditional project management follows a linear, sequential and relatively predictable problem-solving-process, which can be organized in hierarchical tasks, like e.g. stage-gate-process [10]. The theoretical planning of the project is based on existing knowledge and takes place isolated from the later execution [9]. Thereby, the main objective is to stick to the project plan regarding time, costs and quality to reach the intended outcome [2, 11].

Because today´s project needs are in many cases more complex and dynamic, the traditional project management reaches its limits recognizing and articulating all relevant variables and their functional relationships). In this context, research and practice have put forth agile project management approaches, which are more flexible e.g. with regard to timing, resources or task completion [12]. The various agile approaches support the iterative and incremental development of the project, which is not predetermined by a project plan [13] Rapid and continuous consumer or user feedback enables an improved needs understanding and an ongoing according project adjustment [12].

A further approach to project management is based on exploration and experimentation. Experimentation, in particular design thinking, is described as a human-centered practice and learn process (experiment) that recommends collaboration and observation, allow rapid learning, and fast execution of ideas via building of prototypes [14]. In comparison to agile project management approaches, which analyze and address in particular existing (conscious) needs and possibilities, experiments explore both new needs (knowledge) and new solution concepts [15]. Based on experiments it allows to design an imaginable, potential solution and the search for a problem instead of planning and sequentially solving a problem or iteratively developing a solution. It can be described as system of spaces that frame solution and problem rather than a goal-oriented spiral or a predefined order of discrete steps [16]. Experiments are used to test derived hypotheses related to the problem and the solution and help to explore this spaces. Thereby, the main objective is on learning and knowledge acquisition to reduce uncertainty [17], which include the potential and frequent reformulation of the problem statement and project objectives. Both agile and design thinking not only describe a project management approach, but also a mindset [18].

In the innovation context, several scientists consider traditional project management as obsolete and redundant [19]. In contrast, supporters criticize the lack of agile management methods and progress assessment of agile approaches [20]. They regard traditional project management as a general standard to develop, control and assess projects without losing track by continuously defining new objectives [21]. Further approaches try to link the advantages of traditional and modern approaches and investigate in hybrid approaches like agile-stage-gate processes [10]. There is a growing understanding that the project method has to be tailor-made: individually selected, customized and implemented [22]. First approaches investigate in project parameters like project size, team size, and expertise of project manager to identify the best methodology [7]. Nevertheless, context and project needs change during the project lifecycle, and few insights have been published on how to tackle these changing needs appropriately [9].

4 A Decision Aid Model for Innovation Project Management

In order to investigate our hypothesis expressed in Sect. 2, we define a simple model that help situate the current management needs of innovation projects, dependent on the type of uncertainty they are confronted with. Our 2-by-2 innovation project management model is spanned on two axes representing the uncertainty regarding the problem, and the uncertainty regarding the solution, respectively. Both axes are binary, i.e. the model differentiates between uncertainty regarding the problem and the solution (high/high), uncertainty regarding the problem (high/low), uncertainty regarding the solution (high/low), and no uncertainty (low/low). Following Ashby's law of requisite variety (1957), which states that to control a situation with certain variety, an approach with the same degree of variety is required [23]; we assigned the four innovation project management approaches (IPMA) proposed in Sect. 2 to the four spaces as shown in Fig. 1.

4.1 Experimentation

If defining the problem and developing a solution is the challenge, the project team has to focus on experimentation to gain a clearer picture of the current situation as quickly as possible. Hence, the current central focus is on experience-based learning and less on the outcome of the project. Based on the experiential learning model of Kolb (1984) project teams learn through "the process whereby knowledge is created through the transformation of experience", which necessitates the four steps of observing and feedback, reflecting insights, synthesizing ideas, and building prototypes.

Experimentation within innovation projects means gaining a deep understanding of the context, the scope and the needs by analyzing the potential users or customers e.g. by observation or feedback. Thus, new ideas can be synthesized and corresponding hypotheses derived and tested. Exploring these ideas by building prototypes allows testing the hypotheses. This experiential learning circle can be repeated multiple times until the project teams eliminate uncertainty regarding the needs or the solution and should move to a more target-oriented approach. Thus, driving an innovation project by experimentation means to fluidly move back and forth between the concrete and abstract perspective as well as between the reflective and active mode. Order and time spent in each mode don´t follow an established standard [24]. In case of a high level of uncertainty (solution and problem uncertainty) this methodical approach of experimentation allows rapid and unrestricted learning from the environment. This explains why this approach is of high relevance in the context of radical innovation.

Experimentation is not based on key performance indicators, it is rather focused on the learning progress which makes it difficult to measure and evaluate the performance of a project team. With this approach managers delegate the definition of the scope and

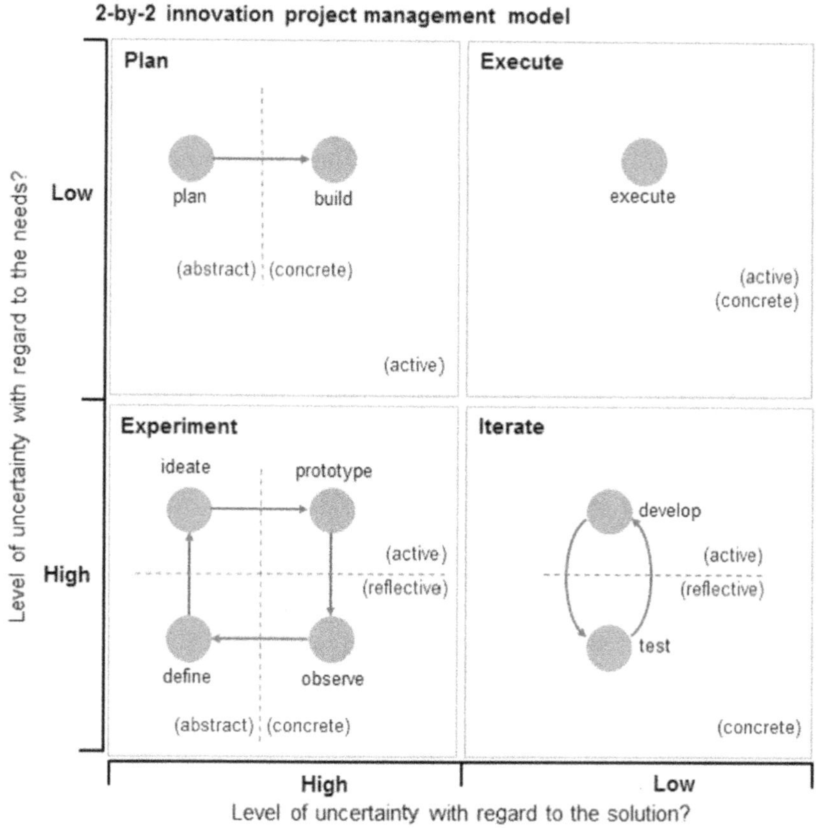

Fig. 1. 2-by-2 model: methodical innovation project management approaches

the problem (allow teams to pivot) as well as the development of a solution to the project teams. To guide teams under these conditions as well as to gain insights about their performance, managers have to make sure that teams always start with the most critical assumption. Furthermore, teams need to move fast and in small steps. This can be ensured by providing short timeframes and a shoestring budget, and/or by the engagement of a coach. Managers can organize frequent feedback sessions or demonstrations in order to ensure that teams don´t remain isolated. Managers have to guide teams as they are moving fluidly between active and reflective mode as well as abstract and real mode (e.g. by placing requirements regarding user exchange intensity). In particular in innovation projects performance is driven by team diversity, which can be presumed by team composition conditions. Basically, the manager has to keep on the sideline to avoid limiting or influencing the possibility space. The key players within experimentation are the project team and the users/ customers.

4.2 Iteration

Iterating within innovation projects means to focus on understanding and defining the needs of the customer to execute the defined solution. As the solution is already well defined there is no focus needed on synthesizing further ideas. In comparison to experiential learning, the learning process through *iteration* is only solution-oriented. To learn as effectively as possible, teams should invest time and resources in building a solution (active mode) and testing their solution through customer feedback and observation (reflective mode). Doing so teams iterate more rapidly in the "express test cycle" between the active and reflective mode and stay in the concrete mode to continuously improve their solution and problem understanding. With regard to the lack of problem understanding, changes within the project are inevitable. Thus, adaptability to change based on learning is a central characteristic of iteration [25–27]. Moving between feedback and solution is often the case of technology push: a new technology is pushed in the organization, whereas the related need still needs to be identified [28].

Iteration like experimentation is focused on learning as it is difficult to measure and evaluate project team performance. In case of iterating the manager delegates how to define the problem. By defining the solution in advance, restricting the budget as well as joint prioritization of features that should be taken into account, the manager is able to provide guidance. Feedback meetings with customers or users ensure the learning progress with regard to the problem understanding. To evaluate the learning progress, dialogues with the team should be focused on the functioning of the solution. In this case, project manager, users and/or customers are key players close to the project team.

4.3 Planning

Planning within innovation projects means to focus on the coordination and prioritization of tasks to develop a solution when the problem is clearly known. Departing from a clearly defined problem, the project team has to link and structure various data to schedule related tasks. Based on experience through preceding and similar tasks, teams are able to abstract the available information and identify patterns. Through the structuring of data, different solution opportunities can be identified. The learning process can be reduced to the active mode: project teams abstract patterns from the available information base to synthesize a plan for the development of solutions.

Planning is focused on the abstraction of given information regarding problem understanding. The manager delegates the development of the solution and project deliverables. Demanding for a specific degree of detail with respect to the project plan or a clear budget restriction, managers are able to provide guidance to the project team. The manager is able to monitor the progress by evaluating if project deliverables have been achieved on time. Optionally the manager is able to summon a steering committee to guide the project. The manager as well as the project team play key roles.

4.4 Execution

Execution means making use of the knowledge about the defined problem and known solution without further learning or planning. Based on a clear understanding coming from available information, prior experience or e.g. a clearly defined guideline, performance is no coincidence. If, for example, an IT expert has to set up a 100 web sites under same conditions, the implementation is a pure execution without further planning (for how to implement each web site) or further feedback loops. In case of a clear understanding of what is needed and how to solve the problem, any experimenting, iterating or planning is considered waste.

Execution can therefore be completely delegated by the manager. Guidance is given by established routine processes and standards. Face-to-face meetings or team meetings can be used as a framework for discussing irregularities. The key players are the operating experts/team members.

In a typical innovation project, these four generic IPMAs have to be applied dynamically at different project stages to strategically tackle uncertainty. The main objective of an innovation project is the outcome, the customer value, which can only delivered by execution. To achieve the intended outcome in an innovation project requires dealing with different sources of uncertainty (regarding problem or solution definition or both), whereas each of the presented approaches is able to deal with one specific source of uncertainty. Due to the continuously changing project needs, managers can neither stick to one single approach nor to a standardized order of approaches. Instead, managers have to ensure that the approach is flexible adapted to the relating subprojects′ needs to drive the project successfully to execution. Further flexibility is required to adapt the basis to assess, guide the project team and their way of communication depending on the selected project management approach.

5 Corporate Innovation Case Study

We applied the 2-by-2 innovation project management model in the context of a German major corporation in the pharmaceutical and chemical industry. In order to analyze the methodical procedure of the teams related the project maturity and context we developed a quantitative questionnaire and a supplementary interview guideline based on qualitative questions. The questionnaire consists of 45 questions, subdivided in questions that address (1) the project charter (2) project maturity (3) project context, and (4) project management approach. The majority of the questions were scored on a 5-item-Likert-scale (strongly agree (1) – strongly disagree (5)) and were reviewed by colleagues and survey experts regarding practical understanding, logic errors, etc. To evaluate the results, we defined an “ideal” answer for each question to develop stereotype context and project management approach profiles (as defined by our model). Based on the ideal answer we calculated the distance of the answer to the ideal answer for each IPMA. For the visualization we plot the inverted results in a network diagram, whereas a value of 0 means a maximum distance (no IPMA characteristic) and a value of 4 means no distance (maximum IPMA characteristic).

The four selected innovation projects analyzed in this present paper have been ongoing for about seven months (A, B, D; 30 months for C) and have reached different technology maturity levels (TRL) [29]: 4 (A), 5 (B), 9 (C), and 7 (D). Two of which are based in the IT domain (C, D). Each of the projects is supported by a corporate innovation initiative with funding and/or consultancy. The projects were intended to be implemented at one individual location (A), at many locations in one county (B, C) and globally (D). The project team size varies between 2 (A, B) and 4 (C, D) team members, which are by the majority located in different departments but similar business units and functions (A, B, D). Only one project (D) consists of 2 external and 2 internal partners located in different business units. All projects were supported by an innovation coach in the beginning (A, B) or throughout the complete duration so far (C, D). Together with the project leaders, we identified 3 (A, B, D) and 5 (C) crucial project phases based on important milestones and turning points. Each project leader and further project team members were asked to evaluate each phase by sequentially using the developed questionnaire.

Team A started their project with a defined problem. The team differentiates three phases derived from central turning points that characterize the project (need definition, ideation & prototyping). In phase 1 the context results state a relatively high and balanced approach of plan, iteration and experimentation and less execution, whereas the results of the used IPMA only state a high level of experimentation and iteration. In phase 2 the results of context and used IPMA are overlapping and balanced at medium level in all four IPMAs. In phase 3 the context results stay on the same extension level, whereas the results of experimentation and iteration state a moderate increase and decrease of experimentation.

Team B started their project with a defined solution to which they originally tried to identify a relating problem. Up to the time of interviewing the team differentiates three phases derived from central turning points during the project (problem definition, development, and prototyping). Starting from balanced values in experimentation, iteration, and planning and a lower value in execution, the characteristics of the results change during the named project phases. Therefore, the importance of experimentation and iteration continuously decreases (context and approach related questions) during the project. On the other hand the importance of execution and planning continuously increases.

Team C started their project based on an identified business problem which the team tried to address by a fitting solution respectively a fitting technology. The team differentiated five project phases (problem definition, ideation, experimentation, developing a working solution, piloting). In the phase 1 the team tried to frame the problem based on different stakeholder definitions. At the same time they were focused on identifying a technical solution. The results in this phase are characterized by a high discrepancy between the context and the used IPMA (see Fig. 2). Whereas the context scores the highest value in experimentation, the team focused mainly on execute and plan, In phase 2 and 3 the team started to involve customers to ensure that the focused technology (solution) fits to the customer needs. In the course of the project phase two to five the values of context and approach results are largely overlapping. In total, the values of experimentation and iteration increase, whereas the values of execution and planning decrease.

Team D had no clear understanding of the user needs neither of the solution at the start of the project. The team differentiates three project phases (experimentation, prototyping/funding, developing a working solution). In the phase 1 the questionnaire results regarding the context state a high level of experimentation, iteration, and relatively high level of plan and a low level of execution. This is in contrast with the

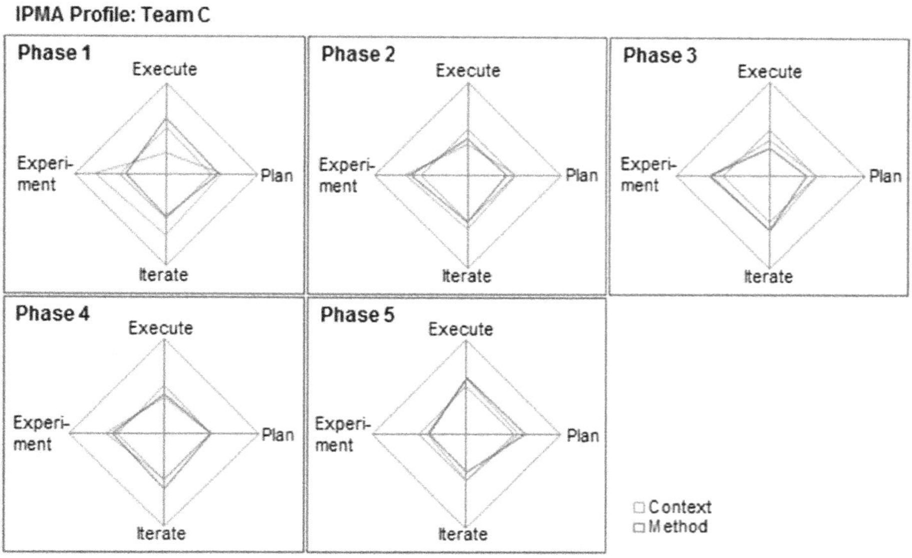

Fig. 2. Results - IPMA Profile: Team C

results of the used approach which indicates a lower level of planning and iteration, whereas the values of experimentation are overlapping. In the course of the project the values of execution, planning and iteration are overlapping, whereas the context results consistently state a higher level of experimentation than the team really used. In sum the values of experimentation and iteration decrease, whereas the values of planning and execution first decrease and later increase.

Summarizing the results of all teams allows comparing the distance of the really used approach to the context stated approach of each IPMA. This indicates a value of 0.42, for execution, 0.40 for planning, 0.34 for iteration, and 0.37 for experimentation with a maximum deviation of 4. In the course of the projects, the outlier values diminish in each IPMA.

Comparing the four innovation projects, there are several patterns that support our hypothesis: (a) the level of experimentation decreases continuously with increasing project maturity; (b) the level of iteration is higher at the beginning of the project than at the last measuring point but can increase during the project; (c) the level of planning is relatively balanced during the project; (d) the level of execution increases continuously with increasing project maturity. The IPMA development of team B, which discarded their first idea, represents one of several events in which a team makes flexible use of IPMAs. In addition to that, the results point out that the teams make use of all four IPMAs in each phase, varying only the strength and focus of the respective IPMA.

6 Implication on Project Management Method Application

The 2-by-2 IPMA serves as a decision making tool for innovation project managers, as their projects moving from one phase to another, and their context change dynamically. In order to provide guidance for the selection of the appropriate IPMA, we provide a mapping of IPMA characteristics and examples to each of the four model areas in Fig. 3.

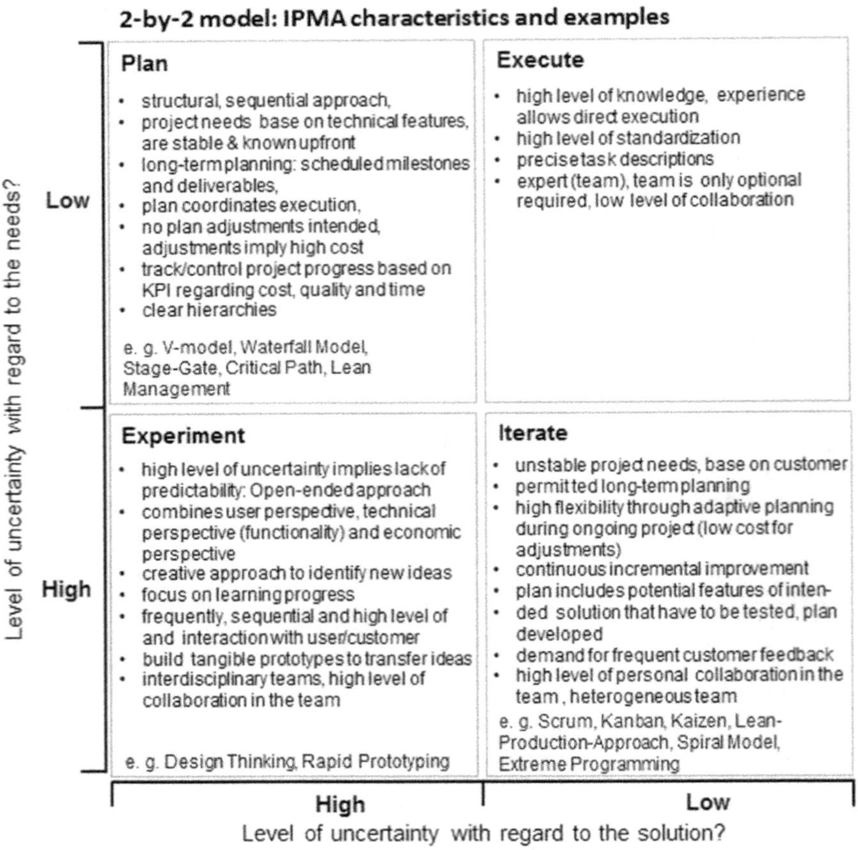

Fig. 3. IPMA characteristics and examples

The 2-by-2 model classifies the IPMA on two axes that characterize the degree and type of uncertainty and, hence, risk in an innovation project. In principle, innovation projects have to deal with uncertainties, whereas each of the four IPMAs represents a portfolio of methodologies that are in particular efficient in dealing with one specific type and level of uncertainty. In other words, the choice and starting point of an IPMA depends on the characteristic of uncertainty. Moreover, the "exit point" of the IPMAs creates a further intersection. Starting from a low level of uncertainty, the IPMA executions starts and ends in executing in the active and concrete mode. Planning also ends in the active and concrete mode by translating the plan to building. Additionally, iteration and experimentation imply the continuously developing or building of a solution/prototype in the active and concrete mode. With decreasing uncertainty the focus in this mode increases. At the end the successful implementation of a project as requirement of creating added value can only become true on the real market with a working solution in the active and concrete mode. When choosing the IPMA, managers have to assess uncertainty which has to be efficiently reduced by fitting IPMA. With decreasing uncertainty the mangers have to ensure an IPMA shift to a more execution-focused IPMA.

7 Conclusion and Outlook

We have proposed a model that supports innovation project managers in selecting an IPMA that fits to the current temporary innovation project needs. The central elements of our model are four fundamental IPMAs *Experiment*, *Iterate*, *Plan*, and *Execute* differing by their level of uncertainty regarding the project´s needs and the solution. The model is complemented by a question catalogue to identify the fitting IPMA derived from the current context and maturity level of the project and its subprojects. We applied our model in a corporate context that is representative for huge and complex organizations. It has to be noted that our results are based on a small sample size and on interviews that underlie subjective interpretations. Our further research will therefore investigate a larger sample of both successful and failed projects in several companies and industries. We will also relate the model to uncertainty and risk management in order to further enlarge its usefulness and applicability as decision aid tool.

References

1. Williams, T.: Assessing and moving on from the dominant project management discourse in the light of project overruns. IEEE Trans. Eng. Manag. **52**(4), 497–508 (2005)
2. Wysocki, R.K.: Effective Project Management, 4th edn. Wiley, Hoboken (2007)
3. Crawford, G.C., Kreiser, P.M.: Corporate entrepreneurship strategy: extending the integrative framework through the lens of complexity science. Small Bus. Econ. **45**(2), 403–423 (2015)
4. Ireland, R.D., Covin, J.G., Kuratko, D.F.: Conceptualizing corporate entrepreneurship strategy. Entrepreneurship Theory Pract. **33**(1), 19–46 (2009)
5. PMI: https://www.pmi.org/-/media/pmi/documents/public/pdf/learning/thought-leadership/pulse/pulse-of-the-profession-2018.pdf. Accessed 01 Apr 2018
6. Cheema, A., Shahid, A.A.: Customizing project management methodology. In: 9th International Multitopic Conference, IEEE INMIC 2005, pp. 1–6. IEEE (2005)
7. Cockburn, A.: Selecting a project's methodology. IEEE Softw. **17**(4), 64–71 (2000)
8. Kolb, D.A.: Experiential Learning: Experience as the Source of Learning and Development. Prentice-Hall, New Jersey (1984)

9. Špundak, M.: Mixed agile/traditional project management methodology – reality or illusion? Procedia - Soc. Behav. Sci. **119**, 939–948 (2014)
10. Cooper, R.G., Sommer, A.F.: Agile-Stage-Gate: new idea-to-launch method for manufactured new products is faster, more responsive. Ind. Market. Manag. **59**, 167–180 (2016)
11. de Carvalho, M.M., Patah, L.A., de Souza Bido, D.: Project management and its effects on project success: cross-country and cross-industry comparisons. Int. J. Proj. Manag. **33**(7), 1509–1522 (2015)
12. Cooper, R.G.: The stage-gates idea-to-launch process: update, what's new, and NexGen systems. J. Prod. Innov. Manag. **25**(3), 213–232 (2008)
13. Lindvall, M., et al.: Empirical Findings in Agile Methods. In: Wells, D., Williams, L. (eds.) XP/Agile Universe 2002. LNCS, vol. 2418, pp. 197–207. Springer, Heidelberg (2002). https://doi.org/10.1007/3-540-45672-4_19
14. Lockwood, T.: Design Thinking: Integrating Innovation, Customer Experience, and Brand Value, 3rd edn. Allworth Press, New York (2009)
15. Sage, D., Dainty, A., Brookes, N.: A critical argument in favor of theoretical pluralism: project failure and the many and varied limitations of project management. Int. J. Proj. Manag. **32**(4), 544–555 (2014)
16. Brown, T.: Design thinking. Harv. Bus. Rev. **86**(6), 84 (2008)
17. Liedtka, J.: Innovative ways companies are using design thinking. Strateg. Leadersh. **42**(2), 40–45 (2014)
18. Serrador, P., Pinto, J.K.: Does Agile work? A quantitative analysis of agile project success. Int. J. Proj. Manag. **33**(5), 1040–1051 (2015)
19. Lenfle, S., Loch, C.: Lost roots: how project management came to emphasize control over flexibility and novelty. Calif. Manag. Rev. **53**(1), 32–55 (2010)
20. Lenfle, S.: Floating in space? On the strangeness of exploratory projects. Proj. Manag. J. **47** (2), 47–61 (2016)
21. Gillier, T., Hooge, S., Piat, G.: Framing value management for creative projects: an expansive perspective. Int. J. Proj. Manag. **33**(4), 947–960 (2014)
22. Charvat, J.: Project Management Methodologies: Selecting, Implementing, and Supporting Methodologies and Processes for Projects. Wiley, New Jersey (2003)
23. Ashby, W.R.: An Introduction to Cybernetics. Chapman & Hall Ltd., New York (1957)
24. Beckman, S.L., Barry, M.: Innovation as a learning process: embedding design thinking. Calif. Manag. Rev. **50**(1), 25–56 (2007)
25. Heck, J., Rittiner, F., Steinert, M., Meboldt, M.: Iteration-based performance measurement in the fuzzy front end of PDPs. Procedia CIRP **50**, 14–19 (2016)
26. de Weck, O.L., Eckert, C.: A classification of uncertainty for early product and system design. In: International Conference on Engineering Design, ICED 2007, 28–31 August 2007, Cite des Sciences et de l'industrie, Paris (2007)
27. McManus, H., Hastings, D.: A framework for understanding uncertainty and its mitigation and exploitation in complex systems. In: INCOSE International Symposium, Rochester, NY, vol. 15, no. 1, pp. 484–503 (2005)
28. Åstebro, T., Dahlin, K.: Effects of expected demand, technological opportunity, appropriability and competitive conditions on invention commercialization. In: DRUID Summer Conference 2003, Copenhagen, pp. 12–14 (2003)
29. Mankins, J.C.: Technology readiness assessments: a retrospective. Acta Astronaut. **65**(9-10), 1216–1223 (2009)

Crises Respondence Strategies for Companies in the Automotive Industry in Order to Maintain Their Reputation

Madlen Doberstein(✉)

3500 Krems an der Donau, Austria
madlen.doberstein@imc-krems.eu

Abstract. Companies face crises. These crises have to be managed in order to keep damage from the firm's reputation. A variety of crises already occurred. As individual as every crisis is, all crises have one common outcome - the learning effect. Organizations can learn from their own crises but also from competitor's crises by adjusting their crisis management strategies. Management practices towards the response of crises were discussed by experts. The experts agreed on a fast response strategy. Furthermore, a wide range of information has to be communicated to the public. The expert's suggestions can adjust crises response strategies in order to keep the negative impact of crises on organizations as minor as possible.

Keywords: Crisis management · Crises · Automotive industry Reputation

1 Introduction

There is no organization what is immune to crises [1]. Especially the automotive industry suffers from crises. From 2000–2011 more than half a billion cars were produced [2]. About one-fourth of these cars needed to be recalled [3]. Crises and recalls in various cases are connected. The crises can affect the company's reputation [4]. The impact of crises towards companies can be minimized or prevented by the learning effect of other crises [5]. This research paper investigates the management methods of past and present crises in the automotive industry.

In order to suggest crisis response strategies, experts regarding the topic were interviewed. The purpose of this research is to adjust former crisis response strategies in order to improve future crisis management actions.

The suggestions towards the crisis management can be applied to crises in the automotive industry. Moreover, these suggestions can also be applied to other business sectors.

X. Larrucea et al. (Eds.): EuroSPI 2018, CCIS 896, pp. 631–639, 2018.
https://doi.org/10.1007/978-3-319-97925-0_53

1.1 Reasons for a Crisis

Several factors can lead to a crisis within an organization. Seymour and Moore narrowed the reasons down to two main triggers [6]. Crises can occur when the company is unprepared and when surprise and weaknesses in an organization come together [6].

Furthermore, comfortableness can lead to crises. Companies face risks on a regular basis. Therefore, it can happen that the companies become too comfortable and familiar with the risks [6]. The risk then can evolve into a crisis [6].

Problematic situations can lead to crises when an individual or a small team tries to manage the situation on their own [6].

Another trigger of a crisis can be not taking action when a difficult situation comes up [6]. The recognition of a crisis which slowly develops is more difficult than suddenly occurring crises. In both cases, the company has to feel responsible and has to take action [6].

An organizational misdeed can also result in a crisis [7]. Three forms of an organizational misdeed exist: The organizational misdeed without injuries, the organizational misdeed which involves injuries and the organizational misdeed which violates the regulatory or legal law [7]. In all three forms decides the management on actions which can bring the stakeholders knowingly in a dangerous situation. Only the outcome of the actions varies [7].

The technical breakdown can be a trigger for a crisis [7]. It is caused by a technical error of the equipment used [7]. A typical reason for a recall is a technical breakdown [7]. The human breakdown is caused by a mistake conducted by a human [7]. Also, the human breakdown is likely to cause recalls [7].

1.2 Crisis Response Strategies

Common crisis response strategies are the integration response strategy, the mortification response strategy, the suffering response strategy, the distance and the denial response strategy [8]. When the integration crisis response strategy is applied, the company accepts the crisis and searches for acceptance of the public [8]. A company applies the mortification crisis response strategy when the company searches for the public's forgiveness [8]. The suffering crisis response strategy is applied when a company tries to represent itself as the victim of the situation [8]. The distance crisis response strategy is a strategy where the company tries to take a step back from the crisis. Distance between the crisis and the company is the aim of this strategy [8]. In case a company denies a current crisis, the company applies the denial crisis response strategy [8].

2 Expert Interviews

For the purpose of this research, it was decided that expert interviews are the most reliable source to gain multiple points of view on the same topic.

Three expert interviews were held. All interviewed experts have specific knowledge, expertise, and experience in the relevant fields of this research.

One crisis and communication management consultant was interviewed in order to apply his professional suggestions. The suggestions of the consultant relate to the crisis management itself and to the communication towards other parties. The consultant contributed suggestions of crisis response strategies he could adapt for several years in his professional career.

The second interviewee is a marketing and communication expert. The professor teaches, inter alia, marketing and communication subjects. With the professor's knowledge and understanding of promotional strategies and customer's aspects, further suggestions could be included in this paper. How to communicate to the public can influence the development of the crisis and therefore the firm's reputation.

To gain a broad range of points of view and in order to gain a reliable result of this research paper, the psychologic perspective of crisis management strategies was included. A business psychologist contributed psychological strategies how companies should act in times of a crisis. The psychological corporate interaction with the public depends on how a crisis will be acknowledged by the public. Therefore psychological interaction has a great impact on the firm's repetition.

Due to confidentiality reasons, the names of the interviewees were changed.

2.1 The Most Appropriate Timing for Taking Action

The timing when to take action is of high importance to the development of the crisis. Therefore, it is also a highly difficult step [9].

The company first should try to gather as much information about the situation as possible. Therefore, internal investigations have to be conducted [10]. As soon as the decision makers know what happened, how the situation transformed into a problem and who was involved, the decision maker can take first actions.

Another difficult and important timing for taking action occurs when it comes to the public announcement of the situation. The point in time when the company can and wants to go out to the public and announces its problems differs. Every crisis and every company is at least a little different [9]. Independent of the company and the type of crisis they face, it is suggested that the company should inform the public as soon as possible in order to minimize the negative impact on the firm's reputation [9].

2.2 The Public Announcement

The way how the public announcement is conducted is from high importance and can have a great impact on the public's opinion towards the crisis and therefore towards the company.

The announcement should happen as soon as possible. In the best case, the organization's internal investigations already conducted enough information to have an overview of the situation. When companies could already gathered an overview of the situation, the managers are more likely to be prevented from becoming panic [10]. If the investigations could not lead to an overview and therefore to an understanding of the crisis, a public announcement is nevertheless suggested [9].

At that point in time, the firm's attitude towards the truth is important. Since saying the truth has a great impact on the customer's reaction towards a crisis [4]. Even if the company could not find out enough information to describe and inform in an adequate manner about the situation, the company still has to go out to the public and announce at least that something happened [10]. Furthermore, the company's spokesperson can calm the public by announcing that as soon as the company finds out more information, the newly gathered information will be then immediately published by the firm [10].

Truth is also important in the opposite way. If a company found out information about the situation it should be published. Concealing the findings in order to protect the firm can sometimes have a greater negative impact when the public finds out about the concealed information as when the firm would have went out with the information by their own [9, 11].

Going out by choice can also help by the apology towards the public. If the company goes out by choice and announces that they feel sorry about the situation and what happened, the public will be more likely to believe and forgive the company [9]. If a third party found out about the crisis and announces the problem to the public the company cannot express in a trustful and believable manner that they feel sorry about what has happened [9]. This will result in a more complex crisis situation since the company has to react to the announcements and cannot shape the message in a way they would have shaped it [9].

In both cases, when the company went out on their own and when another party published their situation, the company has to inform the public about their actions. It is suggested that the company should announce that internal clarification methods were already implemented in order to find out about the problem and to correct the situation [10].

From the psychological point of view, it is also important to add to the announcement of the problem the compensation offers which the firm offers in order to appease the affected customers [10].

2.3 The Apology

The apology is an important part of the crisis management. It should be included in one of the first sentences of the public announcement. Therefore, it has to be conducted at the very beginning of the process of the crisis [9].

The apology is about the profound concern the company feels regarding the crisis. The spokesperson, mostly the CEO of the company has to share the feelings of the whole organization. He should say, and mean, that the organization feels sorry about the circumstances and what has happened [9].

The CEO has to express his feelings in a way that the public and especially the affected stakeholders feel empathy for him [1]. This empathy would lead to a lowered negative impact on the firm's reputation. This furthermore would lead to a less complex rebuilding phase [9].

Moreover, the CEO has to show that he feels sorry about the situation [9]. Visible actions have to be taken. Even if the CEO was not directly responsible for the situation a resignation would be a meaningful action to show his concern [9]. The CEO is in a certain way responsible for everything that happens in his company. Therefore, he is party liable and needs to bear the consequences [9].

Another tactic to keep the harm away from the company is the scapegoat tactic [10]. If only a few people of the company are responsible for the crisis, this tactic can be applied [10].

The few responsible people are fired immediately after the crisis came up [10]. The public should get to know that the responsible people are fired. This will then bring the customer's trust towards the company back since the company seems to be on the right track again.

2.4 The Confession of the Mistake

In order to minimize the impact on the firm's reputation, the confession needs to be taken seriously and with respect. Therefore, the truth must be communicated.

A speech should be held by the CEO of the company which should include the fault, the false ambitions the company was striving for and the bad communication the company used [10]. In case rumors already occurred among this crisis, the misunderstandings have to be named and corrected [10].

The company has to take three actions which are important [9]:

1. The organization has to state that they take the full responsibility and they have to announce that they feel sorry [9].

   The customers need to feel understood in order to forgive the company [9].

2. The sincerity phase is important for the public and therefore for the company [9].

The company has to show that they take the problem seriously. This expresses that the company tries its best to manage the situation to everybody's satisfaction [9].

3. The reflection and learning phase also has to be included in the confession of the mistake [9].

Within this phase the crisis, moreover the problem, will be reflected in order to decide on the best solution for the situation [9]. In the automotive industry, the most common solution is a recall campaign of the cars [9]. The company tries to find out what the problem was, how the problem happened and what to change in order to prevent a repetition of the problem.

The reflection and learning phase is the prevention phase for possible crisis [9].

2.5 The Duration of the Crisis

The duration of the crisis which the company faces has an impact on the firm's reputation [9]. The duration of a crisis can be shortened by the amount and timing of published information. In case the company publishes all the relevant information they could find out, the public would be satisfied [9]. The public will have more trust towards the company due to the fact, that they know the company is honest and does not conceal any information [9, 11].

Furthermore, the newspapers will not have a steady information flow of new facts they can write about [9]. In case the company can and will give a satisfying amount of information at the beginning of the crisis, the newspapers might write about the crisis for a few weeks [9]. During that time the company will be steadily confronted with the crisis. After these few weeks, the media will not have any unpublished facts left what means they will not report about the crisis anymore [9].

Past crises have shown that the customers do not think about crises anymore when the media does not report about them anymore [9, 11].

The shorter the duration in which the crisis is a public topic, the lower the impact on the firm's reputation [9].

2.6 The Compensation

The compensation is an important factor of the rebuilding phase of the firm's repetition [9].

The crisis affected organization should concentrate on the way the crisis harmed the public, moreover, how the crisis harmed the company's affected customers [9].

In case of a crisis caused by a technical or human breakdown, the products should be recalled and the error should be corrected as soon as possible.

In case of an organizational misdeed, the compensation depends on the misdeed. If the organization's core value is part of the crisis, the compensation's focus should be on the core value [9]. Due to the fact that the core value the organization stands for is affected, the customer's trust and the organization's reliability could get harmed by the crisis [9].

If the core value of the firm is the environment and their protection and this value became harmed by the crisis, the company should focus on the environment [9].

Example: This can be done by supporting businesses who focus on the protection of the environment by supporting the deforestation. Furthermore, if the crisis decreased the quality of air, what can lead to lung problems the organization can donate money or equipment to hospitals which focuses on lung problems [9].

Furthermore, concentrate on the customer's concerns. In case of the automotive industry, customers are highly concerned when their own, private car is affected by a crisis and therefore affected by the recall campaign [10].

The purchase of a car is a very personal topic for private households. The acquisition affords for some customers a high financial engagement [10]. This personal engagement leads to emotions towards the recall [10]. These emotions will be affected by the crisis response management of the company. Moreover, the personal emotions will be mostly influenced by the reason of the crisis and by the compensation offered by the organization [10]. Therefore it is important to directly name in the announcement of the situation the firm's compensation offers [10].

Not only the CEO and spokesperson should inform about the compensation actions and therefore positive actions the company offers [10]. Additionally, well trained and well-known people should inform the public. This can be former politicians who know how to communicate with the public [10]. These former politicians are often invited to discussions which are broadcasted on the television [10].

2.7 The Organization's Employees

The employees are important for a company. Not only to create value. Furthermore, to maintain the value during difficult times which companies sometimes face.

A meeting with all employees of the organization should be held early in the process of the crisis [10]. The employees have to be informed about the situation. Third parties what can be family members, friends or the media can confront them and ask them out about the crisis [10]. The employees therefore, have to be trained that they can react to the possible confrontation [10]. The information what the employees give to the third parties can have a impact on the organization [10]. The media could ask complicated questions. In case the employee does not know what to say or says something what she or he thinks might be formed to a statement which will have a negative influence on the firm's reputation. Therefore, the employees have to be informed as soon as possible. Additionally, they need to be taught that it is no problem to be confronted with this topic since there is nothing the employees have to concern about [10].

Furthermore, the employees need to be well informed since they might fear to lose their jobs [10]. Due to that fear, the employees might react to the possible confrontation emotionally [10]. A negative and emotional answer can result in a worst case communication scenario [10].

Additionally, the CEO should emphasize gratefulness towards the employees. This will prevent the employees to feel negative emotions towards the organization. Furthermore, the employees can help with the firm's reputation phase [10]. Employees who stay with the company even in difficult times are important for the company. By conducting their work the employees help the company [10]. Furthermore, the loyalty of the employees expresses to the public that the employees are satisfied with their employer. Even in difficult times they stay loyal. This will be recognized by the public and the company will be recognized as a good employer [10]. This positive employer image will then help the company in different ways. The company might not face a headcount shortage due to a decrease of applications [10].

2.8 The Learning Effect

The learning effect is an essential part of the recovery phase [9]. Furthermore, it is important for the public. In case the company wants to learn from the crisis, the company regrets that situations resulted in a crisis. When a company which faced a crisis tries to learn from the crisis in order to avoid a repetition of the crisis. This willingness to change emphasizes the acceptance of the responsibility.

Furthermore, an improvement of the faulty processes, systems or organizational culture must be shown to the public [10]. What the company has to improve depends on the company and on the crisis they face. Independent from the crisis every company has to show that they learned from the crisis and adapted their processes, systems or culture [9].

2.9 The Competitors

When a company faces a crisis the reputation of the company can be negatively affected [4].

This impact can have many forms. The customers might lose the trust towards the company [11]. The core value of the firm can be affected what lowers the firm's reliability [9]. The overall result of the impact will be shown on the sales numbers of the firm. This furthermore will have an impact on the wellbeing of the company [4].

Competitors might like to take the opportunity to improve their own reputation as long as the competitors are not in the strong competitive market position they used to be [10].

Competitors can influence the crisis situation of other organizations by keeping the crisis alive as long as possible [9].

3 Conclusions

Companies which face crises need to apply crisis response strategies in order to manage the situation with the best outcome possible.

This research paper suggested possible response options. The purpose of the suggested response strategies is to achieve a minimal or no impact on the company's reputation in a crisis situation.

It is suggested that the affected company starts internal investigations as soon as a problem was recognized. Therefore, the company's decision makers have to take immediate actions.

As soon as the first overview of the problem was found out, a statement has to be given to the media and to the company's employees. The media should receive the information at the beginning of the crisis. No important information should be concealed or left out. The media can report about the situation as long as new information comes up. Therefore it is important to offer the information at the beginning of the crisis. After a certain time, the media reported about the crisis and no new information came up, the public will no longer think about the topic.

The employees need to be informed at the beginning of the crisis. Otherwise, they would not feel as an important part of the company. Additionally, the employees could fear their jobs. The employees could also give incomplete or false information to third parties who ask about the crisis. These third parties could than misinterpret the employee's message.

If a third party publishes information about the company's situation first, the company will not be held reliable by the public anymore. Following attempts to gain the public's trust and forgiveness might not be successful.

If the company recognizes that the investigations will need more time to show what happened, the company should not conceal the problem. The company should inform the public that something happened and that internal investigations were already introduced. Additionally, the company should mention that new information will be published as soon as new information could be found.

The announcement should include the mistake. This shows the courage of the company and that the company does not reject their responsibility. Additionally, the announcement of the compensation offers should be mentioned in the same statement where the company informs about the problem. The aim is to rebuild the public's trust.

Furthermore, the learning effect is important for the organization's future. The learning effect should improve the organization's weaknesses in order to prevent possible future crises.

References

1. Coombs, W.T.: Ongoing Crisis Communication Planning, Managing, and Responding, p. 1. SAGE Publications, Inc., London (1999)
2. Worldwide automobile production from 2000 to 2017 (in million vehicles). https://www.statista.com/statistics/262747/worldwide-automobile-production-since-2000/. Accessed 03 May 2018
3. Statistic Brain: Automobile Recall Statistics (2016). https://www.statisticbrain.com/automobile-recall-statistics/. Accessed 03 May 2018
4. NDR Nachrichten: Die VW-Abgas-Affäre: Eine Chronologie (2018). https://www.ndr.de/nachrichten/niedersachsen/braunschweig_harz_goettingen/Die-VW-Abgas-Affaere-eine-Chronologie,volkswagen892.html. Accessed 03 May 2018
5. FPO: Designing Post-Crisis Messages: Lessons for Crisis Response Strategies (2000). http://www.freepatentsonline.com/article/Review-Business/73183466.html. Accessed 03 May 2018
6. Seymour, M., Moore, S.: Effective Crisis Management Worldwide Principles and Practice. Cassell, London/New York (2000)
7. Coombs, W.T., Holladay, S.: Helping Crisis Managers Protect Reputational Assets. Manag. Commun. Q. **16**, 165–186 (2002)
8. Coombs, W.T., Holladay, S.J.: Communication and attributions in a crisis: an experimental study in crisis communication. J. Public Relat. Res. **8**, 279–295 (1996)
9. Wiesinger, A.: Personal Communication, 28 March 2018
10. Vogel, G.: Written Statement, 20 April 2018
11. Müller, P.: Written Statement, 9 April 2018

Theoretical Aspects of Consumer Metrics for Safety & Privacy

Thomas Fehlmann[1(✉)] and Eberhard Kranich[2]

[1] Euro Project Office, 8032 Zurich, Switzerland
info@e-p-o.com
[2] Euro Project Office, 47051 Duisburg, Germany

Abstract. Software metrics are a matter of academic interest. Consumers, software developers, and other practitioners seem less interested in functional size than, maybe, in quality metrics. Functional size is useful for predicting cost of development; however, with today's software development techniques and wide availability of open software, its size has become less important. Today, compliance, usability, and connectivity, are the most important cost drivers when developing software-intense products. However, functional size is essential for software testing. This is not yet widely accepted because today's best practices in testing focus on code coverage. However, software must be tested against functionality. Code is usually not available for cloud functionality such as map services. Software-intense products, for instance when driving autonomous vehicles, or powering robots for daily life, rely on functionality from various origins, not on embedded software alone. This paper sketches the theoretical framework for software metrics that help consumers assessing the level of safety and privacy of their software.

Keywords: Functional size · Software testing · Test goals · Test size
Test intensity · Test coverage · Software metrics

1 Introduction

In 1901, Bertrand Russel detected that any formalization of naïve set theory led to a contradiction (Fraenkel et al. 1973, pp. 156–157). The impact of this discovery is huge but contra intuitive. In intuitionistic interpretation[1], any system that describes a logic for objects without giving strict construction rules for them contains contradictions. The 20th century, but also the past, is full of vain attempts to construct righteous social systems that ended up in horrible contradictions against what was intended. Rule-based systems need arbitration in case its rules no longer apply or no longer provide the intended results.

[1] Intuitionism is an approach where mathematics is purely the result of the constructive mental activity of humans rather than the discovery of fundamental principles claimed to exist in an objective reality. That is, logic and mathematics are not considered analytic activities wherein deep properties of objective reality are revealed and applied but are instead considered the application of internally consistent methods used to realize more complex mental constructs, regardless of their possible independent existence in an objective reality (Wikipedia 2018).

X. Larrucea et al. (Eds.): EuroSPI 2018, CCIS 896, pp. 640–653, 2018.
https://doi.org/10.1007/978-3-319-97925-0_54

This holds as well for software. You cannot decide Turing's Halting Problem (Turing 1937). Consequently, no test suite can exist that, after applying all test cases to the system, will let us unambiguously determine whether the system consistently meets any given specification. The only certainty a test can assert is that all test cases constructed for all test stories found were passed. From this, it is not possible to derive that the system works always correctly.

However, if no system is completely testable, but some systems can do severe harm to humans or things, suppliers and programmers of such systems cannot made liable for all actions of such a system. A consequence of the Russel paradox is that no software-controlled system ever will be able to relieve humans from all responsibility for running such a system. In contrary, these systems will never replace humans but require even more knowledgeability and technical comprehension from its users.

To help understanding the systems in use, consumers of autonomous vehicles and other software-intense products need metrics that allow them judging the system's fitness for doing its tasks. These metrics must give confidence to the responsible consumer that his autonomous system has been, for example, tested for protecting her or his privacy and provides the expected safety. Since consumers bear the ultimate responsibility, never the autonomous system, these metrics matter. Such metrics are the premise sine qua non for autonomous vehicles to go into public operation.

Measuring security, or privacy protection, is not simple. Measuring test coverage for a system using cloud services on containerized virtual machines is far from being current practice; traditionally, testers test code and measure test coverage against code. But there is no code available for these interconnected services, even if it were, only the functionality used matters. And by thinking of map services for autonomous vehicles, this is a very specialized part of the overall map functionality available in the cloud.

This paper recalls existing approaches and shows how they fit together for a framework that can be used to generate autonomous tests in software-intense products used by consumers, and ultimately provide metrics that consumers can use to assess privacy protection and safety level of their products.

2 Research Questions

We remember that the advent of steam engines for locomotion and stationary power was closely linked to two successful news metrics

- Horse Power
- Velocity

The horse power was the unit needed to persuade customers to switch from horses to steam engines because the steam engines exhibited more power than horses for less money. James Watt used a tricky definition, one horse power being what horses could deliver for hours without fatigue (Hart-Davis 2012, p. 121). It helped him to market his new steam engines, persuading customers that they deliver as much or more than its predecessors, steam engines of older making, or horses.

Both metrics are intuitively acceptable by users, and both metrics conform to the VIM (ISO/IEC Guide 99:2007 2007) and the GUM (ISO/IEC CD Guide 98-3 2015).

None of these metrics depend from their environment; they are universal. James Watt was aware of the metrics system and of the modern metrical standards now standardized in the VIM.

Our research questions are:

1. What is the formal logic behind System & Software Testing?
2. What constitutes Safety & Privacy of systems & software?
3. How should the metric be presented to consumers?

The associated paper on practical aspects of consumer metrics (Fehlmann and Kranich, Practical Aspects of Consumer Metrics for Safety & Privacy 2018) addresses the second and the third question. This paper focuses on the first research question.

3 Software Metrics

3.1 Functional Sizing

We observed that testing should not be against code alone but against functionality. For testing complex systems such as those powering autonomous vehicles, code is only partially available, and safety-impacting functionality depends as much from functions hosted in the cloud than from the local controls powered by embedded software.

For measuring tests, it is therefore straightforward to size tests by functional software metrics. Sizing tests against code is inappropriate. Currently, four ISO standards exist that conform to the concepts of ISO/IEC 14143 (ISO/IEC 14143-1:2007 2007). From those, the ISO/IEC 20926 (ISO/IEC 20926:2009 2009), for long years maintained by the International Function Point Users Group (IFPUG), is the most popular.

The IFPUG Model for Functional Counts. The IFPUG model (ISO/IEC 20926:2009 2009) defines a count for functional size (Fig. 1).

The IFPUG model identifies five elementary types of data functions or transaction, categorizing each model element as either low, medium, or high complexity, each with a fixed size number associated. These categories depend from the amount of data handled by each element, and the number of data references. Consequently, the categories define a jumping count.

Thus, with IFPUG, adding data elements can let the complexity assessment jump from one level into another. Or, in contrary, adding new elements to the model sometimes is not reflected in the count. Nevertheless, the IFPUG model can also be used to count *Test Points,* a valid counting method for predicting test effort, proposed by Cagley (Cagley 2018).

The COSMIC Model for Functional Size. In contrary to the IFPUG count, the COSMIC standard (ISO/IEC 19761:2011 2011) complies to the VIM (ISO/IEC Guide 99:2007 2007) and the GUM (ISO/IEC CD Guide 98-3 2015). The VIM and the GUM define the metrics' basic concepts. A key requirement is that one can measure parts, and from the parts one can construct the size of the compose. That does not work with the IFPUG functional size count, but it works with the IFPUG model elements.

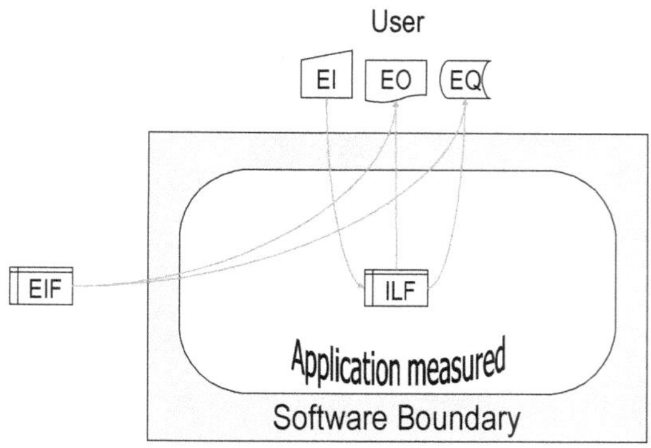

Fig. 1. IFPUG model – three transactions: EI, EO, EQ; two data functions ILF, EIF

The COSMIC standard identifies layers. The layers' boundaries detect the flow of data moving from one objects into another; however, the total count does not depend from how boundaries are drawn. Communication between functional processes require typically an **E**ntry and an e**X**it, with a device in between that connects the two processes, regardless whether data movements cross an application boundary or not (Fig. 2).

A **R**ead or a **W**rite moves data between functional processes and persistent data stores. Every data movement transports a Data Group, identifying the data moved from one object to another. Obviously, the content of those data groups matters for privacy protection; however, it also can affect safety up to some degree.

While IFPUG describes software functionality from a static viewpoint, COSMIC addresses dynamic aspects.

3.2 Strengths and Weaknesses of Software Metrics

Counting Requirements. Software metrics count *Functional User Requirements* (FUR). This makes them independent from implementation details and allows comparing different solutions. Moreover, one does not need a finished product for counting its functional size. If functional size controls development cost, a functional count can be used to predict development cost. Also, it allows managing the scope of a project, e.g., for dealing with deadlines, and controlling budget.
The problem with counting requirements is that today's agile software development process has no clearly defined initial set of requirements. And even if so, they are likely to change. Thus, counting agile development requires counting the backlog in sprints.

Repeatability. Software metrics are independent from the actual counter. Counters are properly educated and certified for the method. A user community maintains a counting practice manual, and provides examination for certified professionals, making it easy to decide whether a count is correct or not.

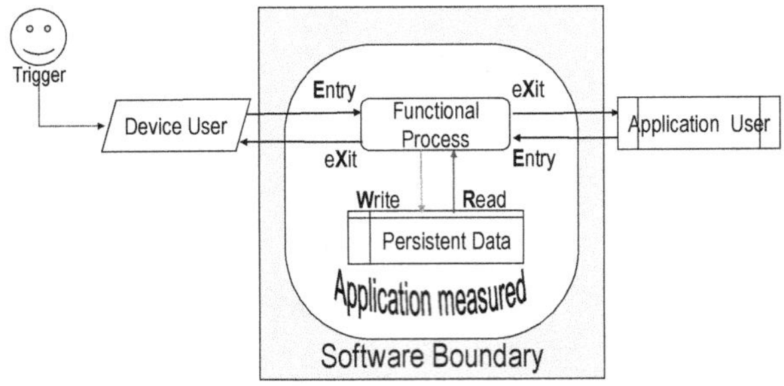

Fig. 2. The COSMIC model, with six data movements **E**ntry, e**X**it, **W**rite and **R**ead

The problem with that approach is that automatic counting is in principle not possible. Nevertheless, automatic counting methods exist but are approximations to the original manual count.

Independent from Implementation. Software metrics do not model implementation details. Functional size is the same for a single-user, closed application as for a mobile app using cloud services to calculate the same.

The concept of counting data movements in COSMIC matches the way modern software is build. Connecting *Docker* container service (Singh et al. 2018) can be modeled as a sequence of data movements between the containers.

For a sample software model, based on COSMIC, we refer to the authors' associated paper on practical aspects of consumer metrics (Fehlmann and Kranich, Practical Aspects of Consumer Metrics for Safety & Privacy 2018).

4 Test Metrics

As already mentioned, test metrics must refer to functionality not code. These days, the lack of internationally accepted test metrics is the biggest obstacle for autonomous vehicles, and for many more software-intense systems such as IoT.

4.1 What Is a Test?

A test is the execution of a piece of functionality with known input (test data) and known response (test response). For example, test data may contain a series of images, or a video; final test response is the action taken with the physical device (actuator).

There are many tests that can be executed to inspect intermediary results. Thus, tests can be combined, or branched. *Test Cases* identify

- Some specific test data;
- A sequence of data movements;
- Some known expected response.

Therefore, each test case has a functional size, given by the number of data movements executed in the test case. The COSMIC rules apply; if a data movement is executed more than once but with the same data group, it counts only once. For testing purpose, this makes sense.

Tests stories are represented by sets of test cases. Test cases are represented by the various test data $\delta_1, \ldots, \delta_n$ and the expected response ρ. For representing test data and response, any formal language $\mathcal{L}$ allowing to express predicates about the scope of the functionality under test will do.

$$\{\delta_1, \ldots, \delta_n\} \rightarrow \rho \tag{1}$$

A test case has a uniquely defined sequence of data movements executed during the test, and thus has a functional size.

Test size is denoted by vertical bars:

$$|\{\delta_1, \ldots, \delta_n\} \rightarrow \rho| \tag{2}$$

Changing test data results in a new test case; executing the same sequence of data movements twice with different test data is considered another, doubled, test, doubling test size as well. Total test size therefore always is much bigger than functional size, but it is the same metric, in case of COSMIC ISO/IEC 19761. The ratio between total test size and functional size is called *Test Intensity*.

4.2 Combining Tests

It is useful to combine tests, both for practical as for theoretical consideration. However, combining test cases with predicate formulas involves logical deductions and thus imposes domain dependencies. For a theory representing tests, applicable to autonomous vehicles and software-intense systems, this is not so useful. Neither is domain always well-defined, nor are logical dependencies between test representations of distinct parts of an autonomous vehicle easily compatible.

Since combinatorial explosion is one of the characteristics of all attempts to model-based testing and test automation (Bringmann and Krämer 2008), it is straightforward to use a mathematical theory that is called *Combinatory Logic* (Engeler 1981). This theory explains how to combine the topics of domain areas that have a cause-effect relationship. Examples for cause-effect relationship include test data and test responses (Fehlmann, Managing Complexity - Uncover the Mysteries with Six Sigma Transfer Functions 2016, p. 319).

The structure that we use for representing tests has been introduced by Engeler in 1979 (Engeler 1981). It generates a rich algebraic structure that generally models the representation of knowledge, and of tests. Compare with neural networks; e.g., van Gerven (van Gerven 2017).

5 The Formal Logic Behind System and Software Testing

The following section is an excerpt from Fehlmann (Fehlmann, Managing Complexity - Uncover the Mysteries with Six Sigma Transfer Functions 2016, p. 319ff) and Fehlmann (Fehlmann, Theorie und Anwendung der Kombinatorischen Logik 1981) and contains the theoretical foundation for testing. Understanding why, and how, tests can be combined and measured, opens a wide field for test optimization and enables test automation. Combinatory logic has so far never be applied to testing.

5.1 The Arrow Term Algebra

Let $\mathcal{L}$ be the set of all predicates about the scope of the functionality under test, as shown in Eq. (1). Predicates about test cases or test responses contain no free variables; i.e., they are propositions about the test stories in the domain addressed with our software model. For more information about formal logic, see Barwise et al. (Barwise et al. 1977).

Denote by $\mathcal{G}(\mathcal{L})$ the power set containing all *Arrow Terms* of the form

$$\{a_1, \ldots, a_n\} \rightarrow b \tag{3}$$

The left-hand side is a finite set of arrow terms and the right-hand side is a single arrow term. This definition is recursive; thus, it is necessary to establish a base definition saying that every proposition itself is considered an arrow term. The arrows of the arrow terms are distinct from the logical imply that some authors also denote by an arrow. The arrows denote cause-effect, not logical imply.

The formal, recursive, definition, written in set-theoretical language, is

$$\begin{gathered} \mathcal{G}_0(\mathcal{L}) = \mathcal{L} \\ \mathcal{G}_{n+1}(\mathcal{L}) = \mathcal{G}_n(\mathcal{L}) \cup \{\{a_1, \ldots, a_m\} \rightarrow b | a_1, \ldots, a_m, b \in \mathcal{G}_n(\mathcal{L}), m \in \mathbb{N}\} \end{gathered} \tag{4}$$

$\mathcal{G}(\mathcal{L})$ is the set of all (finite and infinite) subsets of the union of all $\mathcal{G}_n(\mathcal{L})$:

$$\mathcal{G}(\mathcal{L}) = \bigcup_{n \in \mathbb{N}} \mathcal{G}_n(\mathcal{L}) \tag{5}$$

The elements of $\mathcal{G}_n(\mathcal{L})$ are arrow terms of level n. Terms of level 0 are Predicates, terms of level 1 *Test Cases*. A *Test Story* is an element of $\mathcal{G}_n(\mathcal{L})$ that consists of level 1 terms only and is finite; if it is infinite, we call it *Test Strategy*. Hence, a test strategy is a potentially unlimited source of test cases. This definition is recursive, as before.

To avoid the many set-theoretical parenthesis, and to stress the constructive character of selecting test cases, the following notations are applied:

- a_i for a finite set of arrow terms,i denoting some finite indexing function for arrow terms;
- a_1 for a singleton set of arrow terms; i.e. $a_1 = \{a\}$ where a is an arrow term;
- $\emptyset$ for the empty set, such as in the arrow term $\emptyset \rightarrow a$.

An index always constructs a finite selection from any set of arrow terms. An index is a construction rule.

The indexing function cascades; thus, $a_{i,j}$ denotes the union of a finite number of m arrow term sets $(a_i)_j$

$$a_{i,j} = a_{i,1} \cup a_{i,2} \cup \ldots \cup a_{i,j} \cup \ldots \cup a_{i,m} = \bigcup_{j=1}^{m} a_{i,j} \tag{6}$$

With these writing conventions, $(x_i \rightarrow y)_j$ denotes a finite set of arrow terms having at least one arrow. This generalized form of a test story is called *Rule Set* (Fehlmann, Managing Complexity - Uncover the Mysteries with Six Sigma Transfer Functions 2016, p. 321). Thus, they are level 1 or higher, but still finite, because of the indexing function j.

Each element $x_i \rightarrow y$ of $(x_i \rightarrow y)_j$ denotes one generalized test case of some generalized test story $(x_i \rightarrow y)_j$. Every test story is obviously a rule set within $\mathcal{G}(\mathcal{L})$. The union of all possible test stories is infinite and therefore represents a test strategy in $\mathcal{G}(\mathcal{L})$.

However, many elements of $\mathcal{G}(\mathcal{L})$ do not resemble known test stories, such as $\left((x_i \rightarrow y)_j \rightarrow z\right)_k$. This term consists of arrow terms whose left hands is a finite test story; thus, it is a nested test. It says that when executing test story $(x_i \rightarrow y)_j$, there always holds some arrow term z_k as a test response. This can point at some interesting fail-safe characteristics of software. Another such example is $x_i \rightarrow (y_j \rightarrow z)$. This is a cascade of tests.

Subsequently, the association to the right for arrow terms is used:

$$x_i \rightarrow y_j \rightarrow z = x_i \rightarrow (y_j \rightarrow z) \tag{7}$$

With Eq. (7), tests can be combined, and their size added, as explained in Sect. 5.4 below.

5.2 The Application Operation

Let $M, N \in \mathcal{G}(\mathcal{L})$. Then application of M to N is defined by

$$M \bullet N = \{a | \exists b_i \rightarrow a \in M, b_i \subset N\} \tag{8}$$

In case of M as a rule set, and N as a set of level 0 predicates, this represents the selection operation that chooses those test stories $(b_i \rightarrow a)_j$ from rule set M that are applicable under the test preconditions N. However, the definition applies to all higher–level $\mathcal{G}(\mathcal{L})$ terms as well. As an example, consider $M = (b_i \rightarrow a)_j$ and another rule set $L = (d_k \rightarrow c)_p$, which represent two test stories. Then,

$$M \bullet L = \left\{ a | \exists (d_k \rightarrow c)_j \rightarrow a \in M, (d_k \rightarrow c)_j \subset L \right\} \tag{9}$$

Moreover,

$$(M \bullet L) \bullet N = \{ f | \exists g_j \rightarrow f \in ML, f_j \subset N \} \tag{10}$$

and thus

$$\begin{gathered} (M \bullet L) \bullet N = \\ \left\{ f | \exists (d_k \rightarrow c)_j \rightarrow g_i \rightarrow f \in M, (d_k \rightarrow c)_i \subset L, g_i \subset N \right\} \end{gathered} \tag{11}$$

Therefore, M selects those rules from L that are applicable to the arrow terms in N. Furthermore,

$$\begin{aligned} L \bullet (M \bullet N) &= \{ a | \exists b_i \rightarrow a \in L, b_i \subset M \bullet N \} \\ &= \left\{ a | \exists b_i \rightarrow a \in L, \exists \left(c_j \rightarrow b \right)_i \subset M, c_{j,i} \subset N \right\} \end{aligned} \tag{12}$$

Thus, the result of $L \bullet (M \bullet N)$ are those elements of N that contain test cases $b_i \rightarrow a \in L$ and for each b_i there are test stories $\left(c_j \rightarrow b \right)_i \subset M$. Applying a rule set selects those rules that apply to a given topic.

For the application operator, association is to the right:

$$(M \bullet L) \bullet N = M \bullet L \bullet N \neq M \bullet (L \bullet N) \tag{13}$$

5.3 Universality of the Arrow Term Algebra

Combinatory algebra is the simplest language for describing formal languages (Fehlmann, Theorie und Anwendung der Kombinatorischen Logik 1981). A Model of Combinatory Algebra (Engeler 1995, p. 91) is a structure that contains an application operation between its members and has non-trivial implementations of the two combinators **S** and **K**. The combinator **K** is the *Projection Combinator* and **S** the *Substitution Combinator*. The elements of the graph model are the power set $\mathcal{G}(\mathcal{L})$ of the test predicates $\mathcal{L}$.

Obviously, it is impractical to use the **S**-**K** "assembly language" when testing. However, combining arrow terms $(b_i \rightarrow a)_j$ is quite handy when planning automated tests because this is a constructive framework for generating test cases. We refer to the author's book (Fehlmann Managing Complexity - Uncover the Mysteries with Six Sigma Transfer Functions 2016, pp. 323–329) for further discussions of the fascinating potential of the arrow term algebra for software testing.

5.4 Measuring Test Size

The size of an arrow term is defined such that it still reflects test size. For this, it is not useful to count recursive elements, but only those elements that relate to the base predicate elements, and thus represent executable, testable terms.

$$
\begin{aligned}
|a| &= |\{\delta_1, \ldots, \delta_n\} \to \rho|, \text{if} a = \{\delta_1, \ldots, \delta_n\} \to \rho, \text{where } \rho, \delta_i \in \mathcal{L} \\
|b_i \to a| &= \sum_i |b_i| + |a|, \text{for all } a, b_i \in \mathcal{G}(\mathcal{L}) \\
\left|(b_i \to a)_j\right| &= \sum_j |b_i \to a|_j
\end{aligned}
\tag{14}
$$

The size of a test does not increase with the level of the arrow terms. It always describes the executable size. Data movements that appear in more than one test case are multiply counted.

5.5 Generating Test Cases

Combinatory logic delivers a framework that generates all possible test cases for a test story. While computing power grows, it is still limited and only a finite approximation for a rule set can be used for tests. The problem remains how to select those test cases that are relevant. For this, we need *Transfer Functions* (Fehlmann, Managing Complexity - Uncover the Mysteries with Six Sigma Transfer Functions 2016).

6 Transfer Functions and Eigenvectors

Transfer Functions have become very popular since the last quarter of the 20th century. For instance, the *Fast Fourier Transfer* (FFT) probably made the deepest impact on humankind probably since invention of cooking by a fire; see e.g., Cooley et al. (Cooley and Tukey 1964). It led to the possibility of transferring audio signals in predictable time into digital code. All the music and entertainment stuff that today makes up for a trillion-euro industry started with that invention.

Eigenvector Theory is another achievement of linear algebra that changed the world; however, not before the start of the 21st century. For instance, eigenvector theory is employed in the *Analytic Hierarchy Process* (AHP) developed by Saaty (Saaty 1990) to solve multi-criteria decision problems, in the football teams ranking method proposed by Keener (Keener 1993) or, more recently, for powering Google's PageRank algorithm (Gallardo 2007). Big Data Analytics (e.g., Li et al. (Li et al. 2015)) also relies on Eigenvector theory. The details can be found in Fehlmann (Fehlmann, Managing Complexity - Uncover the Mysteries with Six Sigma Transfer Functions 2016).

The essential feature of transfer functions needed for testing is that transfer functions allow identifying relevant root causes for effects $\boldsymbol{y}$ observed. If a transfer function $\boldsymbol{A}$ has an approximate solution $\boldsymbol{x}$ for the problem $\boldsymbol{Ax} = \boldsymbol{y}$, then the solution $\boldsymbol{x}$ describes the controls that are needed for obtaining the observed effects $\boldsymbol{y}$. If the solution is approximate, the gap $||Ax - y||$ is called the *Convergence Gap*, where $||\ldots||$ is the Euclidian Distance between Ax and y. It describes how well the transfer function A explains the observed effects y.

6.1 Analyzing Cause-Effect Relationships

For analyzing cause-effect relationships and then measuring test coverage, using the techniques of *Quality Function Deployment* (QFD) is necessary (Fehlmann, Managing Complexity - Uncover the Mysteries with Six Sigma Transfer Functions 2016). The reason is that b of the combinatory explosion of test cases, a selection mechanism is needed to focus on relevant tests.

We use *User Stories* to represent requirements. The method of choice is using the Buglione-Trudel matrix (Fehlmann and Kranich, Managing Software Projects by the Buglione-Trudel Matrix 2017), to involve the development team in eliciting detail requirements. This yields a goal profile that can be transformed into a testing goal, using transfer functions.

The following steps are needed:

- Finding an importance profile for the user stories, or *Functional User Requirements*
- Assigning user stories to each data movement – one to many
- Deriving the goal of testing
- Defining test stories, or test scenarios
- Measuring test coverage

Thus, we need two transfer functions to establish cause-effect relationship:

- Mapping functionality from user stories to customer's needs
- Mapping tests from test stories to user stories

The first transfer function establishes a solution profile for the user stories; i.e., the functionality required by the users. This cannot easily be measured directly, because either there are no users available that you can ask, or they are not able to judge priorities because the topic technology is new and unknown to them. And even if you prioritize user stories directly, it is dangerous to believe in it without cross-checking it by the transfer function, mapping the priorities to customer's needs.

In any case, measuring customer's needs, or business drivers in case of products, is a standard QFD practice and used by product managers and marketing for thirty years. The ISO standard 16355 (ISO 16355-1:2015 2015) is an excellent start into this.

The transfer function between user stories and customer's needs that serves testing best is constructed by sizing the functionality of the user stories, using ISO 19761 COSMIC, and analyzing which data movement impacts which customer's need. This impact analysis is subject to experts' judgement. The coefficients in the transfer function matrix thus represent the total of data movements in a user story that impact some customer's need. For a user story, the total of data movements is its functional size. Thus, every data movement is linked to one or more user story.

6.2 Measuring Test Coverage

The second transfer function maps test stories into user stories. The solution profile of the first transfer function becomes the goal profile of the second; in turn, the resulting solution profile represents the importance of each test story with respect to customer's needs. In case customer's needs focus on privacy and security, it is obvious why this mechanism matters for consumer metrics.

The coefficients of the second transfer function represent the total test size of all test cases in a test story, that belong to some user story. Thus, the second transfer function can be calculated automatically.

Now, when extending test stories by adding more test cases, the test coverage transfer function also grows in total test size. By keeping the convergence gap small, the test cases can be selected in a consistent way to keep the tests focused on the user story goal profile, and thus n turn on customers' needs. This enables automatic test case selection; the convergence gap serves as "hash function" to the automated test case generation process.

For more details, the reader is referred to Fehlmann (Fehlmann, Managing Complexity - Uncover the Mysteries with Six Sigma Transfer Functions 2016, pp. 247–270). For a test coverage example, and for the proposed consumer metrics, see the authors' associated paper Fehlmann and Kranich (Fehlmann and Kranich, Practical Aspects of Consumer Metrics for Safety & Privacy 2018).

7 The SPI Manifesto (Korsaa et al. 2012)

Consumer metrics for software have a promising future but are not yet here. For *Software Process Improvement* (SPI), and all the more for the multi-sectoral understanding S(5)P(2)I(3) added to the original definition of SPI, consumer metrics, as needed today, touch *Privacy* and *Safety* (Messnarz et al. 2014).

Consumer metrics involve people actively and affect their daily activities (Value A). To make business successful, software-intense products need metrics for privacy and safety (Value B). Moreover, software development and deployment processes must provide means for consumers to have these metrics at their disposition; not once-upon-a-time, but accurately reflecting the actual system, that has largely evolved from the system originally acquired (Value C).

From the Manifesto's principles, consumer metrics are largely relying upon principle 3: *Base improvement on experience and measurements*. While people aspects (Korsaa et al. 2013) are less important, except for awareness, society and legal aspects regarding liability are of essence (Messnarz et al. 2014).

8 Conclusions

As pointed out by Russo on science history (Russo 2004), techniques based on a strong theory have huge potential for new applications and yield promising metrics. Testing of software-intense systems needs such a strong theory, because the current approach to testing, based on code, is a dead-end. Code-based metrics are neither fit for automated testing, nor for consumers asking for functional safety and privacy.

Our approach requires a merger of very different domains. Mathematical logic, transfer functions, and software engineering usually are considered quite distinct from each other, and now we propose to amalgam them for constructing meaningful and successful consumer metrics. Test automation comes almost for free, as a natural corollary of the theory. This opens a wide field for research and open discussions.

Among the many open points for research, we mention the construction of test generators that focus on narrowing the convergence gap. Even in theory, there must be possibilities to identify where in the matrix to add test cases first, for finding the best ones. But we do not yet know of any suitable method, or algorithm. Moreover, using semantics seems a very promising way of generating good test cases for extending existing test stories fast; however, this seems to be more of a practical application case than just finding and applying a good theory.

We hope our two papers create a community of software process experts, product managers, manufacturers of autonomous vehicles, and other policy makers to push an international standard for consumer metrics on privacy & safety.

References

Hart-Davis, A.: Engineers. Dorling Kindersley Publishers, New York (2012)

Barwise, J., Keisler, H., Mostowski, A., Robinson, A., Suppes, P., Troelstra, A.: Handbook of Mathematical Logic. Studies in Logic and the Foundations of Mathematics, vol. 90. North-Holland Publishing Company, Amsterdam (1977)

Bringmann, E., Krämer, A.: Model-based testing of automotive systems. In: 2008 International Conference on Software Testing, Verification, and Validation, Lillehammer, Norway, pp. 485–493 (2008)

Cagley, T.: Using Size to Drive Testing in Agile. Webinar - Verbal Communication (2018)

Cooley, J.W., Tukey, J.W.: An algorithm for the machine calculation of complex Fourier series. Math. Comput. **19**(90), 297–301 (1964)

Engeler, E.: Algebras and Combinators. Algebra Univers. **13**, 389–392 (1981)

Engeler, E.: The Combinatory Programme. Birkhäuser, Basel (1995)

Fehlmann, T.M.: Managing Complexity - Uncover the Mysteries with Six Sigma Transfer Functions. Logos Press, Berlin (2016)

Fehlmann, T.M.: Theorie und Anwendung der Kombinatorischen Logik. ETH Dissertation 3140-01, Zürich (1981)

Fehlmann, T.M., Kranich, E.: Managing software projects by the buglione-trudel matrix. In: 11th European Conference on Information Systems Management - ECISM 2017, Genova, Italy (2017)

Fehlmann, T.M., Kranich, E.: Practical aspects of consumer metrics for safety & privacy. In: EuroSPI 2018 (proposed), Bilbao, Spain (2018)

Fraenkel, A., Bar-Hillel, Y., Levy, A.: Foundations of Set Theory. Elsevier, Amsterdam (1973)

Gallardo, P.F.: Google's secret and linear algebra. EMS Newsl. **63**, 10–15 (2007)

ISO 16355-1:2015: Applications of Statistical and Related Methods to New Technology and Product Development Process - Part 1: General Principles and Perspectives of Quality Function Deployment (QFD). ISO TC 69/SC 8/WG 2 N 14. ISO TC 69/SC 8/WG 2 N 14, Geneva (2015)

ISO/IEC 14143-1:2007: Information technology - Software measurement - Functional size measurement - Part 1: Definition of concepts. ISO/IEC JTC 1/SC 7, Geneva (2007)

ISO/IEC 19761:2011: Software engineering - COSMIC: a functional size measurement method. ISO/IEC JTC 1/SC 7, Geneva (2011)

ISO/IEC 20926: Software and systems engineering - Software measurement - IFPUG functional size measurement method. ISO/IEC JTC 1/SC 7, Geneva (2009)

ISO/IEC CD Guide 98-3: Evaluation of measurement data - Part 3: Guide to uncertainty in measurement (GUM). TC/SC: ISO/TMBG, Geneva (2015)

ISO/IEC Guide 99:2007: International vocabulary of metrology – Basic and general concepts and associated terms (VIM). TC/SC: ISO/TMBG, Geneva (2007)

Keener, J.P.: The perron-frobenius theorem and the ranking of football teams. SIAM Rev. **35**(1), 80–93 (1993)

Korsaa, M., Biro, M., Messnarz, R., Johansen, J., Vohwinkel, D., Nevalainen, R., et al.: The SPI Manifesto and the ECQA SPI manager certification scheme. J. Softw.: Evol. Process **24**(5), 525–540 (2012)

Korsaa, M., Johansen, J., Schweigert, T., Vohwinkel, D., Messnarz, R., Nevalainen, R., et al.: The people aspects in modern process improvement management approaches. J. Soft.: Evol. Process **25**(4), 381–391 (2013)

Li, K.-C., Jiang, H., Yang, L.T., Cuzzocrea, A.: Big Data: Algorithms, Analytics, and Applications. CRC Press, Boca Raton (2015)

Messnarz, R., Sicilia, M.A., Biro, M., Garcia Barriocanal, E., Garre-Rubio, M., Siakas, K., et al.: Social responsibility aspects supporting the success of SPI. J. Softw.: Evol. Process **20**(3), 284–294 (2014)

Russo, L.: The Forgotten Revolution - How Science Was Born in 300 BC and Why It Had to Be Reborn. Springer, Heidelberg (2004). https://doi.org/10.1007/978-3-642-18904-3

Saaty, T.L.: The Analytic Hierarchy Process – Planning, Priority Setting, Resource Allocation. RWS Publications, Pittsburgh (1990)

Singh, S., et al.: Docker overview. Docker Inc. (2018). https://docs.docker.com/engine/docker-overview/. Accessed 9 Apr 2018

Turing, A.: On computable numbers, with an application to the Entscheidungsproblem. Proc. Lond. Math. Soc. **42**(Series 2), 230–265 (1937)

van Gerven, M.: Computational Foundations of Natural Intelligence, 7 December 2017. https://www.frontiersin.org/articles/10.3389/fncom.2017.00112/full. Accessed 27 Mar 2018

Wikipedia: Intuitionism, 24 February 2018. https://en.wikipedia.org/wiki/Intuitionism. Accessed 8 Mar 2018

ELIC – Building the New Generation of Engineers for Automotive in Europe

Claudia Linditsch[1], Claudia Fussenecker[2], Jörg Niemann[2], Richard Messnarz[3(✉)], Eva Penz[1], Anette Casey[1], and Jakub Stolfa[4]

[1] University of Applied Sciences Joanneum, Graz, Austria
Claudia.Linditsch@fh-joanneum.at
[2] University of Applied Sciences Düsseldorf, Düsseldorf, Germany
claudia.fussenecker@hs-duesseldorf.de
[3] ISCN GesmbH, Graz, Austria
rmess@iscn.com
[4] TUO Technical University of Ostrava, Ostrava, Czech Republic
jakub.stolfa@vsb.cz

Abstract. The Automotive industry is currently undergoing a dramatic innovation. Mechatronic solutions integrate knowledge about mechanics, physics, chemistry, biology, mathematics and informatics. Generations of students were specialising on one field, while current solutions require architects that can combine these different subject fields to one solution in automotive industry. For instance, battery systems require nowadays such a combination of skills, where chemistry is used to build Li cells. Physics is used to create the circuit and resistors to control the loading of cells. Voltage sensors are used as input to an electronic (ECU – Electronic control unit) to control loading and avoid overloading. And temperature sensors are an input to the ECU to identify temperature and avoid overheating and outgasing of explosive H gas. Mathematical models are used in the control algorithms. And Software I developed and executed on the ECU. Etc. The future car industry needs engineers to think outside the box, across different disciplines and who are capable of multi-disciplinary and multi-cultural team-working. ELIC (Engineering Literacy Online - Teachers as Medium for Change) is an EU project supported under the Erasmus+ program which develops an ECQA (European Certification and Qualification Association) compliant skills set and exam for teachers, as well as a MOOC platform to train teachers to teach interconnected science examples for Automotive.

Keywords: ELIC · Automotive · Interconnected sciences · Schools

1 Background – Interconnected Sciences in Schools

Year 2030: The year 2030 [24] is mentioned in many articles nowadays because this is the date where all manufacturers announced to produce only cars with self-driving functionality. The intelligence and control functions in such cars comes from the multi-disciplinary design of complex systems which combine mechanics, physics, chemistry, biology, mathematics and informatics.

X. Larrucea et al. (Eds.): EuroSPI 2018, CCIS 896, pp. 654–665, 2018.
https://doi.org/10.1007/978-3-319-97925-0_55

While generations of engineers had been specialized in one field, a new generation of engineers must be built for this 2030 agenda that can integrate the different disciplines and learn how to manage complex systems. Building such a new generation starts at school. If we train nowadays a student at grammar school (Gymnasium) at 11th and 12th year (4 years primary school, 8 years Gymnasium) it will in average take 8 to 10 years that the new generation finished the study programs and are integrated into work places. So if we start in 2018 this new generation will be just ready for the Year 2030 change.

In ELIC a research across schools in Germany, Austria, Italy and Czech Republic was done to analyse how much the multi-disciplinary approach [5, 17] is supported in school programs already.

MINT (Mathematik, Informatik, Naturwissenschaften, Technik) is a program that started recently in schools in Germany and Austria. In the teaching at schools the combined use of mathematics, informatics, natural sciences (physics, biology, chemistry), and technology is promoted and schools can apply for MINT certificates. MINT is not specialised to a specific domain like Automotive.

STEM (Science, Technology, Engineering, Mathematics) is a term that describes a number of school subjects dealing with natural sciences. STEM is used as term in the English speaking world and is like a catalogue of subjects. STEM teachers is a wording for e.g. mathematics teachers, biology teachers, informatics teachers, etc.

While in Germany and Austria the MINT program is integrated into the educational plans where experiments are done linking different STEM teachers and teaching interconnected science to students, the other countries have STEM teachers but no integrated educational program with mandatory inter-disciplinary experiments in the education. In countries like Czech Republic and Italy the use of such interlinked experiments in teaching is not due to a systematic educational program enforced by the state but depends on single projects and funds which are used in some of the schools.

The MINT program in its current form in Germany and Austria is not specialising in a specific domain. The EU BLUEPRINT approach is that for certain sectors in the EU leadership shall be maintained and extended by contributing key innovation to specific sectors.

ELIC specialises the MINT idea in the fields of Automotive, which is the largest employer in Europe. A MOOC (Massive Open Online Course) will be set up training STEM teachers across Europe to use interdisciplinary Automotive examples in their teaching of mathematics, informatics, natural sciences (physics, biology, chemistry), and technology.

2 Automotive Interdisciplinary Knowledge Elements Concept

The ELIC partners designed a teaching strategy where specific automotive systems [1, 2, 6–12, 14–16, 18–20, 25] are put into the centre and where each MINT/STEM teacher can assign her/his examples in the natural science lecture to specific parts in the automotive example system.

Figures 1, 2, 3, 4 and 5 show the structure of such automotive knowledge elements where each teacher will assign parts of the lecturing and exercises to specific parts of an automotive example. The first version of the MOOC is based on this example pool.

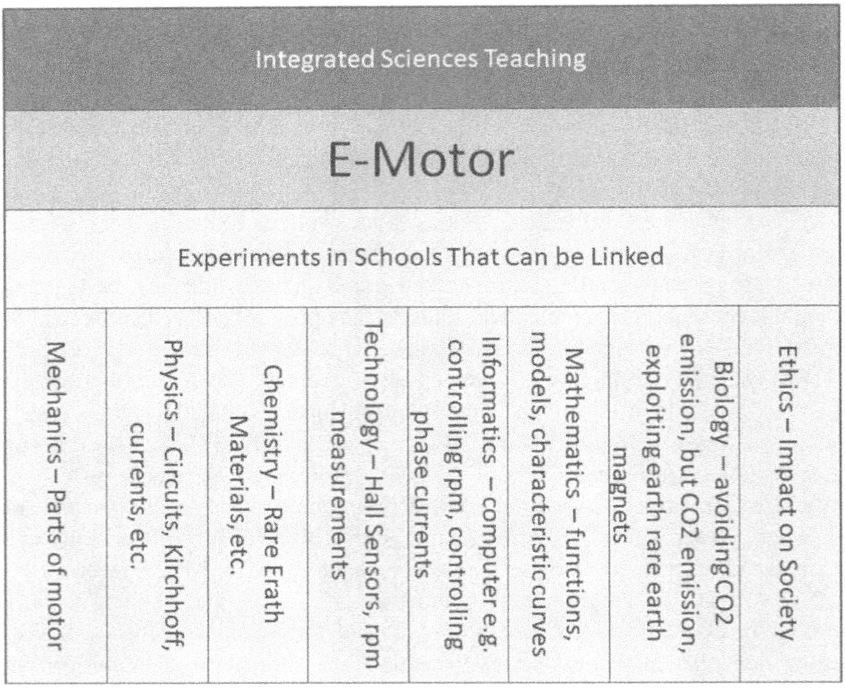

Fig. 1. Automotive E-motor system – STEM approach

For each of the thematic topics -

- E-Motor
- Battery System
- Combustion Engine
- Light System
- Energy Management

- there is a description of the functions of the system, a conceptual design drawing and a system schematic illustrating e.g. sensors, signal flow, control units, actuators, and system engineering design assumptions. STEM teachers can assign the lecturing content and exercises to blocks and interfaces in the system schematic.

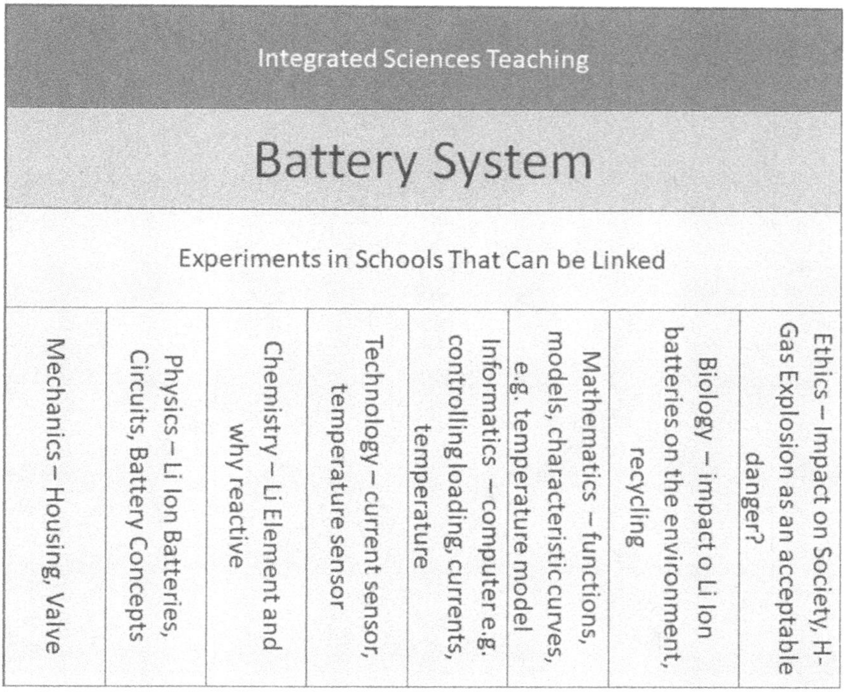

Fig. 2. Automotive battery system – STEM approach

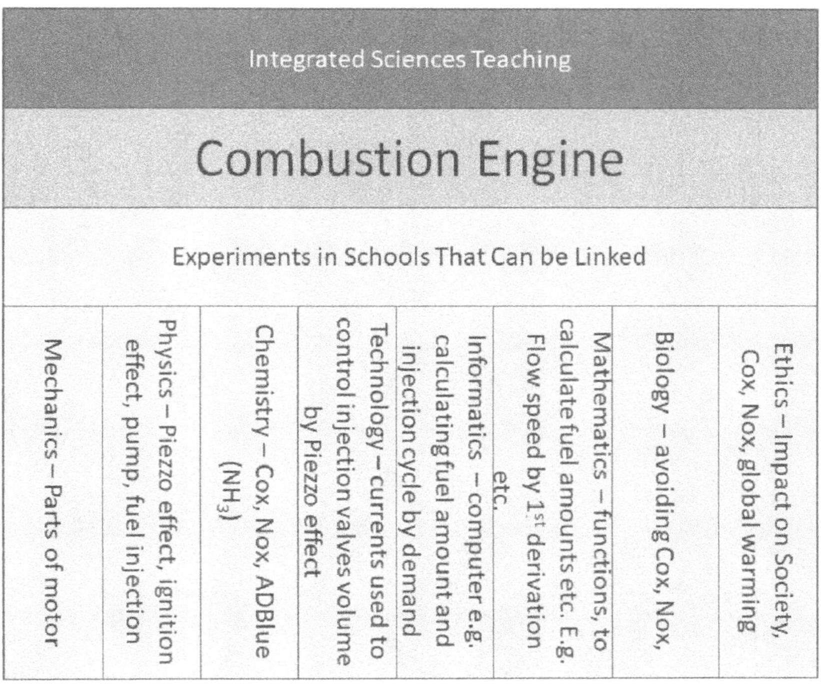

Fig. 3. Automotive combustion system – STEM approach

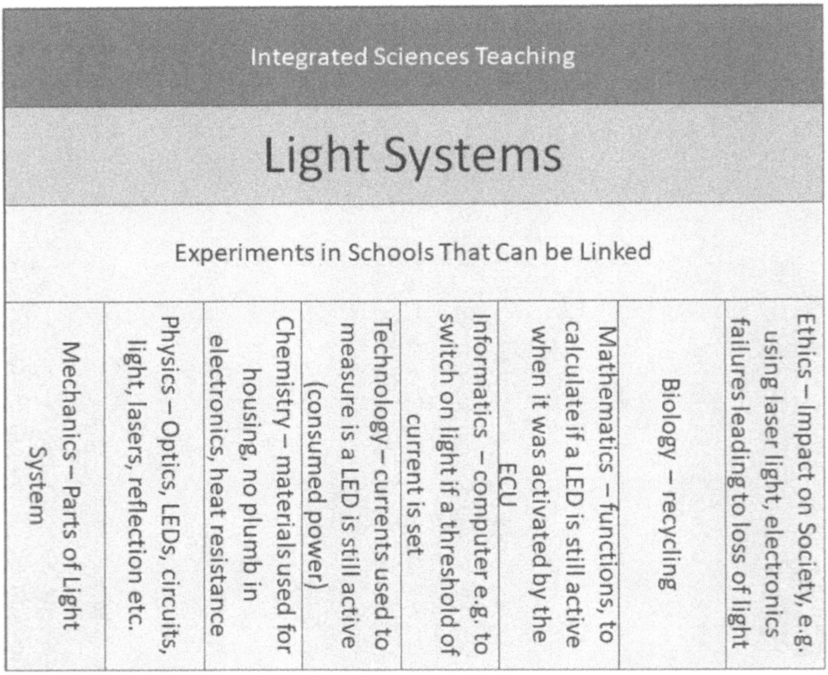

Fig. 4. Automotive light system – STEM approach

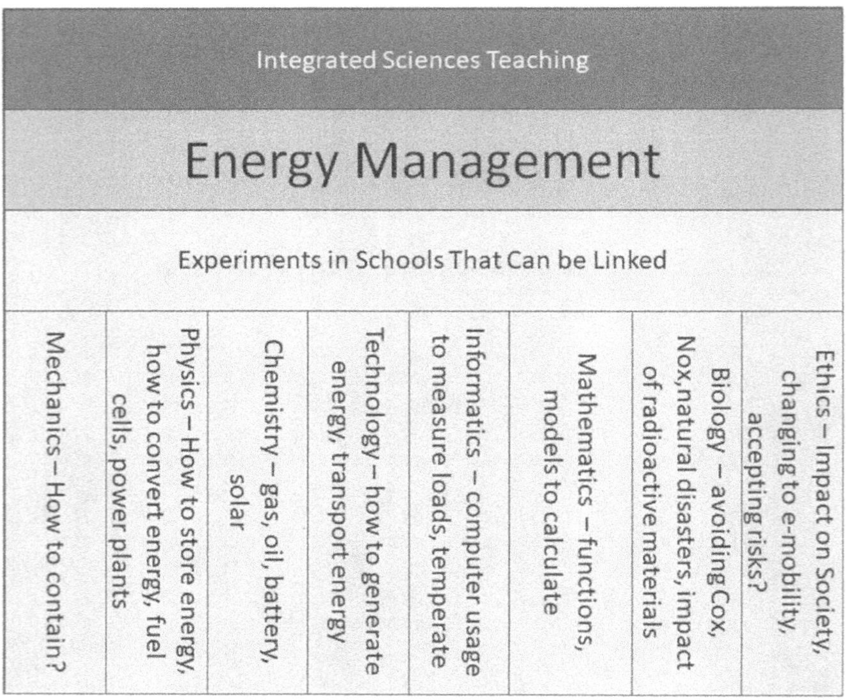

Fig. 5. Energy management system – STEM approach

3 Skills Set for Interdisciplinary Teaching Using Automotive as the Basis

Based on the ELIC research across schools in Germany, Austria, Italy and Czech Republic a skills set based on the ECQA (European Certification and Qualification Association) guidelines has been set up and is currently reviewed by partners from the participating countries. ECQA provides Europe wide procedures for skills definition, skills assessment, exams, and also provides an online campus. More than 30 job roles are integrated into the platform across Europe.

Job Role [4, 13]: ECQA established this term in 2007 in the first EU project EQN (European Quality Network) that led to the foundation of ECQA. One person in a work place can play many roles. For each role specific skills are needed and can be trained and certified. The idea was to select specific job roles and add them to the industry and requalify staff to stay up-to-date and help industry to sustain leadership.

Skills set [4, 13]: A skills set is like a skills tree with a hierarchical model of skills needed for a specific job role. A job role is divided into areas (skills units), each skills unit contains learning elements (concrete knowledge required), and each learning element contains performance criteria/indicators (see PC in Tables 1, 2 and 3) to prove that the learning element is covered. This structure was latter mapped to the EQF and each performance criteria checks a specific learning outcome.

Table 1. Unit 1 introduction

Unit identifier	Unit name	Unit description	Element identifier	Element name	Element description	PC	PC description
ELIC. U1	Introduction	This unit gives an introduction into systems engineering are elaborated	ELIC. U1.E1	Systems engineering	This element introduces systems engineering principles and how they are used in modern car industry	U2. E1. PC1	Understanding principles of systems engineering
						U1. E1. PC2	Knowing systems engineering examples in car industry integrating different disciplines into mechatronics

Tables 1, 2 and 3 describe the skills set for ELIC teachers. For each element in the skills set there is a training module in the MOOC. For each performance criteria of an element there will be exercises for teachers in the MOOC to demonstrate their understanding and competence.

Teachers become multipliers in schools across Europe creating motivation for interdisciplinary natural sciences examples and prepares students for the automotive

Table 2. Unit 2 automotive case studies

Unit identifier	Unit name	Unit description	Element identifier	Element name	Element description	PC	PC description
ELIC. U2	Automotive case studies	This unit investigates different automotive case studies where engineering literacy and networked sciences taught in schools have been applied	ELIC. U2.E1	Battery systems	This element deals with the system engineering of Lithium Ion battery systems	U2. E1. PC1	Understanding the system engineering concept of the Li battery system in cars
						U2. E1. PC2	Knowing how physics experiments and knowledge taught in schools can be mapped onto the battery system
						U2. E1. PC3	Knowing how chemistry experiments and knowledge taught in schools can be mapped onto the battery system
						U2. E1. PC4	Knowing how mathematics taught in schools can be mapped onto the battery system
						U2. E1. PC5	Knowing how informatics taught in schools can be mapped onto the battery system
						U2. E1. PC6	Knowing how biology and environmental issues taught in schools can be mapped onto the battery system
						U2. E1. PC7	Knowing how ethics taught in schools can be mapped onto the battery system
			ELIC. U2.E2	Light systems	This element deals with the system engineering of light systems	U2. E2. PC1	Understanding the system engineering concept of the light system in cars
						U2. E2. PC2	Knowing how physics experiments and knowledge taught in schools can be mapped onto the light system
						U2. E2. PC3	Knowing how chemistry experiments and knowledge taught in schools can be mapped onto the light system
						U2. E2. PC4	Knowing how mathematics taught in schools can be mapped onto the light system
						U2. E2. PC5	Knowing how informatics taught in schools can be mapped onto the light system
						U2. E2. PC6	Knowing how biology and environmental issues taught in schools can be mapped onto the light system
						U2. E2. PC7	Knowing how ethics taught in schools can be mapped onto the light system

(*continued*)

Table 2. (*continued*)

Unit identifier	Unit name	Unit description	Element identifier	Element name	Element description	PC	PC description
			ELIC. U2.E3	Combustion engine	This element deals with the system engineering of combustion engine systems	U2. E3. PC1	Understanding the system engineering concept of the combustion engine in cars
						U2. E3. PC2	Knowing how physics experiments and knowledge taught in schools can be mapped onto the combustion engine system
						U2. E3. PC3	Knowing how chemistry experiments and knowledge taught in schools can be mapped onto the combustion engine system
						U2. E3. PC4	Knowing how mathematics taught in schools can be mapped onto the combustion engine system
						U2. E3. PC5	Knowing how informatics taught in schools can be mapped onto the combustion engine system
						U2. E3. PC6	Knowing how biology and environmental issues taught in schools can be mapped onto the combustion engine system
						U2. E3. PC7	Knowing how ethics taught in schools can be mapped onto the combustion engine system
			ELIC. U2.E4	E-motor	This element deals with the system engineering of e-motor systems	U2. E4. PC1	Understanding the system engineering concept of the e-motor in cars
						U2. E4. PC2	Knowing how physics experiments and knowledge taught in schools can be mapped onto the e-motor in cars
						U2. E4. PC3	Knowing how chemistry experiments and knowledge taught in schools can be mapped onto the e-motor in cars
						U2. E4. PC4	Knowing how mathematics taught in schools can be mapped onto the e-motor in cars
						U2. E4. PC5	Knowing how informatics taught in schools can be mapped onto the e-motor in cars
						U2. E4. PC6	Knowing how biology and environmental issues taught in schools can be mapped onto thee-motor in cars
						U2. E4. PC7	Knowing how ethics taught in schools can be mapped onto the e-motor in cars

industry. This way ELIC uses the MINT ideas and helps to prepare the next generation of engineers that will work in Automotive industry hen the 2030 goals are close to be achieved.

Table 3. Unit 3 hot topics – dependent vehicles

Unit identifier	Unit name	Unit description	Element identifier	Element name	Element description	PC	PC description
ELIC. U3	Hot topics - dependent vehicles	This unit puts a focus on systems that are necessary to provide the automotive industry with the necessary infra-structure	ELIC. U3.E1	Energy management	This element explains how energy is created, stored, transported and used to reload batteries in cars	U3. E1. PC1	Understanding the system engineering concept of energy management connected with car industry
						U3. E1. PC2	Knowing how physics experiments and knowledge taught in schools can be mapped onto energy management
						U3. E1. PC3	Knowing how chemistry experiments and knowledge taught in schools can be mapped onto energy management
						U3. E1. PC4	Knowing how mathematics taught in schools can be mapped onto energy management
						U3. E1. PC5	Knowing how informatics taught in schools can be mapped onto energy management
						U3. E1. PC6	Knowing how biology and environmental issues taught in schools can be mapped onto onto energy management
						U3. E1. PC7	Knowing how ethics taught in schools can be mapped onto onto energy management
			ELIC. U3.E2	Cyber-security	This element deals with cybersecurity topics in cars	U3. E2. PC1	Understanding the system engineering concept of cybersecurity in cars
						U3. E2. PC2	Knowing how informatics taught in schools can be mapped onto cybersecurity design
						U3. E2. PC3	Knowing how ethics taught in schools can be mapped onto cybersecurity design
			ELIC. U3.E3	Autonomous driving	This element deals with autonomous driving cars	U3. E3. PC1	Understanding the system engineering concept of autonomous driving cars
						U3. E3. PC2	Knowing how informatics taught in schools can be mapped onto autonomous driving cars
						U3. E3. PC3	Knowing how ethics taught in schools can be mapped onto onto autonomous driving cars

4 MOOC

The project develops a MOOC (Massive Open Online Course) which will be hosted by the University of Applied Sciences Joanneum, Graz. For each automotive case study there are introductory system concept explanations. Teachers (dependent on their subject, e.g. physics) will receive guidance about which experiments are related to this case study and get tests to answer questions concerning the experiments correctly. Once teachers have successfully passed the online tests for all case studies they can generate a certificate online. The system will be made available to many teachers online from 2019 onwards. In case of interest you can contact the authors of the paper who also are representatives of the EU ELIC project.

5 The SPI Manifesto Revisited

The SPI manifesto [3, 21–23] describes values and principles which need to be considered to make improvements work in an organisation. One of the approaches is to support change by an innovation and include all affected stakeholders. The principle "**We truly believe that SPI is inherently linked with change**" means that change is natural and people should not fear change because if change is correctly handled it will lead to more business opportunities. Especially in car industry a change is happening which was there in the mobile area before, when moving from a cell phone to a smart phone. Not changing might lead to losing business.

The principle "**Create a learning organisation**" means that best practices and knowledge need to be shared and that knowledge of practical value for engineers and which shows commercial advantage of the company shall be maintained as a defined service. ELIC shares automotive examples and best practices with teachers in schools.

An additional principle proposed for the SPI manifesto is: "**Support the organisation's vision and business objectives**" [3]. ELIC has a vision to support the 2030 goals for Automotive by forming the mindset of the future engineers and thereby strengthening the automotive industry longterm.

Acknowledgements. We are grateful to the European Commission which has funded the Erasmus+ project ELIC (2017–2019). In this case the publications reflect the views only of the author(s), and the Commission cannot be held responsible for any use, which may be made of the information contained therein.

References

1. Riel, A., et al.: EU project SafEUr – competence requirements for functional safety managers. In: Winkler, D., O'Connor, R.V., Messnarz, R. (eds.) EuroSPI 2012. CCIS, vol. 301, pp. 253–265. Springer, Heidelberg (2012). https://doi.org/10.1007/978-3-642-31199-4_22
2. Bachmann, V., Messnarz, R.: Improving the software development for multiple projects by applying a platform strategy for mechatronic systems. J. Softw.: Evol. Process **24**(5), 541–549 (2012)

3. Messnarz, R., Biró, M., Koinig, S., Reiner, M., Vajde-Horvat, R., Ekert, D.: The future of SPI knowledge and networking in Europe – a vision. In: O'Connor, R.V., Pries-Heje, J., Messnarz, R. (eds.) EuroSPI 2011. CCIS, vol. 172, pp. 268–277. Springer, Heidelberg (2011). https://doi.org/10.1007/978-3-642-22206-1_24
4. Draghici, A., Draghici, G., Izvercianu, M., Riel, A., Tichkiewitch, S., Messnarz, R.: Qualification and certification of research-entrepreneur skills using the ECQA platform. In: Quintela Varajão, J.E., Cruz-Cunha, M.M., Putnik, G.D., Trigo, A. (eds.) CENTERIS 2010. CCIS, vol. 110, pp. 249–258. Springer, Heidelberg (2010). https://doi.org/10.1007/978-3-642-16419-4_25
5. Feuer, É., Messnarz, R., Wittenbrink, H.: Experiences with managing social patterns in defined distributed working processes. In: European Software Process Improvement, EUROSPI 2003, Graz (2003)
6. Kreiner, C., Messnarz, R., Riel, A., et al.: The AQUA automotive sector skills alliance: best practice in an integrated engineering approach. Softw. Qual. Prof. **17**(3), 35–45 (2015)
7. Messnarz, R., et al.: Integrating functional safety, automotive SPICE and six sigma – the AQUA knowledge base and integration examples. In: Barafort, B., O'Connor, R.V., Poth, A., Messnarz, R. (eds.) EuroSPI 2014. CCIS, vol. 425, pp. 285–295. Springer, Heidelberg (2014). https://doi.org/10.1007/978-3-662-43896-1_26
8. Kreiner, C.J., et al.: Automotive knowledge alliance AQUA – integrating automotive SPICE, six sigma, and functional safety. In: McCaffery, F., O'Connor, R.V., Messnarz, R. (eds.) EuroSPI 2013. CCIS, vol. 364, pp. 333–344. Springer, Heidelberg (2013). https://doi.org/10.1007/978-3-642-39179-8_30
9. Macher, G., Sporer, H., Brenner, E., Kreiner, C.: Supporting cyber-security based on hardware-software interface definition. In: Kreiner, C., O'Connor, R.V., Poth, A., Messnarz, R. (eds.) EuroSPI 2016. CCIS, vol. 633, pp. 148–159. Springer, Cham (2016). https://doi.org/10.1007/978-3-319-44817-6_12
10. Macher, G., Messnarz, R., Kreiner, C., et al.: Integrated safety and security development in the automotive domain. Working Group 17AE-0252/2017-01-1661, SAE International, June 2017
11. Messnarz, R., Kreiner, C., Riel, A.: Integrating automotive SPICE, functional safety, and cybersecurity concepts: a cybersecurity layer model. Softw. Qual. Prof. **18**(4), 13 (2016)
12. Messnarz, R., Kreiner, C., Riel, A., et al.: Implementing functional safety standards has an impact on system and sw design - required knowledge and competencies (SafEUr). Softw. Qual. Prof. (2015)
13. Messnarz, R., Ekert, D., Reiner, M., Sicilia, M.A.: Europe wide industry certification using standard procedures based on ISO 17024. In: Technologies Applied to Electronics Teaching (TAEE). IEEE (2012)
14. Messnarz, R., König, F., Bachmann, V.O.: Experiences with trial assessments combining automotive SPICE and functional safety standards. In: Winkler, D., O'Connor, R.V., Messnarz, R. (eds.) EuroSPI 2012. CCIS, vol. 301, pp. 266–275. Springer, Heidelberg (2012). https://doi.org/10.1007/978-3-642-31199-4_23
15. Messnarz, R., Kreiner, C., Riel, A.: Integrating automotive SPICE, functional safety, and cybersecurity concepts: a cybersecurity layer model. Softw. Qual. Prof. **18**(4), 13–23 (2016)
16. Messnarz, R., Much, A., Kreiner, C., Biro, M., Gorner, J.: Need for the continuous evolution of systems engineering practices for modern vehicle engineering. In: Stolfa, J., Stolfa, S., O'Connor, R.V., Messnarz, R. (eds.) EuroSPI 2017. CCIS, vol. 748, pp. 439–452. Springer, Cham (2017). https://doi.org/10.1007/978-3-319-64218-5_36

17. Messnarz, R., Nadasi, G., O'Leary, E., Foley, B.: Experience with teamwork in distributed work environments. In: Stanford Smith, B., Chiozza, E. (eds.) Proceedings of the E2001 Conference, E-Work and E-commerce, Novel Solutions for a Global Networked Economy. IOS Press, Amsterdam, Berlin, Oxford, Tokyo, Washington (2001)
18. Much, A.: Automotive security: challenges, standards and solutions. Softw. Qual. Prof. (2016)
19. SOQRATES, Task Forces Developing Integration of Automotive SPICE, ISO 26262 and SAE J3061. http://soqrates.eurospi.net/
20. Stolfa, J., et al.: Automotive quality universities - AQUA alliance extension to higher education. In: Kreiner, C., O'Connor, R.V., Poth, A., Messnarz, R. (eds.) EuroSPI 2016. CCIS, vol. 633, pp. 176–187. Springer, Cham (2016). https://doi.org/10.1007/978-3-319-44817-6_14
21. Korsaa, M., et al.: The SPI manifesto and the ECQA SPI manager certification scheme. J. Softw.: Evol. Process **24**(5), 525–540 (2012)
22. Korsaa, M., et al.: The people aspects in modern process improvement management approaches. J. Softw.: Evol. Process **25**(4), 381–391 (2013)
23. Messnarz, R., et al.: Social responsibility aspects supporting the success of SPI. J. Softw.: Evol. Process **26**(3), 284–294 (2014)
24. GEAR 2030, European Commission, Commission launches GEAR 2030 to boost competitiveness and growth in the automotive sector (2016). http://ec.europa.eu/growth/tools-databases/newsroom/cf/itemdetail.cfm?item_id=8640
25. Automotive SPICE 3.1. German Automotive Association, November 2017. www.automtivespice.com

Author Index

CPSIA information can be obtained
at www.ICGtesting.com
Printed in the USA
LVHW08s0352170818
587195LV00021B/353/P

9 783319 979243